Descriptive English

For **Compulsory English Language** Paper
in IAS (Mains), State PCS & PCS (J), IFS
IES, CISF, CAPF, TGT & PGT (English)
SSC CGL

SP Bakshi • Richa Sharma

 ARIHANT PUBLICATIONS (INDIA) LIMITED

ARIHANT PUBLICATIONS (INDIA) LIMITED
All rights reserved

ॐ © Publisher
No part of this publication may be re-produced, stored in a retrieval system or distributed in any form or by any means, electronic, mechanical, photocopying, recording, scanning, web or otherwise without the written permission of the publisher. Arihant has obtained all the information in this book from the sources believed to be reliable and true. However, Arihant or its editors or authors or illustrators dont take any responsibility for the absolute accuracy of any information published, and the damages or loss suffered thereupon.

All disputes subject to Meerut (UP) jurisdiction only.

ॐ Administrative & Production Offices

Regd. Office:
'Ramchhaya' 4577/15, Agarwal Road, Darya Ganj, New Delhi -110002, Tele: 011- 47630600, 43518550; Fax: 011- 23280316

Head Office:
Kalindi, TP Nagar, Meerut (UP) - 250002 Tele: 0121-2401479, 2512970, 4004199; Fax: 0121-2401648

ॐ Sales & Support Offices
Agra Ahmedabad, Bengaluru, Bhubaneswar, Bareilly, Chennai, Delhi, Guwahati, Haldwani Hyderabad, Jaipur, Jhansi, Kolkata, Kota, Lucknow, Meerut, Nagpur & Pune

ॐ ISBN 978-93-8598-077-0

ॐ Price : ₹ 285.00

PO No. : TXT-59-T051124-12-22

PRINTED & BOUND BY
ARIHANT PUBLICATIONS (I) LTD. (PRESS UNIT)

For further information about the products from Arihant log on to www.arihantbooks.com or email to info@arihantbooks.com

PREFACE

The new, revised and comprehensive edition of Descriptive English is infront of you, various competitive examinations require testing of English Comprehension, Communication and Writing Skills of the aspirants. The present edition has been prepared keeping in mind the needs of those who are appearing for Civil Services Aptitude Test (CSAT) and Civil Services (Mains) English Papers, IES, CAPF, IFS, PCS and SSC CGL Exams.

The book is also beneficial to those who wish to appear for Probationary Officers Bank Exam held by SBI or TGT, PGT English (Teacher's Eligibility Test) and also other competitive examinations. The Grammar portion extensively covers the areas which are essential for future teachers to understand the subtle significance of English subject.

We have tried to maintain an objective, critical and frank approach to all the current topics covered under essay or expansion writing. In today's competitive environment writing skills need to be perfected. We are sure that the present edition will certainly help the aspirants in making their writing skills exact and perfect. The topics covered are dealt comprehensively and in comprehension passages, multiple choice questions have been done away with according to the latest requirements of these examinations.

The book contains enough practice material in the form of workbook and cumulative exercise, previous years' questions.

We are hopeful that this revised edition would certainly serve the purpose it is intended for.

We would like to extend our gratitude to the management of Arihant Publications (India) Ltd. extended to us in bringing out this book in its present form.

Authors

CONTENTS

PART A WRITING SKILLS

1. Essay Writing 3-140

- Reservation for Women in Legislature
- Uniform Civil Code
- Judicial Reforms
- Public Interest Litigations— An Integral Part of Judicial Activism
- Electoral Reforms
- Police Reforms
- National Language of India
- Corporal Punishment
- Freedom of Press
- Trial by Media
- Politics of Coalition
- National Integration
- Nexus between Politicians and Criminals
- Second (Poorna) Swaraj
- Corruption in Public Life
- Right to Information (RTI)
- Why not Elected Governors?
- Political Gerontocracy (Retirement of Politicians)
- Religion and Politics
- Presidential System of Government in India
- Transparency in Administration
- Secularism in India—A Myth
- The Politics of Communalism
- Middle-East—A Zone of Turbulence
- Empowerment of Women
- The Problems of Urban Working Women in India
- Crime Against Women in India
- Gender Biased India
- Women Officers in Armed Forces
- The Reservation Policy
- Child Labour
- The Lost Childhood
- Homes for the Aged
- AIDS—A Dormant Volcano
- Drug Addiction
- Alcoholism in India
- Smoking in Public Places
- Euthanasia—Mercy Killing
- Surrogate Motherhood
- Capital Punishment
- Narco-Analysis Test
- Terrorism in India
- Red Terror
- Global Population
- Discipline in Public Life
- Rights of the Differently Abled Persons
- Consumer Protection Laws in India
- Honour Killing—Shameful to the Country
- The Menace of Drug Addiction
- Social Networking Sites—Blessing or Curse for the Society
- Gender Discrimination in India

- Superstition is the Religion of Feeble Minds
- Dowry—A Curse to Indian Society
- Global Disarmament
- India and China
- India and Globalisation
- Indo-US Nuclear Deal
- Inclusive Growth in India
- Reforming the Public Sector
- Poverty in India
- Population Explosion in India
- The Role of Multinationals in Indian Economy
- Special Economic Zone (SEZ)
- Floods in India
- Disaster Management
- Policy on Land Acquisition
- Global Warming
- Non-Vegetarianism and Climate Change
- Biodiversity
- Conservation of Water Resources
- Twenty-20 Cricket
- Social Values— Survival of All
- Humanism— The True Worship of God
- Indian Cinema and its Social Responsibility

- Police Reforms— A Need of Time
- News Channels have Turned into Entertainment Channels
- Role of Media in Generating Public Opinion
- Affirmative Action
- Does Indian History Needs—to be Rewritten?
- Art for Life Sake
- National Healthcare
- Nanotechnology
- Human Cloning
- The Mobile Revolution
- Net Neutrality— A Public Demand
- Our Education System
- Right to Education
- Brain Drain
- Distance Education—Its Future in India
- Entry of Foreign Universities in India
- Ragging— An Evil
- Sex Education in Schools
- Grooming Teachers for Tomorrow
- Swami Vivekananda— My Favourite Spiritual Leader
- Bhagat Singh— A Sublime Martyr
- Rabindranath Tagore

2. Expansion Writing 141-168

- Spare the Rod and Spoil the Child
- All that Glitters is Not Gold
- The Child is Father of Man
- Handsome is He That Handsome Does
- There is Nothing Good or Bad but Thinking Makes it So
- Actions Speak Louder than Words
- Reading Maketh a Full man; Conference a Ready Man and Writing an Exact Man

- There is Least Friendship and Least of All Between Equals
- Paths of Glory Lead but to the Grave
- Proper Study of Mankind is Man
- Without Bread Liberty is Meaningless
- Knowledge is Power
- Art of Living
- We Live in Deeds Not in Years
- All the World is a Stage
- A Thing of Beauty is a Joy Forever

- He that hath Wife and Children hath given Hostages to Fortune
- A Friend is Another Himself
- There is a Silver Lining in Every Cloud
- Rome was not Built in a Day
- Where there is a Will, there is a Way
- A Rolling Stone Gathers no Moss
- Revenge is a Kind of Wild Justice
- Failures are Stepping Stone to Success
- The Pen is Mightier than the Sword
- Beggars cannot be Choosers
- Peace hath her Victories, no less Renowned than War
- Pride hath a Fall
- Character is Destiny or Man is the Architect of his Own Fate
- Example is Better than Precept
- Poetry is the Criticism of Life
- Our Sweetest Songs are those that Tell of Saddest Thoughts
- A Bad Workman Quarrels with his Tools
- Sweet are the Uses of Adversity
- War is Vanity than Valour, it is Cowardice than Courage
- Hope Springs Eternal in Human Breast
- When Money Speaks, Truth remains Silent
- If Winter Comes, Can Spring be Far Behind?
- The Old Order Changeth, Yielding Place to New
- The Hand that Rocks the Cradle Rules the World
- A Little Knowledge is a Dangerous Thing
- Honesty is the Best Policy
- Time and Tide Wait for None
- Virtue has its Own Reward
- Man does not Live by Bread Alone
- United We Stand, Divided We Fall
- Who Lives if India Dies?
- Prevention is Better than Cure
- Only the Wearer knows where the Shoe Pinches
- Speech is Silver, Silence is Gold
- Work is Worship
- Look before You Leap
- Strike while the Iron is Hot
- As You Sow, So shall You Reap
- Slow and Steady Wins the Race
- Travel as a Part of Education
- Necessity is the Mother of Invention
- The Face is an Index of Character
- Familiarity Breeds Contempt
- God Helps Those Who Help Themselves
- The Sins of Fathers Visit upon their Children
- Money is a Good Servant but a Bad Master
- Practice Makes a Man Perfect
- Might is Right
- Justice Delayed is Justice Denied
- Charity Begins at Home
- What cannot be Cured must be Endured
- A Friend in Need is a Friend Indeed
- Do unto Others as You Wish these to be done unto You
- A Stitch in Time Saves Nine
- Fools Rush in Where Angels Fear to Tread
- Conscience Makes a Coward of us All
- Brevity is the Soul of Wit
- To Err is Human; to Forgive is Divine
- When in Rome, do as the Romans do
- Fortune Favours the Bold
- Make Hay while the Sun Shines
- A Bird in Hand is Worth two in the Bush
- Waste not, Want not
- To Run with the Hare and Hunt with the Hound

3. Report Writing — 169-189
  4. Precis Writing — 190-227
  5. Letter Writing — 228-264

PART B COMPREHENSION SKILLS

  1. Subjective Comprehension — 267-304

PART C GRAMMAR SKILLS

  1. The Function of Tenses — 307-327
  2. Voice — 328-344
  3. Clause Analysis — 345-357
  4. Non-Finite Verbs (Infinitives, Gerunds, Participles) — 358-371
  5. Narration — 372-392
  6. Synthesis — 393-427
  7. Transformation — 428-468
  8. Prepositions — 469-497
  9. Miscellaneous — 498-518

PART D VERBAL SKILLS

  1. Paronyms and Homonyms — 521-542
  2. One Word Substitutions — 543-559
  3. Synonyms and Antonyms — 560-590
  4. Foreign Words and Expressions — 591-596
  5. Legal Vocabulary — 597-613
  6. Phrasal Verbs — 614-629
  7. Idioms and Phrases — 630-660
  8. Words Used as Verbs, Nouns and Adjectives — 661-689
  9. Miscellaneous — 690-696

PART A
WRITING SKILLS

The need for expression in English has become imperative with the advent of globalisation the world over. The multinationals are always on the look out for the young men and women with command of written and spoken English.

Writing Skills is the ultimate in English Language and requires quite comprehensive basic knowledge. Before attempting to express an idea in English a student has to grasp the approach to attaining Writing Skills.

Examinations on national level have started laying great stress on descriptive language to test the Writing Skills of an examinee. The present portion of the book is prepared with a view to helping the students to put their ideas in words in simple, easy and effective manner.

CHAPTER 1

Essay Writing

What is an Essay?

An essay is a literary composition, usually in prose. However, literal meaning of the word 'essay' means to attempt. An essay can be written on any subject on Earth. Therefore, the subjects of essays are not confined to any specific area. That is why the scope of writing essays is unlimited. Therefore, an essay is a prose composition. This is an exercise in composition on various subjects divided mainly under the following headings:

(a) Personal, (b) Descriptive, (c) Narrative, (d) Reflective, (e) Biographical.

How to Write an Essay?

Introduction is the most important part of an essay as it introduces the readers to the main theme of the composition. A student can write good introduction only if he is clear about the subject he is writing about. He is supposed to have collection of ideas and then selection of the material for a particular subject is the most significant exercise of mind. The ideas must not be rambling. They must be to the point. It is better if a student can illustrate his ideas with facts, figures and examples in short.

Logical Arrangement

However, these ideas must be arranged logically to make a piece of writing effective. For this purpose the essay should be divided into paragraphs dealing with a single idea convincingly. The body of an essay comprises these ideas arranged logically.

Conclusion of the essay is supposed to satisfy the readers and they should be convinced when they have gone through the essay. Abrupt ending leaves the readers dissatisfied. The effect of the whole essay is marred.

Style, last but not least, leaves a lasting impression on the readers. It gives insight into the character of the writer. It has not been said in vain that "style is the man". It is better to be direct, simple and precise. The students should not labour under wrong conception that the use of difficult words is rewarding. Unnecessary repetitions and ambiguous language should be avoided at all costs. Therefore, the style of the essay should be natural, concise and clear. Adhere to the length of the essay as is required of you by the examiner. However, an essay is normally 400-500 word long composition.

Sample Essays

Directions *Below are some essays with their solutions.*

1. Reservation for Women in Legislature

In a significant step, the Rajya Sabha on 9th March, 2010 voted to amend the Constitution to reserve for women one-third of seats in the Parliament and the State Assemblies. The Bill known as 108th Constitutional Amendment now has to be passed by the Lok Sabha to become an Act. First, the bill seeks to reserve one-third of the seats for women in the Parliament and Legislative Assemblies. Secondly, the reserved seats may be allotted by rotation to different constituencies in a State or a Union Territory. Thirdly, the reservation of seats, however, shall cease to exist 15 years after the commencement of the Act.

Reservation to ensure fair representation to women in parliament and state assemblies is a most welcome step. India has lagged behind her neighbours and other countries when it comes to gender balanced legislatures. In Pakistan, 22% of the National Assembly seats are held by women. With 12% women in Indian parliament, India lags far behind Asian region where women representation stands at 18.5%. Nepal boasts of 33% of women members while Bangladeshi parliament has 19% of women members. When the Bill seeking to reserve one-third of the seats for women in Indian parliament and state legislature is passed, we can ensure fair and just representation to women. Certain objections to the Bill have been raised. Provision for rotating constituencies means that women cannot nurse their constituencies. Secondly, reservation does not extend to the Rajya Sabha. Thirdly, there is no female sub-quota within existing quotas. Above all this kind of quota will favour upper caste women at the expense of backward castes.

According to the bill one-third of the seats in the Lok Sabha and State Assemblies reserved for women will be allotted by rotation. It means that once in every three elections a seat will be set aside for women and for the other two elections revert to a general seat. A woman who wins in a reserved seat, does not have the security to run against a woman in the next elections. Critics say that a woman or man MP will have no incentive to nurse her/his constituency. But analysts point out the serious flaw elsewhere. Women suffer numerous forms of discrimination. Will this discrimination change with more women in the legislature? Reservation for Dalits and the Tribals in the past have failed to end their discrimination meaningfully. On the other side these provisions have merely created a creamy layer. It is estimated that there is only a trickle down from the creamy layer to ordinary Dalits, Tribals and Backward Castes.

In due course of time reservation of women is sure to create a creamy layer, a hurdle to the progress of women in general. The demand for quota within quota indicates that women are more loyal to their castes and community than to gender based equality. Empowerment must be the right of all women, not of just a few privliged women. Demand for sub-quota is made because advantages of reservation are generally cornered by the creamy and the well organised layers among backward castes. It is undeniably true that the reservation for women is likely to be extended indefinitely. Quota has become the life-line for the survival of a government. Even after sixty-five years no political party dare to ease out creamy layer.

Reservation is no means for women's meaningful empowerment. Political parties on their own should have long back increased women's representation. It would have been the ideal way to uplift the status of women. Enlarging women's role in politics is done by the political parties they belong to, not the state. Leaders of all political parties have been insensitive to the neglect of women. Quotas for women can bring about only cosmetic transformation. Only a fundamental change in the character and composition of political parties can do away with their discrimination. It is for the party to pick women candidates on merits and dispense with the criteria of dynasty and class. Voluntary political party quotas can serve the purpose of their empowerment better than the complicated Bill on women's reservation. The trouble is that our government is addicted to hog limelight to cash in on every political and economic measure.

2. Uniform Civil Code

India is a land of diversity, intermingling of different religions, creeds, provinces and languages. Inspite of 68 years of independence the diversity of the country is not bound with a unifying force. There is a lack of emotional and national integration. Article 370 relating to Kashmir is an anomaly. It accords a special status to the state of Jammu and Kashmir. People living in a nation are supposed to have one law based on the concept of one nation. India is not a tribal polity. To unify country into one healthy nation we have a Constitution that gives equal rights to all Indians.

Then why should uniform civil law not be brought into effect? Uniform Civil Code is indispensable for emotional and national integration. The fundamentalists have even gone to the extent of saying that Article 44 should be deleted. Article 44 enjoins upon the government to try to bring into form Uniform Civil Code.

If law is to serve its purpose in real sense, it must be progressive. In 1955, Hindu personal law was reformed. It is largely based on *'Manusmriti'* and other Brahamnical Law Books. Before reformation there were many discriminatory and oppressive elements in it. Bigamy for men, *sati* system, child marriage, discrimination against Women and Dalits were done away with. *Varna* system was abolished.

Then why can the Muslim Personal law not be reformed? The Muslim women in India are struggling for liberation while in most of the Islamic countries they are emancipated. Jordan has abolished the triple *talaq*. Pakistan did the same in 1961 by enacting Muslim Family Law. There are scores of other examples.

Two objections were raised in the Constituent Assembly regarding the framing of Uniform Civil Code. *Firstly,* it was alleged that enactment of Article 44 of the Constitution will amount to violation of Fundamental Right of Freedom for Religion under Article 25 of the Constitution. *Secondly,* it will amount to an attack on minority who were not ready for change in their personal laws.

But both these objections stand no ground. How does a Common Civil Code hurt one's religion? How about Hindu Code Bill? The second objection can best be answered in the words of Dr KM Munshi that he spoke in the Constituent Assembly, "There is no such recognition in personal law of Muslim in the advanced Muslim countries which is beyond change or amendment."

If law is really to serve its purpose, it must be progressive. The lack of clarity has affected Muslim women most adversely. Unfortunately, the All India Muslim Law Board has challenged the judicial verdicts by terming them the "miscarriage of justice" and "propaganda against Islam". Let us be clear about our national objectives instead of parochial interests. No man is above the law of the land. All must realise that one law will definitely help the cause of national integration, humane, progressive and rational society. India has done well to have achieved uniformity in most of the branches of law. In order to bring about equality in all sections of Hindus' Untouchability Act, 1955 was passed. Through this act, the age-old evil of untouchability was done away with. We have almost succeeded.

In Shah Bano Case (1985), Supreme Court had held that a divorced Muslim woman was entitled to maintenance from her husband under Section 125 of the Criminal Procedure Code. But protection of Right on Divorce Act 1986 was enacted in order to appease the Muslim fundamentalists. It is quite clear that political parties are not prepared to annoy the minorities for fear of hurting Muslim factor in their vote bank. Some prominent Sikhs are also in favour of enacting a separate personal law. Of late voice is raised by prominent Sikhs to delink their personal law from that of the Hindus for their community. As the conditions stand today in India, the question of Common Civil Code appears to be dead for all practical purposes.

3. Judicial Reforms

Judicial Reforms in India is a subject that is quite wide ranging in its magnitude and have been pending since long. Judicial Reforms are required for the following components–Speedy disposal of pending cases, Accountability of the judges, Declaration of Judges assets and Procedure of Judges appointment.

Speedy administration of justice is the one aspect that hurts the common man most. In a malfunctioning democracy, judiciary is the last refuge for the redressal of one's problems, "Something is rotten in the State of Denmark." It is as true of India as Hamlet had remarked about his own country. It is horrifying to note that 70% of those in Jails are made up of under trials awaiting justice. It is estimated that approximately 3 crore cases are pending in our courts. As per figures available till 2015 there were 1.94 crore criminal cases pending as opposed to 76 lakh civil cases. Around 5 lakh murder cases form part of the pending criminal court cases. Around 61300 cases were pending in the Supreme Court alone till 2015. The causes for the increase in pending court cases must be addressed fast. The enormity of the job calls for filling in the vacancies, making new appointments, constitution of Fast Track Courts and curtailment of lengthy vacation in the judiciary. The government is determined to reduce the average life of a litigation from 15 to 3 years. Computerisation of court records, quick action at the end of the police and constitution of Rural Courts are the other steps that are proposed for clearing the backlog of pending cases.

The other field that needs immediate remedial measures is the unfair privileges preserved by the judiciary for itself. The Chief Justice of India constantly maintained that his office did not come under transparency law and therefore it was not required to give information like disclosure of a judge's assets. A situation arose when the Delhi

ESSAY WRITING

High Court held that Chief Justice of India is no less accountable than the judicial officers of the Lower Court who are bound by service rules to declare their assets. The High Court stated that the judicial independence of an individual judge was not the personal prerogative of the individual judge. Though most of the judges of the Supreme Court and High Courts declared their assets voluntarily, their declaration of assets, infact, should be governed on a regular basis by a set of service rules because the Chief Justice of India is a public authority and his office is subject to the purview of the Right to Information Act.

Judiciary is one of the three pillars of our democratic structure. But of late the record of the judiciary has not been without blemish. Cases of corruption and scams allegedly involving judges have tarnished the image of judiciary. Judicial Delivery System is getting costly and complicated. As a consequence it is rather difficult for the poor to expect justice.

In view of the unhealthy practices in both lower and higher judiciary, the government has decided to do with the present system of appointment and transfers of judges. Presently, the Collegium decides the transfers and appointments of the judges of the Supreme Court and High Courts. National Judicial Appointment Commission (NJAC), however, was proposed to replace the collegium system for appointment. But a constitutional bench of Supreme Court upheld the collegium system and struck down the NJAC as unconstitutional. The Judges' Standards and Accountability Bill, 2010, seeks to allow common man to file complaint against judges and also provides crucial right to the Government to investigate the complaints against judges.

Judicial Reforms are essential for a civilised society with a view to achieving overall development. The Law Commission submitted a report in August, 2009, wherein it suggested exhaustive reforms so as to take justice to the people and ensure that all people have equal access to justice. There has been acrimonious debate between the Judiciary and the Legislature about their respective primacy. It does not speak well of Indian Democracy. For the common man, it is immaterial who is who. What matters most is that both are vital parts of a democracy. Despite the blemishes in Judiciary, it is still the only oasis in otherwise chaotic state of democracy. The scams relating to Common-wealth Games and 2G Spectrum have been brought to logical conclusion under the supervision of the Supreme Court.

4. Public Interest Litigations—
An Integral Part of Judicial Activism

The concept of Public Interest Litigation (PIL) is in consonance with the objects enshrined in Article 39A of our Constitution namely to protect and deliver prompt social justice with the help of law. Now the courts, under the impulse and motivation of the concept of PIL, are bound to provide access to courts to large number of poor masses. Article 50 of the Constitution stipulates that the state shall endeavour to separate the judiciary from the executive in the public service of the state. It implies that the judiciary should be kept independent of the influence of the executive.

As the things have turned out, Public Interest Litigation has taken upon itself the role of the executive. It goes to the credit of former Chief Justice of India PN Bhagwati (retired in 1986) that the term judicial activism gained currency. It was he who would act on the receipt of post-cards or letters containing complaint from the members of weaker sections. It is how Public Interest Litigation came to stay as a relief to those who could not get justice for years. In his own words, the significance of PIL is well defined, "This was to vindicate the rights of weaker sections because I found that justice was totally denied to them by our legal system." In our country, there are about 3 crore civil cases pending in various courts—2.5 crore cases in lower courts, 50 lakh cases in High courts and 17 thousand cases in the Supreme Court. The poor section of our society is the worst affected."

Judicial activism steps in when the attempts of the aggrieved fails to secure justice from any other source. In fact PIL has been in practice since 1977. The Supreme Court exercised pressure on Government bodies to stop infringement of human rights, investigated the custodial deaths and other related matters.

In recent years, PIL has broadened the sphere of judicial activity. Any one can bring a public grievance direct to the notice of the Supreme Court. The record of the Supreme Court in the field of PIL is very impressive because it has been able to solve a number of problems related to bonded labour, ecology pollution, corruption in high places etc. In a case filed by a lawyer in 1995 Chandra Swami was prohibited from going abroad.

Corruption in the allotment of Govt houses, LPG outlets and petrol pumps were brought to the notice of the Supreme court. As a result of this, 72 VIPs were served notices for eviction. Minister for petroleum was indicted of favouritism and nepotism. Many units in and around Delhi releasing effluents in the Yamuna were ordered closed by the Supreme Court. The DTC buses older more than 8 years were ordered off the roads with a view to checking the menace of pollution.

Thus, the Supreme Court has offered a viable solution in the form of Public Interest Litigation by which any public spirited man or woman can get social justice. The greatest judicial activism recently shown by the Supreme Court in the case of 2G Spectrum, Commonwealth Games, Cash for Vote case in the Parliament and black money is a great service to the nation. But for the intervention of the Supreme Court these mega scams would have rested under the carpet like major Bofors scandles. The case of Hussain Ali of Pune would also have been overlooked. Billions of money of common man having been sent to the drain, the Government was proscrastinating in apprehending the culprits.

The spurt in judicial activism has raised the question how far the court can encroach on the rights of both the executive and the legislature. The judiciary is accused of taking upon itself the role of government. PIL has indeed been degraded by unscrupulous elements for a variety of things.

People are approaching the Supreme Court for violation of human rights in the case of terrorists and criminals. Most of the social activists take to PIL for the sake of their own publicity. In fact, PIL movement started for helping the poor and to vindicate the rights of the weaker section.

However, one thing is certain. Instead of criticising the role of judiciary let the government at the centre and state level show efficiency and solve the problems of the people expeditiously at administrative level. It will not be out of place to state that the active role of the judiciary should awaken the administrative bodies to shed their laxity and casual approach to the problems of the poor and common citizens. They have to shun the attitude of "playing on the fiddle while Rome is burning."

There are no two opinions that the Apex Court has enlarged the scope of Fundamental Rights making them meaningful for the poor masses. It is often said that we are in the era of judicial activism. It is, in fact, an essential part of judicial review because judicial activism helps to advance the cause of law. There are, however, fears in some quarters that the judiciary in overstepping its authority and in the process tresspassing into the spheres reserved for the executive and the legislature.

5. **Electoral Reforms**

Elections are essential part of democracy because democratic form of government is run by elected representatives of the people. Therefore, elections are periodically held to decide which party is favoured by the people. Democracy pre-supposes elections after certain period to avoid rule by one party for a long period.

In fact, the success of democracy requires enlightened electorate. So far we have been complimenting our people for continuing electoral process since the first elections in the country. But the fact is that with massive illiteracy and politically ignorant masses we do not have quality democracy. Elections are fought on caste, community and religious lines. Elections are not over wider issues of corruption, terrorism and economic issues. It is said that even Nehru had to find a safe Muslim dominated constituency for Abul Kalam, our first Education Minister. Today our political leaders win elections by money and muscle power. Crime in its worst form is at full play. In our last general elections in 2014, our democratic process threw up 186 elected MPs with criminal records. Cases against 1/3rd of the winners were registered or pending. About 82% of the MPs were fabulously rich. The politics of communalism and muscle power supported by money is at its ugliest.

Therefore, to make democracy the strength of the people we need reforms. Democracy is hijacked by our leaders and they determine its character. People follow what our leaders in their efforts to retain power propose. There are many laws for fair election process but the problem rises when they come to implementation exercise. First there was the Representation of People Act, 1951 to govern the process of holding just and fair elections. Since then our political thinkers have suggested many reforms through Dinesh Goswami Report in 1990, Inderjit Gupta Committee 1998, Law Commission Report 1999, National Commission to Review working of the Constitution. But their recommendation have gone in vain.

Recently, M Lyngdoh Committee on social electoral reforms suggested a number of reforms. The M Lyngdoh Committee recommended restoration of Section 77 of the People Representative Act and limiting and auditing the expenditure made by a candidate during elections. 50 % of the votes +1 are required to be made compulsory for declaring a candidate successful. A candidate should be debarred from contesting elections until cleared by the court.

Restriction on opinion polls, regulating the internal democratisation of working of the political parties : these are some of the reforms recommended but not implemented. In fact, electoral reforms are the need of the day. The voters will, thus become part and parcel of the entire electoral process and contribute largely to the success of democracy. Realising this need Election Commission has made several proposals for electoral reforms. The commission is for clear provision against surrogate advertisements. The commission has also suggested to include a column in the ballot paper 'None of The Above'. The none of the above (NOTA) has now been introduced by the Election Commission of India. It almost amounts to 'the right to reject'. The most important proposal relates to the publishing and auditing of the accounts of the political parties.

Our election process during the course of time has thrown up many flaws. Bureaucratisation of politics, rewarding the Election Commission by giving them political posts post-retirement, dependence of Election Commission on the centre to a large extent, identity politics, remission of loans, reservation to communities ahead of elections are sessions flaws. Above all, we must take stringent measures to reduce the political parties and make our democracy a two party system. There are a number of leaders strolling on periphery of Indian politics waiting a call by the ruling party to bale it out. In the bargain inquiries against them are either suspended or closed. These leaders are those who have been rejected by the people on criminal, financial or political grounds. A strict law should be passed so as not to allow them to join government at any cost. For the last few years, they are having a field day. The people perceive them to be cheer leaders of corruption, communalism and ugliest part of democracy. The best remedy lies in their retirement. We should fix a tenure for our leaders to give up politics at a certain age. The shortcomings of our electoral system have been virtually institutionalised.

Our Constitution is a sacred document, our democracy is ideal one, our voters cherish a dream of good fair and honest governance. Then where have we gone wrong? Only the wholesome process of elections is the panacea for the ills of our democracy. What about human shortcomings–the ignorance of the people. The poverty, unemployment, illiteracy in the country which made it impossible for democracy to flourish quality democracy. We have just managed to survive as political entity. Inefficiency of our political system has spread disillusionment among the people.

6. Police Reforms

India is still following the Police Act, 1861 enacted just four years after the mutiny of 1857. One can imagine as to what kind of law it would have been then. The Act must have recommended provisions for administrative interference and draconian orders from the above to keep foreign hold over India as strongly as possible. Police is such an indispensable subject as it affects the security of the common man most. The Police Act, 1861 must have intended to impose a police regime. Unfortunately, after independence the political system changed but the police force retained its colonial character.

The need for Police Reforms has long been felt. But no body wants to do any thing about it. The independent India witnessed the enactment of many acts in many states right from 1947. Bombay Police Act, 1951 was passed and then other states followed. Unfortunately, all new Acts have retained the characteristics of the Police Act, 1861. No significant improvement in the performance and the behaviour of the police has been noticed.

The need for revamping the outdated Act has not enthused any well meaning politicians. The arbitrary attitude of the police more than often dictated by their political masters is annoying to a common man. All the pleas for a radical change in the Police Act have fallen on deaf ears since the Police System in the present form suits our political leaders. The National Police Commission, 1981, made comprehensive recommendations to make the police more autonomous and more accountable. Hardly any action worth the name on the reforms has been taken so far.

However, in 2006, the Supreme Court came forward to break a 25 year old deadlock on Police Reforms. With the States and Centre Governments dragging their feet on the issue, the Supreme Court had to intervene and issue comprehensive guidelines to the governments, both the States and the Centre. The Apex Court directed them to give the police functional autonomy and make them more accountable with a view to insulating the police from extraneous pressures. The Supreme Court directed that investigation process be separated from law and order duty. Among other guidelines the Supreme Court advised exercising of transparency in the selection of police chiefs, including Constitution of National Security Commission and upgrading of the service conditions of its personnel.

The fact of the matter is that the Central Government that is in-charge of the police in the capital has failed to set an example to the States. As an escape some state governments have set up their commissions to review the working of the police force. Bihar, Tamil Nadu and Maharashtra are caught in legal imbroglio. Interestingly, smaller states like Arunachal Pradesh, Assam, Manipur, Nagaland, Sikkim, Uttarakhand and Tripura have complied with the judicial directions. Other states have taken half-hearted measures in this direction.

Now afflicted with indigenous and cross border terrorism revamping the police is crucial to our fight against terrorism. Naxalism has to be tackled by the police. Modernisation of police force in the face of crime going hightech is indispensable. Sophisticated weaponry, communication technology and training module has to be of international grade. Without stringent laws to deal with the terrorists and the *Mafia* the police force is fangless. In matters of internal security our country faces an extra-ordinary situation. And extra-ordinary situations need extra-ordinary laws also. Post 26/11 terror is embroiled in the political wisdom of our leaders.

Corruption is a great hurdle in humanising the police force. We need social workers in uniforms. Such an image of the police is cherished by every Indian. But the question is that those who pay to be recruited cannot be expected to be honest with their performance. Policemen need an environment that is conducive to healthy performance. Today, no one will disagree, that police force is dehumanised. Such a mind set kills one's inner voice. Good policing should accord top priority to human values.

Trafficking in children, women, drugs and threats from the road bullies can be dealt with a sense of service to society : Hence, the appeal for both legal and ethical reforms in the police force. The existing system is unacceptable. The nexus between the politicians, bureaucrats and vested interest in the police establishment has to be destroyed as a requisite on the road to reforms.

7. National Language of India

India is a country without a National Language. Article 351 says that it is the duty of the union to promote the spread of Hindi language so that it may serve as a medium of expression for all the elements of the composite culture of India. But nowhere Hindi has been mentioned as the National Language.

Article 343 of the Constitution says that the official language of the Union will be Hindi. Watch out, Hindi is an official not a National Language of India. Hindi as the official language was vehemently opposed by non-Hindi speaking states. The opposition turned violent and English was allowed to serve as official language for 15 years. Later on the act was amended in 1967 to allow continuation of the use of English for official purposes. We have 22 state languages included in schedule VIII of the Constitution. India being a multilingual country, there is no National Language as such. Large states with non-Hindi speaking population proved a destructive hurdle in the spread of Hindi. They heaped contempt and spurned Hindi and treated it as an imposition of the rule from the North over South. In recent years, the prejudice against Hindi has deepened instead of abating.

What an irony! They had no objection against a foreign language. The All India Council for Education in 1956 recommended the adoption of the three language formula. It was adopted as a programme of action by the Parliament in 1992. The lack of political will, opportunistic and divisive kind of politics failed three language formula. The formula, if followed sincerely, would have developed Hindi and helped it to take its rightful place.

Amidst this chaos English has flourished and endured. It is not wrong to say that today it is unofficially the National Language. It is Lingua Franca for success. There is a great demand for English education in India. The poor have taken up the challenge because they know that knowledge of English is a passport to success in the economic and social sphere.

The Census 2011 data are quite revealing. The English speakers in India out number those in Britain. We have more English speakers than twice the UK population. Hindi with 551.4 million speakers tops the list of speakers in any language in India. Data collected by the National University for Education Planning and Administration show that demand for English as a medium of instruction has risen by 150% between 2003 to 2008. So English has stolen march over other languages and become the second largest medium in India's primary schools after Hindi.

There is no escaping the truth that every parent has a longing to send their children to English medium schools. They know that only English can provide access to better jobs. What is more, English is probably the only language which is spoken all over the world and has taken roots in the soil of India.

There is nothing to write against the official regional languages. Rather it is to be pitied that Indian children of every shade and hue are struggling with a foreign language at the grass root level. That we are deprived of our rich culture is quite disappointing. The compulsive need for economic empowerment has led us away from our spiritual urges. Little wonder, our basic needs have driven us to accept a world where English reigns. There is no ambiguity in the statement that "without knowledge of English, progress for a middle class or poor youngmen is a far cry".

However, culturally and spiritually we are losers. Western values have overtaken us and being an Indian in the real sense is no longer a matter of pride. In fact, retention of English language has had adverse effect in that it has taught us to think like a Western. Undoubtedly our contact with English has made us liberal. But it is ironical that our country has not been able to protect its heritage.

India has the richest collection of great works of art and architecture. But inheritance has fallen apart for lack of study of Hindi and Sanskrit. Political factors have denied the status of classical language to Sanskrit. If modern culture has overwhelmed our valuable traditions it is because there is no vehicle to propagate our own traditions.

Today India is engaged in redefining morality regardless of our past values and cultural life. Whenever we try to talk of our past heritage, the secularists term it as the saffronization of India. This is the most perilous and confrontationist attitude of those in power. National Language is the most suitable mode of expression of our cultural heritage. No culture can flourish without a National Language. Past cannot be modified and improved by the present because there is no National Language in India. Our own culture rooted in our traditions is likely to go extinct soon.

8. Corporal Punishment

The law is quite clear on the issue of corporal punishment. On December 1, 2000 the Supreme Court imposed a ban on corporal punishment in schools. Right to Free and Compulsory Education Act, 2009 also declared corporal punishment illegal in schools. Clause 17 of the Act states that no child be subjected to physical punishment and mental harassment in any form.

Apart from legal aspect corporal punishment is not a psychologically corrective measure. There are various acceptable means to inculcate discipline in the young kids. Discipline in life is an indispensable part of a normal personality. A school is a place where the foundation of disciplined life is laid. Children are amenable to the advice. In most of the cases children are anxious to win the favour of their teachers. Only a few children may pose a problem.

First and foremost, a teacher should be equipped to handle the students. It pays to spare a rod, after all. Counselling is the best part of corrective measures. Instead of complaining against the teachers, parents should regularly monitor the behaviour of their children. What is more, there are a number of passive punishments by which kids can be corrected. Unruly children may be banned from participating in games and entertainment programmes for a certain period.

Teacher-Parents meeting can strike at the root of the problem. These meetings should not be treated as monthly rituals. Indiscipline among youngsters is a cause for anxiety. However, school going children in the age-group of 6 to 16 years feel wide ranging influence in the form of television, advertisements, breakdown of joint family system, working parents etc. They need love and care from loving teachers. The mediocre teachers who take up teaching as a career, when all other options are closed, cannot be expected to do their duty well as a teacher.

The government may have imposed ban on corporal punishment but the practice of corporal punishment is still prevailing. The fact is that no action is taken against the erring teachers. Otherwise how else can one account for the reports of ripped ears, damaged eardrums, broken knuckles, bruised organs and sometimes even death? The ultimate truth is that the concept of corporal punishment is deeply rooted in the psyche of Indian teachers.

A slap for a 10th or 12th standard child is not just a slap. Unable to show resentment his confidence is dented. The slander sticks on him like a mud. Corporal punishment is prevalent even in Britain, Canada and many states of America though it has been abolished on paper. It is still believed that the use of corporal punishment leads to immediate compliance. In the 21st century we need to adhere to new technique under which children should be effectively disciplined and should learn in the process. Then there will be no justification for using physical punishment for enforcing discipline in schools.

9. Freedom of Press

The record of freedom of the press in India has been laudable with the exception of emergency era in 1975-1977. Indian Constitution does not specifically mention freedom of the press. But freedom of expression under Article 19(2) has been interpreted by the courts to include freedom of the press. All the same the freedom of press does not mean a licence. It is subject to reasonable restrictions in the interest of the security of the state, friendly relations with foreign states and public order.

Our newspapers are protected against action in the courts for publishing the proceedings of parliament. There are many acts to protect freedom of the press. However, there is no law that restrains the press from publishing information which may be considered as an invasion of the privacy of private citizens. Indian newspapers generally recognise citizens rights to privacy. Then there is the Press Council of India that was established in 1966. It looks after preserving the freedom of the press and raising standards of newspapers, magazines and news agencies by developing a code of conduct. But electronic media does not come under the purview of the Press Council of India.

The government is expected to limit its freedom in due course of time. The press is the fourth estate of any democracy in the world. Free press is a reflection of public opinion and also the plans, policies and programmes of the government. Press is like a barometer. It shows the rise and fall of the fortunes of the ruling class. No doubt free press builds the bridges of understanding between the people and the govt. The press is supposed to expose the misdeeds of the govt. through fearless and impartial expression.

ESSAY WRITING

The press should not play in the hands of a particular political party to reap financial benefits. It is often seen that press has lost its credibility just as judiciary has lost its credibility in the eye of the public. It is charged against the press that they plant stories to destabilise a government at the behest of opposition parties. Even the press is alleged to be playing in the hands of foreign countries. If freedom is the breath of healthy press, a healthy press is the basis of a healthy democracy.

The days are gone when a newspaper would force a corrupt minister to resign overnight. The newspapers of today are willing tools. They join in chorus to defame a person who dare to point at the dishonest dealings of the government. They are no more voice of the people. On most of the national problems they spread misinformation among the people. They seem to conceal more than expose when it comes to the powers that matter. A few newspapers and channels have taken upon themselves to see that the opposition parties should be represented in unfavourable light. Each appears to be the member of some families of the government in power. They never question the apparent motivated investigations of the premier agencies. Electronic media has entered the bed-rooms of the people.

Trial by media is at once a function of an accuser, a prosecuter and a judge. The victim dies a social death long before the decision of the court. The general perception of the people is that the fourth pillar of democracy alone is preventing the government from sagging. Our press is not only free but enjoy licence to write arrogantly, advising the ruling party how to win elections. This is not journalism, enlightened, corrective and informative. Apart from the editorial we read for views of the press, their headlines and bylines exhibit worst kind of prejudiced reports. We do not have illustrious journalists of the past– free, frank and fearless.

Freedom of press should not be considered as a licence to write and say anything against anybody. A free press is supposed to provide free flow of knowledge. Even a free press is supposed to have its code of ethics and conduct. They must not act against the national interests. It is misconstrued that press is omnipotent. It must not indulge in witch-hunting. Instead it should provide free and impartial knowledge and healthy criticism of the activities of the politicians. It must not indulge in yellow journalism and character assassination. The role of Indian press has been praiseworthy and it has done a remarkable job in exposing scams and scandals in defence and other deals.

But the dubious kind of journalism such as *Tehalka* erodes the credibility of the press. With the advent of cable TV and foreign channels citizens must be vigilant to see through the designs of the reporters and the quality of reporting. Just as press needs to be vigilant, the public should also be discriminatory in analysing the truthfulness of the news or otherwise. An enlightened readership is the greatest restraint on misrepresentation of the facts by the information media.

10. Trial by Media

The 'media' is the fourth estate in a democracy. People form the government by handing over their mandate. The media determines the quality of governance and sets the agenda for governance. Media has been rightly described as 'Vox Populi', voice of the people. With internet having been added as an organ of the media, the media has demolished the confines of border lines.

The globalization of media has made the role of media multi-dimensional. Apart from carrying the news to the public, it brings enlightenment to the public too. The enlightened citizenry is the most valuable asset of a democracy. Investigative Journalism and Sting operations are the recent forms of journalism.

Though beneficial, these practices are embroiled in controversy. They are sorts of trial by media. Take Arushi murder case. The media said whatever their investigations revealed on day-to-day basis. Doubt was cast on everyone known to the Talwars. Their sympathisers turned away. The pity is that once an incident involving a person takes place, the media, electronic and print, swing into action. They virtually leave little for the prosecution and the courts. The over enthusiastic media performs the role of prosecution and the judiciary at the same time. It cannot be denied that no one is above law and therefore, mass media should not be allowed to go unchecked. Freedom of speech and expression enshrined in Article 19(1) of the Indian Constitution is restricted by Article 19(2) in the interest of, inter alia sovereignty and integrity of the country.

Apart from restriction of speech the Constitution of India guarantees the fundamental right to privacy under Article 21 of the Constitution. Over-activism of the media is hindrance to a citizen's right to privacy and right to life. There is no doubt that right to privacy is an essential ingredient of personal liberty. In their various observations the courts have drawn the attention of media in the following words "abysmal levels to which the norms of journalism have drifted". In another case they blamed the media interfering with the administration of justice.

One has not to go deep to find out that media has not acquitted itself well while selecting stories for exposure. They might label these stories as authentic reporting in the interest of the viewers but many of them are gimmicks at boosting the viewership of their channel. Media cannot assign to itself the role of judiciary. It must work within the limits of moral and legal frame-work. The media has to eschew sensational stories. Pre-trial publicity should not result in the miscarriage of justice. Media is obliged to respect the rights of a person. To hit a person when he is down and out goes against the doctrine of justice. Half cooked stories flying round may cause life long trauma. Aarushi murder case is an example when distinction between honest journalism and voyeurism got wiped away. Media is the hope of a harried common man. When every right thing has taken political beating, objective, unbiased and ethical reporting can save the media from being sullied. The government is planning to check 'violation of the privacy of individuals'. But in the process it may be an attempt on the part of the government to block investigative journalism.

Therefore the fourth estate must do introspection and act by volunteer self-regulation. The press have virtually gone berserk in many cases where the accused is powerless to retaliate and clarify his/her action. The damage caused to the life and reputation of the accused is irreparable. The victims are blotted out of social life. In the case of irresponsible and reckless reportage the courts can and should protect the rights of the citizens. It is in the fitness of the things that the Supreme Court has suggested that there should be guidelines for the media for the coverage of the news. The media should know how the cases pending investigation should be covered. They should discriminate between what needs to be reported about and what not.

11. Politics of Coalition

When no clear majority appears through elections, coalition governments are formed because another election is not a viable option at all. Government based on a coalition with a larger party is stable and long lived provided the partners hold national interests close to their hearts. In fact coalition politics is a process of democratic accommodation and sharing of power for doing common good. A coalition made before or after elections should be given a chance since frequent elections are deleterious to the developments of the country.

Pluralistic democracy is our great strength but it has thrown up many operational problems. Politics of coalition has undermined our parliamentary system of government. It was fine as long as Congress could monopolise power at the centre and the states but the system began to degenerate from the 70s onwards. Dr Ram Manohar Lohia was the first politician with whom the idea of coalition originated. Enthused by Socialist concerns he put forth the idea of forming a Non-Congress Government. After 1967, coalition governments were formed in many states with a view to averting elections. At the centre the opportunity came as an aftermath of the infamous emergency (1975-77).

In 1977, for the first time there was a coalition government at the centre under the Prime Ministership of Sh. Morarji Desai. Raj Narain, the health minister in the government was lured into toppling Morarji Bhai. Ch. Charan Singh was propelled to the post of the Prime Minister who ironically did not have the opportunity of facing the Parliament. Thus, Raj Narain torpedoed the coalition with the active support of Indira Gandhi who was the chief player in the sad story. Again, Congress was back to power.

The history of coalition government in the states is still worse. Coalition is the most maligned word in Indian democracy despite brilliant performance by the NDA under Sh. Vajpayee and UPA under Dr Manmohan Singh. Nevertheless coalition politics is replete with deceit. India has been through coalition politics for over about two decades. Our wily politicians have perfected the art of political survival, their sole intention is to extract maximum for supporting a government. India witnessed one of the ugliest side of coalition politics over the Nuclear Deal.

All the regional satraps, the likes of Lalu, Karunanidhi, Ramvilas Paswan, Mayawati and Sharad Pawar indulged in every kind of bargaining for every thing. Mulayam Singh Yadav came to the rescue of the Congress when the CPM fell off. There was a chaos. The Coalition reached at its lowest ebb for obtaining majority at all cost. Nothing else could have highlighted better the current Indian Political scene over the Nuclear Deal, the most crucial and controversial issue of the day. Even today we do not know about the views of the small regional political parties in relation to the Indo-American Nuclear Deal. As a matter of fact they had no views at all.

Survival for the rest of the term (6 to 9 months) was the main concern. Sharad Pawar summed up the concern of all small parties. So, deal was passed while keeping the Government in power. To be fair both the CPM and the BJP were clear about their stand. There is no doubt that coalitions in a country like India can provide effective governance. But the sore reality is that the smaller parties have no ideology.

Nor they have the capability to represent the culture and the interests of their states. The coalitions could succeed only if the partners have shared political and policy vision in the context of the national interests.

Coalition Governments in India are run with the help of unprincipled politicians that are conferred with political immortality. Most of them are chargesheeted. But action against them is held in abeyance with a view to settling the scores with their opponents. This kind of Machiavellian Politics gives the impression of a manufactured coalition. To the dismay of Indians, the then Prime Minister Dr Manmohan Singh blamed the compulsion of coalilion for the corruption in the government. In a sum, there is something ominous about the coalition governments in our country.

12. National Integration

India is a land known for unity in diversity. Diversity is there but where is unity? It finds echo only in the speeches of the wily politicians. In fact even such ideals are uttered with an ulterior motive. The seeds of distrust and separatism were laid in 1916 in the Lucknow Pact. The Congress party accepted the principle of separate electorate for Hindus and Muslims. Communalism became victorious resulting in the partition of India. Then there was bitterness among Sikhs and Hindus in 1984. The divisive forces took the ugliest turn in the form of reservation for OBCs in 1993.

Divide and rule is perhaps the best that Indians could learn from their erstwhile masters. Factionalism is the bane of Indian society. Religion, nationality and principles of secularism are expected to generate harmony in society. It is a stark tragedy that these very ideals have been exploited to divide people to perpetuate dynastic rule for over about 65 years.

Integration and promotion of nation building process is not difficult in a homogeneous society. At least religion is not an obstacle. However, there might be divisions in the society on ideological basis. But adoption of common and uniform values becomes difficult for the people belonging to different religions. India represents such a society where fanatic elements of religions are subject to divisive forces. Thus, secularism is thought of from the minority point of view.

Linguistic diversity divides a nation in terms of regional languages. India has no national language of her own. After independence, state organisation was undertaken on the basis of languages. Hindi is not acceptable to southern states. English finds no mention in the VIII Schedule of our Constitution. Yet it is a pity that it has taken the role of our national language.

For genuine national integration, the fruit of economic development should be shared by each and every section of the society. Otherwise the have-nots never think in terms of National unity. Tension and sense of injustice among people is bound to hinder the progress of national integration. Economic development and removal of economic disparities play a vital role in the interest of national integration. Therefore, economic integration will certainly lead to national integration. There must be psychological, emotional, cultural and economic integration among the masses. This implies that people must change their loyalties from petty issues to the nation as a whole. Who lives if India dies?

This kind of awakening is essential. With hostile neighbours on our borders, we must understand that united we stand; divided we fall. As a matter of fact, India was never a nation with common national fabric to unite people. However, a sense of national unity is not entirely inherited. It has to be constantly guarded against and zealously pursued. It is necessary that spirit of unity should be inculcated in the minds of youth through education. Above all, our political leaders should realise that time is running out for the nation. They must think of India, and not of their loaves and fishes. National integration does not mean imposing uniformity or removing differences of identity. Education of the youth on the right lines can bring about national unity based on emotional integration.

To sum up, massive efforts have to be launched at the grass roots level of the society to inculcate importance of national integration in the people. National integrity is possible only if people are aware of national integration. People will have to shun the tendency of asking what their country can do for them. Instead they have to think in terms of knowing what they can do for their country. India is passing through a very difficult phase. Even the greatest sacrifice is too small. Our very survival as a nation is at peril. It is today or never. Anyone striking at the concept of national integration has to be looked upon as an enemy whether he is living in the country or across the borders.

13. Nexus between Politicians and Criminals

There was a time when *mafia* helped the politicians to win elections. Now, for some years the *mafia* want their share in power. Certain political leaders are stalking the government. They come to the help of the ruling party to bale it out inside or outside the Parliament. In 2014 General Election, 186 MPs with criminal record were elected to the Parliament. Over 68 years of independence are mired in corruption. The country needs meaningful change in governance. India ranks near the bottom of the International Corruption Index.

Indian polity is in a sorry state. Politics has become synonymous with unethical practices. Today no party is free from the influence of criminals. Though there were never any doubts that such a nexus existed, the findings of the Vohra Committee have highlighted this nexus. It is not surprising that the Vohra Committee Report was not released by the government for about 2 years. And when it was released it was only in fragments.

The situation has grown so much out of control that the nexus between the criminals and the politicians is not limited only to making money or fighting elections. Now this nexus has crossed national border connections and is giving rise to cross border terrorism. Both Pakistan and America have been able to lure Indian *Mafia*. Through this connection they have been able to trap ministers and politicians to gain access to Indian security forces. The crime-politics nexus has become a national risk. However, in the wake of Bombay bomb blasts in 1993, people have rightly realised the risk that such a nexus poses to the nation. As a matter of fact it is unfortunate that democracy in India has been high-jacked by the criminal elements. The use of money and muscle power in elections is the order of the day.

Eternal vigilance is the price of freedom. On this account Indians have miserably failed. This kind of nexus is helpful to the politicians. But the things took ugly turn when the criminals started demanding their share in the exercise of political powers. Now, the criminals have themselves become politicians. They take the place of pride beside their masters. This is the worst that could happen to Indian democracy. When the criminals become the leaders of a party, the whole society is affected down to the common man. Government agencies investigating the crimes reveal that the criminals are law unto themselves.

How unfortunate it is that the politicians charged and convicted of crimes and sent to jail run the government. from the prisons because they put their favourites as Chief Ministers. Legislatures of all the states, according to a conservative estimate, have anything between one-third and one-fourth of history sheeters as members.

It is tragic that almost all the political parties have collectively rejected the mandate of the Supreme Court regarding the electoral reforms. In accordance with it a candidate for election is required to give the detail of his trials, convictions and financial status at the time of filing the nomination papers. What a hypocrisy on the part of our custodians of democracy?

In any democracy citizens always have the last laugh. Only those leaders should be voted to power as long as they are not tainted and mired in criminality. Indians must realise that it is now or never. In short, criminalisation of politics and politicisation of crime has become all pervasive in the Indian polity. Crime is rewarded and virtue is out of favour. Therefore, the voters should rise to the occasion and throw the criminal elements out of politics.

Crime and corruption are the two ingredients that make up modern politics even at the highest level in our country. While Anna Hazare was on fast in August 2011, the political leaders of every hue and shade showed remarkable unity in meeting the threat by calling Anna's challenge as a threat to democracy. His call for reforms in governance was termed as anti-national and anti-constitutional. Every Indian wishes that the political class showed this rare solidarity in doing away with politics of the kind that crime and corruption fosters.

14. Second (Poorna) Swaraj

India has been a witness to six decades of independence. It is time to pause and introspect whether the aspirations of our forefathers have born any fruit as they had cherished. How have generations born in an independent India braved the problems of young India? We are in the thirteenth decade of freedom struggle as struggle for independence began with the founding of Indian National Congress in 1885.

Poorna Swaraj became the goal of millions of Indians in 1930. Independence for Indians was not a dominion of status on the lines of other British colonies. Our core demand was complete independence that came to fruition in 1947. Sadly, it was a fractured India, India divided into two parts, India for Hindus and Pakistan for Muslims. This division of the country on racial lines has proved very unfortunate for us.

In our own country it gave rise to mythical problems and mythical concepts of India and Indian independence. The dreams of our forefathers have gone sour. We have just managed to survive as a political entity. Our strength has been our Constitution that has given us the frame-work of democracy. In a right spirit we are struggling to sustain our democratic institutions. We have not to look far around us to conclude that we have shamed those who died so that the masses might breath freedom in an equitable system.

In fact power of the people has passed on to the rich and elite class, the sons and daughters of political leaders, and the scions of erstwhile rulers. The democratic dynasts are at the helm of national affairs behaving like Crown princes. Yet we are a democracy. Elections are held regularly. We have fairly honest higher judiciary. Everything is fine on paper.

A simple fact about the last general elections in 2014 is quite revealing. What has a common man to go through in such a kind of democratic system? Our democracy 'by the people' elected 186 MPs with a criminal record. Criminal cases against 1/3rd of the MPs are already registered.

There are about 300 millionaire/billionaires MPs in the present Lok Sabha. Reservation for the Dalits was planned as a unique experiement to nourish a just and equitable system in the country. As a means of vote bank it has proved most potent tool for garnering votes. How the whole community or a caste or a class can be poor is not understandable. The benefit does not filter to the lowest rung of that society. A new class known as creamy layer is a common phenomenon.

There is a sharp communal and casteist divide in the country alongwith 20.6 per cent number of poor persons. It is on the basis of ₹ 32 a day expenditure by a poor person. If we take the international standard of measuring poverty ($2 a day) the number of the poor might go upto 74%. India is still ranked 130th among 188 countries in terms of poverty (UNDP report).

The fruits of development have been siphoned off by the political system and bureaucracy working hand in hand with criminals. The kind of growth in terms of GDP has not done equitable favour to the most deserving. On the social front the laws made have been ineffective because of mammoth corruption in the country. The spoils of freedom are still being distributed among those who are partners in the brazen dealings of kickbacks, bribes, laundering of money and foreign banks. Complete education is still a dream and quality education for the poor is nearly an impossible goal.

On the strength of GDP figures our elite class, Media and vested politicians have spread the notion that India is on the threshold of becoming a super power. On the contrary we are hardly on the way to becoming a power worth the name. We need a second independence on the way to social, economic and national *Swaraj*. *Political Swaraj* was won in 1947 but the fruits of independence have been cornered by a neglegible minority. Until we get rid of the yoke of *'Desi'* imperialism to bring about an equitable system, our cherished goal for *Poorna Swaraj* will remain unrealised.

15. Corruption in Public Life

Independence ushered in an era of development in the history of our nation. Large dams, steel plants, multipurpose projects and large scale public sector undertakings came into being. As a result huge funds were needed. Huge amount of money fell into the hands of politicians, their henchmen and middle men. This created countless opportunities for corruption. But a common man in the street did not know what was happening in the corridors of power.

Contracts and licences were sanctioned to the relatives, friends and those close to the ruling party. The dream of freedom had started turning sour when politicians shunned morality in public life. In fact value based politics was given a good bye. The bureaucracy joined in merry making and minted money at their will. Those who were willing to do the bidding of the politicians grew richer. Prime lands in the Capital were allotted to them. In fact the looting and plundering started the day India won freedom. The so called freedom fighters turned into vultures living on the flesh of poor men.

When the attention of the first Prime Minister Sh. J.L. Nehru was drawn to the misdeeds of the politicians and bureaucrats, he brushed aside the patent fact. He had just to say, that corruption was a worldwide phenomenon. What a pity! A nation at birth was mired in the muddy waters of corruption.

Apart from these political and economic changes, even the changed social values also contributed to the rampant corruption in the country. Lure for money, status and achievement of ends at every cost are some of the factors responsible for spreading corruption. The worst kind of corruption has been in the form of scandals and defence scams. It is the most shameful aspect of our national character. Bofors scandal still remains unsolved.

Narcissim of the political class is to be wondered at. In 2014, general elections our people elected 186 MPs with criminal records. Mega scandals such as Satyam, Wolker Commission, Bofors, 2G, Common-wealth Games scandals, stashing away of black money in tax havens are the few scams that would have toppled many a government and sent a number of leaders to jails in any other country. No wonder then, India ranks near the bottom of International Corruption Index.

In fact corruption is a multifaceted problem giving rise to numerous social, economic, political and moral crises in the society. Today politics is a lucrative career. Individuals take to politics as a profitable career to secure easy money. However, politics without ethics is a disaster. Today's leaders are hypocrites and have betrayed the country and the people. Immorality in politics has become so pervasive that a common man has no social security, medical facilities, efficient public transport system and freedom from exploitation. Can this situation be rectified?

Over 68 years of independence are mired in corruption, scams, scandals and stashing away of national income in foreign tax havens. Now, at least leaders should understand the mood of the public. The country needs meaningful change in governance. Anna Hazare has come to symbolise the voice of the people. The crowds all over the country were on the roads to protest against corruption following the clarion call given by the social activist Anna Hazare.

While Anna Hazare was on fast in August 2011, the political leaders of every hue and shade showed remarkable unity in meeting his threat by calling Anna's challenge to Parliament as a threat to democracy. His call for reforms was termed anti-national and anti-constitutional. Now, that the Anna Movement has lit the spark for strong authority over the politicians, it is for the people to arouse themselves in support of a strongJ *Jan Lok Pal* Bill. The public servants (a name given to the politicians by Mahatma Gandhi) should rise above personal ambitions and serve the people in the spirit of social service.

Where does the solution lie? Just as a country gets the government it deserves, similarly every country gets the leaders it deserves. After all the leaders are a part of our own society. Therefore, silence and indifference of the people would silently encourage corruption. People should rise to the occasion and demand a probe into the politician's financial transactions that have made them billionaires. The system cannot be cleansed by half hearted means. Each political party, leader, bureaucrat and businessman should be forced to give account of their financial status. Those found guilty should be legally punished and voted out of power. Let public should be the arbiter of the destiny of the people.

It is ostensible that no political leader is willing to show political will to bring the investigations to a logical end. They can talk and indulge in breast beating but not expose the facts of corruption. The fact deserves the attention of the people as to how all the political parties got united in objecting to the verdict of the Supreme Court. They objected to filing the detail of their assets, sources of incomes and their criminal records at the time of filing nominations. Worse, Judiciary itself is in collusion with corrupt politicians and bureaucrats. Criminals in public life are ruling the roost. In present circumstance no light is visible at the end of the tunnel.

16. **Right to Information** (RTI)

Right to Information is a part of our Fundamental Rights to the freedom of speech and expression as well as right to life and personal liberty. They are secured in our Constitution in the Articles 19 (1) (g) and 21 respectively. The Fundamental Right to freedom of speech and expression is meaningless unless we have right to information. The right to information will provide us information to express and form our opinions on the subjects.

Right to Information Act was passed on 15th June, 2005 and came into force on 13th October, 2005. It is expected to usher in a new era in the process of governance and performance in the corruption ridden Indian Polity. It has the widest reach covering Central and State Governments, *Panchayati Raj* Institutions, Local Bodies and Government funded NGOs. Even the Judiciary has been put under the purview of this Act. On these lines state information commissions have been set up at Central and State levels. The RTI Act, 2005 seeks to override the Official Secrets Act 1923 and replace the old Freedom of Information Act. This Act provides 30 days deadline for providing information. However, the deadline is 48 hours, if information concerns life and liberty of a person. All the citizens are entitled to any kind of information.

The procedure for securing information has been clearly laid down. First appeal has to be made to the superior of Public Information Officer referred as Appellate Authority. In case the information is not forthcoming, one can appeal to the Information Commission. To make the RTI Act effective penalty for delay in providing information without reasonable cause shall be ₹ 250 for each day up to the maximum of ₹ 25000. Thus, the most important feature of the RTI is the independent appeal mechanism.

The RTI Act provides for access to extensive information with minimum exemptions. There is no denying the fact that the benefits of growth would flow to all sections, eliminate corruption and improve the much needed quality of governance. It is hoped that the concerns of the common man will be addressed by the government in a fair and just manner. Thus, the access to information would strengthen Indian democracy. The Right to Information Act is really going to change the way of governance. However, every thing is not rosy about RTI. A survey was conducted by RTI Assessment and Analysis Group and National Campaign for People's Right to Information. Few would dispute that the RTI Act is one of the most people friendly legislations. But road to accessing information remains difficult. 40% of rural Information seekers complain of harassment. Over 30% of Public Information Officers admitted that they did not know the Act's provisions.

Any attempt to dilute the act might send a wrong signal. The government seems to have made their intention clear to amend the RTI Act. They have already mooted amendments to exclude file notings from disclosure and maintain anonymity for officials. The agitation led by social activist Anna Hazare and present Information Commissioner might deter the government from diluting the Act. There is already a long list of exemptions attached with RTI Act.

It is a matter of great concern that in June 2011 Government has excluded Central Bureau of Investigation from the purview of the RTI Act. It is crystal clear that Government does not want to lose hold over the premier investigating agency. The CBI is already a much maligned agency working under the control of the politicians. This step of the government is quite a serious set back to its often repeated determination to wage war against corruption. It does not speak well for the future of democracy. In fact, RTI Act 2005 is a major step forward towards openness and transparency in governance. Democracy requires an informed citizenry because only an enlightened citizen can make a force that democracy is. It is expected to go a long way in changing the substance and quality of our democracy.

17. Why not Elected Governors?

Of late there have been glaring instances on the part of governors to interfere in the affairs of the elected State Governments. The reason is that they work at the behest of the government at the centre. The machinery of government in the state closely resembles that of the Union. The Governors in the states are the nominal head of the administration in the same way as the President in the Union is. The Constitution lays down that the executive authority in a state will be vested in the Governor and he will be appointed by the President of the Union.

The post of a governor is an integral part of quasi-federal polity. Various anomalies and controversies have come to surround this office of considerable dignity. As soon as there is a change of government at the Centre the existing Governors are the first to go since they hold office during the pleasure of the President. It happens particularly in the case of states run by the parties opposed to the party at the Centre. In the name of break down of constitutional machinery the Central Government imposes President Rule on the report submitted by the Governor under Article 356. Such removals are opposed to the federal structure of our Constitution. Ironically there is no provision for impeaching a Governor. Governors fail and falter only when they use their discretion because it is not their discretion but the obedience to the will of the Centre.

Till 1967, when a single party ruled at the Centre as well as in most states, Governer's role seldom stirred controversies. There were much less litigations. Since 1970, specially after the birth of Coalition Politics the scenario has changed drastically. "Who should be invited to form government and which Chief Minister is to be dethroned, which bill is to be stalled or not"—such material issues are thrashed out in Delhi. And Governors are required to carry out the agenda of the Centre using their own discretion. Discretion is a much abused word in dubious dealings.

Supreme Court, on various occasions, has made adverse comments on the style of their working. Their duties, powers and the style of working do not strengthen the democratic norms. Choosing and dismissing democratically elected Chief Ministers and dissolving the assembly by a person who is the only de jure head is senseless. The Governor also enjoys powers to deny assent to the bills passed by the elected representatives of the people. This power is undoubtedly illegitimate in the context of democratic norms.

Strangely, the people of the state have no voice in the process of his appointment, though he is the head of the executive and the legislature of the state. In fact, the appointment of a Governor is a mere rehabilitation exercise for ageing politicians who are either not willing to retire or have been rejected by the people in the elections. They are appointed and used as a source of settling disputes within the party. Retired bureaucrats are rewarded for their services rendered. That is why our former president APJ Abdul Kalam stated in 2006, "The office of the Governor has been bestowed with the independence to rise above the day today politics and override the compulsions emanating either from central system or the state system."

These sinecure posts involving crores of money to maintain the white elephants in palatial buildings have to be dispensed with in the present form. They date back to the colonial rule. Presently we need an elected de jure head of the state with provisions for his impeachment by the State Assembly. It may take time. Meanwhile a collegium consisting of State and Centre politicians as well as intellectuals should be formed to regulate the appointment of the Governors. However, the goal of having elected Governors should not be lost sight of.

18. Political Gerontocracy
(Retirement of Politicians)

Is there anyone happy with the present day politics? Answer is 'No'. For everyone is sick of the style of political functioning in the country. The majority of the politicians are out to squeeze maximum out of the system prevailing in the country. That is why those who have tasted power once are reluctant to give it up. The system allows them to remain in power as long as they can manage.

The very leaders who struggled for freedom have not acquitted themselves honestly. Even within a year or so the struggle for loaves and fishes by the then leadership started. The problem with our political system is unique. When we talk of youth leadership the scions of old political leaders, earstwhile kings and industrialists are waiting on the bench. Our democracy has created political families like corporate houses.

There are certain classes of politicians who know that they are indispensable to India's political system. Nexus between criminals and politicians have made politics a haven for so-called veterans. That is why pot bellied politicians are ubiquitous in the Indian political system. With no restraint on their age they are endless part of the system. None of the present politicians would like to forgo the power that comes with a sense of supremacy. When a politician has ruled for years he becomes a power addict. "Power tends to corrupt and absolute power corrupts absolutely."

For having walked for years in the corridors of power they learn to make politics a family profession. Today our leaders are in power for years and enjoy the patronage of powerful political families. How can we make two or three terms binding on a legislator while they nurse life long dream from the cradle to reach the top most political post in the country?

The US Constitution provides that no president can run for more than two terms. In India, our Governors and even Presidents do not mind serving as ministers. The lure of power is so great. We have adopted British Parliamentary System but hardly any healthy practice has found way in our political system. Even the most corrupt politicians have certain responsibilities to keep the ruling party glued to their chairs. The active political careers of American Presidents such as Reagan, Bush, Clinton ended before they were sixty. But our politicians are jugglers, they can surface whenever the nation needs 'their services'.

Today our politicians enter the corridors of power for the sake of power. Thanks to the Supreme Court that now we have a bit of transparency in the matter of their assets. The top most politicians travelling in helicopters do not have cars of their own. Are they epitome of Gandhian Philosophy?

We have miserably failed in nursing genuine talent for national leadership. Hoodlums ruling the roost from behind the bars shame us no more. *Lalu Rabri* syndrome is a great political jugglery of our times. The creation of extra constitutional posts in a democracy is undesirable and derogatory to the norms of democracy. Such tactics are a threat to a democracy and smacks of autocratic attitude.

Change is the only alternative to cleanse the cesspool of Indian politics. If the trial of the tainted politicians is precise and fast, no politician would dare have longer innings. Bureaucrats begin their political innings after they have retired. That is their time for being rewarded for the services they have rendered to their masters. Even retired election commissioners and chiefs of the investigating agencies reap profits by joining active politics. The result is that most of our politicians are past the age of retirement. In fact we need an amendment to our Constitution to limit the terms and age of a politician. Else politics will degenerate into a mercenary profession. Senior politicians need to act as a sane voice while the younger generation makes decisions.

19. Religion and Politics

There is no doubt that in the making of our present civilisation religion has contributed a lot more than any other institution. Yet it is an irony that more blood has been shed in the name of religion and more people have lost their lives in communal riots than in all the epidemics or other natural calamities that have struck mankind. What a pity that our politicians and fundamentalists have destroyed the true spirit of religion.

Religion is a personal affair that has nothing to do with public matters including politics. Religion is a force that teaches man the norms of humanity, tolerance and spirit of charity. On the other hand politics is a means to achieve wordly power. But the prevailing political culture has polluted the social and moral standards of politicians. They use religion as a potent weapon to rouse and inflame the religious passions of the people to achieve their political ends.

After independence, India adopted a secular form of polity. We have specifically provided for religious freedom to all religions to propagate their religions. Right to freedom of religion is one of our Fundamental Rights enshrined in Articles 25, 26, 27 and 28 of our Constitution. Then where have we gone wrong that today every religion in India is politicised? In this context the Indian polity presented a very dismal picture from the very beginning while our leaders professed delinking of religion from politics, they created the bogey of majority ruling over the minority. In this clandestine manner they continued to keep their hold on the Muslim vote bank. It is historically true that Nehru was in search of a safe constituency dominated by Muslims for Maulana Abul Kalam Azad. The haven for him was found in Rampur (UP).

However, Indian politics has suffered in the process. Today political atmosphere is charged with communal divide. It is not out of place to mention that the communal divide has become so alarming in the country that the integrity and the unity of the country is at peril. The nation is often caught in communal conflagrations and killings and burning of properties. During communal riots the people of different religions are converted into a blood thirsty mob.

As a matter of fact the country was divided on communal lines right in the year 1909 when Minto-Morley reforms were introduced. The Muslims were granted separate electorate. Two nation theory propagated by the Muslims was obviously welcome to the English. Again the country was partitioned on communal lines. Then how can one expect that the Indian politics will remain free from religion. The political conditions in J&K have further aggravated communal tension in the country.

The atmosphere in the country is already charged with religious tension. Religion and politics relationship poses no threat to country's polity as long as politicians do not misuse religion for their political ends. The problem of communalism is peculiar to India because of parliamentary form of govt. How is it possible to delink religion and politics particularly in a country like India?

"Religion is my heart and soul above my economic activities. What do we mean mixing religion and politics" said Gandhiji. Gandhiji was a secularist but a staunch Hindu. Nobody objected to his being a Hindu because he loved man, not his religion. What about our modern politicians? The root cause of what ails our country lies with politicians.

Media is equally responsible when it sensationalises the news relating to discord between religions communities. Deaths, rapes or any other irreligious act is identified by the name of caste and religion. Communal harmony among the people means the banishment of wily politicians. India needs a sagacious leader at the top who should bring about healing to festering sores of Indian society. Opportunistic politicians which are unscrupulous in the matter of money and human lives must be dealt with a final blow. Religion and politics are a fatal cocktails that go to the heart of those who practise this heady combination.

20. Presidential System of Government in India

We need to have a kind of government whose leaders can focus on governance rather than on staying in power. As the things stand today elections are not bound to throw up a single party majority to form a government. Coalitions at the centre and states are inevitable. Election of a Prime Minister lies in the hands of king-makers who will leave no stone unturned to have a Prime Minister of their choice. People who voted them to power are conveniently forgotten.

Pluralist democracy is our strength but the way it is operated is a matter of serious concern. The system has given rise to the bane of defections and king-makers who can exist and flourish only in a system working in India. A party with just one or two members can shake the Parliament. The debacle over Indo-American Nuclear Deal sank our political system to an abysmally low level. The government, the parties forming the coalition and opposition were found wanting in the principles of governance. A small party can hamstring the policies of the government. Here elections are not fought for policies but for individuals.

The Parliamentary System in India has outlived its utility. What's more, it has retarded the growth of healthy political practices. Yet our politicians are not prepared to discredit it. Democracy is our strength but in the process it has unleashed the forces of communalism, casteism, regionalism and worst form of corruption in public life. We need another kind of democracy i.e. presidential form of government in the interest of the country. The question is whether with a number of political parties, presidential form of government would succeed?

If there has been mushrooming of parties in Parliamentary System, Presidential System would see them merging with larger parties for survival. We have an American model with well organised two party system. There is a French model combining Presidential Rule with a Parliamentary Government with a Prime Minister. However, the President enjoys power over the Council of Ministers.

The primary benefit of a directly elected chief executive will be that he is a national figure. Against this the Prime Minister is a figure propelled by a handful of king-makers. We will be no more defined by narrow identities of caste. He will represent India, stand for India and never be influenced by dynastic or regional preferences. Under our present Parliamentary System we are defined by parochial identities and regional interests.

Anyone aspiring to be the President of India will have to win the support of people beyond his home state. He will have to represent 125 billion people across the length and the breadth of the country. He will be the idol of the nation. We have had Prime Minister representing a party or a coalition of parties. He is propelled to the post of the Prime Minister by king-makers with extra-constitutional authority.

Our parliamentarians have got accustomed to the existing kind of democracy. But Presidential System will emphasise governance and voters will elect directly the head of the State. The most of the sinecure and decorative posts resembling colonial days would have to be done away with. There are people who say that if our public had been educated, Indian democracy would not have survived so long. Illiteracy, ignorance and poverty have come as a boon for our politicians.

The second factor responsible for vote bank democracy is obviously reservation which is a very powerful tool. The privileged among the *Dalits* and the Other Backward Classes have taken charge of reservation. Then there is a minority quota based on religion not approved by our Constitution.

The third factor responsible for vote bank is the dynastic politics. The son of a Prime Minister should be a Prime Minister and a Minister's son should be a Minister. Again in Presidential System we will not have a situation where 24 political parties are sharing a coalition government at the centre. Such type of opportunism will not surely affect governance.

On the other side directly elected chief at the centre could work freely unhampered by the gimmics of the foxy politicians. He will appoint his own cabinet and is answerable directly to the people. At the next elections his performance will be put under scanner. Parliamentary System was opted for because of the pluralism inherent in our society. But we had not asked for this kind of governance which this system has thrown up.

What's more, Presidential System would not require to fit in itself the foxy old politicians hunting on the periphery of Indian Political System. They come to the help of the government whenever a particular brand is needed. "You help me and I will help you" is a kind of incremental politics played by our elected members of Parliament. We are hapless onlookers. Presidential System would at least do away with opportunistic politics because the President is answerable to the people.

21. Transparency in Administration

The UN declaration on Human Rights maintains that freedom of information and transparency in public functioning is an important Fundamental Right. India is one of the signatories to this declaration. Our government is therefore, morally committed to ensure transparent, responsive and accountable administration. Democracy means meaningful participation of people in the administration of the state. Such meaningful participation comes from transparency in the functioning of the government from *Panchyat* to the Prime Minister's office.

Corruption and inefficiency are bred in dark places. All over the world the need for openness and access to information is considered vital for the welfare of the people. Government in sunshine is preferable to the shady affairs in the name of security and safety. In the wake of Right to Information, bureaucrats are getting uneasy about the openness of 'file notings' to public scrutiny. In protest, social activist Anna Hazare had threatened to return his *Padma Bhushan*. The irony of the Indian system of governance is that we have democratic form of government but the participation of common man is at the lowest. Democratic institutions, public departments, government run hospitals, the police and the judiciary are in the service of the rich and the politically powerful people. Media can play a major role by making the common man aware of his rights and exposing the misuse of facilities by the rich and the people in power.

There is hardly objective coverage of news relating to the functioning of the government. The only effective means of information the Right to Information Act. The preamble to the RTI Act passed on 15th June, 2005 emphasises the significance of transparency of information. Transparency is vital to the successful functioning of the RTI Act that may in turn hold government and their instrumentalities accountable to the governed.

It is, therefore, imperative to have transparency in administration for a responsive and accountable governance. Transparency helps the citizens to perform their duties in an enlightened manner. Democracy can work well only when the citizens are well informed. We can eradicate corruption only when we are well informed about the scams to the tune of millions and billions of rupees. Governments cannot escape by sweeping these scams under the carpet. We need to know the truth about fodder scam in Bihar, Volcker Commission's food for oil, Jay corridors police recruitment scams, Bofors, truth about Quattrochei's acquittal, court bonds scam of Telgi, Satyam scam, Buta Singh bribery case and Madhu Koda.

All these and more scams are taxing the common man's minds. Appointments of justices, heads of investigating agencies, judges of inquiry of commissions need to be an open book so that when they say something, people would believe it. Scams involving crores of rupees relating to the Commonwealth Games and 2G would have toppled any other democratic government in the world. Serving governments have their own henchmen to serve on commissions relating to communal riots, corruption and conversions. The citizens are helpless before the might of the powers that be. Tax payers have right to know where their money goes.

Once the governing bodies are held accountable, they are bound to desist from dishonest practices. At the very heart of good governance lies transparency. The enlightened citizenery is capable of electing responsible and clean leaders. Only such a process can cleanse our democracy of the cobwebs of corruption and opportunism.

22. Secularism in India—A Myth

Secularism is defined as something concerned with the affairs of this world. It is opposed to any kind of theocratic culture. As a secular state, therefore, no religion in India has been given the status of state religion unlike in Pakistan and other theocratic states. Indian Constitution has ensured freedom of religion to an individual under the provisions of Articles 25-30. To make matters more emphatic, the word 'secular' was incorporated in the preamble to the Constitution by way of the 42nd Constitutional Amendment of 1976. It is obvious to every right thinking citizens of India that the co-existence of various religions in India is the core of Indian polity. 'Sarva Dharma Sama Bhava' concept has guided the founding fathers of Indian Constitution.

Indian society is basically a religious one. The partition of India was also based on religious divisions resting on two nation theory. The then Indian leaders did not accept the two nation theory concept. As a result of this the Muslims were allowed to stay in India while all the Hindus in Pakistan were made to leave their hearths and homes. Therefore, the controversy about the secularism in India has its roots in the nature of its society. Now the question arises as to why secularism has not been accepted by various religious leaders. As the matter stands today, secularism has not caught the roots and flowered as a healthy way of social and political life. For the last over 68 years no political party seems to have taken unselfish and national view of secularism. Today it is not difficult to describe secularism in India as a cult of minorityism. Each and every political party has tried to create its vote bank in the name of secularism by supporting the minorities in India.

For them secularism has always served as sheer political expediency. They have not allowed healthy growth of secularism in the country. Minorities have never been allowed to merge with the main stream of nationalism. *Dalit* class and minorities have been the main stay of one single party for about half a century. Then in 1984, the brave race of the Sikhs were alienated. It is unwise to blame the majority community for the failure of true secularism in the country. In fact it is a lust for power on the part of every political leader that has lead to the tragic failure of genuine secularism.

Secularism is a very noble ideal enshrined in our Constitution. In recent years certain section of media and government have turned Hindu baiters. *Hindutva* is condemned in derisive terms with an intent to garner votes of other communities. So called liberal voices have, in fact, set in degenerating forces in society. *Bharatmata* and *Vande Mataram* are the symbols of saffronisation. Denigrating the majority, the main stay of Indian society has become of second habit with English bred intellectuals and left parties to please the powers that be.

Secularism could have flowered in Indian soil only by integrating the minority in the national mainstream allowing their religion, culture and ways of social life to prosper. It is unfortunate indeed that secularism is compromised in Indian society.

How ridiculous and non-secular it is that Hindu and Muslim women are governed by two different sets of laws in divorce matters? Even the concept of minority and allowing it to have certain privileges goes against the true character of secularism.

The problem is that the followers of secularism, the politicians and the media are themseleves the invisible violators of secularism. For short-term gains they have invested the minorities with the colour of victimhood. They look at secularism from the point of minorities. Threats to secularism in India originate from a lot of factors. Politics of vote is practised by all and one. Those who profess to be secular exercise subtly the politics of vote bank. No political party thinks in terms of Indianism. The role of caste and religion, a perpetual bane of Indian society, is sharpened and has come into open. India is a multi-racial and multi-religious society. Confrontation among religions and castes is often practised by national and regional parties. The state must deal with individuals as citizens and not as a member of a religious group or community. Their writings are definitely not inspired by some noble purpose. What is being practised, written and preached should be analysed to see through their diversionery gimmicks and arrive at a sober, meaningful and ideal concept of secularism acceptable to all with a view to living up to the dreams of Gandhiji, not a pseudo-secularist in the garb of motivated politicians.

It is high time that the Indian leaders thought about the matter seriously. There is no doubt that we can uphold the image of a united India only when Indians are allowed to think of themselves as Indians first and Indians last. Religion is a matter of private faith, not to be displayed in the streets. It is also time we realised that socio-economic development should be the goal of the political parties to make India a great power.

23. The Politics of Communalism

There is no denying the truth that communalism fostered and grew up with the advent of the British Rule in India. Before Britishers came to India the minority had the genes to subjugate. The majority were divided on the norms of caste, subcaste, regionalism and most of all the neglect of 'the Dalits'. There was no collective rising against the Moghuls. It is not a place to deal with distorted history being written round. But it is true that communalism as a trait of Indian politics manifested during the British Rule. It definitely sharpened even when Indian leaders were waging struggle for freedom. Communal riots became a kind of ritual from that time on. With Britishers as umpires both the sides could indulge in arson and destruction.

When freedom came, the freedom was given on a platter of two nation theory. The two nation theory prevailed with the Britishers and they left India partitioned. They had to because the second world war was the last nail in the coffin of the British imperialism. The rest is modern history.

Had Mahatma Gandhi continued to live long enough during Independence era he might have guided us securely on the road to secularism. His was a disinterested concept of secular India. Unfortunately he was gunned down by a mindless person. If alive, he would not have allowed ideal concept of secularism to be used as a tool of political ascendency.

It is a pity that even after 68 years of Independence communal forces are still on the rampage. There are various factors that have kept on fanning religious frenzy of one community against the other. The discerning analysts have come to the conclusion that all parties practise communalism. Their hues may differ but hands of all are dyed in the shades of communalism. They patronise one or the other community by looking upon them as a promising vote bank. We win or lose elections on the two pillars of our democracy: Reservation and Communalism including Casteism. These forces come into play as ruthlessly as they could during elections. The element of fundamentalism is kept alive by the political parties. For short term gains they lose sight of United India.

The politics of Communalism has given rise to serious problems of internal security of the country. In 2004, the Home Minister declared that by 2001 one crore twenty lakh Bangladeshis had intruded into India. One can easily imagine the horrible state of affairs in 2010 since the intrusion has been continuing uninterrupted. These intruders are working as king-makers in many states and cities besides fomenting communal tension in the wake of change in the balance of population. Our fight against terrorism is hampered but our government and political parties have different concept of unity and integrity of the nation. Religious conversions of the poor tribals by missionaries and opposition by other religions is a matter of great concern. The phenomena of conversions, as all of us know, has generated heat among the people of the area. Conversions have to be stopped because communal peace and conversions cannot exist.

Communalism is regarded as an inevitable product of plurality of religions, cultures and traditions. Enlightened communalism is the part of a thinking that the various interests of various communities are opposed to those of others. The sum and substance of the politics is that India has had a communal past, the major religious communities being ever in conflict. There is no dearth of well meaning citizens in the country. But the political parties in search of power would not spare any means to gain political ascendancy. Post independence period should have brought happier days for our nation. Instead, politics has played havoc with the future of our country. It has, undoubtedly sharpened the contours of confrontation and social prejudices. Pseudo secularists are having a field day because it does not pay to be an open communalist. Hidden hand of communalism is keeping some safe in power. Communalism is at the roots of divide and rule.

People will have to wait for another Mahatma, a disinterested secularist.

24. **Middle-East**—A Zone of Turbulence

Middle-East is an area comprising the countries of Asia and Africa. There are 2 definitions of middle-East: traditional middle-East and the modern middle-East. The traditional middle-East comprises of 16 countries: Saudi Arabia, Bahrain, Qatar, UAE, Oman, Yemen, Iraq, Iran, Kuwait, Egypt, Turkey, Israel, Lebanon, Cyprus, Syria, Jordan. Middle-East with the modern classification includes: traditional middle-East plus Morocco, Algeria, Libya, Tunisia, Mauritania. These are the North African Arab states, sometimes also referred as the MENA (Middle-East North Africa) countries.

The following countries are not recognised as Arab States: Israel, Turkey and Iran. Middle-East since mid-1940s has been involved in wars, civil strife, in recent time Islamic fundamentalism and terrorism. The turbulence middle-East can be attributed to various factors : Arab Spring; crude oil interest of West and US in particular; strategic interest of the region and the associated geopolitics; proximity of Russia and the spread of communism by erstwhile Soviet State; on destruction of Israel the entire middle-East stands united; on the issue of terrorism, there are explicit and implicit support and opposition to various warring and violent groups. All these issues can be analysed with their historical perspective and the current scenario in the region.

Arab Spring started in 2011. The first nation which started the Domino effect was Tunisia, where due to an authoritarian regime, the subjects rose in protest. Instances of self-immolation underlined how deep the discontent was. It eventually spread like a wildfire in the region. The Syrian Civil War which has lingered for over 5 years was as a result of the same. Arab Spring was a call for granting proportionate rights to the common public and remove the highhandedness of the state authorities. It toppled many governments including those in Egypt, Libya, Yemen etc. The most prolonged war which is still continuing has been in Syria. Syria has been under the rule of Bassar Al-Assad a Baathist. The Baath regime in the area has been for a long time, Iraq under Saddam Husain was also under Baath party.

The support to Baath regime comes from the Shia block and Iran in particular. As the West has tacit support for the Sunni block led by Saudi, therefore it was a natural choice for Russia to support Shia block. This balancing of power by the 2 world powers has resulted in a war which has stretched for a long time. Moreover, US had bloodied its nose after Iraq and Iran misadventure. Therefore, it mended its modalities and did not commit any ground troops. However, because of innumerable splinter groups in the region with diverse interests it was difficult to stop the war. Meanwhile, IS also entered the scene and degraded the situation beyond repair.

The swift entry and exit by Russia resurrected the position of Assad regime and gave them an edge over IS and rebel groups. Recapture of Palymyra by Assad army is a case in point here. Arab Spring gave a glimmer of hope, but it did more harm than good. It embroiled the entire region in an unending war. Loss of life and property was incessant and has harmed the region beyond repair.

The area of middle-East is a vast repository of crude oil and natural gas. The deposit in this area is a result of marine-transgression towards the land and consequent inundation of the land for a very long period, geologically speaking. In the 20th century, due to the two world wars the economies of the world were shattered to ground. In order to resurrect these economies there was need for fast paced growth of economy, manufacturing sector in particular.

This growth required energy source. During the same time, crude oil deposits were discovered in this area. Subsequent world powers were interested in this area from UK to USA to USSR. Moreover, the Cold War escalated the situation as both the blocks led by USA and USSR scrambled for taking the region under their own military blocks. Joining of NAM by Iran vindicates the above point. However, the centre-stage was always hogged by the greed of crude oil.

Organisation of Petroleum Exporting Countries (OPEC) was established in 1960, to coordinate and unify petroleum policy regarding its production, price stabilisation, regular and efficient supply to its consumers and to appropriate fair return on capital investment. OPEC is led by Saudi Arabia as it is the largest producer. In the recent times, we have seen the crude oil price plummet to almost $ 40 USD per barrel. Despite this, the production by Saudi was not cut down, notwithstanding the daily limit prescribed by OPEC. The 2 Gulf wars in the past were responsible for the rising crude oil price at that time. But, in spite of the fact that the region has been embroiled in war for almost 5 years, the prices have remained stable. The main reasons for this are: the increase in production by USA and the production of shale gas by fracking. US has therefore less interest in the region now and is therefore, trying to get itself dissociated with the region.

The region is very strategically placed on the world map. The associated geopolitics of the region has made this a volatile ground. This has resulted in nations other than middle-East moving its naval infrastructure in the area. Also, the movement of oil tankers required security and protection from pirates and other violent groups. The Persian Gulf (Strait of Hormuz) has a very strategic position in the area, therefore US navy is anchored in Bahrain in this area to protect their assets. Similarly, Russia also has its interest in the middle-East. Its only warm water port outside Russia is in Syria in Tartus.

Therefore, the interest of Russia in securing the regime in Syria in the recent times fits the puzzle of prolonged Syrian Civil War. Gulf of Aden is another area, which has very high strategic significance. As large number of trade takes place through this area, therefore it is important to secure the area. In 2012, there was a rise in piracy in the area. Pirates from Somalia and the other countries from the horn of Africa were involved in piracy. Recently, in 2015, the civil strife in Yemen made this area more volatile. Therefore, in order to secure this trade route the benefactor states were considering shifting their naval assets to this area.

Similarly, other choke point in the area is the Suez Canal. It has witnessed large scale war in the past. UK and France had interests in the area during the world war. However, during the reign of Gamal Abdel Nasser the Canal was nationalised and UK and France lost control. In order to restore control, Suez War took place in 1956. The British influence ended, Israel captured Sinai Peninsula, ceasefire was mediated by US and USSR and the influence of USSR increased in the area. Also, the significance of the area is important as we can see the high influx of refugees from the strife torn area to Europe. They are migrating to Europe for 2 major reasons: one because of its proximity and the other because of the lure for a better lifestyle.

Russia or the erstwhile USSR has territorial proximity to the region. During the entire Cold War, US was paranoid about the spread of communism in the region. Therefore, in order to contain communism it established military alliances with the region. Iran was to be maintained under the influence of USSR in the North and Britain in the South. However, USSR tried to install a Communist Government in Iran. A puppet government was installed with the support of US. The control of crude oil was tacitly taken by US.

In 1953, a coup took place at the behest of US and oil was sold to US an art accepted discounted rate. In 1955, Baghdad Pact was signed which formalised the military agreement among UK, Iraq, Pakistan, Turkey and Iran. US signed individual treaties with these nations. The main idea was to contain communism. In 1979, Iranian Revolution took place and Khomeini became the supreme leader and ties with US were severed. Iran became part of NAM and opposed any foreign interference.

Israel has been a contentious issue for the whole of middle-East. The question of Jerusalem as a holy place has bound the Arab State with the same string. The root of this conflict can be traced to AD 71 when the Jews were driven out by Romans from their homeland. In 1897, the Zionist Movement started, which called for return of the Jews to their homeland. US pressure allowed the Jews to settle in the area. The proposal of 2 state solution in 1948 was rejected by Arabs. Meanwhile, UN recognised Israel. A brief war in 1948 resulted in, Israel capturing three-fourth of Palestine.

Again in 1967, Arab countries ordered troop mobilisation, but Israel launched pre-emptive strikes and repealed the Arabs. Israel occupied West Bank, Gaza and Golan heights and pushed the Arabs further away. In 1973, propelled by the supply of arms, Arabs attacked Israel on the day of their festival, Yom Kippur. The result was: oil supply glut; Suez Canal was blocked by Israel. With the signing of the Camp David Accord, Israel withdrew from the Suez Canal and swore not to give back the hitherto occupied territories. Oslo accord was signed between Israel and Palestine Liberation Organisation, but, was kept on the backburner and the solution seemed farfetched.

Terrorism has been associated with middle-East for the last few decades. Although, the definition of terrorism is not appropriate for the different violent groups active in the area, as the history of their violence in almost every case is related to extraneous factors. The violence of groups in these areas is retaliation of the unsolicited unilateral interference of West in the region. Rise of IS (Islamic State) is as a result of US led NATO interference in the area and the vacuum left after its withdrawal from Iraq.

Similarly, Al-Qaeda was a result of the Western interference. Terrorism as defined by West is heavily biased. In the Western discourse, the debate on terrorism has blurred the line between Islam and terrorism. Also the region has fault line, where Shia and Sunni factions are at loggerheads with each other. In this chaos, West is taking the advantage. Sunni faction led by Saudi is backed by West implicitly; similarly, Shia faction led by Iran is backed by Russia implicitly. In the recent times, this fault line was conspicuous in Yemen Civil War, 2015, continuing Syrian Civil War, the rise of IS and its pledge to exterminate all Shias and establish a Caliphate with Sharia law.

Middle-East has been a turbulent zone because of various, aggravating factors. The only binding, factor has been their culture. In order to preserve the region, the role of Gulf Cooperation Council, United Nations and Amnesty International are of importance. The region has immense scope for development, but its full potential can only be actualised when they are allowed to grow on their own terms without external interference. Artificial imposition of democracy to realise the human rights will do no good, unless it comes from the residents of the area.

ESSAY WRITING

25. Empowerment of Women

Women all over the world are treated, if we use the words of Aristotle, "an inferior type of man". Long before this, Manu, the ancient Hindu law-giver, used derogatory remarks to define the status of women in the society. It is so because it is the world that is controlled and dominated by men. It is often said that status of women in India suffered with the advent of the foreign rule. The truth is that women all over India have always played a subordinate role. But the last fifty years have seen tremendous transformation in the status of women. The status of women in a society is determined by the quality of participation by women in various nation-building activities. In this regard, India presents a unique paradox. While we have the distinction of having women as President, Prime Minister, Chief Ministers, Governors, Justices, Police Officers, their status is still inferior. There are a number of Indian women CEOs in corporate sector and women representatives in International fora. As a matter of fact all women have not been lucky to enjoy the fruits of emancipation.

The truth is that the last fifty years have witnessed some essential changes in the status of women. National Commission for Women (1998) was established as watch dog to protect their rights. The Hindu Code Bill (1956), Hindu Succession Act, Anti Dowry Act, Equal Pay Requirements, Right to Divorce all these laws have been formulated as corrective steps for their empowerment. There are number of laws to correct gender bias at grass root level. 73rd Amendment (1993) to the Constitution has provided for reservation of seats for women in the Panchayats. Today women empowerment is an important feature in our plans at every level. Women's Reservation Bill is expected to be passed in the Parliament very soon. It was introduced in Rajya Sabha as 'Women's Reservation Bill 2008' (108th Amendment) to provide reservation of one-third of all the seats for women in the legislature at centre and states level. The bill has been passed in the Rajya Sabha on 9th March, 2010, but is pending in the Lok Sabha. When passed, the bill would spark of thousands of opportunities for women to show their skill at decision-making level.

"*Tum yahaan aa jaogi to roti kaun banayega*", wondered a male MP and asked a fellow female MP. This is the crux of the problem and sums up the attitude of men in a male dominated society. Patriarchal attitude and traditional norms of our society are a great obstacle in the path of women's empowerment. Many fear the proliferation of *Lalu-Rabri* syndrome as has been witnessed in the case of Panchayat Raj System.

The Indian women have played a silent and self-effacing role in sustaining Indian civilization. Since Independence with the support of law they have steadily but surely progressed. Fortunately, the question of women empowerment has captured the imagination of the nation and it is quite encouraging.

26. The Problems of Urban Working Women in India

The problems of women belonging to different strata of society are different in nature. Their problems need to be tackled at various levels. The hazards faced by the upper class womens differ from their counterparts in the lower strata of society. Like wise the dilemma of women in cities differs from those of rural women. In the same manner the problems of urban working women in India are different from those of housewives or those engaged in self-employment. The problems that the working women face are because of age old obsessions. Therefore, the major cause is gender bias.

In fact the origin of the problems faced by women folk are gender based animus. How can a society dominated by men tolerate women as their equal in the professions so far controlled by men? Men are unable to accept them as equals in their professions. It is well-known that many industries offer those jobs to women that men hate to do. Excepting modelling, advertising and film industries their beauty is a curse because they are taken to be at their face value.

Once a woman has stepped into the male's world she is expected to shun her feminity and inhibitions. Her going out for a job adds to her vulnerability. It is not safe for her to go out by her private vehicle. Even her travelling by public transport exposes her to every kind of eve-teasing, molestation and obscene remarks.

The lack of security is faced by every working Indian woman. Once she steps out of the confines of her house, she is subject to every security problem. Apart from her insecurity on the roads and streets, there is a security problem at their workplaces. Sexual harassment and unwelcome sexual advances may make hell of her life. In case she tries to uphold her dignity, everyone around her will be hostile to her. It is by far the most condemnable problem faced by the working women in the urban areas. Inspite of their high education and professional achievements they cannot feel a sense of security that is her birthright.

Even at home she is a victim of male chauvinism. Time management between her official duties and domestic duties is her biggest problem. Every man wishes for a working partner. But in practice the same man becomes an exploitative husband. He expects her to do domestic work, look after children and perform other duties efficiently.

Many a time working women are victims of nervous break-down. A study conducted by a sociologist, Hochschild reveals interesting aspects about working women. Working women work roughly 15 hours longer each week than men. Inspite of this many a time she suffers from guilt complex thinking that she has not performed well both at home and office. Husbands think it beneath their dignity to co-operate with their wives in their domestic duties.

The problems faced by urban working women in India are many but they are not insurmountable. We must have laws specifically dealing with sexual harassment. How many Indian working women can dare to lodge a complaint against their employers? They are afraid lest they should be ostracised from society. As a matter of fact, the social scientists must come out and realise their responsibilities. Proper studies on the subject should be conducted and facts should be brought to the notice of the public and the media. According to a Sakshi survey, 28% of India's workforce are women. Only 3% of senior management posts in corporate India are held by women. 80% women confess that sexual harassment exists in their workplaces.

According to the same survey 53% women complain that they don't get equal opportunities and are treated unfairly by supervisors, employers and co-workers. The sexual harassment of women at workplace (Prevention, Prohibition and Redressal) Act, 2013 is a legislative act in India that seeks to protect women from sexual harassment at their place of work. The act will ensure that women are protected against sexual harassment at all the work places, be it in public or private sector.

In addition, stalking is a serious problem faced by women. India records over 36 per cent of stalking related deaths. Urban working women including school and college going girls are subject to the immoral and illegal practice of eve teasing. But the law is silent on the subject. Even if the police have to record an FIR, they file the complaint under sections covering obscenity or criminal intimidation.

The stalkers take to variety of acts such as SMSes, letters, frequent calls at odd hours and sometimes threatening warnings. It is not that cases of stalking go unnoticed but for want of stringent laws women and girls continue to be harassed. In the age of social networking stalking has acquired a menacing new facet. We should stand by hapless women on the streets. The Criminal Law (Amendment) Act, 2013 has included stalking under Indian Penal Code Section 354D.

A sociologist GK Karanth has aptly summed up the position of urban working women, "The social, economic and political fields of Indian women is increasing. But the mechanism for protection of their basic human rights is yet to take shape."

27. Crime Against Women in India

Atrocities on women is a global truth and our Indian society is no exception. The rate of atrocities on women is very high in India. Female foeticide, female infanticide, sexual harassment, rapes, child prostitution, molestation, eve-teasing, *sati*, dowry deaths—all are the crimes against women which prevail in our so called civilised and cultured society. In India, according to a survey by Sakshi, a woman is raped in every 54 minutes. Around, 15468 women were raped some time in the past. Today, the number of rapes has increased to an unimaginable level. There are various laws for the protection of women. Inspite of this 1651 rape cases are pending trial in Delhi courts. Due to these conditions, Delhi has become the most unsafe metro followed by Mumbai, Kolkata and Chennai. The news of dowry death is a common feature of every daily newspaper.

Woman is the greatest enemy of woman. Even before the birth of a female child she is killed in the womb of her mother. The condition of widows is very heart breaking. She cannot enjoy any kind of freedom. Her second marriage is not acceptable in the society. Without any reason she is punished by the society. Trafficking of girls and women is flourishing in the society. The Devdasi system is a stigma on Indian society. Newspapers and social magazines are replete with the shocking news such as father raping his own daughter or of incestuous relationships. There are various laws which the Constitution of India has given to women but these laws are not beneficial for women because our society is socially and economically backward. To ameliorate the condition of women there is a great need of change in the attitude of men. Without changing attitudes of men, even thousands of laws will not improve the degrading lot of women. There is no use of celebrating International Women's Day on 8th March. A society which does not learn how to behave with women, has no right to call itself civilised.

There are various Government and non-Government institutions which are working for women empowerment. But their efforts are not sufficient. Money factor is the greatest hindrance in the path of justice. Many parents are not in a condition to take steps against these crimes. They have no option but to tolerate the condition of their daughters and sisters.

India is facing a paradoxical situation. 28% of India's workforce are women. It was just 13% in 1987. One million women have been elected to Panchyats since 1993. There are women chief ministers, MPs and ministers. Yet violence against them is on the rise. It is strange that our leaders talk of women empowerment but they are not prepared to allow political reservation for them. They are still considered a weaker sex in a male dominated society. The capital of India has the highest molestation cases. According to Sakshi survey, 23.6% of the total molestation cases in Delhi speaks for itself.

Increasing number of women going out for education and jobs has made them more vulnerable to violence and atrocities. It is high time that Indian society adjusted to the phenomenon of women taking the place of men in corporate sector and Government. jobs. It is no use worshipping them and then exploiting them to one's advantage. They should be treated as human beings. For this purpose women have to come forward themselves and solve their own problems on equal footing.

28. Gender Biased India

India has not been a girl child friendly country. The adverse child ratio has come to stay in the country while the social status of women is on ascent. The declining sex ratio has its roots in the practice of sex selection that can be explained as a practice of determining the sex of the foetus and aborting it if it is a girl.

In certain parts of the country there are less than 800 girls for every 1000 boys. On the whole it stands at 914 girls to 1000 boys (Census 2011). Since 1961, there has been a sharp decline in gender sex-ratio which was then 927 girls to 1000 boys. It is a matter of deep concern that inspite of Prohibition of Sex Selection Act, the misuse of technologies such as ultrasound that enable testing the sex of a child before it is born is on the increase.

We honour our girl children on 24th January on the occasion of National Girl Child Day. The day is a sort of grim reminder that India is already missing millions of girls and women. The decline in sex-ratio is most obvious among children of 6 years old. Once it was a shameful secret kept within the confines of the labour room. But with the advance of Genetic Engineering shame came to be replaced by the greed of doctors. The matter does not end here. A girl child is aborted but when born, she is abandoned, sold or murdered after birth.

The most disturbing fact is that the practice of foeticide and infanticide is prevalent in every strata of society. Even highly educated couples indulge in illegal practices to avert the birth of a girl child. The problem is the result of deep prejudices against women that have persisted for centuries. The criminal neglect of girl children is to be studied in the context of patriarchal social framework. In a 'son preferring society' the position of a girl child is that of dismay.

Their neglect is to be studied in terms of scanty nutritions and no access to educational and entertainment facilities. They are kept confined to kitchen chores and up keep of the homes. In 'a son prefering society' the birth of a son is considered a bonanza. The belief that the family name will be carried forward by the son. In terms of economic terms girl is a *'Paraya Dhan'* and the spectre of dowry is attendant on her. On the contrary the birth of a son brings the image of a post dated demand draft to mind. Such concepts about girls deny dignified living to every girl in the society.

These disturbing trends have to be eliminated lest girls should be eliminated unendingly before they are born. It is heartening to note that girls in every section of society are being looked after well now. There are a number of schemes in the field of education and nutrition for the girls. The government is rolling out many new schemes for the girls. The government has launched special deposit schemes for the future of the girl child in India. It has introduced *Sukanya Samriddhi* Account, a saving instrument that could be operated by the girl child after the age of 10. This account can be opened in a post office or any public sector bank. Apart from this the government is also running schemes to provide education to young girls and women in India since gender discrimination in India begins in the cradle.

Laws against gender discrimination are there and the enlightened citizens can contribute to the amelioration in the condition of little fairies. We should learn to love our daughters and shun prejudices against them and change our mindset. We have to convince others to stop gender holocaust. Each girl like a boy, has a right to live and become an equally respected member of the great family i.e. India. It is high time that a movement should be started and we all should be a part of it. It is time we rise from the slumber and support the voice of gender equality.

29. Women Officers in Armed Forces

The status of women in a society is defined by the quality of their participation in the affairs of the nation. Economic equality for women is a potent means to bring about quality of life in their condition. Education and equal employment opportunities for women can do wonders. The question of women's joining armed forces has to be studied in a larger context. Till 2008, women were selected for Short Service Commission for a limited period of service in certain wings of Armed Forces. In 2008, the government's decision to grant permanent commission to women in education and legal branches was most welcome for more than one reason. They got identical career span of service along with their male counterparts.

There are about 2200 serving women officers in all the wings of Armed Forces. The shortage in armed forces has been much talked about issue for quite sometime. Now we hope to compensate to some extent for the shortage when women officers serve at par with men officers. A number of men officers seek premature retirement on account of prevailing promotion policy in defence forces. Therefore, the place of women in armed forces at par with men would play a significant role for them. Now they may be encouraged to opt for careers in defence. For women, employment in defence forces is much better option than a job in a private sector. Here they can serve with dignity, assurance and sense of job security.

However, a controversy has been raging round the question whether or not women should be assigned operational duties on the war front. Women are still fighting for permanent commission as combatants in defence. But the fears are voiced because of their physical parameters and medical fitness. It is therefore, asserted that women should be confined to medical, administrative, education and legal duties. If viewed impartially, there might be some truth in it.

Modern warfare is a very complex affair in every sense. Besides, operational duties there are a lot of far more important things during war. Women are competent enough to look after a number of strategic jobs while men are engaged in actual fighting. War is now a hightech affair. Brain more than the brawn is needed to win wars. Medical, nursing and welfare activities alongwith salvage operations are indispensable part of active warfare.

They can perform their duties with specialised skill. In March 2010, the Delhi High Court handed over a landmark judgement directing the government to grant permanent commission to the women serving as Short Service Commissioned Officers. The Court, however, turned down the plea for allowing women in combat operations. In August 2010, the government finally decided to abide by the verdict of the Delhi High Court. The question of their joining operational wings has been decided in the Supreme Court. The Supreme Court of India in 2015 said that it was in favour of permanent commission of women officers in all wings after they complete their short service stints. The open court's decision came after hearing an appeal filed by the Navy and Defence Ministry.

30. The Reservation Policy

Highly disgraceful blots on Indian social structure in the course of history must, of course, be removed. For this purpose the interests of social justice of scheduled castes, scheduled tribes and other backward classes have been sufficiently safeguarded in our Constitution. Article 46 of the Constitution specifically mentions that the state shall promote educational and economic interests of SC, ST and weaker sections of the people. Before the recommendations of Mandal Commission were announced, there was already provision of 22.5% of reservation for SCs and STs in Union and State Government services.

Besides reservation in jobs, Article 334 of the Indian Constitution, makes a provision for the reservation of seats for scheduled castes and scheduled tribes and nomination of Anglo-Indians to the Lok Sabha. However in 1990, the then Prime Minister Sh. VP Singh through notification made 27% reservation applicable for Other Backward Classes (OBCs) as well. The Mandal Report identifies 27% of the total population of India as Other Backward Classes (OBCs). They are over and above 22.5% who are SCs and STs. Never before in the history of the world, the reservation in state services has been prescribed for around half of the population.

The Mandal Commission recommendations apply to all jobs in the government all public and private sector enterprises and also to admission and appointment in universities and colleges. It also applies to all level of promotions in the areas covered above.

In 1991, Rao government adopted the notification of VP Singh government into except with two amendments (a) Within the 27% reservations, preference should be given to the candidates belonging to the poorer sections of the backward classes. (b) An additional 10% reservation should be given to economically backward classes.

On 16th November, 1992, Supreme Court pronounced its decisions on the Mandal case. The Supreme Court rejected both the notifications of VP Singh and Narsimha Rao. The most welcome aspects of the verdict are, (a) The reservation will not apply to promotion in services, (b) The quota system shall apply irrespective of faith so that the backward sections among the non Hindu communities can also avail the benefits of the reservation (c) The reservation should not exceed 50%, (d) A family could avail itself of reservation only once. (e) The Supreme Court laid down minimum qualification for taking advantage of reservation policy of the government by excluding creamy layer from the list of beneficiaries. Originally, reservation to the Dalits was granted for 15 years. But it has managed to continue till now. A noble ideal has become an irreparable casuality in the hands of wily politicians. It has become very necessary to review the entire gamut of reservation policy since the third generation in a single family has come to enjoy the fruit of the occupancy.

A family should be restricted to one chance for availing the benefits of reservation policy. Let us make a beginning by excluding creamy layer among the Dalits. Now, reservation should be made applicable to only those that are economically backward irrespective of caste and community. No religious or linguistic group can claim to be economically backward in entirety.

The review of the policy on reservation cannot be overlooked because despite the reservation continuing for more than sixty years the problem of social and economic inequality has deepened. The government recently announced that the government policy is clear and the reservations will continue. The solution lies somewhere else, not in reservation. Equal educational opportunities at school level would ensure the upward mobility of the socially and economically backward. That the new elite class among the Dalits is still enjoying the benefits of quota system, is a matter of grave concern. Reservation in a worse form as it is today, cannot be allowed to continue.

If considered from national point of view the politics of reservation has given rise to the divisive forces. It has not served the purpose which it was supposed to have served. As a matter of fact the weaker sections should denote that class of people who are economically poor. But no such protection is available to the poor sections of higher classes. Poverty is not endemic to a particular class. It is mockery of reservation to extend benefits of reservation to a class as a whole. Many states have exceeded the limit of 50% fixed by the Supreme Court. Voicing RSS this year demanding no reservation in jobs and education for the affluent, the government in power stated that there is no rethink on the present social and caste based reservation policy. It is rightly said that our politics has been marginalised and the interest of the poor forgotten. A chance of noble service to the poor has been sacrificed and killed at the altar of mean and petty politics. There is a desperate need to redress the imbalance in the country.

31. Child Labour

There is no universally accepted definition of child labour. Generally speaking a work done by a child under the age of 14 years is said to be child labour. India has the highest number of child labourers and the number continues to grow. They are estimated to be over 17 million.

Child labour means lost childhood. Childhood is the most sensitive part of the life of every human being. The impressions received in this period of life are indelible. Psychologically, the character of a person develops during this part of life. Wordsworth has wisely stated, "Child is the father of man." Children, all over the world, are the future of mankind. What they get from society today will be returned in the same coin when they are grown up. In addition to Universal Declaration of Human Rights of 1948, our own Constitution provides certain rights to children and prohibits child labour. Article 24 prohibits children below the age of 14 years from being employed.

Article 39 (e) and 39 (f) also take care of children. Article 21 A added by the 86th Amendment Act 2002, provides that state shall arrange for free and compulsory education to all children of the age of 6 to 14 years. This very amendment has also added Article 51 A (k). It has made incumbent upon parents or guardians to provide education to their children.

Education is the most potent tool to combat the evil of child labour. In 2010, the government adopted Right of Children to free and Compulsory Education Act (RTE). The government is also spending a lot on Mid-day Meal Scheme with a view to universalising primary education. For all these measures, a study by Child Rights and You (CRY), reveals that 35 million children in the 6-14 age group are out of schools.

Compared to many developing countries, children form 5.2% of the total labour force in India. Poor system of education and poverty are the two chief sources of child labour. Campaign for 'Common School System' blames the miserable and deplorable quality of education for increasing child labour in India. The present system imparts minimal skills to children inspite of tall claims on paper. The State Governments have failed to impart meaningful education to children. Chairperson, National Commission for Protection of Child Rights, says that most laws on education do not cover 15-18 year age-group. Most of the children are dropouts and unskilled and end up as part of casual and untrained workforce. This sector of labour force is fed mostly by child labourers.

Secondly, poverty forces children of all age-groups into work to supplement their family's income. Sometimes parents mortgage their child's labour to local money lenders and wealthy families. Moreover, child labour is cheap and safe. Children are trouble free and their wages are no problem. Hunger and povetry drive these children to do any kind of menial or hazardous task.

The government formulated national policy on child labour in 1987. A National Authority on Elimination of Child Labour was set up in 1994. There are large number of laws to check employment of children as labourers in households, factories, roadside *dhabas*, tea shops. But the problem remains unabated. A nation that cannot look after its children has no right to dream of growing its stature in the comity of nations.

32. The Lost Childhood

India is a home to one-fifth of the world's children. Admittedly, it is a Herculean task to look after them. Their condition should be a matter of grave and urgent concern to all. Exploitation, insecurity, child labour, malnutrition besides social evils like child marriages are some of the problems that ail them. In the report issued by the State of Asia Pacific Children (2008), it is stated that child mortality below 5 years is the highest in India. The latest UNICEF report has also stated that 5000 children under the age of five die daily due to preventable diseases. 15% deaths are caused by malnutrition and 3.5 crore children are without shelter. A report by National Human Rights Commission has revealed a heart rending fact that 4500 children disappear every year.

Data on missing children shows that over 3.25 lakh children went missing between 2011 and 2014 at an average of nearly 1 lakh children going missing every year. Not all the children who are separated from their parents are missing children. Unable to afford food and treatment their parents abandon them. Most of the children wander off and are lured by traffickers. They may be used as forced labour, exploited sexually or sent to the Gulf countries as camel jockeys or child brides. Many of them are pushed into begging rackets and drug peddling. In the end they may become part of organ trade.

Nithari (Noida) killing was a wake-up call for the government and a committee on missing children was formed by National Human Rights Commission. Child labour is another area of grave concern for children. India ranks 80th in the Global Hunger Index of 104 countries. Hunger drives children out to earn food for themselves and supplement the income of the family. Working children in india forms 5.2% of the total labour force in the country according to a study by Child Relief and You (CRY). Around 35 million children in the 6-14 group are out of schools. Will Right to Education be able to free them from forced labour?

More than often, poor parents mortgage their children's labour to money lenders or some rich household. Child labour denies the joy of childhood to children. Children are naturally deprived of mental and physical development. Working for long hours and unable to voice their protest against exploitation they are subject to retarded mental growth. They lack social contacts and are denied emotional support from their family and society.

Child marriage is a social evil. Child marriage prevention measures in our country stand no ground before religious customs and orthodox opinions. According to one estimate 45 lakh marriages take place in our country every year. The average age of girls in the case of 30 lakh marriages range from 15 to 19 years. The inevitable effect is early motherhood resulting in deteriorated health of both child and mother. The most effective measure to prevent child marriage is to provide education to both boys and girls. Despite the existence of Child Marriage Acts since 1929, we have hardly heard of any family being convicted. While 70% of our population lives in villages, the concerted efforts are not made to target the most vulnerable section of rural population. Child brides are quite common sight on the rural side of our population.

Childhood is the most innocent and beautiful beginning of human life on earth. As sapling grows into the fruitful tree, so childhood grows open into life full of opportunities and potential hopes. It is very simplistic saying. But the truth is that future fate of mankind is reflected in the quality of life they get from us today.

They will give back tomorrow what they get today. They are our priceless investment. We must try our best never to deprive them of their innocent smiles and joys. The National Commission for the Protection of Child Rights was established by the government in March, 2007 and now five state commissions have been added. Could these commissions restore the days rolling out of the life spans of these children? A day lost cannot be recalled.

33. Homes for the Aged

Next to God parents are to be loved, respected and obeyed. When they are old, they are to be served. A dutiful son is a joy to his parents. A dutiful daughter is an asset. We need parents when we are young, parents need us when they are old. Parents need their children most when they are in the twilight of their life.

Ironically, science has prolonged the average age all over the world complicating the survival into old age. Today in India a person can survive beyond the age of 80 years. Here lies the crux of the problem. It gets difficult for old persons to plan for the rest of life say for about 10 to 20 years after thier active life. By this time their children are settled, married and living their own life. Coupled with this, change in social and cultural outlook of their children have broken down the institution of joint family system. It is, therefore, hard for old parents to spend the last crucial years without the physical, mental and financial support of their children.

Forced by circumstances and in search of success and status, educated young men and women settle far away from their parents. Some go abroad. The very education that the parents manage to give to their children turns against them in the end. Their children go away in search of green pastures leaving them alone. International community as well as our Government is aware of their problems. The UNO proclaimed the year 1999 as 'International Year for the Aged'. In our own country too the year 2000 was proclaimed 'The Year for the Aged'.

Article 41 of our Constitution clearly makes it incumbent on the state to look after the aged. There is a social welfare ministry responsible for the welfare of the aged. Laws are made from time-to-time to protect the rights of senior citizens. For example under law parents cannot be evicted from a house without due process of law under section 105 of the Criminal Procedure Code. A magistrate can order a person to maintain his/her old parents under the Maintenance of Parents Act. The Hindu Adoption and Maintenance act says that the aged parents can demand for maintenance from their children. The Domestic Violence Act also provides parents with the rights to seek relief from any kind of abuse.

Indira Gandhi National old age pension scheme is dedicated pension scheme for people in the BPL category in the age of 60 years and above. Beneficiaries receive a pension of ₹ 300 per month. Person above 80 years of age receive ₹ 500 per month.

ESSAY WRITING

The present system is unable to deliver old age income security. The Government of India passed Maintenance and Welfare of Parents and Senior Citizens Bill, 2007. The act provides for three months jail term and penalty up to ₹ 5000 to those who abandon their parents or maltreat them in their old age. This legislation has made provisions for claiming maintenance speedy, simple and inexpensive. The act also provides for setting up of a tribunal in each district for helping the old in distress.

The tribunals are invested with powers to disinherit the children if the senior citizens desire so. Moreover, the act also provides setting up of homes for the aged in all districts. Will the litigation under the various laws bring about harmony among the members of the family? Will the fear of punishment not fill their hearts with rancour? The fact of the matter is that the spate of materialism is to grow with more fury. Family system is set to collapse completely. Homes for the aged is the only option and hope for the hapless senior citizens. There they will have to learn to relive their second childhood and achieve emotional stability with the world.

34. **AIDS**—A Dormant Volcano

The Acquired Immuno Deficiency Syndrome (AIDS) is spread by HIV—the Human Immuno Deficiency Virus. This virus slowly attacks the immune system of the body and soon a person loses his capacity to fight any disease. There are only three ways in which the disease can spread—through sexual contact, infected needles and infected blood. In addition to this hospital wastes have been identified as potential cause for the spread of AIDS in India. As a matter of fact AIDS is basically a Sexually Transmitted Disease (STD).

According to experts India's position is quite grim. If it is left unchecked, it could bring about social and economic devastation in the country. Six years after the first case of AIDS was detected in India (1986), WHO estimated that in India around five lakh people are infected with this virus. The highest incidence of HIV infection has been reported from Maharashtra. The survey conducted by National AIDS Control Programme reveals that Manipur heads the list in North Eastern states. India will have the largest number of people infected by HIV within a very short period if adequate precautions are not taken. Every fifth person carrying sexually transmitted disease in the world is an Indian. The largest number of HIV positive cases in India are in the age group of 20-40, the most productive period in the human life cycle.

The National AIDS Control Organisation formed in 1993 is the leading organisation for the implementation of National AIDS prevention and control programme. It deals with all the aspects of the problem from supervision to education on the subject. There is a lot of misinformation on the subject in the public because of which AIDS victims suffer social humiliation. This kind of discrimination is not going to help the infected individual. The person prefers to die untreated rather than reveal his identity before undergoing testing and treatment. Refusal to accept HIV cases as a matter of policy for hospitals is discriminatory. It is against the spirit of Article 14 of the Constitution. To refuse treatment to AIDS patients is irrational and inhuman. Therefore, ignorance and lack of discrimination are great hurdles to tackle the problems sanely.

Women have now been recognised as one of the major groups requiring a help. 30%-50% of infected population has been found to be among women. In many countries specially in South-Asia, women have little control over sex, when and how they have it. A woman infected with HIV is bound to pass on the infection to her child.

A report by United Nations on AIDS has been released to assess the achievements and set future goal to tackle the dreaded disease on global scale. Based on data submitted by 182 countries the report assesses progress and gaps in the global response. The report provided for measures to achieve universal access to HIV prevention care and support by 2015. The report laid stress upon harnessing the energy of young persons and respecting the dignity of women and girls in a fight against this global epidemic.

Since 1981, when the word first witnessed the emergence of this strange disease, significant gains have been made against HIV/AIDS but the achievement is fragile. The epidemic may have claimed 25 million lives and left more than 60 million infected in the last 30 years but the UNO's report has confirmed 25% drop in the number of new infections globally recently. Inspite of the reported decline of 25% in new infections in the top ten countries suffering from the epidemic, the results have not been desirable. Against this 25% decline in number of people acquiring infections, it is on the rise in Eastern Europe, Central Asia, North Africa and Sub Saharan Africa.

In 2014, an estimated of 5 million people were living with HIV. Out of these, a vast majority of people live in low and middle income countries. As of March 2015, 15 million people living with HIV were receiving antiretroviral treatment representing 41% of those in need. Significant progress has been made in prevention of mother to child transmission. But still winning against the epidemic demands great amount of discovery and effective treatment as epidemic has continued to outpace the response. In fact, there is need for continued vigilance in view of the fact that the epidemic is easily transmitted.

Prevention policy is the potent form of dealing with the epidemic. Hope lies in the fact that the world has moved "from the state of denial to action for achievement". We have almost overcome psychological and social barriers in the name of stigma, discrimination, human rights and gender inequality. It leaves a lot of scope to take the problem by its forelock. It is tragic that such a dreaded disease requires huge expenditure for the treatment of the patients. Azidothymidine (AZT), the only drug known to prolong life by about 36 months, has to be imported and costs rupees 3 lakh a year per patient. If meanwhile the patient develops blindness, an additional rupees 6.9 lakh per year needs to be added to the cost of the treatment.

The poor are more prone to it rather than those who are economically better off. The projected world wide spending on AIDS amounts to epic proportions. This would eat up the entire health budgets of the most third world countries. The poor section of the society has made it imperative on the part of the Government to provide facilities for treatment to the poor. Right now, the best cure is prevention and spreading education and awareness among the masses. The more awareness among the people, the less incidence of this fatal disease.

35. Drug Addiction

The menace of drugs has spread fast among the youth of India. Both the affluent as well as those living in poverty are vulnerable to drug abuse. Unfortunately, India is a happy hunting ground for drug pedlars. It is so because it is sandwiched between the so called Golden triangle and the Golden crescent. The former area comprises Thailand, Myanmar and Laos and the latter is covered by countries—Pakistan, Afghanistan and Iran.

The World Health Organisation (WHO) has defined drug abuse as persistent or sporadic excessive drug use. Addiction or physical dependence is a state whereby the body requires regular doses of a drug both legal or illegal such as heroin, cocaine, alcohol, tobacco etc. The drug users use these drugs for variety of purposes. Some use them for forgetting unpleasant surroundings, experiencing kicks and easing tension and depression. Some may use them for improving their physical stamina, sexual potency and entertainment at rave parties. Drug addiction has given rise to ever increasing illegal trade amounting to 400 billion dollars. The United Nations has put the number of drug users all over the world at about 200 million. The reasons are not far to seek. The family bond is gradually loosening. The parents are busy in their profession. Mostly the youth residing in hostels, fall easy prey to drug addiction. They are ever in search of thrill and excitement. Drug taking has often been attributed to uncertain future, unemployment, family problems and academic pressures. Moreover, new values in the form of free sex, drug abuse, false notion of independence are the new substitutes.

Those addicted to drug taking lose agility of mind, sense of friendliness, warmth and social awareness. In the long run, they suffer from schizophrenic state. They may also suffer persecution mania, an obsession of being tortured. They also develop tendency to commit suicide. But above all, they don't hesitate in indulging in any anti-social or anti-national activity at the cost of procuring drugs. The sudden boom in the infection of AIDS is a result of unsterilised needles used by the drug addicts. The spread of HIV has made drug addiction a menace to the health, life and peace of many families.

The problem cannot be dealt with in piecemeal measures. Multifarious strategy is required to tackle this problem. The parents, teachers, doctors and social workers need to work in tandem. An abuser cannot be forced to give up the habit. The initiative has to come from him. They require genuine love, concern, counselling and sacrifice on the part of family members. On medical management level, it is very important to cure withdrawl symptoms. Rehabilitation programme may include provision of suitable employment, prayer, meditation and involvement in gainful activities. However, there is Narcotic Drugs and Psychotropic Substances, Act 1985. The Act provides for a minimum punishment of 10 years and a fine of ` 2 lakh for dealing in banned narcotics.

The NDPs Act was amended in 1988 to include punishment for financing illicit trade and sheltering the offenders. The Narcotic Control Bureau is also in operation to oversee the problem at the centre and state level. Due to corruption, traffic in Psychoactive drugs is run in connivance with the police and other enforcement agencies. As such drug addiction is a problem that we have to overcome from different angles at different level. Drugs and crime go hand-in-hand.

Addicts resort to crime to pay for drugs. Incidence of impulsive murders, physical assaults, sexual misconduct, domestic violence etc are the common traits in the behaviour of drug users. The abuse of drug have given rise to night club life and culture of rave parties. Most of the drug users belong to the productive age-group of 18-35 years. Therefore, the loss in terms of human potential is tremendous. Around 7-10 % of the workforce is affected by addiction. HIV has come to stay as a dreaded disease as a result of drug abuse all over the world.

Drug addiction is the most potential menace for the youth, the society and the country. The enemies of the country find the youth soft target and bring about ultimate ruin of the country. There are enemies within the country in the form of anti-social and anti-national elements. The menace of drug is not related only to taking drugs. It is a problem relating to sale and purchase of drugs in the country itself. There are many types of psychoactive drugs according to their properties and the major responses they bring about. There are a number of drugs and India is the happy hunting ground for those becoming rich overnight at the cost of the future of the country. It is such a lucrative business that the political leaders interested in making money are part and parcel of the crime world.

36. Alcoholism in India

The permissible drinking age in Delhi and the whole of India is 25 years. Delhi State's excise department has recommended the lowering of this age to 21 years. These recommendations have raised many an eyebrow despite the truth that in India age is no bar for going to a bar or a pub, neither for boys nor for girls. In fact the permissible drinking has become a force in Indian society.

"What has the age to do with drinking? Neither have the bar owners nor have the police prevented us from drinking", says a youngster. What is the use of such rules? Why a boy or a girl who is mentally fit to vote and drive should not be considered mature enough to drink and pub? They cite the example of Italy and Cuba where the permissible drinking age is fixed at 16 years. In India they are old enough to vote but too young to consume alcoholic drinks. Certain actors like Imran Khan has filed a PIL against the orders of the Maharashtra government raising the permissible drinking age to 25 years. Is it out of conviction or just a pass time?

The basic question of addiction to liquor is not related to permissible drinking age. The disturbing fact is how global market economy has taken charge of Indian culture. Our own liquor manufacturers have targetted India's upwardly mobile boys and girls. The findings of Alcohol Atlas of India are alarming. Near 625 million people in India drink alcohol with per capita consumption being around 4 litres per adult per year. For every six men one woman drinks alcohol in India. India has also grown as one of the largest alcoholic beverage industry in the world producing 65% of alcohol in the South-East Asia. The studies say that Indians hit the bottle at 19 now and soon the age is estimated to decline to 15 years.

These disturbing facts made the then Union Health Minister Ramados voice the national concern about the dangers of indiscriminate alcoholism in India. As a first step he made an appeal to the film industry to avoid glamorising alcoholism on the screen.

The first to react was the then Censor Board Chief, Sharmila Tagore, who asked the Health Minister to attend to other far more serious problems than glamorising drinking. We do not need a crystal ball to foresee where we as a nation, are heading for. We have established hundreds of de-addiction centres, the revenue generated from liquor industry is far less than the revenue loss due to alcohol related health problems all over the country.

India is estimated to account for 60% of the people suffering from heart diseases in the world. Of the total road accidents, 40% are caused by drunken driving. In every slum, there is a proverbial drinking husband blowing up his daily wages on liquor. Why forget that alcohol is an addictive drink? The studies have revealed that alcohol is a tool for sexual conquest and gives rise to 'acquaintance rape'. A health advocacy group in UK has found liver related damage disease in young people. Addiction to drinking has by far the most serious economic and social ramifications. The poor families afflicted with the scourge of drinking are cause of tension in the society. Unemployment, preventable diseases and social stigma have their inevitable toll.

The lowering of the permissible drinking age would definitely add to the complexities of the problem by aggravating poverty, diseases and crimes. In a country as poorly governed as India, age limit has a lot to do with drinking. If we cannot do away with alcoholism, the teenagers can at least be protected. We should not be taken in by the frivolous arguments that alcoholism should exist, flourish and add glamour on the screen because it was a popular drink in ancient India. No one is so naive to believe that alcoholism can be done away within modern times. But we owe to our children the responsibility that they should not take to it at the school level age. They should be so guided that they remain away from it until they are mature enough to understand what drinking is.

37. Smoking in Public Places

Government of India revised the rules relating to smoking in public places from 20th October, 2008. Now smoking is strictly prohibited in all public places. The public places included in the notification are : auditoriums, hospital buildings, health institutions, public offices, court buildings, airports lounges, railway stations, bus stops, work places etc, and even places of entertainment such as amusement centres, cinema halls, refreshment centres, pubs, bars, discotheques, shopping malls, coffee houses. However, some of the places are allowed to have separate smoking areas or space. Hotels with 30 or more rooms and airports can have smoking areas.

Any violation of the act is a punishable offence with fine. Proprietor or anyone managing the public place will ensure that instructions are prominently displayed. Anything symbolic of smoking such as ashtrays, match boxes and lighters that help in smoking should not be provided in public area. In case of violation of rules or failure to report this violation the owner or the manager of a public place will be liable to pay a fine equivalent to the number of individual offences at ₹ 200 per offender.

The policy on smoking ban is commendable for the reason that the ban will make people think twice before they hold a cigarette in their hands in a public place. It is a spirit behind the ban that deserves kudos. We all know that evil of smoking cannot be eradicated root and branch but the constructive step on the part of the then Health Minister Ramadoss deserve to be highly praised.

The film stars and Chairman of Censor Board have come out against ban on smoking on silver screen. Pro-smoking lobby has resorted to flimsy grounds to criticise this ban in the name of democracy, fundamental rights and pre-occupation of the police with other important national issues. They believe that smokers do not need any sermons because they know what they are doing. Even if they are killing themselves, who are we to exhort and warn them? What a funny argument ! Censor Board Chief and top most film stars have come out heavily against the ban. It they are told that drinking and smoking should not be encouraged on the screen, they would say that they are not teaching institutions. They forget that they are an entertainment industry only because of the people. If people do not like to be entertained by the cinemas, they are bound to end as clowns whom people would not like to look at. Questions are raised about the feasibility of the ban.

Right to smoke is not individual. By eschewing smoking smokers can contribute to a clean atmosphere and the health of the nation. A medical journal study survey says that in coming years smoking will cause one death in every ten in our country. The passive smokers are more endangered than believed earlier. Inhaling second hand smoke may lead to asthma and lung-breast cancer, heart diseases and premature births and deaths. Children are the worst affected.

Ban on smoking may not be successful like all other well meaning measures. But awareness of the problem across the country is very important. Tobacco is a risk factor for six out of eight preventable causes of death. India is the second largest consumer and third largest producer of Tobacco in the world. Around 50% of all cancer deaths in the country are due to tobacco consumption. Ban on smoking in public places is a first step on the way to a complete ban on smoking itself.

38. Euthanasia—Mercy Killing

'Euthanasia' is simply a Greek word meaning 'good death'. Literally translated into English it means mercy killing. By the gentle act of mercy killing the death is caused to a person who is terminally ill and whose continued existence might cause untold sufferings to the ill person, family and the society. In this case death is caused either by passive or active euthanasia.

Passive method involves deliberate withdrawal of life support systems so that a patient is allowed to die naturally. Active euthanasia is caused by the use of lethal drugs and it is the most controversial. For years mercy killing has been the subject of fierce debate in various countries. Doctors around the world are not allowed to assist their patients to die. The Netherlands was the first country to legalise Euthanasia in 2002. Belgium also passed a law to this effect. Mercy Killing is legalised in a very few European countries and a few states of America. In Asia, Thailand is the only country that permits mercy killing.

In India, a sort of beginning was made in 1994 when the Supreme Court in a verdict declared that attempted suicide is not a crime. The verdict amounted to declaring euthanasia legal. But in 1996 five-judge Constitution Bench declared an attempt to commit suicide illegal. In a more recent development, the government has decided to delete Section 309 of the Indian Penal Code that criminalises attempt to suicide. In 2008, Law Commission took the first step towards legalising mercy killing.

The Commission recognised the validity of the statement 'life does not mean animal existence' and recommended to the government to make euthanasia legal. If a person is unable to take normal care of his body or has lost all the senses, he cannot be compelled to continue with a torturous and painful life. In such cases it will indeed be cruel not to permit him to die. It is quite sound logic to save a person from the torture and agony of life.

In a landmark judgement in 2011, the Supreme Court legalised passive euthanasia giving thousands of patients living a vegitative state all over the country the right to have artificial life support systems withdrawn to enable them to end a life of misery. However, the Supreme Court ruled out active euthanasia which involves giving terminally ill patients lethal drugs to end life. The verdict clearing the way for passive mercy killing is a big leap forward. Now it is for the government to make a law on the subject. Besides, saving terminally ill patient's right to die will lighten the burden of the society. The time of doctors and the space in hospitals can be utilised for those whose life could be saved.

However, it is feared that mercy killing will open the flood gates of abuses. Can doctors be relied upon to do justice and honour to their profession? How many of them abide by the Hippocratic oath in normal circumstances? They may misuse their powers and knowledge in collusion with the relatives of the patient or outsiders. But we all know that every law is subject to misuse.

There have to be stringent safeguards to prevent the misuse. Those against mercy killing say that a doctor should not be invested with the power of providence. He should not play God. Despite all this it is the wish of many to die a painless death. Dying by inches lowers the dignity of a patient. The basic concept of good death means that a man should be able to exercise free will to choose alternatives to die if life becomes an unbearable and torturous.

39. Surrogate Motherhood

Surrogacy is the practice of giving birth to a baby for another woman who is unable to have a baby for herself. In simple words, surrogate motherhood is defined as mothering by proxy. A surrogate mother rents her womb to get a child for an intended mother. Female infertility or any other medical problem that makes a woman unfit to bear a child are the chief reasons of surrogacy. There is another reason for making 'mothering by proxy' popular.

American and European busy couples who cannot undergo the bother of pregnancy hire a womb. And a surrogate mother is willing to rent a womb for financial considerations.

There are childless couples across the world. Surrogacy is a viable option for childless couples if they choose to overcome biological limitations. In case they cannot bring a child to life, there is assisted conception to help them. Parenthood is a rare experience for such couples and science can do miracles in such cases.

However, surrogacy is one controversial issue that has many supporters. There are many grey areas of which we are not even aware. Surrogacy has the potential to convert the normal biological function of a woman's body into a commercial machine.

There are several agencies that advertise their services. They make huge profits out of women's bodies. Surrogacy degrades pregnancy to a profitable business. India is emerging as a leader in international surrogacy. It is reportedly a 500 million dollar industry in India. India has virtually become a destination for medical tourism but often it is a destination for wrong reasons. Indian surrogates are cheaper and foreign couples save a fortune while choosing them. So long as surrogacy is voluntary and altruistic act, there is no problem. The problem begins where money comes in. In the case of a baby Manji born to an Indian surrogate there were no takers. Many a time the partner changes his/her mind. Sometimes surrogate mothers get emotionally attached to a child in her womb and refuses to hand over the baby.

India legalised commercial surrogacy in 2002 and the Supreme Court unequivocally ruled that "Commercial surrogacy is legal". Yet there is no law to check its malpractices. Many poor Indian women are tempted to risk their lives while carrying a child. These highly secretive and unregulated baby factories are only concerned with the baby and not the surrogate mothers health and sufferings. 25000 children are now being born in India every year to support an industry worth 2 billion. Since the cost of womb and fertility treatment in India is cheaper, would be parents are flooding in.

But most of the industry is operating unchecked. Indian Medical Research watch dog drafted regulations in 2010, but it still awaits presentation in the Parliament. And even many of the supposedly well run clinics do not appear to be transparent in their dealings. The guidelines issued in 2005 by Indian Council of Medical Research are not in the nature of binding. Therefore, in India, the controversial fertility market is growing into surrogacy supermart. Surprisingly, it is legal by default. There is much more invisible than meets the eye in the lucrative practice of surrogacy. Surrogacy laws in each country differ and is important to understand the same before embarking on this important decision.

There is no substitute for one's own baby in a womb. A woman has divine experience in motherhood but for childless couples, surrogacy is the last resort. While surrogacy is used to provide a child for a childless couple, genetic engineering may go a step further. The day is not far for made to order babies. Liza Mundy in her latest book on surrogacy sums up the whole issue "what is at work in assisted reproduction is often not science but business".

40. Capital Punishment

Crimes that can result in death penalty are known as 'Capital Offences'. There are conflicting opinions about the relevance of Capital Punishment in a civilised society. Those who are against capital punishment believe that every sinner has a future. We cannot write off the man who has committed a crime. We should hate the sin, not the sinner. Liberalisation of views in every field has made capital punishment a controversial issue. In the past, the execution of criminals and political opponents was carried out frequently. In modern times, all European Countries including America and Canada have abolished capital punishment. The United Nations have already passed a non-binding resolution calling for a moratorium on capital punishment.

Those who favour the abolition of capital punishment believe in *'Operation Valmiki'*. Every sinner has a future. 'Eye for Eye Policy' sends a wrong message. Killing a criminal signifies that a society does not have any means other than capital punishment to control crimes.

When a state kills a criminal, all his kins and relatives experience death by proxy. Why kill a person when life in a prison is itself a continuous torture? What's more he may reform himself in the process? Death for death is a kind of wild justice. Civilised societies believe that hanging is a primitive and barbaric practice. Rigorous life imprisonment is much more harmful than death by hanging or electric chair. A death by capital punishment is a sort of deliverance for the deceased, a deliverance from thousands of physical ills and pricks of conscience. The abolitionists consider capital punishment a savage and immoral institution.

Besides judges, being human beings, are liable to err in their judgement. And many a time murdered persons have reappeared after his alleged murderer has been hanged. Such ludicrous situations can be avoided by abolishing capital punishment. Death sentence, as it is claimed, is no more a deterrent. Justice Iyer has substantiated this statement while observing that abolition of death sentence has not increased the number of crimes in the United States and Britain. On the contrary there have been a fewer murders where capital punishment has been abolished. It is not the man but the society that should be on trial.

On the contrary those who wish to retain capital punishment believe that it is better to deter a criminal from committing a crime than to let him strike. Today, if the number of crimes is small, it is because there is a provision for death penalty. Those who kill must be killed in the larger interest of the society. Otherwise the habitual murderers and dreaded terrorists will be the biggest gainers. India is the only country that is affected by both indigenous and cross border terrorism.

While our soldiers die as martyrs, the terrorists are awaiting hanging endlessly. In the process they earn more limelight for the wrong reasons. Human Rights Organisations, NGOs, Champions of liberty of various hues and shades start taking cudgels on their behalf. Even exalted martyrdom is politicised. Justice Iyer has put this aspect of justice lucidly in these words; "Plurality of forces come to play a significant part in the administration of justice, the forces of subjectivism, behavioural emphasis, social background, human rights perspective, outdated social and psychological concepts. Firm guidelines on death penalty are needed. We cannot afford to leave the question of death punishment to the discretion of the judiciary and the politicians. We must have established principles governing the issue of capital punishment. So that politicians should not be given a chance to avoid the inevitable."

In India, death sentence is constitutional. A judge cannot, therefore suspend death penalty in favour of life punishment. The power to grant pardon in cases of death penalty lies with the President of India. As the matter stands today capital punishment should not be politicised. When the judge has performed his duty, the politicians should not make a mess of law. It is better that one man should die than the whole people perish. Bestial murderers, dreaded terrorists and rapists should be put to death. We cannot risk experimenting with the abolition of capital punishment.

41. Narco-Analysis Test

Narco-analysis may be defined as a process of 'psychotherapy' that is conducted on a suspect or a witness by inducing a sleep like state in him. The suspect is then interrogated by investigating agencies in the presence of doctors. In May 2010, the Supreme Court ruled that non-voluntary narco-analysis and brain-mapping tests are violative of the Constitution. They cited Article 20(3) that protects the individual's choice to speak or remain silent. The Supreme Court has held such tests as illegal whether they suggest the subject to be guilty or innocent.

The criticism against the judgement is irrelevant because constitutionally an accused cannot be compelled 'to be a witness against himself'. Moreover, both narco-analysis and lie-detector tests produce divergent outcomes from interrogator to interrogator. In fact narco-analysis, brain-mapping and polygraph tests are no substitutes for interrogation skill. These tests have been growing dangerously though they are unreliable short-cuts in investigation. Moreover, it is highly objectionable that the suspect is administered a mind altering drug that is nothing short of a torture.

It is true that normally no court would convict an accused unless there is some corroborative proof to the statement made during narco test. Indian Journal of Medical Ethics have termed narco-anlaysis as 'pharmocological torture'. In narco-analysis a trance-like state in a suspect is obtained with the help of medicines. He starts blabbering about everything, may be his fantasies and truth. And it is a problem to distinguish truth from fantasy.

There are some who defend narco-analysis on two grounds. First, the police can't go berserk doing such tests on all and one. Permission has to be obtained before subjecting the accused to narco test. Secondly the statements so obtained are not admissible as evidence. The statements of the accused under narco test are just 'leads' that help the police curtail time involved in investigation. Such leads help in large scale recoveries of arms and ammunition and discovery of dangerous conspiracies. But there is no substitute for smart investigation. There are a number of cases in the recent past where repeated but unproudctive narco tests have not revealed any result. Aarushi Murder Case is the one in question. The conditions of Indian policing and the investigative agencies are below par. Increasing reliance on narco-analysis, brain mapping, lie-detector and third degree methods have lowered the image of the Indian police. Their very approach to investigative methods has disgraced the name of the chief investigative agencies. They are bargaining agents for those in power.

Since psychotherapy and third degree tortures have been declared illegal, it must be realised now that the police should become totally professional and efficient with modern scientific apparatus. Enough of such investigative system that fall in the realm of pseudo science. They may produce occasional flash in the pan. By the time the judgement of the Supreme Court declaring narco tests illegal came a large number of applications for carrying out narco tests were pending before the courts. However, there is nothing to suggest that such tests have no scope. The Court has disallowed only forced use of narco tests. Whenever a suspect in his own interest volunteers to undergo such tests with a view to clearing his name of certain allegations, such tests may come to his aid. Despite all this such tests are not scientific and are no substitute for evidence gathering in a traditional manner.

42. Terrorism in India

Terrorism is basically a 'Political Weapon' used by those who aspire after political power. In India, Terrorism started in 1984 in Punjab and then in Jammu & Kashmir as Separatist Movements. Assam and other North-Eastern States are ripped by their own local Separatist Movements. Immigration of Bangladeshis into our states have altered the social and political character of the region. Their support has become a crucial factor for winning elections.

Besides, Red terrorism has come to afflict the 5 states of the country : Bihar, Jharkhand, Chhattisgarh, Odisha and West Bengal. Of the 676 districts in India 60 districts are threatened by Naxalites. A country that is the target of every shade of terrorism; political, religious, cultural and economic; cannot be expected to deliver justice to the people. The fact is that all Separatist Movements in India have global dimensions supported by international players. Pakistan, Bangladesh, China, Nepal and Islamic countries are engaged in destabilising the nation. We are not secure and safe while China, Pakistan and Bangladeshis are breathing over our shoulders. America had always wanted to see Pakistan as counter power to India to enjoy South-East Asian hegemony. Only after 9th September, 2001 America, suddenly conscious of the ramifications of the Islamic Terrorism, awoke to reality when Al-Qaida Power gave a mid-day knock at its door.

In 2015, there has been a number of terrorist attack including the Udhampur attack, Gurdaspur attack and Manipur attack from across the border. Islamic Terrorism is an international movement which cannot be tackled by playing ostrich. There is cross border terrorism but it has penetrated into India with the support of indigenous elements. They know that they have safe hideouts and political parties would blame only one another tracking aside the real issue. The voices of sanity would be drowned for lack of political will. No body talks of the killing of 50 thousand persons including security forces killed by the Terrorists. About 3 lac Kashmiri Pandits have been rendered homeless in their own country. Still no body talks about it as if some inevitable historical event has come off which is irreversible.

India is a soft target. Even when there is no war on our borders in the West, North, South and East our security forces are tense. Our security personnel are killed at regular intervals. Enemy forces enter our land and paint it red. Whenever we talk of stopping influx of Bangladeshis, almost all secular political parties start demanding Citizenship Rights for them. Some politicians have silently built up their vote bank. Bangladeshis have started their own terrorist outfits. There are regular local violent conflicts between them and the Indian citizens. Red terror in the country has assumed horrendous dimensions. In 2005, about 1600 Naxal attacks struck the vulnerable targets. During the last five years our country has been struck by Naxals more than 7400 times killing more than 7 thousand persons including security persons. Since, the end of monarchy in Nepal it has been the epicentre of every kind of Naxalite and Islamic terrorism.

It is misfortune of the country that the grave question of dealing with terrorism in India has been politicised, just for the sake of preserving vote bank. Our leaders see votes in the form of terrorists. People are being taken for a ride in the name of secularism.

Strong laws such as Pota and TADA were maligned for the possibility of their being misused. If they were misused, it means India is not a land of law. The country cannot be run for fulfilling the ambitions of a few families. We are now one and a quarter billion nation waiting helplessly for the good times when political interest of the nation will be delinked. We cannot win this war unless we expose those faces who have tried to subvert the unity of the country. Unless we win the war on terrorism, we cannot win economic war against poverty, illiteracy and disease. Empowerment of relations with Israel and America has put India in direct and open line of global terrorism. We have to put our home in order to enable ourselves to face the threat to the country from international forces.

However, Naxal Terrorism is a human problem. We are paying high price for the neglect of the most deprived section of our society : the tribals. It is our duty to bring them back to the mainstream of national life. There could not have been a better instance to highlight the causal relationship between poverty and Naxalites. Red Terrorism has to be fought on economic ground.

Islamic and Red Terrorism have to be fought on different levels. The Pune blasts in the wake of Mumbai blasts have once again shook the nation. This time one of Indian Islamic terrorist outfits has been put under scanner. The role of America is as dubious as ever on the question of our access to David Headley. The government is not forthcoming.

The confusing statements being issued by America and Pakistan do not tally with the statements of our government. We have lost plot at the centre of terrorism issue. Besides, we are weighed down under American pressure. There is ambiguity all round us on the burning problem of terrorism. Recently in January 2016, a heavily armed group attacked the Pathankot Air Force Station, which is a part of Western Air Command. It is a grim remainder that in fact we are living in terror.

43. Red Terror

Red Terror has come to stay and our security scenario is very fragile with internal threat from two types of terrorism, *Jihadi* and Left wing terrorism. The latter has also been given the name of 'People's War' that is waged by the Maoists. Red Terror is a national challenge and a continuous war like situation exists in two thousand police stations of 60 districts in India. In March/April 2010, Dantewada and Chintalnar Talmetra attacks shook the nation. In the latter attack 76 CRPF persons were ambushed and killed. In March 2016, a powerful landmine blast struck a truck filled with para-military forces in central Chhattisgarh.

Whether our para-military forces are equipped to deal with insurgency is a question of different kind. Are they trained to deal with insurgency ? There is no doubt that Red Terror is not a law and order situation. The Police are trained to deal with a situation where the people to be controlled are not armed. In the case of Red Terror we are dealing with our own people who have risen in armed resistance. They are group of people who are fighting for equality guided by their social and economic philosophy. They are tribals who have been left far behind. They suffered perpetual neglect at the hands of successive governments. Their backward areas are now their strongholds. Yet they are armed and out to destroy our sense of security.

ESSAY WRITING

How has such an outfit develop and why? It is not an overnight development. In simple words, it is an economic problem arising from failure on the part of our leaders. The problem has in fact, its origin in the struggle against the atrocities of the landlords of the village Naxalbari (West Bengal). This unheeded outcry for justice in 1967 founded Naxalism in the country.

How Naxalites should be dealt with? Are they terrorists? Or they are to be treated as citizens fighting for economic and social equality. One view must be clear in one's objective before dealing with a problem that is vital for the internal security of the country. We believe that Naxalism is an armed struggle and we must fight it with the help of the police. At the end of the day along with the police operations, elemination of poverty is one of the inevitable operations.

From this stand point both good policing and economic development should go hand-in-hand. Naxalites are not the intruders who have captured our land. It is primarily a human problem. Good policing needs good intelligence for the success of anti-terror operations. Unfortunately, the police in India like other security and revenue agencies, is a highly politicised force. The new political masters after independence have made the force subservient to their own requirements. Their need is to remain glued to the chair and the police successfully break the back of the opponents of their masters. Poverty is the breeding ground of Naxalites. Red Terror can be tackled only by doing away with the causes of poverty. The use of Force is the last resort in a democratic society. A sensible government will desist from using force and also create conditions not to allow citizens to do the same: This kind of approach was developed by Andhra Pradesh. They built police units called Greyhounds who spoke the language of the people and earned trust by acting as their protectors and not their conquerors.

However, there is a compelling need to have a unique civilian para-military force with military grade training to overcome the obdurate resistance. And when overcome, they need human touch. It is obvious that Maoists are well trained, highly motivated and well equipped groups. They are mobile squads of more than 100 persons, Locals are their mainstay and guerrilla tactics in the dense forests are their unique technique. Partly we are facing insurgency and untrained and ill-equipped police is no answer to the armed insurgents. Therefore, we need a unique para-military force with a human face. It has to be civilian with military training in infantry system. At the same time, it should be people friendly. The two pronged strategy is the sole situation we should aim at. The political will is a pre-requisite to win battle against Naxal menace. The result will not arrive over night. But all political parties including regional interests, cutting across party lines will have to come forward to safeguard the integrity of the country. The very idea of India has been jeopardised. In fact fight against Maoists is a litmus test for the very idea of India.

44. Global Population

Global population touched the 7 billion mark on 31st October, 2011. In India, Nargis was born at 7: 20 am as the symbolic 7 billionth baby. Since the origin of life on earth till 1800 there were only 1 billion people all over the globe. But the second billion was added during the next century. Worryingly, in the first half of the 20th century (1900-50), we were 3 billion. But the pace of population growth onward since 1950 has been astounding. From 3 million in 1950 to 4 billion in 1974, 5 billion in 1987 and 6 billion in 1998. And on 31st October, 2011 globally we are 7 billion. India's share alone is more than 1.2 billion. Thus, the world has been growing 1 billion every 10 to 12 years recently. Standing with almost 7.5 billion in 2016, where are we heading?

Should this growth not be brought under control? The crucial question for our survival is whether the earth can support the seven billion plus the estimated 3 billion making them 10 billion, by the end of this century. The economists are hopeful that the earth is capable of supporting many more in the short term. There is no substance in Malthus' theory of population that rising population can be the cause of massive starvation. Coupled with this increase is the fact that life expectancy over the world has gone up to about 70 years.

Amidst the present scenario, we have been witnessing favourable aspects for the last 40 years. The growth rate of world's population has declined to 1.1% from 2.2% in the 1960s. The average number of children born per woman in India has fallen. It was 5 in 1950 but now it is about 2.5. Nearly two-thirds of women under 50 married or in union use contraceptives. In the process, a large number of deaths in childbirth and millions of abortions are averted each year. This news is welcome.

Joel E Kohen, the author of 'How Many People can the Earth Support', has placed two alternatives before us. He asks "Is economic development the best contraception? Or is voluntary contraception the best?" In other words, do we need bigger productive technologies? or do we need to have fewer mouths to feed through voluntary contraception? Whatever the economists say, there is no panacea for the ills of population growth. So far our economic growth has not kept pace with the growth of population.

No wonder that our growth should be measured in prosperity, not in numbers and flawed indicators in the form of GDP. We have to see how we satisfy basic human needs and how well we develop dignity, cooperation and brotherhood. We have not been able to achieve even one of the indicators of prosperity. Nearly half of the world lives on US $2 a day or less. More than 8 million people in India live in slums. A total of 842 million people in the world were estimated to be suffering from chronic hunger in 2013 not getting enough food to conduct an active life.

Despite the fact that the world produced 2.3 billion metric tonnes of food capable of sustaining 9 to 11 billion people, only 46% of the produce was available for human consumption because 34% of the total production went to domestic animals and 19% was utilised for industrial purposes. Earth can definitely support our seven million and even more people. But the future population scenario is changing. The numbers will not matter. The number of households will matter. People will like to look after their children well and establish small households. The need of more energy and more public utility services will place a huge burden on our productive technologies and natural resources.

In fact, we need a strategy to make the world liveable so that those who are living in it may lead a life supportive of their basic needs. For achieving this desirable goal one strategy cannot do all. However, there are some priorities to be kept in mind. Voluntary contraception, support services, universal primary and secondary education, alleviation of hunger, food for lactating and pregnant mothers as well as for children under 5 years head the list of priorities.

45. Discipline in Public Life

Discipline is one of those values in life that give direction to life and it adds joy and harmony to life. Discipline in life guides us to do the right things and helps us to be morally upright. Discipline is one of those ideals which a family, a society and a country expects us to follow in the larger interest of life.

Institutions of family, society and religion were evolved by man to bring about discipline to anarchist conditions in society. Without the evolution of these institutions, it is hard to think of discipline. In fact, discipline is the core of law and order in society that leads to the development of civilisation in the larger interest of society. A life without discipline will become chaotic and disastrous because indisciplined life poses a great threat to law and order in society.

Discipline for countries like India is the most immediate prerequisite to economic, social and political progress. In the present context, indiscipline is all pervasive in society. Negligence in the performance of duty by paid public servants, teachers and doctors should make us sit up and do some serious soul searching. The steady decline in discipline among elected representatives of the people is a deplorable fact of our public life. They use their rights more to flout the principles of discipline than to follow the path of *dharma* that leads to the performance of duty. Unprincipled alignments, defections, floor crossings etc are painful reminders of the near collapse of discipline in public life.

There is a total loss of value-based life. Responsibility towards one's goal of life is lacking in every field. A responsible person would follow a disciplined way of life and he will be prompted to be careful, reliable and efficient. Responsibility means involvement in a dutiful way of life for the betterment of humanity. It is no exaggeration to say that discipline comprises many ingredients of life.

Brotherhood is a common bond of discipline among human beings. Disciplined life can be led only if we recognise the rights of others and follow our duties. Care for our surroundings and environment comprising air, water, soil, animal world etc is part and parcel of discipline in public life. Concern for the environment is an indispensable ingredient of discipline because it prompts us to lead life within norms laid down by society. Further, sympathy makes us share the afflictions and distress of others. In other words, feelings of sympathy inculcates love for others that is the anti-thesis of violence and indiscipline in life.

Thus, a civlilised society expects all of us to abide by simple rules of peaceful living lest the feelings of our fellow beings should be hurt. Therefore, discipline is a comprehensive form of life—it touches all aspects of human life. Accordingly the need of discipline is imperative in a civilised society.

The most important point is that discipline is relevant to every field of life, be it family, school, society or public life. Lack of discipline in any institution leads to disorder and a violent attitude on the part of people. Administration in society breaks down and there is a shift in moral values. Unethical practices take root in society. Everyone is a sufferer. There is no substitute for discipline in life. In fact, discipline implies order in public life.

46. Rights of the Differently Abled Persons

A disability may be generally defined as a condition which may restrict a person's mental, sensory, or mobility functions to undertake or perform a task in the same way as a person who does not have a disability. Disabilities affect people in different ways. People have the attitude that people with a disability are totally different and therefore need to be treated differently. Unfortunately, this kind of stereotyping is in itself a form of discrimination,

The only thing that separates a person with a disability is that, for one reason or another, they are unable to do certain things in the same way as the mainstream of society. They may require some form of adaptation or alteration to assist them to overcome the effect of their disability.

The Disability Discrimination Act (DDA) identifies and defines the following categories of disability :

- **Physical** It affects a person's mobility or dexterity.
- **Intellectual** It affects a person's abilities to learn.
- **Psychiatric** It affects a person's thinking processes.
- **Sensory** It affects a person's ability to hear or see.
- **Neurological** It results in the loss of some bodily or mental functions.

A disability may be present from birth or occur during a person's lifetime. However, when one thinks of names like Einstein, Helen Keller, Stephen Hawking, Sudha Chandran, Arunima Sinha, Rajendra Singh Rahelu and many more, one realises that these are not just disabled people they are, in fact, people with very special abilities.

As per the census 2011 conducted in India, disability includes the following physical and cognitive impairments:

1. Blindness
2. Low vision
3. Leprosy-cured
4. Hearing impairment
5. Loco motor disability
6. Mental retardation
7. Mental illness

The census shows that the population of disabled people has increased by 22.4% from 2.19 crore in 2001 to 2.68 crore in 2011. The increase is more in the rural areas and in Maharashtra, Andhra Pradesh, Odisha, Jammu and Kashmir and Sikkim, the disabled account for 2.5% of the total population. In rural areas, people with disabilities are ostracised and not included in the society. They are denied basic education or vocational training and thus do not have any scope of employment. Lack of rehabilitation turns them poverty-stricken and the disabled people in the rural areas are therefore caught up in a vicious cycle of disability and poverty. It is time to make inclusive policies with action on the ground to stop further discrimination.

There are cases where the disabled are harassed and discriminated, like the disability discrimination row over Jet Airways failures to provide for passengers with reduced mobility. Buildings in India do not cater for the requirements of the disabled, with no provisions for ramps for the wheelchairs.

It is as though the society has become visually impaired, turning a blind eye towards them country India's Disability Act of 1995 provides various facilities for both children and adults with disabilities in the country.

They are as follows :
1. Children with disabilities have the right to free education until they reach the age of 18 in schools that are integrated or in special schools.
2. Children with disabilities have the right to appropriate transportation, removal of architectural barriers, as well as the restructuring of curriculum and modifications in the examination system.
3. Scholarships, uniforms, books and teaching materials are all provided to children with disabilities for free.
4. Children with disabilities have access to special schools that are equipped with vocational training facilities and non-formal education. India provides training institutions for teachers in order to establish manpower.
5. Parents of children with disabilities in the nation can move to an appropriate court for the redress of grievances in regards to their children with disabilities.
6. Parents of children with disabilities are required to obtain a 'disability certificate' from 'Office the Commissioner for Disabilities,' in order to access the facilities.
7. Every 'panchayat' is provided funding by the government in order to build roads, schools and public ramps for people with disabilities.
8. 3% of all government jobs in the country are reserved for people with disabilities and the Disability Act includes affirmative action for people with disabilites.

As act has been enacted under Article 253 of the Constitution read with item no. 13 of the Union List. It gives effect to the proclamation on the full participation and equality of the persons with disabilities in the Asian and Pacific Region and provides for their education, employment, creation of barrier free environment, social security etc.

Differently-abled persons are entitled to the realisation of all human rights and fundamental freedoms on equal terms with others in society, without discrimination of any kind. The human rights of differently-abled persons include the following indivisible, interdependent and inter-related human rights:
1. The human right to freedom from any distinction, exclusion, restriction or preference based on the status of differently-abled, which has the purpose or effect of impairing the enjoyment of human rights and fundamental freedoms.
2. The human right to active participation in all aspects of social, economic, political and cultural life of society and in shaping decisions and policies affecting him or herself and community, at the local, national and international levels.

3. The human right to freedom from discrimination in access to housing, education, social services, health care or employment.
4. The human right to equality of opportunity.
5. The human right to full equality before the law and equal protection of the law.
6. The human right to the highest attainable standard of health, medical, psychological and functional treatment, including prosthetic and orthotic appliances, medical and social rehabilitation and other services necessary for the maximum development of capabilities, skills and self-reliance.
7. The human right to work, according to capabilities, to receive wages that contribute to an adequate standard of living and to receive equal remuneration for equal work.
8. The human right to economic and social security and to an adequate standard of living.
9. The human right to be treated with dignity and respect.

Disabled persons have to visit the office of the Commission for Disabilities to seek information. If a school is not found to be disabled friendly, parents can take up the matter with Disability Commissioner.

The government in February, 2014 introduced a bill in the Rajya Sabha to add to the rights and privileges of the disabled in India.

The bill had the following points :
1. Respect for inherent dignity, individual autonomy, including the freedom to make one's own choices and independence of persons.
2. Non-discrimination.
3. Full and effective participation and inclusion in society.
4. Respect for difference and acceptance of persons with disabilities as part of human diversity and humanity.

Prime Minister Narendra Modi said the mindset towards differently-abled people must change and the word 'viklang' (disabled) should be replaced with 'divyang' (endowed with special faculties).

In his 27th December, 2015 'Mann ki Baat', Prime Minister, Modi had based his concept of 'Divyang' on the premise that the people with physical disabilities tend to develop special faculties that even the fully 'able' lack.

The Department of Disability Affairs has since given a serious thought to changing the official teminology.

It is important for every citizen to realise the need for including the disabled people into the society. One never knows in whom a Stephen Hawking or an Albert Einstein is hidden. As we forge ahead into a brighter and a better world, we need to hold the hands of the disabled people and take them alongwith us. It is time to make India a discrimination-free and inclusive society where the disabled have the right of space like all others. It's time for a better tomorrow.

47. Consumer Protection Laws in India

Globalisation has led to growing interdependence and increased connection among economies of the world. The positive outcome of this trend is that there is universal emphasis on consumer rights protection and promotion. Consumers are now increasingly being made aware of their right and protection mechanisms available to them. Consumer protection laws are being designed and updated to ensure fair trade competition and free flow of genuine information in the market place. In India, focus on consumer protection laws is being renewed.

Consumer protection has its roots in the rich soil of glorious Indian civilisation. Human values and ethical practices were kept at highest pedestal in the ancient India. Dharma-sutras and Vedas were primary sources of law in ancient India. Manu Smriti prescribed a code of conduct for traders and specified punishment for various crimes committed against the consumers. Kautilya's Arthasastra was another text that dealt with consumer protection. This text describes the role of the state in trade regulation and also deals with its duty to prevent crimes against consumers.

In medieval period too, consumer protection continued to be of prime concern to the rulers. A large number of units of weight were used in India during this period. There were mechanisms for price enforcement in the market. There were incidents of shop-keepers being punished for under weighing their goods.

In the modern period, the British introduced the legal system that replaced the age old traditional system of India. The system however, adopted to the Indian conditions and combined best of the Indian and the British system. Some of the laws that dealt with consumer protection during the British era includes the Indian Contract Act (1872), the Indian Penal Code (1860), the Usurious Loans Act (1918), the Sale of Goods Act (1930), the Agriculture Procedure (Grading and Marketing Act) (1937) and Drugs and Cosmetics Act (1940). These laws provided specific legal protection for consumers.

The Sale of Goods Act of 1930 was considered as 'consumer charter' and remained an exclusive source of consumer protection for more than 50 years. In addition, the Indian Penal Code (1860) contains a number of provisions to deal with crimes against consumers. With the adoption of the Constitution, a new dimension was provided to legislation dealing with 'citizens' in general and 'consumers' in particular. The Constitution provided the philosophical ground on which structural edifice of the consumer protection laws in Indian stands today. Experts have equated the word 'consumer' with the word 'citizen' in the Constitution. Now as the Constitution deals with welfare of all the citizens, it inevitably includes the interests of consumers. To give concrete legal status to the constitutional mandate, various legislation/ laws has been enacted in India since independence for protecting the rights of consumers.

Consumer protection legislation enacted after independence includes-Essential Commodities Act (1955), Prevention of Food Adulteration Act (1954) and Standard of Weights and Measures Act (1976). Food adulteration is prevalent in the country and has emerged as a grave Menace for health and well-being of the consumers. The Prevention of Food Adulteration Act, 1954 that become operational in 1955 and later, amended in 1976 and 1986 came as a great relief for consumers.

The Essential Commodities Act, 1955 was enacted to regulate the production, supply and distribution of commodities which are considered as essential for the people and, to ensure that exploitative element of the trade do not indulge in stockpiling or deliberately inflating the prices.

However, inspite of all these legislations, the consumers still find themselves at a disadvantage, they are still victims of unscrupulous and exploitative practices. Besides adulteration of food, exploitation of consumers assumes numerous other forms such as spurious drugs, unregulated and inflated pricing, poor quality products, deficient services, deceptive advertisements, hazardous products and black marketing among other things.

This all forced the legislators to look for, "A more holistic and comprehensive law to deal with such unfair practices in the market place". A major development towards this come on 9th April, 1985, when the General Assembly for Consumer Protection of UN adopted a set of guidelines for consumer protection. Members countries were required to adopt these guidelines through national laws.

The guidelines included :
- Protection and promotion of consumer's economic interest.
- Standards for safety and quality of consumer goods and services.
- Measures enabling consumer to obtain redress.
- Consumer's education and information programme.

Though these guidelines were not legally binding, they certainly provided an internationally recognised set of basic objectives for countries to strengthen their consumer protection policies and legislations. In India, the Consumer Protection Act (1986) was enacted to this end and was specifically designed to protect consumer's interest. This act is a social welfare legislation with two main objectives.

Firstly, this act gives consumers the right to be protected against the marketing of hazardous goods and services. This means that consumers have right to know about the quality, quantity, purity, standard and prices of goods and services. *Secondly*, the act aims to provide speedy redressal to consumers related to disputes arising out of unfair trade practices.

The Consumer Protection Act aspires to clear all bottlenecks in promoting competition among business units. It endeavours to provide better protection of the interests of the consumers, to make provisions for establishment of consumer councils and other related authorities for settlement of consumer disputes. The provisions aim to provide effective safeguards to consumers against exploitations and harassment. Unlike other laws, the Consumer Protection Act is also compensatory in nature. The advantage of this act lies in it being flexible with wider jurisdiction and inexpensive justice mechanism.

The Consumer Protection Act is applicable to all goods and services unless specifically exempted by the Central Government. It covers all sectors including public, private and co-operatives. It provides adjudicatory authorities, which are simple, speedy and less expensive. It also provides for consumer protection councils at national, state and district levels.

Among the major focus of the act are the areas that includes prohibition of anti-competitive agreements, prohibition against abuse of dominant position, regulation of combinations and advocacy of competition policy. Under this act, every district houses atleast one consumer redressal forum, also known as a Consumer Court. These are first point of contact to get grievances heard. Above the district, forums are the state commissions. The National Consumer Disputes Redressal Commission, New Delhi sits at the top of the hierarchy. Claims of less than ₹ 5 lakh are to be filed with the district forum, claims between ₹ 5 to ₹ 20 lakhs with the State Commission and claims over ₹ 20 lakh with the National Commission. If a consumer is not satisfied with the order of the district forum, he can file an appeal against the order with the State Commission within 30 days of the order, which is extendable for further 15 days. An appeal against the order of State Commission lies in the National Commission. Final appeal can be made with the Supreme Court.

With around 20 years of its existence and going through a number of amendments, the Consumer Protection Act has stood the test of time. But still there is a lot of scope for further improvement. The act deals only with the problems of an individual consumer. It does not specifically deal with the issues related to maintainly or increasing supplies of any essential commodity or for securing their equitable distribution. However, inspite of its shortcoming, the Consumer Protection Act of 1986, which provide easy access to justice, has brought a legal revolution in India as a result of its cost-effective mechanism and popular support. In this age of consumers, the regime of Indian consumer protection law will undoubtedly rule Indian markets and should maintain the balance between forces of globalisation and interest of the consumers.

48. Honour Killing—Shameful to the Country

Recently there has been an increase in the instance of honour killing in the country. Everytime we open the newspaper, a number of cases of honour killing can be viewed. In the town of Jhajjar in Haryana, a father allegedly strangled his 21 years old daughter to death because she was in love with a man. In yet another brutal act of tyranny, a man in Rajasthan had beheaded her daughter with a sword etc.

India is a country of mixed cultures and heritage. The proverb 'Unity in Diversity' aptly suits our nation. But, the unfortunate thing is that all these things are now becoming matters of the past. We are heading towards a future that is darkened with things like religion and caste. Killing someone in the name of prestige is gaining precedence over love and affection towards others.

Honour killing is defined as a death that is awarded to a woman of the family for marrying against the parent's wishes, having extramarital and premarital relationships, marrying within the same gotra or outside one's caste or marrying a cousin from a different caste. According to statistics from the United Nations, one in five cases of honour killing internationally every year comes from India. Of the 5000 cases reported internationally, 1000 are from India. Non-Governmental organisations put the number at four times this figure. They claim it is around 20000 cases globally every year.

Honour killings have been reported in Northern regions of India mainly in the Indian states of Punjab, Rajasthan, Haryana and Uttar Pradesh. They are rare to non-existent in South India and the Western Indian states of Maharashtra and Gujarat. The Indian state of Punjab has the largest number of honour killings.

There are various misconceptions regarding the practice of honour killing. The first misconception is that this is a practice that is limited to the rural areas. The truth is that it is spread over such a large geographical area that we cannot isolate honour killings to rural areas only, though one has to admit that majority of the killings take place in the rural areas. Many cases have been recorded from the metropolitan cities like Delhi. The second misconception regarding honour killing is that it has religious roots. Even if a women commits adultery, there have to be four male witnesses with good behaviour and reputation to validate the charge. Furthermore only the state can carry out judicial punishments, but never an individual vigilance. So, we can clearly see that there is no religious footing or religious roots for this heinous crime.

The other side of the story points fingers towards the role played by Khap Panchayats in honour killing. These Panchayats are self driven setups that have gained wicked popularity for having paved a way for honour killing. Boycotting families from villages that chose to allow their children's marriage to their choice, supporting the families in honour killing are some of the naive activities of these so called Panchayats. The unlawful laws of the Khap Panchayats are imposed through social boycotts where the victims are killed or forced to commit suicide. All these inhumane activities are done in the name of brotherhood and honour. Love marriages are considered taboo in these areas, which is highly unfortunate.

It is important to note that honour killing is not specific to India only. It continues to be prevalant in other parts of the world too. Reports submitted to the United Nations Commission on Human Rights show that honour killings have occurred in countries like Bangladesh, Great Britain, Brazil, Ecuador, Egypt, Israel, Italy, Jordan, Pakistan, Morocco, Sweden, Turkey and Uganda.

'Honour killings' are a recognised form of violence against women in international human rights law because they violate women's rights to life and security of the person. Honour killings are an extreme and brutal abuse of human rights, violating the most basic of human rights-the right to life- as well as every other article in the Universal Declaration of Human Rights (1948). Honour killings also violate the convention on the Elimination of All forms of Discrimination against Women (1979). This convention has been signed by 185 countries worldwide— over 90% of the members of the United Nations—including most countries where 'honour killing occurs'. India is also a part of the signatories.

In India honour killings are homicide and murder which are serious crimes under the Indian Penal Code (IPC). The perpetrators can be punished as per Section 302 of the IPC. The members of the family as well as community can also be prosecuted under Section 302 of IPC for instigating suicide. Apart from this, honour killings also violates Articles 14, 15 (1) and (3) 19, 21 and 39 (f) of the Constitution of India. On the other hand, the Supreme Court in a judgement on 19th, April 2012 has termed the Khap Panchayats illegal and has directed the State Governments to take strong measures to prevent any atrocious acts by the Khap Panchayats.

ESSAY WRITING

Alarmed by the rise of honour killings, the Government of India assigned the National Crime Records Bureau (NCRB) to collect data on honour killings since January, 2014. The law commission has submitted its 242nd Report titled as "Prevention of Interference" with the Freedom of Matrimonial Alliances (in the name of Honour and Tradition) and has recommended for bringing a legislation namely "The Prohibition of Interference with the Freedom of Matrimonial Alliance Bill" to curb the social evil of the caste councils/Panchayats interference and endangerment to the life and liberty of young persons marrying partners belonging to the same gotra or to a different caste/religion. Marriage, as defined by the draft, also includes proposed and intended marriages. The offences under it will be cognisable, non-bailable and non-compoundable.

The need of the hour is to check such incidences with full force and at any cost. The problem must be tackled at several fronts. *Firstly*, the mentality of the people has to change. When we say that the mentality has to change, we mean to say that parents should accept their children's wishes regarding marriage as it is they also have to lead a life with their life partners. *Secondly*, the government should make very sincere efforts to educate the people and formulating the policies thereby strengthening the governance of rule of law. There is a need for media to lend a hand in creating local awareness about the horror of honour crimes. One must keep one thing in the mind that humans do not have the right to write down death sentences of innocent fellow human beings.

49. The Menace of Drug Addiction

It is a matter of great concern that the menace of drug addiction has been prevailing all over the globe. Drug addiction has become a matter of major concern in recent years for the society and the nation alike with the number of youngsters getting addicted to the vice at an alarming rate.

Originally the term 'drug' was used for medicines but it has now been given a new connotation. It now not only refers to medicines but also the fatal narcotics such as cocaine, heroin, brown sugar and the list goes on. All these drugs have their evil effects on the mind and body cells of the addicts.

Drug addiction is a condition characterised by an overwhelming desire to continue taking a drug to which one has become habituated through repeated consumption. Addiction is usually accompanied by a compulsion to obtain the drug, a tendency to increase the dose, a psychological or physical dependence and detrimental consequences for the individual and society.

Like most other mental-health problems, drug addiction does not have a single cause. There are a number of biological, psychological and social factors that can increase an individual's vulnerability to developing a chemical use disorder. Some of the psychological causes of drug addition are sexual abuse, neglect, chaos at home, a mental illness such as depression, inability to connect with others, poor performance at work or school etc. Other cause includes a person's environment where drug abuse is seen or where it's seen as permissible. Children who grow up in homes with drug addicts often become drug addicts themselves.

Another factor for drug addiction is genetic aspect. In fact, in studies of twins it appears half of someone's risk of becoming addicted to drugs is genetic. Other risk factors which can cause drug addiction are peer pressure, anxiety, loneliness and lack of family involvement.

According to a survey conducted by the UN, around 16 crore people across the world consume illegal drugs. There has been a rise in the incidents of illicit drug trafficking. Another report by the State Crime Records Bureau, India, the number of drug related cases are currently on hike.

The number is much high as compared to the total number of similar cases recorded in the previous years.

The profile of a majority of drug addicts is the same. They set off during teenage years by smoking cigarettes and gradually move on to opium and smack. The first experience with drugs is not very pleasant, but the kick it provided to the brain makes the user dependent on it. It is believed that the use of drugs provides great peace and tranquility which has led many people to fall prey to this habit. Studies have shown that consuming drugs increases the risk of heart attack and causes kidney failure and other diseases. People addicted to opium tend to loose weight and fertility. Heroin addicts suffer from muscle cramps, diarrhoea and perspiration.

Lysergic acid die thylamide (LSD) can cause severe damage to the central nervous system. Failure of getting the daily dose due to the shortage of money can make or drug users resort to crime and murder. A drug addict in due course gets alienated from the mainstream of the family and society in general.

Drug trafficking is the root cause for the continuation of drug addiction. Drug trafficking is a global illicit trade involving the cultivation, manufacture, distribution and sale of substances which are subject to drug prohibition laws. Asia is the major production centre of drugs. There are two areas in Asia where drugs are cultivated and produced. One is called the 'Golden Triangle' which includes Thailand, Laos and Burma and the other area is called the 'Golden Crescent' which includes the area of Pakistan, Iran and Afghanistan. Drugs are taken out illegally from the Golden Crescent by various agencies and taken to different countries. From Golden Triangle drugs are mainly exported to Australia, Canada and USA.

If we talk about India, its proximity to the Golden Triangle and the Golden Crescent has made its border vulnerable to narcotic trafficking. The Northern region is the hub of growers, suppliers and couriers. Cultivation of poppy and extraction of opium is legal in UP, Rajasthan and Madhya Pradesh for medicinal purposes, but a large part of it finds its way into the illegal trade. In Kerala too, the 'drug culture' has become highly rampant. Goa can pretty much be called a hotspot for drugs. The illegal trade has flourished in Goa largely due to the high amount of Russia mafia influence in the state and is now known as 'Little Russia' by the locals.

Many international and national laws have been enforced to curb the menace of drug addiction and trafficking. The Government of India has enforced the Narcotic Drugs and Psychotropic Substances Act of 1985 which has made drug offences non - bailable. The Narcotics Control Bureau has on several occassions intercepted huge hauls of drugs.

Apart from this, the 1988 United Nations convention Against illict Traffic in Narcotic Drugs and Psychotropic substances is one of three major drug control treaties currently in force. It provides additional legal mechanisms for enforcing the 1961 single convention on Narcotic Drugs and the 1971 convention on Psychotropic substances. Apart from this, the United Nations Office on Drugs and Crime (UNODC) is leading the international campaign to raise awareness about the major challenge that illicit drugs represent to society as a whole and especially to the young.

The problem of drug addiction can be resolved if the addicts are provided proper treatment. For the total recovery of the addict, psychological treatment alongwith medical treatment through individual counselling, group therapy, re-education and yoga is of immense help. The planning of treatment must focus on self-exposure and self-help. Unless an individual wishes to get rid of this habit and has a strong will power, it is really difficult for him to give it up. Awareness campaigns may also be used to good purpose. The media, the NGOs, self-help groups and other governmental agencies can play an influential role to educate the people about the abuse of drug addiction.

50. Social Networking Sites—
Blessing or Curse for the Society

The biggest gift that mankind has got is technology and more so, it is the information technology that has brought this world closer. While growth, development and speed of progress have increased due to this, a special bonding is taking place between human beings. This is through the social networking. The invention of social media has changed our lives tremendously.

With instant messaging, unlimited access, lower communication costs, raising awareness, and generating income by promoting goods and services, social media has revolutionised modern day society. However, by developing addition, changing the definition of privacy, creating scams and developing addition spreading anti-social messages, social media can also prove to be harmful to mankind. Thus, social media can be either a blessing or a curse to the world. It is left up to the public to decide.

Social networking is fundamentally shifting the way we interact, communicate, organise, form opinions and even shop to an online platform. It is blurring boundaries, increasing transparency and creating fluidity in everything we do. Companies, large and small, can no longer ignore or block social networking in their environment. The reality is that you need to go where your target audiences are and people are more likely to participate in a social media forum than any other venue. Customers, partners and employees, alike expect to engage with you *via* social media — it is a way for you to stay connected, gather feedback, recruit and collaborate. As a result, you need to support social media in your environment to enable innovation, increase productivity and accelerate growth that will drive your business. It all depends on how these sites, like Facebook or Twitter, are being used. Social media itself can be abused, overused and taken advantage of. However, the power of social media itself is probably greater than the power of any person, any novel, any ruler or even any country.

The power of social media can be something extremely influential. At first, this served as a revolution. For the very first time, people's voices and opinions were coming together to form something larger than themselves. This first took a huge role in the beginning of 2011 with the political upheaval of Egypt. The internet's far reaching speed combined with social media websites to create something unforgettable. The voices of Egypt stood together to overthrow the regime of Egyptian President Hosni Mubarak, and they spread all through the world. The power of social media was also noted when Mexicans turned to it for survival, not too long ago. Internet has got many social networking sites such as Facebook, Instagram, Twitter etc., and this has become a special platform for strangers to become friends and a powerful tool of communication.

With instant messaging, people can get in touch with their family and friends anywhere across the globe in seconds. And all we need is an internet connection. e.g. whatsapp is a social networking service that has drastically changed the speed of communication across the world. In the past, people used to send messages through letters and telegrams that would take days to reach their destination. Thanks to social media we do not have to wait for such a long time to hear from our loved ones.

Social media is the most effective way for businesses to conduct market research about the goods and services they promote to the public. Businesses can use the constructive criticism expressed by consumers to enhance their products and satisfy the demands of the public. e.g. opinions.com is a specially designed website for consumers to rate, appreciate and criticise new products and services that have recently been launched to the public. The other advantages of social networking sites are listed herewith:

- **Finding New Talent** Social networking sites like LinkedIn are a great resource for business owners to find new talent or even partners for a new venture.
- **Free Business Promotion** This is probably the biggest advantage for business owners using social networking sites. Facebook, Twitter, Linked in, Google + and many others are great forums to talk about your business, your services and even exhibit your industry expertise.
- **Low Cost Advertising** Some social networking sites provide a business owner with the opportunity to advertise to a very specific demographic for very little money. So you can advertise to exactly the customer that you want to attract and save money *versus* other forms of advertising.
- **Application** Through social networking sites, we can get the attention of huge number of target customers at a time, so it can be used to promote business, to advertise for our business, to take opinion of the customers that what changes they want. It can be used as a platform to promote and advertise business.
- **Build your Credibility** By consistently interacting and posting a person can build trust and credibility amongst their audience which in turn can lead to more business.
- **Ease of Communication** Social networking sites allow you a fast and free resource for communicating with customers and potential customers. Sales, promotions, special events can be announced by simply typing your message and posting it to your page or profile.

On the other hand, social media brought some shortcomings along with its advantages. One crucial disadvantage is the fact that young people have become isolated. To explain it better, even if teenagers communicate with other people, they do this *via* their mobile phone or an electronic computer. That way, they lose all contact with the outside world and become addicted to the internet. There has been an increasingly disturbing behaviour found in students and youngsters after their exposure towards such sites.

Another drawback is the fact that adolescents may talk to someone they don't know. Internet is full of dangers and one of them are people with malevolent intentions. More than 5000 young people fall victims in the hands of these people.

Another way in which social media can act as a curse is through its changing the behaviour of our society. Some say social media sites can lead to a shorter attention span and less efficient work. Not only that, but teenagers, tend to abuse social media and use it for popularity. Despite social media being a term with the connotation of connecting us, it is the thing it seems to be doing the least. People who abuse Facebook, e.g. by requesting and accepting as many 'friends' as possible, up to thousands, are giving those relationships artificial traits. Those relationships are so scattered and insignificant that many people don't even know some of their 'friends.' These relationships have no value, and are illusions of genuine relationships. In this abuse of social media, values of building relationships and making new connections, as were the intentions of social media, are being taken away and transformed wrongfully.

Social media has changed the definition of privacy. In the past, mankind was careful not to share any private information over the internet. But now, we have become so accustomed to social media that we provide all our private information to our loved ones across the internet. This can lead to identity theft which poses a serious problem to our lives. Strangers can steal our money, property and other assets in a moment. Therefore, we must be careful not to disclose our private information on the internet. Social media can be used to scam people for personal benefit. For instance, the Nigeria Letter 419 Advance Fee fraud is the most commonly known scam. Therefore, we have to be aware with whom we interact through social media. All in all, people have to weigh the pros and cons of social media to decide for themselves whether social media is a blessing or a curse to modern day society. The difference in your actions may be small, but the end result varies greatly and it is up to you to decide social media's role in your life. So folks, wake up and use technology as a boon and not a bane.

51. Gender Discrimination in India

Gender discrimination in India means health, education, economic and political discrimination between men and women in India. Today's India offers a lot of opportunities to women, with women having a voice in everyday life. Nevertheless India is still a male dominated society, where women are often seen as subordinate and inferior to men. Even though India is moving away from the male dominated culture, discrimination is still highly visible in rural as well as in urban areas, throughout all strata of society. While women are guaranteed equality under the Constitution, legal protection has a limited effect, as patriarchal traditions prevail.

According to the Global Gender Gap Report released by the World Economic Forum (WEF) in 2015, India was ranked 108 on the Gender Gap India (GGI) among 145 countries. When broken down into components of GGI, India performed well in political empowerment, but it scored poor on sex selective abortion. India also scored poorly on overall female to literacy and health rankings. India with a 2015 ranking of 108 had an overall score of 0.664 while Iceland topped the list with an overall score of 0.887. Similarly, UNDP has published Gender Inequality Index and ranked India at 130 out of 188 countries in 2015.

The Constitution of India has tried to provide equality status to women. Article 14 states that the state shall not deny to any person equality before or equal protection of law. Article 15 says that no women can be discriminated against on the ground of sex. Article 15 (3) emphasis that the state shall make special provisions for women and children and Article 16 provides equality of opportunity in matters relating to employment by the state. Article 39(a) emphasis that the citizens men and women equally, have the right to an adequate means of livelihood whereas Article 39(d) states that the state should secure equal pay for equal work for both men and women. Even though the Constitutional provisions provide equality between men and women, there is gender discrimination in India. There are many spheres of life where women are denied opportunity. Discrimination against females starts with their birth and continues throughout their lives. This is evident from the declined child sex ratio of India. According to 2011 census, the child sex ratio in India was 919 females to 1000 males which declined from 927 females to 1000 males in the previous decade.

The important factor for the declined sex ratio is female foeticide. Poverty, dowry and preference to son in the society are few reasons for female foeticide.

The economic gender discrimination can be viewed in the labour participation of women. As per census 2011, the workforce participation rate for females is 25.51% against 53.26% for males. Rural sector has a better female workforce participation rate of 30.02% compared with 53.03% for males whereas for urban sector the participation rate of females trails at 15.44% against 53.76% for males. 41.1% of female main and marginal workers are agricultural labourers, 24% are cultivators and 5.7% are household workers. Apart from this, certain jobs are decided to be done by females, which has stereotyped it. For instance, a reception job is always offered to a female, it is the mindset of the society that for a girl teaching job is more than sufficient and last, but not the least in few advertisements also, females are portrayed as if they are the once to perform it (washing machine ad or any perfume ad). On the other hand, women are not regarded to perform combat roles in the armed forces. Recently, a case was filed by few women officer to get permission for permanent commission in the defence.

Moving on to the other factor of discrimination is the field of education. According to the census 2011, the literacy rate of females is 65.46% compared to males which is 82.14% only states like Kerala and Mizoram have a high female literacy rate. The main reason behind the low female literacy rate is the mindset of the parents for whom girl's marriage is more important than her education. According to them, household work is a vital role to be played by a female rather than educating herself. For them spending money on girl's education is a wastage because they keep the money to be given as dowry.

The gender discrimination could be seen on the issues of health too. There are more men than women in India and this is due to sex selective abortion. The main reason behind the ratio is female foeticide wherein unborn girl child is killed in the womb of her mother. Another health factor which leads to discrimination is the nutrition given to the male child. It is the male child who gets all the nutritious and choicest foods while the girl child gets whatever is left behind after the male members have taken their meals or food. One of the main reasons for the high incidence of difficult births and anemia in women is the poor quality of food which a girl always gets either in her paternal home or in her in-laws.

Apart from this, the other measure for gender discrimination is the political participation of women in India. Women's participation in politics is not very impressive. The number of women politicians is small as compared to men. The majority of women are indifferent to politics, this is clear in their low participation in voting, in public demonstrations and in public debates. Women turnout during India's 2014 Parliamentary general elections was 65.63% as compared to 67.09% turnout of men. Whatever participation there is, it is mostly limited to women from the urban elite groups. The poorer women are more preoccupied with daily bread issues rather than the broader questions of women's development and national politics. Even though we had the first women Prime Minister and President of India as Indira Gandhi and Pratibha Devisingh Patil respectively, but the members are few. The bill to provide 33% reservation of seats for women in Lok Sabha is still pending in Parliament.

One field where gender discrimination in India is rampant in sports. Although, India boasts of several sports women like PT Usha, Sania Mirza, Jwala Gutta, Deepika Kumari, Saina Nehwal and so on, who have achieved accolades and made India proud, female discrimination is for more common in the field of sports than in other field. Where sports and women are concerned, many believe that males are better sportpersons than their counterparts as the male body on an average is of bigger built and weighs more than the female body. Major problems faced by female sportpersons are social, psychological, financial and family issues. Sexual harassment by the coaches is nothing new.

All these indicators points towards the sorry state of affairs in India regarding gender justice and women's human right. Various protective legislations have been passed by the Parliament to eliminate exploitation of women and to give them equal status in the society. For instance :

1. The PC and PNDT Act, 1994 is a major step taken by the government against female foeticide.
2. The Dowry Prohibition Act, 1961 eliminates the practice of dowry.
3. Schemes like 'Beti Bachao Beti Padhao', 'Kasturba Gandhi Balika Vidyalaya' and others promote girl child education.
4. The Government of India also initiated schemes for mother care which includes 'Mother and Child Tracking System', 'The Indira Gandhi Matritva Sahyog Yojana' etc.
5. The sexual harassment of women at workplace (Prevention, Prohibition and Redressal) Act, 2013 is a legislative act that seeks to protect women from sexual harassment at their place of work.

6. Hindu Succession Act, 1956 gives equal inheritance rights to daughters and sons.
7. 33% of seats are reserved for women in the Panchayats by the 73rd Constitutional Amendment Act. Few states including Bihar, Kerala, Rajasthan and Maharashtra have decided to provide 50% reservation for women in Panchayat.

Apart from these initiatives taken by the Government of India, many organisations are working against gender discrimination in India. These include:
- All India Democratic Women's Association
- National Commission on Women
- Ministry of Women Children and Development

So there are varied legislative safeguards and protective mechanisms for women, but the ground reality is very different. Despite all these provisions, women are still being treated as second rate citizens in our country. Therefore, what is needed is the movement for women's empowerment where women can become economically independent and self-reliant, where they can fight their own fears and go out in the world fearless.

Let's hope and wish that our participative democracy in times to come and with the efforts of both men and women would be able to find solutions to the problem of gender discrimination and would take us all towards our cherished dream of a truly modern society in both thought and action.

52. Superstition is the Religion of Feeble Minds

Since times immemorial superstitions have prevailed on the Earth and millions of people believe in them, while many laugh and ignore them. Superstition is a credulous belief or notion, not based on reason, knowledge or experience. The word is often used pejoratively to refer to folk beliefs deemed irrational. This leads to some superstitions being called 'old wives tales'. It is also commonly applied to beliefs and practices surrounding luck, prophecy and spiritual beings, particularly irrational belief that future events can be influenced or foretold by specific unrelated prior events.

Superstitions are the legacy of every civilisation and are inherited by the following generations. It originated perhaps, when man was at the mercy of natural elements. He respected and worshipped the forces of nature like the Sun, the Moon, water etc. He worshipped fire because of its destructive ability. When man started falling prey to diseases he started appeasing the Gods with offerings, penance and sacrifices to ward off evil spirits.

It is important to understand the various reasons for the birth of superstitions. Illiteracy, lack of knowledge and inability to reason out are the basis which generate superstitions. What is mysterious, unknown, unintelligible and inexplicable generates awe and fear. The fear in its turn gives rise to blind faith and superstitions. The sense of some insecurity, fear of ill luck and the dread of the unknown forces in the universe are ingrained in the human nature. It is believed that only illiterate people and villagers believe in superstition. But highly educated people living in urban areas are not free from these. They are educated but not enlightened and so rationality has been marginalised.

All the people in the world share some common superstitions. Belief in spirits, ghosts and witches, the cries of owl and ravens and mewing of cats are superstitions followed all over the globe. Walking under a ladder is believed to bring bad luck in some countries. Sneezing is also considered a bad omen by many people. The breaking of a mirror is supposed to bring bad luck to the family. People in the West still regards number '13' as an unlucky number. The reason behind this is that at 'The Last Supper,' Lord Jesus dined with his twelve disciples and was later crucified.

Salt spilled on the table on which they dined and therefore, even now spilling of salt is considered unlucky. Apart from this, Friday is considered as an inauspicious day to start a new work.

Looking at a country like India, a country of diverse culture and traditions, as well as a lot of superstitions. A cat crossing one's path, a sneeze or when someone interrupts or calls while one is going out are considered as bad signs. Similarly, there are auspicious and inauspicious days. People consult astrologers and priests to know the auspicious hours and days to start their work, projects and journey. The time and date of marriage, inauguration are fixed according to the advice of astrologers and the position of the planets and stars. Apart from this, the worst form of superstition followed in India is human sacrifice. Small children are sacrificed in the name of offerings to God and to become wealthy.

Even animals are sacrificed for the same purpose. Thus, it is not wrong to say that superstitions have made human beings more or less inhuman. Superstition can sometimes lead to horrifying crimes. Women, who are suspected of practicing witchcraft are tied and burnt alive. Apart from this, superstitions rule the minds of people. They poison the minds fatally and suppress the basic instinct to think and act. They implant an ideology of slavish servility and paralyse the will and mind. They stifle self-reliance and deter people from living creatively and productively.

Now the question arises that even after vast scientific developments, what is the place of superstition in the society? The Indian Constitution talks about the eradication of superstition through the Fundamental Duty in Article 51 A. It states to develop scientific temper, humanism and the spirit of inquiry and reform. To completely eradicate superstition from the society, it is important to change the mindset of people. Apart from this, spiritual leaders, cutting across religions, should be the helmsmen in creating awareness among the public about various ill effects of superstitions.

For the first time in India, the state of Maharashtra, approved a bill to curb superstitious practices after the assassination of Dr Narendra Dabholkar, an anti-superstition activist and author from Maharashtra. The Act titled as 'The Maharashtra Prevention and Eradication of Human Sacrifice and Other Inhuman, Evil and Aghori Practices and Black Magic Act, 2013' criminalises practices related to black magic, human sacrifices, use of magic remedies to cure ailments and other such acts which exploit people. The offences are non-bailable and cognisable.

However, mere amendments in law cannot ensure a permanent solution to this persistent problem. Stringent enforcement of the law, collective responsibility taken up by the government, activists and public play a crucial role in eradicating superstitions. In today's scientific world, it is necessary that we do not blindly follow all the superstitions passed on by our ancestors. We are modern, both in our outlook and the age we are in. It is important for us to have a judicious look or some logical reason behind every superstition before accepting it. We would then be able to give up those superstitions which have no rationality and applicability in today's life. It is only in this way that we can lead a normal life.

53. **Dowry**—A Curse to Indian Society

"Gods reside there where women are worshipped."

Even we are using the quotation since ancient era, it has its aspect in the present time as things have turned upside down in the society.

The dowry system is as old as the institution of marriage. It is a social evil prevalent not only in India, but also in other parts of the world. Many of the traditional customs have been given up but the custom of dowry has not only continued but flourished over the years. It reflects and perpetuates man's superiority over woman and hence is a mockery on the very idea of gender equality.

In India, dowry refers to the durable goods, cash and real or movable property that the bride's family gives to the bridegroom, his parents, or his relatives as a condition of the marriage. It is essentially in the nature of a payment in cash or some kind of gifts given to the bridegroom's family along with the bride and includes cash, jewellery, furniture, crockery and other household items that help the newly - weds set-up their home.

The system of dowry also prevailed during the ancient period. Parents of the bride provided gifts, money, property and other household items to the girl out of their own wish. It was known as 'streedhan' and was justified as the premarital right of the girl. She was the absolute owner and even the husband had no right over it. But with the passage of time, the definition of dowry changed. It became an important factor in marriage. It became necessary for the parents of the girl to give a good dowry to her whether they could afford it or not. The married life of a girl came to depend upon dowry. Several girls, whose parents could not afford a good dowry, had to commit suicide as their greedy in-laws made their lives miserable. The worst part is that this evil led to the birth of another evil of female foeticide.

It becomes important to understand what causes such an evil practice to prevail in the society when we are moving towards modernity. There are multiple reasons for this :

1. The social custom and tradition is one of the reasons for dowry. It is a feeling that practicing customs generates and strengthens solidarity.
2. A few people give more dowry just to exhibit their high social and economic status.
3. Dowry system is related to caste system as it is paid in order to marry a girl to a boy of the same caste.

4. Most of the people believe that their daughters should live happily with their husbands and hence provide dowry.
5. Illiteracy is an important cause because most of the people are unaware of the effect of dowry.

With the passage of time, dowry has evolved many characteristics when compared to the traditional practice of giving gifts. It is no more a voluntary exercise rather it is demanded diplomatically. These days the boy's family will say "Oh! we don't need anything, we need only your precious daughter" but will not hesitate to accept if the girl's parents offer precious articles on their own. On the other hand, the rate of dowry changes according to the qualification of the boy. There are 'rates' fixed for IAS, IPS, PCS, IES officers and qualified engineers and doctors. In a number of cases, the bridegroom and his family shamelessly present a list of things which they want at times, they haggle with bride's parents to get maximum amount of money and costly gifts as dowry. Today, marriage has become a stepping stone to acquire more wealth and social status. There is no other social institution which has been as commercialised as marriage.

Hardly is there a day when one does not read of dowry deaths in the national daily newspapers. Dowry is considered a major contributor towards violence against women in India. Some of these include physical violence, emotional abuse and even murder of brides and young girls prior to marriage. The predominant type of dowry crimes relate to cruelty, domestic violence, abetment to suicide and dowry death which includes bride burning and murder. In India, total of 24771 dowry deaths have been reported in past 3 years with maximum of them occurring in Uttar Pradesh with 7048 deaths. It is followed by Bihar and Madhya Pradesh with 3830 and 2252 deaths during the same period.

As per National Crime Records Bureau data, the country has recorded 3.48 lakh cases of cruelty by husband or his relative and West Bengal tops the chart with 61259 such cases in past 3 years followed by Rajasthan (44311) and Andhra Pradesh (34835).

The government has taken many steps to stop the abominable practice of dowry. The Dowry Prohibition Act, 1961 marked the beginning of a new legal framework of dowry harassment laws. It prohibits the request, payment or acceptance of dowry and provides penalty for the same. Apart from this, Section 304 B was added to the Indian Penal Code (IPC) which made dowry death a punishable offence. Further Section 113 B of the Evidence Act, 1872 creates an additional presumption of dowry death when it is shown that before her death, the woman had been subjected to cruelty. Section 498 A IPC was included in 1983 to protect women from cruelty and harassment. In 2005, the Government of India passed the 'protection of women from Domestic Violence Act' to provide a civil law remedy for the protection of women from domestic violence.

India is also party to several international human rights instruments which provide theoretical remedies to the dowry problem. These include the Universal Declaration of Human Rights (UDHR), the Convention on the Elimination of All Forms of Discrimination Against Women (CEDAW), International Covenant on Civil and Political Rights (ICCPR) and the International Covenant or Economic, Social and Cultural Rights (ICESCR).

Apart from this, several women's organisations have come into being in order to check this evil. Media is also playing an important role in curbing this disease from the society. State Governments have come forward with better legislation. Even our young boys and girls are taking an oath not to follow this evil custom. Much has been done, but much more needs to be done.

It may be concluded that the abolition of the dowry system would be a landmark social reform. With whatever intentions this custom may have been started, it cannot be denied that it has failed to give equal status to women in the society. The time has come to scrape the roots and branch of dowry system. Unless we become more progressive in our outlook, less orthodox in our ways and more revolutionary in our ideas, dowry will remain the bane of our society.

54. Global Disarmament

Global disarmament is the dream of a number of pacifists and many a weak nation. We have heard a lot of the advantages of disarmament and have cherished a dream of a world without arms and weapons. The United Nations has been constantly striving to achieve the goal of disarmament since its inception.

Once again on 24th September, 2009, the United Nations Security Council adopted the resolution sponsored by US calling for global disarmament. President Obama said, "It enshrines our shared commitment to a goal of a world without nuclear weapons." It is a laudable statement by the President of a supreme power. In fact when we talk of disarmament, the problem relates only to non- proliferation of nuclear weapons. It is sheer hypocrisy on the part of nuclear weapon states who are permanent members of the Security Council. They never talk of complete disarmament.

That is itself enshrined in Nuclear Non-proliferation Treaty that came into being on 5th March, 1970. America has been after India since 1970s when America, China and Pakistan axis during 1960-70 was working against India in full fury. India has serious objections to being asked to sign the NPT. Our national concerns are supreme. China, Pakistan and America with ambivalent attitude are tremendous threat to India's security. This time India asked America not to ask her to sign the treaty. Rather it was feared that India was being targeted. However, Obama assured the Indian Prime Minister that UNSC resolution asking the non-NPT states to sign the treaty was not directed against India.

The NPT (1970) was quite discriminatory. According to the treaty Non-Nuclear weapon states could not acquire nuclear weapons or technology related to such weapons. They are required to place all their existing weapons and technologies under the supervision of International Atomic Energy Agency. Nuclear Weapon States were not subject to any of such obligations. These unfair provisions have created virtual nuclear apartheid. In fact, the attitude of the Nuclear Weapon States (NWS) is self-serving and defeats the objectives of disarmament. Nuclear disarmament, by no means, is total disarmament; it is partial and concerns only to proliferation of nukes. The NPT was signed in 1970 for 25 years under which Non-Nuclear Weapon States (NNWS) could not acquire nuclear arms. Moreover, the countries having nuclear weapons before 1967 were termed as NWS. It also did not spell out time bound programme for NWS. The result was that in 1995 when NPT came up for review surprisingly it was extended indefinitely in the form of CTBT (Comprehensive Test Ban Treaty).

The step amounts to virtual legitimisation of the nukes of NWS. Ironically, NNWS had been desisting from carrying out nuclear explosions all along while NWS developed through a series of tests over 35000 nuclear weapons.

Apprehensive of nexus between America, China and Pakistan, India was forced to conduct Pokharan I in 1974, with a view to equipping itself with nuclear deterrent. Again seeing through the designs of N5 states in 1995 (the review of NPT) India gave up voluntary moratorium and conducted Pokhran II in 1998. However, in accordance with her responsible nuclear policy, it declared that it would develop minimum credible nuclear deterrent and not engage in arms race. At the same time no first use and no use against NNWS also form parts of Indian Nuclear Doctrine.

Now, when NWS have extended the tenure of CTBT in their favour indefinitely, the nukes of these countries have got legitimised. What is more, they will not be deterred from developing and refining the technology in future. They are now in a position to perfect weapons, without any further tests. A test ban, therefore, will not affect N5 powers adversely while NNWS will ever be at the mercy of these powers. The irony is that CTBT does not offer any time bound programme for nuclear or total disarmament. Like NPT, CTBT is also discriminatory. Therefore, India has objected to the Article 14 of the CTBT that lays down that the treaty will not come into existence unless all the 44 countries with nuclear installations sign it. The Clause also threatens severe sanctions against those who veto it.

India's security scenario is dismal. China has been helping Pakistan since long to make her a strong nuclear power with collision of China and Myanmar and no guarantee of nuclear umbrella from super powers. India has no other option than reject CTBT outrightly. India has always been taken for a ride by America. Despite the signing of Indo-American Nuclear Deal, India should be wary of the designs of American nuclear policy. The efforts of the UNO to achieve total disarmament are expressive of hypocrisy on the vital question of disarmament. Sometimes it appears that through disarmament America and other NWS are interested in perpetuating their supremacy.

55. India and China

Indio-China relations have a history of chronic strife that India would like to forget but which China would not let us forget. Way back in 1950, after the Communist Revolution, the US offered China's UN Security Council seat to India. Pt. Nehru, India's first Prime Minister turned down the offer on the advice of USSR lest China should be offended. Within a year, the process of annexation of Tibet by China began. What is more, today China is stoutly opposing India's inclusion in the UN Security Council. Our first Prime Minister, Nehru, visited China on October 1954 and he was overwhelmed with the amazing reception he got on his first visit. The doctrine of *Panchsheel* (Five principles of coexistence) was established. Yet the ties between the two became strained with border skirmishes and discovery of Chinese road in Aksai Chin. In 1959, Dalai Lama, fled Tibet and was granted political asylum by India. In 1960, the conflict between the two countries came into open. When Chinese Prime Minister Zhou Enlai visited India, India rejected the Chinese claim over Arunachal Pradesh. In 1962, Chinese troops entered deep into India with orders to conquer. Within fifteen years of Independence India experienced two wars, one with Pakistan and the other with China. Both these wars were designed to serve some purposes and they have proved their psychological purpose successfully. China came and smeared an indelible stigma on our national honour. Our ill-equipped soldiers lost their lives and were subjected to the trauma of dishonour.

China still has not given up its claim on Arunachal Pradesh. China helped Pakistan to achieve nuclear status in the 1990s. In return, Pakistan acknowledged China's suzerainty over Aksai Chin. China is helping Bangladesh to develop its Missile System. Its closeness to Nepal and the rise of Maoism there do not bode well for India. China has bought Coco islands from Burma in the vicinity of India. China continues to enter 4,057 km long India border at its will painting it red. Now China has openly come out claming 2.1 sq km finger area as the Northern most tip of Sikkim, almost a settled issue for India. After 68 years of Independence, India is as pathetic a country as it was in 1962. It was squarely proved when China entered our territory at will and painted it red.

The pity is that India is in no position to bargain with China both in economic and military might. China's GDP at Current Price is 11385 (billion USD) whereas India's GDP is at 2183 (billion USD). On the other hand, China's GDP per capita at current price is 14189.5 and India's GDP per capita is 6209.5. In every field India lags woefully behind. The world was petrified with display of China's military might on its national day in 2015. Gold rained on China in 2012 London Olympics.

China got 38 Gold Medals whereas India didn't win even a single. In military might, India pales into insignificance. China is possessed of stock pile of nuclear arms that compares well with America and Russia. China has all the ingredients of a super power to impose its will on other countries. For decades China has been projecting itself as the motherland of Himalayan provinces. They claim Arunachal Pradesh as part of Tibet. Since 1984, China has not issued visas to the residents of Arunachal Pradesh claiming that visas are issued to foreign nationals. The same kind of trick they have tried to play with J & K nationals. The Chinese soldiers are reported to be present in large number in Pakistan Occupied Kashmir.

Will New Delhi ever respond to Beijing? When our media and few interested optimists fix a particular year for India emerging as a super power, they must be knowing that the question of super power can be settled among other things on the sweet will of China. China being our neighbour for centuries understands our defeatist mind set. In every field we have to do much of catching up with the Dragon. China is fighting water war covertly. China's sinister plan to divert the water of Brahmaputra to feed its parched north-east region is a matter of great concern. In fact China is fighting a multi-pronged war with India—psychologically, economically and militarily. India can no longer shy away from making hard diplomatic choices against Chinese expansionist and revisionist policies. But the most important question is whether China will loosen its hold on Indian territory?

56. India and Globalisation

Integration of national economies on global bases has become indispensable. The term liberalisation is synonymous with globalisation and privatisation. Liberalisation implies shift from command economy to market economy. Its relationship with socialism is over all over the world. During the last ten years sweeping changes have been going on in the economy of the world. Under the new economic order no nation can survive in isolation. Therefore, no country can escape the process of globalisation. Globalization implies that a government must introduce liberalisation in its economy. It points out the phase of globalisation in the economy which aims at unification with the global economic order. For this purpose, free imports, curtailment of custom duties and free and direct in-flow of foreign investment should be allowed. In addition to this, full convertibility of Indian rupee has also been undertaken as one of the measures under the present phase of globalisation.

For developed economies, globalisation is an aspect where there are no constraints in dealing with national and international trade policy. Globalisation has not only affected the economic order of the world but the also the social and cultural aspect of the countries. America is the leader in the process of Globalisation since the last decade. It is now clear to one and all one that no country can survive without abiding by the process of globalisation. Liberalisation is the natural outcome of the policy of globalisation. The 19th and 20th centuries belonged to England and the 21st century belongs to America. It is no exaggeration to state that economic imperialism is the cult of American policy. Every big and small country has to follow the dictates of economic policies laid down by the United States of America. The result is very obvious.

WTO is the manifestation of this policy and almost every country falls to be a member of WTO. In the Indian context, the year 1990-91 was an unprecedented year. Indian economy was under stress. Our economic growth was at an all time low level of 1.1%. Foreign investors had lost faith in the Indian market. Capital was flowing out. So it was very essential for us to form a multi-directional programme. As a result of this we decided to do away with the licence system. We undertook Operation Globalisation with a view to bringing our economic policies in line with the developed nations in the world.

The first step towards globalisation was taken in the form of devaluation. By this the value of the rupee declined by 18 to 19% against major currencies in the world. Secondly, sweeping changes were made in the trade policy. In 1991, the Government of India announced a package of trade policy reforms. Under this, exports and imports procedures were simplified.

Even 51% foreign equity was permitted in trading houses. Thirdly, India undertook the policy of convertibility of rupee, under which foreign exchange access was liberalised for current business transactions. Fourthly, Industrial policy reforms were also under taken. These positive signals gave further thrust to our economy. The encouragement to private enterprises was adopted as a matter of policy. The disinvestment in public sector undertakings was also encouraged. Golden hand shake policy was introduced to get rid of surplus staff.

Undoubtedly, globalisation has played a great part in increasing the role of foreign investment through Foreign Direct Investment and Foreign Institutional Investment. US played a major role in international capital market till the crisis in 2006. Since globalisation slarted everything around world economies had been optimistic. But at the end of 2006, international melt down (financial crisis) set in with the beginning of sub-prime market crisis in the US.

As a result the mortgage companies in loaning business suffered when the number of defaulters increased. Lehmen brothers, the oldest investment bank in the US, was the worst sufferer. USA is yet to recover fully from the 2006 melt down. In fact the shadow of another meltdown is looming large and European economies are cracking. When the economies of the world are integrated the hazards of international economic depression cannot be wished away.

Many financial experts are of the opinion that there would be a slowdown in the world economy. In the era of global integration none of the markets will remain unaffected. Globalisation and WTO too are criticised on the grounds that these organisations are the tools for economic imperialism. World Trade, which used to grow faster than the GDP, seems to have turned sluggish. There have been reports stating decline of exports from Taiwan, Egypt, Indonesia, Jordan and China to name as few.

But if analysed overall, the process of globalisation has changed the industrial pattern and social life of people and has immensely impacted the Indian Trade System. Though the pace is fluctuating, India has seen the positive side of the coin and may overcome obstacles to adopt global procedures to expand business at an international scale.

57. Indo-US Nuclear Deal

In July 2005, the then President of the United States George Bush visited India. It was agreed between the two countries that henceforth civilian and military nuclear facilities would be treated separately. This agreement became the basis of an agreement between India and America in October 2008. The agreement signed was intended to govern a Civil Nuclear Deal between two countries. The bill had to pass through various tortuous stages: IAEA safeguards, Nuclear Supplier Group and approval of American Congress and Senate Houses.

The Indo-US Nuclear Deal witnessed the most controversial Indian Lok Sabha session. It had all the trappings of a mystery fiction leading to a trust vote. The changing statements of the Prime Minister did not win the trust of the people. The government was never candid about the draft treaty. The principal opposition party was not taken into confidence. Instead, government preferred to be bullied by the CPM, who had taken up the Chinese viewpoint by proxy. Yet government miraculously survived courtesy the Samajwadi Party who now regret having saved the ruling coalition headed by the Congress Party. The Indo-US Nuclear Deal is the key to developing nuclear power in India. Nuclear power is an important option for the future. Just 3% of energy in India is generated by nuclear power while the agreement would help India to aim at 10% nuclear power.

The Nuclear Supplier Group waiver is truly a global opportunity. India is no more an isolated nation in the field of nuclear technology. India is now virtually a nuclear powered nation. It is expected to generate a US $ 40 million trade opportunity. India might be able to set up 24 imported light water reactors in the next 50 years. Additionally, 12 indigenous heavy water plants would be set up. All the imported reactors will generate 10000 MW each by the year 2020. India is likely to achieve a 52 thousand MW target from the present 4120 MW.

The nuclear deal is expected to usher in self-sufficiency in the energy sector. The alliance with the USA should prove all-pervasive from political, military and economic considerations. Since the announcement of the proposal about the deal in 2005, there has been increasing adjustment of our economic policy to enable flow of American capital into India. India badly needs an infrastructure and manufacturing base.

Despite all this, one question remains to be answered by the government-has the deal ended India's 34 years isolation since Pokhran I in 1974? Now America wants to universalise NPT membership. As of now, the deal is yet to become fully operational. Yet the historic agreement has certainly opened the door of opportunity for India. India has signed civil nuclear deals with many countries including France, Russia, Mongolia, Namibia, Kazakhstan, Argentina, UK, Canada and South Korea. India has definitely emerged as a nuclear power, but a nuclear power without a right to conduct a nuclear test. In future, such a move by the US would undermine the letter and spirit of the agreement and the clean waiver accorded by the NSG.

However, it has become more evident that America wants the NPT signed. India is the obvious target. China is said to have offered to Pakistan a nuclear deal on similar lines to what America has signed with India. The future would unravel the mystery of that deal. Let us wish India well.

58. Inclusive Growth in India

Inclusive growth is synonymous with pragmatic justice. Sense of justice is not confined to idealistic justice. What is more, pragmatic justice is opposed to fixed or dogmatic way of justice. The society that is ever expanding cannot be governed by transcendental justice. If we want a gentle and compassionate economic growth, it cannot be achieved through charity. Inclusiveness is the key to pragmatic justice. It is the exclusiveness of the rich that have rendered the world unjust. In an unjust social order, people have the right to be angry.

Founding fathers of our Constitution have done yeoman service to the nation by providing for inclusive growth. Economically weaker sections and disadvantaged sections of our society are sufficiently provided for. Since Independence, our government has come out with various schemes to dispense pragmatic justice to the millions of the poor and deprived sections of society.

There has been, of course, awareness in the nation about the injustice done to those who have been left behind in receiving the benefits of economic growth. With this end in view Indian Government has launched various schemes from time-to-time. Besides reservation policy, the schemes like National Rural Gurantee Act are in operation.

The largest Public Distribution System in the world was introduced in 1965. Mid-day meal scheme in the schools was started for providing food and education to children under one roof. There are separate schemes for girl children and adolescent girls. *Antyodaya Annayojna* and *Annapurna* yojana provide rice and wheat at subsidised rates to the poor. In a nutshell, there are number of poverty alleviating programmes launched by the Government of India. At the same time, it is right to be worried about where populism could take politics.

Protests in the West is a right type of warning to market driven economies. Occupy Wall Street movement caught the hearts and minds of everyone in Europe. It needs no blast to spark the idea of revolution in developing countries like India where crony capitalism coupled with corruption in public places can do worse. We are in the nascent stage of development. In America and Europe, it happened after two decades of stable growth. Now the streets of these developed nations are resounding with the slogans "We are the 99%". In their capitalist economies the wealth in said to have concentrated in the hands of 1% people. Such are the dangers of exclusive growth. By one estimate 58% of the real economic growth in America of the past 30 years was captured by 1% people.

The concentration of wealth in India among the rich is alarming. According to one estimate 17.2% of GDP amounting to 11 lakh crore lies in the hands of 44 Indian capitalists. The world has come to believe that capitalism is no more at fault. It is crony capitalism that is at fault. Money spent by Indian Government on welfare schemes is mind boggling. The Food Security Act in the making may involve an astouding amount. Despite all this, poverty-line for India is at an average level of ₹ 32 in rural areas and ₹ 47 per day in urban areas a day. Among the average non-poor, the average consumption per day was just ₹ 44, per person per day in rural areas and ₹ 80 in urban areas (NSS Survey).

Urban areas comprise besides others, the mighty rich class of politicians, Industrialists and higher bureaucracy. This fact should be kept in mind in the calculation of average urban consumption.

However, equality in consumption is not achievable. One wonders where goes the huge money of the tax payers spent to make economic growth inclusive in India. In the case of India "the best way to sell corruption is if it is disguised with human face." says Surjit S. Bhalla of the Oxus Investments. What he means to say is that all our plans to bring about inclusive economic growth expire half way in the hands of cronies responsible for the execution of state administered and state directed poor programmes.

The problem with Indian political leaders is that they swear by the interests of the people but in disguise they aim at political gains. The specialists in the principal ruling party devise crony ways to win elections. They believe that they will win the next elections because where else will the poor go? Indian political system has to devise a system to do away with cronyism and corrupt, the formidable obstacles in the way of Inclusive Growth.

59. Reforming the Public Sector

Today privatisation is a worldwide phenomenon. The privatisation of PSUs in India has already been accepted as a matter of Government policy. But remember, privatisation is not a panacea for the economic ills of the country. Reforms in public sector undertakings will save our huge infrastructure. The PSUs number no less than 300 as on today. We must look into the causes of their failure and rectify them.

Instead of talking about the privatisation of the public sector units it may be more useful to talk about reforms. First we must make a distinction between commercial units and public utilities units. Hotels, steel and textile mills etc are bound to earn profits. Why should a steel mill or a hotel not earn any profit? Why should government start all these if it cannot manage such units efficiently? If that is so, let government provide good administration to the country and not take to commercial activities. Then there are units to serve the people such as hospitals, education, transport and medicines.

After independence the government invested in steels mills, heavy engineering and other industries because private sector was not willing to invest in them. After a reasonable time these industries should have started showing profits. Instead, these units came to survive on subsidies. We should assign a new role to select public sector enterprises within the framework of the new economic order in the areas given below.

Increased autonomy should be given to these units. Just as we have started with the Navratnas, these companies should be granted autonomous status. Accountability should be made compulsory, as is expected of managerial staff in private sector. Obsolete technology should be replaced. Political and official interference should be eliminated. A competitive spirit in production, price fixation and marketing should be developed. There should not be import restriction or controls in the wake of the recent liberalisation.

In fact the concept of public sector undertaking is obsolete in the days of WTO. But in view of the peculiar Indian conditions, public sector should not be considered obsolete when globalisation is the order of the day. Obviously, the steps taken so far are half-hearted. No concrete steps have yet been taken to improve the technology and efficiency of the public sector. At the same time, privatisation should not be considered a panacea for the ailing public sector. Reforms are possible but political will is needed.

In fact private sector should also be roped in. Forgetting ideological differences, a healthy national sector needs to be developed, Public and private sectors should be complementary. The need of public enterprises in public utility areas cannot be denied. In the areas of transport, railways, hospitals and medicines, government should bring about reform earnestly. Let those undertakings with commercial overtones be privatised lest they become a drain on the Indian economy. Therefore, the ideal solution lies in developing a robust national sector without making a distinction between private and public sectors.

60. Poverty in India

Poverty is the greatest threat to social life and political stability of a country. It is a social phenomena in which a section of society is unable to fulfil even its basic necessities of life. Earlier poverty was defined in nutritional terms of per capita daily intake of 2400 calories in rural areas and 2100 calories in urban areas. India had 27.5 per cent poor in the country in 2004-05.

The economic adviser to the then Prime Minister, Suresh Tendulkar had come up in 2009 with an estimated 37.7 per cent number of the poor in the country. According to the expert group appointed by plan panel chaired by Suresh Tendulkar, a person is poor if he spends ₹ 20 a day in cities and ₹ 16 a day in villages (at 2004-05 prices). At today's prices it comes to ₹ 32 a day in cities and ₹ 26 a day in rural India. It means that a family of four, living in Delhi with a monthly income of ₹ 3890 is not to be considered poor. These facts embodied in an affidavit were submitted to the Supreme Court with a footnote that one could also buy health with this amount of income. On the contrary protestors carrying placards outside the Planning Commission had a different story to tell about this spending figure to determine the number of the poor: "Poor person allowed to eat only half a katori every day." Another placard said: "Poor person allowed to spend on vegetables ₹ 36 a month, the cost of only two cauliflowers."

These absolute rock bottom indicators of poverty point to a starvation line than to a poverty line. The expert group, therefore estimates that a third of our people are poor. If the government adopts the internationally accepted US $ 2 a day figure (prices adjusted), the numbers are likely to be closer to 74 per cent as estimated by the World Bank. The figures given by the Tendulkar Committee are disturbing because the kind of life led by the poor does not include access to public services. Forgetting any solutions, government is busy projecting the success of the economy in terms of GDP per annum.

In fact poverty has many dimensions. We are yet to decide upon the criteria to measure dimensions of poverty. Our experts take into consideration only economic aspects such as consumption and household expenditure to determine poverty. But poverty also involves social concerns and one's access to public services like clean drinking water, sanitation and healthcare. Whatever the truth about the figures. India still ranked 130th among 188th countries on the Human Development Index (HDI) in 2014 (UNDP report).

In short, anyone who lives in dehumanising conditions in which one is unable to look after one's basic needs such as economic, social etc, is poor. Moreover, poverty is socially generated, reinforced and perpetuated under an inequitable economic system. The economic growth under a global economy does not necessarily reach the poorest people and vulnerable sections of society. The concentration of wealth in a few hands is an indispensable part of a market-driven economy. Disparity in income is inevitable. It is also a hard fact that no progress is feasible without rapid GDP growth. But this is only half the story. The other half of the story has to be social policies, inclusive policies and agricultural policies aimed at helping out the poor. The Indian Government has launched several poor-oriented policies such as subsidised food, free medical care, social security schemes, cheap housing and free education.

These schemes are for those who the government identifies as poor. The rest are left out. The problem is further compounded when government is unable to identify who is actually poor because official studies indicate another story. Worse, the help is reduced to a trickle by the time it reaches the impoverished.

The most crucial factor in our poverty alleviation strategy involves evaluation of our plans made for the purpose from time to time. Let us take the example of the Public Distribution System. We spend ₹ 60000 crore under this scheme to provide relief to the poor. A huge amount is also being spent on Integrated Child Develop services. But no evaluation of the programmes has been made for the past several years. The benefits of the programmes are not reaching those who they are meant for. At the time of independence, there were 20 crore poor people in the country against the population figure of 33 crore. Today the poverty figures have drastically risen. Where have we gone wrong?

Whatever the different reports on the number of poor or non-poor say, all are biased, subjective and controversial. There is no uniformity, even near-uniformity between the figures. Estimates are, therefore, useful only as broad indicators which can help government to formulate policies for alleviation of poverty. We should be fair with the poor and not play with their lives. It is more important because, according to one estimate, 17.2% of GDP amounting to ₹ 11 lakh crore lies in the hands of 55 Indian capitalists.

61. Population Explosion in India

India's population is the second largest in the world, the first being that of China. We have already crossed the 1.2 billion mark. Needless to say, this is a horrible scenario, perhaps more horrible than a nuclear flare up. Population is the mother of all evils in our country. Poverty, diseases, violence, unemployment, pollution and corruption are some of the evils that are obstacles to our progress. No wonder, India has 17.84% of the world's population covering only 2.4% of the land area in the world.

India is faced with a paradoxical situation. Birth rate has actually come down. According to 2011 census, birth rate has fallen, but this advantage has been neutralised by the fall in death rate. Coupled with this, life expectancy has also increased to 68 years.

The number of women in the reproductive age group and average age of marriage among women is also a potential factor in determining the birth rate in the country. The reproduction span for Indian women is about 35 years. Migration from neighbouring countries has further aggravated the problem. In 1971, about 10 million refugees found their way into India.

Linked with the population problem is an essential question of food supply. Capital and land availability have also come down. Large scale deforestation is now occurring at the rate of 15 million hectares per year. At this rate, by 2050 India is expected to be a forestless country. The rising income of India gets distributed among the rising population. Thus, the overall increase in national income has no real impact on the standard of living.

India adopted the National Population Policy 2000 to check population growth. But it took five years to hold the first meeting of the National Commission on Population constituted to implement government's agenda on population. In fact, our population policy has taken a political beating.

Some humorous proposals by the Indian Health Minister are in circulation. When light reaches villages, 80% population growth can be reduced through TV. So the entertainment contraceptive will bring down population growth because the minister says that when there is no light, people engage in activities of population growth. It appears as if light and entertainment depresses the libido!

The fact is that over 18 million people (officially) are being added every year. If we have to achieve the goal set by United Nations, which is the eradication of poverty by 2050, we cannot afford to indulge in entertainment contraceptives. According to United Nations Population Fund, India will overtake China by 2050. China's strict family planning measures such as 'one family one child' has paid a dividend. Our government has been confusing between strict and coercivue measures. The reasons are obvious.

Why forget that India's population increase has largely been among the poor and least educated sections of people. With negligible investment in primary education and public health, we cannot continue to add mouths to feed and expect government to rolling out charitable schemes. Census 2011 has revealed an alarming growth in our population, about 18 million people. Now, they have to be fed, educated and housed.

This is a huge burden on our developing economy. Moreover, our population has resulted in overcrowding the Indian cities and encouraging a growing culture of violence, terrorism and corruption. Poverty and illiteracy are traceable to our increasing numbers. At the time of independence, our population was 330 million. Today we are over 1.2 billion. The increase has led to massive environmental damage. A major effort on a very huge scale needs to be made towards stabilising our population. India is sitting on a volatile volcano.

62. The Role of Multinationals in Indian Economy

Multinational corporations, as the name implies, are large corporate institutions. They have a variety of business interests. With their headquarters in one country, they carry on their business in more than one country. There are a number of criteria to define a multinational company. But the only criterion that comes to mind is their global and transnational activities.

Globalisation since its advent has been looked at suspiciously as a means of the developed nations bringing the developing nations in line with their own interests. Globalisation and economic liberalisation came as a pioneer of new hopes and developing nations were promised economic prosperity. In isolation, they could not survive, they were told. The World Trade Organisation (WTO) is the organisation which ensures that globalisation works in favour of developed countries. Various WTO ministerial conferences show that globalisation has not proved what it promised to be. MNCs from the economically developed countries establish their outlets in the areas that benefit them. They would not invest in the sectors beneficial for the developing countries. Even in India, production is guided by MNCs. In international conferences the developed nations defend the interests of their own MNCs with authority.

What is the real truth about the multinational operations in the context of India? Multinationals are not an unmixed blessing for developing countries like ours. Do they really contribute to the economic stability and progress of the host countries? As a matter of fact, their utility lies in the field in which they are working. They must not be allowed to work in non-priority areas indiscriminately.

In the case of India, foreign investment has flowed in non-priority areas in a significant proportion. Around 40% multinational companies in India are operating in sectors like hotels, tourism, food processing, service sector etc. There are very high rates of return in these sectors. Out of the total foreign investment in India by various countries, the share of USA alone is about 40%. Again, out of a total of 3700 collaborations, almost half of them are financial in nature. The result is that financial sector in India remains erratic.

Foreign investment in non-priority sectors has resulted in a new kind of consumerism in the form of colas, ice-creams, music systems, potato wafers, expensive bikes and cars. These items serve the need of only about 20% of population living in urban areas. On the other hand, the rest of the population is suffering from the lack of basic amenities. Again the portfolio investment in India is in the form of 'hot' money. This money can be easily diverted to their own countries. So, it is a mistake to treat portfolio investment as a stable factor. The increased Foreign Direct Investment (FDI) leads to inflationary trends. It is again a mistake to think that the entry of multinationals would ensure the transfer of high technology to India. There is no indication that technology is being transferred to the country. We just get the taste of screw driver technology.

At present multinational companies are operating in the areas where they get an excessively high rate of return. Take the example of Colgate Palmolive. Their rate of an return is estimated to be 80%. It is strange that we have not got a response from multinational companies engaged in oil production, power generation and other priority areas. They have, in fact, only made three solid contributions to our national economy.

Firstly, they have used indigenous raw material instead of imports. *Secondly*, a cadre of professional managers have been trained. Thirdly, they have set up an efficient trading infrastructure.

In conclusion, one can say that a multinational corporation is a mix of virtues and vices, boons and banes. Therefore, the government should adopt a pragmatic approach to them because multinationals have come to stay in the present day world. We will have to learn to live with multinationals under the new global economic order.

63. Special Economic Zone (SEZ)

Special Economic Zones are the areas demarcated specifically for private companies to carry on production and trade activities. The units operating in these areas are entitled to various benefits such as exemptions in taxes, lesser tariffs and less customs duties.

In the wake of enactment of the SEZ law in February 2006, a number of SEZs have been approved in many states. On the whole, 86107 hectares of land was acquired for 237 SEZs in 19 states in 2008. Under this law, a ceiling on total amount of land to be used for an SEZ has been fixed. As of now, limit for construction of SEZ is 5000 hectares of waste an and barren land and 200 hectares of cultivable land.

The development of an SEZ requires a large tract of land. Urban land supply is already under pressure because of increasing population and trade and commerce activities. Therefore, most of the areas acquired for SEZ constitute rural areas or suburbs of cities. Agricultural land has also been taken over by builders, increasing the pressure on land. However, many agro-processing industries and agricultural economic zones are to be built to boost the agricultural sector. The moot point is whether such developments will be commensurate with the agricultural land foregone for this purpose. If all the SEZs are constructed, we need more than 0.12% of total agricultural area. This area, if cultivated, could feed millions and would serve as a basis for the livelihood of many villagers.

In fact, land is fixed in supply. As the population increases, the price of land goes up. Had the land acquired so far been cultivated and properly utilised, it would have been more profitable than the construction of SEZs, says an estimate.

From this point, the land acquisition is not as simplistic as it appears to be. The fact is borne out by the furore over the land acquisition issue in Nandigram. Even though rural land is the only option left for acquistion, obstacles faced are no less monumental. For villagers, land is both a question of survival and traditional belief of ownership leading to status in society. To overcome these difficulties, some of the provisions of both Land Acquisition Bill and Rehabilitation and Resettlement Bill have been amended.

Acquisition of land for public facilities and infrastructure can be forced by government. In that case, the socio-cultural environment is vitiated. Above all, the political fallout is a most important factor for the ruling party. However, rehabilitation and resettlement of the uprooted people is intrinsic to development. Government has come up with Rehabilitation and Resettlement Bill, which is an improvement on the previous bill. Confrontation in West Bengal over land acquisition has thrown open a great divide between the objectives of development and the traditional belief of land ownership.

The gulf has to be bridged to the satisfaction of our farmer community that has already been suffering for long. The pressure on agricultural land acquisition has further increased on account of urban building activity. In many cases private builders lure the villagers with false promises. In a nutshell, land acquistion by government deserves to be carefully handled lest our farmers should suffer in the end. In the wake of the Allahabad High Court judgement on acquisition of land in NOIDA, a

ESSAY WRITING

threatening situation has come up. Farmers are up in arms against the UP Government. The sale of land to the private builders has been declared null and void.

Millions of rupees of the builders and the home-buyers is likely to be wasted unless some solution is found. Hence acquisition of rural land is no more simple for any purpose. Finally, the Land Acquisition Policy in a new form has been incorporated in the revised LARR 2011. Now the govt has proposed the clubbing of acquisition of land and resettlement in the proposed Land Acquisition and Rehabilitation and Resettlement Bill 2011.

64. Floods in India

Floods are regular features in India. Years and years have passed by but the situation has gone from bad to worse. In the beginning the floods spreaded only in a few kms, now they affect acres of land and millions of lives.

Recently, 2015 Assam floods in the State of Assam were triggered by heavy rainfall is neighbouring Arunachal Pradesh State through Brahmaputra river and its tributaries. The floods are reported to have caused the death of 42 people and resulted in numerous landslides and road blockages and affected 1.65 million people in 21 districts. Flooding affected 2100 villages and destroyed standing crops across an area of 180000 hectares (440 000 acres).

In India, flood conditions may take place on account of:
- rivers in spate,
- melting of snow,
- storm surges,
- short storms causing flash floods.

Floods in India are caused by many reasons : inadequate capacity within the banks of the rivers, river banks erosion, landslides, poor natural drainage, heavy rain fall etc. Nature of the flood problem in India is complex. Floods are mostly confined to the northern bank of the river Ganga. The tributaries of Ganga like Kosi, Gandak etc. over flow and often change their course.

The problem of drainage congestion causes floods in the Western and North-Western areas of Uttar Pradesh. Some time the floods are caused in Ghaghra and the Gandak rivers as a result of erosion and silting of river beds. In Bihar, the floods are confined to the rivers of north Bihar. In fact Assam, Bihar, West Bengal, Uttar Pradesh and Odisha are more prone to floods almost every year. Other states like Arunachal Pradesh, Andhra Pradesh, Maharashtra, Tripura and Himachal Pradesh are also affected by floods on account of drainage congestion. Brahmaputra river regions are also devastated by flooding every year because of over flowing.

The region is prone to earthquakes causing landslides in the hills and forests. The flood problem in Assam is therefore, very acute. Rain on the snow packed mountains or water from the melting snow is also one of the causes of floods. The water does not infiltrate into the soil. Infiltration takes place only when the snow melts. Till that time for several months water is accumulated above the soil surface. Another cause of floods in coastal areas is due to storm surges. The sea is driven on the land by meteorological forces. A storm with intense low pressure causes the level of sea to rise. As a natural result floods take place. Then there are flash floods of short duration. They arise from the high concentration of rainfall on a small area. Flash floods are common in arid and semi-arid areas. Mountain areas are often prone to thunder storms.

As a matter of fact no permanent measures are adopted to control the flood situation on permanent basis. The Government of India has always taken ad hoc measures. But disaster response alone is not sufficient. It yields only temporary results at a very high cost. Disaster prevention, mitigation and preparedness are better than disaster response. Disaster management in advance before we are struck is the only viable and permanent step in the right direction. The results achieved are of lasting nature.

65. Disaster Management

Disaster is a sudden calamity bringing great damage and devastation to life and property. The damage caused by disasters occur in the form of floods, droughts, volcanic eruptions, cyclones and conflagrations. From time-to-time they keep on reminding man of the might of nature. Man proud of his mind intellect and achievements has often found himself helpless in the face of disasters. We tend to forget that all human beings are the children of nature first and last.

India is a vast country and much of its area is prone to disaster of one kind or the other. 60% of the total land mass is prone to Earthquakes. Forty million hectares of land is flood prone, 68% of the area is susceptible to droughts and eight thousand kilometer of our coastline is threatened by cyclones. In 2015, South Indian floods resulted from heavy rainfall by the annual North East monsoon in November-December.

More than 500 people were killed and over 18 lakh people were displaced. It affected the State of Tamil Nadu and Andhra Pradesh. It is the most recent example of how our current disaster 'mitigating mechanisms' are nowhere near the vision of being 'effective'. God forbids, worse situation can occur any time.

There are four aspects to Disaster Management : means of information, preparedness, response to disaster and mitigation. The last is rebuilding of damage, resettling of uprooted population and restoring normalcy. Awareness about the disaster is the most important factor in Disaster Management. This keeps people alert and they can face the disaster when it strikes. Effective Warning System and regulated human activity can definitely help in minimising its impact.

We were so ill-equipped in 2008 that the 8-9 Richter earthquake could not be communicated by US Geological Survey to the countries of the Indian Ocean. India has 27 operational satellites. There are about two hundred seismic observatories in the country. We have some 82 seismic stations. Inspite of this the country presently has neither emergency response capacity nor effective warning system.

Indian Government enacted the Disaster Management Act in 2005. Subsequently, National Disaster Management Authority under the Prime Minister and State Disaster Management Authority under the Chief Minister of the state were formed.

The central Relief Commissioner is the Nodal Officer who handles all Disaster related problems at national level. Under this act every district is required to have a District Management Cell headed by Disaster Management Officer under the District Collector. Eleventh Finance Commission has ensured that each State has its own Calamity Relief Fund. The Central Government shall contribute 75% and the remaining 25% share will be funded by the State Government. The 14th Finance Commission has recommended that upto 10% of the funds available under the State Disaster Response Fund (SDRF) can be used by a state for occurrences which state considers to be 'disasters' within its local context. The 10th Five Year Plan had outlined comprehensive frame-work for national disaster. It deals with means to achieve coordination among Disaster Prevention Strategy, preparedness, response and the cooperation of the people. The 12th Five Year Plan rightly observes that investing in prevention of disaster is for more economical and socially more beneficial than expenditure on relief and rehabilitation. The plan believes that the disaster risk reduction needs a 'whole of government, whole of society' approach.

In the aftermath of Tsunami there has been paradigm shift in the approach to Disaster Management. However, state of readiness and quality of response to disaster is incomplete until there is co-operation from the civil society. So far our planning revolves solely around government strategies. Trained local teams should be equipped to act swiftly and efficiently in any emergency.

66. Policy on Land Acquisition

A fair comprehensive land acquisition act is most needed now as the recent agitations across the country have underlined the need for equitable acquisition. The present unrest among the farmers is obviously caused by their rising expectations over compensation and other benefits on being deprived of their ancestral land. But at the same time the need of the industrialists and urbanisation of land has to be addressed rationally. In fact the efficient use of land is crucial to the economic growth of the country.

The recent controversy resolves around the role of government in acquiring land for the industrialists or private builders. Therefore a new Land Acquisition Resettlement and Rehabilitation Bill (LARR) was tabled in September 2011. There is no doubt that this bill is much improved upon the previous coercive take-overs. The draft bill positively recognises the demands of all farmers, infrastructure development, urbanisation and industrialisation. The bill has been passed by both the houses of Parliament. The present bill passed in Parliament seeks to replace the 117 years old Land Acquisition Act, 1894. The new act has wisely combined the questions of acquisition with resettlement and rehabilitation. In its earlier attempt, the government had passed two separate bills that treated acquisition of land different from resettlement and rehabilitation. However, as is clear from the nomenclature of the draft bill, all the problems have been clubbed together. The act ensures that LARR Act is in addition to the existing laws and shall not apply to existing central laws governing mining and special economic zones. The Act also allows the state governments to make any law governing acquisition or other subjects related to it provided these laws do not interfare with the provisions of the LARR.

The acquisition of land for public purpose is also well defined along with the package of rehabilitation and resettlement. As proposed, minimum compensation would be four times the market value. For landowners, the bill has provided for a subsistence of ₹ 3000 per month per family for 12 months. Affected families will be entitled to a job for one family member or ₹ 5 lakh per family or ₹ 2000 for 20 years, indexed to inflation. The bill also provides for awarding one acre of land to each family if the land is being acquired for an irrigation project.

There is a special provision for SC and ST families who lose their land. They will be offered 2.5 acres of alternative land against 5 acres of land proposed earlier. There are certain provisions for the acquistion of multi-cropped land. The bill also proposes that the land acquired, if not used within 10 years, will not be returned to the original owner but will become the part, of that state's land bank. The bill has defined unambiguously the term 'public purpose' for the acquisition of the land.

Accordingly the bill further stipulates that no change from the purpose specified in the land use plan at the time of the acquisition will be allowed. All said and done, the most remarkable feature proposed in the LARR is that both acquisition and RR (Resettlement and Rehabilitation) process will be carried out simultaneously.

A sane land acquisition policy is indispensable in a country where 18% of the world population exists on a mere 2.4% of world land. In view of the increasing population, per capita land availability has declined to 0.2 hectare from 0.9 hectare in 1901. It is envitable that the young population dependent on land so far may have to seek jobs outside land related jobs. In addition to this urbanisation, mobility of rural population to the cities in search of jobs has added fuel to the fire.

The construction of national highways, hydel projects and development of infrastructure are the need of the day. When the Indian economy is growing at around 7 to 8%, the proposed land acquisition bill is expected to address engagement between the sellers and the buyers to foster a healthier climate for all round development.

67. Global Warming

Global warming is a great threat to the very survival of our planet. The human induced global average temperature is rising constantly. It has increased by about 0.6 °C in the 20th century when compared to the late 19th century. The United Nation's Inter-government Panel on Climate Change has predicted that global temperature could rise further by 1.4°C to 5.8°C by the end of the present century. The decade 2000 to 2010 has been the warmest on record, while the year 1998 has been the warmest since 1961. The prospect is quite frightening. The emissions of greenhouse gases beyond the tolerable point has triggered off global warming. The greenhouse effect is caused by the role played by greenhouse gases such as carbon dioxide, methane and nitrous oxide.

These gases effectively trap energy from the heat of the Sun within the Earth's atmosphere. This phenomenon keeps the earth warm. But the emission of these gases beyond a tolerable limit has brought about the problem of global warming. The concentration of carbon dioxide, a major greenhouse gas, has risen by more than 30% since 1980.

A 2° temperature rise over the current level in India would result in a change in the rainfall pattern. It would displace millions of people living in the foothills of the Himalayas and in coastal areas on account of melting ice, landslides, floods and rising sea level. As a result of global warming, the polar ice caps have shrunk. The glaciers that feed many major rivers have retreated.

Arctic ocean could be mostly open by 2050. The climate change is projected to increase extreme weather events such as floods, droughts, storms and imbalance in earth's temperature. Man is heavily dependent on fossil fuel consumption, not just for its development but for its very survival. The future is quite grim because population is projected to double by 2050. The increase in greenhouse gases is therefore an inevitable factor.

There is no decline in the growth of population. Population activists believe that the world can support only two to three billion population at present. The alarming increase in birth rate is supposed to double the population by 2050. We would need more commercial energy not only to run factories but also to pump water and light up our homes. Energy is indeed the driver of the global economy.

In fact the solution to the problem of global warming lies in transition to a less energy intensive world. We need a universal consensus to turn the tide. As a major step, developed countries possessing clean energy should transfer it to developing countries, since climate change affects us all. Only a sincere global effort can change the world and avert an inevitable disaster. A warmer climate is creating conditions for the spread of infectious disease. All in all, the problem of global warming is universally ominous.

There are blames and counter blames by developed and developing countries. In all fairness, industrialised nations should bring their per capita emissions down before they ask us to do so. India, China and G-77 countries are pressing their views to arrive at a balanced solution.

The United Nation's Climate Change Conference was held in Poland in December 2008. All countries had agreed to shape and form an effective response to climate change at the Copenhagen meet at the end of 2009. Unfortunately the meet proved a damp squib. The Copenhagen Climate Accord is just a token agreement, as it is legally non-binding. The deal acknowledges the need of limiting global temperatures. But it is silent on some important specifics and is unlikely to yield results which are urgently needed. It is dismaying to note that we have not learnt any lesson from the past.

COP 21 was held is Paris in 2015. Negotiations resulted in the adoption of the Paris Agreement, governing climate change reduction measures from 2020. The adoption of this agreement ended the work of the Durban platform, established during COP 17. The agreement will enter into force only if 55 countries which produce at least 55% of the world's greenhouse gas emissions ratify the agreement.

68. Non-Vegetarianism and Climate Change

Dr RK Pachauri, the then head, UN Inter-governmental Panel on Climate Change, virtually stirred a hornet's nest when he called upon the nations of the world to eat less meat to fight climate change. He asked the people to abstain from meat once a week. People wonder what meat eating has got to do with climate. We know that the rich countries are more responsible than the poor ones for emissions.

So the quantity of meat consumed by them is quite large. The Food and Agricultural Organisation estimates that meat production accounts for nearly a fifth of global greenhouse gas emissions. Emissions are caused when the land for animals and feed for them is prepared and grown. The methane emitted by livestock has been proved to be 23 times stronger as a climate change agent than carbon dioxide.

An average Indian eats just 2.1 kg of poultry products per person per year. A UAE citizen consumes about 100 kg of poultry products per person per year. An average American eats 46 kg of chicken in a year. These figures are in addition to beef that comes to 41.7 kg consumed by an American on average every year.

As meat eating related activities are potent agents of global warming, there is complete sense in the advice tendered by Dr Pachauri for the survival of mankind. The most interesting conclusion arrived at by Dr Pachauri was that meat consumption would double by 2050, implying that methane emitted by livestock would also double. There are no two opinions that the cattle being grown for human consumption are part of the climate change. Then what about dairy cattle? Do they not contribute to climate change? Milk, butter, cheese and yoghurt are the best source of protein to our children. Should we not abstain from them to avoid adverse impact on climate change? Why not? Those who cannot understand what sacrifice means cannot tolerate even a day's abstention. Dr Pachauri has not spoken ill of non-vegetarian food. Nor has he touched upon the ethical concept of eating meat.

Dietary patterns since the evolution of mankind have been changing under the stress of various circumstances. Calls for eating less meat are made on moral grounds also. This is not a place to discuss the moral aspect of the problem. Our dietary patterns are closely related to our culture, geographical conditions and the basis of our religion. There is no question of disputing the dietary habits of our fellow beings.

Developed countries in the West would continue contributing to global warming as long as they do not change their way of life. Those in favour of vegetarianism say that non-vegetarian dishes are dietary diversions, not mainstream food items. On the other hand, for non-vegetarians genuine culinary delights can be found in animal food. India is a vast country; still non-vegetarianism is not that much spread when compared with China and European countries.

None has a right to be derisive about the non-violent sensibilities of communities. The words of Dr Pachauri, that the world should exercise some kind of control over consumption of meat, should not be taken lightly. Their substance should not be allowed to be lost in futile argument for and against non-vegetarianism. Every year 25th November is observed as 'International Meatless Day'. The observance of Meatless Day shows that the nations are already seized of the problem. Respect for animal rights coupled with Environment Day once a week instead of once a year can go a long way in generating awareness about less meat and less emissions.

69. Biodiversity

Biodiversity or biological diversity refers to the variety and viability among living organisms including the ecological complexes in which they occur. So we can include in biodiversity different genes, species and ecosystems. In fact it is as wide as all life. India is one of the 12 mega biodiversity centres in the world. India has 10% of the world species and is 10th among the plant rich countries.

Though India has just 2.4% of world area, it has over 47000 plant species, 89000 animal species containing 7% of the worlds flora and 6.5% of its fauna. Indian flora comprise amazing variety: 15000 flowering plants. Zoological Survey of India has identified 350 species of mammals, 420 reptiles, 2000 amphibians, 2546 fishes, 67000 insects, 1224 birds and variety of other species of living organisms.

Loss of biodiversity makes ecosystems less stable. All living creatures supported by the interaction among organisms and ecosystems make them viable. Imbalance in biodiversity, therefore, makes ecosystem unstable, weak and vulnerable to natural disasters. For instance, water cycle depends on forests. Forests regulate water flows by recycling rain water. Energy cycle helps green plants to convert sunlight, water and carbon dioxide into carbohydrates, nitrogen, carbon and oxygen cycles help all organisms to live and that is a large component of earth's, atmosphere. Carbon and oxygen provide us with a breathable atmosphere. In fact the balance in all these cycles moderates the climate and temperatures of the earth. Thus, the natural cycles provide us with food, clean water and air to breathe.

The economic values of biodiversity are no less important than its biological value. Everything that we eat, buy and sell come from the world of nature. Nature provides the material for our survival. Nature is also the source of many medicines. A significant proportion of drugs are produced from biological sources.

The increasing population requires a large number of resources to sustain it. On account of population pressure, biodiversity of species is now vanishing faster than at any other time in world's history. Overexploitation of natural resources, pollution and habitat destruction are great threats to biodiversity. India's present framework for conservation of these resources is constituted by laws governing forestry and wildlife like Water (Prevention and Control of Pollution) Act, the Environment (Protection) Act etc.

Nature's biodiversity is a unique spectrum of earth's ecosystems, species and their genes which proves its worth by sustaining life itself. It has come under grave man-made threats as a result of overexploitation of natural resources. Climate change and decreasing resistance to floods and earthquakes threaten loss of biodiversity. Nature has to recover itself and it is only man who can help nature do it.

70. Conservation of Water Resources

World water resources are drying up fast and therefore growing population and global warming will combine to reduce the average person's water supply. By 2050, water scarcity is estimated to affect 2 to 7 billion people the world over. The water scenario, water therefore, presents a grim future. The World Bank Report says that per capita availability of water in India which was 5000 cubic meter per year (cu m/yr) at the time of independence in 1947 has come down to 1545 cu m/yr. India gets approximately 4000 billion cubic meters (Bcm) every year from all natural resources.

A large part of this, 1500 Bcm flows into the sea, 1400 Bc m is lost in evaporation during flow along the ground and 430 Bcm is used in ground recharge. Out of the balance of 670 Bcm, only 370 Bcm is utilised and 300 Bcm is yet to be harnessed. This grim scenario requires to harness without delay 1500 Bcm of water that flows into the sea as a result of floods. Floods and droughts are regular annual events in India affecting over 400 million people.

It is an irony that India is one of the few nations that are gifted with rich water resources and is yet struggling with the water crisis. Water requirement is closely related to population rise, demand for food and industrial needs of the country. The total water requirements for irrigation to produce the required foodgrains accounts for 85% of all fresh water available.

Apart from availability of water, there is a serious problem of clean drinking water. Forget the villages, even in our National capital people are sometimes made to drink sewage through water pipelines. Almost 95% of rural habitations are covered with water supply but most of them are facing a quality problem. 78% of rural population still have no access to sanitation. Needless to say, lack of such facilities in rural areas have caused serious health problems. Indian cities are not far behind.

The national water requirements for domestic use and municipal needs is projected to be 62 Bc m in 2025, whereas population is estimated to rise to beyond 1.5 billion by 2025. Correspondingly the water requirements will increase, for which current water availability and respective capacity building seems highly inadequate. The situation is further aggravated because all major river water systems in India are facing problems of pollution and mismanagement.

Let us take the example of the Ganga Action Plan. A comprehensive survey of pollution in Ganga was made in 1979. Central Ganga Authority was constituted in 1985 to oversee the implementation of the plan. The Comptroller and Auditor-General of India has clearly stated, "The GAP has not been able to achieve its objectives despite a total expenditure of ₹ 901.71 crores over a period of 15 years."

Rainwater harvesting and water recycling should be made compulsory for all the states. We need to build check dams, develop watersheds, desilt ponds and rivers and recharge the wells. Recycled water may be used for agricultural needs and other purposes other than drinking. Our country will face incalculable consequences in the next few years if we are not careful in conserving and preserving precious water resources. Water is most likely to be a rare and precious accommodity which will lead to conflicts within nations and among the nations at an international level.

71. Twenty-20 Cricket

Twenty-20, a recent phenomena is a diminutive form of one-day cricket. Some have called it a 'pocket book edition'. To many this new format is not cricket. They have called it a 'crudely edited version' of the game and 'low grade rubbish'. The fear that test matches will be gradually eased out continues to haunt them. So they resist any innovation in the form of cricket. It is well-known that Twenty-20 is a movement of the twenty-first century and it cannot be wished away. It is symbolic of speed and energy.

"There is no doubt that 20 overs do not seem to be much of a cricket", writes Greg Chappell, and goes to ask "What is cricket then?" He replies as well saying that cricket is a contest between bat and ball. Chappell is right because Twenty-20 Cricket offers this contest in a heightened form.

Fielders are always on springs, the bowler is expected to get a break-through at every ball. The batsman is not his worth if he does not earn a sixer with every strike, flick or drive of the ball. Slip or no slip, silly point or no silly point batsman must flash and explode. Such is the Twenty-20 Cricket. There are as many Ohs, Ahs, Wovs and Fies as are the balls. Where is a game that moves so majestically towards its climax? It is certainly a cricket of power, skill, strategy and improvisation. There are no Sachins out on the pitch in their nervous nineties contriving to play leisurely into eternity. It is a game for Sehwags, Gambhirs, Yuvrajs, Kohlis, Dhonis and Rainas.

Twenty-20 is all bang, prowess and speed. When the One Day International (ODI) version (of 50 overs) of cricket was introduced by Kemy Packer there was similar hue and cry by the purists of the game. India walked into that kind of cricket very late. But this time Indian cricket has taken the world by storm. Indian Premier League has attracted adverse criticism. But it is more out of envy than any logic. It has been dubbed as a decadent form of cricket. Some have called it 'rustic'. In our Indian context it has injected fresh life, zest and speed into the game. Indian Premier League was rightly hailed as the block buster of the decade. Four million spectators were estimated to have watched the IPL in stadiums of different states. More than one billion viewers had tuned into watch IPL matches spread over 44 days. It was IPL time at 8 pm for the whole of India. The matches offered excitement far from the madding serials, insipid reality and laughter shows.

Financially IPL1 had done extremely well. It is said to have enriched the coffers of the BCCI by ₹ 350 crore in 44 days in the very first year of its inception. In comparison BCCI had earned ₹ 235 crore as profit for the whole year. In 2010, IPL expanded its ambit. With two new franchisees IPL in 2011 displayed the magnificence of cricket with 10 teams. The Pune and the Kochi based teams were sold together for staggering amount at the auction.

Despite the pretensions of the team owners the financial dimensions of the IPL are stunning. After all, it is money and money makes the mare go. Thanks to Kapil Dev's ICL. Its establishment spurred the BCCI to score over Kapil Dev. Given the financial and political clout of Sharad Pawar, IPL has come to stay as symbolic of India's youthful cricket. IPL2 in South Africa in 2009 created a history of a sort.

The way the tournament was organised on a foreign soil with meticulous care enhanced India's stature in the cricket world. The 2016 session of the IPL (IPL 9) started in April 2016. This season has two new teams, Gujrat Lions and Rising Pune Supergiants. Interestingly, the IPL, contrary to the apprehension, expressed by critics, has not taken away from the charm of conventional cricket, though the IPL has been a runaway success in all the seasons.

None should grudge resounding success to the IPL because the ultimate winner is cricket. The discovery of new talents and spinning out of the unfit and the misfit players will brighten up Indian Cricket. Change is the law of nature and the elderly people should not grudge entertainment to the youth. We fear lest IPL should be a political victim. The bigger worry is the floating around of charges of match fixing, rigging, money laundering, kick-backs, shady foreign deals etc. Despite all this we hope to keep on enjoying cricket in its latest edition as it is supposed to be a good sport.

72. **Social Values**— Survival of All

Values are a set of principles or standard of behaviour which are held in high respect in society. Value means something worthwhile and precious. Thus, values give meaning and strength to a person's character. There are personal values, moral and spiritual values and social values. Social values are always practised in relation to society in which we live.

Responsibility, duty and service are the core of social values. The sense of brotherhood leads us to the essence of living. It recognises the principle of 'live and let others live'. Social values are the epitome of moral and personal values. The field of social values is so vast that it comprises all the basic principles of good living. Those who value the social values work for the betterment of society. It makes one compassionate to others and selfless in the service of other members of society. The sense of brotherhood can be cultivated through respect for rights of others, the principles of other religions and social customs of other communities.

Politeness and amiable behaviour leads one to be kind and helpful to others. It helps one avoid rudeness to others and be courteous and helpful at the time of need. A good human being does not believe in evil for evil. A life of quality is touched with tenderness and selfless service. Merely uttering the words 'please' and 'thank you' does not make one courteous in the real sense. On the contrary, one should learn to pay compliments even when one is hurt.

Humanism is a great quality that makes one realise the right of others to live in society with dignity. We are not living in tribal civilisation. We have travelled far from the times of barbarism. Man has evolved religion to control one's baser instincts.

Those who can do it have a right to be called humanists at heart. Cruelty not only to human beings but also to animals has to be avoided. One must refrain from cruel misdeeds and come to the help of the sick, the old and the needy. Such persons are willing to grant freedom of soul and action to those around them.

Lasting relationships between man and man are based on friendship that is reciprocal and trusting. All of us need friends on a personal level. But those who are the friends of the other members of society are beneficient and followers of basic values make society worth living. Concern for others and gratitude for their good deeds make one a true friend. Love is the greatest boon God has conferred on us. We can return this love by showing love to those around us by spreading the message of justice, equality and service.

In fact, service born out of sympathy is the essence of good life. Service means concern for the problems of others and helping them tide over their difficulties. True service implies giving others without expectation from others. The image of society is reflected in the character of the members who inhabit it. Today India is passing through the worst phase when the place of social values is at a nadir. Our leaders are after their own loaves and fishes. They sow the seeds of discord to maintain their own positions. They indulge in flouting personal, moral and social values. The high profile bureaucrats have taken to immoral and corrupt practices. The judiciary is meant to hand out justice but they are mired in corruption. It is no exaggeration to say that lost to every sense of value based life, our society presents a tribal look. It is a bleak scenario for those living in present times.

73. **Humanism**— The True Worship of God

Tagore has best described the term humanism when he says that God cannot be realised through renunciation but through oneness with humble humanity and participation in their humble activities. In one of his lyrics he expresses his faith in these words.

"Leave this chanting and singing and telling of beads! whom dost thou worship in this lonely dark corner of a temple with doors all shut? Open thine eyes & see thy God is not before thee!" —*Gitanjali*

Tagore admonishes the priest who tries in vain for deliverance. Deliverance does not mean renunciation. It is to be found in toiling with the poor and sharing their labour. Religious practice does not lie in ritualism, as most of us have come to believe. For ages man has been in quest of the discovery of the ideal form of religious practice. To some, knowledge of scriptures is the best form of worship. Still there are those who consider establishing personal relationship with Him the highest form of worship. This is the path of a mystic.

However, there is another class of lovers of God. They would accept service to society or mankind as the best kind of worship. Different methods have been preached by different religions causing chaotic conditions even in the field of realisation of God. Conflicting religious opinions have caused violence and unprecedented bloodshed in the name of God. Which religion is superior to which? This is the fundamental question which has deviated man from the true path of religion. Such questions are the seeds of discord that will never blossom into harmony.

The religions may be numberless; God is one and so are the ideals of every religion. God can at best be realised by following the basic truth that God is one and He has created every one alike. That is why great thinkers have come to the conclusion that complete realisation of God can come only through love of man, service to man and general welfare of man. Man comes closest to God because He created every one alike. There is no other way to establish our contact with God than in serving his creation.

Therefore, humanism is a doctrine that is rooted in the earth— a deep concern for a number of human problems and sufferings. The road to heaven lies through service, selfless service. The lines quoted from Gitanjali is the core of humanism. God is among those who sweat and toil, suffer and starve. The highest kind of worship is what makes the universe a better place for living. Humanism is the form of worship that leads to the betterment of human life on earth. Realisation of God through service of man is an undisputed tenet of every religion. Once we realise this imperishable truth, we can establish heaven on earth.

74. Indian Cinema and its Social Responsibility

The cinema has remained the most powerful media for mass communication in India. It has the ability to combine entertainment with communication of ideas. It has the potential appeal for its audience, leaving other media far behind in making such appeal. The cinema has produced much which touches the innermost layers of man. It is very handy in breaking the monotony and boredom of life and rejuvenates us from the everyday chores of life. Thus, it will not be wrong to say that cinema is like a mirror reflecting the hopes, aspirations, frustrations and contradictions of the society which leads to an attachment of social responsibility to it. It becomes important to avoid such stories which may lead to erosion of social morals and values.

The influence of cinema cannot be underestimated as it helps in learning process. Thus, what is seen on the cinema screen is automatically absorbed by those who see the picture. The person laughs with films and cries with them. Our dress, hair style, shape and design of footwear, even manners and habits are influenced by cinema. We all know that the deepest influence of the cinema is on the young and illiterate. For an educated person; the cinema might be just an art but, the influence on the illiterate and children is seen in their trying to copy or imitate what they see. e.g. scenes of film like 'The Legend of Bhagat Singh' made people patriotic and sentimental. In the same way, film 'Lajja' focused on the condition of Indian women in the society.

From the 30s, right through the 60s, Indian cinema has developed in focusing on different aspects of Indian life. It has not only presented but tackled with burning issues from freedom to unemployment, from dowry to women's emancipation, from poverty to exploitation, from social conflict to national integration and so on. With the transformation of the society, the issue confronting it kept on changing and so also the themes adopted for film-making.

It is worthy to mention some of the Indian films that have sensually touched the audience and the society through their messages.

Indian cinema talked about upliftment of untouchables in 'Acchut Kanya' (1936); fought against marriage of young girls with old persons (Duniya Na Mane, 1937) highlighted the problem of alcohol in 'Brandi Chi Batti' (1939), raised the issue of dowry in 'Dahej' (1950). Films like 'Do Bigha Zameen', 'Mother India' and 'Mujhe Jenne Do' focused on the socio-economic causes of the Indian problem.

However, over the years cinema has lost its educative and social aspect. Film producers and financers are merely concerned for the commercial value of the films and thus, pack the films with the ingredients of sex, violence, 'item number' etc. Such scenes has a great impact on the minds of children who are seen using abusive language often. Apart from this, women in cinema are protrayed as an object of entertainment. Movies like 'B.A Pass,' 'Girlfriend', 'Grand Masti', 'Murder', 'Hate Story' and so on merely focuses on exposure and thus are against the moral values. These kinds of movies increase the percentage of crimes like rape, murder, kidnapping in the society.

But the story has its other side too. With the passage of time, there were movies made to have positive influence. Movies like 'Rang De Basanti' encouraged people to take up things in their own hands, 'Taare Zameen Pe' and 'Three Idiots' helped you to accept what are you as you are; 'Swades' portrayed the problem of brain drain in the country, 'Aarakshan' was based on controversial policy of caste-based reservations in Indian Government jobs and educational institutions and 'My brother Nikhil' dealt with the stigma associated with HIV/AIDS.

This deviation of Indian Cinema from its social responsibility is a matter of concern. This growing tendency of the film industry to exploit sex and violence must be firmly curbed. In a developing country like India, the cinema has a major role to play due to the high percentage of poverty and illiteracy. Cinema has the ability to inform and educate apart from just entertainment. Hence, this ability of cinema should be ensured by lying down guidelines for the people involved in its making and there must be provision of stringent action against those who violate them.

Instead of presenting life as it is and as it should be in a country such as India, our film producers creates false values, generally present stories of the affluent class, of life in bungalows and palaces, gorgeous dresses and costumes and artificial situations for removed from the actualities of Indian life. Hence, for filmmakers it is important to understand that they too have social responsibility and they must not forgot their duty towards society in their craze for making profits by all popular techniques.

To conclude, we may say that the cinema has the power to influence the thinking of the people. It has changed the society and social trends rather introduced new fashions in the society. Films can go a long way towards arousing national consciousness and also in utilising the energies of the youth in social reconstruction and nation-building. If cinema industry produces noble and inspiring films, the cinema would be a true friend, philosopher and guide of the masses.

75. **Police Reforms**— A Need of Time

"We are bound by law to be free, not to be subjugated." However, in this nation of a billion plus people, where we empower a few to make laws for the country and ensure its enforcement, those few themselves flagrantly violate laws with impunity. State and citizens have existed based on the foundation of the Theory of the Social or Political Contract given by Jean-Jacques Rousseau. Social contract arguments typically-potray that individuals have consented, either explicitly or tacitly, to surrender some of their freedoms and submit to the authority of the state in exchange for protection of their remaining rights.

The question of the relation between natural and legal rights, therefore, is often an aspect of Social Contract Theory. It is that point when state itself starts to trample on these rights, police in this case, that clamour for Police Reform gets stirred up. Police who are supposed to be the protectors of common public and custodian of law and order of the state becomes subservient to their political master. It stands to reason, why this unholy nexus between the politicians and police exists in the system; parochial interests, pecuniary gains and such other diabolical activities top their 'list of duties!' and not 'protecting and serving'. One of the major reasons why this hand-in-glove relation between the politicians and police exists is because of the extant laws still prevalent in the system.

The Police Act, 1861 remains the central piece of legislation that governs all aspects of policing in India. It is a British legacy which our legislators find hard to cast off. Among other things IPC, CrPC, Indian Evidence Act, 1872 etc also help in much of the policing function. The 1861, Police Act came into being immediately after the 1857 mutiny, solely to perpetuate and consolidate British rule and to keep a check on such civilian upsurge.

However, to start with, Charles Napier, the then Governor of Punjab was the one, who felt the need of a civilian policing system in 1843. Before setting up a Police Organisation in his province he had two models in mind- London Policing System and Irish Constabulary System. London Policing System was based on the philosophy- Police is public, public is police. Whereas the latter was meant to exercise a coercive control and perpetuate exploitation. Irish Constabulary Policing System dovetailed with the Indian requirements. This system was later emulated in other provinces also, but it gained a pan-India face only after the introduction of the umbrella Police Act of 1861.

Policing, for any democratic set-up is a vital function. It ensures law and order in the society; protects rights of citizens, women and backward sections of the society; nips corrupt activities of the system; provides security at times of emergancies etc. Law and order, is the cornerstone of any civilised society. Anarchy and chaos will be the order of the day if 'Rule of Law' is absent in a set-up. Police doesn't just ensure law and order, but is also the facilitator of justice. Therefore, it is imperative that we make the transition from being a quasi-police state to a welfare state, where policing is citizen friendly and not antithetical to their needs and demands. The cases of violence with religious colours and the police interference to restore normalcy in the area is pertinent in this regard. Other very important aspect of policing is protecting the rights of citizens. Police needs to be sensitised towards women and the weaker sections of society *viz.* backward castes, SC, ST, children, transgender. This will ensure that we move towards a more egalitarian society, where every section of society is able to achieve their full potential.

Recent cases of temple entry of women in Shani Singnapur temple is a case in point. Another aspect of policing is weeding corruption from our society. With a torrent of scams in the recent past, it can be said that polices' pro-activeness accompanied with executive, legislative and judicial actions would have kept a check on them. However, things have come to such a passe that bureaucratic-executive nexus have made such scams possible. CBI has come down hard on the accused by leaving no stone unturned and bringing the accused to justice. Similarly, police paraphernalia is used for ensuring security of vital installations and respite at the time of exigencies *viz.* disaster management, terrorist attacks etc. The duty of police is to ensure a sense of security among the citizens. Therefore, it is important that public places like airports, railway stations, markets be kept safe from any untoward incidents, where the role of police becomes very important. Role of police during 26/11 attacks, rescue relief operation during Uttarakhand floods are relevant in this regard.

However, the image of police is not so respectful in India. Instances of police excesses; custodial deaths; indifference towards public complaints; high handedness in dealing with the weaker sections of the society; insensitive attitude towards women; profligate use of force etc have been irritants in public-police relations. Supreme Court in 2014 said that the menace of police excesses on women and helpless people must be stopped by all and sundry, as it reproached the recent episodes of police excesses on a woman in Punjab's Tarn-Taran district and on contractual teachers in Bihar. Police excesses don't command respect in the mind of public, rather it makes their relation more acrimonious. Custodial deaths is another area which remains a cause of concern. Every accused needs trial and any attempt to extract information by torture is a grave violation of the Right to Life and other tenets of human rights. Amputation of male organ of Shri Jugtaram in police custody in Barmer, Rajasthan in 1994 is a case in point.

Similarly, cases of indifference of police towards general public is appalling. The reluctance to register FIRs, casual attitude towards pursuing any case without any a case in point. Cases like, filing of FIR against 3 students in JNU on charges of sedition and in the same instance, refusal to file named-FIR against perpetrators, when these students were beaten with impunity in High Court premises is relevant in this regard.

Police authorities display high handedness in dealing with the weaker sections of society. Policing, far from being the professional imposition of a coherent moral consensus on society is an intensely political activity with policemen often facilitating and participating in the violence not just against these 2 communities, but against minorities, other weaker sections and women. Naxalism, which today is the greatest internal security danger to the country can trace its origin to police high handedness on weak and the denial of justice. Time and again we have heard cases of women not being treated appropriately by police officials and their modesty being breached. Similarly, in a recent Supreme Court directive, the court was of the view that 'good Samaritans', helping during road accidents should not be harassed and police should be sensitive in handling with these cases. Police brutality is also manifested as the use of force is applied with profigacy. Riot control requires use of baton or water cannons to disperse violent mobs. But the use of force against peacefully agitating crowd is uncalled for. In 2012, Nirbhaya Case Force was used by police to disperse peacefully agitators. These incidents instill a sense of fear in the minds of citizens demanding justice.

Since the police organisation still runs under the overall rubric of the 1861, Police Act, it carries certain characteristic to the disadvantage of the common public: search, seizure and arrest at discretion, distancing and grandeur, authoritarianism, brutality, feudal attitude etc., to list a few. Flouting all canons of moral and legal propriety, they indulge in shameless sycophancy and shenanigans. There is another breed of pernicious corruption which although is said and done for larger public interest, but is in violation of law per se and sets a wrong precedent, i.e. Noble cause corruption. Police empowerment is another area which needs attention. Bad service conditions; overworked and underpaid lower functionary etc, needs immediate attention.

Taking a leaf from some of the successful police organisations *viz.*, Singapore, the Netherlands, New York Police departments may serve the purpose. Delegating and devolving more power to the lower, intermediate and field officials can also bring about agility and swiftness in operation. Training of the officials is largely pedagogic rather than being andragogic. Appraisal system is subjective and lacks scientism. Introduction of latest technology in policing is also long due. Computer statistics, biometrics, GPS tracking, smart-gun, visionic facelt system, e-policing etc., can be handy tools. There exists a mismatch between the modus operandi of police and the problems of 21st century. Issues like human trafficking, organised crime, cyber crimes, illegal drug cartel and such other crime syndicates are thriving because of the lax, unsystematic, infructuous nature of police operation. Police start rearranging deck chairs only when the problem balloons to the point of explosion. Police reform is imperative to mitigate such gaps existing in the system.

Government in 1977 set-up Shah Commission to look into the police excesses committed during the 1975 epoch National Emergency. The JP Government could not act on the recommendation because of its ouster in 1980. Dharamveera Committee was also formed in this period to suggest reforms, but government couldn't act because of the same reason, notwithstanding the fact that it had certain very effective recommendations.

In response to a PIL filed by Prakash Singh, Julio Ribeiro Committee was formed. Government remained steadfast in bringing about any change. Amidst mounting pressure government again set-up a committee, Padmanabhaiah Committee under the then Home Secretary. The vortex of suffering of the common public by the hands of despotic police and capricious politicians will continue and the Police will keep carrying the tag of 'Criminals in Uniform'.

The recommendations of this committee were also put on the backburner. Supreme Court taking cognizance of government's intent hardened its stand and did not mince a word. In response, government pointed out that, hitherto there were around 600 recommendations and government was finding it hard to formulate a Bill. To gauge into and suggest relevant ideas from these 600 recommendations, government again set-up a committee, Kamal Kumar Committee.

After the recommendations of this committee also, government remained indifferent. Finally, the Supreme Court set-up a monitoring committee and outlined seven important attributes around which the government should bring out Police Reform as soon as possible. The vortex of suffering of the common public by the hands of despotic police and capricious politicians will continue and the Police will keep carrying the tag of 'Criminals in Uniform'. The present status is that government still has not taken any prudent step.

76. News Channels have Turned into Entertainment Channels

There is an old quote – "Quality is better than quantity". This is something which Indian news channels of the present era need to understand. As the media sector is seeing a cut-throat competition, the news channels now-a-days resort to anything and everything they could possibly do to fetch high TRPs. There are several dedicated news channels that broadcast information round the clock. But now, these channels are taking the form of entertainment rather than real NEWS. They are more concerned about the celebrities personal, lives, rather than highlighting the real issues.

This is despite the fact that there are more news channels than those of any other genre. There have been some changes in the number of channels as the total number of news channel has grown up from 393 to 397 and the general entertainment channel has been reduced from 402 to 401. If mass entertainment channels are falling short of enough entertainment value for viewers, news channels are doing their bit to make up for the shortfall with dramatic and sensational content.

For the sake of definition as given in the policy documents: "News and current affairs channel means a channel which has any element of news and current affairs in its programme content." This definition has served as the point of entry of news channels into the entertainment genre. However, the genre of news has taken a different meaning altogether.

Time was when news channels were largely focused on hourly news bulletins comprising major political and other news events, human interest stories, sports and entertainment stories. But news channels now-a-days have moved from serious news reporting and analysis to tabloid television-a sensational, impactful and dramatic –format which relies more on breaking news of every kind rather than serious news. The prime time has become a platform for political debates where representatives of major political parties speak less on merit of issues and more about party view point, thus making their presence redundant as far as the issue is concerned.

We already have health and cookery shows on news channels that technically do not fall under the entertainment genre. But now, we also have special programmes on various channels on entertainment available on other channels –so we have special shows to catch up on the daily television soaps such as 'Saas, Bahu aur Betiyan' on Aaj Tak and 'Saas, Bahu aur Saajish' on Star News. Then we have special shows to catch up with celebrities and their partying ways, much like the Page 3 coverage in newspapers, on special shows such as 'Night Out' on NDTV. On some Telugu news channels, special programmes even showcase functions where the sound tracks of movies are released. Apart from this, till a decade ago, news channels were known for their news content, editorial standards and degree of impartiality. News readers and weekly debate anchors that were also news readers on week days were known as professional television journalists working for a certain channel. They were known for their reading skill, presentation style, language proficiency and other professional skills. Today, news readers are old hats or non entities to be more precise.

They have been replaced by prime time news hour anchors that are the face of their respective channels. In fact, they are not only just the face of the channel but celebrities and brands bigger than the channel. As a result, today certain channels are known by their star anchors like Arnab Goswami, Rajdeep Sardesai and Rajat Sharma, to name just a few, just as daily soaps are known by their main characters and TV stars that play them. Now the question arises that why the news channels have deviated themselves from their primary duty? On most news channels, political/government news is given prominence, followed by crime/law and order. Crime/Law and order enjoys the maximum share on English and Hindi channels at 28 and 26% respectively followed by sports at 24% (Hindi 16%), political/government at 19% (Hindi 13%) and entertainment news at 13% (Hindi 14%).

The time has come when some introspection by the Indian media is required. The defects should ideally be addressed and corrected in a democratic manner. Such irresponsible journalism or rather 'un-entertainment' cries for a government regulation for creating a journalism framework. Democracy and freedom of speech are for mature people and not for irrational kids and immature persons creating unnecessary sensation about useless and trivial news as they have to understand that India is still 26% illiterate.

77. Role of Media in Generating Public Opinion

Media plays a vital role in a democratic country like India where public opinion has major respect. Media is regarded as the fourth pillar of the society, the other three being legislative executive and the judiciary. It is even said to be a 'mirror' and 'moulder' of public opinion. In other words we may say that the public replicates or follows as well as accumulates opinions and decisions through the media and the information displayed by it. People not only obtain real information about public matters from the news media, but also pick up how much prominence to assign to a subject on the basis of the highlighting done on it in the news.

Internet including e-mails and blogs, television, radio and newspapers play a significant role in the formation of outlooks and opinions of the general public. News media highlights the personalities (politicians, film industry people and other celebrities) and issues and the common man believes and forms an opinion about them according to the news. Today's picture of the media is entirely different. Public can talk about the incidents happening not only in the country, but also outside the geographical boundaries only due to awareness created by media.

Media also plays a crucial role in enlightening and educating the people. It can aid public involvement through advocating issues and transferring knowledge, skills and technologies to the people. Awareness about various rural development programmes, propagation of family planning could be spread by using the media. Media awakens the people against many evils prevalent in the society. Apart from this, it covers many students on a single platform through its educational programmes.

The impact of media can be seen on the youth also. Youth exposure to media has increased evidently in past few years. The usage of personalised forms of media, comprising text messages and social networking sites has exponentially expanded. It is also contributing to greater awareness of political issues and prospects for public activities. Posting a blog or using twitter to create awareness amongst the youth about any incident makes them more involved with the incident and its consequences or aftermath. Today, individuals not only get information about government from news sites, but they also respond by posting their opinions on the news and initiate discussions on various forums or by joining groups on Facebook. Young people are at ease in forming their opinion about any incident as they learn about then in detail through the media.

It is important to mention an example to show the positive effect of media on public opinion. Media played a significant role in pacing up the movement led by Anna Hazare. Round the clock coverage and upholding the pitch, media ensured that the protests occur throughout the country and there is a mass rage and frenzy. TV and newspapers were noticeably the driving force behind the Anti-Corruption Movement. The Indian media voluntarily became a party, a sort of participant in the drive for Jan Lokpal Bill. It is true that channels have given extreme coverage to Anna Hazare, but that's what happens in case of all major movements. It gave Anna Team the power and brought people on the streets and forced government to become flexible and agree to talks.

But it is important for media to report in a fair and unbiased manner. The media should apprehend the consequential importance of events happening around and report issues in an impartial and dispassionate manner. It should bring all aspects of incidents before the public. Ignoring this point of conduct will lead to severe damage to democracy as hiding any part of the story results in creation of wrong and prejudicial public opinion. For instance, some channels start showing such scenes and images, which are of no importance and have an adverse effect on the mind of viewers. Showing of sexual and rape cases, with minute details given by the anchor and showing brutal scenes of murder, crosses the limit of ethics and morality. Few media groups have even started daring to produce news on their own. Media often use the phrase 'from highly placed sources' to give things a realistic shade. It is thus important to understand that media plays a crucial role in generating public opinion. It affects the mindsets of people and hence it should present the matter in an unbiased way.

The information reaches door to door through the media. Hence, it is their social and moral responsibility to present a factual and authentic picture of any incident without thinking much about money-making or TRP generation. With such a huge responsibility towards the people, media should be more sensible and alert instead of a casual approach towards an event because it is they on whom the general public is relying.

78. Affirmative Action

Affirmative action lies at the root of democracy. It is the flesh and bone of democracy because the basis of affirmative action is tantamount to 'equality of opportunity'. Founding fathers of our Constitution have made adequate provision for the uplift of the poor and *Dalits* who from time immemorial suffered injustice at the hands of the so called upper class. India's social system has ever been mired in caste based complications.

In the interest of the socially and economically depressed classes, Article 46 secures their uplift and equal opportunity in all the benefits granted by the government. Besides for their political empowerment, Article 334 of the Constitution has made a provision for the reservation of seats in the legislature and government jobs.

In fact, Reservation Policy is the most judicious and far-sighted act of our founding fathers. But there are objections if the benefits of the quota system do not go to those who deserve it. Creation of Creamy Layer and third generation enjoying the benefits have created hurdles in the way of reaching the benefits where they are needed most. Besides, in the hands of our wily politicians, it is an unfailing key to the vote bank.

However, we have made tons of economic policies for making affirmative action a success. Mahatma Gandhi National Rural Employment Guarantee (MNREGA) Act, 2005, is a huge scheme providing employment on demand to Below Poverty Level (BPL) (rural) families. It is expected to serve the twin purposes of rural development and employment. (For further detail refer to the essay on the topic)

Our Public Distributing System sometime back fell to pieces. This was the most important system because it benefited the urban poor too. It is however, on the way to universalisation. It is argued that targetted system cannot avoid the error of exclusion and it is divisive too. The universalisation of system is being favoured by the majority of the economists. But the financial dimensions are daunting.

We have already a number of programmes running as a part of affirmative action. These programmes relate to the various sections of society and to different age groups.

Antyodaya Anna Yojna, Integrated Child Development Services, Mid Day Meal Scheme, National Old Age Pension Scheme are few of the schemes that are meeting the objectives of Affirmative Action. The proposed National Food Security Act for the poor is in the making.

Women empowerment has been taken up seriously to provide equality of status and economic freedom. Their empowerment through their one-half reservation in Panchayat institutions has been instituted and one-third reservation in state and central legislatures is taking shape. Child Labour, Right to Education and various poverty alleviation schemes have been in progress. Successive governments have made commendable contribution to the success of affirmative action. In the wake of globalisation, market driven economy and crony capitalism affirmative action is the imperative need.

Social audit have been made mandatory into all food related schemes through Right to Information Act to enable the government to take action against the erring personnel. Despite all this we have damning reports from Comptroller and Auditor General. The help, it is said, becomes a trickle when it reaches those who deserve it.

In fact, affirmative action taken by government is flawed because it revolves round the idea of moral compensation for the injustice to socially and economically weaker sections of the society. Today it makes no sense in granting benefits on caste, community or class basis.

79. Does Indian History Needs to be Re-written?

History is considered the most important part of any country's culture and heritage. It gives us true picture of our past.

British wrote Indian history to suit their imperial designs. And then after independence history written highlighted the sacrifice of certain powerful segment of national leadership. It is time now to correct these wrongs in an objective manner. Distortions in history need to be set right. It is strange that the struggle of Indians against the Muslim rulers and the British rulers is presented as the misdeeds of terrorists. How can an Indian mind digest the idea that Guru Teg Bahadur was a looter and rapist? Shivaji waged struggle against Aurangzeb just because it was the growth of Maratha national sentiments. The martyrdom of Guru Teg Bahadur was due to the conspiracy of some members of his family. No body has objections if Aurangzeb is called *Zinda Pir*. The attacks of Allaudin on Chittor to get Rani Padamani are not acceptable to many so called secular leaders. It is irony that Khudi Ram Bose, Lala Hardayal, Bhagat Singh, Vir Savarkar and Bhai Parmanand are presented as terrorists. According to self-styled secular historians, they were terrorists.

If India is a secular state, it became secular only after the Britishers had departed. Secularism in the past was an unknown concept during the Muslim and British Periods. History should not be used to extol one dynasty or one community. Nor should it be used to denigrate any one particular segment of society. At the same time it is a mockery what is taught in the text books for class V in West Bengal. According to the Marxist Government it may be correct to teach children, "Islam and Christianity are the only religions which treat man with honour and equality." Such half truths and half lies have distorted modern history.

The teaching of the Vedas and astrology don't go against the interest of any particular community. If the Vedas are not taught in Indian schools and are not respected in India, should it be expected that other countries will do it? What a ridiculous Idea! One should have no objection if there are references to the evils of *Varna* system, plight of widows, the sufferings of the Dalits and women and so many other evils of Indian society.

It should not be considered as profanation of Hindu Religion. It is tragic to note that such a subject as History has come to be politicised. One should be honest enough to admit that Indian National Movement has not been projected in true colours. Most of freedom fighters have not found a place of honour in the pages of Indian History.

Has any body heard the name of Durga Bhabhi, the steadfast companion of Bhagat Singh and other martyrs? Is there any statue of hers or any institution named after her? Definitely not.

The reasons are obvious. The name of Udham Singh should have been glorified in no uncertain terms. His daring deeds should have been highlighted to make the youth of the country manly in their outlook. Tragically, it is not so. Who will unveil the mystery surrounding Netaji and his monumental sacrifice? It is unpardonable historical error. History is not a moral fable and description of glorious events. The facts must be brought out so that we may develop scientific temper and learn from the mistakes of the past. All those living in India are Indians. They must learn to accept the facts of History. They cannot grow up as part of the nation if they shut their eyes to the past. Past is a mirror and we must look in it and remove the distortions in our thinking.

It is more important function of history not to ignore unpleasant facts. Therefore, keeping this fact in mind truthful and objective history is the need of the day.

Indian history dates back to more than 4000 years. History has proved beyond doubt that Indian civilisation was highly developed and scientific in comparison to its counterparts. India had a rich culture, very rich indeed, notwithstanding certain flaws common to every society. In the wake of independence, Indian society took to reforms as fish takes to water. For political reasons one may say that the majority of Indians are casteists, communal, orthodox and what not. Since independence the majority has undergone material change in their mindset. The coming years will add more to the transformation.

To denigrate the majority in the variety of ways has become second habit of certain political parties and so called liberal and the marxists. For the communists a special kind of history needs to be written so that the past of Indians could be written in derogatory terms. This kind of mindset to destroy what is our past is reprehensible on the part of those who plan to rule the country perpetually. How can the leftists call themselves the voice of liberalism? Their interpretation of history and godless society has long been consigned to dust across the world.

80. Art for Life Sake

Essence of art is sublimity, a quality to elevate life and living. Sublimity is the echo of a great soul. A mean and ignoble person cannot produce a sublime work of art because stately thoughts belong to the loftiest minds. In fact a richer and more varied life is opened up through art. An artist recreates a concrete fact that comes to receive universal recognition.

In the process higher truth that has been unknown until now to is mysterious. An artist sees the life as a whole, not in fragments. Therefore identification of beauty and truth is the long endeavour of an artist. This is what we call eternity in art. One can explore beauty in ugliness and ugliness in beauty. Pain and misery can be described in the moments of joy. This is the integrity of life that artist tries to attain.

Great writers wrote with an eye on man and society in an objective manner and interpreted it subjectively. Art preaches no divisions. Human impulses and instincts cannot be classified by the name of caste, creed and nationality. They are similar in their throbbings. Love, joy, pangs of separation, hunger, failure, deprivations etc. evoke the same kind of emotions and responses in human beings living in diverse societies. In fact art, as Mathew Arnold wrote, is the criticism of life i.e. the application of sublime ideas expressed in art to daily life. Hence an art of revolt against moral ideas is art of revolt against life.

There are some who believe in the idea of 'Art for Art's Sake'. Art, they say, has nothing to do with morality, art is its own end. Art cannot deny its own nature by taking over the functions of a preacher. An artist is not a preacher and moral discourse is not the domain of art. Art is not designed to teach people a moral lesson since art has no end other than impart pleasure to the reader by inviting them to share artist's joy. Experience of an artist itself is an end. There is increasing insistence on the autonomy of art. Yet the supporters of this concept have not been able to present very convincing agruement in favour of art for art's sake.

There has been a long drawn conflict about the aim of art. Artists of every hue and shade have fought over it endlessly and will continue to fight till eternity. But the fact remains that the artists have moral grounds to defend. Art is the nearest thing to life and is of an account of deep and lasting human impulses. Art grows directly out of life. Artists, therefore, are shaped by zeitgist, the spirit of the age but in turn he also shapes it. He is of his age and yet above it. They are the unacknowledged legislators of mankind. It is an artist who can propagate the lofty ideas and ideals. Art cannot be divorced from life. Art is the breath and spirit of life. The question 'how to live' can best be interpreted by art. An artist cannot afford to hurt in the name of art for art's sake and claim immunity on the plea of freedom of expression.

Those who bat for art and literature as means of apprehending life in its entire gamut believe that art is the nearest thing to life. Man is a social being. He cannot therefore, ignore his obligations to the society. The artist and the society are dynamic. Writers are the cultural ambassadors of their countries like Prometheus, the fire giver and the liberator of mankind. Every great artist has a social responsibility. He unravels the complexities of his age and helps us understand the pulse of the people. Art is a mirror to life and not an expression of nudity in the things most sacred.

81. National Healthcare

India, a country of more than 1 billion, spends only 5.2% on healthcare with more than 80% of this being spent in the private sector. Indians have to depend on private sector, making a huge a dent in their personal resources. While India ranks among the top 10 countries for communicable diseases, it is a world leader in diseases like diabetes, hypertension and cardiac ailments.

Malnutrition of children is a matter of major concern: 15% death among children is caused by malnutrition. The latest UNICEF report says that 5000 children under the age of five die daily due to preventable diseases. 900 people die of tuberculosis daily. Taking into account the magnitude of public health problems, spending on healthcare is negligible. India ranks at 171 out of 175 countries in public health spending (WHO).

National Health Policy in India was not framed until 1983. The objectives of the draft National Health Policy 2015 are as follows:
- It proposes a target of raising public health expenditure to 2.5% of the GDP in five years.
- It also suggests making health a fundamental right; a National Health Rights Act would be enacted.
- The government also plans to rely on general taxation for financing healthcare expenditure.
- Plans are also afoot for creation of a health cess, similar to education cess, for raising funds.

The draft document highlights the urgent need to improve the performance of the health system with focus on improving maternal mortality rate, controlling infectious diseases, tackling the growing burden of non-communicable diseases and bringing down medical expenses.

However, widening economic and regional disparities are posing serious problems for the health sector. About 75% of health infrastructure is concentrated in urban areas where only 32% of population lives. Thus, only 25% medical services are available to 68% of the population, which lives in rural areas. Therefore, healthcare is a serious problem for Indians, specially for rural population.

Earlier, the National Rural Health Mission (NRHM) was set-up with special focus on 18 states which were backward in health status. The NRHM covered these states through 2.5 lakh villages based on 'Accredited Social Health Alternatives' (ASHA). These acted as a link between the health centres and the villages. The ASHA workers were trained to advise villagers about sanitation, hygiene, contraception and immunisation. They received performance based compensation for promoting universal immunisation.

The government is also looking after healthcare of the nation through other programmes like National Vector Born Diseases Control Programme, Leprosy Eradication Mission, AIDS Control Programme, National Mental Health Programme etc. In spite of all these programmes, the health status of the nation is grim. No matter what we say, India has one of the most privatised healthcare systems in the world. It is estimated that in 2004-05, 39 million people were pushed into poverty on account of expenditure on medical treatment.

In fact, rural Indians spend nearly 27 per cent of their income on healthcare. The Union Cabinet with its decision dated 1st May, 2013, approved the launch of National Urban Health Mission (NUHM) as a sub-mission of an overarching National Health Mission (NHM), with the NRHM being the other sub-mission of the NHM. The NRHM will receive ₹ 15000 crore to put the crumbling public health infrastructure in order. These are significant developments, but are hardly adequate because they touch only the fringes of the problem. Population growth rate is still a challenge, as it has taken political beating. We know well that medical care is not all about curative measures. Preventive measures in the form of providing safe water, better sanitation, nutritious food to children and mothers and preventing the onset of preventible diseases are also required.

82. Nanotechnology

The dictionary meaning of 'nano' means one billionth unit of measurement. The important fact about nanotechnology is that, it deals with physically small, really small structures. Nanotechnology deals with structures that are less than 100nanometres long. In technical terms, a nanometre is one thousand millionth of a metre. Scientists often build nano structures using individual molecules of substances.

The scientist Eric Drexler popularised the word 'nanotechnology' in the 1980's. He used this word for building machines on the scale of molecules, a few nanometres wide. Nanotechnology is a highly disciplinary science in the field of chemical, biological, mechanical and electrical branches of engineering, applied physics, chemistry, medicine, robotics and many other fields.

Eric Drexler was the first person to popularise nanotechnology. He was interested in building fully functioning robots, computers and motors that were smaller than a cell. In the early stages, the success of nanotechnology was doubted. However, today this kind of technology means something different. Instead of building microscopic motors and computers, scientists are interested in building superior machines atom by atom. Nanotech, therefore, has come to mean that each atom of a machine is a functioning structure on its own, but when combined with other structures, these atoms work together to perform a larger purpose.

The ability to see nano sized materials has opened up a world of possibilities in a variety of industries and scientific fields. It is so because nanotechnology is essentially a set of techniques that allow manipulation of properties on a very small scale. As nanotech continues to develop, consumers will see that it is being used for several different purposes. This technology may be used in energy production, medicine and electronics as well as other commercial uses. The application of nanotechnology in medicine, drug delivery and tissue engineering will open up a new concept of medicinal treatment. It is going to tackle the problem of air pollution and water pollution. This technology will surely address our environmental and health concerns.

We are in the first generation of nanotech, when structures created are passive and carry out one specific task. Scientists are entering the second stage, when the structures created are able to carry out multi-tasks. The third generation is expected to introduce systems composed of thousands of nano structures. The last and fourth generation will be defined by nano systems designed on the molecular level.

We have not seen much of nanotech being fruitful at present. But its future is bright. The first wave of its application is only now beginning to break. As it does, it will affect everything from the batteries we use to the clothes we wear and to the way we treat cancer.

The sum and substance of nanotechnology is that materials begin to develop odd properties when they are of such a small size. Substances behave magically at this scale because that is where the essential properties of matter are determined. For instance, an aluminium foil torn into tiny strips may continue to behave like aluminium. But at some point, aluminium strips measuring 20 to 30 nanometres may explode. There is a talk of adding nano aluminium to rocket fuel. It is like one shrinks a cat and keeps on shrinking it and then at some point, all at once, it turns into a dog.

83. Human Cloning

Genetic engineering is a highly advanced branch of science and comprises complicated techniques for modifying the character of an organism by manipulation of genetic material. This technique involves taking the DNA out of one organism and putting it back in the same or another organism after changing it with the help of chemicals. Genetic engineering is the science of the 21st century. First, it was nuclear physics and now it is genetic engineering. Gene therapy is one of the most promising areas for genetic engineers. Gene therapy is the technique of altering DNA within cells in an organism to treat or cure a disease. New genetic therapies are being developed to treat diseases like AIDS and cancer.

Science is a bad master. With the manufacture of atom bombs, the world stands on the edge of disaster. In the same way, genetic engineering has given rise to surrogate motherhood and human cloning, though its uses to cure fatal diseases are immense. Cloning is a scientific device and, as a part of genetic engineering, it was a great feat performed in the 1990s in the UK. Cloning means producing an exact copy of an animal or a plant from its cells.

In other words, a clone is a plant or an animal that is produced naturally or artificially from cells of another plant or animal and is therefore exactly the same as the original is. In 1997, Ian Wilmut and his team cloned a sheep called Dolly. At the same time he admitted that for cloning, one had to experiment a number of times on foetuses. When he cloned Dolly, he had to discard four hundred foetuses before he could get it right. However, he had no hesitation to state that human reproductive cloning is immoral and should not be resorted to. He was charged with playing God. The charge is not without truth. Creation is an act of nature. Let us leave it to God alone. Instead of devoting our precious time and resources to human cloning, efforts towards human welfare should be made.

Subsequently in 2001, Advanced Cell Technology (ACT), a US company, claimed to have cloned the first human embryo. They assured the anxious world that they had no intention of carrying on human cloning. Instead, they were interested in stem cell research with a view to providing treatment for a number of organic diseases.

Whatever the truth is, research is welcome with a purpose to make human life painless and comfortable. Man is already a victim of various incurable diseases such as cancer, Alzheimer's, Parkinson's, diabetes and AIDS. Genetic engineering holds hope for millions of patients.

Science is an amoral subject. Those who consider cloning immoral forget that surrogacy in practice is gaining currency. Even healthy mothers are avoiding to conceive as usual. It is a horrifying idea to think of humans replicated by the scientists in a laboratory. While opting for surrogate motherhood, embryos are transplanted in other volunteer women. As such, scientific human cloning is not far away.

Man is well-known for using science for unethical purposes. Take the practice of female foeticide that has been made possible with the help of the ultrasound device. The idea of hundred abortions to clone a person is not only unethical but also contemptible. It is feared that genetic engineering is capable of making babies to order. Parents in search of perfect babies are likely to encourage human cloning.

The fact is that only living human beings can be cloned. It is impossible to clone the dead. After the ACT claim in 2001, Colonaid Company in 2002 also claimed human cloning but no further details were forthcoming. Most of the scientists believe that it has not been done at all. Going by the history of science, human cloning will certainly take place in the near future. Those in denial mode today would find some excuse for human cloning, as the manufacturers of the nuclear bomb have done.

84. The Mobile Revolution

'*India bol raha hai*', the cellphone as arrived in India. Every age has its own lifestyle. The advent of the 21st century is the age of the mobile phenomenon. Television in the 90s of the last century revolutionised the world of entertainment and domestic life in India. Summer or winter, watching serials in the evenings became a ritual. Evening prayers by the elderly, dinners, evening call-ons had to be adjusted with the timing of one's favourite serials. Family gatherings became imperative for watching movies and the weekly *Chitrahaar*. Today it is the mobile, a tiny machine. A few years ago one could not think of being near if separated by a long distance physically. The cellphone has proved a boon for maintaining one's personal and social connectivity every minute. It has added to the mobility of the Indian masses. One can talk into it the whole day. Above all, we feel a strange sense of freedom from babus and linemen who had to be called, requested, cajoled and gratified till our contact on stationary telephone handsets with the world was restored. Today we have hassle free connectivity. The cellphone is more than a phone today. There is hardly any activity that cannot be handled by this small magic box. Sending money to overseas has became as easy as drawing money through an ATM. In fact, the tiny machine is a combination of phone, camera, radio and internet. No wonder then, tomorrow we may come upon a handset that can telecast programmes. Letter writing has lost its charm and sending SMS is easier and faster. It does not impose any restraint on selection of words. 'Hinglish' is both at its best and worst. 'SMSing' is a favourite with youngsters. The matter does not end here. Most required information can be found.

Telemarketing is a new phenomenon in the world of marketing and advertisement. No place is unsafe for women if they are wise with their handsets. Travellers can call for help wherever they are stranded. Parents are providing cellphones to children and young girls due to safety concerns. Sensing danger, they can press the 'call' key unobserved. In solving crimes, the cellphone has done wonders. At times, it is our lifeline.

Cellphones have been a boon to us, as every minute a person has an important thing to convey or receive. It is a common sight to see a young boy or a girl with legs astride mobikes engaged in whispers while earning the abuses of passers-by. Car drivers resting their ears on shoulders with cellphone sandwiched is not uncommon. Rich or poor, you must have one because SMS contacts are part of one's daily chores in India. The growth of mobile phones is very high and has already crossed 4.61 billion.

It is yet to be ascertained how much exactly in our life cellphones is relevent. Is our preoccupation with cellphones going to contribute to the quality of time we pass? What is more, cellphones pose a great health risk. Mobile phones and relay towers of mobile signals radiate radio frequency energy that heats up tissues which may be possibly harmful to human health. Particularly pregnant women, heart patients and children are at great risk, but at present who cares? Therefore, one cannot afford to be careless with the small machine in our hand or pocket. The innocuous looking cellphone may, by radiation exposure or electronic discharge, cause potential health hazards.

All over Europe the governments have issued warnings about electronic radiation. European Environment Agency wants exposures to be minimised and advises limited use for children, pregnant women and persons with certain diseases. It is time our government adopted safety measures with the cooperation of the cellphone industry.

85. **Net Neutrality**— A Public Demand

Network neutrality is the principle that ensures competition in the online world. All content on the internet travels in the form of data packets across the telecommunication networks around the world. Net neutratlity requires that all data travelling over the network be treated equally. Telecom companies, who own the infrastructure through which data packets passes inter alia argue that they should have a right to control this data flow and the 'freedom' to charge accordingly (to ensure that certain data gets priority over another or that certain data is not carried at all, etc.)

Their argument is that since telecom companies spend large amounts of money building the infrastructure (or the tubes through which data packets pass), they should have a say over what content travels over or through it and of course make more money from it. Network neutrality is the principle according to which internet traffic shall be treated equally, without discrimination, restriction or interference regardless of its sender, recipient, type or content, so that internet user's freedom of choice is not restricted by favouring or disfavouring the transmission of internet traffic associated with particular content, services, applications or devices.

In the layman's term, net neutrality means internet that allows everyone to communicate freely. It means a service provider should allow access to all content and applications regardless of the source and no websites or pages should be blocked, as long as they aren't illegal. It's like a fixed-telephone line, which is equal to all, and no one gets to decide who you call or what you speak. Another aspect of net neutrality is level playing field on the internet. This means, all websites can co-exist without hampering others. All websites are accessible at the same speed and no particular website or application is favoured. For instance—like electricity, which is common for all. Net neutrality also means all websites and content creators are treated equal, and you don't have to pay extra for faster internet speed to a particular site/service.

Why should one bother or what will happen if there is no net neutrality? To put it out straight, if there is no net neutrality, the internet won't function as we've known it too. It will mean internet Service Providers (ISPs) will be able to charge companies like YouTube or Netflix as they consume more bandwidth, and eventually the load of the extra sum will be pushed to the consumers. Similarly, ISPs can then create slow as well as fast internet lanes, which will mean all websites cannot be accessed at the same speed and one can do so only on paying an additional sum. For instance, currently, you have a standard data package and access all the content at the same speed, irrespective of whether it's an international website or an Indian one. Similarly, ISPs can also charge extra for the free calls you make using services like WhatsApp, Skype and others, and eventually, the load of additional payable sum by the OTT players will be pushed onto consumers.

Net neutrality is extremely important for small business owners, startups and entrepreneurs, who can simply launch their businesses online, advertise the products and sell them openly, without any discrimination. It is essential for innovation and creating job opportunities. Big companies like Google, Twitter and several others are born out of net neutrality. With increasing Internet penetration in India and given that we are becoming a breeding ground for startups and entrepreneurs, the lack of net neutrality should worry us greatly. Besides, it is very important for freedom of speech, so that one can voice their opinion without the fear of being blocked or banned. In the West, in 2010, Federal Communications Commission (FCC) had passed an order to prevent broadband internet service providers from blocking or meddling with the traffic on the web, known as the 'Open Internet Order'. It ensured the Internet remained a level playing field for all.

However, in 2014, the court said the FCC lacked the authority to do so and enforce rules. This means, telecom companies who were earlier forced to follow the rules of net neutrality strarted adopting unruly ways. This also paved way for ISPs to monitor data on their networks and also allowing governments to ban or block data. Besides banning or blocking data, we also had the high profile Netflix-Comcast tussle.

Recently, FCC has approved 'Net Neutrality Rules' that prevent internet providers such as Comcast and Verizon from slowing or blocking web traffic or from creating internet fast lanes that content providers such as Netflix must pay for. European Union member states have also been striving for net neutrality.

In India, there is no law that expressly mandates the maintenance of a neutral internet. As of August 2015, there were no laws governing net neutrality in India, which would require that all internet users be treated equally, without discriminating or charging differentially by user, content, site, platform, application, type of attached equipment, or mode of communication. There have already been a few violations of net neutrality principles by some Indian service providers. The government has once again called in for comments and suggestions regarding net neutrality and has given the people one day to post their views on the mygov forum. After this, the final decision regarding the debate will be made.

The debate on network neutrality in India gathered public attention after Airtel, a mobile telephony service provider in India, announced in December 2014 additional charges for making voice calls (VoIP) from its network using apps like WhatApp, Skype etc.

On 10th February, 2015, Facebook launched internet.org in India with Reliance Communications. It aims to provide free access to 38 websites through an app. Only Bing was made available as the search engine. Sunil Mittal, CEO of Bharti Airtel, criticised the concept.

In April 2015, Airtel announced the 'Airtel Zero Scheme'. Under the scheme, app firms sign a contract and Airtel provides the apps for free to its customers. The reports of Flipkart, an e-commerce firm, joining the 'Airtel Zero Scheme' drew negative response. People began to give the one-star rating to its app on Google Play. Following the protests Flipkart decided to pull out of Airtel Zero.

The Communication and Information Technology Minister, Ravi Shankar Prasad, later said that a committee will be formed to study the net neutrality issue. Rajeev Chandrasekhar, a member of the Parliament, had also supported net neutrality. The Competition Commission of India (CCI) Chairman, Ashok Chawla, said that they were examining whether these practices were unfair.

In March, 2015, Telecom Regulatory Authority of India (TRAI) had already released a formal consultation paper on Regulatory Framework for Over-The-Top (OTT) services, seeking comments from the public. The consultation paper was criticised for being one sided and having confusing statements. It received condemnation from various politicians and Indian internet users. The last date for submission of comment was 24th April, 2015 and TRAI received over a million e-mails.

In response to this, TRAI issued another consultation paper on differential pricing for data services. This was seen as a major improvement over the previous consultation paper. However, the debate between telecom regulators and OTT players refuse to die down.

While telecom regulators complain that OTT players like WhatsApp, WeChat etc., are eating up their main revenue without investing in networks; OTT players, on the other hand, defend themselves by demanding access to web services without any discrimination. On 8th February, 2016, TRAI took a revolutionary decision, prohibiting telecom service providers from levying discriminatory rates for data, thus ruling in favour of net neutrality in India. This move was welcomed by not just by millions of Indians but also by various political parties, business persons, industry leaders and the inventor of the World Wide Web, Tim Berners Lee.

However, the debate over net neutrality is far from settled telecom companies that wish to discriminate between applications argue that in the absence of an internet that has completely permeated all strata of society, an obligation to maintain neutrality is not only unreasonable on the companies, but also unfair on the consumer. After all, if nothing else, Airtel Zero and Free Basics bring, at the least, some portions of the internet to people who otherwise have no means to access the web. What we have, therefore, at some level, is a clash of values: between access to the internet (in a limited form) and the maintenance of neutrality in an atmosphere that is inherently unequal. This makes tailoring a solution to the problem a particularly arduous process.

The internet, in its purest form, is a veritable fountain of information. At its core lies a commitment to both openness and a level playing field, where an ability to innovate is perennially maintained. It is difficult to argue against Facebook when it says that some access is better than no access at all. But one of the problems with Free Basics and indeed with Airtel Zero too, is that the consumer has no choice in which websites he or she might want to access free of cost. If this decision is made only by Facebook, which might argue that it gives every developer an equal chance to be a part of its project as long as it meets a certain criteria, what we have is almost a paternalistic web. In such a situation, information, far from being free, is shackled by constraints imposed by the service provider.

Those who are arguing in favour of net neutrality sees this move as a laudable end that follows unethical means. They aren't resistant to the idea of greater penetration of the internet. According to them, negating net neutrality, in a bid to purposely achieve greater access to the internet in the immediate future, could prove to be profoundly injurious in the long-run. But the history of markets tells us that we have to be very careful in allowing predatory practices, devised to achieve short-term goals, to go unbridled. As citizens, each of us has a Fundamental Right to Freedom of Speech and Expression. If we were to get the balance between these two values wrong, if we were to allow the domination, by a few parties, of appliances that facilitate a free exchange of ideas, in a manner that impinges on the internet's neutrality, our most cherished civil liberties could well be put to grave danger

86. Our Education System

With 32 million children in the 6-14 age-group out of schools and 26% of illiterate population, where does the question of becoming a super power arise? To make matters worse female literacy is dismally low at 65.46% while total literacy is no better at 74.04%. The problem is further compounded by illiteracy in our villages. After 68 years of Independence it is disheartening that there is a vast gap between literacy and genuine education. Before 1976, education was the exclusive responsibility of the States. In 1986, it was placed on Concurrent List by way of constitutional amendment. The Union Government, thus, accepted a larger responsibility to evolve an effective meaningful and qualitative system of education.

The Central Government developed National Policy for Education (NPE) in 1986. It envisaged free and compulsory education of satisfactory quality to all children upto the age of 14 years. Historic National Mission in the form of *Sarva Shiksha Abhiyan* was launched in 2001 to provide 8 years of quality education to all children in the age-group of 6-14 years. In 2002, the Parliament passed 86th Constitutional Amendment Act to make education a fundamental right for children in the age-group of 6-14 years. In 2009, the Government adopted Right of Children to Free and Compulsory Education Act that came into force in April, 2010.

The Act makes elementary education not only compulsory but also stipulate. duties for parents, private schools and local communities. They should ensure that children in the age-group of 6-14 years get free education. National Programme of Nutritional Support to Primary Education (Midday Meal Scheme) was launched in August, 1995. The main purpose of the scheme was to give boost to universalisation of primary education and to improve nutritional status of the children.

The Secondary Education Sector prepares students in the age-group of 14-18 years for entry into either higher education or employment. Yashpal Committee has recommended very effective guidelines to deal with the problem of secondary education.

The Central Government launched *Rashtriya Madhyamik Siksha Abhiyan* to check the drop out rate as a part of the proposed Education Reforms. The aim of the scheme is to take forward the mission of *Sarva Siksha Abhiyan*. Drop out rate increase is a perennial problem in our system.

There was also a proposal to introduce CBSE degree for Skilled Education (class 10th or 12th) as many children want jobs immediately after completing school education. Secondary Education has great importance because they prepare the pupils for universities. It also provides terminal education for those who will wish to enter upon some career in life. That is why Skilled Education is required to be imparted to students. Today after Secondary Education our young men are on their wit's ends for lack of professional qualifications. They are compelled to take up university education.

Our university system is in a state of despair. Major criticism levelled against the university education relates to quality of higher education. Of the total 14000 colleges under the jurisdiction of University Grants Commission (UGC) 61% of them do not satisfy assessment norms. It is necessary to bring them under a defined system to improve the standard of education. The University Grant Commission was established in 1956 with a view to coordinating and promoting university education all over the country. Of the total colleges only 8% have achieved the quality parameters.

The bulk of them impart low quality education affecting the system of education in totality. Therefore, the first step to improve university education is to bring 92% of colleges of the total 744 universities under the fold of UGC but only after they have met with the standard of education laid down by this apex body.

As of now higher education has concentrated on academic pursuits. It is neither innovative nor creative. Skill based training institutes are avoided by the students. Yashpal Committee has, therefore, recommended revolutionary reforms in higher education system. The recommendations of the committee are as follows:

National Commission for higher education and research will be set-up and it will be directly responsible to the Parliament. It will subsume as many as 13 existing professional regulatory bodies including UGC and the Medical Council of India. The accredition of deemed universities will be stopped according to its recommendations. The committee has recommended that all institutions combine academic and research programmes.

The fake foreign universities should be barred strictly. Most importantly multi-disciplinary approach to learning has been recommended at under graduate level. The recommendations of Yashpal Committee could not have come at a better time to lift the education system out of chaos.

87. Right to Education

The Right of Children to Free and Compulsory Education Act, 2009 came into effect on 1st April, 2010. The coming into effect of the Right To Education (RTE) marks a historic moment for all the children of India. The Right of the Children to Free and Compulsory Education had been recognised in 2002 by passing the 86th Constitutional Amendment. The 86th Constitutional Amendment added a new Article 21, (A) making education free and compulsory to all children of the age-group of 6 to 14 years. A new fundamental duty was also added making it mandatory for parents to send their children to schools. The Act is likely to serve a launching pad to ensure that every child has the right to guranteed quality elementary education. The best part of the legislation is that the parents and the society have a legal obligation to fulfil this duty.

The Act is quite a wide ranging document and all pervasive to ensure quality compulsory and free education to children in the age-group of 6-14 years. The world had set itself the millenium development goal of educating every child by 2015. In India alone there are about 32 million children out of schools and about 220 million children get very poor quality of education. The world cannot achieve the millenium development goal as long as Indian children are out of school.

The RTE strives for quality with equity and is likely to improve quality of school education that at present is at the lowest ebb. The morning in every city presents a very depressing scenario of education in India. One need not stretch one's neck to see different children going to different kinds of schools depending on their economic and social status. This act seeks not only just to ensure elementary education to all but also to reform the system. It stipulates duties for parents, private schools and local communities to ensure that children in the age-group of 6-14 years get free education. Besides, the act seeks to improve the quality of school education that at present is miserably at the lowest.

Even those running unrecognised schools are liable to punishment. If recognised schools do not adhere to certain standards, they are subject to derecognition. These standards have been set in terms of teacher's qualifications, their duties and pupil-teacher ratio. Teachers are forbidden to take up private tuitions. Nor will they be used for non-educational jobs except for population census, election duty and other national emergency purposes. In case of holding tests and interviews of parents for admission a school may be fined ₹ 25000 for first violation and ₹ 50000 for subsequent violation. The bill also seeks to do away with capitation fee charged by schools. Moreover, schools cannot deny admission to a child for lack of age certificate nor can he be expelled or detained until he has completed elementary education. Corporal punishment has been prohibited in the schools too.

The private schools have also been roped in as a joint effort. 25% of seats in private schools are required to be reserved for disadvantaged students. The minority schools are allowed to allot 50% of seats to their own communities. Besides, the schools need to maintain pupil-teacher ratio 40:01. The urban-rural divide among students and teachers has to be bridged. So, a provision has been made to impart elementary education in a child's mother tongue. Few countries in the world have such a huge national agenda to ensure both free and child friendly education to all children. So far our stress has been on quantity rather than on quality. Government has so far directed efforts to increase enrolment numbers without ensuring quality learning. But RTE would not only help bring all our children into schools but also ensure quality education for all of them, the half of whom continue to be pushed out of the system.

However, the success of the RTE hinges on the crucial question of quality teachers. Educational Reforms are meaningless unless teachers are geared up to implement them, as to educate a child we need good teachers. The RTE would yield results only if we have dedicated and qualified teachers. The Right to Education Act, indeed, poses a serious challenge to all of us.

88. Brain Drain

Brain drain may be simply defined as flight of talent from India. It is a pity that the most talented students and trained professionals are absorbed by the Western countries. India is just a training school for the industrially advanced countries. According to an estimate the annual brain drain from India to all the countries of the world is said to be around 10000 trained personnel. A significant number comprising those who migrate to foreign countries are engineers trained at various IITs of the country. They are mostly computer science graduates. In addition to this, doctors form another large chunk of those going to foreign countries in search of money and material success.

In fact, India suffers from brain-drain in terms of superior talent because India has a fairly well developed infrastructure. The irony is that the most qualified professional graduates of high quality institutions find lucrative posts abroad and the country is deprived of their services. In fact the system of employment and promotions is unhealthy in India. Those belonging to influential families having political and bureaucratic links get preferential treatment. Corruption in bureaucratic and administrative machinery is a great obstacle to the progress of genuinely qualified candidates. Talented workers make way for sub-standard workers resulting in frustration among deserving and capable candidates. It is just like the working of Gresham's law according to which bad money drives the good money out of circulation.

As a matter of fact we have not been able to develop work ethics. The employers are not interested in talented persons because they would not have to pay higher salary to those who deserve to be rewarded. As a result of this frustrated young men in India would look to the West where they might get recognition for their talent. Examples of Sir JC Bose, Dr Hargobind Khurana and S Chandrashekhar should serve as an eye opener to Indians. Today in the context of progress in the field of information technology brain-drain has become an alarming problem.

Even in medical profession the problem of brain-drain is all pervasive. It is said that the British Health Services are largely run by Indian Doctors. We have very effective infrastructure for medical education. How unfortunate Indians are that those trained at public expense go out of the country to serve the foreigners. One can conclude very easily that the two most important causes of brain-drain are fascination for the West and corrupt bureaucratic and political culture in our own country.

Unless talent gets proper recognition in our country the problem of brain-drain will continue to eat into the vitals of Indian society. The entire socio-economic scenario needs to be changed drastically so that a genuinely talented person does not become the victim of frustration. First, we have to explode the myth that the West is superior to the East. Self-employment has to be encouraged. The industrialists will have to learn to respect the talent by paying salaries commensurate with the talent.

Myth is already exploded. Though we always decried the brain drain but were not able to lure our experts to return home. That appears to be changing fast. The reason lies in our strong rate of growth and dismal performance of American and European economies. European countries can retain foreign talent only if they relax immigration policies. India is likely to draw on its brain bank in due course of time.

PM Narendra Modi during his visit to California in 2015 said "the brain drain that we discussed for many years has now actually become brain gain."

Indian migrating to the US was once criticized as brain drain. Now, it is renamed as brain bank or brain circulation. Of late, new dimensions have been added to Indian migration to the US. It has become apparent that the diaspora played an even bigger role in the economic and social life of the US. The brain drain gradually increased the number of influential Indians in the US. The size and the clout of the diaspora grew fast in Silicon Valley. The trend now encompasses all walks of US life. This has raised India's profile in the US. One-third of Silicon Valley engineers are Indians. The rise of Indians in the US is a story that has kept on growing. Indian Americans are the fastest growing ethnic group, now estimated at almost three million.

But one thing is clear that a big shift is underway. India would not remain content to allow the flight of indegenous talent. What is more, with India's rapid growth, home will offer a number of incentives not available in the past and brain drain might be put in reverse gear. With ten per cent unemployment and depressed spending the US will find it difficult to hold Indians back for a long time.

89. **Distance Education**—Its Future in India

Distance education is a highly welcome step because in a country like India, overcrowding of schools, colleges and universities is a chronic problem. The infrastructure in the field of education is on the verge of break down. The prospects of distance education have been made more fruitful because of the development of information technology. Moreover the field of conventional education may be limited because the students interested in higher education may like to earn while acquiring education. For want of financial constraints students will not have to cut short education.

The development of distance education will make education accessible to all irrespective of financial, social and age factor. Equality in the field of education can be achieved for the rich and the poor, the urban and the rural population. In 1966, the Kothari Commission made a very meaningful observation on distance education. It said that the home study or correspondence method does not provide the opportunity for inspiring contact with the teachers. Interestingly, it remarked that inspiring teachers are rare these days. In correspondence system of education there is a strong motivation to learn. It is a fact that distance education does not provide effective kind of close relationship between the teacher and the taught, but this shortcoming has been overcome by providing contact classes and study centers for the guidance of the students.

Everything said and done, the inspiring ideal behind distance education is self motivation of the learners for betterment of their own prospects. The Kothari Commission has also observed that important vocational programmes can be taken up in the field of industry, commerce and agriculture, to help the workers improve their efficiency.

Even the Indian Education Commission (1964-66) was also of the opinion that there must be a method of taking education to the millions who depend upon their own efforts to make advancement in the educational field. The International Commission on education has also strongly supported distance learning system. Open university system has come to assume immense significance as a viable alternative to conventional system of education. The Indira Gandhi National Open University (IGNOU) was established with these objectives and it has proved quite useful in its scope to encourage open school system.

Most of the universities in the country have come up with distance learning programmes in accordance with National Policy on Education. In India, we have a kind of dual system of distance education—Distance education Directorates and Open Universities. The advent of open education in India came up with the establishment of Andhra Pradesh Open University in 1982. Indira Gandhi National Open University (1985) and Kota Open University (1987) have given fillip to distance education in the country.

However, the system of distance education in our country is not free from the problems. Most of the distance education directorates are poorly funded by the states. In some cases they have to support themselves. It is therefore, important that these directorates should be given autonomy within the university system so as to plan new courses and enhance their financial status.

The distance education system has not been able to make full use of electronic media as a means of two-way communication between the students and their tutors. Moreover the material provided by these directorates is sub-standard and the study material is not received in time. There is a need of closer examination of the study material so as not to lower the standard of education provided by distance education directorates. Inspite of these shortcomings, in a country like India only distance education can bring education to the door of all and one.

90. Entry of Foreign Universities in India

Higher Education is getting increasingly global the world over; the opening up of foreign universities in India is quite a viable step. The Foreign Education Provider's Bill is intended to facilitate their entry. Now, the institutes for Higher Education are looking beyond the borders of their countries. Will the entry of foreign universities make any improvement in the quality of routine education in India? It is a crucial question.

According to UNESCO, Global Education Digest, 2012 almost 200600 students from India, highest after China go abroad for higher studies. With 744 universities and millions of students studying in them, quantity has never been a problem in India. Giving quality education, on the contrary, has always been a problem. Secondly, India needs many more colleges and universities due its large population

Granting entry to foreign universities has to be, therefore, an integral part of meeting with shortages and quality education. There is no doubt that there is a huge demand for quality higher education among Indian students and foreign universities in India can surely come upto their expectations. But if foreign universities come over to India to exploit student demand and make quick money, they cannot contribute to quality education. India has to be realistic about which university can deliver the goods. There are about 150 off-shore universities around the world and all are not competent enough to impart education on an international scale. We have already plenty of franchisees working in India through partnerships and collaborations. They couldn't perform as per the expectations.

The experience of entry of foreign universities in other universities has not been qualitatively successful. China opened up to foreign universities in its unique style. A Foreign University intending to come over to China has to join a Chinese partner. It helps to keep a watch on the kind of education being imparted. In the nineties, Israel invited Foreign Universities but was disappointed with their performance. So, ultimately they were asked to close down.

In the Indian context objection to the entry of foreign universities are many. Will it not amount to the creation of another elite class in a country that lives by the faith of equality for all? The common objection to the opening up to foreign universities is that the only inferior universities may enter into the Indian education system to make quick money by imparting sub-standard education. Why will Harvard Business School open a branch in India? They believe that Boston itself is an essential part of Harvard MBA experience. We cannot expect to establish Oxford or Cambridge in NOIDA and Gurgaon.

Every Indian nurses an ambition to go to America or Great Britain for higher study. Some of the Foreign Universities have stood as brand names for real education. As the degrees from these universities are unfailing passport to success, they are hard to be lured into India. However, the common perception is that living abroad for study gives an advantage beyond education. Living abroad enables the students to face the global challenges on strong footing. It imbibes confidence, the most potent adjunct of education. The sanest views heard so far is that we should open up to the best universities. If not possible we should upgrade our educational system and put our own house in order to enable the system to impart innovative education.

91. **Ragging**— An Evil

Once a kind of harmless interaction between the seniors and the freshers, now ragging has degenerated into a dangerous entertainment where, there is so much pain and agony for one party in a game, the game that is senseless. Thus, a freshers' party tends to become senseless. The Supreme Court has rightly defined ragging as "any disorderly conduct, whether by words spoken or written or by an act which adversely affects the physique or psyche of a fresher or a junior student, is an act of ragging." Oxford dictionary defines ragging first an act of laughing or playing tricks on some body. But these acts should not be allowed to go to the extent of causing death. Sometimes, deaths have been caused due to ragging or the students unable to cope with ragging commited suicide or just dropped out. Today, ragging amounts to intimidation of the freshers into submission for the rest of their time in the institution. In co-ed institutes the practice of ragging has become inhuman.

Girls have to bear the brunt of ragging that continues for months. The worst form of teasing, abusing, threatening, molesting and practical jokes on students are the manifestations of the evils of ragging these days. They are bound to leave a lasting scar on the psyche of a bewildered fresher or Junior. One thing is quite clear that students should learn where to draw the line. Three pronged approach has been advocated by Co-alition to Uproot Ragging from Education (CURE). (a) Ragging should be regularly monitored and the offenders punished. (b) Social awareness should be created since society has not accepted ragging as a social evil. It is regarded as a necessary initiation ritual. (c) We should find out amiable ways and means of welcoming freshers. The repulsive ways are not compatible with the places of learning.

Ragging has always been a problem on college and professional institutes and campuses. But ragging in schools is rampant too. Central Board of Secondary Education (CBSE) has taken serious note of the menace of ragging. There have often been incidents of physical and sexual abuse in schools which are not reported for fear of shame and to protect the reputation of the institution.

CBSE board has warned such schools saying that they have their own source of information network regarding such ugly happenings.

Now, there is a law to punish the offenders. A student or his/her parents can lodge a complaint against the offenders. Even abetting the act of ragging can lead to dismissal or suspension in addition to penal action against the staff members. If the head of the institution does not take action against offending students, he may be seen as an abettor and face the punishment. This extreme punishment is only the last resort.

The other ways to overcome this problem include counselling, suspension for a certain term, heavy fine or expulsion. Ragging should be placed on the report card of the students as one of the measures for the student's evaluation. Students should be sensitised on the adverse effect of ragging. Above all, ragging should be included in college ranking system so that the college authorities may always be watchful. Punishment to erring students is not a lasting solution.

As college authorities have not been successful in imposing discipline on the raggers, UGC has came out with a proposal recommending three year imprisonment or a ₹ 25000 fine to check growing hooliganism in the college and university campuses. The punishment may serve a deterrent so as not to allow things to go out of hand. Many students feel that UGC should not serve as kill-joy and drain-off fun and joy out of college life.

Instead of imposing fine it would be better to take the help of serious minded senior students in preventing the criminal elements to take charge of ragging. Committees of responsible students should be constituted to keep a watch on irresponsible elements.

Secondly the principal and the professors should exercise moral authority over the mischievous students. Those who take up teaching profession by choice are expected to know their duties as well. They have responsibility towards society in addition to their teaching profession. Therefore, the best course to deal with raggers should remain invested with the teachers. Let no outside authorities interfere in the interest of long term harmonious relationship between the teachers and the students.

On the healthier side, ragging is a part of growing up and facing upto challenges that a college life opens up to a student. It is considered a part of college life. If you respond with courage, you make seniors your life long friends. Ragging is a kind of introduction to one's seniors in an informal manner and this kind of interaction is quite harmless, if ragging is done within limits.

92. Sex Education in Schools

Sexual behaviour has recently been included in the area of social psychology. Sexual behaviour involves interaction with the opposite sex. It has become a topic of academic and research interest. In modern times, it has received scientific respectability and acceptability. One can say that Freud and Darwin have totally revolutionised the concept of our living. As a result of change in attitude to sex, it is proposed that India should also introduce sex education in schools.

So far sex behaviour and discussion about sex were regulated and disciplined by means of customs, religions, taboos and laws. The earlier generations learnt about sex through instinctive learning. Sex was never considered a healthy socio-biological concept. It resulted in perverted habits, crime against women and resentment against social norms. Studies in this field show that sexual behaviour in human beings also involves factors at emotional level. Thus, the subject has entered a new phase.

Need of sex education appears to be imperative because of co-education at school level. Boys and girls get more opportunities to mix with one another. They must be enlightened about the effect of early sex, emotional damage, mental and physical abuse. The child must be taught what is acceptable behaviour. Children must be taught the values of sublimation of sex upto certain age level. Regulation of sexual behaviour does not mean repression.

Boys must be more aware of civilised behaviour towards girl students. Strict vigilance is needed both at home and at school. Parents and teachers must encourage them to ask questions and, in turn, satisfy their curiosity. Counselling cells in schools can help in removing certain misconceptions from young minds.

Today progress and concept of modernisation is considered synonymous with Westernisation. The unscrupulous advertisers and widening role of electronic media has promoted obscenity. This definitely has made pernicious effect on the mind of the youth. Nudity, ultra modern fashions, display of female body have confused the unemployed youth, girl students and poverty ridden families. Boys and girls must be taught value based social behaviour. So, role of media has to be more educative. Most importantly, sex education should be ultimately connected with the hazards of unsafe sex. The youth must be made aware of the contagious ailments. It is the duty of parents at home and teachers at school to protect children from child abuse. Education should be given so that the victims of sexual abuse may not feel the pressure of guilt.

In a nut shell, the right communication is very important. The subject should be handled by specially trained teachers. It should aim at promoting ethical and spiritual values in relation to sex. It should bring about empowerment of women. This may enable them to fight violence against them. The findings of John Hopkins University should serve as a guideline in this field. According to the findings it has proved successful in the West.

However, it has failed in promoting the values of healthy sex education. Sex education should be inevitably linked with moral values and sense of social responsibility among the students. The top priority, however, is to take the stigma out of the word sex validity.

Sex education in schools is a Western concept. But has it succeeded in the West in promoting social awareness and moral values among the school and college going students? The only answer is in negative. It has not reduced the cases of violence against women, teenage pregnancies and has not promoted the values of healthy sex education. Therefore, the question of teaching sex in schools in India should be linked with moral & social sciences. India is a traditional country and such a revolutionary education will not find favour with Indians.

A sex education programme and syllabus developed by the Ministry of Human Resources Development, National Aids Control Organisation, UNICEF and NCERT have not found favour with people across on religious ground. Most of the states have imposed ban on teaching sex education in schools.

The often cited reason in favour of sex education in schools is that teen sex is on the increase all over the world. Therefore its focus on HIV/AIDS. Child sexual abuse is a serious problem in India. South Asia, particularly India is known to be one of the biggest sources for human trafficking. Young children both boys and girls are trafficked for commercial sexual exploitation. Sex education will enable them to understand and respect their bodies for the rest of their lives.

93. Grooming Teachers for Tomorrow

Government has made education compulsory and free for all the children of the age-group of 6-14 years. We have already had National Programme of Nutritional Support (Mid-day Meal Scheme) at primary and middle level. Prior to this government had launched various schemes and made a large number of laws to make education universal at primary and middle level.

If we go by what we see around us all the schemes have failed to meet with desired results. The simple reason is that our nation lacks the will to do so. It is impractical to think of quality education without a dedicated class of teachers. We have often heard that 'Education should be a right'. We need schools for all our children but the question is who will teach them?

We should understand the essence of having dedicated teachers. They should be trained in the art of imparting quality education at primary level. Primary education is the life-line of higher education. Without quality primary education it is unthinkable to have good engineers, good doctors, good leaders, good professionals etc in the future.

What a paradox? We are a country where half the population is illiterate but which has produced world's second largest pool of trained scientists and engineers. Our primary school system has become one of the largest in the world with 150 million children enrolled as students. To educate a child we need a good teacher. So far our stress has been on quantity rather than on quality. Governments have raised enrolment numbers without ensuring quality learning. There is no effective answer unless we groom our teachers for tomorrow.

We have a nationwide shortage of 25 lac teachers. Several of the teachers who exist do not teach. Most of the schools, colleges and professional institutions and even universities have employed teachers who are not fully qualified. These institutions employ teachers who do not measure up to the standard laid down by University Grants Commission. The ritual of honouring teachers have continued for years. Teacher's day is an occasion for celebration whereas it should be a day of reflection. The function of true education is to build an integrated personality of the students. What our youth think today, the nation will think tomorrow. The roads to building a nation passes through the portals of schools and colleges. It is an irony that people who could not perform well in schools opt for teaching as a career. And mediocre teachers would impart mediocre education.

Give good incentives to teachers so that really capable teachers are attracted to the field of education as a career. There should be an all India teachers service to provide better incentives and status so that quality people can be attracted. The training of AITS on all India level has to be scientific, uniform and modified to meet with the essence of quality education. Educational Reforms are meaningless unless teachers are geared up to implement the reforms. Teachers are the strongest link between the present and future and this link has to be strengthened. Without dedicated teachers any attempt to reform the present education set-up is akin to putting a cart before the horse.

94. Swami Vivekananda— My Favourite Spiritual Leader

Born on 12th January, 1863 as Narendra Nath Vivekananda was one of those few divinely inspired souls who tried to revive the lost glory, values and traditions of ancient India, which were first suppressed by the Muslim rulers and then the British masters. In almost one thousand years of slavery, Indians had lost esteem and self respect. It is no exaggeration to say that he emerged as a pole star to guide the stranded Indians to their destiny. As a founder of the Rama Krishna Mission, Narendra Nath was christened as Swami Vivekananda and was one of the greatest religious reformers of India. Charisma reflected on his face spoke of his inner strength and purity of his soul. As a humanist, reformist and harbinger of Vedantic Revolution, his place in the history of our country is irreplaceable.

Swami Vivekananda acquired initiation into the spiritual world at the feet of Swami Ram Krishan Parmahans. He inspired the youth with his positive outlook and taught them to have iron muscles and nerves of steel. It is possible only by following the ideals of the Upanishads. A positive outlook can be developed only by the native wisdom of ancient India. However, his own speeches and writings can inspire the youth of the country that has fallen prey to wily politicians. Most of them, in the garb of freedom fighters, have climbed up to the zenith of their political careers by spilling the blood of innocent citizens and by exploiting their credulity.

In a modern context, charismatic and sagacious leaders like Swami Vivekananda can mould the destiny of India. Under such a leadership and guidance, the youth can redeem their honour. Emancipation from the shackles of communalist and casteist leaders can be achieved by exposing their ulterior motives. The relevance of Swamiji today is greater than what it would have been a few years ago. He made us realise what kind of India we need.

Swami Vivekananda brought out the validity of vedantic philosophy in application to life. He worshipped God not for his own *moksha* in parochial terms of Hindu religion. The realisation of divinity within oneself makes one a Karma Yogi, lover of humanity and compassionate to every living human being. His thundering words at the Parliament of Religions at Chicago on 11th September., 1893 resounded and spread all over America. Their echo does not seem to have died down; nor will it ever die down. It is the voice that every human being ever longs to listen to. Tagore rightly said about Swamiji "to know Vivekananda is to know India". He was a great awakener of India at a time when the spirit of every Indian was at its lowest ebb.

As a champion of the women's cause, his unforgettable words should never be lost on those who think them inferior human beings: "If you do not raise the women who are the living embodiment of Divine Mother, do not think you have any other way to rise."

In the last, one can say that Swami Vivekananda represented the best of both East and West. He identified himself with a universal outlook : 'The world as one family'. What a pity that he passed away in the prime of his life at the age of 39 on 4th July, 1902. 12th January is rightly dedicated as 'Youth Day' to keep his memory perpetual in every Indian heart.

95. Bhagat Singh— A Sublime Martyr

The Indian nationalistic movement, from its very inception, remained divided between moderate and extremist elements. The path of extremism is laid with hardships, blood, sweat, tears and death. The difference between the two streams of thought existed right from 1907. The moderate views suited the Britishers and they did their best to placate them while declaring the extremists as terrorists. The repressive measures against the extremists were not effectively and sincerely opposed by the moderates. The Revolutionary Movement was led by leaders like Aurobindo Ghose, Savarkar and Bhagat Singh. Bhagat Singh was imbued with an ardent desire to drive the Britishers out of India. Born to Kishan Singh and Vidyavati at Banga in the Lyallpur district of the West Punjab in 1907, Bhagat Singh grew up as a patriotic young man.

He became a leader of the student community and later joined the National College, Lahore founded by Lala the Lajpat Rai. In 1925, he established Nav Jawan Bharat Sabha at Lahore. He came in contact with other revolutionaries like Sukhdev, Chandra Shekhar Azad, Jatinder Nath Das and others.

The decisive moment in the life of Bhagat Singh and other revolutionaries came in 1928 when Lala Lajpat Rai was seriously injured by the police. A huge procession in the form of a protest against the Simon Commission was being headed by Lala Ji who later on succumbed to injuries sustained in police atrocities on the procession. His death infuriated young men like Bhagat Singh, Azad, Raj Guru and many others who decided to avenge the death of Sher-i-Punjub. They shot dead Saunders, Asstt. Superintendent of police. Then Bhagat Singh had the courage to throw a bomb in the Central Assembly on 8th April, 1929. Bhagat Singh, Sukhdev and Raj Guru were sentenced to death and hanged on 28th March, 1931. Thus ended a tempestuous career at the age of 24.

Bhagat Singh was inspired by his uncle Sardar Ajit Singh. Patriotic fervour ran in the family blood. Vidyalankar, a lecturer at National College and Lala Lajpat Rai had a tremendous impact on his thoughts. Nav Jawan Bharat Sabha established in 1925 by Bhagat Singh was entirely aimed at social welfare. But soon it took up the cause of the country's freedom and served as an outlet for preaching revolutionary ideas to the young men. Bhagat Singh was no less a political and social thinker. Nav Jawan Bharat Sabha was renamed as Hindustan Socialist Republican Association. It was an organisation of about 60 young men and 5 women.

Durga Bhabhi, a courageous woman, played a historic role in the organisation. Sadly enough, her name does not find any mention in the history books. Her saga of courage can serve as an inspiration to the young women of today. Bhagat Singh has left a legacy of revolutionary ideals which are relevant even today. Though the revolutionaries did not succeed, they made a dent in the British empire. Today we owe a debt to him and countless young men and women who sacrificed their comforts and embraced an arduous path to freedom.

96. Rabindranath Tagore

Rabindranath was a born poet who began composing when he was barely seven years old. But he wrote great poetry after the 'Great Illumination' which gave him a new insight into the universe. It happened when he was just eighteen. He describes this experience akin to lifting of an ancient mist from his sight, "That which was memorable in this experience was its human message." Rabindranath Tagore was born in Calcutta on 7th May, 1861. He was lucky in the moment of his birth. The second half of the 19th century was the period of full flowering of the Indian Renaissance. It was an age when, in contact with the English, India was struggling to come out of hibernation, isolation and backwardness.

In fact, the Muslim rule had come to an end. The medieval slumber was over. What happened to England in the 16th century during the great renaissance happened to India after about three hundred years. The Muslim culture was barren in the field of creation, education, social development and humanism.

The English arrived and brought along with them the revival of learning. Those were stirring times when men of genius like Tagore could make their presence felt. A humanist to the core, he was a nationalist who dreamt of India as a nation free from superstitions. He strove to develop scientific spirit among Indians. He was lucky in his birth in more than one way. His grandfather Dwarkanath was called the prince. His father Dabendranath was called Maha Rishi. His brother Satyendranath was the first Indian to enter the civil service. At the age of seventeen he was sent to England for higher study.

On his return from England he was married to Mirnalini Devi in 1883. He became the Secretary of Adi Brahmo Samaj, of which his father was a great leader. He was a tireless critic of the caste system and upheld the dignity of every caste. He was a true humanist. He came into touch with the life of the people and wrote from experiencing actual life. He established himself as a great lyricist. Even his prose had the ring of lyricism.

In 1901 Tagore made a great contribution in the field of education. At Bolpur his father established an Ashram called Shantiniketan. Here, Rabindranath founded his open-air school which later on developed into a famous university, Vishwa Bharti. The year 1905 witnessed the partition of Bengal and Tagore took an active part. In 1911, partition of Bengal was revoked. But the English had succeeded in creating a permanent communal divide. Tagore composed *Jan Gana Mana*, the national song, on the eve of reunification of Bengal.

Guru Dev, as Tagore was affectionately called, won the Nobel Prize in 1913 for his Gitanjali and was knighted in 1915. However, Tagore renounced the knighthood in 1919 in protest against the Jalianwala Bagh massacre. At the age of 80, the end of his fruitful life came in 1941. As a humanist, poet and true nationalist, he will always be remembered.

Essays for Practice

Directions *Write essays on the following topics given below with the help of the given points.*

1. **E-waste—The Digital Darker Side**
   - Points
     - electronic waste
     - network fanning
     - precautions
     - threats of misuse
     - unnecessary exploitation of resources
     - irrelevant storage and improper dumping
     - virus and detection

2. **Green India—Need for Sustainable Growth**
   - Points
     - green India
     - moderation is in resource usage
     - government initiatives
     - benefits : health, infrastructure and economy
     - sustainable growth
     - plans and programmes

3. **The Value of Sports**
   - Points
     - sports
     - mental benefits
     - team player and leadership qualities
     - physical benefits
     - personality development traits

4. **FDI in Retail : Good or Bad**
   - Points
     - FDI in retail
     - increase in foreign currency
     - competitive environment and prices
     - economic decentralisation
     - discouragement for the local retailers

5. **Environmental Pollution**
   - Points
     - pollution
     - harmful effects
     - man-made causes
     - giving rise to diseases
     - motor, air, noise etc
     - danger to health and nature
     - effects on living beings

6. **Cyber Crime**
   - Points
     - increasing number of cyber crimes
     - morphing, frauds, theft
     - groups and institutions
     - rising reports for blocking leak of private information
     - need of the hour
     - safe and reliable browsing

7. **Students and Politics within Universities : Is It Healthy or Not?**
   - Points
     - political parties behind students
     - often leads to violence
     - tremendous inefficiency owing to political interference
     - political wars
     - prejudiced behaviour instigated

8. **Virtual Learning : Can it Replace Teachers?**
   ↘ Points
   - virtual learning
   - electronic learning
   - no personal touch-rigid terms
   - set standards
   - no alternative methods for children with different IQ
   - beneficial for only one set of students with same intellect

9. **Dream of Smart Cities—Myth or Reality in India**
   ↘ Points
   - Indian dream
   - urban development vision
   - information and communication technology
   - aimed at improving quality of life
   - enhance quality, interactively of urban services
   - reduces costs and resource consumption etc

10. **Role of NGOs in India**
    ↘ Points
    - NGOs
    - lending voice to the weaker section
    - supporting social causes
    - funded by government or run on donations/charity
    - effective work
    - not 100% reliability or accountability of functioning

11. **Should Animal Testing be Banned?**
    ↘ Points
    - animal cruelty
    - for cosmetic chemical or medical research
    - right to live freely as humans
    - painful experiments leading to fatal results
    - steps to make it offensive and illegal

12. **Indian Agriculture : Achievements and the Way Ahead**
    ↘ Points
    - supports 58% of rural population
    - largest exporter and producer of spices and spice products
    - governmental initiatives helping the sector grow
    - plans for better momentum and increased funding

13. **Nelson Mandela**
    ↘ Points
    - South African President and philanthrophist
    - member of African National Congress
    - devoted champion for peace and social justice
    - civil rights activists

14. **Reservation Policy in India**
    ↘ Points
    - based on caste system
    - prevails in higher education institution, public sector unit and aided government bodies
    - benefitting the physically disabled under certain circumstances.
    - 33% seats for women in parliamentary forces

ESSAY WRITING

15. **Sachin Tendulkar**
    - **Points**
      - former Indian cricketer and captain-known as greatest batsman of all times
      - part of Indian winning team of 2011 World Cup
      - receiver of Arjuna Award, Rajiv Gandhi Khel Ratna award, Padma Shri and Padma Vibhushan award and Bharat Ratna award
      - nominated in Rajya Sabha and named a honorary member of order of Australia

16. **Participating in Sports Help Develop Good Character**
    - **Points** [Civil Services (Mains), 2014]
      - value of life skills
      - team spirit and competition
      - development of self confidence
      - develops persistence and patience
      - provides exposure

17. **Should Students be Allowed to Grade their Teachers**
    - **Points** [Civil Services (Mains), 2014]
      - best first hand feedback
      - personal experience
      - freedom of speech
      - develops analytical skills
      - builds sensitivity and maturity among students

18. **Impact of Politics on Society** [Civil Services (Mains), 2015]
    - **Points**
      - collective shrug on society
      - rise of corruptive behaviour
      - misuse of potential
      - exploration of power and authority

19. **Eco Tourism and Challenges-It Faces** [IES, 2014]
    - **Points**
      - environmentally sound tourism
      - a global sector and need for the country
      - ensuring survival of attractions of nature and culture for tourism

20. **Use of Social Media in Politics** [IES, 2014]
    - **Points**
      - surveyed to be positive in association with political participation but weaker in comparison to civic engagement
      - transformational effects
      - better for creating awareness
      - independent variability with politics

21. **Pro Active Indian Judiciary** [CISF, 2014]
    - **Points**
      - executed when democracy is threatened
      - authority saving authority
      - running when the in house mechanism fails to operate on certain issues

22. **Computer Literacy to Para Military Forces** [CISF, 2014]
    ⇒ **Points**
    - call for urgent requirement for advancement
    - aiming for self reliability
    - easy employment and income generation

23. **Save the Earth-Save Life** [IFS, 2014]
    ⇒ **Points**
    - green earth
    - better life
    - freedom from manual cruelty and actions
    - over exploited resources
    - efforts and awareness needed
    - sustainable development
    - need of the hour

24. **Communication-Face to Face or Facebook** [IFS, 2014]
    ⇒ **Points**
    - loss of personal touch and meaning
    - virtual living
    - insignificance of body language and voice inflection
    - bridging a yet widening gap

25. **Indian Women in International Sports** [Civil Services (Mains), 2012]
    ⇒ **Points**
    - laurels to the nation
    - breaking gender stereotypes
    - Sania Mirza, Saina Nehwal, Saba Anjum, Mithali Raj, Mary Kom etc
    - establishing records on international platforms

CHAPTER 2

Expansion Writing

Candidates and aspirants appearing at various Competitive Examinations are tested in their expression skills. They are asked to deal with Essays, Descriptive Comprehensions, Precis including expansion. The expansion means elaboration of certain statements or famous sayings or meaningful poetic or prose statements. Say, for instance,

"Revenge is a kind of wild justice." "The child is father of the man."

These are profound sayings implying wealth of ideas. Sometimes, students are asked to elaborate paradoxical and metaphorical statements into an independent paragraph. Such statements need fuller and detailed explanations. A candidate is required first to discover the implication and then to enlarge upon the meaning in not more than hundred and fifty to two hundred words. Expansion Writing tests the candidate's power of expanding and enlarging upon the ideas. In a precis writing, he is asked to comprehend and compress the ideas within the limits fixed by the examiner.

☑ Useful Hints

- A student must stick to the old principle of writing on a subject according to the following divisions
  1. Exposition   2. Argument   3. Conclusion
- Expanded paragraph should be comprehensible, simple and easily understood in its meaning.
- The clarity of the views expressed must be given utmost importance.
- A student is advised to be brief in dealing with the subject relevant to the theme.
- Arrangement of ideas is essential so that the expanded idea is read as a whole. As such, thinking is a process through which a student can construct a paragraph. It should not be rambling. It must have coherence and continuity.
- No need to say that the expansion should be free from grammatical errors. Writing makes a man perfect. A student must write on his own and get matter checked by an experienced teacher.
- **Limit of words** A student should limit himself to the number of words set by the examiner. A paragraph should not exceed the limit nor fall below the limit. In the book, we have not set any limit of words because we have kept in view the need of the students according to different examinations. Most of the topics can be further enlarged and given the shape of an essay, if required.

Samples of Expansion Writing

Directions *Below are some expansion writing with their solutions.*

1. Spare the Rod and Spoil the Child

The child is as restless in the growth period of childhood as he was in his infancy. His interest in the objects around him is on the increase. In the maturity period, the child specially develops social consciousness. Therefore, it is high time he learnt the disciplined way of life at every level—home, school and society. It is the duty of both the parents and the teachers to guide him properly by persuasion and teaching. A child should not be pampered by adulation of parents. Mothers are more culpable in this regard. In case, a child shows a sign of taking up a wrong path, parents and teachers should not refrain from enforcing discipline on him.

It may also require punishment. He should never be allowed to become petulant, vagabond or truant. These are not healthy habits. Today, corporal punishment is prohibited in schools. Teachers are taken to task for thrashing a child even though the latter has grossly violated discipline. However, a good teacher or responsible parents should not refrain from punishing a child with a view to discipline him.

2. All that Glitters is Not Gold [IES, 2015]

We should not go by appearances as they are often deceptive. A well dressed man may not necessarily turn out to be a gentleman. The same is true of a man, whose sweet words may charm you at first sight, but whose actions may repel you later on. Wicked persons conceal their true intentions in the beautiful garbs with the help of sweet words. Gold is to be judged not by its glitter. Its intrinsic purity determines its worth. So is the case with every man.

It requires strenuous efforts to judge of a man and his character. We can't dismiss a person giving him a label that suits our caprice. Just as touchstone brings out the worth of gold, so the worth of man is measured by his deeds and intentions. It is a good principle to go slow in making friends till we have seen through his inherent qualities. Never take a person at his word. Watch him, test him and be sure of his worth before entering into steady and stable relationship.

3. The Child is Father of Man

The word 'child' means here superior, wiser, more innocent or nearer to heaven, where we all come from. A child is nearer to heaven and retains divinity around him. It is how Wordsworth glorifies childhood. The heart of a child is the seat of noble human qualities. In fact, his soul is in direct communication with God. In our childhood, we have the recollections of the divinity. This vision of a blessed divine world makes the child see on Earth the light of heaven. But as the child grows up, the celestial vision fades away.

A grown up man cannot see the vision of the divine. He gets immersed into worldly affairs. This makes the soul of a man ultimately oblivious of the bliss that was once his. It is how the child is father of man. However, as a child grows up, the influence of the world begins to corrupt him. Thus, he is no more as innocent as he was in his childhood. The child is the father of man because he is superior to his elders.

4. Handsome is He That Handsome Does

Appearances are deceptive. Handsomeness of a person should not be considered in terms of physical features. A worthy life comprises worthy deeds. The nobility of life depends on noble character. Those, who are taken in by physical beauty in the beginning have often rued their lot. Our character depends on honesty, stability of ideas, faithfulness and attitude to others. These are precisely the qualities that constitute handsome deeds, not by wealth or physical beauty. Only such persons as do good deeds win permanent place in our hearts. Beauty is a nine days' wonder, fickle and transient. Only truthful deeds and ideas are beautiful. A character of man is summed up by what he has done worthwhile and only such a person deserves to be called handsome.

5. There is Nothing Good *or* Bad but Thinking Makes it So

Man is the only thinking animal. He is supposed to live by his own ideals and good deeds. It is possible, only if, he has learnt the art of mastering his thoughts. For a pessimist, the results of our acts, however good they may be, are pre-determined by some mysterious power. On the contrary, men of actions face life with indomitable fortitude. Life is a challenge to them. They would never give in willingly. So, life is a blend of both good and evil.

It depends on us how we look at it. It is our thought-process conditioned by external impressions that determine our behaviour. Nothing is either good or bad. Both are the two sides of the same coin. It depends upon how we look at it. It is just to say that an optimist sees the rose, a pessimist sees the thorn. In a sum, one should develop a healthy attitude to life and men so as to lead life better.

6. Actions Speak Louder than Words

A man is best known by his deeds but not by what he professes to be. Self-praise is no praise. The braggarts are not to be taken seriously. Judge a person by the qualities of his actions. Actions reveal the character and intrinsic worth of a person.

True nature of man hardly remains hidden for a long time. It is bound to find its expression in his deeds sooner or later. If education is a boon for some, others exploit it for the attainments of their ulterior motives. Unfortunately, demagogues have ruled the world. Gullible masses are taken in by outward appearance and oily tongue of those in power.

An intelligent person knows the value of deeds. Education ought to make us realise the distinction between words and actions of those, who come into contact with us. Deeds and deeds alone are the criteria to judge the character of a man. Actions are eloquent than the words of a man because nobody likes to disparage himself in his own words.

7. Reading Maketh a Full man; Conference a Ready Man and Writing an Exact Man

There are different forms of studies—reading, discussing and writing, which perfect human understanding in different ways. Reading develops faculties of comprehension and judgement of a man. It makes him a scholar full of wisdom. The habit of discussion leads him to exchange of ideas with others. This sharpens his intellect and makes him quick witted. He gets mental acumen and can argue with others with confidence.

In the same manner, the practice of writing makes a person disciplined, precise and correct. It is through reading that a person imbibes new ideas and reaps the wisdom of sages contained in the books. Discussion with others helps him to put up his ideas well before others. While writing, a person has to be very careful because whatever he writes goes on record in black & white. He can't afford to be wrong or mislead others lest he should be considered ignorant. One cannot write at random. One has to weigh an idea before he writes.

8. There is Least Friendship and Least of All Between Equals

There is hardly true friendship in the world. It is generally believed that friendship is based on mutual needs, which friends fulfil for each other. That is why, it is remarked that true friendship can exist alone among equals because on material plane one can repay in kind what one has received. The friendship between a rich a˙ a poor person is very rarely heard of. If there is any, its basis might be the exploitation in the name of friendship.

Such friendship is looked upon with suspicion by the world. In fact, friendship is rare in this world. There are only acquaintances that are guided by practical consideration of mutual benefits. We are apt to give the name of friendship to general socialisation. By the same criterion, true friendship hardly exists between equals. It is fraught with jealousies and rivalries that ultimately give rise to feuds. Fortunate is the man, who has even one true friend because the test of friendship is the hardest to pass through.

9. Paths of Glory Lead but to the Grave

The moral of this poetic line is plain and universal. The rich, the wealthy and the ambitious should not be proud of their wealth and high aspirations. Death is the ultimate goal of humanity. It is the eternal abode of all the living beings.

Then, why feel proud of ones achievements? Why should one mock at the underdog and the deprived? Many talented persons die unhonoured and unsung because they are poor. But, the successful persons have to keep in mind that whatever they have achieved in life is doomed to come to end. No one and nothing can escape the destined end—death. Glory is bound to fade and so what you are proud of is subject to oblivion.

10. Proper Study of Mankind is Man

The age, in which Alexander Pope wrote, held the belief that literature must follow nature. However, nature does not imply the gushing streams, the lofty mountains or the tranquility of the dusks and the dawns. To the age of 18th century of England, nature signified human nature rather than the nature that we enjoy in the forests. The vices and foibles, good and noble in human nature make a perfect subject for study.

The study of man as well as the study of society in which he lives, ought to be the subjects of art and literature. This kind of study alone enlightens man and widens his horizon of understanding. This ultimately leads to improvement in morals and manners. The study of man in relation to universe, to himself and to society can alone portray man in true colour. To understand man, it is indispensable to study human nature in totality.

11. Without Bread Liberty is Meaningless

The awareness of human rights and liberty in modern age, is definitely a milestone. The tyranny of the rulers, so common in the Medieval Age, is a thing of the past. Today, the Rule of law prevails almost in every country. There are many liberals in international arena to protest against the oppression and gagging of freedom of speech. However, in almost all the countries the rich rule the roost. Wealth is concentrated in a few hands.

There is economic exploitation everywhere in every form. We have yet to evolve a system, whereby the rights and economic justice should co-exist. Rights are meaningless, when the poor have no economic means to enjoy them. Rights are worthless for a hungry person, an unemployed youngman and exploited class of people. While one is hungry and deprived of necessities of life, liberty is futile.

12. Knowledge is Power

"Know Thyself" is a dictum preached by the sages. Knowledge of one's own self can lead a person to the right path of truth and goodness. This path is ultimately conducive to the society as a whole. A man has to think of the problems of his own existence and of the universe in which he lives. Only then, he can strive for the betterment of the society. However, it is often seen that man misuses his knowledge. The power gained through knowledge makes him insolent. In fact, right kind of knowledge is needed. This knowledge "Samyag jnana" secures salvation and liberates man from ignorance.

Today, modern civilisation is heading for self destruction. The stockpiles of nuclear arsenals will inevitably cause nuclear holocaust. We require neither this kind of knowledge nor power. The knowledge of spirit, eternity and ultimate truth is the right kind of power to enable man to lead contented and peaceful life.

13. Art of Living

A few persons know the art of living. Most of us, waste away the time and energy in finding faults with what we have. The real art of living implies a healthy development of mind, body and intellect. Fortunate is he, who takes pleasures and sorrows with mature attitude to life. Sanity in outlook means that man is never bothered by unfounded fears. Groundless hallucinations will never haunt his thoughts. He is bound to look on life with optimistic view. Worries and cares are never going to unnerve him. Those, who are not satisfied with life always grumble. They are foolish enough to turn the blessings of life into incurable curse. Modern life is highly complicated. In fact, art of living may be given the name of science of modern living. So, right way of living has to be evolved by man so that his spirit and material needs may not clash against each other. His spirit may not starve, while he is busy in materialistic pursuits.

14. We Live in Deeds not in Years

It is undeniably true that in the ultimate measure, the deeds done by man in his life time sum up the quality of his life. The span of life is meaningless, when measured in years alone. It is often seen that great souls, who achieved something notable in their short lives command a sacred place in history. They become legendary figures to be emulated. Good deeds, not the number of years, carve a niche for them in history.

A long life without a single deed worth, the name is insignificant. Such a life does not leave any impact on mankind. Just to eat, sleep and exist is no life at all. Noble deeds alone entitle him to be cast in the mould of a real man. A real man suffers, for mitigating the miseries of others and for the good of humanity. A man is remembered by his deeds long after he is dead and not by the criterion of longevity. In other words, one crowded hour of glorious life is worth an age without a name.

15. All the World is a Stage

The world is often compared to a stage, where like actors, we enter, perform our allotted role and then have our exit. In other words, the role of man is predestined. The invisible director of our lives decides our roles—tragic or comic. We are born in the world to perform what is expected of us. From cradle to pyre, we are to play different roles. Only those are honoured, who perform their roles to the best of their ability.

They alone are remembered in the annals of history, who perform exceptionally well. One should not grudge the role one is offered to perform. It is a part of larger universal design envisaged by God. In fact, drama is an imitation of life. A character has to do different roles at different times. So has man, in reality, to do right from infancy to the old age, what he is destined to do. We should not be deterred by the brickbats of the audience nor elated at their praise.

16. A Thing of Beauty is a Joy Forever

A lover of beauty is haunted by idea of beauty in everything. He seeks beauty everywhere—in human body, in nature, in life around him, in ideas and spirit. Here, the concept of beauty stands for truth—the beauty of truth that does not exclude the idea of ugliness. Ugliness is an essential part of life just as evil is. Even, the ugly in facial features may inspire the lover of beauty. His idea of beauty is not skin deep. Artists live with the abstract idea of beauty. For them, once one has understood the real meaning of beauty, it is for ever. Physical beauty is mortal, it is transient. But, the creation of an artist born of beauty is immortal. The concept of beauty in the works of Kalidas and Shakespeare is universally valid till today. This concept will go down as truth as long as the universe exists. So is true about Kabir, Nanak and other great sages. The beauty inspired by their sagacious thoughts is a source of perennial joy to mankind.

17. He that hath Wife and Children hath given Hostages to Fortune

A married man with children is a prisoner of fortune. They are obstacle to his progress. He is unable to take risks in life and enter upon bold ventures. Those, who are not married, are in a better position because they can set their sights high. Being free from shackles of matrimony, unmarried persons can devote themselves to the service of society. The philanthropic works can easily be undertaken by them for the welfare of the society. On the contrary, a married person develops a myopic view of life. His vision of future is confined to the future of his family alone. He is just like a prisoner, whose spirit of enterprise is restrained by his wife and children. However, it must not be taken as a rule of life that unmarried persons are better equipped to accomplish high deeds.

18. A Friend is Another Himself

A true friend is, in fact, more than himself. There are many problems, which a person cannot solve himself. His friend can do so and may complete and perfect the actions of a person. A friend illuminates the mind and dispels the gloom of confusion. The chief fruit of friendship is that a man can share his thoughts with another person. By doing so, he can understand himself better. A friend need not be from outside the circle of kith and kin. She may be a wife or a daughter or he may be a husband, teacher or a son. A friend is a blessing both on the material and spiritual level. A man without a friend is without the benefit of a free, frank and honest advice. A friend is another himself may imply that a friend is a complement. He compensates one for one's shortcomings and relieves man of sufferings and miseries.

19. There is a Silver Lining in Every Cloud

Though the sky is overcast with clouds, it will not be long before the clouds disperse. The whole world will be enveloped in light and joy. No one can deny this universal phenomenon. So is the case in our personal lives.

Disappointments and failure in life are like clouds that make our life bleak. But, one should take heart from the fact that misfortunes are apt to disperse giving place to good days. Such a hope should make man cheerful even while the going is not good. The cycle of life consists in this very fact that nothing is permanent in life. This fact of life is heartening and cheering enough to breed eternal hope in human breast for the good days to come. Joy and woe are woven fine and the texture of real life comprises both these alternating with each other.

20. Rome was not Built in a Day

Success is a long tale of travails and tribulations, sweat and perseverance. It cannot be achieved overnight. There is no royal road to success. Miracles are the theme of fairy tales. Boons granted by angels are mere myths. One must realise that hard work is the only key to success. Those, who burn midnight oils, taste the sweet fruit of success. So, impatience would lead us nowhere. Great achievements require greater efforts and patience. Great creations take time to come into being. Therefore, one should not despair of hopes if success is belated. Our efforts are undoubtedly crowned, sooner or later. Unmindful of results, one should continue one's efforts with a hope that success is a certainty. Patience is the talisman to success. Impatience leads a man astray from his goal of life. No success worth the name can be achieved within a short time. The greater the success, the longer the time.

21. Where there is a Will, there is a Way

If a man has a will to do a thing, he will find a way to do it. No obstacle is insurmountable enough to deter him. Nothing can shake his faith. A man of will is never discouraged by physical infirmity, poverty or lack of support from his kith and kin. Such a man can achieve anything in teeth of stiff opposition. He can mould inhospitable circumstances to his liking. Hardships and sufferings are naturally unwelcome. But, life is not a bed of roses.

One can achieve his aim of life by hard work. Those, who are weak willed buckle under the pressure of circumstances. They flounder against the rocks and are destroyed in the long-run. It is the will that makes man improvise, manipulate and devise ways and means. So, strong will is the last means of a man if he is to achieve his cherished goal of life. He has talent to carve his own way if he has the tenacity of will.

22. A Rolling Stone Gathers no Moss

Fickleness is the worst frailty in human nature. Those, who are not firm in their thoughts drift here and there. They are directionless in their aim of life. Those, who can't stick to their resolution come to grief. Moss grows only on stagnant stone and it gets heavier. Similarly, a man engaged in a particular work regularly gains some experience. Contrary to this, a man, who is constantly switching on from one job to another fares worse in the world of competition. Perfection is the fruit of constancy and cause of success in life.

Capricious actions make the life of man like a rudderless boat that is drifting here and there. As a rule, man should not change his professions too often. The constant change may make a man jack of all trades but master of none. Those, who are prudent, act patiently to achieve their hearts' desires. Only a determined person tastes success by following the determined path.

23. Revenge is a Kind of Wild Justice

Revenge is a natural instinct in man. It is ingrained in his nature. He is inclined to take revenge on others for the wrongs done by them. But, it does not behave a civilized man to take law into his own hands. If a man does so, he undermines the value of law that is the hallmark of modern civilization. Revenge is definitely to be discouraged because the wrong that has been done cannot be undone. It is a glory of man to let bygones be bygones. Forgiveness is the noblest virtue that a man should learn to practise. It exalts him over the brute and the beast.

Vindictiveness is the unforgiving nature of the devil. Just as we pluck out the thorn that pricks us, we should ignore the wrong doer. This is the noblest course of life. Eye for an eye is the rule of jungle law that man has left far behind. In fact, revenge is the poor delight of little minds because avenger is moved by animal instincts.

24. Failures are Stepping Stone to Success

Man acts with a view to achieving his goal in whatever field he is engaged. Obviously, he dreams of success and he will never bargain for less than success. But, success is not always the result. All his efforts may end in fiasco.

The lesser men would give in to the pressure and throw their hat in. But, a man of fortitude will persevere realising that his failure is a stepping stone to success in future. He learns from his failure. The failure provides man an opportunity to analyse its cause. Having realised his shortcomings, he will adopt prudent course on way to success.

The ascent to Mount Everest and landing on the Moon are the rare achievements of the recent past. Do we think that the only first attempt brought the success to the adventurers? One shudders to think of the amount of failure they must have encountered to be at last on the top of the world. It is the indefatigable spirit that ultimately leads to success.

25. The Pen is Mightier than the Sword

[IES, 2014]

Both, the pen and the sword, symbolically stand for intellectual power and the physical power of the brute. Both are powerful in their respective fields. But, the question is which of the two is more conducive to the welfare of mankind. In the realm of intellectual field, the pen is supreme. The poets and the philosophers have blessed man with imperishable truths. They have unravelled the inscrutable laws of nature. Guided by them man has attained to the present height of civilisation.

On the other hand, conflict is inherent in human nature. The Greeks and the Romans built empires by dint of swords. They trampled the weak and plundered the hapless innocent members of mankind. Now, the conclusion is obvious. The victories won by the sword are subject to ruins. But, the thoughts expressed by the intellectual persons, are enduring and lasting. Hence, the pen is mightier than the sword.

26. Beggars cannot be Choosers

The world is ever ruled by the rich and the mighty. They have always enjoyed the right to dispense the fate of those over whom they rule. So, the high and mighty decide the quality and quantity they like to dole out to those, who are under them. The poor and the weak have never enjoyed the right to choose for themselves. The beggars are forced to accept whatever is given to them in alms. They have no courage to remonstrate with the donors, nor have they the rights. On the contrary, they are expected to express their gratitude for what they have been given. Why should a donor take the trouble of knowing the choice of a donee? Donor is giving something in charity that is not required by himself. He is not inspired by the spirit of sacrifice. The needy have no alternative but to accept what is given to them. So, those, who give, decide what is to be given to the needy.

27. Peace hath her Victories, no less Renowned than War

The word victory is associated with war. But, we are aware that war is a weapon of the brute. Victories of war are won at the enormous cost of destruction. The weapons of war unleash fatal fury on innocent men, women and children. The tremendous cost has to be paid by the warring nations in the form of devastation. On the other hand, peace brings happiness and prosperity. The victories of peace are renowned more than war. They imply victory over poverty, suffering, ignorance and disease.

The glories of peace are numerous. Peace and prosperity usher in an era of progress.Recent history is a witness to the fact that during the last fifty five years after the Second World war, the attainments of the countries in the field of science and technology are amazing. We have achieved what could not have been achieved even during thousands years of war. Peace alone encourages man's constructive activities. So, victories of peace are far more worth winning than the most famous military triumphs.

28. Pride hath a Fall

"Pride hath a fall", says the Bible. Lucifer fell from the grace of God because he had aspired to be His successor. When denied the favour, he revolted against the Almighlty, was vanquished and was damned to hell. One, who flies on waxen wings, is bound to have a fall. The wings would melt near the sun resulting in a head strong fall.

History is replete with instances, when the proud, intoxicated with power and money, had to bite the dust. The proud are despised though they may extort respect from others. But, the meek win genuine respect. They are loved and respected. The mighty have to eat humble pie sooner or later. Pride results in brutal and unabashed use of power. On the other hand, the humble spread sunshine wherever they are. They rule over the soul of human beings. The proud are bound to face humiliation in the long-run.

29. Character is Destiny
or Man is the Architect of his Own Fate

The ancient masters like Aristotle propounded the theory that the tragedy in the life of man issues from flaw in his own character. The rebound of his own acts contribute to his ruin. Man himself is the architect of his destiny. Whether, a man suffers or prospers will depend upon a man's temperament, his actions and his doings. Good actions usually lead to good results.

Whereas, ill-considered actions have unpleasant and even disastrous consequences. Nothing can tie down a man of fortitude. However, the debate has been unending for those, who believe that man is ranged against predestined forces of life. To them, fate determines our joys and sufferings. Yet, how far fate meddles with the affairs of man is an unanswerable question. Those, who succeed, owe their success to their efforts. On the contrary, failure is attributed to destiny.

30. Example is Better than Precept

The best form of advice is to translate it into one's own action and set an example before others. There is no dearth of preachers in the world. The pity is that mere advice cannot be expected to have the desired impact on those, whom we wish to guide. If one lives upto one's belief, it might have tremendous effect on others. They are more than willing to follow you. A commander, who leads his army by his own deeds of valour, is far better than him, who leads his troops by words of valour.

A teacher, who practises what he teaches, is likely to be emulated most. Mere words of advice and laying down rules can lead society or country nowhere. Mere advice to others without following oneself is meaningless and may sound hollow. It will make one look ridiculous in the eyes of others. Therefore, it is better to show the way by following what one wishes to preach.

31. Poetry is the Criticism of Life

Poetry should interpret life faithfully and truly. It should not dabble in futile subjects unrelated to life. Art is for life's sake. It must point out the ills and present the true diagnosis of suffering humanity. It is the function of the poetry to place before us the ailments of the age and preach what makes life worth living. Poetry must not be divorced from morality. At the same time, poetry goes a step farther. It does not present life as it is.

Rather, a poet gives in his poetry, what he really and seriously believes in. A poet teaches through poetry the noble and profound application of ideas to life. In other words, it answers the question how to live life nobly. Such kind of poetry makes life richer because a poet speaks from the depth of his soul. He creates beauty, a perennial source of joy that finds its expression in the dictum what life ought to be.

32. Our Sweetest Songs are those that Tell of Saddest Thoughts

There are moments in the life of man, when he is confronted with the hard realities of life. All his hopes are dashed. A sense of loneliness and desolation overtakes him. It is the mood in which an artist expresses his sorrow in his songs. But, the emotion of pleasure is momentary. Happiness is just an interlude in the tale of sufferings. The reality of life is hard and it just breeds pessimism in man. Those, who overcome it, are optimists but those, who are unable to overcome feel a sense of melancholy.

They try to express the truth of life in their songs, which are bound to be sad but also sweet. The appeal of comedy is skindeep while that of tragedy goes into the innermost depths of our hearts. That is why, sad songs are sweet. They make us sensitive and realise all that is touching about the fate of mankind. In fact, poetry saw the light of the day inspired by a bleeding heart.

33. A Bad Workman Quarrels with his Tools

Seldom does a man blame his own imperfections. He blames either someone or circumstances for his own failure. Instead of analysing his own short-comings, he criticises others. The reason is that man is essentially an egoist and never admits his faults. This is true of an imperfect artist and artisan. They will blame the tools and equipment they use for the accomplishment of their job.

On the other hand, practical men will analyse their faults and try to rectify them to the best of their own ability. Instead of criticising others, they will see to it that their next effort should be made with precision. Blaming one's tool may be likened to deceiving oneself. In a sum, practical course of life, in the event of failure, is self-analysis and self introspection with a view to achieving one's goal.

34. Sweet are the Uses of Adversity

Adversity has its own virtues. It should not be dismissed as something abominable. The period of adversity in life discovers the virtue of fortitude, the hidden qualities, which man has never known before. It will not be exaggeration to say that prosperity reveals the evil in man and attract many vices. On the other hand, adversity brings out the best in man. The real test of man's character lies in the manner, he overcomes the problems.

If a man buckles in, his whole life passes in miseries. If he has the capacity to tide over the misfortunes of life, he is in for glorious days. Adversity is the time of self introspection and spiritual progress. Fair-weather friends desert whereas only genuine friends stand by you. No ground of suspicion is left for the days to come. In a sum, adversity makes man wiser about men and matters and inculcate wisdom in him.

35. War is Vanity than Valour, it is Cowardice than Courage

The vanity of man knows no limits and his cowardice is without confines. One cannot help saying that war is the enemy of society. Yet, man is a victim of vanity and has often pushed mankind to the brink of catastrophe to satisfy his ego. It is an irony that man uses wonderful creations of his own to annihilate himself. In the name of valour, he falls prey to vanity to fulfil his unlimited ambitions of proving his own dominance over others.

He forgets that war is an act of cowardice and not of courage. It is the lack of self-confidence that makes him believe that attack is the best means of self defence. War requires courage but only physical courage. Valour consists in moral courage. The former is vanity but the latter is real courage. War is an act of cowardice on the part of tyrants and vain rulers.

36. Hope Springs Eternal in Human Breast

Both fortune and misfortune are inescapable facts of life and we term it luck or ill luck. Mysteries of life are inscrutable. Many a time, the governance of life seems an irrational act of impersonal forces. However ruthless the miseries of life may be, a man is saved by hope.

A little bird of hope ever sings in us. We are encouraged to face adversities with a hope that better time is in store for us. In fact, hope is the only saviour of man that encourages him to look forward to future with invincible faith. It is his hope that eggs him on to continue struggle against misfortunes. While groping in darkness, he is ever hopeful to see light at the end of a tunnel. Hope implies those ideas and ideals that enrich life and give strength to the heart and mind. Hope never deserts a man of courage and fortitude.

37. When Money Speaks, Truth remains Silent

One need not go deep to find out the truth why money is a potent weapon today. As a matter of fact, it has always been so. The might has ever ruled though its form has kept on changing. The poor and the weak stand helplessly, when the rich wield their power. Ideals of truth and honesty is a thing of the past. Plundering the nation by unscrupulous politicians, killing and extortions by their henchmen are the order of the day. Which corrupt politician has been convicted and jailed? The poor are being crushed daily under the heels of justice.

The ill starred human beings with no money are stuffed into prisons. It is not the indictment of the legal system. This reality speaks of the power of money that gags the truth. "Satya Meva Jayate" is the chief good of life and it, of course, pays when one has lost every thing. Power-play in international, national and even in the social and domestic spheres is evident. Money lends glory to man's life, though for a moralist, it may be transient.

38. If Winter Comes, Can Spring be Far Behind?

Nothing is permanent in life. Just as dawn follows night, so joys follow despair and sufferings. Cloudy sky must give place to sunny day. Misfortunes of life are bound to vanish giving place to happier days again. The message of hope is held out by the poet in this line. Optimism encourages man to face adversity boldly and convert misfortunes into success.

Only those, who believe that texture of our life is woven of joys and woes, have right to live in true sense of the word. They hopefully believe that miseries will be dispelled by good times. This is a universal truth of life and those struggling in adversity should gain hope from failures of life. They should take human imperfection and evil as part and parcel of virtues and goodness. To define black, you have to contrast it with white. Therefore, an optimist derives hope from failures. A person has to change his attitude towards evil, pain and misery by accepting them as essential part of human life. A man with this eternal truth of life would never lose confidence in himself and his bright future.

39. The Old Order Changeth, Yielding Place to New

Change is the law of nature. Nothing escapes the ravages of time. Rightly it is so. Change implies progress. In the absence of change, there may be stagnation that starts giving out foul smell. There is cycle of seasons, days and nights, life and death and so on. Since the dawn of civilization, man has travelled in terms of physical time millions of years. Evolution has always been in process. Change of old order is inevitable for the continuity of the world. Every institution, however useful and good it may be, gets corrupt and loses its significance and utility. Nature has ordained that outmoded order has to give place to some new system for the progress of mankind. The progress of new ideas and innovations are inevitable for evolution in society.

40. The Hand that Rocks the Cradle Rules the World

The influence of mother on a child is undeniably tremendous. As goes the saying, maternal influence begins the day the mother conceives. The example of Abhimanyu as narrated in the Mahabharata is witness to this fact. When a child is born, the role of a mother as a nurse and teacher begins forthwith. If a mother imparts right kind of education to her child, the child will definitely imbibe it. The very early impressions of childhood go a long way in making or marring the character of the children.

The seeds of future growth are laid in infancy and childhood when mother is the constant companion of her child. Mother rules the world by proxy through her son. Fortunate are those, who have loving, understanding and wise mothers to share their joys and sufferings.

41. A Little Knowledge is a Dangerous Thing

This statement is universally true. A man of a little learning is prone to flaunt his knowledge. Empty vessels make much noise while deep water runs silently. So far so good. But, when it comes to imparting it to others, it is awfully dangerous. Take the example of a teacher with a little knowledge.

He can only misguide his credulous students. An incapable doctor may leave his patient in a condition worse than he went to him for treatment. An ill trained soldier may imperil the survival of his regiment. Such persons have rightly been called quacks, who move around in hordes in this world. They are exploiters and they prey on the gullibility of the innocent. They are the worst enemies of mankind. Surprisingly, only such persons are in the fore front of society. They know the tricks of the trade. It is the duty of society to expose them. Unfortunately, false propaganda is potent enough to silence the truth. Beware of such sharks in the garb of scholars, teachers, doctors or preachers, who sail under false colours.

42. Honesty is the Best Policy

Honest course of life is paved with difficulties but it certainly leads to one's cherished goal. Means are more important than ends. In the rat race, man considers ends more important. It hardly matters whether means are fair or foul. Nobody bothers about the questionable methods, which a person uses to achieve his goal. What you have achieved, is more important than how you have achieved it. Success at every cost, is the major concern of modern man. However, honesty pays in every walk of life though the path is definitely an arduous one. Honest means bring success and a feeling of elation as well. It cannot be felt by a man with guilty conscience. In fact, honesty should be learnt and practised as a principle of life. Success achieved by dint of honest means, is durable and matter of honour.

43. Time and Tide Wait for None [IES, 2015]

Time is fleeting. It never waits for anyone. Those, who let the time slip away, repent. Someone has correctly said that procrastination is the thief of time. So, one must make use of it. Only those, who realise this truth, succeed in life. Time is precious. It cannot be recalled. Once gone it is gone for good. The prudent course for a man of action is to utilise each and every moment. If we waste minutes, we may be wasting hours and years in cumulative term. The clock keeps on ticking and its hands are continuously moving. They know no break, no respite and no rest.

People, who are lazy, fritter away their energy and while away their time. Those, who make the best of time, succeed in the long run. Take care of the minutes, for the hours will take care of themselves. As a rule, we must make use of every minute of our limited time span. The very idea finds expression in another wise saying "Take time by forelock."

44. Virtue has its Own Reward

It has been well said that man's greatest virtue gives him greatest bliss. A virtuous act itself is a matter of joy and reward in itself. An evil mind is ever haunted by fear and guilt, that denies peace and joy to man. Virtuous persons experience the bliss of doing virtuous deeds. They do not need any reward other than contentment.

They do not care what world thinks of them. They do good for the sake of doing good. It elevates the character of a man and raises him in self esteem and self-confidence. Cheerful spirit guides him to be scrupulous in his deeds.

If it is no reward, then where reward is to be found? On the contrary, punishment of vice is vice itself. In fact, evil deeds recoils on the evil doers. It does not let the soul of man enjoy rest. Evil deeds are satanic and invite agony and anguish, whereas virtue brings peace and bliss to the soul of man.

45. Man does not Live by Bread Alone

Human life would be meaningless if its sole purpose were gratification of physical desires. Since, man is akin to God and superior to lower animals, he has noble and lofty aspirations. Thus man has the divine in him. Man was not created to eat and drink and indulge in physical pleasures like the lower animals. If he had no higher purpose in life, his life would be futile and aimless. Man is superior to animals, who are satisfied with mere gratification of physical desires. As man is created in the image of God, he is both a doer and creator. He ought to engage himself in the improvement of the world in its moral and spiritual content. He is not supposed to be selfish and ungrateful to his fellow beings and above all to his creator. So, he must work out his spiritual salvation and realise aspirations of his soul. Man does not live by bread alone; he has a spirit with higher yearnings of its own.

46. United We Stand, Divided We Fall

We all have heard that union is strength. In other words, a house divided against itself cannot stand. Such statements have universal ring of truth about them. Seeds of discord lead to destruction and miseries. Nations and leaders, who do not realise this, are likely to fall prey to slavery. Unity, in every field, is a source of strength, joy and prosperity. However, in the case of nations, this truth requires strict following. Unity is the only weapon that can keep enemy away from united people. Fissiparous forces can not raise their head and encourage the division of people. Integrity of a nation depends upon the unity of the people irrespective of their caste, creed and religion. Short-sighted and selfish politicians are more interested in perpetuating their rule by creating wedge among the people.

They inflame their prejudices against one another to grind their own axe. They forget that the nations exist only when they are united. Take the example of our country. Who lives if India dies?

EXPANSION WRITING

47. Who Lives if India Dies?

For a strong and united country, there must be psychological, emotional cultural and economic integration among the masses. This implies that people must change their commitments and loyalties from petty principles to the nation as a whole. Who lives if India dies? This kind of awakening among the masses is essential. With hostile neighbours on our borders, we can ill-afford to sit around and wait. United we stand, divided we fall. We must learn it from history. The personal rivalry between Porus and Ambi led to the success of Alexander the Great. Divisive forces in the form of religion, regionalism & casteism are bound to lead to disintegration of India.

48. Prevention is Better than Cure

From time to time our elders, on the basis of their experiences, keep on guiding us to learn the Art of living. Still, experience is the best teacher. As a rule, man must try to nip undesirable habits in the bud. This saves him from the labour of overcoming the consequences that are obstacles to his success. Certain preventive steps taken at the very outset, help a patient to check his disease from becoming incurable.

Similarly, if a person is not in the habit of cutting his coat according to his cloth, he is forced to lead a life of poverty and shame. If evils are allowed to go unchecked, they soon become alarmingly great. No one gets into a bad habit all at once. But such habits, if not checked at the earliest, can ruin a man. So, one has to learn to control one's passion and resist one's evil desires. This prevents one from falling prey to certain vices in life.

49. Only the Wearer knows where the Shoe Pinches

It is undeniable that world is full of all kinds of evil and hardships. Power and responsibility are accompanied with a lot of care and worries. A crown is never without a thorn of responsibility. There are persons, who have very difficult duties to perform. Only such persons know the meaning of suffering and responsibility. It is not easy to enjoy the glory of success because it involves a lot of suffering and sacrifice of one's efforts.

Those, who don't have to face the difficulties, problems and responsibilities don't know the value of their duties and obligations. It is just true that there is a thorn with every rose. There is no gain without pains too. Therefore, those, who are bound to discharge duties, realize how difficult it is to meet with the problems that arise in their way. A person in power is always haunted with the fear of losing it. So the wearer of the crown knows, where lies the real problem. If one aspires after fame and gain, one should always be prepared to face the pinches of difficulty as a necessary evil.

50. Speech is Silver, Silence is Gold

It has been rightly said that silence is more eloquent than words. Speak, when you have to speak and be silent, when you are not required to speak. This is the golden rule that one must follow in life. Meaningful silence is better than worthless talk. Even, while one talks one must be discreet to use words. Unnecessary words have no effect on others and people don't pay heed to such persons. Those, who speak at a proper time are respected, feared and heard with respect. Babblers and talkers are ignored. Just as empty vessels make much noise, so shallow men indulge in useless talk. Silence on the part of a wise man gives the impression of the depth of his mind. There is profound wisdom in the saying that "silent waters run deep".

51. Work is Worship

A man can fulfil all his ambitions, if he sets his eyes on his goal. He is an architect of his own fate. One, who puts in hard-work in his ventures, always tastes success. His zest for work can bring wonders to life. Thus, the wise thing is not to put off till tomorrow. Those, who shirk work often repent. Real life consists in realizing dreams. Work is real worship. Man's true salvation lies in work, useful and creative work done for the welfare and happiness of mankind. Idle persons are parasites on society. They run away from the struggle of life. Work is divine. Fortune also favours those, who believe in the principle of hard work. Name and fame cannot be earned by a sheer stroke of luck. One has to strive for getting a respectable place in society. It is possible only through useful work. It is the highest kind of worship.

52. Look before You Leap

Practical men are those, who act prudently. They weigh pros and cons of every opportunity that knocks at the door. They know that haste makes waste. On the other hand, foolish people are governed more by emotions than by reason. Their approach to life and opportunities is not pragmatic. They don't ponder over before taking hasty decisions. As a result, they act thoughtlessly and suffer later on. But, such rash decisions seldom yield good results. However, in certain circumstances man requires to take quick decisions. But, at the same time, he is expected to be rational in his approach. In normal circumstances, a sensible man makes a proper planning and decides his line of action. One must not jump to conclusions and decisions. Our actions must be the result of our foresight lest we should repent later on.

53. Strike while the Iron is Hot

There is a tide in the affairs of men and they should take advantage of it. One must not let a chance slip out of one's hands. Opportunity knocks rarely at one's doors and it must be seized, when it happens to knock. Just as one can give shape to hot iron, so one can change the opportunity to his own way. Wise men realize that opportunity utilized at the right moment lead to success. It is no use wasting time in wild goose-chase.

One must look about proper time to act. Once it comes, it should be seized and used to one's advantage to achieve success. Those, who have the foresight to discover the right opportunity at a right time are bound to succeed. Those, who are lazy enough to ignore the opportunity in life are bound to suffer in the long run.

54. As You Sow, So shall You Reap

One is rewarded or punished in one's life according to what one does. Youth is a period to cultivate good habits so as to reap good rewards later on. This world consists of both good and evil, noble and ignoble, constructive and destructive powers. If God is there to guide noble souls, the devil is not far behind to encourage the evil spirits. A God fearing person knows that he is on earth to serve humanity.

He believes in truth, peace, happiness and constructive ideas. In fact, every action has a reaction. We must do good to others to enjoy the benefits of our deeds at the later stage of our life. It is a hard fact of life that one cannot escape the consequences of his actions good or bad. It is a very sound advice to the young persons to inculcate good habits and character that can be useful to them, when they face the hard realities of life.

55. Slow and Steady Wins the Race

Speed is the hallmark of modern civilisation. In this world of cut throat competition, he sets endless aims. But, success always results from steady pursuit of aim. The work done by fits and starts leads one nowhere. As a rule, for the proper execution of work, both constancy and steadiness are necessary. A diligent person is not discouraged by difficulties.

He continues to march towards his goal of life. Thus, he steals a march on a person, who believes that success is sudden and effortless. The haphazard manner of spending hours on one's project may not yield satisfactory results. A persistent man keeps his head cool and achieves his goal steadily. Thus, to be successful, one must move on and on steadily though slowly. In fact, persistence is a key to success.

56. Travel as a Part of Education

Travelling is now rightly considered an indispensable part of education. Bacon remarked, "Travel, in the younger sort, is a part of education; in the elder, a part of experience." Thus, man acquires both practical education and experience, when he travels. Travelling serves both the young and the old. Travelling helps a man in enhancing his knowledge by learning different languages, customs, manners and morals. A traveller can add to his experience.

Travelling is, by no means, a source of whiling away one's time. Such travel contributes nothing to education. As a rule, a traveller must gather some information about the language and the people of the country he is planning to visit. The knowledge of the language helps him in interacting freely with the people and acquiring new acquaintances. Thus, one needs to keep one's eyes and ears open to make one's travel successful.

57. Necessity is the Mother of Invention

While a person passes through a difficult phase of life, he discovers his own hidden qualities. In happier days, a man is not aware of the qualities lying dormant. A man of courage is bound to find out ways and means to overcome the problems. Man is gifted with dormant energy, which comes out only when one is in difficulties. The history of man is a witness to the fact that he has always been making constant effort to overcome nature to make his life worth living. Modern civilization is a monument to the success of man in discovering and inventing ways and means to overcome the hurdles of nature. If man is at the height of achievements today, it is all because of his own power to invent ways and means to overcome even nature.

58. The Face is an Index of Character

Character is a sum total of feelings and thoughts that are part and parcel of habits. Man's character is reflected on his face. It is easy to read out the mind of man by studying the expression on his face. Noble character is the result of noble feelings and deeds. By the same criterion, wicked thoughts give a wicked look to the face. The truth or falsehood, of what we say, can easily be observed by a careful observer. Gestures of a man themselves speak of his character. Constant thoughts, good or bad, are bound to be reflected on the face. Mere a beautiful face cannot be the index of character. Soothing beauty, sympathetic actions and real concern for others are the index of one's mind. However, appearances are deceptive. The smile of a villain may hide his villainy. But, for a keen observer, there is always something in the face that will reveal the hypocrisy of the other person.

59. Familiarity Breeds Contempt

Distance lends charm. Unknown persons may inspire love and admiration in us. But, when we become familiar with them, we come in contact with their shortcomings. That is why, the kings, the officers and the rich like to maintain distance from the commoners. Familiarity in every field of life leads to disrespect for others. As long as we strive for ideals, they appear to be worth achieving. But, once we have achieved them, they may lose their attraction. However, familiarity does not affect true relationship based on mutual respect. Rational approach to relationships in life leads to intimacy instead of contempt. It is wrong to say that familiarity always breeds contempt. Yes, it cannot be denied that familiarity affects the quality of selfish relationships. But, sincere and selfless familiarity never turns to contempt, however close one may get.

60. God Helps Those Who Help Themselves

Hard work is key to success. No gains without pains–is universally true. Those, who believe in destiny alone are idlers. They don't achieve anything worthwhile in life. One must realize that the success is the result of only diligence. Destiny, of course, plays a part in making man's life. But, destiny is not the sole factor that determines our future. Only those have right to rely on destiny, who work hard. As a matter of fact, God will come to the help of only those, who help themselves.

Great men achieved success by dint of hard work, not by waiting for miracles. Success results from sincerity of purpose and integrity towards one's goal of life. Those, who think of God's help without labour, are day-dreamers who find an excuse for being idle. They would blame God and curse destiny instead of working hard.

61. The Sins of Fathers Visit upon their Children

This wise saying is both moral and instructive. The elders are always blaming the younger generation for the acts of omission and commission. But, they forget that their own acts have inevitable effect on the younger generation. Their noble deeds are a source of benediction and joy for their offspring. On the contrary, their misdeeds sow seeds of destruction and curse for them. Even if they may get away with their sins and crimes in their own life time, the posterity has to suffer. It is their children, who have to pay for their sins. Their evil nature is reflected in the character of their children. The curse of their misdeeds befall them.

What children learn from their parents, play a dominant role in their lives. As such, it is obligatory on the part of the elders to be exemplary in their conduct lest their children should go astray. It is universaly true that example is better than precept. The same is true of a nation. What the leaders of today sow, the coming generation will have to reap. The benefits or the harms befall the future generation. History is witness to the fact that the rise and fall of civilization revolve round this simple but undeniable truth.

62. Money is a Good Servant but a Bad Master

Money is indispensable in life. Without money, we cannot stand upright and face life with dignity. As ever, money makes the mare go every time and everywhere. It is the duty of a person to earn and provide for those, who depend upon him. There is nothing wrong in earning and saving for unfavourable days. Yet, money is not the be-all and end all of life money should not be allowed to dominate our life.

When money becomes obssession, man is a slave to money, Let money not master our thoughts since excessive desire for money makes a man mean, greedy and dishonest. Fast for money is dehumianising. We should not be exploters and blood suckers for the sake of money. Money spent on humanitaran projects ennables man's life. Money should serve as a means to an end. Money itself is no end. This fact should be clear to all of us that money should not be our ruling passion.

63. Practice Makes a Man Perfect

Perfection in art and craft comes after long practice. One may learn easily but perfrctions attained with practice. It is by practice, one is able to achieve skill. Even with limited abilities a person can move mountains by sustained efforts. The abilities are like tools. They must be oiled and kept in use else they get rusted. Regular and efficient practice shape one's still and improve performance. Constant and dedicated practice is the core of a player's or an artist's art.

The more he practises, the better he performs. Practice involves perserverence and perspiration, constaney brings teried experience to man. A write perfects his art by regular writing and so does a musician. The lives of great men & women are tales of tool and presistence that brings out the best in them. while the sloppy have hundreds of exeuses for their failure, only those blaze the trail, who burn mid might oil.

64. Might is Right

Survival of the fittest is the central truth of our existence. Struggle for survival is every where...in air, in sea, on land and in the heavy nook and corner of the innverss. The mighty are the kings of all that they survey, they have right over everything and they have the andacity to claim it.Justice does not carry and weight the weak, who have no alternative but to submit. In the primitive age, it was physical power that was on display to intimidate the weak and the helpless.

Gradually the form of power was transformed and became synonymons with economics means and political power. We talk high of our civilisation in terms of democracy, equal rights, fair distribution of means. We swear by law, order and safety. But, the fact is that civilisation is a this veneer under which has the economic power is the most dominating factor in life. Money decides and money rules. Law and power are on the side of the rich. Today, right is ironically, not independent of might.

65. Justice Delayed is Justice Denied

Justice to all...the weak and the mighty, the rich and the poor...is the corner stone of modern civilisation. Justice to all is the quality of being impartial and prompt in dispensing justice. Delayed justice devalue the spirit of law. Timely justice upholds the honour & dignity of the aggrieved party and punish those, who violate the law. Delayed justice defeats the purpose of law while causing untold sufferings to those, who need justice.

Justice done in time has positive effect on other institutions of the society. If justice is delayed, the sufferings continue to pile on till the time justice is done. The fact is that delayed justice is no justice at all. Doing justice is one thing and doing it in time is another. Delayed justice amounts to dehumanizing the institutions of our society. The sooner justice is done, the better it is. Else justice loses its soul and essence.

66. Charity Begins at Home

Charity is the noblest attribute of our life. Those are blessed, who are chartiable. They will inhert renown in life and blessings of those, who need charity. The world is better today because there have been quite a good number of philanthropists. Charity is opposed to materialism. Those, for whom, money itself is an end, do not practise charity. Charity is opposed to materalistie ways of life. The farmer teaches us to live for others while the latter, for ourselves.

World is not short of mercenaries and money sharies. On the contrary, charity is rare. Practice of charity is divine, no doubt. But, a charitable person should not exceed the limits of charity lest he should himself suffer. It is our prime responsibility to take care of those, who are bound to us by ties of flesh & blood. In other words, a man cannot be charitable at the cost of those, who depend on him. Charity is the most acceptable religion but to begin charity at home is a sane and most responsible way of life.

67. What cannot be Cured must be Endured

When one is in a mess, endurance is that sole option. There is no escape from adverse circumstances. One is to face them with strength till they are overcome. There is no alternative but to pass the bad time and wait for good days to come. The days of adversity are transitory and so, it is wise to endure difficulties while hoping for good days. Nothing is permanent.

Change, for better or for worse is the law of nature. One must live with assured optismgm, "If winter comes, can spring be for behind." Only such positive attitude can stand in good stead amids bad ones. One must not lose patience. Why blame oneself for the misfortiunes even though one cannot turn the tide of events. Optimism is the only cure for adverse days since through optimism comes the quality of patience. Optimistic persons are not cowed down by and don't field to hardships of life. Life is a compound of joys to sorrows. One needs to imbibe this unalterable truth of life.

68. A Friend in Need is a Friend Indeed

Prosperity gains friends, adversity loses them. Friends are tried, when one is amidst the misfortunes of life. In prosperity, a host of people profess their friendship. They form a crowd around you. Fair weather friends are the hallmark of a prosperous man. No sooner does a man fall on bad days, than they start deserting one by one. Adversity loses them. Our adversity is the touchstone of true friendship. False friends donot stand by us.

They fall off and vanish, when we need them most. A true friend lend ear to your woes and sufferings. He is sources of solace and help. A true friend is not a time server and neither is a sycophant. The pity is that it gets too late before we are in a position to discrimmiate between a true and a false friend. Therefore, We should exercise utmost caution while making friends. Those, who have friends around them in their difficulties, are fortunate.

69. Do unto Others as You Wish these to be done unto You

We eternally wish others to be kind, helpful and polite to us. As we live in society, its other members too wish as we wish. We all are bound by lies of mutual relationship. In a family, there are fillial, parental and praternal bonds. These bonds are nurtured by mutual love, respect and understanding among the members.

Love & respect is not a one way passage. Reciprocal attitude is the theme of any healing relationship. Good relations are embedded in mutual love for one another. If we don't follow this simple rule of human conduct, how can we expect others to do so? We often complain against others? Have we ever given a bit of thought to our own actions? We never confess, where we went wrong. But, once the truth is revealed to us and we rectify our behaviour, life is sure to become worth living. Most of our troubles arise, when we blame others and overlook our blemishes, love begets love, hate begets hate. Give love and feel the power of love in your life. It is the invaluable principle of art of living. Respect others if you wish to be respected.

70. A Stitch in Time Saves Nine

'Take time by forelock' is a wise saying. Procrastination is the worst thing in a character. Timely action is a key to success. Problems should be tackled as soon as they arise. With the passage of time, they get complicated. Those, who make the best of time, succeed in the long run. The delay in solving problems, cost a lot of damage in terms of time, money and prestige.

Time lost once cannot be recalled. Neglect of small things may spoil the labour of the years. Thus, the most effective motto of life should be : Do it now. Do not put off till tomorrow what you can do today. Delay is the theft of time. Those, who have the habit of delaying matters, look back on life with regret. They are bound to lose all that they possess just by ignoring a small hole in a garment. With the passage of time, the hole will become too big to be repaired. Better to nip error in the bud.

71. Fools Rush in Where Angels Fear to Tread

Prudent persons refrain from rectless actions. They do not jump to conclusions and decisions. Actions of such persons are the result of foresight. They are discreet enough to understand what is the right time to act. On the contrary, a fool is not used to sound and timely actions. He is supposed to act in haste regardless of the consequences. But, a thoughtful person weighs the pros & cons of the situation before he decides to act. He is calculative and is ready to withdraw, if he is not equal to the task. Such persons act with conviction of faith. A fool is apt to take a leap in dark and repent later on. A fool throws his coins to winds.

Thoughtless actions bring misery in their trail and make one's actions miserable. A fool is seldom rational and often acts impulsively, whereas a wise person is rational enough to plan his line of actions Needless and senseless exhibition of physical courage does not amount to valorous deeds. A wise man knows well, how to discriminate between bravado and true courage.

72. Conscience Makes a Coward of us All

Man is superior to animal in that he is not only a rational but also a spiritual being. He is capable of discrimination between good and evil conscience is indeed our inner voice, divine and transcendental. While conscience guides man to do good, it also deters him from doing evil and such a man is surely a coward. Better be a coward than take an evil course of life. Unscrupulous persons have tendency for acting regardless of what is moral or immoral.

They may cheat, defraud and act dishonestly. They can easily override moral compulsions. This kind of boldness is undesirable part of character. In this context, cowardice is preferable. Good persons are guided by noble promptings of soul. It is universally true that noble deeds are the expression of a noble mind and these deeds can never go wrong.

73. Brevity is the Soul of Wit [IES, 2015]

Brevity is a synonym of 'brief', which means short and wise. This phrase as used by Shakespeare supports that the most humorous and convincing flashes are often the shortest. The ability to express ideas in a concise and short manner requires much intelligence and tact. This needs the skill to put together the most appropriate words in an impactful way. Long sentences or speeches may make a person lose interest. One should condense the essence of the thought into a short and meaningful sentence to let its purpose be served as best.

It is often successful in making a place in the listeners mind and in fact is easier to remember. The right words, when used, are capable of explaining something as deep as the sea. Many famous writers as Socrates, Aristotle etc, understood this concept well and used it effectively to serve and influence the masses.

74. To Err is Human; to Forgive is Divine [IES, 2015]

This proverb, used by Alexander Pope in his poem 'An Essay on Criticism' holds a deep moral meaning. It justifies the inevitability of human beings to make mistakes and the presence of extraordinary self of human beings to forgive as divine. Alexander conveys that it is almost impossible for a human being not to make mistakes. It is natural. A person may try his/her best to avoid making mistakes, but the fact that no one is perfect, justifies the unintentional errors. Since, it is unavoidable to make mistakes, it is possible to grant forgiveness for the same. A person, who is hurt or at loss because of a mistake done by others, may find it difficult to forgive and forget the accused. It is indeed very hard to forgive as it is a Godly attribute and thus, Alexander calls it divine. One needs to be at peace to be able to forgive the other and that only comes by eliminating the imbalance in mind . Forgiveness depicts the high spirited attitude in a person as it is a sign of greatness. Thus, the proverb teaches us to treat the accused as oneself and forgive and forget the wrong and the wrongdoer. **(199 Words)**

75. When in Rome, do as the Romans do [IES, 2014]

The idiom 'When in Rome, do as the Romans do' assists the advantages one receives by abiding the customs of a society/place, where one is new. It is said to be polite to follow the customs of a foreign land. It morally means that, when one is in an unfamiliar situation, he/she should follow the lead of those, who know the ropes. This expression recommends people to behave in a certain manner that is respected and respectful according to the place or situation.

It is indeed polite to adapt your way of behaving, when you're in a different culture. We should be open to adjust in and according to the situation for our own benefit and of that of the people around us. This way, we not only learn about new tactics, culture, customs etc, but also build trust in people to confide within us. Therefore, acting and reacting according to the situation and following proven steps, is helpful.

76. Fortune Favours the Bold [IES, 2014]

This proverb means that one cannot achieve great heights or success without taking risks. It is not all, who have the courage to take risk and step out of the secure zone. It is people with firm determination, who risk the secured and attain success.

It is true in every walk of life. Great achievements involve great risks. Overcautious people never take risk. Some people complain and blame the fate, when unable to achieve all that they want, but in reality, they fail to realise that is demands more than they are ready to give to achieve their dreams. Fortune favours those, who are bold and daring enough to fight for what they want at any cost. But, it is important to remember that a man should be reckless in the name of bravery.

He should only take risk, where there is a great likelihood of success. The decision of risking everything must only be taken after taking into consideration all the prospects of the situation. The fortune can only shower more, when one is ready to take. For, if a man, ventures nothing, he will have nothing.

77. Make Hay while the Sun Shines

This proverb is a piece of advice for people, who suggests one to take advantage of good circumstances. In other words, we should make good use of favourable time and most of an opportunity while we hold a chance. It can be used as a supportive substitute. Opportunities may not come very often, thus, we should make sure that we take full advantage of it, before the chance slips away. Hay should be gathered, while the Sun shines as it gets ruined, if wet. We must act upon an opportunity, when it presents itself, else, we will be left empty handed. Its always good to take stock of the situation and hammer it in the appropriate time to reap benefits. Therefore, realising and making an opportunity turn around in your favour can only be done, when one answers the knock at the door but most importantly, in time.

78. A Bird in Hand is Worth two in the Bush

[IES, 2015]

This proverb is a gentle warning against losing what one already has because of greed or irresponsible risk taking behaviour. This depicts the meaning that it is better to keep what you have than to risk it for something greater. Giving up on an advantage that you already have for more, is mere foolishness because there is no certainty of success. A bird, which you already own, is much more valuable than the two in the bush.

It is always wise to utilise the opportunity that is at hand than look forward to some other that may come in future with more advantages. This proverb applies in every walk of life, to people around us as well. Those, who are near us and willing to help, are more valuable than those, who are away and not willing to help. Thus, it is foolish to reject whatever help is at hand. The wise always relies on the present instead of laying his hopes on future.

79. Waste not, Want not

This proverbial saying means the wise use of one's resources will keep one from poverty. Wilful wastage gives rise to woeful wants. The message, this proverb conveys, is not to waste anything as you may always have enough or because you may need it in future. It is advisable not to throw away or waste anything as you do not know the likeliness of the need of that thing anytime later. The chances may be odd but the fact the need might be urgent should be considered practically. If one is not wasteful, one will not be needful. We don't just require changes in consumption patterns, but also in the discarding patterns. This change will not just save various 'still usable' resources but shall also save our hard earned money by avoiding the mere situation of needing to buy that resource again. Thus, it is rightly justified that if we use a commodity or resource carefully, moderately and without extravagance, we will never be in need.

80. To Run with the Hare and Hunt with the Hound

If someone is running with the hare and hunting with the hound, they are trying to support two opposing views, causes and factions at the same time. It is a deceitful behaviour of one, who fights in favour of one party, but secretly helps the opposing party as well. Such people are termed as double dealers. It is physically impossible to be at termed places at one time. Similarly, it is impossible to curtail truth for a long period. Sooner or later, one's intentions are revealed and these tricksters are exposed. Therefore, one should be loyal to one side only.

This saying, in a metaphorical sense, implies that someone is trying to do two things at the same time. It teaches us how to have firm and clear opinion about a situation and have the courage to support our viewpoints openly without fear/pressure. Being loyal to our feelings and thoughts, is an important part of building our character in a positive light without fearing the consequences.

Expansion Writing for Practice

Directions *Write the expansion writing on the following topics given below.*

1. Failures are the pillars to success.
2. Money is a good servant, but a bad master.
3. We learn little from victory, much from defeat.
4. A lie has many variations, the truth none.
5. Smooth seas do not make skillful sailors.
6. The fool speaks, the wise listens.
7. There's no such thing as free lunch.
8. Don't bite the hand that feeds you.
9. Ambition is the greatest enemy of peace.
10. Habit - A good servant but bad master.
11. Ideas rule the world.
12. Knowledge without character is dangerous.
13. Bite off more than you can chew.
14. Picture paints a thousand words.
15. Don't give up the day job.
16. Kill two birds with one stone.
17. Walls have ears, shoes have tongues.
18. Virtue is its own reward.
19. Wilful waste makes woeful want.
20. Behind every great man there is a great woman.
21. Trust yourself to get success.
22. Preparedness for war for preserving peace.
23. Where there is a will there is a way.
24. A contented mind is a blessing kind.
25. Greatness or success was not built in a day.

CHAPTER 3

Report Writing

Report writing is concerned with reporting events or incidents for a newspaper. Newspapers are the best medium to convey information that requires the attention of the people. So, its main purpose is to pass information to the readers.

Now, reports are also telecast on T.V. for the information of the viewers. Visuals accompany the reading of the reports for the benefit of the viewers.

Writing reports for newspapers or T.V. requires objectivity on the part of the correspondents and reporters. It should be free from personal prejudices. The subjective approach is likely to distort facts. Therefore, factual description needs balanced and unbiased information.

An objective reporter talks to eye witnesses and persons involved in the events and gives pros and cons of the case. The task of the reporter is really difficult because he has to meet people from the cross sections of the society and government officials and present their viewpoints impartially.

Their versions of the events should be factual in order that the people may get true information. The facts should be neither suppressed nor highlighted excessively since this effort on the part of the reporter is likely to mislead the people.

In a nutshell, a report should be informative, objective and factual.

Specimen

Here we are giving a report published in a newspaper as it is. Look at it.

DELHI
THE HINDU • FRIDAY, MARCH 2, 2012

UIDAI glitch forces adivasis to pay for free enrolment

Barwani tribals told UID is mandatory to avail PDS coupons

Mahim Pratap Singh

- "This is a peculiar situation wherein the poor adivasi must pay for the free UID service."
- The UIDAI has suddenly stopped reimbursing cost of enrolment: State Civil Supplies Commissioner

BHOPAL: While the Madhya Pradesh Government is very excited about linking the State's crumbling Public Distribution System (PDS) to the much talked about Unique Identification (UID) scheme, beneficiaries are clearly unhappy with the new arrangement that not only makes it mandatory for them to register for the UID but also to pay for it.

Several beneficiaries from the backward tribal-dominated district of Barwani have approached Chief Minister Shivraj Singh Chauhan requesting him to scrap the existing system and initiate a comprehensive consultation programme with beneficiaries.

However, if the Chief Minister fails to do so, they have warned of launching a mass agitation.

The new system, put in place last year, is being implemented by a corporate consortium led by HCL Infosystems along with Edenred India Private Ltd, a subsidiary of corporate meal voucher provider and multinational hospitality giant Accor — and Virgo Softech Pvt. Ltd., an Indore-based IT firm.

Under this system, PDS will be implemented through the use of food coupons linked to the UID.

However, tribal beneficiaries from Barwani have objected to this as they have been asked to pay Rs. 275 for the registration. Further, they have been told that registering for the UID is mandatory, and that without it they will not be eligible for the PDS.

"UID is supposed to be free, but not the food coupons. But since food coupon surveys are being used to capture data for UID, beneficiaries are also being charged for the UID cards. This has resulted in a peculiar situation whereby, for example, a well-off executive from New Delhi gets the UID/Aadhaar card for free, but poor adivasis from Madhya Pradesh are forced to pay for the same card," says Madhuri Krishnaswami of Barwani-based tribal-rights group Jagrit Adivasi Dalit Sangathan.

"Further, due to irregularities in the BPL survey methodology and implementation, thousands of poor families have been wrongly categorised as APL and therefore cannot afford to pay for a service they were, till now, getting for free. Many families have had to sell their poultry, cattle, etc. to meet this new expense," adds Ms. Krishnaswami.

The authorities confirm the situation but say this is a minor glitch that will solve by itself soon. Till that happens, the beneficiaries will have to pay up. "According to the contract, the Government was supposed to pay the service provider [the consortium] Rs. 275 upfront for UID enrolments, to be reimbursed to us by the UID Authority of India [UIDAI]," State Food and Civil Supplies Commissioner Dipali Rastogi told The Hindu.

"Recently the UIDAI suddenly stopped the reimbursements and so the beneficiaries will now have to pay the amount only for the period till the UIDAI sent the reimbursements — which they have told us should be done by April," said Ms. Rastogi.

Once the UIDAI starts reimbursing the State Government again, the fee will be returned to the beneficiaries, she said. However, she also admitted that the State Government was not clear as to how much would be reimbursed by the UIDAI. "Earlier the amount to be reimbursed to us was Rs. 275, but now if UIDAI lowers it, then there is nothing we can do about it," she said.

Samples of Report Writing

Directions *Below are some report writing with their solutions.*

A. Prepared Report as Correspondent of a Newspaper

1. Sale of New Born Babies

Express News Service
Aligarh, 28th January

    A staff nurse pretending to be a doctor has been selling new born babies in the city. She adopted the modus operandi that continuously hoodwinked the hospital authorities. However, the police is trying to establish whether any doctor or hospital authorities were in collusion with her. Sheela Singh would deliver babies of poor or unwed mothers in her illegal clinic run in the heart of the town besides her employment in district hospital. She would sell them to childless couples at a price ranging from ₹ 20000 to 40000.

    The interrogation revealed that she had sold over 20 babies. She had her contacts, who would bring the women for delivery to her clinic. They would locate buyers for a child not wanted by the parents. She would make the foster mother stay at the clinic for about a week and then hand over a baby to her. She did it to provide a bonafide birth certificate and then discharged her. The police have also arrested the two touts operating for her. On receiving information on telephone about Sheela Singh's nefarious activities, the police sent a decoy. While, she was handing over the baby to the woman, she was caught red handed. The baby's mother made the statement, "The baby would go to a business man's house and would be treated well. We are poor and cannot afford to have the fourth daughter."

    She expressed her unawareness about the selling of the babies for monetary benefits. Sheela Singh revealed the names of the couples, who had bought children from her. However, the police say that they have no plan to separate these children from their foster parents. When contacted, Sheela Singh admitted the sale of new born babies by her. At the same time, she said that it was a humanitarian activity to help ladies to get rid of unwanted children and give them to childless couples. She did not understand what was wrong in this practice. As for money, whatever she got, she got it as a gift for the help she was rendering to childless couples. However, the police have arrested her and sent her to lock up.

2. Cyclonic Storm

Times News Service
Ludhiana, 5th June

    A cyclonic storm struck the city and the adjoining areas last evening. For the last few days, the mercury had shot up to 40°C and there was depression in the area. Official sources from the state capital Chandigarh said that the storm had lasted over 40 minutes blowing off a large number of houses. Approximately over 4000 people were rendered homeless.

The eight villages were flattened by the cyclone. 35000 farmers inhabiting these villages, were taken unaware by the storm. Their mud houses and thatched roofs were blown off. In the city, 24 women were reported to be killed. The toll of death has been estimated at about 50 persons apart from a number of domestic animals. The strong winds raged at a speed of 100 kilometers per hour. The situation was further complicated, when the city and the adjoining areas were lashed by heavy rains.

Official estimate confirmed that nearly 5000 people were affected by the storm. The rescue operation was hindered by torrential rain that accompanied the storm. Those injured by flying debris and falling of roofs were admitted to the various hospitals. Being a wedding period of the year, many marriage processions underwent quite a heavy loss in the form of lives and injuries. The cars and scooters were tossed up by speeding winds.

Electricity and telephone lines snapped. The whole city was plunged in darkness. The traffic came to a stand still. In some places, there was stampede causing panic in the city. When contacted, the D.M. Prabhat Kumar said that it would take 2 to 3 days to restore normal electric supply in view of the devastating damage.

3. Bomb Explosion

Kanwal Kalra
Sonipat, 23rd January

A mysterious explosion rocked Netaji Square on Monday morning, injuring at least ten persons and killing as many as two children. The toll is likely to rise. The damage caused to the shops in the main market of the town is yet to be correctly estimated. However, unofficial sources claim that the loss in terms of money and goods may amount to lakhs of rupees.

The police have discounted any terrorist angle to the tragedy saying that the blast was caused by an oxygen cylinder. It is a matter of concern that the blast has taken place just two days before the Republic Day celebrations. The police are at a loss to identify the cause in view of the statement given by a witness that the blast was triggered off by the hidden bomb in the dickey of a scooter.

The theory is supported by the fact that a charred scooter was found near the site of the blast. Besides, Pearl Gas Agency just opposite the site of the blast remained unaffected. The shopkeepers thank heavens that a major tragedy has been averted if the gas agency was singled out to trigger off the series of blasts in the area. It appears that the blast was aimed at the Agency stocked with gas cylinders.

The SP told this correspondent that even though they had ruled out any subversive angle to the blast, they would begin a probe into the incident to establish any such possibility. The condition of the injured persons admitted to district hospital is said to be improving.

4. Lack of Civic Amenities

Meenakshi Sudan
Agra, 5th May

The historical city has paid heavily for being a major tourist centre in the form of damaged roads, erratic electric supply and lack of other basic amenities of life. Instead of providing the best of comforts, the Municipal Corporation has been neglectful of this aspect of life.

The promise made by the newly elected Mayor has roused a ray of hope among the residents of the city. He assured of an immediate attention to the sloppy drainage and sewerage system, a scourge for the residents of the area. The residents brought to his notice that the old drainage pipes need to be immediately replaced. The broken roads and depressions are a result of water logging caused by silted and choked drains and sewers. Half hearted measures like desilting and cleansing the sewers will not serve any purpose. The problem needs to be tackled from the roots.

Alongwith this, the roads in damaged conditions also require immediate attention. Since, the rainy reason is about to set in, the condition of the roads on account of water logging is expected to worsen. The stagnant water in the depressions of the roads is a fit place for breeding mosquitoes. In such conditions, accidents cannot be ruled out causing loss of life and limbs. The epidemics are most likely to break out.

The statement by the Mayor is most welcome. If implemented, it would go a long way in alleviating the miseries of the citizens. Besides, the unavoidable electric breakdowns put extra strain on the residents. The transformers are not up to the mark and electric wires need replacement on large scale. Two school going children were electrocuted, when a high tension wire snapped and fell on the children, who died at the spot. The parents of the children have accused the Hydle department of criminal neglect and lodged an FIR with the police. The police are investigating the case.

5. Traffic Jams and Reckless Driving

Siddharth Rao
Ambala, 5th January

Travelling, either in a public bus or in a private vehicle, is a living nightmare in the city. Travelling by scooters is more dangerous as a result of sudden increase of the four wheelers in the city. Given the conditions of the roads, travelling is hazardous. Traffic jams and crossing the intersections take away most of our time and energy. The work that one can do in two hours takes the whole day to complete it. Most of the areas in the city are prone to traffic jams. It is no exaggeration as it takes two hours to reach the central market from clock tower. Otherwise, it is a matter of only one hour drive.

The citizens have the habit of doing everything on the roads. It may be a marriage procession or mourning. They are unmindful of the inconvenience caused by vehicular traffic. They do not mind parking scooters and cars in front of the shops which often results in bottlenecks. Dharnas, rallies and public demonstrations are held on the busy routes in the city.

During the peak hours of traffic in the morning and evening, the conditions are even worse. Encroachments are the order of the day. The congestion on the roads is caused by disobeying the rules of the road. In the last two years, three flyovers have been constructed to make travelling safe and comfortable. As a matter of fact, the traffic police do not take stern action against illegal parking and encroachments and reckless driving. The condition of the roads adds more problems to traffic jams.

No wonder, accidents, mostly fatal, make one wary of driving. School boys and girls are driving vehicles without license. They are reckless drivers. Being young, they don't care about the hazards they pose to others. School authorities and traffic police need to conduct training classes in schools for teaching the young the traffic rules. The training, they are supposed to get, will have lasting impression on their minds. Ultimately, the safety on the road depends on the police as to how they enforce law. Strict checking and stringent enforcing of already existing law can instill fear in citizens. Otherwise, the chaotic conditions on roads are likely to continue.

6. Bomb Hoax

Hindustan Times Correspondent
<u>Aligarh, 10th January</u>

Security forces at Aligarh railway station were in panic last night, when the police received a phone call stating that bombs had been planted in Toofan Express. The passengers were confounded, when they were asked to vacate the compartments in no time. Chaotic conditions prevailed at the railway station. Numberless jawans and police officers were running here and there at the railway station. It appeared that the whole station was under siege. A bomb defusing squad in military uniform was standing alert to meet with any emergency arising out of bomb blasts. The passengers were asked to move far away from the compartments. They virtually ran helter and skelter leaving their bag and baggage at the station. There was a stampede and an old man was crushed to death. The cries of children rent the air. Meanwhile, frantic search was on. Sniffer dogs in every compartment were trying to detect the planted bombs. It took almost an hour to complete the search. Inspite of extensive search, the security forces did not come across any thing suspicious. When satisfied, the police declared the phone call as a hoax. The train was two hours late. The whole railway schedule for incoming trains was thrown out of gear.

7. Drug Gang Busted

Express News Service
<u>New Delhi, 10th March</u>

The Delhi Police (Narcotics Branch) raided last night the residence of a builder, who is said to be the kingpin of cocaine dealers. Three persons including a foreign woman have been arrested. On receiving information on telephone from an anonymous caller, the police sent a decoy to verify the correctness of the information. According to the police 1.5 kg. of hashish and 20 gm of cocaine were recovered from the residence of Sameer Ali. All the accused, present at the residence, have been arrested.

One of their accomplices is absconding. The trap was laid under the supervision of Inspector Nagpal. When, 1 gm of cocaine was delivered to Ram Singh, the decoy, the officers swung into action and arrested the accused. The contraband was ceased from them. During the interrogation, it was revealed that all the accused were law-graduates. They took to trafficking in drugs under the cover of property business. The foreign woman (Nationality not disclosed by the police) was their 'live-in companion'. The police told this correspondent that the foreign woman has been into drug trafficking for the last 7 years.

She is alleged to have been also arrested earlier. She had been eluding the police since she jumped the bail. The police are trying to locate the source of their supply. The police claim to have seized a diary containing the names of elite members of society, who are said to be their regular customers.

8. Massacre by Terrorists

Hindustan Times Correspondent
<u>Jammu, 20th April</u>

In the worst ever massacre committed by Kashmiri militants, 40 persons including three security personnel were killed in the sensitive area of Rajouri. The terrorists came at night and sprayed bullets on the inmates on Tuesday night. The militants entered a cluster of huts and asked the men to come out. They segregated the group of Hindus, lined them up and shot them dead. One Inspector and two constables of the BSF, who challenged the militants were also shot dead.

Indefinite curfew was imposed in the area including Jammu district as well as Rajouri, Punch and Udampur towns. The State Government claimed that safety measures have been tightened to avert any further mishap. Among the victims, there were also tourists, who were on visit to their relatives. The victims were from Delhi and Kanpur. Their dead bodies were flown to their home towns by Indian Airlines.

In view of impending rush of pilgrims to Vaishno Devi, security measures have been beefed up. The Jammu and Kashmir cabinet held an emergency meeting to review the law and order situation and passed a resolution condemning Pakistan having failed to stop cross border terrorism. The cabinet also ordered ex-gratia payment to the next of kin of the victims. So far, no militant group has owned responsibility for the killing. However, an official spokesman in Srinager claimed that the identity of the militant group has been established.

The army has taken control of the management of route leading to the shrine. Taking no chances in this regard, the Inspector General of Police has ensured security for the pilgrims. The incident is likely to adversely affect the inflow of the pilgrims. Moreover, any further attack on the pilgrims may lead to communal riots in Jammu as well as other parts of the country.

9. The Menace of the Political Rallies

Hindustan Times Correspondent
<u>New Delhi, 28th February</u>

The political rallies appear to have become a necessary evil in our social and political life. The rallies held by the party in power in a state or at the centre are sheer nuisance for the common citizens. The Congress rally held at New Delhi is the witness to the fact, how the ordinary life of an ordinary citizen, commercial and business activities come to a stand still. The Congress rally at New Delhi was held to celebrate the completion of five years of Sonia Gandhi as the President of Congress party. The daily commuters on public and private transport were the worst affected. Most of the commercial houses and banks remained closed for want of access of the employers to their working places. Non-availability of transport added to the woes of the citizens needing immediate medical attention.

The citizens out on very important tasks had to go back. The route leading from adjoining districts, towns and villages of Haryana, Punjab, Rajasthan and Uttar Pradesh were choked with over crowded buses, public carriers, tractors and bullock carts. It is horrible to imagine that how a political party can afford to look over the financial loss to the govt. ex-chequer, private industries and inconvenience to the public. It was observed that there was hardly any respectable and educated citizen taking part in the rally. The lure of daily allowance and food and sight seeing bring the villagers and the poor to the city. Their transportation is managed by rich party leaders and capitalists owning political affiliation with a political party. Private buses owners are forced into doing the bidding of powerful mafia. The mob returning from the rally caused chaos in the city. The New Delhi dwellers preferred to remain inside because of slogan shouting. Crowd was in a menacing mood and could have turned violent under slightest provocation.

10. Inadequate Fire Fighting Arrangements

Hindustan Times Correspondent
<u>Noida, 23rd January</u>

A fire, in one of Noida's multistoreyed buildings last week, has not made Noida fire department any wiser for any such mishap in future. The apathy of the fire department and the State Government is appalling. Fire tragedy that took place in Noida's Phase-I, caused crores of loss in terms of money and infrastructure. 20 lives were also lost but fire department has yet not woken to reality.

What is worse, the breathing apparatus available with the Noida Fire Department is outdated. Fire personnel cannot go through thick smoke or gas to rescue victims even from the ground floors. During the holocaust in the last weak, many shortcomings of the fire department came to light. There are four fire engines in Noida Phase-I. Two of them are over 15 years old and need immediate replacement. Noida Phase-II has only one fire engine. Strangely enough, Noida fire brigade has no turnable ladder. Without these devices, meant to fight fires and conduct rescue operations on the higher floors of multistoreyed buildings, fighters find themselves quite helpless. It was clearly revealed last week. Even the Phase-I fire station's phone is a one way connection as the bill is unpaid.

REPORT WRITING

Fire department sources states that there are 30 buildings in Noida that are tall enough. It is mandatory requirement to install wet risers, down comers, underground tanks, pumps and fire extinguishers but all these buildings violate these mandatory rules. Fire department is required to inspect the buildings at the time of their completion. But, nobody bothers about their inspection. According to them, the Noida authorities are not doing anything to upgrade the fire brigade. When contacted, a senior Noida official said, "I am sorry but I am not aware of these things because fire brigade does not come under my jurisdiction."

11. Red Alert on Independence Day
Press Trust of India
Meerut, 13th August

A red alert has been sounded in Meerut as a part of a special alert in connection with Independence Day celebrations to prevent any untoward incident. This is being done because the State Government has issued special instructions to the district administration to remain extra vigilant. The intelligence agencies have warned the state Govt. that the militant groups operating in the major towns of the state have chosen this state as a major target for subversive activities. A large number of terrorists visiting India on the pretext of meeting their relatives have gone in hiding. Even after the expiry of their visa tenure, their whereabouts are mystery for the police.

Senior Superintendent of Police, Arnav Sharma has issued instructions to all police officials to remain extra alert. Sensitive localities, public buildings, power houses, thickly populated areas, busy market places, cinema houses, railway stations and bus stands have been placed under extra vigil.

Instructions have been issued to police stations to guard academic institutions. Utmost precaution should be exercised at all functions being organised in connection with Independence Day. A door to door campaign has also been launched to round up all suspicious persons.

The encouraging aspect of the arrangement, according to the Police Chief Arnav Sharma, is, that a number of voluntary organisations and ex-service men of all communities have come forward to exercise vigilance in their localities.

12. Dowry Death
Hindustan Times Correspondent
New Delhi, 15th March

The Delhi Police have registered a case of murder against Mohit Kumar, the proprietor of a jewellery shop. Mohit and his family members have been accused of poisoning their daughter-in-law. The police registered the case following a statement by the victim, who was admitted to a local nursing home. Shalini made a statement before the SDM last night at the nursing home, where she was being treated.

The SHO of Karol Bagh police station said that the accused had not been arrested so far because they had fled their homes. However, frantic search is on to nab them.

According to Shalini's statement, her in-laws were demanding dowry and always threatened her with dire consequences. They often asked her to get more money from her parents for expanding the business and opening a new show room in South Delhi. Shalini's father is a well known property dealer. Shalini was married with Mohit last December. Her parents gave expensive presents to her in-laws. When contacted, Shalini's father Sailesh Mohan alleged that the in-laws of Shalini forced his daughter to consume poison and then they left home.

If a neighbourer had not accidently dropped in at that time, Shalini would have died within half an hour. The neighbourer, Ram Singh rushed her to the nursing home. The doctors diagnosed it as a case of poisoning and informed the police. The police arrived and the statement of Shalini was recorded before the SDM, when she had partially recovered her senses. Later on, her position got out of control and she succumbed to the effect of poisoning.

13. Communal Riots

Indian News Service
Rampur, 19th July

Last evening, communal riots broke out in Rajpur locality. Most of the people living in this locality are Muslims. Last evening, a rumour spread like wild fire that a city mosque had been desecrated as some of the pieces of pork were found in the mosque. The rumour kept on doing the rounds of the city. About 20 youths gathered at the mosque and started shouting anti Hindu slogans. Gradually, the group of youth took the form of agitated mob and marched towards Shiv Mandir in the Hindu dominated locality. They shouted provocative slogans. The Hindus of the locality also came out of their homes.

On receiving the information, the police immediately swung into action. They pacified the Muslims and persuaded them to go back and verify the facts. They had themselves sent a police party to the mosque and had received the report that there was no act of desecration as alleged by anti-social elements wanting to disturb the communal harmony in the city. But, shortly in another Muslim dominated locality of Khanpur, a house was set on fire. Stabbing cases were also reported from the same area. When the Hindus came out they shouted anti Muslim slogans and hurled stones at the Muslim mob.

The police re-enforcement was ordered by the District Magistrate. Tear gas shells were fired to disperse the crowd. In turn, the police were also attacked. The mob stoned the policemen and as a result two policemen were injured. The situation was getting out of control. The reports of killing and stabbing from other areas started pouring in. The police at once imposed curfew in the city. There was heavy patrolling in the area. The fire brigade was pressed into service as cases of arson and looting increased. The fire in certain areas could not be brought under control because of narrow lanes and by lanes.

The DM Prabhu Singh claimed that the situation was under control but admitted that the coming days were very crucial to bring peace and normalcy to the strife torn city. Meanwhile, 50 persons of both the communities were arrested.

# REPORT WRITING

14. Drought

Focus News
Jhansi, 20th June

On account of delayed rains, the whole region of Eastern U.P. is affected by drought conditions. Jhansi is the worst affected district due to lack of water. The state is reeling under the dark tragedy of drought. Standing crops are withering away. Describing the situation in the Malwa region, the Commissioner stated that the situation was out of control. Crops had dried up, animals were dying from lack of fodder and the farmers alongwith their families and cattle were leaving the villages. Despite the efforts of the government to send water tanks for drinking water, food supply and fodder, the villagers were in panic.

There are reports of violence from Jhansi. The police are said to have resorted to lathi charge to scare away the demonstrators.

When contacted, the DM Jhansi denied these reports but admitted that the situation was likely to go out of control any day. The large scale migration of the villagers to the district is posing law and order problems. There is no immediate solution in sight. This region was identified as a drought prone area long ago. Never in the past, has the administration tried to avert the avoidable tragic situations.

According to one source, the local MLAs and MP have never tried to approach the authorities to take remedial steps beforehand to the chagrin of many villagers. They have not visited the area since the drought conditions started affecting the villagers. As many as 40 villages are in the grip of drought. A large number of cattle are languishing for want of fodder and water. The situation is not likely to improve until the rain sets in.

15. Transport Strike

Hindustan Times Correspondent
New Delhi, 18th April

Truckers' strike has adversely affected the supply of vegetables, fruits, milk and raw materials for industries. There is spurt of prices all over the city. The strike has entered the 7th day and the effects of the strike are visible in every sector. Even the medicines have not been spared by the wholesale stockists. The patients have to pay through their nose because they must buy essential medicines. Inspite of the appeal of the government that essential services to the public should not be affected, it has had no impact on the transporters. The figures released by the Agricultural Produce Marketing Committee, a Delhi government body, managing the mandies show that the supply of vegetables and fruits to wholesale markets has remained largely constant and the wholesale prices have not gone up.

The supply line has not been affected in Azadpur. The supplies continue pouring between midnight and 8 a.m. It is obvious that the strike has not affected supplies. Tempos and light cart vehicles have come to the rescue of the people. The shortage is said to be artificial created by wholesale dealers to take advantage of the situation. Even the supply of LPG cylinders has been maintained to Delhi and nearby towns with the help of the trucks owned by the companies.

There is a panic among the consumers and hoarding of vegetables, food grains and other food products has contributed to the situation getting out of control, if the strike enters the second week. Seeing apprehension, the truckers made an appeal to the tampo owners to join the strike. Striking truckers claim to have won the support of tempo owners. The ongoing trucker's strike is likely to worsen for the consumers, the retailers are taking full advantage of the situation. The prices vary according to the economic status of the consumers. In the posh colonies of South Delhi and West Delhi prices have rocketed high because consumers living in these colonies can afford to pay high prices.

The Azadpur Mandi will remain closed tomorrow as a token of solidarity with the truckers. The government is in no mood to decrease the prices of diesel. The State Transport Minister has appealed to the Union Government to view the demands of the truckers sympathetically. The Union Government has also turned down the demand of toll-tax on highways. So far, the strike is peaceful. The transport owners have arranged free langars for truck drivers and the labourers. There is apprehension lest the unrest among the drivers and labourers should turn violent. So, the government has taken every step to check the violence beforehand.

16. Child Marriages

Hindustan Times Correspondent
Durg, 5th May

National Women Commission has expressed concern at child marriages being celebrated with the connivance of the authorities and political leaders. Akti or 'Akshaya Tritiya' is a festival meant for marrying dolls. It is celebrated all over Chhattisgarh by weddings of hundreds of children, particularly girls. It is an annual ritual and government finds itself helpless in rooting out this evil. The enforcement of Sharda Act or the Child Marriage Restraint Act 1978 is very difficult on account of political reasons. If parents find suitable match, the age of the bride and groom is insignificant.

The administration does not deny that the practice of child marriage exists in the area. The officials are on alert to stop any such proceedings. "We are trying to visit every marriage venue and checking buses and other vehicles to apprehend the offenders and the bridegroom party. We can take action only on specific complaints," says Ranjit Singh, the district magistrate of Durg. An NGO, Forum for Fact Finding Documentation filed PIL alleging that states including Rajasthan, Madhya Pardesh and Orissa have failed to implement the Child Marriage Restraint Act. As a result, the practice of child marriage is widely prevalent in the states.

17. Robbery in a House

Times Network
Siroha, 15th March

Dacoits intruded the house of a famous jeweller Ram Chauhan in the wee hours on Saturday and robbed him of about 2.2 lakh in cash, jewllery, a revolver and a mobile phone. The intruders were armed with edged weapons and sticks. They beat up the jeweller badly. When his wife tried to intervene, one of the dacoits hit her with the bullet of the revolver. Leaving both of them drenched in blood, they soon fled with the booty. Ram Chauhan is said to be an influential person of the town. The police swung into action in no time. More than 2 dozens suspects have been rounded up by the police after the incident. No breakthrough has been achieved yet regarding the criminals.

There is panic in the area. Mr Ram Chauhan, 60 is an influential leader of the ruling BSP. Many leaders including Mr Bhanu Pratap, MP have visited the victims and asked the police to nab the criminals immediately. While talking to the Times of India, Ram Chauhan said that it was a providential escape for him and his wife. While dacoits were grappling with Ram Chauhan, the watchman rang the bell as a routine check.

Fearing detection and arrest, the robbers fled through the back door of the house and disappeared under the cover of darkness with the booty. Police suspect the hand of the domestic help and artisans working for Ram Chauhan because Ram Chauhan had just received large amount of payment last evening, which was known to those working in his shop. All of them have been taken into custody for interrogation.

18. Water Logging

Hindustan Correspondent
Mathura, 29th July

Severe rains lashed Mathura on Monday evening leading to water logging and traffic jams at many places. Delhi road had about a foot deep water causing many vehicles to stop. Water logging under Bhagat Singh bridge in the main market also caused many motorists to stop in the midst of water resulting in disrupted traffic and traffic jams. Many vehicles particularly two wheelers got stuck and sank in the accumulated water under the bridge. Even traffic lights stopped working. Traffic at Krishan Nagar intersection also got disrupted because of heavy downpour. It was difficult for the pedestrians to pass through knee-deep water. The passengers on the Bus stand were stranded.

When contacted, the District Magistrate blamed the unusual heavy rain in the city. According to him, every drainage system has an optimum capacity beyond which, it cannot handle rain water. To prove his point he cited the example of Mumbai, which has the best drainage system in the country. He denied that the municipal authorities maintained the drains unproperly. According to him, whenever it rains, the additional load affects the sewers and when they are full, the rain water starts spilling over to drains and streets. However, water logging is a common sight during rainy season. Non-functional street lights add to the number of accidents on roads. The failure of street lights add to the woes of the common man. Drainage and sewerage system coupled with damaged roads pose a serious threat to the life and property of the citizens.

Town planners have miserably failed on this account. They make promises every year and by next rainy season, they are transferred. There is lack of accountability on the part of the authorities that amounts to criminal negligence of duty.

19. Seminar on Adult Education

By Garv, Special Correspondent, The Indian Express
New Delhi, 20th January 20XX

A seminar on Adult Education was held from 10 am to 4 pm on 17th January, 20xx at VKT Public School.

It was organised by the CBSE. 150 representatives from 15 different schools attended the seminar. Most of the attendees were from government schools and those schools, which conducted classes for working people in the evenings. These teachers have faced many practical difficulties in spreading adult education. The purpose of the seminar was to chalk out plans for spreading adult literacy in North district of Delhi. The seminar was presided over by a well-known educationist Dr VK Rao from the Directorate of Education.

In his address, he referred to the extent of ignorance and illiteracy that prevails in our state and how damaging it can be for those adults, who are not educated, especially in the slums. Principals and teachers representing various schools gave suggestions regarding steps that could be taken to eradicate illiteracy.

20. North-East Students Protest Death of Nido Tania

By Staff Reporter Amrit Singh, The Hindustan Times
New Delhi, 6th February, 20XX

A group of students from the North-East staged a protest against the death of an Arunachal Pradesh MLA's son after being allegedly thrashed to death in Lajpat Nagar.

This protest at the Union Home Minister's residence followed the earlier demonstration held in front of the Lajpat Nagar police station, under whose jurisdiction the beating up of the student occurred. The 19 years old student Nido Tania was allegedly beaten up by some shopkeepers following an altercation sparked by their taunts on his hairstyle. Police reached the spot and brokered compromise after which, Tania returned home with friends.

However, he did not wake up the next day and was declared brought dead at AIIMS. Protestors in large numbers gathered outside the Lajpat Nagar police station and raised slogans against the police. Police have registered a case of murder and are probing the matter. A magisterial inquiry has also been ordered.

21. Automobile Industry Dominates International Trade Fair

By Karun,
Special Correspondent, Times of India
New Delhi, 15th November, 20XX

International Trade Fair at Pragati Maidan takes place every year from 14th to 27th November. This year, it was inaugurated by Dr Manmohan Singh, the Prime Minister. The theme of the fair this time was automobile industry. Well-known Indian companies like Maruti Suzuki, Tata, Eicher, Mahindra, Hero, Bajaj, Kinetic and others had large stalls managed by knowledgeable staff, who impressed all the visitors. Apart from Indian automobile companies, many car companies from abroad participated in this fair. Giants such as Ford, BMW, Mercedes, Audi etc., launched their luxury cars for the Indian market.

Apart from automobiles, there were other stalls displaying their artifacts, electronics, textiles etc. Pavilions of different states could be seen. The exhibition showcased India's progress in numerous fields. All the stalls drew large crowds and their exhibits were sold in no time. Such fairs help in strengthening business and cultural ties with other countries and thus should be promoted.

22. Constitutional Amendments Necessary for Stability

Hindustan Times
Delhi, 24th March

The Union Minister for Parliamentary Affairs convened a press conference at his residence on the proposed changes in the Constitution of India in order to provide a Stable Government to the country.

India, being a democratic country, elects its representatives to run the government. In case, any single political party fails to get the absolute majority to form a government, it has to get the support of other political parties to form a government. Thus, a coalition government is formed. At present, we have a coalition government, but its success is neither certain nor admirable, as the allied parties, in general, force their motives and decisions on the government. This poses great hurdles in the smooth functioning of the government. Sometimes, the coalition partners start working against the government. In order to put a check over such actions, certain changes in the Constitution are under process.

23. Environmental Pollution

Times Correspondent, New Delhi,
25th October, 20XX

Environmental pollution has assumed alarming proportions. It has resulted in a serious health hazard. Not only air, but water also has become dangerously polluted. Smoke pollutes the air, sewage pollutes the water and solid wastes (garbage and junk etc.) pollute the land. Industrial units throw their industrial and chemical wastes into the rivers. Sewages of big cities are being dumped into rivers. This has resulted in spreading of gaseous chemicals in the environment, which are harmful for the living organisms. Plants, animals and human beings are suffering from many known and unknown diseases because of this pollution. The polluted water causes dangerous diseases like cholera, jaundice and diarrhoea etc. The smoke coming out of the chimneys of factories and vehicles causes serious health problems.

The public must be made aware of the harms and the problems caused due to environmental pollution. Public must be advised to use anti-pollutant measures in their vehicles and regular tuning and pollution check should be made compulsory.

24. Students Demonstrates Against Fee Hike

The Times, New Delhi,
29th August

The students of senior secondary classes of Government School, Moti Nagar walked out of their classes and held massive demonstration against the hike in board fees. They raised voice against the government decision of increasing board fees and abolishing the compartmental examinations altogether. They were seen waving hand bills and many posters. They demanded restoring of compartmental examination and maintaining the status quo in the matter of board fees. This peaceful procession proceeded towards the office of the Education Minister.

The police tried to disperse the students but they did not budge even a single inch. There was complete chaos that resulted into heavy traffic jam.

The minister arrived on the spot and had discussion with the students leaders and assured the students of a prompt and positive action, The situation was thus controlled and then the students left the place willingly and peacefully.

25. International Womens' Day Celebration

The Times, New Delhi
9th March, 20XX

From workshops to burning effigies of politicians and seminars to puppet shows, women activists organised a wide range of programmes in the capital to mark 'International Womens' Days on Monday.

The 'Joint Action Forum for Women' organised a seminar on 'Necessity of Women's Empowerment for the Development of the Nation in which, Union Human Resource Development Minister was the Chief Guest. Several other political leaders also graced the occasion with their presence. Most of the speakers asserted the need of passing the bill on providing Womens' reservation in Parliament and State Assemblies. The minister informed that the bill on reservation had already been introduced in this budget session of Parliament and the government is trying to get the bill passed with the support of the opposition. The member activists exemplified the role of women in the freedom struggle and in the development of the nation. The President of the forum Mrs Kidwai told that by giving 33% reservation for women, no political party was doing any favour to the women.

26. Acid Attack on Women

The Times
New Delhi, 25th October

The Delhi police on Monday evening was registered with an acid attack on a 21 years old, North Delhi girl, Suhana Malik. Suhana was reported to be heading back home from college on her two wheeler in late evening, around 1900 hours, when two guys, faces covered, spilled burning acid on her face. The victim was immediately admitted to Safdarjang Hospital and is currently being treated for third degree burns. The accused were nowhere to be found afterwards.

Revealed in the investigation through the sources, the boys had been following Suhana for quite a few days. She had opposed and confronted them of not doing so. This seems to be a case of eve-teasing and revenge rising from public humiliation. This incident has again raised the question of women security in the state leaving everyone dumb struck on the cruel and inhuman acts on rise.

27. Penetration of Left Wing Extremism in Tribal Areas

Express News Service
Monday, 13th May

Prime Minister Narendra Modi in the LWE meet asked various ministries to work in coordination to develop strategies for stopping the spread of Left Wing Extremism and instructed the newly established NITI Aayog to plan the development of tribal areas. One of the objectives should be to work towards 'technology penetration'—for instance, electricity and mobile phone reach in the tribal areas, Modi said.

He also asked the Ministry of Tribal Affairs to identify growth centres within tribal areas and ensure proper development of education, health and sports facility in the country. Another important objective should be to link relatively undeveloped tribal areas with developed areas through good infrastructure, he added. Minister of Tribal Affairs Jual Oram and other senior officials were present on the occasion.

28. Uttarakhand Disaster and the Role of Indian Military

The Indian Express,
Uttarakhand 2nd December

Nature's fury hit the North Indian state of Uttarakhand leaving thousands of pilgrims and locals stranded. People lost hope after the routes connecting the areas of safety were destroyed by the flash floods, until they saw the men in patriotic hearts and uniforms. The Indian armed forces were the first to reach the state. They formed human walls as they helped thousands of people pass through the rough mountainous areas and landslides during their rescue operation. They did all they could–be it helping people to cross the river with ropes or carrying the weak on their shoulder.

"Our forces are conducting a heroic task in rescue and relief work in Uttarakhand. The accident, during relief operations, has come as a huge shock to me. My heart goes out to the families of those, who have lost their lives. The nation mourns with me the loss of our heroes, whose selfless efforts has saved thousands of lives. Continuing the good work would be the best homage and tribute to these martyrs", said the Prime Minister in a statement.

B. Reports for College Magazine and Television

29. District Hospital

Ruchi Gupta
MPS, Meerut

The mushrooming of private hospitals and nursing homes in Meerut is much talked about issue in the city. The patients have just two choices. They have either to pay through the nose and get good care or depend on unreliable government health care. During the last many years, non-governmental medical facilities and private hospitals have earned reputation. But sad enough, the same is not true of public medical infrastructure and the district hospitals. It is a pity that quality health care is a distant dream for the poor and the middle class.

The existing government hospital was allotted 5 acre of land for its expansion and provision of modern facilities. It is a pity that construction has not started yet. The land has been illegally occupied by the land mafia operating in the city and nearby areas. In fact, land has been allotted but funds have not been made available for the hospitals. The fee for out-door patients, admissions and treatment are constantly going up. There is shortage of medical and para-medical staff. There is also lack of friendly attitude. The attitude of the staff at the civil hospital is callous to the patients. It is a serious problem because private medical facilities and treatment at private hospitals is unaffordable for a common man. Those needing special medical treatment fall prey to the private medical practitioner. Those, who are self employed cannot meet with the rising health care costs.

Dr Murthy, the Chief Medical Officer has shown his helplessness. According to him, it is very difficult to compete with private sector only on the strength of government grants. He suggests that the insurance sector must step in to make quality health care affordable for all.

He has another valuable suggestion to offer. Medical council of India should come forward to regulate the treatment and admission fee in the private nursing homes. The government should exercise control and regulate the functioning of private hospitals. In the present circumstances, government is not in a position to pose any challenge to hospitals in private sector.

30. Doping Evil in Indian Sports

Vijeta Singhania
SD Girls' School, Raipur

In the wake of National Games, disturbing news is published and telecast on the media that weightlifter, Charu, who won three gold medals at last Commonwealth Games has tested positive for the second time in her career and is likely to face a life ban. The test was conducted at last month's National Weightlifting Championship in Lucknow. Ironically, Sports Minister, Vikram Verma had denied only last week that no top athlete had been caught. Charu was last caught in 1995. Now, she has again tested positive for doping and it is a life-ban offence under international rules.

For the past couple of years, weightlifting in India has seen the most cases of doping. The Indian Weightlifting Federation has been run by an ad hoc committee. The committee is charged with laxity in enforcing punishment. Last year, Sunita Rani was charged with violation of a steroids related offence. Faced with the biggest ever drugs controversy in the past month, the news has come that 45 athletes tested positive in two separate cases.

When contacted, the Sports Minister dismissed the dope scam saying that the sports persons had performed well. He appeared to be unconcerned and overlooked the fact conveniently that the large list of Indians caught at top international events dates back to 1986. Sad enough, more than a year later, it still has not announced the names of 19 athletes, who had tested positive at the National Games held in Punjab. He, however, stated that India would soon sign World Anti-Doping Code that has already been signed by 80 countries in Copenhagen. Will it solve doping evil at national level?

31. Pollution in Your Town

Abhinav Goel
DM Academy, Shimla

For the last 5 years, the city is plagued by all sorts of pollution. The environmental health of the city has degraded to a large extent. The slums clusters and industrial units and the use of generators have affected the environment of the city.

Meerut, next to Kanpur and Ghaziabad is one of the most polluted cities in the state. An estimated 300 ton of pollutants are emitted by vehicles. The vehicles are major source of nitrogen oxide, carbon mono-oxide and hydro-carbons. The effluents discharged into the nearby rivers is the result of polluting industries. Suspended particulate matter as a result of industrial pollution and gases have direct effect on the health of the citizens. Diseases relating to lungs function, brain, liver, kidney etc. adversely affect the health of the children and the old citizens. Water pollution and sewage disposal are the major problems. Sewage material has been often found in the drinking water supply because of the defective drainage and sewerage system. The citizens do not get clean water. The infectious diseases are very common among those living in unhealthy conditions. The residents of slums, pavement dwellers and unplanned colonies have made these problems worse.

The same is the case with noise pollution caused by automobiles, generators and public address system. The noise pollution level has crossed the permissible limits. As Meerut is developing into one of the major industrial towns of the state, there is an utmost urgency to manage the problem of pollution. The district authorities have not paid any heed to the pollution caused by the use of generators in the residential areas. It is a menace to the peaceful and quiet living conditions for the citizens. Immediate steps should be taken to curb the use of generators in the residential areas. Moreover, the effluents discharged from the local Distillery into Abu open drain passing through the heart of the city give out foul smell causing discomfort to the citizens. Inspite of many protests by the citizens, the Mayor of the city is unconcerned.

32. Damage Caused to Life and Property Because of Recent Floods

Sania Gupta
Dewan School, Meerut   [CAPF, 2011]

Floods are annual ritual in our country. In 2010, there was unusual rain in Delhi and Yamuna rose to danger level all of a sudden that week. The rain continued relentlessly. The warning was sounded and hundreds of villages were evacuated. Those, who could not be shifted in time, had to suffer the ravages caused by flood. On the night of 10th August, hundreds of villages in rural Delhi and Haryana were submerged in water. The carcasses of animals and also living animals were floating on the river. Many people were seen sitting on the roofs of their houses and waving for help and rescue operation. Damage caused to the buildings could not be accounted for but the authorities got them vacated with the help of para-military forces. Three lakh people become shelterless and shifted to improvised tent huts and camps.

The crops to the tune of crores of rupees were destroyed. Many bikes and motor cars sank. There were injuries caused to thousands of the residents. Hundreds of hectares of cropped area was affected. Kharif paddy and crops were totally destroyed. The loss caused on this account was estimated to be running into crores of rupees. Floods around Delhi, on account of the release of flood water in Haryana, is an annual threat and causes huge loss of limb, life and cattle every year. Disaster management is a pre-disaster planning including relief management strategy.

33. Implementation of National Rural Health Mission in Your District

Karan Kapoor
DMA, Kanpur   [CAPF, 2011]

There has been great improvement, though insufficient, in providing health services in our villages. India is second most populous country of the world. About 75% of our population live in villages. Contagious, infectious and water-borne disease for the most part abound in rural areas. Ironically, around 75% of health infrastructure, medical man power and other medical facilities for treatment are concentrated in urban areas with mere 27% of population. Our district Rampur falls in Uttar Pradesh, one of the 18 states targeted under National Rural Health Mission (NRHM) that seeks to provide effective healthcare to rural population. Now, we often come across a female health activists visiting rural households and interacting with women and even young girls.

Health and sanitation committees are making efforts to strengthen the rural hospital to provide curative and preventive treatment to fairly large number of the rural population. The integration of vertical Health and Family Welfare Programmes on local level with NRHM has proved very useful for optimal utilization of funds and infrastructure. There is District Plan for Health to look after the need of sanitation, safe drinking water and prevalence of hygienic conditions. During 2005-12, the access of the rural people of the district, specially poor women and children, to primary healthcare has definitely improved all over even over distant places. What's more, the NRHM has played the supervisory role to the existing programmes of Health of Family Welfare establishing an effective network of health services.

Report Writing for Practice

Directions *Write the report writing on the following topics given below.*

A. *Prepare a report as a correspondent of a newspaper on the following.*
1. Ineffective drainage system of the city during monsoon.
2. ATM fraud in your area.
3. Terror threats to the country.
4. Pending bill against job reservation quota.
5. Rise of child exploitation cases in your state.
6. Damage due to severe earthquake in your state.
7. Production of directed weapon banned.
8. Evidences of life on mars.
9. Raise in pay scale of government employees
10. Rise in fatal cases due to impure drinking water.
11. Successful implementation of raise the girl child programme 2016.
12. Changes for balanced budget 2016.
13. Introduction of hybrid engines to save the environment.
14. New laws to fight against cyber crime.
15. Success of lasik surgeries fiber optics.

B. *Prepare a report as a columnist of a magazine on the following.*
1. High cut off list released raises stress among students.
2. World Book Fair 2016.
3. Odd-Even success declared.
4. International artist in Indian music concert.
5. Contemporary art exhibition.
6. Increasing options in distant education institutes.
7. United Nation questions energy reservation techniques.
8. Accident during river rafting.
9. Survey reveals : Caffeine addiction raising chances of skin cancer.
10. Car free day reintroduced.
11. Robotic surgery in India by 2021.
12. Indian space expedition in 2018.
13. Apple launches new 3D touch technology.
14. Reservation quota for disable children increased in educational institutes.
15. India ranked fourth in global slavery survey.

CHAPTER 4

Precis Writing

Precis (Pronounced 'presse' in French) is a derivative from 'prezisi', a Latin word. Precis is an art of compression or giving the gist of a passage. However, precis is entirely different from paraphrasing.

A paraphrase is normally a substance of the passage in detail touching upon the points in order of sequence. But, a precis is different in matter and contents rather than body and soul.

☑ Useful Hints

- A student must read a passage again and again till he is able to digest the full significance of the passage.
- No hard and fast rule can be laid down for the length of a precis. However, a precis should not normally exceed one-third of the number of words in the original passage.
- The use of first person in a precis should be avoided.
- A precis need not express the idea of the original passage in serial order. A student should be intelligent enough to find out a key sentence in the passage and begin the precis with it. One may find the key sentence in the beginning, middle or in the end of the passage.
- The ideal precis is concise, self contained and written in one's own language comprising a paragraph.
- Once a student comprehends the underlying meaning of the original passage, it is not difficult for him to supply a title to the precis. It must be kept in mind that title is an integral part of the precis. Title has to be given, whether or not it is specifically asked for by the examiner.

Till a student has gained enough writing skill, he should prepare a rough draft encompassing all the main points. Final precis should be developed on the rough outline.

Last, but not the least, remember that the ideal precis is a true summary and nothing should be added to the original theme from your side.

Samples of Precis Writing

Directions *Below are some precis writing with their solutions.*

Q. Write a precis on the following passages in about 100 words. The precis should be as far as possible, in your own words. Suggest a suitable title for your precis.

Passage 1

The ease with which democratic government has given way to authoritarian regime in one Asian country after another has made many persons ask in despair whether the parliamentary system based on the western model is suited to underdeveloped countries. People, who do not know how to read and write, they argue, can hardly know how to vote. Popular elections often bring incompetent men to the top, they contend and the division of party spoils, breeds on corruption. What is worse, the system of perpetual party warfare obstructs the business of government.

They point to the dismal results of the last ten years. The pace of social and economic change has been far too slow and the governments in most of the under developed countries have failed to come to grips with the problems, which face the people. What they say is, no doubt, true to some extent but it is pertinent to remember that every alternative to democracy while it, in no way, guarantees integrity or efficiency in the administration, lacks even the saving merits of regimes, which are based on the suffrage of the people, leave it to the people to find out, by trial and error, who is their best friend.

The people can peacefully get rid of a democratic government, which has failed to keep its promise. They can overthrow a dictatorial regime only through a violent revolution. Those, who feel sore over the ills from which, democratic regime suffers should beware, therefore, of suggesting a cure, which is likely to undermine the democratic structures of the state. The people can at least raise their voice in protest against the injustice of a democratic government; they can only suffer in silence the tyranny of a regime, which is responsible to no one but itself.

Answer   **Democracy v/s Dictatorship**

Precis Generally democracy is regarded to be unsuitable for underdeveloped countries. This fact is supported by the experience of failures of democratic government in these countries. The obvious reasons cited are illiteracy, election of inefficient leaders, internal dissensions, corruption and slow tempo of progress. Dictatorship is, therefore, considered a panacea for the ills of democracy.

But dictators, the world over, have not been able to provide efficient and clean administration, For all the faults inherent in democracy, it provides for smooth change over of government, thus replacing the inept administration without violence and bloodshed. Such a smooth change is foreign to autocratic regimes.

Passage 2

If by some magic, you could be granted one quick wish, perhaps you might wish to be popular. Being popular means being liked by a lot of people instead of just a few close friends and that is a big order. All the same, you too, can be well liked if you are willing to be on guard against the perils of popularity.

Let us consider some of these. You cannot be polite and friendly to some and not to others without the word getting around as to what kind of person you really are. When you are considering other people, take time to be friendly with the folks older than you are, your neighbours, teachers, parents and other relatives. If you treat them with respect, they are going to think of you as a like-able person, not as a good for nothing boy. And do not forget to be kind to the 'little kids' too. Again, you must think of others and consider their wishes. A majority win, you know, and if you are out-voted in the discussion of what to do and where to go, remember that being a good spirit is another way to help your popularity. A good lover does not complain when the plans do not go his way. At some time, do not be afraid that you are risking your popularity to stand up for what you think is right. It takes courage to say so, and is appreciated.

Answer   **On Popularity**

Precis Everyone wishes to be popular in life. But, one should not hanker after popularity and sacrifice the truth one stands up for. Popularity means that one is liked by a majority of the people. Therefore, one should be friendly specially to one's teachers, neighbours, parents and children. It may help a person to earn name as an amiable person. The greater number of persons admire him, the more popular he is. However, one must cultivate a sportsman spirit and one must not complain if the response is sometimes cold. One must persist in being likeable to others.

Passage 3

Whatever may be true of other countries, in India at any rate, where more than eighty per cent of the population is agricultural, and another ten per cent industrial, it is a crime to make education merely literary and to unfit boys and girls for manual work in after life. Indeed, I hold that as the larger part of our time is devoted to labour for earning our bread, our children, must from their infancy be taught the dignity of such labour.

Our children should not be so taught as to despise labour. There is no reason, why a peasant's son after having gone to a school should become useless, as he does become as an agricultural labourer. It is a sad thing that our school boys look upon manual labour with disfavour, if not with contempt. Moreover, in India, if we expect, as we must, every boy and girl of school going age to attend public schools, we have not the means to finance education in accordance with the existing style nor are millions of parents able to pay the fees that are at present imposed.

Education, to be universal, must, therefore, be free. Even under an ideal system of Government, we shall not be able to devote two thousand million rupees, which we should require for funding education for all the children of school going age. It follows, therefore, that our children must be made to pay in labour partly or wholly for all the education they receive. Such universal education can be made possible only by (to my thinking) hand spinning and hand weaving. But, for the purposes of my proposition, it is immaterial whether we have spinning or any other form of labour so long as it can be turned to account. Only it will be found upon examination, that on practical, profitable and extensive scale, there is no occupation other than the processes connected with cloth production, which can be introduced in our schools throughout India.

Answer **The Need of Vocational Education**

Precis India is a country, where 90% people are engaged in manual labour. Ironically, our present literary educational system does not teach the young men and women the dignity of labour. Children should be taught the dignity of manual labour from the very beginning of education. If India wishes to attain the goal of total literacy, every boy and girl is expected to earn while he/she learns. Parents cannot afford huge expenditure on education. On the part of government, funding of education, to make it universal requires 2000 million rupees. This is also not possible. The need of the hour is vocational education. The activities relating to cloth manufacturing will teach the students to pay expenditure on education themselves.

Passage 4

The cinema is a outstanding wonder of this modern age. Apart from the great pleasure it gives us as a means of entertainment, it is many ways an education in itself, and no regular patron of the cinema can ever be called illiterate. The cinema is also a very valuable asset to educationists in imparting knowledge. The film companies, from time-to-time, produce historical pictures and their pictures are of great importance to the teacher of history.

A couple of hours spent in the company of historical personages dressed in the proper dress of that period can teach us far more than we can learn from a whole weak's browsing in a history text book. Even some of Shakespeare's dramas and comedies have been filmed and we thereby gain a much better idea of the play than would be possible from a casual reading of it. But, of the far greater importance is the use of the film in the teaching of science and industry. There are educational film companies, which devote their time to the filming of the habits and customs of animals, insects, fishes, germs and numerous other branches of scientific life.

We can see the hatching of the eggs of fish and their gradual development into large fishes; we can watch the unceasing activity of many kinds of germs and their effect on water, milk or blood. We can watch the opening and closing of flowers and leaves and the growth of grass and weeds. All these actions and movements are greatly magnified on the screen. Such pictures are intensely interesting and are a great help to the cause of education.

Answer **Education Through the Cinema**

Precis The cinema is a means of entertainment. But, it is an education in itself. Historical pictures contribute both to entertainment and our education. They are useful even to a teacher of History. The cinema produces historical characters as if they were living creatures. They appear to be so well dressed in the proper dress of that period. Time spent in watching historical pictures widens our perspective about history and literature. Besides, pictures are very useful in imparting knowledge about science and industries. In this kind of educational films, one can learn about the environment, animals, insects, germs and their behaviour and effects on human life.

Passage 5

The test of a great book is whether we want to read it only once or more than once. Any really great book, we want to read the second time and every additional time that we read it we find new meanings and new beauties in it. But, we cannot consider the judgement of a single individual infallible. The opinion that makes a book great must be the opinion of many. For, even the greatest critics are opt to have certain dullnesses, certain inappreciations.

Carlyle, e.g. could not endure Browning, Byron could not endure some of the greatest English poets. A man must be many sided to utter of trustworthy estimate of many books. We may doubt the judgement of single critics at times. But, there is no doubt possible in regard to the judgement of generations. Even if, we do not at once preceive anything good in a book, which has been admired and praised for hundreds of years, we may be sure that by trying, by studying it carefully we shall at last be able to feel the reason for this admiration and praise. The best of all libraries for a poor man would be a library entirely composed of such great works, only books which have passed the test of time.

This, then, would be the most important guide for us in the choice of readings. We should read only the books we want to read more than once, nor should we buy any others, unless we have some special reason for so investing money. The second fact demanding attention is the general character of the value that lies hidden in all such great works. They never become old; their youth is immortal. A great book is not apt to be comprehended by a young person at the first reading expect in a superficial way. Only the surface; the narrative is enjoyed.

No young man can possibly see at first reading the qualities of a great book. But, according to a man's experience of life, the text will unfold new meanings to him. The book that delighted us at eighteen, if it be a good book, will look to us different at 30 years of age. At forty, we shall re read it wondering why we never saw how beautiful it was before. At 50 or 60 years of age, the same facts will repeat themselves. A great book grows exactly in proportion to the growth of the reader's mind.

Answer   Definition of a Great Book

Precis The test of a great book lies in the universality of ideas that are applicable in every age. The judgement of one person does not determine the real value of the book because this judgement is likely to be prejudiced. The greatness of a book is determined by the judgement of the posterity. A reader wishes to read again and again and discovers a new meaning contained in such great works.

It is likely that the real significance of a great book may not be understood at first reading. As man grows older, the context of our interest in a book also changes. The ideas of a great book are always changing as man advances in years. Therefore, the best of all libraries should contain such great works, which have passed the test of readers of various generations. The ideas of a great book are perennial and truthful in all ages.

Passage 6

In the United States, they have opened their first rehabilitation centre for Internet Addicts. De-addiction camps in China were in the news recently for the death of a teenager because of the brutal methods used to cure 'Internet Addiction' (IA). Our country must seriously think about such centres that help de-addict compulsive Internet-users, both young and old.

IA for now is a catch-all term that not only stands for addiction to specific activities such as gambling or gaming, but also refers to longer hours devoted to the computer network at the expense of other activities. Though, the Internet is only a medium of communication and information transmission and retrieval (like the printed book or television), 'addiction' is being used in this case with concern because of a fundamental dialectic : 'quantity becomes quality.'

A whole new world is just a click away with the Internet. It is a medium just like books and television, but the amount of interaction it makes possible with others, sometimes replacing the need for real-world interaction, makes it vastly different. Educators, neuroscientists and those others having public health concerns in all developing and developed countries have woken upto this reality.

According to expert neuropsychiatric opinion, IA is somewhere between Obsessive Compulsive Disorder and addiction due to substance abuse. Substance abuse led addiction focuses on gratification, which this form of attachment provides, though there is no chemical ingestion.

At the same time, the behavioural modifications are similar to those with Obsessive Compulsive Disorder. It is almost like the 'rush' gamblers get out of a purely gratification-oriented repetitive action. [IES, 2013]

Answer **Internet Addicts and Cure**

Precis Internet addiction is an all new term circulating around the globe post the identification of rising number of people falling into the trap of the world wide web. US and China are running rehabilitation centres for the internet addicts, but our country is still new to this concept.

This change shall be executed for all age groups considering the worsening condition of addicts, both old and young. Internet has now become much more than just a medium of communication. The health threats it poses on addicts due to negligence of other life activities are serious. A major cause of Internet addiction is the instant gratification it offers in each and every aspect, that leads to behavioural modifications and many other problems.

Passage 7

The greatest fact in the story of man on Earth is not his material achievements, the empires he has built and broken, but the growth of his soul from age to age in its search for truth and goodness. Those, who take part in this adventure of the soul, secure an enduring place in the history of human culture. Time has discredited heroes as easily as it has forgotten everyone else; but the saints remain. The greatness of Gandhi is more in his holy living than in his heroic struggles, in his insistence on the creative power of the soul and its life-giving quality at a time, when the destructive forces seem to be in the ascendant. Gandhi is known to the world as the one man more than any other, who is mainly responsible for the mighty upheaval of the Indian nation, which has shaken and loosened its chains.

Politicians are not generally reputed to take religion seriously, for the values, to which they are committed, such as the political control of one people by another, the economic exploitation of the poorer and weaker human beings, are so clearly inconsistent with the values of religion that the latter could not be taken too seriously or interpreted too accurately. But for Gandhi, all life is of one piece. "To see the universal and all-pervading Spirit of Truth face to face one must be able to love the meanest of creation as oneself. And a man, who aspires after that cannot afford to keep out of any field of life." [IES, 2013]

Answer **Truth and its Course**

Precis Growth of soul in search of truth and goodness is credited as the greatest fact of human life. Time waits for none but the journey of people walking on the path in search of the purpose of the existence is immortal. As an example, Gandhi is known for his spiritual and moral preachings more than the sacrifice he made and pain he suffered during his struggle to independence. It is because he adopted holy living and went against the wind of destructive forces. Politicians are rather not reputed on a religious front because their belief cannot be interpreted through their political actions. It is rightly depicted through a quote by Gandhi that one can travel far distances and achieve great heights provided they aspire to face the spirit of truth in an optimistic light.

Passage 8

There is a fatal imbalance between what man is and what he wishes to be. This discord is responsible for our unrest. We talk like wise men but act like lunatics. We cannot prepare for war and at the same time for a world community. We are tormented by inner uneasiness and pangs of conscience. The warring sides of our nature require to be reconciled. If, we are to defeat fratricidal tendencies in us, we must break our self-will, the pride of egoism, which is widespread in all sides of our life. In man, there is always an urge to self-transcendence, but until it becomes absolute unselfishness, narrow loyalties and destructive rivalries will prevail. The unrest in the world is a reflection of our inner disharmony.

People are saved not by their military leaders or industrial magnates, or by their priests and politicians, but by their saints of implacable integrity. Religion is the discipline by which we are helped to overcome the discord in our nature and integrate our personality. If, we reflect on the history of religious development, we will be surprised at the amount of intellectual ingenuity, passion and zeal spent on the task of defining the Supreme, to which silence or poetry would seem to be the most appropriate response. Self-righteousness breeds fanaticism. None but fools and fanatics are quite certain of their views of God with crusaders, there is no arguing.

Before God, there is neither Greek nor barbarian, neither rich nor poor, neither master nor slave. They are all citizens of the one commonwealth, members of one family. A truly religious person cannot hold back but should lead. He cannot remain silent, when he should speak up. He should not compromise, when he should stand fast. Ethical values have relevance to social facts. We must face up to the ugly facts of sin, pride and greed.

Human nature is essentially good and it is opposed to tyranny, injustice and authoritarianism. Religion appeals to the hearts of men to root out fear, guilt and faith in force. The tradition of tolerance, not merely in a negative, but in a positive sense, that is an appreciation of other faiths, has been with us for centuries. Tolerance is not apathy, but is conviction without condescension. Aggressiveness is not an essential part of human nature. Combativeness can be replaced by meekness and gentleness. The Cross indicates that the love, which suffers is more powerful than the force, which inflicts suffering.

Answer **The Godly Virtues**

Precis If a person is determined to achieve what he wishes, the difference of peace in his mind and heart must be resolved. He/She must find a balancing technique to take a practical decision. In the process of self-betterment, we need to realise the importance of inner harmony. It is impossible to work towards peace and prepare for war at the same time. Saints are the saviour, who guide people to follow the religious and spiritual path.

The efforts taken by them to define the supreme power of divinity are reflected in the history of religion. No matter, what religion does one belongs to, God is unbiased and loves all equally. A truly religious person is filed with ethical values. It is human nature to oppose tyranny, injustice and domination. Tolerance on the other hand is also graded high as it takes high spirit to respect other faiths.

It is, thus said, that love that suffers and is polished after facing troubles is more powerful than the evil forces.

Passage 9

The belief that fashion alone should dominate opinion has great advantages, It makes thought unnecessary and puts the highest intelligence within the reach of everyone. It is not difficult to learn the correct use of such words as 'complex,' 'sadism,' 'Oedipus,' 'bourgeois,' 'deviation,' 'left'; and nothing more is needed to make a brilliant writer or talker. Some, at least, of such words represented much thought on the part of their inventors; like paper money they were originally convertible into gold. But, they have become for most people inconvertible, and in depreciating have increased nominal wealth in ideas. And, so we are enabled to despise the paltry intellectual fortunes of former times.

The modern-minded man, although he believes profoundly in the wisdom of his period, must be presumed to be very modest about his personal powers. His highest hope is to think first what is about to be thought, to say what is about to be said, and to feel what is about to be felt; he has no wish to think better thoughts than his neighbours, to say things showing more insight, or to have emotions, which are not those of some fashionable group, but only to be slightly ahead of others in point of time. Quite deliberately, he suppresses, what is individual in himself for the sake of the admiration of the herd. A mentally solitary life, such as that of Copernicus, or Spinoza, or Milton after the Restoration, seems pointless according to modern standards.

Copernicus should have delayed his advocacy of the Copernican system until it could be made fashionable; Spinoza should have been either a good Jew or a good Christian; Milton should have moved with the times, like Cromwell's widow, who asked Charles II for a pension on the ground that she did not agree with her husband's politics. Why should an individual set himself up as an independent judge? Is it not clear that wisdom resides in the blood of the Nordic race or, alternatively, in the proletariat? And, in any case, what is the use of an eccentric opinion, which never can hope to conquer the great agencies of publicity?

The money rewards and widespread though ephemeral fame, which those agencies have made possible places temptations in the way of able men, which are difficult to resist. To be pointed out, admired, mentioned constantly in the press and offered easy ways of earning much money is highly agreeable; and when all this is open to a man, he finds it difficult to go on doing the work that he himself thinks best and is inclined to subordinate his judgement to the general opinion.   [CAPF, 2014]

Answer   Intellect-The Modern Way

Precis It is believed that learning the correct use of complex or difficult vocabulary is all that is needed to become a brilliant writer or talker. A modern and intellectual man is said to be modest and quicker than his neighbours. He thinks, says and feels ahead of people around him for the sake of admiration. Modern standards do not approve adoption of solitary lives like that of Copernicus, Spinoza or Milton. The question arises whether it is known or not where the wisdom resides. It is of no use to think and hope to conquer against the publicity agencies. A common man is lured and trapped by these agencies that offer tempting rewards, but when these are offered to him in lieu of the work, he deemed the best, the judgement merges with the general opinion.

Passage 10

Honesty in business dealings or in other areas are not the only measures of morals and values. The strength of character of a person is also measured by uncompromising aversion to cowardice, intrigue, envy, ambiguity, falsehood, disloyalty, treachery, in short, all undignified actions. There are, in reality, few human beings endowed with a truly spotless character. This is because an almost immaculate character does not exist until the last lives in human form. Educated individuals are not necessarily endowed with good morals and values. In fact, some of them use education and their intellect as a tool for deceit. However, the advantages and the need for education and culture cannot be denied.

They contribute largely for the development of intellectual ability and the power to reason, which are the means by which the spirit analyses, compares, infers and arrives at conclusions in the search for truth about the meaning of life. The most precious assets of the soul are its morals and values, but they are not easy to build. The character of each person requires longer periods of thoughtfulness, reasoning and the practice of those values, during many reincarnations, in the course of which, ideas sink in under life experiences.

PRECIS WRITING

It is only after enduring much disillusionment, grief, injustice and ingratitude for many successive corporeal lives, that a person will be able to measure, in the innermost recesses of his soul, the extent of human moral misery. Then, disgusted, he rebels against it and opens the door to a more ethical and honourable life. Thus, having known and experienced suffering, the spirit, in countless reincarnations, gradually frees itself from evil actions and, through enlightenment and conviction follows the rigid tracks of a flawless conduct.

It is of great significance to talk about morals and values but it is also crucial to define the lines of character that everyone should consider in their lives. Some of the most important ones are good judgement, fairness, common sense, punctuality, loyalty, courage, magnanimity, dignity, gratitude, politeness, faithfulness, moderation, truthfulness, self-respect, respect for others etc. All these qualities, if properly cultivated, compose a prime set of dignifying virtues, which accounts for a refined character. e.g. we all make mistakes and to err is human. However, once an honest person is advised and becomes convinced of his mistake, he should admit it and try not to repeat it. Unfortunately, it is common practice to conceal one's mistakes, instead of avoiding them.

This is very detrimental to spiritual growth. Most people seldom use impartiality and justice in the innermost evaluation of their own actions. Even those, who are too harsh in the judgement of other people's actions, for whom they always have words of criticism and reproach, do not escape the usual tendency. When their own faults are concerned, they find a full, lenient, absolvent, justification.

In this way, not only it denotes lack of character, but mistakes often end up incorporated to human habits. By acting this way, an individual loses his self-respect and his sense of character and dignity and becomes corrupted. What everyone should do, is to face up his mistakes and avoid new mistakes, by improving his sense of morals and values, with the help of his will-power.   [Civil Services (Mains), 2013]

Answer   **Building Characters**

Precis A character cannot be graded first on the basis of honesty in business dealings. A vast ground is laid for its measurement. Standing up for truth and justice, and against the undignified acts are some barricades, one need to pass through to have a polished character. It is not necessary that educated individuals are blessed with moral and values. Although, education is a must for development of intellect but it does not guarantee transparency of character, for morals and values are the food for soul.

As easy to say, it is very difficult to practice the morals and values a truthful human should possess. It is only after undying passion of learning, patience and countless suffering of many lives that one is able to free its soul from the materialistic desires of this world. Though, there is no set of values laid for a refined character, some important qualities one should have are loyalty, judgement, courage, honesty and truthfulness.

Making mistakes is inevitable but acceptance of the mistake requires courage. It is a very important trait of a fair person to be able to accept his/her mistake with dignity and try not to imitate it in future. One should treat others as oneself while judging, when others are at fault and oneself as others, when oneself is at fault. Trying to escape justified consequences in ones own case depicts cowardice. Thus, one should learn from mistakes and never give up on being a better person with a good character by practise.

Passage 11

People write and publish autobiographies and autobiographical sketches for a number of reasons. One of these reasons is to put on record the events of a famous or influential career. But not all autobiographies, not even the autobiographies most frequently and widely read, are by famous or extraordinary men. Another reason is to hand on to others, wisdom won through experience and hard labour. Yet, many fine autobiographers seem to have little concern to teach or to persuade. A third reason is to distill from past experience events, persons and situations, which hold a firm place in memory, and to put true values on them.

In this sense, autobiography is, as Somerset Maugham has said, a 'summing-up', and its first utility is to its author himself. Whatever its purpose or the fame of the man who writes it, autobiography is a thing created out of the recollections of life. It is not life itself. Whether it be valuable or useless depends upon whether it is well or ill-made. Good autobiographies can be mined from inconspicuous lives. For, autobiography is the inclusive and summary form of what we call 'themes of experience'. It may contain reminiscences, descriptions of places, of animals, of people, the identification of characteristic preferences and prejudices, and other matters as well. It has the traits of all these minor forms.

An autobiography is objectively true, but is not indiscriminately inclusive. It presents a selection of detailed episodes with sufficient fullness to preserve their essential qualities. It is usually written within the framework defined by a consistent point of view. It presents its subject in more than two dimensions, fusing the person and his actions with setting, manner and purpose. One further trait of autobiographical writing raises a few special problems: by its nature autobiography tempts its author to proceed chronologically. The events sort themselves. by the calendar, and it is a natural impulse of every autobiographer to begin with the words "I was born on ..... ."

Strict chronological arrangement poses a discipline of some force. It is by no means easy to "begin at the beginning, go until you come to the end, and then stop." Considerations, other than the calendar, have a way of forcing their way to notice. With due care, however, a chronological autobiography can be accomplished.

It is important to remember that chronology is not the only principle, by which autobiography can be organised. Benjamin Franklin, whose procedure in his autobiography is basically chronological, does not hesitate to recognise the Philadelphia girl, who laughed at him as the very one, who subsequently became his wife. Joseph Conrad prefers the pattern of walking tour to that of the calendar, and his richly imaginative account is stored with pertinent associations of the past with the present and future.

Often, to the autobiographer, it seems that life does not pass so much as it accumulates. Qualities emerge as identities independent of time. For this reason, we should not, as we write feel compelled to maintain a steady rate of advance through the time marks of our stories. Like Hazlitt on his journey, we linger over a choice adventure or a valued friend, and then; if we choose, we skip a few years to catch up.

[Civil Services (Mains), 2013]

Answer **Dimensions of Biography**

Precis People write autobiographies for various different reasons. Some write to record the events of life of someone famous, some to handover lessons learnt from experiences and some to add values to the incidents of life. Autobiography is a summation of incidents that hold special place in the heart of the writer. The efficiency of an autobiography depends upon how well it is written. It consists of opinions, reactions, descriptions and conclusions of different things. It is written with a biased perspective of the writer. An autobiography is not all inclusive.

It does not include details that the writer feels are unimportant. An autobiography is deemed to be preceding chronologically by all as it is presumed to be a recollection of events of life from one leading to another. It is important to follow the order of events to form a well comprehended association with the reader. But, it is equally important to note that it is not the only way to present an autobiography. Benjamin Franklin, apart from following chronological order, mentions his thoughts and aspirations of realisation and future. Joseph Conrad chose to tour along his way while remembering past events and relating it to his present and future. Thus, it is upon us to choose the way we want to connect and present the stories of our life.

Passage 12

The real implication of equal distribution is that each man shall have the wherewithal to supply all his natural needs and no more. e.g. if one man has a weak digestion and requires only a quarter of a pound of flour for his bread and another needs a pound, both should be in a position to satisfy their wants. To bring this ideal into being, the entire social order has got to be reconstructed.

A society based on non-violence cannot nurture any other ideal. We may not perhaps be able to realise the goal, but we must bear it in mind and work unceasingly to go near it. To the same extent, as we progress towards our goal, we shall find contentment and happiness, and to that extent too, shall we have contributed towards the bringing into being of a non-violent society.

It is perfectly possible for an individual to adopt this way of life without having to wait for others to do so. And if an individual can observe a certain rule of conduct, it follows that a group of individuals can do likewise. It is necessary for me to emphasise the fact that no one need wait for anyone else in order to adopt a right course. Men generally hesitate to make a beginning, if they feel that the objective cannot be had in its entirety. Such an attitude of minds, is in reality, a bar to progress.

Now, let us consider how equal distribution can be brought about through non-violence. The first step towards it is for him, who has made this ideal part of his being to bring about the necessary changes in his personal life. He would reduce his wants to a minimum, bearing in mind the poverty of India. [IES, 2014]

Answer **Equal Distribution of Resources**

Precis A non-violent approach advocates contribution with contentment by each for the society. It holds the idea of realisation by each and every man in the society to realise its needs, satisfy it and give up the want for more. This way, one can be complacent while moving towards the goal to achieve equal distribution and eliminate poverty.

The concept of equal distribution shall be revised and should now be based on the needs of an individual as the needs of each man may differ. It should discard the equal ratio distribution system. It is definitely possible for an individual to accept this way of conduct irrespective of its social acceptance by far. One should not feel the hitch to take initiative as it proves to be the only barrier towards progress. Equal distribution can be brought to literal existence in the most appropriate terms by bringing about changes in needs and consumption in personal life while considering social issues and benefits.

Passage 13

Mining companies are dumping more than 180 million tonnes of hazardous mine waste each year into rivers, lakes and oceans worldwide, threatening vital bodies of water with toxic heavy metals and other chemicals poisonous to human beings and wildlife. The amount of mine waste dumped annually is 1·5 times as much as all the municipal waste dumped in US landfills in 2009.

Mine processing wastes, also known as tailings, can contain as many as three dozen dangerous chemicals including arsenic, lead, mercury and processing chemicals such as petroleum by-products, acids and cyanide. Waste rock, the extra rock that does not contain significant amounts of ore, can also generate acid and toxic contamination. The dumping of mine tailings and waste rock pollutes waters around the world, threatening the drinking water, food supply and health of communities as well as aquatic life and ecosystems.

In a world, where climate change, ocean acidification, overfishing and recurring tragedies like the Gulf of Mexico oil spill are already disrupting water and food supplies, polluting the world's waters with mine tailings is unconscionable and the damage it causes is largely irreversible. No feasible technology exists to remove and treat mine tailings from oceans; even partial cleanup of tailings dumped into rivers or lakes is prohibitively expensive.

There is but one workable solution: Mining companies must stop dumping into natural bodies of water. In some cases, safer waste management options exist: putting dry waste in lined and covered landfills (a process called dry stacking) and putting tailings back into the pits and tunnels the ore came from (called backfilling). In other cases, even land-based tailings disposal is too risky. Some places, where companies want to dump tailings are simply inappropriate for mining and should be no dumping zones. The protection of such areas must be coupled with more efficient use of metals and support for sustainable development and livelihoods that do not endanger communities' health and safety.

A number of nations have adopted prohibitions or restrictions on dumping mine tailings in natural bodies of water. Nations with some restrictions on dumping including the United States, Canada and Australia - are home to major mining companies that use practices internationally that they wouldn't be allowed to use at home. Even these national regulations, however, are being eroded by amendments, exemptions and loopholes that have allowed destructive dumping in lakes and streams.

Non-governmental initiatives to promote responsible- mining by corporations can play an important role in helping close regulatory loopholes. Civil society organisations working to encourage more responsible mining are calling on mining

PRECIS WRITING

companies to end water-based tailings dumping. In turn, the mining industry as a whole must, share our collective responsibility to protect water and aquatic ecosystems by pledging not to dump mine wastes in Earth's most precious resource: water.

[IFS, 2013]

Answer Mining and Environmental Problems

Precis Mining companies have become major contributor of environment pollution through water based tailing dumping. These companies have risen to dump five times more waste with heavy toxic metals and chemicals that pose danger to the aquatic ecosystem. Mine processing waste, tailings, contains number of hazardous chemicals that pollute the natural water bodies, thereby, threatening drinking water, food supply and health of communities.

With uncontrollable problems like climate change, ocean acidification etc. mining companies should rise to alter their dumping patterns to cease the irreversible harm they are causing to the environment.

The only helpful solution is for the mining companies to adopt safer waste management. They should segregate their dumpings depending upon its kind; dry waste in the landfills and tailings to be backfilled in the mines. There should be specific zones, where such activities can take place and these places must be endowed with better use of metals, so that they do not endanger communities' health and safety.

We should join hands with nations, who have prohibited water based tailings dumpings. Though the regulations and laws enforced has certain loopholes that allow partial water based dumpings, mining companies all around the globe should rise as one and realise this social and environmental responsibility to protect the aquatic ecosystem by pledging not to dump mine waste into natural water bodies.

Passage 14

We are the failed generation - we, who are now in our 40s and 50s. We do not have to look far to realise that our generation has failed. The India, we inherited, was wonderful, but the one that we have bequeathed our children is degraded in every ways. We are the citizens of transition, with personal memories of our childhood, when we lived in a good, simple world, where laws and morals had their place. And now, we have first hand experience of an India stifled by corruption and injustice, with breakdowns on every front.

There is no point getting defensive about our failure. There is no point denying it either. Perhaps, time has come for us to face up to reality and to try and understand why we failed. We were good and talented and grew up in a relatively safe and protected environment, then why and where did we go wrong? Perhaps, we must rewind a bit.

Our grandparents were the generation of freedom fighters. They were brave and committed men and women fired with a vision of free India. They made sacrifices, donated money and property, their youth and even lived, to achieve their goal. They were incredibly disciplined. And then came our parents' generation. They wanted to build a new India, a modern India, where all citizens were equal. They were incredibly thrifty.

They worked hard and saved money and believed the best they could give their children was a good education. And then came my generation, born in safety and security. We benefited from a good education. Our nationalistic goals had whittled down - we only wanted to make a difference. But, we did not manage to, because we were incredibly ambitious. We wanted to create a separate identity, push the frontiers of our personal capabilities and professional parameters to a new height. That hurt the social fabric - we wanted the best for our family, but community and country could look after itself. ...

And our children, they worship money. And when, it is their parents' money, they do not care for it. Nowhere, in the world do teenagers' spend their parents' money as freely and without compunction as they do, here. We are to be blamed for that too because we are permissive, not liberal. Parents are so involved in their work that they do not have time for their children. They buy children's affection with guilt-money. So kids, now have cars, electronic gadgets, designer clothes. India is a fading figment of their parents' nostalgia.

But, can you blame them? Look at the India they are living in - pollution is high, crime is endemic, brute power is law, civic amenities are deplorable, justice non-existent. It is caste or connections that work. There are cases of affluence amidst unbelievable deserts of deprivation. How long is India really sustainable? Can it really remain stable and peaceful amidst such grotesque ills and inequities.

Often, we are optimistic because we are afraid to be pessimistic. Impending scenarios scare the living daylights out of us. So, we collectively believe that things will improve and gladly cite a variety of instances to prove that there are areas of growth and excellence. We want to be optimistic because we do not want to be pessimistic or lapse into despair. After all, what is life without hope? [CISF, 2014]

Answer   Generation Gap : The Indian Prospect

Precis We, the middle aged generation, have failed. We inherited a beautiful country but could not pass on a more refined one to our kids. Though, our memories of childhood are that of a simple society, where morals were worshipped, our childrens' childhood floated with evidences of injustice and violence. We cannot argue over our efforts as it is better to accept our defeat and search the cause.

We grew up in a safe environment. Our ancestors were passionately patriotic, who spent their lives fighting for the country. Our parents worked hard towards building a modern India by laying the foundation of equality. But our generation, who were blessed with a silver spoon failed to maintain its pride. We did work hard, but not selflessly. We prioritised our personal goals over social issues that needed to be addressed. These self-centred acts had a negative impact on our national objectives.

We made up for the time we could not devote to our children with money. It is not our children, who should be blamed. It is merely because of us that once a heritage, is now, a corrupted and unjust nation. The question of the hour is whether or not we can achieve our goals while the situations are not ideal. We are optimistic just because we don't want to fall in the pessimistic trap of depression. Being optimistic without actions, is illusionary, but we still cling onto the hope of rope for betterment.

Passage 15

The means may be equated to a seed, the end to a tree; and there is just the same inviolable connection between the means and the end as there is between the seed and the tree. I am not likely to obtain the result flowing from the worship of God by laying myself prostrate before Satan. If, therefore, anyone were to say; 'I want to worship God; it does not matter that I do so by means of Satan', it would be set down as ignorant folly. We reap exactly as we sow.

If I want to deprive you of your watch, I shall certainly have to fight for it; if I want to buy your watch, I shall have to pay you for it; and if I want it as a gift, I shall have to plead for it; and according to the means I employ, the watch is a stolen property, my own property, or a donation. Thus, we see three different results from three different means. Will you still say that means do not matter ?

Let us proceed a little further. A well-armed man has stolen your property; you have harboured the thought of his act; you are filled with anger; you argue that you want to punish that rogue, not for your own sake, but for the good of your neighbours; you have collected a number of armed men, you want to take his house by assault; he is duly informed of it, he runs away; he, too, is incensed. He collects his brother-robbers, and sends you a defiant message that he will commit robbery in broad daylight.

You are strong, you do not fear him, you are prepared to receive him. Meanwhile, the robber pesters your neighbours. They complain before you. You reply that you are doing all for their sake, you do not mind that your own goods have been stolen. Your neighbours reply that the robber never pestered them before, and that he commenced his depredations only after you declared hostilities against him.

You are between Scylla and Charybdis. You are full of pity for the poor men. What they say is true. What are you to do ? You will be disgraced, if you now leave the robber alone. You, therefore, tell the poor men: 'Never mind. Come, my wealth is yours. I will give you arms. I will train you how to use them; you should belabour the rogue; don't you leave him alone.' And so, the battle grows. The robbers increase in numbers; your neighbours have deliberately put themselves to inconvenience. Thus, the result of wanting to take revenge upon the robber is that you have disturbed your own peace; you are in perpetual fear of being robbed and assaulted; your courage has given place to cowardice. If you patiently examine the argument, you will see that I have not overdrawn the picture. This is one of the means.

Now let us examine the other. You set this armed robber down as an ignorant brother, you intend to reason with him at a suitable opportunity; you argue that he is, after all, a fellow man; you do not know what prompted him to steal. You, therefore, decide that when you can, you will destroy the man's motive for stealing. Whilst you are thus reasoning with yourself, the man comes again to steal. Instead of being angry with him, you take pity on him.

Henceforth, you keep your doors and windows open, you change your sleeping place and you keep your things in a manner most accessible to him. The robber comes again and is confused as all this is new to him; nevertheless, he takes away your things. But, his mind is agitated. He enquires about you in the village, he comes to learn about your broad and loving heart; he repents, he begs your pardon, returns you your things and leaves off the stealing habit. He becomes your servant and you find for him honourable employment. This is the second method.

Thus, you see, different means have brought about totally different results. I do not wish to deduce from this that robbers will act in the above manner or that all will have the same pity and love like you. I only wish to show that fair means alone can produce fair results and that, at least in the majority of cases, if not indeed in all, the force of love and pity is infinitely greater than the force of arms. There is harm in the exercise of force, never in that of pity.

[Civil Services (Mains), 2015]

Answer   **Methods do Matter**

Precis The medium and means are directly proportionate to the end results. It is your actions that lead you to your destination. Your present situation is the justified result of your past actions and this is not arguable, means to do something largely effects the results you see.

If someone wants to achieve something, it is very important to study the and means of effort. One can fight for it, plead for it, work hard for it or adopt illegal and unfair means to achieve the same. He/She may reach the destination but the ownership will differentiate on various levels of gratification.

Lets take an example of a robbed man. A robbed man reaction to the unfortunate situation can bring about huge changes. Consider the robbed man to be agitated and filled with vengeance. He may take aggressive steps to provoke and challenge the robber to catch him for other's benefits. He is already robbed of his values but it endangers his neighbours to suffer in the name of help. This may lead to danger and violence, if taken further.

It may help in catching the robbed, but it won't decrease any amount of fear in the society. But, if the robbed man reacts with a calm mind and tries to rob the reason of robbery, it can infuse great changes in the robber. With the power of reasoning and pity, if the robbery is invited and made easy, it might stir the mind of the robber. It can shake him up out of his ill-deeds and spark his soul to rectify and change his path of life.

Now, it is clear that our actions and efforts can change the results we come across. There is no certainty of results, but fair means always bring fair results. It is rightly said that we reap exactly what we sow.

Precis Writing for Practice

Directions *Write a precis of the following passages in not more than 100 words. The precis should be as far as possible in your own words. Suggest a suitable title also.*

Passage 1

If we look back at India's long history, we find that our fore-fathers made wonderful progress whenever they looked out on the world with clear and fearless eyes and kept the windows of their minds open to give and receive. And, in later periods, when they grew narrow in outlook and shrank from outside influences, India suffered a setback, politically. What a magnificent inheritance, we have, though we have abused it often enough.

India has been and is a vital nation, inspite of all the misery and suffering that she had experienced. That vitality in the realm of constructive and creative effort spread to many parts of the Asian world and elsewhere and brought splendid conquests in its train. Those conquests were not so much of the sword, but of the mind and heart, which bring healing and, which endure very vitality. If not rightly and creatively directed and may turn inward and destroy and degrade. Even during the brief span of our lives, we have seen these two forces at play in India and the world at large. The forces of constructive and creative effort and the forces of destruction, which will triumph in the end? And on which side do we stand? That is a vital question for each one of us, and, more especially, for those from whom the leaders of the nation will be drawn, and on whom the burden of tomorrow will fall. We dare not sit on the fence and refuse to face the issue. We dare not allow our minds to be befuddled by passion and hatred, when clear thought and effective action are necessary.

Let us be clear about our national objective. We aim at a strong, free and democratic India, where every citizen has an equal place and full opportunity of growth and service, where present day inequalities in wealth and status have ceased to be, where our vital impulses are directed to creative and co-operative endeavour.

In such an India communalism, separatism, isolation, untouchability, bigotry and exploitation of man by man have no place and while religion is free, it is not allowed to interfere with the political and economic aspects of a nation's life. If that is so, then all this business of Hindu, Muslims, Christian and Sikhs must cease in so far as our political life is concerned and we must build a united but composite nation, where both individual and national freedom are its cure.

Passage 2

The word 'adventure' embraces a company of great words, including courage, tenacity, selflessness and faith, but its most potent ingredient cannot be expressed in one word. It is the spirit that urges men to volunteer to undertake hazardous tasks, for adventure implies the readiness and desire to embark on a course of action that entails risk. A young child may display an instinct for adventure by climbing out of his play pen to explore the mysteries of the nursery, but this kind of adventure is hardly laudable because the child has not yet sufficient reasoning power to realise the potential risk in such an action.

As we grow older, however, the spirit of adventure tends to be restrained by caution; the fire is often smothered by reason, which gives warning of impending dangers and coldly counsels safety first. Yet, in some men, the urge for adventure may be so strong that it overwhelms the primary instinct of self-preservation and inspires them to attempt the impossible.

To evoke our admirations, adventure need not be successful; it is enough if the adventurer is impelled by courage. Indeed, the failure of a gallant enterprise often touches our hearts even more than its success. Success in dangerous enterprises often bring material rewards, but a glorious failure that inspires those, who follow after brings a greater honour than any material reward.

It was said of Mallory that "a fire burnt in him that caused his willing spirit to rise superior to the weakness of his flesh." Yet it would be a fallacy to assume that the conquest of the flesh is easier for such adventures than for is humbler mortals. There has never been a man, who knew no fear, but the finer the courage of a man, the less will he betray his fears. When we imagine that men, who deliberately set out on perilous adventures are endowed with a disregard for danger, let us remember that their bodies are sensible of the same pains as ours and that their minds suffer the same anxieties.

What they have that we lack is the ability to call up some impelling force from within that we all possess but that lies dormant in most of us, although we admire its manifestation in others. To summon the power, the individual must fight gigantic battles within himself; reason, hunger, love of life, the insistent call of home—all these present vast obstacles, which he must surmount and which yet rear up before him again and again.

Passage 3

The Capital city with its slum and polluting industries, is plagued by all sort of environmental degradation, says a report. "Continuous migration of people into Delhi, whose population has already crossed the nine million marks, has strained the existing infrastructure within the city to the point of no return", says the report ⊦ A.K. Lal, the planning engineer at the environmental planning division of town and country planning organization here. The 1,100 slum clusters, 94,000 industrial unit, over 22 lakh vehicles and 4,400 metric tonnes of municipal solid wastes have thrown the city's environmental health out of gear, Lal reported in the Indian Journal of Environmental Protection.

"The most serious problem is air pollution with Delhi ranked fourth among 41 polluted cities monitored worldwide. As estimated, 1,280 tonnes of pollutants are emitted by 22 Lakh vehicles, and vehicular pollution accounts for more than two-thirds of Delhi's total air pollution. Almost 2 lakh vehicles are added in Delhi each year, two thirds of them being two wheelers", Lal reports says. The vehicles are major source of nitrogen oxide, carbon monoxide and hydro carbons.

The next major contributor to the city's air pollution are the industries with the Central Pollution Control Board (CPCB) having already identified five major and 22,000 significantly polluting industries in the capital. The prime source of pollution includes thermal power plants, brick kilns, potteries, steel rolling mills and induction furnace. Data collected between 1988 and 1993 indicates that the Suspended

Particulate Matter (SPM) usually exceeds permissible limits, the report says. Studies from 1987 to 1993 also show that particulate lead level have exceeded that limit prescribed by the World Health Organisation (WHO) at some busy intersections in the Capital.

Air pollution caused especially by emission of poisonous gases such as nitrogen oxides, carbon monoxide and lead oxide, has been linked to lung cancer, asthma and bronchitis. In fact, four out of every five cancers are linked to toxic and hazardous chemicals in the environment. Nitrogen oxides emitted by vehicles are respiratory irritants that cause breathing problem, while sulphur dioxide and Suspended Particulate Matter (SPM) damage lung function. SPM also affects larynx, brain, liver, kidney and stomach. Increasing lead pollution from industries and automobiles can cause cancer. On inhalation, lead can be absorbed in the brain, liver, kidneys and blood leading to brain damage, muscle paralysis, convulsions and even death.

Delhi is facing formidable problems of water pollution and sewage disposal too. The Yamuna picks up nearly 1,800 Millions Liters Daily (MLD) of domestic and industrial waste waters, while only three quarters of the city are covered by sewage facilities. Majority of Delhi is unauthorised and resettlement colonies and squatters settlements do not have a sewage system, while about 40% of Delhi's sewage is discharged into the Yamuna without treatment, the report says.

The city is also ridden with noise pollution caused by automobiles, railways, aircraft, industrial machines, public address system and social and religious activities. A recent study by CPCB has shown that noise level in several industries and commercial areas were higher than the stipulated levels. However, the most disturbing trend was in silence zones, where noise levels exceeded permissible limits not only during day but also in the night.

Passage 4

The union cabinet's approval of an information and Broadcasting ministry proposal to bring forward legislation to regulate cable television is belated but a necessary step. The boom in cable television following the satellite invasion of the skies has revolutionised the medium in ways that are still not fully appreciated. And the full potential of multiple and free choice, in viewing that satellite and cable television represent, has far from been realised as yet.

With millions of homes being inundated with entertainment and information programmes from all kind of sources, it is obvious that some degree of regulation is essential in the public and national interest. But, the precise nature and means of regulation are bound to be contentious. It is as well that the Government appears to be proceeding carefully.

The bill will require cable operators to register themselves and their operations will be monitored. All operators will be obliged to telecast one Doordarshan channel for purposes of important public information and to use equipment conforming to ISI standards. All operators will also have to observe programme and advertisement codes, which have still to be evolved.

Just how the programme content and equipment of tens of thousands of neighbourhood cable operators are to be monitored remains to be seen. If it leads to an army of local inspectors it is bound to lead to petty corruption without any real efficiency. And of what use would such a monitoring agency be in a few year's time, when technological developments put small and cheap satellite dishes within reach of individual household? Similar problems are presented by the other objectives of the proposed Bill.

Some kind of minimal programme and advertisement codes are obviously necessary to protect audiences against things like pornography, inflammatory propaganda and misleading information. The difficult question, as always in these matters, is who is the best judge of what audiences should or should not see, governments or private citizens? It must be hoped that the intended programme codes will be drafted with the greatest care so as to protect rather than infringe individual rights.

As general rule, regulatory bodies will have to rely on complaints from audiences rather than their own inspectors to be able to intervene promptly. At the same time, there should be no occasion under the guise of enforcing programme codes to interfere with the freedom of expression and information as has been the case all too often with the programmes of independent producers supplying Doordarshan.

The I and B Ministery would do well given the many difficulties in drafting its new Bill to consult informed public opinion, television producers advertising professional and other experts on the mechanisms for regulating cable television as well as programme codes. It should also encourage the formation of self-regulating bodies for cable and network operators.

Passage 5

The truth is that husband's success depends more upon his wife than he ever admits, if he has a good wife. And many a man fails completely because he married a pullback. If a wife takes a keen interest in her husband's business and encourages him to talk about it, this is tremendous help to him. If he can talk out his troubles, they will not worry him so much. He will not brood over them. A wife's advice in almost any matter of business is valuable. Why?

Because, women are the money power of the world. They are the chief spenders. In nearly every problem of marketing, a woman's opinion is more valuable than a man's. A sales manager, for instance, can learn more from his wife than from any one else. Many times, I have increased the sales of a firm by making it present its goods from the woman's point of view.

Then, there is the matter of the husband's feelings and temperament. His wife has more control of these than any one else has. She can start him out right in the morning. Many a man remembers all day long for better or worse what his wife said to him at breakfast. The great thing is to keep him in money-making humour. And, no one can do this for a man as well as his wife can.

Passage 6

We have three valuable sources of information about those distant times and each of these has given us a great deal of historical knowledge. The first is 'archaeology'. This word has come to have a special meaning. It means the study of the material remains and ruins of the past, of the tools, weapons, pots, house foundations, ancient settlements and towns that have been left behind by the people, who have vanished.

The second source of historical knowledge is 'oral tradition'. This is the history-partly legend and partly truth-which generation of our ancestors have passed down by word of mouth. West Africa, like other regions of Africa, is rich in such historical traditions. These remembered traditions are sometimes very useful to historians. But, care has to be taken, for these old traditions also tell things, which did not happen the way they are said to have happened, or not for the reasons that are given in the story.

Then, there is a third source of knowledge about the distant past of West Africa. This is generally less valuable than the other two. It consists of the books that were written by North African and Arab travellers and historians. Many such books were written by scholars, who wrote in Arabic. Some of them are of great value. Much later, Europeans also began to write books about West Africa, in Portuguese, English, French, Dutch and other European languages and a few of their books, too, are full of useful information.

Passage 7

First and foremost among the blessings of civilisation are order and safety. If today, I have a quarrel with another, I do not get beaten merely because I am physically weaker and he can knock me down. I go to law, and the law will decide as fairly as it can between the two of us. Thus, in case of disputes between one and the other right has taken the place of might. Moreover, the law protects me from robbery and violence. Nobody may come and break into my house steal goods or run off with my children. Of course, there are burglars but they are very rare and the law punishes them whenever it catches them.

It is difficult for us to realise how much this safety means. Without safety, those higher activities of mankind which make up civilisation cannot go on. The inventor could not invent, the scientists could not find out or the artist could not make beautiful things. Hence order and safety, although they are not themselves civilisation, are thing without which civilisation would be impossible. They are necessary to our civilisation as the air, we breath, is to us and we have grown so used to them that we do not notice them any more than we notice the air. For all that, they are both new things.

Except for a short period under the Roman Empire there have been order and safety in Europe only during the last two hundred years and even during that time there have been two revolutions and a great many wars. Thus, it is a great achievement of our civilisation that today civilised men should in their ordinary daily lives being practically free from the fear of violence.

Passage 8

Under the present system of mass education by class, too much stress is laid on teaching and little on active learning. The child is not encouraged to discover things on his own account. He learns to rely on outside help not on his own powers, thus losing intellectual independence and all capacity to judge for himself.

The overtaught child is the father of the newspaper reading; advertisements believing, propaganda swallowing, demagogued-man—the man, who makes modern democracy the force it is. Moreover, the lessons in class leave him mainly unoccupied and therefore, bored. He has to be coerced into learning what does not interest him and the information acquired mechanically and reluctantly by dint of brute repetitions is rapidly forgotten.

Quite naturally, the child being bored and unoccupied, is also mischievous. A strict external discipline becomes necessary unless there is control. He loses moral as well as intellectual independence. Such are the main defects in the current system of mass education.

Many others could be mentioned but they are defects in detail and can be classified under one or other of the three main categories of defects—sacrifice of the individual to the system, psychologically unsound method of teaching are irrational methods of imposing discipline. We need a new system of universal education of the same kind as that which has proved itself so successful in the training of defectives and infants but modified so as to be suitable for older boys and girls. We need a system of individual education.

Passage 9

The behaviour of young boys is the subject of comment the world over. Particularly, distressing is the manifestation of insulting conduct towards school and colleges going girls in university towns. While no condemnation can be too severe for such ungentlemanly conduct, whereever it may take place, a general enquiry is called for into the cause that has led to this kind of behaviour. Lack of reverence for women is only an off shoot from a larger evil. The real tragedy is surely the complete lack of self-discipline evident in the behaviour of those youngesters. This lack of control needs to be dealt with broadly. We can hope to see improvement in its narrower aspects.

We all know that the best way to teach a child any thing is by example. But cases of children, who misbehave prove too clearly that many parents and teachers undoubtedly fail calamitously in their duty. Both at home and at school far too many children are brought up to do only what they want at the expense of other people's convenience. Parents say they cannot manage their children.

It grows more and more difficult to find a teacher, who can manage a class. And then the behaviour of parents and teachers is not always calculated to inspire respect. But, perhaps the greatest harm is done by the perpetual rousing of sense of posters, films, magazines, advertisements etc. Society will have to make a much more determined effort to mould the character of the children, if this moral deterioration is to be halted.

PRECIS WRITING

Passage 10

It is the height of selfishness for men, who fully appreciate in their own case great advantages of a good education to deny these advantages to women. There is no valid argument by which the exclusion of the female sex from the privilege of education can be defended. It is argued that women have their domestic duties to perform and that if they were educated they would bury themselves in their books and have little time for attending to the management of their households. Of course, it is possible for women, as it is for men, to neglect necessary work in order to spare more time for reading sensational novels. But, women are no more liable to this temptation than men and most women should be able to do their household work all the better being able to refresh their minds in the intervals of leisure, with a little reading.

Education would even help them in the performance of the narrowest sphere of womanly duty. For, education involve knowledge of the means, by which health may be preserved and improved and enables a mother consult such modern books and will tell her how to rear up her children into healthy men and women and skillfully nurse them and her husband, when disease attacks her household.

But, according to higher conception of women's sphere, women ought to be something more than a household drudge. She ought to be able not merely to nurse her husband in sickness, but also, to be his companion in health care. For this part of her wifely duty, education is necessary.

There cannot be congenial companionship between an educated man and uneducated wife, who can converse with her husband on no higher subject than cookery and servants wages. Also, one of a mother's highest duties is the education of her children at the time, when their mind is most amenable to instruction. A child's whole future life, to a large extent depends on the teaching, it receives in early childhood, and it is needless to say that this first foundation of education cannot be well laid by an ignorant mother.

Passage 11

The habit of reading is one of the greatest resources of mankind and we enjoy reading books that belong to us much more than if they are borrowed. A borrowed book is like a guest in the house; it must be treated with punctiliousness, with a certain considerate formality. You must see that it sustains no damage; it must not suffer while under your roof. You cannot leave it carelessly. You cannot mark it, you cannot turn down the pages, you cannot use it familiarly. And then, some day, although this is seldom done, you really ought to return it.

But, your own books belong to you, you treat them with affectionate intimacy that annihilates formality. Books are for use, not for show; you should own no book that you are afraid to mark up, or afraid to place on the table, wide open and face down. A good reason for marking favourite passages in books is that this practice enables you to remember more easily the significant sayings to refer to them quickly, and then in later years, it is like visiting a forest, where you once blazed a trail.

You have the pleasure of going over the old ground, and recalling both the intellectual scenery and your own earlier self. Everyone should begin collecting a private library in youth; the instinct of private property, which is fundamental in human being, can here be cultivated with every advantage and no evils. One should have one's own book shelves, which should not have doors, glass windows, or keys; they should be free and accessible to the hand as well as to the eye.

The best of mural decorations is books; they are more varied in colour and appearance than any wall paper they are more attractive in design, and they have the prime advantage of being separate personalities, so that if you sit alone in the room in the firelight, you are surrounded with intimate friends. The knowledge that they are there in plain view is both stimulating and refreshing. You do not have to read them all. Most of my indoor life is spent in a room containing six thousand books; and I have a stock answer to the invariable question that comes from strangers. "Have you read all of these books?" Some of them twice. This reply is both true and unexpected.

There are, of course, no friends like living, breathing corporeal men and women; my devotion to reading has never made me a recluse. How could it? Books are of the people, by the people, for the people. Literature is the immortal part of history; it is the best and most enduring part of personality. But, book-friends have this advantage over living friends; you can enjoy the most truly aristocratic society in the world, whenever you want it.

The great deads are beyond our physical reach and the great living is usually almost as inaccessible. As for our personal friends and acquaintances, we cannot always see them perchance they are asleep, or away on a journey. But, in a private library, you can at any moment converse with Socrates or Shakespeares or Dumas or Dickens or Shaw or Galsworthy. And there is no doubt that in these books you see these men at their best. They wrote for you. They 'laid themselves out', they did their ultimate best to entertain you, to make a favourable impression. You are necessary to them as an audience is to an actor, only instead of seeing them masked, you look into their inmost heart of hearts.

Passage 12

It is not a nation that counts for me, what counts for me is whether a man is good or bad; this is only criterion, which I recognise. I do not think that every one outside my nationality, whom I regard as alien, is wicked or bad; nor do I think that all men, who belong to my nationality are good. I do not adopt such ideas. If you wish to have a symbol of the true universal spirit, the spirit which in the western world has been put forth by Socrates, and which was exemplified by many others in later years–it can be sought in intellectual sincerity and universal love.

Whatever one may say of the great achievement of science and technology, and their possibilities for bringing an end to this world, the one good thing that they have done is to bring the nations, races, cultures and civilisation of the world together. They have come together—never again to part. We have to settle down and work together as member of one community. Our true nationality is the human race, the world is our home. It is the kind of society that is emerging today. We will see that the tumult, the agitation, the violence, the anger, which we come across in the world are all the birth-pangs of a new world order.

This world has progressed from a state of molton mass of fire to that of life, first of animals then of human beings. But, men have now to the state, when they are divided by doubts and discord. The revolution, however, is not complete; men have to become perfect before they can become citizens of a world community. We are accustomed to the nation-state, and also to the military method of solving our international disputes. Both have now become out of date. With all its nuclear weapons, the military method is not likely to help us in achieving our ends.

Secondly, conflicts are inevitable in the very concept of the nation-state, which our belief that we are the elect of God and designed to be the educators of the human being. We have to settle down to a situation, where we think that we are all the children of Supreme, and that every nation has a particular contribution to make to the richness, variety and the wealth of human society. It is the kind of society that we have to work for.

Passage 13

In the highest sense, and from the point of view of truth, religion is an intensely individual issue. Every man and woman must find the answer in his or her own heart. But, there is a national question also. And a national question may be deemed to be always a question of high expediency, through not a question of conviction or conscience. We must hold together and we cannot hold together only on the strength of police regulations.

An internal regulator of conduct is absolutely necessary. Will men and women be good and wise without the aid of religion, i.e. without an attempt in their lives to practise the presence of God. Have we become self-sufficient by reason of scientific knowledge and become capable of maintaining character without the sanctions and discipline of some religion or another?

I do not believe it. I believe the truth is far from it. Enlightened concern for society's welfare has not taken the place of religion as people hoped in the 19th century. Far from this having happened, what do we see in the whole world? We see the most advanced people preparing for so-called defence, new weapons that when used will surely end in disaster to mankind. Is any further demonstration necessary to show that human welfare does not appear to appeal with any degree of force as a result of greater scientific knowledge? Whatever honesty of compassion or nobility remains in the world, it is due to other cause, not the advance of science.

Forgetting world politics and thinking in terms of our own people, the enemies of good character, of humanity, of equanimity, of tolerance and kindliness, of purity of thought and rectitude, are avarice, lust and anger. Modern life has not simplified but multiplied desires and with that multiplication the greed and anger that are associated with those desires have assumed various and intensified shapes.

As desires are multiplied without the corrective of a sense of spiritual values, without developing the inner ear for the voice of conscience, knowledge of modern science or technology does not reduce either greed or lust. Indeed scientific and technological knowledge has nothing to do with these criminal disturbances of the mind. On the contrary, it finds fresh tools for evil and actually facilitates greater indulgence in all form of greed, lust and anger.

The only thing that can prevent or restrain these evils is the religious sense. Out of reverence and awe for the divine power that rules the universe, man developed a sense of spiritual values. This sense has taken the shape of civilization. It can be maintained in effective, potent condition so as to shape man's thought and action, only by religion, by the continuous practices in our lives in the presence of God.

Passage 14

Though the US prides itself of being a leader in the world community, a recent report shows that it lags far behind other industrialised countries in meeting the needs of its youngest and most vulnerable citizens. The US has a higher infant mortality rate, a higher proportion of low birth–weight babies, a smaller proportion of babies immunised against childhood diseases and a much higher rate of adolescent pregnancies. These findings, described as a "quiet crisis" requiring immediate and far-reaching action, appeared in a report prepared by a task force of educators, doctors, politicians and business people.

According to the report, a fourth of the nation's 12 million infants and toddlers live in poverty. As many as half confront risk factors that could harm their ability to develop intellectually, physically and socially. Child immunisations are too low, more children are born into poverty, more are in substandard care while their parents work and more are being raised by single parents. When taken together, these and other risk factors can lead to educational and health problems that are much harder and more costly to reverse.

The crisis begins in the womb with unplanned parenthood. Women with unplanned pregnancies are less likely to seek pre-natal care. In the US, 80% of teenage pregnancies and 56% of all pregnancies are unplanned. The problems continue after birth, where unplanned pregnancies and unstable partnerships often go hand in hand. Since 1950, the number of single parent families has nearly tripled. More than 25 per cent of all births today are to unmarried mothers. As the number of single parent families grows and more women enter the work force, infants and toddlers are increasingly in the care of people other than their parents.

Most disturbingly, recent statistics show that American parents are increasingly neglecting or abusing their children. In only 4 years from 1987-1991, the number of children in foster care increased by over 50%. Babies under the age of one are the fastest growing category of children entering foster care. The crisis affects children under the age of three most severely, the report says. Yet, it is this period—from infancy through pre school years—that sets the stage for a child's future.

Passage 15

Judiciary is the backbone of a modern civilised society. It is rather the corner-stone of a democratic system of Government. Independence of judiciary is also a modern development. From the days of summary trials of arbitrary rules till today's notion of social justice and rationality of Judgement-writing is a long journey.

The aim of independence of judiciary is to ensure supremacy of the law of a democratic state. In other words, the ultimate objective of the independence of judiciary is to make the juristic sense of the people as a whole.

Despite the fact that several precautions are taken to ensure independence of judiciary with the object of defeating the arbitrariness of man, there have been certain limitations of guaranteeing the independence of judiciary. Certain checks are provided in the procedure for appointment of judges, so that men of juristic eminence are chosen as judges. It is normal in all the democratic countries to make the appointment and removal of judges beyond the reach of the arbitrariness of the executive.

In India, there are constitutional provisions regulating the appointment and removal of judges of the High Courts and the Supreme Court. In USA, the appointment of judges to the Supreme Court is subject to the approval of the Senate. In Switzerland, judges are elected by the legislatures. The Swiss legislators show exemplary wisdom in selecting men of juristic eminence to serve as Supreme Court Judges. We can not even think of such a practice being given a trial in India. It requires the political maturity of the people and their representatives.

In India, the major part of its population is illiterate, Citizens are not capable of defending their democratic rights; rather they are unaware of them. Under these circumstances, it is essential that there must be some independent and impartial Institution capable of protecting the individuals against atrocities. If the judges are chosen for appreciation of Government Policies and their willingness to give judicial support to them, who will protect the individual from the tyranny of the State.

Passage 16

Except for countries, where minimum necessities of life are met on the whole, most of the crimes all over the world are committed due to want. Of course, the lure of anti-social activities due to want is not alike in all men at all places. Some crimes vary in intensity or magnitude in accordance with degrees of moral strength of an individual. Nevertheless, however, strong the sense of morality be, most of the people try to attack the extent social structure, when want threatens their very existence. In such a circumstances, the reasonings that they adduce, in defence of their acts. I can hardly discard in the name of humanism. They demand only the minimum right to live and on this bare human right depends the well-being of the society – the justification for its existence.

Of course, in the history of the world, millions of people have died of starvation, caught in the fangs of man-made famine. Although an extraordinarily strong sense of morality is one reason for their not making the last desperate bid for self-preservation, yet it is not the only reason. The starving people keep on losing their vitality by slow degrees and do not retain the guts for a fight.

Failing to keep up their mental equilibrium for the time being under pressure of want, men of integrity and character, who hate immorality from the cores of the hearts, also at times fall victims to criminality purely for the sake of self-preservation. What will be the effect in such circumstances; should the judges take only their crimes into account of show even a bit of callousness towards the principal of casualty? Such offenders-most of whom are more honest than the so-called well fed, well dressed honest men are thrown behind the bars as criminals only due to social disparity in production and distribution.

If anybody commits theft or robbery out of hunger or indulges in any mean act driven by any of his sensuous faculties, it is the duty of the society to know the nature of his want and then to remove it. But, should the society fail to carry out its obligations and punish him instead, taking only the magnified view of his crime, the sense of contributions for his past misdeeds gets obliterated from the mind of that criminal and there awakens a 'come what way' attitude in its place.

So, the fundamentals of solution of these various deeds centering round 'want' lie in the sound economic and social structure.

Passage 17

My uniform experience has convinced me that there is no other God than Truth. And, if every page of these chapters does not proclaim to the reader that the only means for the realisation of Truth is *Ahimsa*. I shall deem all my labour in writing these chapters to have been in vain. And, even though my efforts in this behalf may prove fruitless, let the readers know that the vehicle, not the great principle, is at fault. After all, however sincere my strivings after *Ahimsa* may have been, they have still been imperfect and inadequate, the little fleeting glimpses, therefore, that I have been able to have of Truth can hardly convey an idea of the indescribable luster of Truth, a million times more intense than that of the sun we daily see with our eyes. In fact, what I have caught, is only the faintest glimmer of that mighty elegance. But, this much I can say with assurances, as a result of all my experiments, that a perfect vision of Truth can only follow a complete realization of *Ahimsa*.

To see the universal and all-pervading Spirit of Truth face one must be able to love the meanest of creation as oneself. And a man, who aspires after that, cannot afford to keep out of any field of life. That is why, my devotion to Truth has drawn me into the field of politics; and I can say without the slightest hesitation, and yet in all humility, that those who say that religion has nothing to do with politics do not know that religion means.

Identification with everything that lives is impossible without self-purification; without self-purification the observance of these law of *Ahimsa* must remain an empty dream; God can never be realized by one, who is not pure of heart. Self-purification therefore must mean purification in all the walks of life. And purification being highly infectious, purification of oneself necessarily leads to the purification of one's surroundings. But, the path of self-purification is hand and steep. To attain to perfect purity one has to become absolutely passion free in thought, speech and action; to rise above the opposing currents of love and hatred, attachment and repulsion. I know that I have not in me as yet that triple purity, in spite of constant ceaseless striving for it. That is why, the world's praise fails to move me, indeed it very often stings me. To conquer the subtle passions seems to me to be harder far than the physical conquest of the world by the force of arms.

Ever since my return to India, I have had experiences of the dormant passions lying hidden within me. The knowledge of them has made me feel humiliated though not defeated. The experiences and experiments have sustained me and given me great joy. But, I know that I have still before me a difficult path to traverse. I must reduce myself to zero. So long as a man does not of his own free will put himself last among his fellow creatures, there is no salvation for him. *Ahimsa* is the farthest limit of humility.

Passage 18

The individual is the passenger in the chariot of the material body, and intelligence is the driver. Mind is the driving instrument, and the senses are the horses. The self is the enjoyer or sufferer in the association of the mind and senses. So, it is understood by great thinkers. The individual consciousness or the life particle is compared to the passenger because he is the chief occupant and thus enjoyer or sufferer of the journey. The horses indicate the sense that always drag the chariot of the human body to the objects of the senses. Intelligence is compared to the driver

PRECIS WRITING

because the driver employs necessary discrimination for a successful and comfortable journey. Reins are compared to the mind because they are directly connected to the horses (senses) and are guided by the driver (intelligence).

An able driver (intelligence) takes to guide the chariot properly towards its destination by discrimination. In this way, the passenger or the soul can reach the desired destination by proper use of all the faculties. On the other hand, if any of the faculties are not controlled and coordinated properly in the hierarchy, sooner or later there may be an accident.

Many spiritual traditions of the world, specifically the Vedic tradition of India have proclaimed that consciousness is a distinct reality in nature other than particles and waves. Some modern scientists have also supported this ancient wisdom. For example, Thomas Huxley remarked, "It seems to me pretty plain that there is a third thing in the universe, to wit, consciousness, which... I of either." Similar observation is echoed in the words of the renowned physicist, Eugene Wigene Wigner, who started, "There are two kinds of reality or existence; the existence of my consciousness and the reality or existence of everything else."

According to Vedanta, human activities are carried out by the will of the conscious life particle, which is then translated through the intelligence and mind to the human body. Mind interacts with body through the brain. The brain is like the central processing unit of a computer, where all signals for activities come in and also go out; but it functions according to the will of the programmer. John Eccles suggested phychon as the fundamental unit of the mind and it interacts with the brain through dendrons.

Karl Pribram has suggested that psychon is something like a Gabor function, a wave function. However, Vedanta indicates that the life particle lies beyond particle and intelligence, is a highly complex interaction and may well lie beyond the scope of modern science. It will be natural that modern biologists and biochemists should include the study of mind vs body.

Passage 19

The handy polythene bags just refuse to go. Government apathy and public connivance – (don't forget they are your life-line in the bazaar) – have perpetuated what looks innocent but poses a serious threat to the environment. Despite numerous directives by the courts to check their spread, use of plastic bags has only gone up. Plastic is non-biodegradable and 90% of its recycling in the capital takes place in unauthorized units. Sewers choked with plastics, cows munching on bags in garbage dumps, rubbish piles dotted with the colourful material and small laminated gutka and sweet pouches littering the road are common enough sights – yet, no one gives a damn.

According to scientists, the thickness of the plastic bag is important not because that reduces toxins but because the thickness makes it that much easier to collect. Thinner bags tear easily, are not handy and thus, disposal is that much quicker. Even rag pickers, who are responsible for 90% of plastic collection for recycling, won't bother with thin bags since it takes too much effort to collect a sizeable amount.

These bags cause the most problems since they lie about, clogging sewers and pipes with no state mechanism for recycling plastic in place, about 50% of it is just lying about in the city. Chemicals come out of the polythene bags over time. In case of PVC, heavy metals are emitted. These toxins contaminate ground water and agricultural land. If burnt, they release more chemicals. Other than that, our animals are at a huge risk because once consumed they line their intestines and the animals die a slow death.

Passage 20

Political films challenge the status quo and raise question about how we are controlled. They create a dissonance that makes people uncomfortable. The marketplace does not like such films; what it promotes are comfortable films, which have happy situations and reaffirm the belief of happily-ever-after. This is one of the main difficulties of making a political film. Political films also challenge establishments. I remember going to the Censor Board with *Hazaaron Khawaishein Aisi* (2005). The Bhartiya Janata Party was in power at the Centre then. They objected to my take on the declaration of the Emergency by the Congress. It was a historical fact but I was forced to change the shot. The difficulty is not in the attitude of the audience; people are constantly asking me to make a film like *Hazaaron Khawaishein Aisi*. The young people liked it. But, if I write a film like that today, no one is going to fund it.

The Supreme Court upheld the screening of *Aarakshan* in Uttar Pradesh and just the fact that it stood by the films gives hope to filmmakers. It's a wonderful thing. But, there are two sides to it. Courts have upheld the film so it will embolden film-makers but seeing the trouble that the film went through, businessman will run away from political films. The filmmaker is left to fend for himself at such troubled times.

It is those in power, who pretend to speak on behalf of people, who create problems for political cinema. The main political parties lack an agenda, and they don't win elections on their own. There are vested interests the parties can't ignore. When Sudhir Mishra made *Dharavi* in 1992, the censors didn't have a problem with it but the Shiv Sena protested. It is the duty of the state to protect you but it doesn't; everyone just stands by and watches.

It entertains such pressure groups even when a film has been passed by the censors. *Aarakshan* is a balanced film. It tries to understand the pain on both sides; it is not an anti-reservation film as it is being made out to be. The groups opposing it don't even understand what they are opposing. In a political film, everything is not said out loud in words; some things are meant to be understood. Soon, they will be telling us how to make films.

There is a big problem with the expectation that a political film is a propaganda tool and that the filmmaker will provide solutions to the problems he is showing. It is not their job to find solutions. Their job is to open minds and provoke people to recognize problems as well as spur them to think of solutions. A political film is the filmmaker's analysis of his times and his job is provocation.

Passage 21

Hampi Bazaar, an example of living heritage with hotels offering budget accommodation, restaurants serving kosher food for Jews and vegetation fare of Jain, hawkers selling harem pants and silver trinkets, all within the splendour of the ruins around the 16th century. Virupaksha temple, is now a thing of the past. In a quick operation on 29th July, the district administration of Bellary, armed with a Karnataka High Court order, brought in three bulldozers to demolish the renowned bazaar —a series of shops built over 20 years — attached to the 500-year old pavilions of the temple. "We were given less than a day to pack up. The bulldozers arrived even before dawn," says R. Suri, a shopkeeper, who has been selling silver trinkets in the bazaar for over five years.

In their zeal to complete the operation in record time, the bulldozers damaged portions of the heritage pavilions of temple, including a stone arch at its entrance. The entire stretch in front of the temple has been razed to the ground, leaving hundreds of people with no means of livelihood.

The bazaar is on a street lined with pavilions of the Virupaksha temple. They once housed of the nobles of the court of King Krishnadeva Raya of the Vijaynagar kingdom. All 26 sq km of Hampi was put on the endangered list by UNESCO's world heritage committee in 2004 on account of a bridge that was to built on the Tungabhadra river and posed a danger to the monuments in the town. The state government was forced to shift the bridge 6 km downstream. It also came up with a master plan, after which UNESCO took Hampi off the endangered list. According to the plan, shops that were illegal and posed a threat to heritage were to be phased out.

While everyone, including the encroachers, agree that the shops were illegal, the manner, in which the demolitions were carried out by the Hampi World Heritage Area Management Authority, a committee under district administration, is what has locals as well as historians fuming. "The master plan included rehabilitation of all the people operating in the bazaar, something even the High Court ordered, but the demolitions were carried out in a hurry. There should have been more discussion", says Shama Pawar, founder of Kishkindha Trust and convener of INTACH in Hampi.

Passage 22

Today, business school graduates have their sights set on international careers, and rightfully so. Yet in recent years, there has been a growing recognition that leaders operating in a global arena are facing increasingly complex challenges that call for a new and varied set of skills. The challenge confronting business schools collectively is how best to prepare future leaders for this global environment.

One important step is to have a global strategy. The MBA population is increasingly international. Most students have spent at least a few months living, studying, and working abroad. Many speak multiple languages. Schools must create a learning experience that meets the needs and expectations of this changing population. At HBS, our global strategy is to chase knowledge, where it exists in the world and bring it back to the classroom. Thirty per cent of the case studies we teach to MBA students focus on overseas business issues, and the percentage of our faculty members doing global research is rising. We invest in this strategy by operating research centres in Japan, China, India, Europe, and Latin America.

Bringing a global focus into the classroom is critical, but that alone is not sufficient. Students also need a broader set of skills to cope with the challenges of managing in a multitude of environments. Over the decades, MBA curricula have been effective as a means of transferring knowledge to students.

Yet, extensive research conducted by HBS faculty looking at dozens of MBA programmes around the world, has shown that there is a gap, when it comes time for students to apply that knowledge. We call that the 'knowing-doing' gap. It is critical for business schools to give students the tools they will need to act effectively in a global context.

Passage 23

Information technology and library services are two faces of the same coin. In a village set-up, mostly the young and the old use libraries and the middle-aged make little use of these libraries. They need job related information to update their skills and knowledge. The library and information services play a dominant role in catering to education, information and recreational requirements of society. Library is an instrument of social change.

All along, the concept of library has been associated with literacy and books, and the librarian was considered the keeper of books. Concurrent with changes in society, the concept of library has changed. It is a multimedia centre and a place for learning resources for the literate as well as the illiterate. Education is the key to individual achievement and national strength.

Integrated approach in starting at least a reading room in every hamlet is the need of the hour. Co-ordination, between the Department of Education and Panchayati Raj, in spreading the library movement is of paramount importance. Amalgamation of adult education programmes with the library programmes also needs to be given a greater thought. The school can function in a hamlet or a village serving the common needs of students and pupil.

The massive permanent building programmes for weaker sections in rural areas should earmark at least one house for every 1,000 houses or in every cluster for library purpose. The services of a retired teacher or a retired employee in that hamlet can be availed. A person residing in the same hamlet is more useful with inherent advantages than an outsider for library works as the library has to function in the evening hours and to be extended for TV and Internet operations also.

Information technology, Internet and e-commerce have great potential in catering to public needs. However, we have to be pragmatic in our approach in terms of electronic access to information in rural areas. Availability, affordability, accessibility, acceptability and sustainability of the service should also be kept in view. Once a common service place is identified, the IT based services can conveniently be cushioned on. It is hoped that the State and Central Governments will give top priority to this minimum facility.

[SSC, 2004]

PRECIS WRITING

Passage 24

Love of play is the most obvious distinguishing mark of young animals. Whether human or otherwise. In human children, this is accompanied by an inexhaustible pleasure in pretence. Play and pretence are a vital need of childhood, for which opportunity must be provided if the child is to be happy and healthy, quite independently of any further utility in these activities. There are two questions, which concern education in this connection: first, what should parents and schools do in the way of providing opportunity? And second, should they do anything more, with a view to increasing the educational usefulness of games?

Let us begin with a few words about the psychology of games. This has been exhaustively treated by Gross. There are two separate questions in this matter:

The first is as to the impulses, which produce play, the second is as to its biological utility. The second is the easier question. There seems no reason to doubt the most widely accepted theory, that in play the young of any species rehearse and practice the activities, which they will perform in earnest later on.

The play of puppies is exactly like a dog-fight, except that they do not actually bite each other. The play of kittens resembles the behaviour of cats with mice. Children love to imitate any work they have been watching such as building or digging: the more important the work seems to them. The more they like to play at it. And they enjoy anything that give them new muscular facilities such as jumping, climbing, or walking up a narrow plank-provided the task is not too difficult. But, although this accounts, in a general way for the usefulness of the play-impulses. It does not by any means cover all its manifestations, and must not for a moment be regarded as giving a psychological analysis.

Some psycho-analysts have tried to see a sexual symbolism in children's play. This, I am convinced, is utter moonshine. The main instinctive urge of childhood is not sex out the desire to become adult, or perhaps more correctly, the will to power. The child is impressed by his own weakness in comparison with older people, and he wishes to become their equal. I remember my boy's profound delight, when he realized that he would one day be a man and that I had once been a child: one could see effort being stimulated by the realization that success was possible.

From a very early age, the child wishes to do what older people do, as is shown by the practice of imitation. Older brothers and sisters are useful, because their purposes can be understood and their capacities are not so far out of reach as those of grown-up people. The feeling of inferiority is very strong in children; when they are normal and rightly educated, it is a stimulus to effort, but if they are repressed it may become a source of unhappiness.

[Civil Services (Mains), 2008]

Passage 25

Erosion in Nature is a beneficent process without which the world would have died long ago. The same process, accelerated by human mis-management, has become one of the most vicious and destructive forces that has ever been released by man. What is usually known as 'geological erosion' or 'denudation' is a universal phenomenon, which through thousands of years, has carved the earth into its present shape. Denudation is an early and important process in soil formation, whereby the original rock material is continuously broken down and sorted out by wind and water until it becomes suitable for colonisation by plants. Plants, by the binding effects of their roots, by the protection they afford against rain and wind and by the fertility they impart to the soil, bring denudation almost to a standstill. Everybody must have compared the rugged and irregular shape of bare mountain peaks, where denudation is still active with the smooth and harmonious curves of slopes that have long been protected by a mantle of vegetation. Nevertheless, some slight denudation is always occurring.

As each superficial film of plant-covered soil becomes exhausted, it is removed by rain or wind, to be deposited mainly in the rivers and seas, and a corresponding thin layer of new soil forms by slow withering of the underlying rock. The earth is continuously discarding its old, worn-out skin and renewing its living sheath of soil from the dead rock beneath. In this way, an equilibrium is reached between denudation and soil formation so that, unless the equilibrium is disturbed, a mature soil preserves a more or less constant depth and character indefinitely. The depth is sometimes only a few inches, occasionally several feet, but within, it lies the whole capacity of the earth to produce life. Below that thin layer comprising the delicate organism known as soil, is a planet as lifeless as the moon.

The equilibrium between denudation and soil formation is easily disturbed by the activities of man. Cultivation, deforestation or the destruction of natural vegetation by grazing or other means, unless carried out according to certain immutable conditions imposed by each region, may so accelerate denudation that the soil, which would normally be washed or blown away in a century, disappears within a year or even within a day. But, no human ingenuity can accelerate the soil-renewing process from lifeless rock to an extent at all comparable to the acceleration of denudation.

Passage 26

"The teacher, like the artist, the philosopher, and the man of letters, can only perform his work adequately, if he feels himself to be an individual directed by an inner creative impulse, not dominated and fettered by an outside authority. It is very difficult in this modern world to find a place for the individual. He can subsist at the top as a dictator in a totalitarian state or a plutocratic magnate in a country of large industrial enterprises, but in the realm of the mind it is becoming more and more difficult to preserve independence of the great organized forces that control the livelihoods of men and women. If the world is not to lose the benefit to be derived from its best minds, it will have to find some method of allowing them scope and liberty in spite of organization. This involves a deliberate restraint on the part of those, who have power, and a conscious realization that there are men to whom free scope must be afforded.

Renaissance Popes could feel in this way towards Renaissance artists, but the powerful men of our day seem to have more difficulty in feeling respect for exceptional genius. The turbulence of our times is inimical to the flowering of culture. The man in the street is full of fear, and therefore unwilling to tolerate freedoms for which he sees no need. Perhaps, we must wait for quieter times before the claims of civilization can again override the claims of party spirit. Meanwhile, it is important that, some at least continue to realize the limitations of what can be done by organization. Every system should allow loopholes and exceptions, for if it does not, it will in the end, crush all that is best in man."

[CAPF, 2009]

Passage 27

There are, of course, many motivating factors in human behaviour, but we would claim that nationalism is particularly worthy of study. Why is it particularly significant? Its significance lies in its power to arouse passionate loyalties and hatreds that motivate acts of extreme violence and courage; people kill and die for their nations.

Of course, it is not alone in this: people are driven to similar extremes to protect their families, their extended families or 'tribes', their home areas with their populations and their religious groups and the holy places and symbols of their religions. However, these other loyalties are often rather easier to understand than nationalism. Parents making supreme sacrifices for their children can be seen as obeying a universal imperative in life forms, the instinct to protect one's own genetic material.

This instinct can also be seen at work in the urge to protect one's extended family: but then the extended family, or on a slightly larger scale the 'tribe' can also be seen, in perhaps the majority of circumstances, in which human beings have existed, as essential for the survival of the individual and the nuclear family. The nation is not generally essential to survival in this way. Of course, if the entire nation were to be wiped out, the individuals and their families would die, but the disappearance of the nation as a social unit would not in itself pose a threat to individual or family survival; only if it were to be accompanied by ethnic violence or severe economic collapse and such cataclysmic events are not an inevitable consequence of the loss of political independence.

Devotion to one's religious group, like support for one's nation, is much less obviously to the individual's advantage than is defence of the family, but we would maintain that it can be more comprehensible than nationalism. It can be seen in ideological terms as the defence of a world views, and its symbols against views is olds, which are considered to be fundamental erroneous and which, if successful, would force the conquered to act in ways abhorrent to then beliefs.

While the defence of one's nation has often been seen as the defence of one's religion, and while modern hostilities between nations frequently do have a religious dimension, there are many serious national, conflicts that have no clear religious element; the two world wars were fought in Europe with Catholic France, Protestant Britain, and Orthodox Russia opposing Germany with its mixed Catholic and Protestant population.

Thus, while modern nationalisms may be linked to religion, many cases can be found without any clear religious dimension. Not only do modern nationalisms lack a religious element; there is often (to outsiders) no obvious ideological difference between rival nations. Hence, while defence of one's nation, religion can be seen as defence of an entire system of beliefs.

[Civil Services (Mains), 2009]

Passage 28

In the many respects, 'Sakuntala' is comparable to the more idyllic comedies of Shakespeare, and Kanva's hermitage is surely not far from the Forest of Arden. The plot of the play, like many of Shakespeare's plots, depends much on happy chances and on the super-natural, which, of course, was quite acceptable to the audience for which Kalidasa wrote. Its characters, even to the minor ones, are happily delineated individuals. Kalidasa makes no pretence to realism, but his dialogue is fresh and vigorous.

In fact, the dialogue of the better Sanskrit plays generally seems based on vernacular, and is full of idiomatic expressions. Indian playgoers did not demand the conflict of feelings and emotions, which is the chief substance of serious European drama, but Kalidasa was quite capable of portraying such conflict effectively. His beauties and merits are tarnished by any translation, but few, who can read him in the original would doubt that, both as poet and dramatist, he was one of the great men of the world.

There were many other dramatists. Sudraka, probably Kalidasa's approximate contemporary, has left only one play 'The Little Clay Cart' (Mrcchakatika). This is the most realistic of Indian dramas, unravelling a complicated story, rich in humour and pathos and crowded with action, of the love of a poor Brahman, Carudatta, for the virtuous courtesan Vasantasena; this story is interwoven with one of political intrigue, leading up to the overthrow of the wicked king Palaka, and the play contains a vivid trial scene, after which the hero is saved from execution at the last moment.

Visakhadatta (6th century) was the dramatist of politics. His only complete surviving play, 'The Minister's Signet Ring' (Mudraraksasa), deals with the schemes of the wily Canakya to foil the plots of Raksasa, the minister of the last of the Nandas and to place Candragupta Maurya firmly on the throne.

Second only to Kalidasa in the esteem of the critics was Bhavabhuti, who lived at Kanyakubja in the early 8th century. Three of his plays survive : 'Malati and Madhava', 'The Deeds of the Great Hero' (Mahaviracarita), and 'The Later Deeds of Rama' (Uttararamacarita).

[Civil Services (Mains), 2010]

Passage 29

Nations are built by the imagination and untiring enthusiastic efforts of generations. One generation transfers the fruits of its toil to another, which then takes forward the mission. As the coming generation also has its dreams and aspirations for the nation's future, it therefore adds something from its side to the national vision, which the next generation strives hard to achieve. This process goes on and the nation climbs steps of glory and gains higher strength.

Any organisation, society, or even a nation without a vision is like a ship cruising on the high seas without any aim or direction. It is the clarity of national vision, which constantly drives the people towards the goal.

Our last generation, the glorious generation of freedom fighters led by Mahatma Gandhi and many others, set for the nation a vision of Free India. This was the first vision, set by the people for the nation. It, therefore, went deep into the minds and hearts of the masses and soon became the great inspiring and driving force for the people to collectively plunge into the struggle for freedom movement. The unified dedicated efforts of the people from every walk of life won freedom for the country.

The next generation has put India strongly on the path of economic, agricultural and technological development. But, India has stood too long in the line of developing nations. Let us, collectively, set the second national vision of Developed India. It means the major transformation of our national economy to make it one of the largest economies in the world; where the countrymen live well above the poverty line, their education and health is of a high standard, national security is reasonably assured, and the core competence in certain major areas gets enhanced significantly so that the production of quality goods, including export, rises and brings all-round prosperity for the countrymen.

Passage 30

We all know, what we mean by a 'good' man. The ideally good man does not drink or smoke, avoids bad language, converses in the presence of men only exactly as he would if there were ladies present, attends church regularly, and holds the correct opinions on all subjects. He has a wholesome horror of wrong doing, and realizes that it is our painful duty to castigate Sin. He has a still greater horror of wrong thinking and considers it the business of the authorities to safeguard the young against those, who question the wisdom of the views generally accepted by middle-aged successful citizens.

Apart from his professional duties, he spends much time in good works. He may encourage patriotism and military training; he may promote industry, sobriety and virtue among wage-earners and their children by seeing to it that failures in these respects receive due punishment. Above all, his 'morals', in the narrow sense, must be irreproachable.

It may be doubted whether a 'good' man, in the above sense, does, on the average, any more good than a 'bad' man. I mean by a 'bad' man the contrary of what we have been describing. A 'bad' man is one, who is known to smoke and to drink occasionally, and even to say a bad word, when someone treads on his toe. His conversation is not always such as could be printed, and he sometimes spends fine Sundays out-of-doors instead of at church.

Some of his opinions are subversive; for instance, he may think that if you desire peace you should prepare for peace, not for war. Towards wrong doing, he takes a scientific attitude, such as he would take towards his motor-car if it misbehaved; he argues that sermons and prison will no more cure vice than men a broken tyre. In the matter of wrong thinking, he is even more perverse. He maintains that what is called 'wrong thinking' is simply thinking, and what is called 'right-thinking' is repeating words like a parrot. [CAPF, 2011]

CHAPTER 5

Letter Writing

The success of any relationship depends on healthy communication. Letters are the best mode of expression of one's feelings. The language used by us reveals our motives and emotions we wish to convey to our friends and near and dear ones. Art of writing letters has not lost its role in promoting healthy relationships inspite of the development of modern information technology.

Invention of telecommunications like telephone, fax, e-mail, e-commerce and even video-phone has not diminished the art of writing letters. With the help of letters a person can be just what he wants to be, a good salesman, a charming friend or a gracious host.

It is true that everyone likes to receive letters but for various reasons no one likes to write them. In modern age, we find hardly a man who can sit down and write a wonderful letter. In fact, writing letters should be made part of our daily life. The principle behind writing letters comprises two important facts. One should be timely and one should be oneself.

It may be a personal, official or a business letter. Applications need more attention of the writer because while writing application you expect that your request will be granted by him for whom the application is addressed.

Kinds of Letters

For the convenience of the students, letters should be placed under the following heads :

Informal

1. **Personal Letters** Personal letters come under the category of informal or social letters. These letters include private letters to relations, friends and notes of invitation.

Formal

2. **Official Letters** Official letters are addressed to newspapers, leaders and high officials.

LETTER WRITING

3. **Business Letters** Business letters are addressed to business houses, managers of the firms, suppliers and customers. Sometime, they are in the form of circulars also.
4. **Applications** Applications are addressed to higher officials designed to achieve a specific object.

Parts of a Letter

Every letter has four important parts. *These are :*

1. **The Heading** The heading of any letter consists of the writer's address and date. *e.g.*

    23, Vasundhara Apartments
    Chandigarh
    2nd April, 20XX

2. **Salutation** or form of address will depend on the kind of letter.

    Informal

    Personal letters
    (i) To members of family
        Dear mother, My dear father
    (ii) To friends
        Dear Rohan, Dear Vishal

    Formal
    (i) Business letters
        Dear Sir, Dear Sirs, Dear Madam
    (ii) Official letters/Applications
        Sir/Madam

3. **Body of the Letters** These are the contents of a letter that form the main theme of the subject of any letter.

4. **Courteous Leave Taking**

    Informal

    Personal letters
    (i) Family members
        With regards/With love,　　　　　　　　　　　　　　Yours affectionately
    (ii) Friends
        With best wishes,　　　　　　　　　　　　　　　　　Yours sincerely

    Formal
    (i) Business letters
        Thanking you, awaiting an early reply,　　　　　　　Yours faithfully
    (ii) Official letters/Applications
        Thanking you, Yours truly/　　　　　　　　　　　　Yours faithfully

Personal Letters

1. **Write a letter to your father who is annoyed with you because of your misbehaviour to your relatives.**

   115/B, Ganga Nagar
   Lucknow

   5th July, 20XX

   My dear father

   I am writing this letter because I have no courage to face you. Therefore, through this letter, I seek pardon of you for the misbehaviour to my uncle and aunt last night.

   I am sure that you will agree with me that their remarks about my being without employment were undesirable. You know that I am very sensitive about this issue. Inspite of my having completed B.Ed, I have not been able to get a suitable job. I am always under stress and it is very considerate of you and dear mother to encourage me. Your very attitude has sustained me during the last two years. But the remarks of my uncle and aunt hit me, where I felt hurt most. I was provoked into using disrespectful words which was never my intention.

   Now I realise that I should have exercised control over my feelings. I was unable to do it and it is quite distressing to me. I know they must have left with very poor opinion about me. They left dining table and went to bed without food. In fact all of us did not take food that night. I am aware that you and mother must have had to cut a sorry figure because of my thoughtless behaviour. I am sure that you understand the feelings under the influence of which I uttered undesirable words.

   I assure you earnestly that I will not let such ugly incident happan in future. I am also writing to uncle Raghu to seek pardon from him.

   With regards,

   Yours affectionately
   XYZ

2. **Write a letter of sympathy to your friend on his failure in the entrance test for CPMT.**

   15, Rohtak Road
   Hissar

   10th August, 20XX

   My dear Ajay

   I was shocked not to find your roll number among the successful candidates in the entrance examination of CPMT. I could not believe and was distressed beyond words. It is still unbelievable that a student with 80% of marks in U.P. Board Examination could not clear the test. All of us thought it an easy cake walk for you. But what is more surprising is the success of those candidates who hardly stand any comparison with you in academic field.

   You have had the best of guidance at the Institute of repute in the capital which has a splendid record of turning out hundreds of students successful. I remember you were confident too. But in the age of cut throat competition, all results are uncertain.

LETTER WRITING

Notwithstanding that you have been studying 16 hours a day, your failure is beyond the comprehension of your friends. You had a dream to become a doctor and share the lucrative practice of your father. I am afraid your father must have been disappointed. However, I have some other idea about this unfortunate incident. It was your first chance. If you persevere and avail yourself of another opportunity, success is bound to come to you. Therefore, please don't take this failure as the end of the road. Competitive examinations have different criterion for success. It is just by slight margin, I believe, you seem to have missed mark. Please keep on your sustained efforts and wait for success.

May God bless you with success!

With best wishes,

Yours sincerely
XYZ

3. **Write a letter of congratulations to your cousin on his success in Punjab Civil Services examination**

229/C, Defence Colony
Allahabad

29th September, 20XX

My dear Rajat

Your father conveyed to us on telephone the news of your success in the PCS Examination just in the morning. We all were thrilled. You deserve every credit for this success. Please accept our congratulations on your distinguished success. It has really added a feather in the cap of our family. We all are proud of you.

You have been burning midnight oil for the last three years. Inspite of your failure last year you did not lose heart. In this direction your father and mother have also played a very supportive role. They kept up your morale and you persevered till you have achieved your goal.

Please don't think this success to be the last step in your life. You have to go a long way. You must set your sight on qualifying IAS for which you are quite capable. This is your first stepping stone towards the success in Indian Civil Services. There are still many miles to go for you. You are young and the age is on your side. We come of illustrious family and you must prove it by aspiring for civil services. At this stage you are in the right frame of mind. You are dedicated and devoted to your studies. Any laxity on your part may prove detrimental to higher goals of life.

I congratulate you once more and pray to God for your further success.

With best wishes and regards to uncle and aunt.

Yours affectionately
XYZ

4. Imagine you are visiting your native village/town after an interval of ten years. Write a letter to a friend describing the changes which have meanwhile taken place.

17/19A, Kavi Nagar
Ajmer
24th February, 20XX

Dear Rahul

I received your letter last month. I am sorry for the belated reply. The fact is that I had gone to my village in Punjab to attend the marriage of my cousin. You will not believe how thrilled I was to visit my native village after 10 years.

My village, situated at a distance of ten miles from Patiala did not look familiar to me. There was tremendous change in all respects. Today it is well connected by mettled roads and public transport system. As I stepped down at Patiala bus-stand, there was a bus bound for my village waiting just near by. Within 20 minutes I reached my village. It was quite surprising. As I took a road to enter my village, I caught sight of a degree college, a co-educational institute serving the needs of thirty odd villages of the Tahsil.

Young men and women were dressed in modern clothes and moving freely here and there. The electricity and telephone wires gave me the impression that the villages are really developing. In every home I found Cable T.V. and telephone facility. Even there was a small book store with latest magazines, newspapers and books for the students.

It being the month of February, wheat crop and mustard crop with yellow flowers provided bright outlook to the background. The sight of lush green fields reminded me of the blessings of nature. Life appeared to be moving at leisure. There was no hurry and worry, hustle and bustle of the commercial cities. Even life up to 10 o'clock in the village was marked with gaiety and laughter.

Ten years back when I visited the village, it was just a sleepy hamlet even at six p.m. Life was not that much attractive. I was amazed at the sea change that has taken over the village. If the development continues at this pace, our countryside will be worth inhabiting for all those desirous of peaceful and healthful living.

With best wishes,
Yours sincerely
XYZ

5. Write a letter to your friend explaining why you could not attend interview at Lucknow on account of a political rally. Describe how political rallies are the bane of Indian Politics.

21, Central Market
Moradabad
10th May, 20XX

My dear Raman

It was a great shock for me for not having been able to attend interview for the Subordinate Services Examination. Unfortunately, on the day of my interview a political rally by BSP leader Mayawati was to be held. For this purpose private buses and public transport were engaged for taking to Lucknow those associated with the party.

When I reached the station, I found that all the compartments of Nauchandi Express were over crowded. Even the reservation compartments were forcibly occupied. The people were huddled together and no one was allowed to enter. All were without tickets. Many genuine passengers were running in panic here and there. The policemen were looking on helplessly. All our entreaties fell on deaf years of the station authorities. The political leaders of the parties had occupied air conditioned compartments. If any genuine passenger tried to enter already over crowded compartments, they were resisted and threatened by the political leaders leading the flocks of people to Lucknow.

Political rallies have been in vogue since the Congress rule. Transporters, truck owners & railway department served the cause of party in power. The same tradition is still continuing. The whole city and the station were under virtual siege. Rallies are held by the political leaders and parties to show off their popularity. Those attending rallies are provided with free journey and free food. The leaders of the political parties in power show off their clout they enjoy with the administration. Even the railway personnel were mishandled by the rallyists. There was total chaos in the city and on the station. Slogan shouting mob posed danger to the safety of peaceful citizens.

The effects of such rallies need not be mentioned because they are well known. There is loss of crores of Rupees all over the country, the business and industrial units almost come to a stand still. I can well understand how the political parties are behaving irresponsibly, using the state money and machinery. What a corruption!

I do not know whom to approach for the redressal of my grievances. Will the SSC be considerate enough to announce another date for interview?

With best wishes,

Yours sincerely
XYZ

6. **Write a letter to your mother about your intention of marrying out of your caste without any dowry.**

10, Old Hostel
City Medical College
Fatehgarh

10th August, 20XX

Dear Mother

Last time when I visited Jhansi I gave a hint to you that you should not accept any proposal for my marriage. I did not have the courage to tell you that I had developed a liking for a colleague of mine, working with me in the hospital. You would like her most when you meet her. She has amiable nature and belongs to a status family like ours. The only drawback from your point of view may be that she belongs to Brahmin caste. To me, caste is no qualification for a compatible marriage. It is the character & the value based life that determine the success in marriage.

Moreover, I have made up my mind not to accept dowry. The reasons are obvious. She is as much qualified as I am. Her parents have already spent a lot of money on her education. Taking of dowry has no justification. Even otherwise you know my views on accepting dowry. I know that the questions of caste and dowry might be disappointing to you but it is I who have to decide about my future and career prospects. Both of us can earn our livelihood honourably supplementing family income. After proper experience we can run our own nursing-home. I know all these considerations have no force for you and dear father because you treat marriage as a social event. But for me its is a personal decision. My choice of a life partner is entirely my own because it is I who have to lead a life with her.

I don't mean to hurt your sentiments. I have conveyed my views about my marriage. If you agree her parents can approach you with the proposal for marriage. Otherwise please don't think of my marriage with any other girl. You suggested few names but I was not in a position to refuse to your face.

With regards to dear father and love to Reena and Varun.

Yours affectionately
XYZ

7. You are Kuku Gidhwani. Write a letter to your pen friend in America about the issue of reservation for women in Indian legislatures.

10, Bandra Road
Mumbai

10th June, 20XX

My dear Andy

You have shown curiosity about the ongoing controversy about Women's Reservation Bill in our Parliament. It is quite amusing farce that politicians have made of this serious issue. You know that atrocities on women is a major problem faced by women all over the world. Indian record in this regard has been a paradox. While there are women Prime Ministers, Chief Ministers and women holding administrative posts, they are still a neglected lot in India. They are subjected to domestic violence and harassment on the roads and their places of work.

Now the reservation for women in the legislature is hanging fire since 1996. Every time the Women's Reservation Bill come up for discussion in the Parliament, the political parties shy away from it on one pretext or the other. It is an irony that every party has welcomed it in the hope that other parties will scuttle it. The BJP insists on consensus knowing well there will be no consensus. The Congress is ready to support it knowing that other smaller and regional parties want reservations for SC, ST and backward class women. And it will not happen.

We have already witnessed a great success of reservation of women in the village panchayats. It is not understood why political parties in India are against the reservation of women in Centre and State legislatures. Indian women have been fortunate enough to enjoy equality with men at least on paper. If we study the history of the world, we will find that women in Switzerland got the right to vote only twenty years ago. Even women in England had to struggle for their political rights. Muslim countries in the Persian Gulf have come forward to give rights to their women very belatedly.

In India, women are free to join any political party and contest elections from any part of the country. However, Women's Reservation Bill will make it mandatory that one-third of the total seats should be reserved for women candidates. It is not in the interest of smaller parties because most of the parties have even less than 5-10 of their representatives. Marxist party, Socialist party of Mulayam Singh, RJD party of Laloo and Shiv Sena are the main objectors to the reservation of women.

In my opinion reservation of women in Parliament or State legislature is just playing with the idea of emancipation of women. Reservation or no reservation, emancipation of women lies within women themselves. Reservation policy is not going to solve the problem of dowry and inferior status of women in the field of marriage. No legal remedy, whatsoever, has been able to curb dowry evil in India. Dowry deaths have been on the increase even among the highly educated women because there has not been any change in the psyche of male dominating society.

Therefore, I personally believe that no amount of higher education, equality for women enshrined in our constitution has been able to confer equality in practice. Women have to wage struggle to achieve equality and awaken the concept of equality in men. They must begin it first with their parents and then parents-in-law and society. Awakening among women is the need of the day.

With best wishes,

Yours sincerely
Kuku Gidhwani

8. **Write a letter of condolence to your friend on the death of his father.**

260/H1, Deep Nagar
Bilaspur

5th January, 20XX

My dear Ritu

I am really shocked to learn of your dear father's death in the prime of life. The news was conveyed to me by your cousin who happened to meet me at the bus stand. It was incredible as to how it could happen to a soul like you.

The news is shocking and heart rending. The pity is that your education is still not complete and the responsibility of looking after the family has befallen you. Your elder sister is married but your younger brother is too young to look after himself. You have dual responsibility at this stage of life. Apart from this, there is a financial aspect. It is always the case when the only earning member of the family passes away.

In my opinion you should take up a job only after graduation. There is one year left for completing your B.Com. degree. Please don't give up study at this stage. For a brilliant student like you there should not be any problem to get a job. You can acquire higher education while earning. When I told this news to my father, he was moved and promised to do something for you after you have completed your study. Meanwhile, I am at your service and you can bank upon me for anything. I shall never disappoint you. I shall be rather glad to be of some help to you.

I will visit you next week and discuss the matter in detail. Kindly convey our heart felt condolence to your mother & other members of the family. My father has asked me to convey his profound sense of loss on the death of your dear father. May God rest his soul in eternal peace.

Sharing your grief,

Yours sincerely
XYZ

9. **You were travelling from Delhi to Amritsar by Frontier Mail. Four bogies of the train caught fire. You were a witness to the tragedy. Describe your traumatic experience to your mother.**

36, Lawrence Road
Amritsar

16th May, 20XX

My dear mom

I telephoned you from Ludhiana at 5 a.m. to inform you that I was safe and sound. Now in the letter I want to tell you how I had to go through trauma of fire and death that I witnessed with my own eyes.

At 4.00 in the morning the train suddenly came to a halt around 10 km ahead of Ludhiana. We heard heart-rending cries of the passengers. I, alongwith other passengers, rushed down the train. It was a horrible sight to see the four compartments burning and people struggling to come out. The passages of the four compartments were blocked by the luggage of the unauthorised passengers travelling in the compartment without reservations. It was because of the agility of the military personnel travelling by that train that saved the rest of the train from catching fire. Army-men pulled the chain and separated the compartments on fire from the rest of the train.

Meanwhile the villagers, the passengers and the railway staff from Ludhiana began rescue operations with lightning speed. By that time huge loss of life and material had been caused. I went into the coach on fire and helped a number of people escape. It was in the fit of horror that I flung the children to the crowd standing on the track. Most of the deaths were caused because the exit of the compartments were blocked. It was difficult to believe that children, women and the old were charred to death. Passengers were searching for their relatives by examining each and every limb among the charred remains. The fire was so intense that the bodies were burnt beyond recognition. Even relations were finding it difficult to identify the bodies.

Many theories are afloat about the cause of the fire. But it is too early to say anything. One fact is still hurting me. Many lives could have been saved. But Indian trains are without extinguishers and emergency exits. Heat expanded the doors which got stuck. Secondly, railway authorities do not impose the rules strictly about carrying stoves, cylinders, fuel etc. I feel that this tragedy is just caused by man's indifference to the safety of others.

The role of army and the villagers was commendable which kept the number of casualties to the minimum. It is estimated that 40 passengers died in the devastating fire. The dead bodies wrapped in white sheets were horrible sight to look at.

There are many heart-rending stories of the individual passengers that I will not be able to forget throughout my life. The cause of fire has not been ascertained so far. But how does it matter to those who have suffered irreparable loss in the tragedy?

With love,

Yours affectionately
XYZ

LETTER WRITING 237

10. **Reproduce a letter that your pen friend in New York wrote to you sometime back about the Occupy Wall Street Movement.**

67, Pine Walk
New Jerssy

10th November, 20XX

Dear friend

I agree with you that what you are reading about Occupy Wall Street Movement is truth but it is not the whole truth. First, there is no need to entertain alarmist views of the economic slow down affecting America. The protestors are none else but those who are trying to focus attention on increasing inequality generated by croxy capitalism. The alarmist view that the protestors are out to destroy American political and economic system is baseless.

Over here we do not think of dispensing with capitalist system, though there is wide spread resentment against croxy capitalism. The point of the Occupy Wall Street revolution has been well brought round to our prolic-makers. The slogan of the Occupy Movement that we are 99 per cent is not lost upon them. What's more, the Occupy Wall Street Movement might have died in infancy but for the thoughtless strategy of the police officials to deal with the protestors. However, one thing is certain that the occupy protests are not anti-capitalists. Asian countries obsessed with the philosophy of socialism would not perceive the mind set of American have nots. They are not campaigning against capitalism.

They are not just rabble rousers at Occupy Wall Street. However, one fact cannot be ignored that there is something wrong with a system, if it allows one to grab more than one's fair share. Too much inequality can harm the efficient operation of the economy and result in poor economic growth. Yes, there is potential threat to our capitalist system. But those protestors are not anarchists, not at all. So what you are reading in newspapers is a distorted view of our economic crisis. There are crisis but there is no break down of economic system on capitalism. Rather these protests are a wakeup call to oust crony from captalism and restore equality and economic justice right not.

It is good to hear that you, in India, are doing well and am sure that your country is well equipped to meet with the situation.

With best wishes,

Yours sincerely
XYZ

11. **Write a letter to your father about your painful experience of college hostel life.**

22/9, Raj Nagar
Jabalpur

7th July, 20XX

Dear father

I have been allotted a seat in hostel. I had not to face any problem in getting seat in the hostel because students were admitted to hostel only on the basis of merit list prepared on the basis of last examination results.

The early days in college were quite taxing because of ragging of the freshers. Ragging in college did not pose any serious problem because freshers moved in groups. Even then the seniors indulged in every kind of nuisance making life intolerable for fresh entrants.

For the last two days, I have been in real trouble. Since I joined hostel, I have not been able to pass a single hour in my room. When I returned to my room two days back after attending college, I was shocked to find that my room had been ransacked. All my clothes, time piece and eatables were missing. I was stunned. There was nobody to tell me what had actually happened. Moreover I could not muster up courage to report the matter to the warden. I was warned that if I did so, I would be thrashed. Even my room partner did not help me in the crisis. He appeared to be in league with the other inmates of the hostel. I was in a dilemma as to what to do. Even money lying in my box was missing. It was raining very hard that day. There was no help from any quarter. The warden also passed by me watching my plight. I was in a fit of rage and lost control over myself at mid night.

Therefore, I had no alternative but to face the challenge on my own. I went to the residence of the Principal and narrated to him what had happened to me. Immediately, the Principal called the warden and ordered him to get my goods restored in no time and punish the guilty. He warned him that if this kind of ragging went on, the students would be scared to join College. He also reprimanded the warden. Only then all my things were recovered at 2 a.m. It is a most painful experience of my life. However, since then ragging has ended both in college and hostel premises. Now every thing is peaceful. There is no problem and I have started devoting time to study.

With regards to respected mother and love to Ritu and Raja.

Yours affectionately
XYZ

12. **A friend of yours has gone abroad. He has read in newspaper reports about frequent incidents of violence in India. Write a letter to him what you feel about these incidents.**

290, Preetam Nagar
Bhopal

13th December, 20XX

Dear Raman

I have heard from you after quite long time. You are away but your heart seems to be in India. It is obvious through your letter that you are much concerned about the reports of violence in our country. No doubt, there are frequent incidents of violent terrorism and communal riots. But they are confined to limited pockets of the country at present. For example Kashmir is torn with violence as a result of cross border terrorism. North east of India is afflicted with separatist movements encouraged by China.

States of UP and Bihar suffer from violence because of communalism and casteism. In fact violence is gradually getting hold of the whole of India. Terrorism seems to have become the destiny of India. As you know, foreign powers are interested in break-up of the country to serve their own ends. Since you left India terrorism and violence have been on the rise. Now these forces are operating throughout the country. Bomb blasts, killings, derailments, kidnappings are just the manifestations of larger evil of terrorism and political motives.

It is sheer folly to blame foreign countries. One must keep one's house in order to keep out siders from interference. For the last over 65 years, India has degenerated from United India to a country where separatists group, political parties and religious leaders are busy with their destructive activities. Our political system has, ofcourse, endured the onslaught of the violent and divisive forces. In the process, the erosion of democratic values has been continuously taking place. Election of incompetent political leaders and their unethical strategy to grab power has demoralised a common peaceful citizen.

The need of the hour is to look beyond the political power at the cost of the unity of the country. Country is on the brink of social disaster. The remedy lies only with the political leaders. A common man is quite hopeful of some sagacious leader emerging out of chaos to save the country from the perils of disintegration. Your concern about our country deserves appreciation. But rest assured that the largest chunk of population cherish peace and prosperity in the country. As long as the majority strive for peace, no harm can come to the country.

I hope you are doing well in your studies. I look forward to your visit. When you come we will discuss these matters in details.

With best wishes,
Yours sincerely
XYZ

13. **Your brother has joined a private company at Srinagar. All of you are worried because of the menace of terrorism. Advise your brother to take precautionary measures for his personal security.**

1002/H, Trinagar
Ganga Nagar

10th January, 20XX

Dear Raj

Last night all of us were disturbed when the news was telecast about the massacre in the Lal Chowk of Srinagar by militants. Mother was greatly disturbed. It is good that you have got a very lucrative job and we are proud of you in this regard. It is not easy to get a job in GE, one of the first 20 multinational companies. The prospects are very bright.

At the same time the family over here is torn with anxiety. It is difficult to say whether it is a right step on our part to permit you to join your first posting at Srinagar. The conditions are getting tougher day by day. No part of Kashmir is unaffected by militancy. Newspapers are full of news of bomb blasts, attack on security personnel, killing of innocent men, women and children of one community. I myself had been in Srinagar for two years. I can well realise how life is insecure and fragile. Any thing can happen to any one. Terrorists choose their soft targets at random and spray bullets to cause killing and panic among the residents.

I once again advise you to take up accommodation in the company guest house where security arrangements are supposed to be foolproof. Living in a private hotel is very risky. You can't distinguish between a terrorist and a tourist. One is likely to fall prey to the designs of the militants. Life in private hotel is marked with anxiety. In a company guest house you will be living among familiar faces and the security arrangements are supposed to be strict. Moreover don't try to move out after dusk and also don't mix with strangers. One is not sure about the identity of the strangers.

Terrorists are lurking in every nook and corner of the city. Please never venture out for any excursion unless you are accompanied by security men employed by the company. I hope you will make note of my advice and comply with it to the letter.

With love from parents and me,

Yours affectionately
XYZ

14. **You have completed M.Sc. (Chemistry) and your father is posted in Bombay. Inform him of your splendid success in the examination seeking his advice on taking up suitable career.**

   250/C, Yamuna Nagar
   Raipur

   19th June, 20XX

   Dear father

   I informed you on telephone about my success in M.Sc. (Chemistry) last night. Thank you for your congratulations and blessings. Father, I understand very well that I could not have achieved the success with distinction without your trust in me and moral support which you and mother have always extended to me.

   Now I would like to seek your advice as to which career I should take up now. Very few options are available. I should join some manufacturing organisation as a chemist. Otherwise I have also an option to undertake sugar or alcohol technology training at Kanpur. This is highly valued qualification in sugar and alcohol manufacturing industry. By obtaining this degree I am sure I can establish myself in private sector very securely.

   It is a matter of two years of education more. Of course, financial aspect has to be considered by you. I will not like to be a burden any more on family resources. I am aware that we are planning to marry Ritu this winter, Raj is also a brilliant student who has an ambition to become a doctor. I am aware of the financial constraints. Therefore, I have to act as you think best in the interest of the family. If you wish me to share your financial burden, I can also get a job in Rampur Distillery as a chemist right now.

   I hope you will guide me in order that we all may be a happy family in the long run.

   With regards from Ritu and Raj,

   Yours affectionately
   XYZ

15. **Write a letter to a friend who has been involved in an accident.**

   20, Mathura Road
   Aligarh

   25th November, 20XX

   Dear Mohan

   Yesterday I received a telephone from my brother informing me that you, your wife and your son met with an accident while travelling by car to Agra. It was indeed a shock and I could not sleep the whole night. I had asked my brother to keep me informed about your condition from time to time. I think he must be by your bed side in the hospital.

   This morning I felt immensely relieved to hear from my brother that all of you are out of danger. In fact no serious injury has occurred. Mohit, your son must be in trauma at the horrible experience he went through in the accident. We should be grateful to God that all of you had a providential escape with no serious injury. My brother told me that your car collided with a truck that was standing by the road side. Trying to save a village boy running across the road, your car skidded off the road and hit the truck. You have been fortunate enough because the truck was not moving. I can guess that your car must have been slightly damaged.

It was also nice of the villagers to put you all in a tractor trolly and admit you to a near by nursing home of the city. This timely help has come as a miracle that saved all of you. I must say that the positive attitude of the villagers helped you to get emergency treatment so quickly. We may just call it a divine help.

My brother gave me detail of the accident. My mother and I will be leaving tomorrow to see for ourselves how you are improving. If you need anything from our side, please don't hesitate to tell my brother.

Praying to God for your speedy recovery.

Yours sincerely
XYZ

16. Write a letter to your landlord requesting him for urgent repairs of the building you are living in.

20, Patel Enclave
Bhav Nagar

10th May, 20XX

Dear Mr Bansal

It is long since I heard from you. I hope you have been getting rent regularly through my bankers every month. I am sure you have no complaint on this account.

When last you visited Bhav Nagar, you promised to get the house repaired, that is in very aweful condition. The roofs are leaking and there is dampness in the house. My wife is a chronic patient of arthiritis and the dampness has further aggravated her disease.

The house gives a shabby look for lack of white washing and painting. The house looks so dirty that it does not seem to be worth the rent I pay.

It is a pity that you have not paid heed to my oral requests. If you have no time I shall get the house repaired myself. I shall send you the estimate of the cost of repairs. The amount will be deducted from the monthly rent till all the bills are adjusted.

In present circumstance, I feel it is an ideal proposal. The amount of instalment to be deducted can be mutually decided.

As an owner you must be knowing that timely repairs enhance the life of the building. I shall send you the estimate on hearing from you as to what course you think suitable for you. Rainy season is likely to set in soon. If the repairs are undertaken soon, I shall feel obliged to you.

With best wishes,

Yours sincerely

XYZ

17. **Write a letter to your friend describing the famine conditions prevailing in one of the regions of MP.**

10, Samrat Hotel
Morena, MP

28th June, 20XX

My dear Ajay

The famine conditions in the drought affected region of Chambal are horrifying. Though I am on a marketing tour in this area, I can not help observing the plight of the inhabitants of the region on account of famine conditions prevailing. Lakhs of people living in the inhospitable ravines, are facing the question of survival. They earn their living by selling wood, making baskets and seasonal migration to places where food is easy to come by.

I am shocked to see the hamlets in remote settlements situated in a desolate valley of Shivpuri District. As we travelled from Gwalior to Shivpuri in the company of our distributor, the poverty and hunger scenario grew darker. Rampant unemployment, dry wells and dead cattle were a common sight.

Our dealer, Mr. Arjun Singh informed us that according to newspaper reports 52 starvation deaths have already occurred in this area in recent months. He gave objective account of the level of hunger and hunger related misery of the people. The chronic poverty in the area is aggravated by the worst famine in living memory.

Crops have completely withered and other traditional sources of livelihood have disappeared. The collection of Mahua and Tendu has virtually come to a stand still. Emaciated children, semi-clad women and wrinkled faces of men tell the story of miseries of the inhabitants.

Inhabitants seem to have accepted hunger as their fate while they see cattle and men dying around them. Some residents stated stoically that they had not eaten food for days. Some of them lived on wild berries but an over dose of these berries appears to cause stomach ailments.

As I returned in the evening to my hotel, I felt disgusted with life. I was at a loss to understand how these people were alive at all. Although Annapurna Cards have been issued to the people, this card entitles a person to 10 kg of grain per month for four. This quantity is hardly adequate to sustain life of a person. It is strange that Government and political leaders can be so callous of the conditions that can rend the heart of any common man.

We have made mockery of our democracy. Freedom from British rule seems to have lost significance. Freedom from hunger and poverty has not been achieved even after 55 years of independence. The hypocrisy of the politicians is very much evident. What more can I write?

With good wishes,

Yours sincerely
XYZ

Official Letters

1. **Write a letter to the Health Officer of your city complaining about the insanitary conditions in your locality.**

   29/2 Arera Colony
   Bhopal

   15th June, 20XX

   The Health Officer
   Bhopal

   Sir

   Reg. : <u>INSANITARY CONDITIONS IN ARERA COLONY</u>

   I, on behalf of the residents of Arera colony, would like to bring to your notice the insanitary conditions prevailing in our locality.

   Once a posh colony, now Arera colony is a store-house of dirt and garbage. The heaps of rubbish are visible at every step. The drains are silted and overflow with foul smelling water. Even sewers are overflowing emitting foul smell. In the absence of dustbins, the residents throw the garbage and domestic rubbish on the roads. Even the educated residents are careless of the sanitary needs of the locality. The streets are often littered with domestic refuse.

   The roads are in very bad conditions. During rainy season, they are source of potential danger for accidents. The manholes are without covers. The rain water collected in the depressions of the roads breed mosquitoes. There is every danger of breaking out of infectious diseases. One has to be wary of going out at night. Many accidents have taken place causing loss of life and limb.

   We have brought these conditions to the notice of the Sanitary Inspector again and again. But he has not taken even a single step. Sweepers are hardly to be seen on their duty. The absence of the sweepers add to the sufferings of the residents.

   In view of the foregoing, you are requested to visit the locality and take remedial steps to improve the sanitary conditions. Rainy season is likely to set in within this month. We would be highly obliged if you could take early action in the matter.

   Thanking you,

   Yours faithfully
   XYZ

2. **Write an application to General Manager of Indo Chem. Ltd. for the post of Sales Manager in response to their advertisement in the newspaper.**

   20/4, Mayur Vihar
   Jalandhar

   18th April, 20XX

   The General Manager
   Indo Chem. Ltd.
   Udaipur

Sir

Reg. : <u>FOR THE POST OF SALES MANAGER</u>

In response to your advertisement in the Hindustan Times of 10th April, 2012 for the post of Sales Manager in your esteemed concern, I am enclosing my Bio-data for your favourable consideration.

The enclosed Bio-data would show that I have had a very successful professional career with a diploma in Pharmacy. I love meeting people and I am sociable by nature. I desire to change the place of my work for better future prospects.

Hope, you will find my qualifications suitable for the job I am applying for and look forward earnestly to hear from you.

Thanking you,

Yours faithfully
Rahul Malik

Enclosures : Bio-Data
              Experience testimonials

Bio-Data

Name	:	Rahul Malik
Date of Birth	:	22nd November, 1978
Marital Status	:	Married
Father's Name	:	Shri VK Malik
Educational Qualifications	:	B.Sc. honours (Bio-group) with Diploma in Pharmacy from Chandigarh college of Pharmacy.
Experience	:	(A) Worked as a Pharmacist in the PGI Chandigarh for two years.
		(B) Took up sales career with my present employers M/s Ranbaxy Ltd. as Sales Supervisor. Have worked with them for 10 years.
Contact No.	:	9712308960

3. **A letter of appointment.**

Indo Chem. Ltd.
Udaipur

Our Ref : AP/PH/IC-4

20th May, 2012

Mr. Rahul Malik
20/4, Mayur Vihar
Jalandhar

Reg. : <u>APPOINTMENT FOR THE POST OF SALES MANAGER.</u>

With reference to your application dated 18th April, 2012 for the post of Sales Manager and subsequent interview on 1st May, 2012, we feel pleasure in offering you appointment for the post of Sales Manager in our establishment.

We are enclosing an appointment letter in original alongwith a duplicate copy. Please keep the original copy with you and return us the duplicate copy duly signed by you as a

LETTER WRITING 245

token of your acceptance of our terms and conditions mentioned therein. We have offered you very attractive and lucrative terms and conditions to enable you to devote your best capabilities to the job.

You are requested to report for duty on 1st June, 2012.

Thanking you and wishing you bright future,

Yours faithfully
for Indo Chem. Ltd.
XYZ
General Manager
Enclosure: Letter of appointment

4. **A letter expressing an apology.**

10, Manali House
Ambala

14th August, 20XX

The Manager
Bharat Tubes Co
Ambala

Sir

Reg. : A SINCERE APOLOGY FOR MY UNBECOMING CONDUCT

Ref : Your letter No. MNS/F/3 dated 12th August, 20XX

You are requested to accept my heartfelt apologies for my irresponsible behaviour and inconvenience caused to you.

Though no explanation will compensate for the irresponsible behaviour, I would like to inform you that I have been undergoing severe depression on account of my domestic problems. But I am determined to face life boldly because I know how precious this job is for the survival of my family. I don't wish to add financial burden to the already existing problems.

I assure you, Sir, that I shall give you no chance of complaint in future and shall update my work within this week.

Thanking you,

Yours faithfully
Vivek Mishra
(Typist-Clerk)

5. **Report to the Inspector of Police Station, Rohini about the disappearance of your younger brother.**

B1/4, Ranjan Apartments
Sector 9, Rohini

10th December, 20XX

The Station House Officer
Police Station, Rohini
New Delhi

Sir

Reg. : <u>THE DISAPPEARANCE OF MY BROTHER</u>

May I draw your attention to the sudden disappearance of my younger brother, Amit Sharma, who did not return home last evening from Holy Angel Nursing Home where he works as a receptionist?

He is twenty five of age, fair complexioned, 5 feet 6 inch tall, a young man of strong built and has a small scar on his right cheek. When he disappeared he was wearing a pink shirt and blue jeans.

We have approached the authorities of Holy Angel Nursing Home. They say that he left at 8 in the evening after the other receptionist had come. We have telephoned all his friends and our relatives. But everyone has shown unawareness. As far as we know he is a boy of good temperament and has no enemies. He never remains absent from home without information.

I request you to take immediate action in the matter for the search of my brother.

I am enclosing his latest photograph.

Thanking you,

Yours faithfully

Ajay Sharma

Enclosure: Photograph of Amit Sharma

6. **Write a letter to the railway authorities bringing to their attention the danger posed by unmanned railway crossing citing the example of recent tragic accidents.**

10, Govind Puri
Hapur

10th July, 20XX

The General Manager
Northern Railways
Delhi

Sir

Reg. : <u>UNMANNED RAILWAY CROSSINGS</u>

I draw your kind attention to the accidents taking place because of unmanned railway crossings all over the country.

There are numberless unmanned railway crossings in the country. But some of them are prone to serious accidents. You must have read about the recent two tragic accidents involving a truck and a Maruti gypsy with in a span of one month. No doubt, in both the cases the drivers of these vehicles were responsible. Yet the railway authorities cannot absolve themselves from their responsibility.

On 1st April, a truck collided with Sangam express at Hapur Garh Road railway crossing. It was 7 p.m. and driver should have been well aware of the speeding of the train. He took the risk of speeding past the train. Unfortunately the truck banged into the railway engine and was reduced to splinters in no time. Both the truck driver and the conductor lost their lives. Their bodies were mutilated beyond recognition.

LETTER WRITING 247

In a similar accident, on 25th April, there was a collision involving Maruti gypsy. This time the car struck against Nauchandi Express killing its driver. It was about 8 p.m. and the lights must be blazing. Obviously the driver was aware of the approaching train. He committed the similar folly of thinking that he would speed ahead of the coming train. This time Maruti was thrown up in the air and fell with a loud bang. The driver was crushed to death in an instant.

Such accidents are very common. When contacted, the Station Master told the reporter that the responsibility for constructing motorable roads lied with the Public Works Department. They should have consulted the railway authorities before making roads that cross the railway lines. This did not appear to be convincing answer. However, unmanned crossings are hazardous even for pedestrians. They are around 25,000 in number. The government must take concrete steps to help check the avoidable loss of life and material.

Thanking you

Yours faithfully

Ashish Mehra

7. **Write a letter to the Editor of a local newspaper of your town to draw the attention of the Superintendent of police to the law and order situation in your locality.**

12/A, Lohia Nagar
Patna

19th December, 20XX

The Editor
The City News
Patna

Sir

Reg. : <u>LAW AND ORDER SITUATION IN SHAKTI NAGAR</u>

Through the columns of your esteemed daily, I may draw the attention of the police authorities to the worsening law and order situation in our locality.

The residents of Shakti Nagar are facing a number of problems because of lawlessness in the area. There is a sense of insecurity among the residents on account of two day-light murders last week. A woman was hacked to death as soon as her husband and children left home. The 30 years old woman was done to death when the intruders asked her to part with valuables and cash in her home. On her refusal they committed heinous murder by stabbing her in stomach. The same noon, an old man was shot dead by the burglars. In both the cases the motive was robbery.

The thefts of two wheelers and motor cars are very common. Only last month the robbers dragged out the owner of a car and drove off in the same car. Eve-teasing is a common feature in our locality. Office going ladies and school going young girls are subjected to obscene remarks and molestation.

All these incidents are duly registered with Police station of the area. The SHO has been personally contacted many times to take remedial steps to check the lawlessness in the locality and restore the confidence of the residents. Sadly enough, no step has been taken so far. A tea stall and a cigarette kiosk are the central points where the unruly elements assemble and pose problems for peaceful citizens. In fact many land lords appear to have let their houses to anti social elements. Being a posh locality of the city the criminal elements are not easily identified by the residents.

Even the request to the SHO for posting police men at vulnerable points has gone unheeded. If done, it would have deterred the anti social elements. There is panic among the residents. Therefore, we are drawing your kind attention to restore sense of security of the law abiding citizens.

Thanking you,

Yours truly
XYZ

8. **A letter to the Editor about preserving the historical monuments in your town.**

The Heritage Society of India
Meerut

27th March, 20XX

The Editor
The Statesman
New Delhi

Sir

Reg. : <u>THE PRESERVATION OF HISTORICAL MONUMENTS</u>

May I, through your esteemed daily, appeal to the Archeological Department of India to look after the heritage of India represented by historical monuments in our district?

Meerut is a historical region. Historical places like Parikshat Garh, Hastinapur, Barnawa belong to the epoch of Mahabharta. In recent excavations many relics of Indus valley civilization have been discovered in Alamgir. Sardhana & Meerut are historically important in the context of the British rule in India. As we know, Hastinapur, Parikshat Garh, and Barnawa conjure up in our minds the memories of the days of our ancient glory. All these places are associated with the dynasties of Pandavas and Kauravas. There are numberless monuments dating from that epoch.

Sardhna and Meerut are associated with modern British era and the first revolt against the British rule. In Meerut itself there are historical places related to freedom struggle. Sardhana was founded by Begum Samru. She built a grand Church there when she embraced Christianity. In Meerut itself, she built a great palace in Begum Bagh named after her. Few years back it was in dilapidated conditions. Later on it was demolished by Meerut Development Authority for building Apartments. If happened through neglect of the Archeological department and district authorities. If preserved, the palace of Begum Samru would have added to the glory of Meerut.

Similarly many ancient monuments are facing extinction. It would be better if government of India took over these monuments and took care of them under its direct supervision.

Thanking you,

Yours truly
for Heritage Society of India
Secretary

9. **Write a letter to the Editor of a leading daily newspaper of India, inviting attention of the authorities concerned to the serious nuisance of cattle let loose daily by the neighbouring villagers to graze in your newly developed colony.**

The Residents Welfare Society,
Kamal Enclave
Ranchi

5th January, 20XX

The Editor
The News Times
New Delhi

Sir

Reg. : <u>STRAY ANIMALS</u>

Through the columns of your esteemed daily, I would like to express the difficulties caused by stray animals in our locality. Ours is a newly developed colony situated on the outskirts of the city. Stray animals are a great threat to pedestrians & vehicle drivers even in the heart of the city. In the city area the dairy owners let loose their domestic animals to graze on the domestic waste and garbage.

Many a time the life of citizens is endangered on account of accidents caused by these animals. Stray animals are ubiquitous in every street and colony of the city. The rabid dogs are a major source of threat to the children playing in the streets and parks. Our colony faces the same problem in a different manner. The villagers let loose their animals to wander about the streets and colonies of the city. Although there should not be any shortage of fodder in the country side, yet the animals stray into residential colonies. The small kitchen gardens and the parks are damaged. In the evening the cows move straight to their owners for being milched.

In the city one may report matter to the municipal authorities but in this case the residents are in a fix about whom they should approach with complaint about the menace of stray animals. The roads are defiled by their dung. Some times the animals fight with each other and rush into homes. When villagers are approached, they are not concerned at all. On the contrary they collectively threaten the residents.

We hope that the authorities concerned would look into the matter and take immediate steps to solve the problems of the residents.

Thanking you,

Yours truly
for Residents Welfare Society
Secretary

10. A letter to the Editor about water shortage.

322, Bapu Marg
Jaipur
10th May, 20XX

The Editor
The Indian Times
Jaipur

Sir

Reg. : <u>WATER SHORTAGE</u>

Through the columns of your esteemed daily, we, the residents of Begum Bagh, wish to draw the attention of the authorities concerned to the severe water shortage that we have been experiencing.

Since summer has set in, as usual we get water just for 30 minutes in the morning and 20 minutes in the evening. The amount of water barely comes to 100 litres a day. How can one cope with the supply so miserably low in quantity?

The civic authorities often send tankers in order to provide temporary relief. But the supply of water by tankers is so inadequate that the residents often resort to capturing tankers forcibly. Such a situation has led to violence many a time resulting in loss of life on one occasion. The police have to be often summoned to quell the riotous situation. There is animosity among the residents who ironically belong to educated and elite class of the city.

The residents of the area have been clamouring for some permanent solution. Summer or winter, the problem is always there, though in summer it gets more acute. In view of the foregoing we would urge the administration to offer proper infrastructural planning to solve the problem.

The D.M. had promised last week that five thousand litre tanks will be set up all over the city. The tanks will be filled up at night by Municipal Corporation tanker to avoid wastage through spillage. The idea is laudable but no action has been taken so far. Though fortnight has passed and the summer is at its peak, there is no sign of construction of water tanks anywhere in the city. Water shortage is acute and is likely to worsen in the coming days.

Thanking you,

Yours truly
XYZ

LETTER WRITING

11. Write a letter to the Editor of National daily bringing out the plight of the residents of a colony developed by a builder in your city.

10/A, Prem Nagar
Bhopal
23rd March, 20XX

The Editor
The Times of India
New Delhi

Sir

Reg. : <u>THE PROBLEMS OF THE RESIDENTS OF A COLONY</u>

May I draw your kind attention?

Prem Nagar is a residential colony for single unit houses. It was developed by Vichal Brothers, the renowned builder in the country in late 90's. It was an attractive alternative for those who preferred spacious living and pollution free environment. But the dream of the residents has turned sour. Prem Nagar roads are broad. Its drainage system is better than that of the other newly developed colonies. It has large parks and a spacious community centre.

To a casual visitor it might be an ideal residential colony. Residents, however have a different story to tell. Even after 12 years of habitation, residents complain about the lack of basic amenities like power and water. Lack of proper approach roads and absence of faultless sewerage system have made the colony uninhabitable. Scores of the roads are full of depressions. The rain water is collected in them, where mosquitoes breed. These depressions are a potential danger to the scooterists and motorists. The erratic electricity supply makes the conditions worse. No doubt, the roads are quite wide but the enroachments by the residents themselves have disfigured the look of the colony. Since the residents in the posh colony are well connected, Bhopal Development Authority is helpless in demolishing the unauthorised constructions which have almost choked the roads.

Another problem with Prem Nagar is that of the scarcity of water supply. During summer season there is a supply of water hardly for two hours at dawn. After that not a drop of water trickles from the taps. Besides, the parks are not well maintained. They have become the haunts of anti social elements and pavement dwellers at night.

In a sum, Prem Nagar residents pay for comforts with bad roads, scarcity of water supply and sense of insecurity. Bhopal Development Authority should take over the colony and maintain it as we are paying house tax to them like other residents of the city.

Thanking you,

Yours truly
XYZ

12. **Write a letter to the Director, Adult Education Delhi, requesting him to help you in planning and organising an Adult Literacy Programme in your area. You are Arvind Singh of Balwal village. Use an appropriate format for the letter.**

Village Balwal
Tehsil Shripul
District Churu

17th May, 2011

The Director
Adult Education
Delhi

Sir

Reg. : <u>ORGANISATION OF ADULT LITERACY PROGRAMME</u>

I am a retired Reader from Hindi Department, Rajasthan University. Having devoted my life to material pursuits and success to a great extent, I am now desirous of contributing a bit to the social service. I have decided to settle in my native village Balwal, Tehsil Shripul, District Churu. Therefore, I have planned to organise adult literacy programme in the Tehsil that will cater to the needs of nearby villages.

In view of this, I hope you will help me in organising the programme by sending me the guidelines for conducting the programme. The SDM has already allowed to conduct classes from 4 to 7 pm in the Tehsil Block office. He has promised to provide all the infrastructure needed for the purpose. I don't need any financial help in this regard. In case there is financial assistance granted to the participants in the programme, it is for you to look into the matter.

As for me, I need only lesson plans and other guidelines. I have contacted the Pradhans of the area and they are very much excited about the programme. They have assured me of motivating the adult villagers to participate in the programme.

Assuring you of my earnest dedication to the literacy programme and thanking you.

Yours truly
Arvind Singh

13. **Write an application to the Principal, Jesus & Mary Convent for admission of your children.**

10, The Mall
Shimla

5th April, 20XX

The Principal
Jesus & Mary Convent
Shimla

Reg. : <u>AN APPLICATION FOR THE ADMISSION OF CHILDREN</u>

Madam

I wish to seek admission of my two children to your esteemed institution.

My daughter Pearl Sharma and son Arnav Sharma have passed 8th standard and 6th standard from St. Mary Convent at Srinagar. Their records, as you will find from their Report Cards, have been outstanding.

Being in Defence forces I received my transfer orders in the last week of March. I was posted at Kupwara and had no means to get the names of my children registered in advance.

Keeping in view the nature of my service and place of posting you will kindly take note of these factors and be kind enough to grant admission to my children to class IX and VII.

Please intimate the date and time when I should bring my children to your school for admission.

Thanking you,

Yours truly
Col. Virendra Sharma

14. You are Vivek Mishra of 105, Hailey Road, Patna. You have just completed your graduation and are keen on joining some institution which may help you in personality development. Write a letter to the Director of the centre, Personality Point, seeking necessary information about admission procedures for an eight week summer course in leadership.

105, Hailey Road
Patna

17th April, 20XX

The Director
Personality Point
Patna

Reg. : <u>SEEKING INFORMATION ABOUT ADMISSION PROCEDURES FOR SUMMER COURSE IN LEADERSHIP</u>

Sir

I have heard a lot about your Centre in the field of helping young men and women in personality development. I have just completed B.A. (Hons.) English from Magadh University. Now I am interested in taking up career in marketing for which communication skill and personality development are indispensable qualifications.

I am preparing for CAT entrance test. Meanwhile I have time that I wish to devote to personality development. I would like to know the comprehensive detail about the kind of training you impart to young persons in the field of personality development. I am keen on joining your institute for which I need to know about the admission procedure. In case you have some brochure containing the information required by me, I would request you to send it to me for which I shall be highly obliged.

Thanking you,

Yours faithfully

Vivek Mishra

15. **A letter about discrimination in promotion policy towards women.**

Women's Equality Forum
5, Safdarjung Enclave
New Delhi

25th February, 20XX

The Chief Personnel Officer
M/s Bharat Petroleum Company,
New Delhi

Sir

Reg. : <u>GENDER BIAS IN PROMOTION POLICY</u>

Let me assure you at the outset that we have no intention to interfere in the official policy of promotion. Promotion is such a sensitive subject that promotion to higher posts cannot be taken for granted. Promotions are based on merits and many other considerations that go a long way in determining the performance of any organisation in the long run. We are writing to you because many instances have been brought to our notice, where gender bias is quite evident.

You don't, we feel, consider women fit for supervisory posts or in your views men are more capable of management of the company. At every cost the promotion policy for the last five years reflect your thinking that women are capable of only working at subordinate jobs. Gender bias is self evident in your recent promotion list issued by your organisation. There is hardly any name of woman in the list. Your policy goes against all norms of equality among sexes. It is a pity that you think that women are not capable of devoting full time to their jobs on account of their domestic obligations.

In view of the foregoing impressions, we request you to change your promotion policy and give chance of promotion to women. They have proved their worth in every field. Why not in your organisation?

Thanking you and looking forward to an early reply.

Yours faithfully
for Women's Equality Forum
XYZ
President

16. **Write a letter to the Wildlife Conservator complaining against the cruelty that the animals in the zoo are often subjected to, suggesting ways of protecting them from teasing spectators and indifferent keepers.** [IFS, 2015]

C92, Jackson Road
Ranthambore

22nd March, 20XX

The Wildlife Conservator
National Wildlife Park
Ranthambore

Reg. : <u>COMPLAINT AGAINST STAFF OF BIGRASH ZOO IN THE CITY</u>

Sir

This is to bring to your notice that I, XYZ, recently visited the local zoo of our city that is registered to be operated under your managerial control. I was shocked to see the undernourished animals and unkept condition of the cages. It was well evident that the staff and trainers at the zoo were negligent to the needs of the animals. It raises a lot of questions on humanity as well as on the management. The trainers did not once stop or warn the on lookers/visitors from teasing the animals. In fact, they did not even pay any heed, when children fed inappropriate food to the animals.

It is very important to point out the management to take necessary steps. The management should train the staff regarding and according to the upkeep and needs of the animals. They should install CCTV cameras to keep a check whether or not the visitors are conducting according to the set standards. They should also enforce law of imposing fine on the spectators at fault and indifferent keepers. These measures are sure to bring about better environment at the zoo and attract more visitors.

Thanking you,

Yours sincerely
XYZ

Business Letters

1. **A letter about opening wholesale drug agency.**
   Medico Drug Agency
   34, Bhagat Singh Market
   Ludhiana
   Ref : MDA/47/12
   5th February, 20XX

   M/s Lifeline Medical Stores
   79, Ganga Plaza
   Ludhiana

   Dear Sirs

   Reg. : <u>OPENING OF WHOLESALE DRUG AGENCY</u>

   We are pleased to inform you that on 1st March, we are opening a whole sale drug agency, under the name and style of Zenith Drug Co. at our above mentioned address. We assure you that we shall always aim at giving you our very best attention at competitive prices.

   The resources at our disposal are adequate enough to enable us to fulfil special requirements of bulk orders of life saving drugs. We trust that you will favour us with your valued trial orders. We assure you to extend our best possible co-operation and services.

   Yours faithfully
   for Medico Drug Agency
   General Manager

2. **A letter of information about appointment as a distributor.**
   M/s Kirti Book Agency
   42, Subhash Market
   Calcutta

   Our Ref : KBA/3/17

3rd April, 2012
M/s Mohanty and Co.
Delhi

Dear Sirs

Reg. : OUR APPOINTMENT AS A DISTRIBUTOR

We are pleased to inform you that we have been appointed sole distributors for the Kirti books for the whole of India.

This publishing house publishes about twenty new titles each year. Kirti Publishing house needs very little introduction to the trade and it is a ready profit for retailers to sell these titles.

We are now ready to deliver their two new titles from stock, and you can make out from the catalogue enclosed that all prices are subject to a very generous trade discount of 33%.

We thank you for your confidence in us in the past. We have always tried our best at serving you with quick-selling books. We hope that you will again give us an opportunity to offer you another series of titles on the most convenient terms.

Yours faithfully

for Kirti Book Agency

Proprietor

3. **A letter of enquiry about supply.**

Chawla and Sons
Rajpur Road
Ranchi

Our Ref : CAS/40

25th July, 20XX

The Sunrise Mills Ltd
Andheri East
Bombay

Dear Sirs

Reg. : ENQUIRY ABOUT SUPPLY OF COLOUR COTTON CLOTH

We will be glad to receive as soon as possible the particulars of your olive green cotton cloth for army unifrom purposes.

It is very likely that our requirements throughout the year will be uniformly heavy. We have been fortunate enough to get contracts for military supplies and so we are interested in cloth of superior quality.

Our needs would be mainly for the above mentioned quality and colour and we should appreciate samples in various forms.

We look forward to an early reply so that we may proceed with placing an order provided the terms and conditions are favourable.

Yours faithfully
for Chawla and sons
Manager

LETTER WRITING 257

4. **A letter of reply to an enquiry of supply.**

   The Sunrise Mills Ltd.
   Andheri East
   Bombay

   Our Ref : SML/279/4
   Your Ref : CAS/40 of 25th July
   5th August, 20XX

   Chawla and Sons
   Rajpur Road, Ranchi

   Dear Sirs

   Reg. : <u>SUPPLY OF COTTON CLOTH</u>

   We thank you for your enquiry of 25th July, and have pleasure in quoting the details of material as desired by you.

   1. Olive green fast colour 64 cms. width in pieces of 45 mts. @ ₹ 30.00 per metre.

   You will find this cotton cloth absolutely unshrinkable and wrinkle-free. The cloth material is of superior quality and is suitable for daily use.

   Orders would be executed promptly from stock. Of course, reasonable notice would be required for unusually large quantities.

   We are enclosing a comprehensive selection of samples, which we submit to your examination with confidence. We trust that we shall have the pleasure of supplying your needs and we look forward to it.

   Yours faithfully

   for The Sunrise Mills Ltd.
   Manager

5. **Circular intimating the new name and style of the firm.**

   Darwin Industries (P) Ltd
   Grand Plaza, Kanpur
   Ref : DIPL/10
   1st March, 20XX

   Reg. : <u>TO WHOM IT MAY CONCERN</u>

   We bring to your kind attention that Darwin Industries is now registered as Private Limited Company with effect from 1st March, 20XX.

   Henceforward, you are requested to mail all your correspondence, bills, orders, Cheques and drafts in favour of Darwin Industries (P) Ltd. at the above cited address.

   Thanking you for your cooperation.

   Yours faithfully

   for Darwin Industries (P) Ltd

   Amit Singhal (Manager)

6. **Write a letter about launching of a new product in the market.**

   Pearl Industries
   Dr. R.P. Road, Jaipur
   Ref : DI/703
   30th June, 20XX

Khanna Electronics
King Bridge Road
Calcutta

Dear Sirs

    Reg. : <u>INTRODUCTION OF NEW RANGE OF COOLERS AND AIR CONDITIONERS</u>

We think you will be interested in the new range of coolers and air conditioners, we have just introduced in the market.

The designs of these products have undergone extensive modifications. Moreover, keeping in mind the recent advances in technology in the field of electronics, we have used the improved machinery in our products. These are light in weight and occupy less space, thus, suitable for both, office and household purposes.

The prices are surprisingly low. In order to popularise these products, we are offering a special discount of 10% for a limited period only to our valued old customers. The price list will be sent only if you are interested in our products.

We trust that our products will justify our claims. We look forward to receiving an early reply from you to allow us to demonstrate the complete range of our products. We shall arrange to send our representative as soon as you write to us.

Yours faithfully

for Pearl Industries.
    Sales Manager

7. **A letter to insurance company for sending an insurance agent.**
Menka Apartments
Sector 9, Rohini
New Delhi

12th January, 20XX

The Manager
Life Insurance Corporation
Karol Bagh, New Delhi

Dear Sir

    Reg. : <u>ARRANGE A VISIT OF AN INSURANCE AGENT</u>

I wish to insure myself and my wife and I am interested in knowing the detailed information of various schemes you offer.

I shall be glad if you send your agent to our above mentioned residence on any day after 5 p.m. so that we may discuss the matter in detail.

Yours faithfully
Anuj Bali

8. **A letter to insurance company for reduction in the insurance rate.**
Pearl Rubber Industries
10, Industrial Estate, Ambala

Our Ref : PRI/246/E
Your Ref : NILC/15/7—2 of 15th March, 20XX
23rd March, 20XX

The Manager
New India Insurance Company
Prem Nagar Branch, Ambala

Dear Sir

Reg. : <u>REDUCTION IN INSURANCE RATES</u>

We are pleased to receive the rate of insurance quoted by you for the insurance of our premises at the above address against theft and fire.

However, we regret that the rates quoted by you are not competitive. The rate of 15 paise per cent quoted by you are not satisfactory. We don't find justification in these rates as other companies are prepared to cover our business premises at 10 paise per cent As a matter of fact, we are still holding insurance cover at this rate. We wish to insure with you because we are interested in distributing the risk over various companies.

If you are willing to reduce your rate to 10 paise per cent, we might request you for an insurance cover of rupees 2 lakh. Therefore, we shall highly appreciate your expeditious reply about our proposal.

Yours faithfully

for Pearl Rubber Industries
Manager

9. A letter of inability to reduce the rate of insurance cover.

New India Insurance Company
Prem Nagar Branch
Ambala

Our Ref : NIIC/15/7—3
Your Ref : PRI/246/E of 23rd March, 20XX
17th April, 20XX

The Manager
Pearl Rubber Industries
10, Industrial Estate
Ambala

Dear Sir

Reg. : <u>INSURANCE RATES</u>

We regret to state that you are under the impression that the rate of 15 paise per cent quoted for the insurance of your business premises is excessive. We take this opportunity that the rate is a general one adopted by all the insurance companies. The rates have been raised uniformally by all companies recently because the incidence of fire and theft has increased. Therefore, no other alternative was possible than to increase the rate of insurance cover.

It is surprising that you have been able to cover your premises at the old rates. It is, however, a tempting offer that you have offered in the form of such a huge business but we are not in a position to reduce the rate of insurance cover because it is not commercially viable.

Yours faithfully

for New India Insurance Company
Manager

10. **Write a letter requesting for reservation of a room in a hotel.**

   S Kumar and Co.
   Bhagat Singh Road
   Chandigarh
   Our Ref : SKC/R/87
   23rd August, 20XX

   The Manager
   Hotel Oberoi
   New Delhi

   Dear Sir

   Reg. : <u>RESERVATION OF ROOM</u>

   You are requested to reserve one single room for our Managing Director, Mr Sachin Bakshi from 19th September, 2012 to 23rd September, 2012.

   Mr Bakshi will clear all his bills in cash.

   A line of confirmation through fax or E-mail will be much appreciated.

   Yours faithfully
   for S Kumar and Co
   Personnel Manager

11. **Write a letter to a company for supply of electronic goods.**

   M/s Kumar Electronics
   Minto Bridge Road, Delhi
   12th June, 20XX
   Our Ref : KE/47/Orders

   M/s BPL Electronics Company
   Gole Market
   Saharanpur

   Dear Sirs

   Reg. : <u>ORDER FOR SUPPLY OF GOODS</u>

   We shall very much appreciate your sending us the following goods purely on sale and return basis :

1.	BPL Television (21")	12
2.	BPL Television (28")	10
3.	BPL Semi-Automatic Washing Machine	15
4.	BPL Fully Automatic Washing Machine	12
5.	BPL Microwave Oven	15
6.	BPL Refrigerator (Medium)	12

   It is understood that as per our terms & condition in the past, goods will be sent F.O.R. destination. Documents comprising Advice & Bill will also be sent direct, allowing us a credit of one month.

   Yours faithfully
   for Kumar Electronics
   Manager

LETTER WRITING

12. A letter of complaint about supply of defective wrist watches.

M/s Time Centre
Napier Road, Hyderabad
Our Ref : TC/NR/H-5
Your Ref : OS/TT/119 of 20th March, 20XX

10th April, 20XX

M/s Oberoi Watches Ltd.
Faridabad

Dear Sirs

Reg. : SUPPLY OF DEFECTIVE WRIST WATCHES

We have already taken delivery of the consignment of 150 wrist watches from M/s Jaipur Golden Transport Co. The payment has been duly made to the PNB, The Mall, Hyderabad for obtaining GR & other consignment documents.

On opening the package, we were shocked to find that watches were not supplied according to the specifications mentioned in our order form. We had strictly instructed your sales representative. not to supply the watches with golden frame & black dial because they are not popular with the customers here.

Secondly, we had never placed an order for watches in square & rectangular shape.

We regret carelessness on the part of your packaging department. Otherwise, a company of repute such as yours, is not expected to act in a careless manner. There has never been any record of negligence during the last ten years we have been dealing with you.

You are requested to take prompt action in the matter as the festival season is very much on. Please send your senior representative to rectify the mistake.

Yours faithfully

for Time Center
Manager

13. Write a letter to your client to clear the pending payment.

M/s Current & Current (P) Ltd.
15, Industrial Estate
Gurgaon
Our Ref : Orders/45/CC
Your Ref : TBL/69-H dt. 5th December, 20XX

10th March, 20XX

M/S Tirath Breweries Ltd
Gole Market
Vidisha

Dear Sirs

Reg. : OUR PENDING PAYMENT OF ₹ 40,000 AS PER OUR
A/C STATEMENT ENCLOSED HEREWITH

We wish to draw your attention to our letter of 27th February requesting you for clearing up your payment of ₹ 40,000 pending for about three months.

We supplied two air conditioners on consignment basis and sent the Invoice and delivery papers direct on your request.

As the financial year is coming to a close, it has become urgent for us to get the pending amount cleared up well in advance.

You have been our most reliable clients and we have never had any financial problem while dealing with you. Therefore, we expect you to expedite the payment and favour us with a bank draft by return of post.

Hoping for an earlier action,

Yours faithfully
for Current & Current (P) Ltd.
Finance Manager
Enclosure—Statement of A/c

14. A letter of regret for inability to make payment in time.

M/s Tirath Breweries Ltd.
Gole Market
Vidisha
Our Ref : TBL/80-H
Your Ref : Orders/45/CC of 10th March, 20
20th March, 20

M/S Current & Current (P) Ltd.
15, Industrial Estate
Gurgaon

Dear Sirs

Reg. : <u>PENDING PAYMENT OF ₹ 40,000</u>

We thank you for your letter of 10th March, alongwith the statement of account.

We regret very much that we have not been able to make payment of ₹ 40,000 in time in respect of the two air conditioners supplied by you. In fact, they are lying packed in our godown on account of our workers going on lightning strike. The delay in payment is, of course, unavoidable and we are under great financial strain. For the last three months, crores of our finances are stuck up with our own customers, for our failure of execution of their full and final orders.

Now, that a compromise with the workers have taken place, we are expected to speed up our production & commercial activities on war footing. We are quite hopeful to remit your pending amount within this fortnight. We appreciate your patience and would request you to bear with us for a few days more.

Assuring you of an early action in the matter.

Your faithfully

for Tirath Breweries Ltd.
General Manager

LETTER WRITING

15. A letter from a wholesale distributor to the manufacturers.

M/S Variety Store
Begum Bridge Road
Meerut

Our Ref : VS/A/C-5
Your Ref : CIR/47 of 2nd February, 20
19th February, 20XX

M/S Royal Hosiery Ltd.
Ludhiana

Dear Sirs

Reg. : <u>INCREASE IN RATE OF COMMISSION</u>

We are pleased to receive your circular of Feb; 2 intimating the introduction of fancy items of undergarments both for ladies and for gents. We are immensely satisfied that you have come up in the area, where you have been lacking in the past.

On our part, we have fully co-operated with you during the last five years and have pushed up the sales of your products almost to double.

These outstanding results have been achieved only because of our sustained advertisements in our franchise of trade. It has caused us heavy financial strain. As, you are aware, we have to bear extra expenditure in view of the competition we have been facing by your competitors.

In view of this, it will not be out of place to request for the increase in the rate of commission to enable us to face the competition with confidence. The increase by 2% will compensate our extra expenditure on advertisements.

Trust me, you will appreciate our point of view and do the needful in the matter.

Your faithfully
for M/s Variety Store

Proprietor

Letters for Practice

Directions *Write the following letters given below.*

1. Write a letter to your friend residing abroad inviting him to your parents 25th wedding anniversary celebration.
2. Write a letter to the post office in your area complaining about your lost letter sent a month ago to your sister.
3. Write a letter to your office applying for a months medical leave to recover from a prolonging illness.
4. Write a letter to your client reminding them about renewal of after sale service contract in order to avoid restricted/ceased maintenance services.
5. Write a letter to your grandmother consoling her with love and informing her about your visit as your grandfather passed away recently.
6. Write a letter to muncipal corporation of Delhi registering a complaint against certain officials taking undue advantage of their posts by demanding bribe from people in your area.
7. Write a letter to your official bank informing them to put stop all the payments on standing instruction basis due to financial loss incurred by the company.
8. Write a letter to an old client congratulating them on completing 10 long years of fair correspondence and business with your company and achieving a loyalty badge with raised benefits.
9. Write a letter to your sibling telling him about your new hostel life away from home.
10. Write a letter to your university requesting them to issue a reference letter for future career purposes and prospects.
11. Write a letter to the General Manager of Patanjali Ayurveda Pvt. Ltd. seeking a franchise license in your name. You are Mr Rustam from Indore.
12. Write a letter to the District Magistrate of your district requesting him to open a library in your village under the government schemes.
13. Write a letter to the minister of tribal affairs seeking his help to run a pilot project on the awareness of their rights.
14. Write a letter to the Executive Engineer of BSNL requesting him to repair the mobile tower which is out of order for a couple of months.
15. Write a letter to the Block Development Officer (BDO) of your area seeking some information regarding start-up India Project.

PART B
COMPREHENSION SKILLS

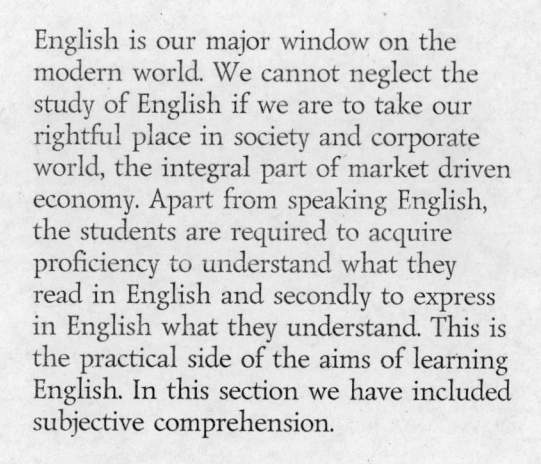

English is our major window on the modern world. We cannot neglect the study of English if we are to take our rightful place in society and corporate world, the integral part of market driven economy. Apart from speaking English, the students are required to acquire proficiency to understand what they read in English and secondly to express in English what they understand. This is the practical side of the aims of learning English. In this section we have included subjective comprehension.

CHAPTER 1

Subjective Comprehension

The progress of a student in language is judged by his power of comprehension. It is done through the comprehensive understanding of an unseen passage. The passage given for comprehension is followed by questions through which the students' grasp of knowledge and power of expression is tested.

Before attempting a paragraph on comprehension, a student is advised to read it more than once to grasp the meaning of the passage in detail. It would help the student answer the questions correctly in accordance with the requirement of the examiner's intention.

Points to be kept in mind while attempting subjective comprehension
- A student should write answers in complete sentences in his own language.
- For this purpose a student is supposed to possess a knowledge of function of Tenses, Modals, Voices, Clauses and Non-finite Verbs.
- The knowledge in this field is very important to write correct and to the point answers.
- While writing about the theme of the passage, one is to state only what the passage is about. A summary of the passage is uncalled for.
- However, the title of the passage should also be derived from the main theme. The title should never be in the form of a sentence.
- In some competitive examinations, the students are also required to answer questions on synonyms and antonyms given in the passage. It is very important to note that the meaning of the words should be chosen in the context of the passage. A student must not take into account only the literal meaning of the word, their figurative use should also be kept in mind.

Sample Passages

Directions *Below are some passages with their solutions.*

Passage 1

What is the future which awaits our children? The underlying assumption of the questions that Indian children have a common future is itself dubious. It can legitimately be asked whether a student who is well fed, attending a boarding school in the salubrious climate of the hills, and learning to use computers has any future in common with a malnourished child who goes to a school with no black boards. The latter may have no worthwhile future at all. And it might be worthwhile to analyse the significance of this marginalisation of more than 75 % of the children of this country.

The failure to provide an infrastructure for primary education in the villages of India more than 68 years after Independence is in sharp contrast with the sophisticated institutions, for technical institutes of higher education are funded by Government, which essentially means that the money to support them comes from taxes. And since indirect taxation forms a substantial part of the taxes collected by the Government, the financial burden is borne by all the people. LK Jha put it graphically when he observed that 25 paise of every rupee spent on education of an IIT student comes from the pockets of men and women, whose children may never enter a proper classroom.

Questions

1. Why can there not be equality among Indian children?
2. How does the writer bring out the disparity in educational system for children?
3. What is going to be the effect of such difference in future?
4. What is the opinion of LK Jha on education?
5. What does the author want to convey?

Answers

1. There can not be equality among Indian children because there are two classes of children. One is the rich class which gets good education and the other is the poor class which do not get proper education.
2. Those belonging to affluent class get superior education in boarding schools of the hills and learn the use of computers. Whereas the poor children go to school without a black board.
3. The effect will be that 75% of the children of the country who belong to the poor would not have a bright future.
4. According to LK Jha, most of the money for higher education comes from indirect taxes which every citizen of the country has to pay. In fact, the funding of higher technical education by the government is the result of contribution of largely that section of the society whose children cannot dream of proper schools.
5. The author wants to convey that the education of 75% of the children of the country is neglected. Most of them go to a school with no blackboards. Government has failed to provide necessary facilities for the education of the children. The author wants to emphasise that the Indian children are not expected to have a common future.

Passage 2

We do not realise adequately to what extent our minds are moulded by books we read especially in youth. We have several means by which we acquire knowledge today i.e. radio, cinema, newspaper and television etc. But reading of books is the most ancient and effective of them all. Reading a book is different from mechanised instruction. We are never alone when we have books as our companions.

A great writer has said that religion is what a man does with his solitariness. It is not merely religion but art and literature, scientific discovery and technological invention that are the outcome of what a man does with his solitariness. In the modern world we tend to be gregarious beings. When we have a little leisure we run to parties, clubs or other social activities. We are afraid to be alone with ourselves, afraid to stand and stare, much less to sit and think. We are happy with others not with ourselves. Pascal tells us that all the evils of the world arise from the fact that men are unable to sit still in a room. Reading a book gives us the habit of solitary reflection and true enjoyment.

Questions

1. What is the best means of acquiring knowledge?
2. How has man produced great art, literature, scientific discoveries or technological inventions?
3. What is man by nature and how does he use his leisure?
4. What is the cause of evils in this world according to the author?
5. What are the views of Pascal on the loneliness of man?

Answers

1. The best means to acquire knowledge is through books. While reading a book, we cultivate the habit of solitary reflection which is otherwise not possible.
2. Man has produced great art, literature, scientific discoveries or technological inventions by utilising his solitariness.
3. Man is gregarious by nature. He does not like to use his leisure as a time for reflection. On the other hand, he seeks the company of other men in parties or clubs.
4. In the opinion of the author, most of our evils are because man is unable to sit still in a room.
5. Pascal shares the view that man is not capable of sitting alone and reflect upon himself.

Passage 3

A recent report in 'Newsweek' says that in American colleges students of Asian origin outperform not only the minority group students but the majority whites as well. Many of these students must be of Indian origin, and their achievement is something we can be proud of.

It is unlikely that these talented youngsters will come back to India, and that is the familiar brain drain problem. However, recent statements by the nation's policy makers indicate that the perception of this issue is changing. 'Brain bank' and not 'brain drain' is the more appropriate idea, they suggest, since the expertise of Indians abroad is only deposited in other places and not lost.

This may be so but this brain bank, like most other banks, is one that primarily serves customers in its neighbourhood. The skills of the Asian now excelling in America's colleges will mainly help the USA. No matter how significant, what non-resident Indians do for India and what their counterparts do for other Asian lands is only a by-product.

But it is also necessary to ask, or be reminded, why Indians study fruitfully when abroad. The Asians whose accomplishments Newsweek records would have probably had a very different tale if they had studied in India. In America they found elbow room, books and other facilities not available and not likely to be available here. The need to prove themselves in the new country and the competition of an international standard they faced there must have cured mental and physical laziness. But other things helping them in America can be obtained here if we achieve a change in social attitudes, specially towards the youth.

We need to learn to value individuals and their unique qualities more than conformity and respectability. We need to learn language of encouragement to add to our skill in flattery. We might also learn to be less liberal with blame and less tight fisted with appreciation, especially.

Questions

1. What is the benefit of the high level of competitions faced by Asian students in America?
2. What are the limitations which the brain banks have to face?
3. According to the author what do non resident Indians do for India?
4. What would be the ways of making the situation better in India?
5. What is the concept of brain bank according to the writer?

Answers

1. High level of competition faced by Asian students in America brings out the best in them. They are able to give up mental and physical laziness.
2. Brain banks are likely to serve only those countries in which they are working. This is the limitation.
3. Non-Resident Indians cannot benefit India by their talents. Whatever they can do is insignificant because the country where they are residing is benefited most.
4. Indian students can do better in India if we learn to value individuals and their unique qualities. They must be encouraged and it requires a change in our social attitude.
5. The flight of Indian talent was considered an evil in the form of brain-drain. The concept of brain-drain has undergone a change. Talented students working in foreign countries are considered a brain bank as their expertise is only deposited in other places and not lost.

SUBJECTIVE COMPREHENSION

Passage 4

The villager has customarily been very conservative in his attitude and approach. He is reluctant to change his traditional way of thinking and doing things. His attitude, in many respects is 'home made is best' for instance, most cattle farmers in the villages, prefer to feed their cows and buffaloes with a home-mix comprising of local oil cakes like mustard or cottonseed, pulses, jaggery, salt etc.

It takes numerous visits, hard convincing, daily trials and experiments to convince the rural cattle farmer that compound feeds, scientifically formulated, improve the yields of milk, without any incremental costs. The age old values and attitudes towards caste, creed, women, time and money take time to change. The villager has traditionally been a believer in the philosophy of *Karma* or fate. He has found it more convenient to blame his economic destitution, poor living conditions and strained social status on *Bhagya*, *Karma* or fate.

The security that the villagers find in the 'status quo' acts as a disincentive to change and experiment, in the short-run. Many of these antiquated attitudes, value systems and outlooks are changing due to improved levels of awarness and education. However, the rate of change is sluggish. Attitudes that have fossilised over the centuries, do take time to change.

Questions

1. Why does the phrase 'home made is best' imply?
2. When will you call a person conservative in his attitude and approach?
3. Why does a villager feel secure in maintaining 'Status quo'?
4. What is the best method to convince the average Indian villager about the superiority of a new cattle feed?
5. Find a word from the passage which is the opposite of "Fast" or "Active".

Answers

1. The phrase 'home made is best' implies that the food made or prepared at home by the farmers for their cattle is considered to be the best.
2. A person is considered conservative when he/she is reluctant to change his traditional approach, way of thinking and doing things.
3. The villagers feel safe and secure in maintaining a status quo because it acts as a disincentive to change and experiment and villagers being conservative are not open to change.
4. The best method to convince the average Indian villager about the superiority of the new cattle feed are numerous visits, daily trials, spreading education and awareness and proven experiments on the scientifically formulated compound feeds.
5. Sluggish

Passage 5

Earlier leaders treated Parliament with deference because they believed in the virtue of Parliamentary democracy, in the value of good precedents, and in the laying down and carrying out of policies with the consent of people or their representatives. It was not easy, for with vast burden of illiteracy, the country had started with adult suffrage.

To them, there was no other way. With many limitations, they enabled three general elections to become an impressive demonstration of the working of the world's largest democracy. Any democracy, whatever the forms and the rules is government by deliberation and it demands capacity for debate, and they taught the lesson ceaselessly. Democracy must ensure good government, it must allow criticism and correction, it means balances and checks.

Parliamentary democracy demands many virtues. It demands, of course ability. It demands a certain dedication to work. But it demands also a large measure of co-operation, of restraint, of self discipline. They said that they could claim that Parliamentary democracy had functioned with a large measure of success in the country. They did not claim any credit for themselves, they gave all the credit to the people.

Questions

1. Why did earlier leaders treat Parliament with respect?
2. What do you understand by the phrase 'vast burden of illiteracy?'
3. How should government function in a democracy?
4. What virtues are necessary in a democracy?
5. Why did they disclaim any credit for themselves for the success of democracy in the country?

Answers

1. Earlier leaders treated Parliament with respect because they believed in the virtue of parliamentary democracy, good precedents and in the laying down or carrying out of policies with the consent of people or their representatives.
2. By the phrase 'vast burden of illiteracy', we understand the state of the country where majority of people are illiterate and uneducated. In context to the passage, it refers to the situation where people were unable to understand the concept of democratic government.
3. In democracy, the government must give space for debate and logic. It should ensure that the people of the country are allowed to criticise and correct. It should maintain a balance in every aspect while allowing feedbacks and taking rectifying actions upon it.
4. Parliamentary democracy can be well run only on the foundation of set virtues of cooperation, restraint and self-discipline.
5. Earlier, the leaders disclaimed the credit for the success of democracy because for them, the ability of the masses to understand the process of development and change was difficult. They appreciated the support lended by the people as without it, they could not have given shape to the country's new parliamentary system.

SUBJECTIVE COMPREHENSION

Passage 6

Apropos the article 'Children of a Lesser God' by PK Arun (HT March 28) in the context of the "Public hearing on child labour, organised by the campaign against child labour." It is obvious that more heat than light has been generated on the issue of child labour. One has to find out as to why children are forced to work as labourers. Is it by choice or compulsion?

Leaving aside bonded labour, none will like his/her children to work as labourers. All would like their children to attend school and be educated. And ultimately, it is for the children to pursue studies and not run away from school. However, more often than not, most of the children working as labour in towns and cities are school dropouts because they have found study to be too difficult. I have come across many children, who are unwilling to study despite being provided free tuitions. They consider studying to be the most difficult work. They repent only when it is too late. After all, one can take a child to school, but can not force him to study.

The government is guilty only to the extent that it has failed to provide free and compulsory education to all children between the ages of 6 and 14 years and provide suitable facilities within walking distance of all families. Providing free meals to children has also not succeeded.

In case the children do not study and are not gainfully employed, they become vagabonds and indulge in anti-social activities, thereby becoming a problem for the family and for society. Under these circumstances, it is better for the children to be employed i.e. occupied in their traditional profession or at some other place.

Questions
1. Why does the writer say that the issue of child labour has generated more heat than light?
2. How do children change from students to working labour?
3. Why can't the parents and authorities be totally blamed for child labour?
4. To what extent is the Government guilty?
5. Why should the children work in case they do not study?

Answers
1. The writer says that the issue of child labour has created more heat than light because it is a highly debatable topic which no actual and evident cause of the situation.
2. Children change from students to labourers because they find studies to be difficult.
3. Parents and authorities cannot be totally blamed because children leave school as they find it difficult to study. Despite of free tuitions being provided to them, they discontinue the journey of literacy.
4. The government is guilty only till the extent that it has failed to provide free and compulsory education to all the children between the ages of 6 and 14 years and provide suitable faculties within the walking distance of all families.
5. The children should work in case they do not study because they may indulge into wrong activities and become vagabonds if they are not be gainfully employed.

Passage 7

Religion can be defined as a system of beliefs and practices by means of which a group of people struggle with the ultimate problems of human life. It is the refusal to capitulate to death, to give up in the face of frustration and allow hostility to tear apart one's human associations.

All men experience these unending difficulties to some degree. For some persons, however, they stand out as the most significant experiences of life. These individuals are impelled to try to discover some meaning in what seems to be senseless suffering, some find a road to salvation through the obstacles of human life.

The beliefs and rites that make up a religion are the expressions of those who have felt the problems most intensively, who have been most acutely sensitive to the tragedies of death, the burdens of frustration, the sense of failure, the disruptive effects of hostility, powered by the strength of their feelings, such religious innovations have created 'solutions' that frequently have burst the bonds of man's sense and of nature, that have brought their adherents some relief. Thus religions are built to carry the 'peak load' of human emotional need.

Defined in this way, religion is and seems likely to remain an inevitable part of human life. Although the ways of struggling with these ultimate problems are enormously diverse and seem destined for continuous change, the problems themselves are universal. A society that did not furnish its members with beliefs and practices that sought to deal with an enormous burden of tragedy unalloyed with hostility unrestrained could not flourish, if need, it could survive at all.

Questions

1. How can religion be defined?
2. What, according to the writer, is 'experience' as it is understood by some?
3. What are the religious 'solutions' made in order to overcome the human problems?'
4. Why are religions built?
5. Why are religious beliefs and rites called innovations in the paragraph?

Answers

1. Religion can be defined as a set of beliefs and practices that guides a community or said group of people to tactfully handle and face the problems of life.
2. According to the author, the 'experience' understood by some is realisation and discovery of actual way to salvation by searching the real meaning of their suffering.
3. The beliefs and rites that a religion lays for humans to cope with the acute sensitivity towards obstacles of life are the 'solutions' made that offer relief to people.
4. Religions are built to help people overcome and cope with the unending struggles of human life. They help a person to move on with faith and ray of hope for betterment at an individual level.
5. The beliefs and rites of a religion are called innovations in the paragraph because they were the expressional consequences of people who have gone through severe emotional trauma or sufferings and these 'innovations' have brought them hope and solution to tackle those situation.

SUBJECTIVE COMPREHENSION

Passage 8

An educated man should know what is first-rate in those activities which spring from creative and intellectual faculties of human nature, such as literature, art, architecture and music. I should like to add science and philosophy but in these two subjects it is difficult for any but the expert to estimate quality and many educated people have not the close knowledge necessary to judge their real worth. On the other hand everyone has close and daily contact with the other four.

Architecture surrounds him in every city, literature meets him on every book-stall, music assails his ears on his radio set and from every juke-box; and art in its protean aspects of form and colour is a part of daily life. The architecture may often be bad, the literature and music often puerile, the art often undeserving of the name; but that is all the more reason why we should be able in all of them, to distinguish good from bad.

To judge by the literature offered us in hotel book-stands; and by most of the music played on the radio and by juke-boxes we might be more discriminating in these fields than we are. If it be said that music and art and literature are not essentials of life but its frills. I would reply that if so, it is curious that they are among the few immortal things in the world, and that should a man wish to be remembered two thousand years hence, the only certain way is to write a great poem or book. Compose a great sculpture, or build a great building. [Civil Services (Mains), 2007]

Questions

1. What is it that it necessary for an educated person to know?
2. Why does the author exclude science and philosophy from it?
3. What makes it practically easy for an educated man to be able to know literature, art, architecture and music?
4. How does exposure to ordinary literature and music help us?
5. What is the author's argument to prove that music, art and literature are essentials of life?

Answers

1. It is necessary for an educated man to know the first rate in activities that spring up from the creative and intellectual front of human nature i.e. literature, art, architecture and music.
2. The author excludes science and philosophy from it because according to the author, it is mandatory to have a thorough knowledge about these two subjects to estimate or judge the actual worth of the work.
3. It is practically easy for an educated man to be able to know literature, art, architecture and music because one finds all four of these in their surroundings.
4. Exposure to ordinary literature and music help us discrimate the good from bad in these fields.
5. The author gives the argument that music, art and literature are the few immortal things in the world. He further states that if a person wants to be remembered two thousand years hence, he can write a great poem or book, compose a great sculpture or build a great building.

Passage 9

I went to bed with mixed feelings about the rainy day. Though it had initially started well with the cool breezes and the droplets outside my window, getting to school was an uncomfortable experience. During the free periods we missed the bright sunshine when we used to run about in the playground. Towards the evening, the electricity went off for a few hours and I could not do my homework. The next day the papers reported that many people faced hardships while travelling. Trains are delayed and taxis were charging higher rates than usual at the station. But there are different seasons so we may be in touch with the rhythm of nature. It also makes it possible for us to appreciate what we otherwise take for granted.

The rain and rainy days affect people in different ways at different times. Alexander Frater's book Chasing the Monsoon gives a graphic account of the way the monsoon affects people's lives across India. In places which have a heavy monsoon, rainy days are a way of life and people prepare for the season by stocking up provisions and buying rain gear. However, in recent times the rain has been playing truant. With climate change starting us in the face globally, it could well be that the beauty of the rain will be a thing of the past. **[Civil Services (Mains), 2007]**

Questions

1. Mention three problems that the writer faced on the rainy day.
2. Which three difficulties did the newspaper report the next day?
3. Explain:
   (a) Mixed feelings (b) Rhythm of nature
   (c) To appreciate what we otherwise take for granted
4. How do people living in areas with heavy monsoon prepare for it?
5. Find words in the passage which mean the same as:
   (a) At the beginning
   (b) Give an account of something heard, seen, done
   (c) Visual symbols

Answers

1. The writer found it uncomfortable to reach school, missed the sunshine in the free periods when he used to run about in the playground and also could not manage to do his homework due to the electricity cut off.
2. The newspaper reported that many people faced troubles while travelling, the trains were delayed and the taxi drivers charged more than usual at the stations.
3. (a) Mixed feelings refer to partly positive and partly negative reaction to something, i.e. a mixture of positive and negative.
   (b) Rhythm of nature in the passage indicates the changing flow of weather and nature.
   (c) To appreciate what we otherwise take for granted means to value something that we get without taking it for granted.
4. People living in areas with heavy monsoon prepare in advance by stocking up provisions and keeping their rain gear ready to avoid any sort of difficulty in daily chores.
5. (a) Initially (b) Reported (c) Graphic

Passage 10

There can be no greater example of mankind's creative genius, than for him to move off from his home planet, and extend life throughout the solar system, by creating new abodes for life. Today with an increasing population of more than six billion people and the fear of possible disaster, the need for an alternate home for mankind has become urgent. Mars stands alone as the one planet in our solar system—not including Earth—that might be able to support life as it has all of the ingredients necessary for life. Though the average surface temperature on Mars is frigid and it is a desolate lifeless planet, Mars once had an atmosphere thick and warm enough to allow for the flow of liquid water on its surface.

If it is ever done at all, transforming a dry, desert-like Mars into a lush environment, where people, plants and other animals can survive, will be a huge undertaking that could take several decades or even centuries. Let us examine two methods that have been proposed. One method is placing large orbital mirrors that will reflect sunlight and heat onto the Mars surface. These mirrors would be directed at the polar caps of Mars and they would melt the ice. Over a period of many years, the rise in temperature would release greenhouse gases and heat up the planet.

Another option would be to set-up solar-powered, greenhouse gas producing factories. These would imitate the natural process of plant photosynthesis, inhaling carbon dioxide and emitting oxygen. The Mars atmosphere would slowly be oxygenated to the point that people on Mars would need only a breathing aparatus.

While we may reach Mars this century, it would take several millennia for the idea of transforming it into a planet on which plants and animals can flourish.

[SSC, 2008]

Questions

1. What are scientists planning with regard to Mars?
2. How are Mars and Earth similar to each other?
3. Why is there a need for an alternate home for humans?
4. Describe in your own words how orbital mirrors can raise the temperature of Mars.
5. What role would solar powered greenhouse factories play on Mars?

Answers

1. Scientists are planning to move off people from Earth to Mars due to overpopulation on Earth.
2. Mars and Earth are similar to each other as Mars is the only planet other than Earth in the entire solar system that might be able to support life since it has all the ingredients necessary for life.
3. There is a need for an alternate home for humans as our population has crossed the 6 billion mark and the fear of possible disaster has gone up. So, to avoid any mishappening, it is time to consider a supportive alternative home for mankind.
4. The orbital mirrors placed facing the polar caps may absorb and reflect all the sunlight which after a period of many years may melt the ice on the caps on Mars. After a few years, the rise in temperature would release greenhouse gases and heat up the planet.
5. The solar powered, greenhouse gas factories would imitate the natural process of plant photosynthesis, inhaling carbon dioxide and emitting oxygen. Thus, atmosphere would slowly be oxygenated to a point when Mars could support human life.

Passage 11

More and more as I near the end of my career as a heart surgeon, my thoughts have turned to the consideration of why people should suffer. Suffering seems so cruelly prevalent in the world today. My gloomy thoughts probably stem from an accident I had a few year ago. One minute I was crossing the street with my wife after a lovely meal together, and the next minute a car had hit me and knocked me and my wife. She was thrown into the other lane and was struck by a car coming from the opposite direction.

During the next few days in the hospital, I experienced not only agony but also fear and anger. Over and over I asked myself why should this happen to us? There were patients waiting for me to operate upon them and my wife had a small baby to look after.

As a doctor, I have always found the suffering of children particularly heartbreaking especially because of the total trust in doctors and nurses. They believe you are going to help them. If you can't they accept their fate.

What I witnessed in the hospital one morning opened my eyes to the fact that I was missing something in all my thinking about suffering.

What happened that morning was that a nurse had left a breakfast trolley unattended. And very soon two children took charge of it—a driver and a mechanic. The mechanic provided motor power running along behind the trolley with his head down, while the driver seated on the lower deck, held on with one hand and steered by scrapping his foot on the floor. The choice of roles was easy. The mechanic was blind and the driver had only one arm. They put on quite a show that day. Judging by the laughter and shouts of encouragement from the rest of the patients, it was a great entertainment.

Let me tell you about these two. The mechanic was all of 7 years old. One night his mother threw a lantern at his father, it missed him and broke over the child's head and shoulders. He suffered severe third degree burns and lost his eyes. His face was a mass of flesh. When I stopped by him on that day, he said, "You know we won", he was laughing.

The driver of trolley I knew better. A few years earlier, I had successfully closed a hole in his heart. He returned with a tumour of the bone. A few days earlier, his shoulder and arm were amputated. After that event that day he proudly informed me that the race was a success. The only problem was that the trolley's wheels needed to be oiled. Suddenly, I realised that these two children had given me a profound lesson in getting on with the business of living. This business of living is the celebration of being alive.

[SSC, 2008]

Questions

1. How did the doctor react to his accident?
2. What is his attitude to the suffering of children?
3. What was worrying the doctor when he was hospitalised?
4. What happened to the 'mechanic'?
5. What was the problem with the driver?
6. How did these two children change the doctor's outlook of life?

SUBJECTIVE COMPREHENSION

Answers

1. The doctor reacted to the accident with agony, fear and anger. He was profoundly disturbed as to why had all this happened to them when people waited for him to operate upon them and when his wife had a small baby to look after.
2. The doctor is sensitive towards the suffering of children. He finds it heartbreaking to see them in pain especially because they trust the doctors and nurses blindly to help them.
3. The doctor worried about his patients who were waiting for him to operate upon them and of his small baby who was to be taken care of by his wife.
4. The mechanic was accidentally hit by a lantern on his head and shoulder that his mother was throwing at his father which made him suffer from loss of vision due to third degree burns.
5. The driver was treated for a hole in his heart successfully, but had now returned due to a tumour in his bone which resulted in amputation of his shoulder and arm.
6. The two children changed the doctors outlook towards life. They made him realise that since he was in the business of living, it was his duty to celebrate being alive and able to help people.

Passage 12

Winning the war against France had been a Herculean effort. The conventional wisdom, then and later, attributed final victory to sea-power because, above all, it ensured that Britain stayed in the ring. The ships of the Royal Navy had prevented invasion, they had confined French power to Europe and allowed Britain to occupy nearly all the overseas possessions of her adversaries; they had guarded the convoys which sustained Wellington's Army in the peninsula; and they had guaranteed the survival of Britain's global commerce, which generated the wealth needed to pay for her war effort and underwrite those of the three big European powers with armies large enough to engage Napoleon on equal terms.

There were many reasons for the navy's success. The determination, self-confidence and professionalism of its officers and crews owned much to traditions established in the previous hundred years. Nelson was outstanding as a leader and tactician, but Duncan Jervis and Collingwood also deserve high praise. All understood their country's predicament and how much depended on them, which was why, whenever the chance came for battle, they grabbed at it, regardless of the odds. In the decisive battles of caps St Vincent, Camperdown, Abukir Bay and Trafalgar the British fleets were outnumbered but, trusting to superior seamanship and gunnery, their admirals took the offensive. An aggressive, gambling spirit paid off. As Nelson famously observed, an officer who laid his ship alongside the enemy could never be in the wrong.

Much depended on the individual naval officer's instinctively correct response to an emergency, something which Nelson cultivated among his subordinates to the point where they knew without being told what he expected of them. This quality filtered downwards. During an engagement with the French frigate Topaze off Guadeloupe in January, 1809, Captain William Maude of the Jason saw no need to inform the commander of his consort, the Cleopatra, of his intentions. "I considered it unnecessary to make any signal to him and he most fully anticipated my wishes by bringing his ship to anchor on the frigate's starboard bow and opening a heavy fire." Maude wrote afterwards. The action lasted 40 minutes and was decided by superior broadsides aimed against the French ship's hull. [Civil Services (Mains), 2008]

Questions

1. How did the British Navy defeat the French Navy?
2. What were the reasons for the British Navy's success?
3. How did the British Navy win the battles of Cape St Vincent, Camperdown, etc?
4. What did Nelson cultivate among his subordinates?
5. What was the reason for Captain William Maude's victory in January, 1809?

Answers

1. The British Navy defeated French Navy by occupying nearly all the overseas possessions of French adversaries.
2. The reasons behind British Navy's success was the determination, self-confidence and professionalism of its officers and crews.
3. The British Navy won the decisive battles of Cape St Vincent, Camperdown etc, by trusting their superior seamanship and gunnery and their admirals.
4. Nelson cultivated the factor of trust among his subordinates to instinctively depend and act upon the officers decision in the time of emergency and otherwise.
5. The reason for captain William Maude's victory in January 1809, was his instinctive and quick decision to bring his ship to anchor on the frigates starboard bow and take down a heavy fire against the French ship's hull.

Passage 13

The altogether new thing in the world then was the scientific method of research. Which in that period of Galileo, Kepler, Descates, Harvey and Francis Bacon was advancing with enormous strides. All walls, all the limitations, all the certainties of the ages were in dissolution tottering. In fact this epoch, in which we are participating still, with continually opening vistas, can be compared in magnitude and promise only to that of the 8th to the 4th millennium BC: of the birth of civilisation in the Near East, when the inventions of food production, gain agriculture and stockbreeding, released mankind from the primitive condition of foraging and so made possible an establishment of soundly grounded communities: first villages, then towns, then cities, kingdoms, and empires. Leo Frobenius wrote of that age as the Monument Age, and of the age now downing as the Global:

"In all previous ages, only restricted portions of the surface of the earth were known. Men looked from the narrowest upon a somewhat larger neighbourhood, and beyond that, a great unknown. They were all so to say insular: bound in. Whereas our view is confined no longer to a spot of space on the surface of this earth. It surveys that whole of the planet. And this fact, this lack of horizon, is something new."

It is chiefly to the scientific method of research that this release of mankind is due, and every developed individual has been free from the once protective but now dissolved horizons of the local land, local moral code, local modes of group thought and sentiment. Not only in the sciences but in every department of life the will and courage to credit one's own senses and to honour one's decisions, to name one's own virtues and to claim one's own vision of truth, have been the generative forces of the new age. Their is growing realisation even in the moral field that all judgements are (to use Nen/Sche's words) "human, all too human."   [Civil Services (Mains), 2009]

SUBJECTIVE COMPREHENSION

Questions

1. What is the 'epoch in which we are participating still'?
2. In what way is it comparable to the period of the 8th to the 4th millenniums BC?
3. What is meant by the new 'lack of horizon'?
4. What do you think is implied by 'all the certainties of the ages' that were 'in dissolution during the period of Galileo and his fellow scientists?
5. What is the new freedom we have found and why does it require courage?

Answers

1. The 'epoch in which we are participating still' means the scientific method of research and thinking without limitations.
2. It can be compared to the period of 8th to 4th millenniums BC as the discoveries at that point of time helped mankind to be free from certain problems as the scientific research today is helping the civilisation with the same.
3. This 'lack of horizon' refers to the shift of attention from conferring to small spaces and possibilities to greater ones in terms of physical surfaces on Earth.
4. 'All the certainties of the ages that were in dissolution during the period of Galileo and his fellow scientists' means that the scientists in that era looked and thought beyond certainties and limits.
5. The new freedom that the people have found is from the now dissolved horizons of local land, moral code, modes of group thoughts and sentiments. It needs courage to accept these and stand up to credit ones own senses, honour ones own decisions, to name ones own virtues and to claim ones own vision of truth as these are the generative forces of the new age.

Passage 14

All of us are now aware of the threats facing the Earth of the degradation that man is causing to his own environment. We know that the global temperature is rising, that the ozone layer is being disrupted, that the groundwater level is going down alarmingly. We also know that our air, water and soil are being increasingly polluted, that our forests are being steadily depleted. Our Earth is becoming more and more uninhabitable.

Why is this so? The most important reason is that our concept of development is unscientific and illogical. Our development has made life more complicated and difficult for us.

In fact, it is over-exploitation of our natural wealth that has resulted in the many unsolvable problems we now have, problems of pollution of air, water and soil.

The natural resources of our Earth are being exploited by the developed nations to such an extent that it becomes almost impossible for the rest of the world to meet even their basic needs. The developed nations do this for the sake of change and novelty and this craze has given rise to 'a throw away culture'. They throw away not only cups and plates, paper and clothes and foodstuffs, furniture and cars, but even their homes and old people. This attitude of the developed countries has wrought havoc not only to them, but to the poor, backward nations too; for this is the model of development the developed countries place before them.

Development does not mean piling up luxuries; development does not mean having more and more automobiles on your roads; development does not mean making air, water and soil more polluted; development doesn't mean more and bigger buildings. The mad rush to catch up with the artificial speed of high competition is not development.

Let us take the example of a small state. Kerala was one of the most beautiful places on the Earth, all lush green with the Sahya Mountains on the East and the Arabian Sea on the West. Forty-four rivers and an intricate network of lakes and streams and backwaters and two regular rainy seasons kept this land cool and prosperous. Here we had our own system of agriculture, our own seed and manuring and our own watering methods.

Then came development. The groves were cut down and cash crops were sown. The ponds were filled up because it was considered wastage of land. The people were told that their local seeds were no good and were given high-yielding varieties. Cow dung and leaf manure were also considered primitive. At subsidised rates, chemical fertilizers and pesticides were given. The chemical manure was considered excellent and pesticides a boon. It took time for the people to understand that the chemical fertilizers are not wonderful and that the pesticides do not know when to stop killing. Even the friendly moths, the beneficial bacteria, the earthworm, field spiders and the grasshoppers are wiped out. The soil and water and the network of streams and canals have become polluted.

Likewise, in the name of development we have cleared most of our precious lands. Felling and encroachment, the so-called developmental activities and big dams have almost wiped them out. We have at present not more than 5% good forest in Kerala.

[IFS, 2015]

Questions
1. What is the greatest danger which the Earth is facing now?
2. What does the author mean by 'throw away culture'?
3. What is the real meaning of the term 'development' as explained in the passage?
4. How did the so-called development affect the people of Kerala?
5. What caused deforestation in Kerala?

Answers
1. The greatest danger that the Earth is facing right now is the degradation caused by men, which has led to climate change, ozone layer depletion, decreasing groundwater level and rising air, soil and water pollution.
2. By 'throw away culture', the author refers to the discarding habit or pattern of developed nations. It points out that people in these developed nations throw away various things that can be useful to other people.
3. As explained in the passage, development means optimum use of man-made and natural resources for the sustainable progress of the nation.
4. The so called development affected the people of Kerala by making their soil and water and the network of streams and canals polluted.
5. Deforestation was done in Kerala so that cash crops can be grown in the deforested areas.

SUBJECTIVE COMPREHENSION

Passage 15

A complete reading program, therefore, should include four factors : at least one good book each week, a newspaper or news magazine, magazines of comment and interpretation, and book reviews. If you keep feeding your intelligence with these four foods, you can be sure that your brain cells will be properly nourished. To this must be added the digestive process that comes from your thinking and from discussion with individuals or groups. It is often desirable to make books that you own personally part of your mind by underlining or by marking in the margin the more important statements. This will help you to understand the book as you first read it, because out of the mass of details you must have selected the essential ideas. It will help you to remember better the gist of the book, since the physical act of underlining, with your eyes on the page, tends to put the thought more firmly into your brain cells. It will save time whenever you need to refer to the book.

Above all, never forget that creative intelligence is correlation of facts and ideas, not mere memorising. What counts is what you can do with your knowledge, by linking it with other things you have studied or observed. If you read Plutarch's life of Julius Caesar, think how his rise to political power paralleled the technique of Adolf Hitler or that of your local political boss. If you read a play by Shakespeare, think how his portrayal of the characters helps you to understand someone you know.

In everything you read, keep at the back of your mind what it means to your life here and now, how it supports or challenges the things you were taught in school, in church and at home, and how the wisdom you get from books can guide you in your thinking, in your career, in your voting as a citizen and in your personal morals.

[Civil Services (Mains), 2014]

Questions

1. What are the four things required for a complete reading program and why?
2. What else is required to feed your intelligence?
3. Why does the writer recommend underlining or marking in the margin the more important statements?
4. What use can you put your knowledge to?
5. How can what you learn from books help you in your life?

Answers

1. The four things required for a complete reading program are reading of atleast one good book in each week, a newspaper or news magazine, magazines of comment and interpretation and book reviews. These are required to properly nourish one's brain cells.
2. We need to add a digestive process that comes from our own thinking and from discussion of what we have fed our brains from the four sources with individuals or groups.
3. The writer recommends underlining or writing the important statements in the margin because it helps you select the essential ideas out of all the information the book has to offer and feed it more firmly into your brain cells. It also saves time whenever you need to refer to the book.
4. One can put one's knowledge to correlate the facts and ideas one has learnt and linking it to understand the meaning of life. It can help one to know how the knowledge one gained from the four sources apply, supports and challenges incidences in one's life.
5. The wisdom we gain from books can help us guide our thinking towards every aspect of our life, i.e. career, responsibility as a citizen, individuality etc.

Passage 16

Ever since the dawn of civilisation, class inequality has existed. Among savage tribes at the present day, it takes simple forms. There are chiefs, and the chiefs are able to have several wives. Savages, unlike civilised men, have found a way of making wives a source of wealth, so that the more wives a man has the wealthier he becomes. But this primitive form of social inequality soon gave way to others more complex. In the main, social inequality has been bound up with inheritance, and therefore, in all patriarchal societies, with descent in the male line. Originally, the greater wealth of certain persons was due to military prowess. The successful fighter acquired wealth, and transmitted it to his sons.

Wealth acquired by the sword usually consisted of land, and to this day land-owning is the mark of the aristocrat, the aristocrat being in theory the descendant of some feudal baron, who acquired his lands by killing the previous occupant and holding his acquisition against all comers. This is considered the most honourable source of wealth. There are others slightly less honourable, exemplified by those who, while completely idle themselves, have acquired their wealth by inheritance from an industrious ancestor; and yet others, still less respectable, whose wealth is due to their own industry. In the modern world, the plutocrat who, though rich, still works, is gradually ousting the aristocrat, whose income was in theory derived solely from ownership of land and natural monopolies. There have been two main legal sources of property: one, the aristocratic source, namely, ownership of land; the other, the bourgeois source, namely, the right to the produce of one's own labour.

The right to the produce of one's own labour has always existed only on paper, because things are made out of other things, and the man who supplies the raw material exacts a right to the finished product in return for wages, or, where slavery exists, in return for the bare necessaries of life. We have thus three orders of men-the land-owner, the capitalist and the proletarian. The capitalist in origin is merely a man whose savings have enabled him to buy the raw materials and the tools required in manufacturing, and who has thereby acquired the right to the finished product in return for wages. The three categories of land-owner, capitalist and proletarian are clear enough in theory; but in practice the distinctions are blurred. A land-owner may employ business methods in developing a seaside resort which happens to be upon his property.

A capitalist whose money is derived from manufacture may invest the whole or part of his fortune in land and take to living upon rent. A proletarian, in so far as he has money in the savings bank, or a house which he is buying on the instalment plan, becomes to that extent a capitalist or a land-owner as the case may be. The eminent barrister who charges a thousand guineas for a brief should, in strict economics, be classified as a proletarian. But he would be indignant if this were done and has the mentality of a plutocrat.

[CAPF, 2013]

Questions
1. How is social inequality bound with inheritance?
2. What is the irony in the most honourable source of wealth?
3. What are the two legal sources of property?
4. How does the writer distinguish the three orders of men?
5. Who is a plutocrat?

SUBJECTIVE COMPREHENSION

Answers

1. Social inequality is bound to inheritance since times immemorial as people used to acquire wealth through military prowesses and these successful fighters used to transmit it to their sons.
2. The irony in the most honourable source of wealth is that of the wealth of land is acquired by killing the previous occupant and holding its acquisition against all the challengers. It does not come from any kind of hard work or fair means.
3. The are two legal sources of property are the aristocratic source and the bourgeois source.
4. The capitalist is a man whose savings have enabled him to buy the raw materials and tools required in manufacturing. The land-owner is the one who owns the land and the proletarian is the working class.
5. A plutocrat is someone whose power is derived entirely from their wealth.

Passage 17

Gandhi's experience in South Africa was decisive: not only in his political, family and social life, but also for his culture and religion. Two of his most faithful collaborators there, Henry Polak and Hermann Kallenbach, were secular Jews. Gandhi had occasion to meet exponents of diverse religions and denominations, including Christian ones; he held long discussions with them, and some tried to convert him. It was a Jainist poet and thinker from Bombay, Raychandbhai, who confirmed Gandhi in the faith of his fathers.

Gandhi met him on his return to India from England, and continued to correspond with him from South Africa, until the poet's premature death. In his autobiography, Gandhi wrote that only once in his life had he come close to choosing a personal guru: yes, Raychandbhai. He considered him "the best Indian of his time," and freely acknowledged his debt to the Jain. If his Christian friends in London had awakened in him "the thirst for a religious quest," Raychandbhai had taught him that religion was essentially the control of one's own spirit, and liberation from any attachment or aversion to people or things.

It was principally during his South African years that Gandhi became acquainted with writers whom he would consider masters for the rest of his life: Ruskin, Thoreau, Carpenter, Tolstoy. In 1904 he read Ruskin's *Unto this Last*, a book identifying the individual good with the common good, and speaking of the importance of work as the cornerstone of life; for Ruskin, all types of work have equal dignity and value, whether they be intellectual or manual, noble or humble. In 1907, Gandhi read Thoreau's "On the Duty of Civil Disobedience," and was struck by its central theme: one's duty to refuse to obey a country's laws if one believes them to be unjust. Two years later, while in London, he read a volume written by the idealistic socialist, Enward Carpenter:

Civilisation: Its *cause* and *cure*. He found it "enlightening", excellent in its anaylsis of civilisation.

An advocate of the return to a simple life in harmony with nature, Carpenter condemned modern civilisation as degrading and corrupting; like Ruskin, he exalted the joy of manual work, which industrialism had separated from the creative project.

However, the author that struck Gandhi more than any other was Tolstoy. All during the rest of his life, Gandhi would recognise his debt to the Russian writer. He probably read Tolstoy for the first time during the London years of his youth, when he greatly admired the author's ideas and work.

But his first great encounter with Tolstoy dates back to 1894, in South Africa, when a friend gave him a copy of *God's Reign is Within You*. Gandhi's reading of it left an indelible impression on him. He felt for the book and its author the same admiration that he had held for the Sermon on the Mount.

He found in it an admonition against responding to evil with violence, an exhortation to love one's neighbour and practise pacifism, and a confirmation of the ancient Indian commandment (Jainist, in particular) of *ahimsa*. He also found a brief story of the forerunners of non-violence, and a catalogue of its advocates and "militants" at that time: from the Quakers to Tom Paine, from the American abolitionists to the Russian *duchobors*.

In other books by Tolstoy which he read in the years that followed, Gandhi was led to agree more and more adamantly with the Russian's distillation of Christianity-and of every religious faith-to the commandment to love one's neighbour; the aspiration toward a profound moral rebirth of man; a highly critical attitude toward progress, science, luxury and wealth, as well as toward the city, a place of alienation and destruction of man's deepest values. [CAPF, 2013]

Questions

1. Why was Gandhi's experience in South Africa decisive?
2. Who was Gandhi's personal guru and why did he consider him so?
3. Who were the writers whom he considered as masters?
4. How did these masters influence Gandhi?
5. How much was Gandhi impressed by Tolstoy?

Answers

1. Gandhi's experience in South Africa was decisive because two of his most faithful collaborators were there. He interacted with intellectual exponents of diverse religions and denominations.
2. Raychandbhai was Gandhi's personal guru. Gandhi chose him because it was him who taught Gandhi that religion was essentially the control of one's own spirit and liberation from any attachment or aversion to people or things.
3. Gandhi considered Ruskin, Thoreau, Carpenter and Tolstoy his masters.
4. The masters influenced Gandhi in different ways. Ruskin taught Gandhi about identification of personal good in common good and to respect every kind of work. Thoreau and Carpenter fed him about civil duties, right, causes and cure. Tolstoy refined Gandhi as a non-violent person as he inspired him to not respond to evil with violence.
5. Tolstoy left an impeccable mark on Gandhi. He shook him internally through his advocation of admonition against violence as a response.

SUBJECTIVE COMPREHENSION

Passage 18

Why do some countries get over all the impediments and overcome vested interests with leaders able to mobilise their people to really improve their infrastructure, education, and governance and other countries stall ?

One answer is culture.

To reduce a country's economic performance to culture alone is ridiculous, but to analyse a country's economic performance without reference to culture is equally ridiculous, although that is what many economists and political scientists' want to do. This subject is highly controversial and is viewed as politically incorrect to introduce. So it is often the elephant in the room that no one wants to speak about.

But I am going to speak about it here, for a very simple reason : As the world goes flat, and more and more of the tools of collaboration get distributed and commoditised the gap between the culture that have the will, the way and the focus to quickly adopt new tools and apply them and those that do not, will matter more. The differences between the two will become amplified.

One of the most important books on the subject is *The Wealth and Poverty of Nations* by the economist David Lands. He argues that although climate, natural resources and geography all play roles in explaining why some countries are able to make the leap to industrialisation and others are not, the key factor is actually a country's cultural endowments, particularly the degree to which it has internalised the values of hard work, thrift, honesty, patience and tenacity, as well as the degree to which it is open to change, new technology and equality for women. One can agree or disagree with the balance Lands strikes between these cultural moves and other factors shaping economic performance. But I find refreshing his insistence on elevating the culture question and his refusal to buy into arguments that the continued stagnation of some countries is simply about Western colonialism, geography or historical legacy.

In my own travels, two aspects of culture have struck me relevant in the flat world. One is how outward your culture is : to what degree is it open to foreign influences and ideas ? How well does it 'glocalise'? The other, more intangible, is how inward your culture is. By that I mean, to what degree is there a sense of national solidarity and focus on development, to what degree is there thrust within the society for strangers to collaborate together and to what degree are the elites in the country concerned with the masses and ready to invest at home, or are they indifferent to their own poor and more interested in investing abroad?

The more you have a culture that naturally glocalises – i.e. the more your culture easily absorbs foreign ideas and global best practices and moulds those with its own traditions - the greater advantage you will have in a flat world. The natural ability to glocalise has been one of the strengths of Indian culture, American culture, Japanese culture and, lately, Chinese culture. The Indians, for instance, take the view that the Moguls come, the Moguls go, the British come, the British go, we take the best and leave the rest, but we still eat curry, our women still wear saris and we still live in tightly bound extended family units. That's globalising at its best.

Cultures that are open and willing to change have a huge advantage in this world. Openness is critical because you start tending to respect people for their talent and abilities. When you are chatting with another person in another country, you do not know what his or her colour is. You are dealing with people on the basis of talent-not race or ethnicity and that changes, subtly, over time your whole view of human beings, if you are in this talent-based and performance-based world rather than the background-based world.

[CISF, 2013]

Questions

1. Explain how the economic performance of a country is related to its culture.
2. What according to David Lands are the cultural endowments of a country?
3. What, according to the writer, will happen when the world goes flat?
4. What is 'glocalisation' and how has India glocalised?
5. Explain the benefits of the openness of a culture.

Answers

1. The cultural endowments such as the value of hard work, thrift, honesty, patience and tenacity as well as the degree to which a culture is open to change decides the economic performance of a country.
2. According to David Lands, the values of hard work, thrift, honesty, patience and tenacity are the cultural endowments of a country.
3. According to the writer, if the world goes flat, more and more of the tools of collaborations will get distributed and commoditised. As a result, the gap between the cultures that have the will, the way and the focus to quickly adopt new tools and apply them and those that do not, will matter more.
4. Glocalisation is absorbing foreign ideas and global best practices and moulding them with our own culture and traditions. Indians take the best views from the foreign ideas such as from the Moguls and the Britishers, but still eat curry, wear saris and live in a joint family system.
5. Openness of a culture results in the willingness to change and has a huge advantage in this world. It helps to respect people for their talent and not on the basis of their race or ethnicity. It changes our viewpoint from a background based world to a talent and performance based world.

Passage 19

I had come to Bangalore, India's Silicon Valley, on my own.Columbus like journey of exploration. Columbus sailed with *Nina*, the *Pinta* and the *Santa Maria* in an effort to discover a shorter, more direct route to India by heading West, across the Atlantic, on what he presumed to be an open sea route to the East Indies - rather than going South and East around Africa, as Portuguese, explorers of his day were trying to do. India and the magical Spice Islands of the East were famed at the time for their gold, pearls, gems and silk-source of untold riches. Finding this shortcut by sea to India at a time when the Muslim powers of the day had blocked the overland routes from Europe, was a way both for Columbus and the Spanish monarchy to become wealthy and powerful.

When Columbus set sail, he apparently assumed the Earth was round, which was why he was convinced that he could get to India by going West. He miscalculated the distance, though. He thought the Earth was a smaller sphere than it is. He also did not anticipate running into a landmass before he reached the East Indies. Nevertheless, he called the aboriginal peoples he encountered in the New World 'Indians'. Returning home, though, Columbus was able to tell his patrons, King Ferdinand and Queen Isabella, that although he never did find India, he could affirm that the world was indeed round.

I set out for India by going due East, via Frankfurt. I had Lufthansa business class. I knew exactly which direction I was going thanks to the GPS map displayed on the screen that popped out of the armrest of my airline seat. I landed safely and on schedule. I too encountered people called Indians. I too was searching for India's riches. Columbus was searching for hardware - precious metals, silk and spices-the sources of wealth in his day. I was searching for software, brainpower, complex algorithms, knowledge workers, call centres, transmission protocols, break throughs in optic engineering-the sources of wealth in our day.

Columbus was happy to make Indians he met his slaves, a pool of free manual labour. I just wanted to understand why the Indians I met were taking our work, why they had become such an important pool for the outsourcing of service and information technology work from America and other industrialised countries. Columbus had more than one hundred men on his three ships: I had a small crew from Discovery Times channel that fit comfortably into two banged-up vans, with Indian drivers who drove barefoot.

When I set sail, so to speak, I too assumed the world was round, but what I encountered in the real India, profoundly shook my faith in that notion. Columbus accidentally ran into America but thought he had discovered part of India. I actually found India and thought many of the people I met there were Americans. Some had actually taken American names, and others were doing imitations of American accents at call centres and American business techniques at software labs.

Columbus reported to his king and queen that the world was round, and he went down in history as the man who first made this discovery. I returned home and shared my discovery only with my wife, and only in a whisper.

"Honey", I confided, "I think the world is flat".

How did I come to this conclusion? I guess you could say it all started in Nandan Nilekani's conference room at Infosys Technologies Limited. At one point, summing up, Nilekani uttered a phrase that rang in my ear. He said to me, "Tom, the playing field is being levelled." He meant that countries like India are now able to complete for global knowledge work as never before and that America had better get ready for this. America was going to be challenged but, he insisted, the challenge would be good for America because we are always at our best when we are being challenged.

What Nandan is saying, I thought to myself, is that the playing field is flattened... Flattened? Flattened? My God, he's telling me the world is flat! [CISF, 2013]

Questions

1. What was Columbus searching for on his voyage to India and what did he find?
2. While Columbus found that the world was round, how is it that the writer finds that the world is flat?
3. Why has India become a pool of outsourcing of service and information technology?
4. Why does the writer think that many Indians have become Americans?
5. What does the author mean by "... the playing field is flattened.... Flattened?"

Answers

1. Columbus was in search to discover a shorter, more direct route to India and he found the aboriginal people.
2. While Columbus found that the world is round, the writer feels that the world is flat because he thought that he had encountered more Americans in India, out of which some had taken American names and some imitated American accents and business techniques.
3. India has become a pool of outsourcing of service and information technology because India is abound with the knowledge of software, brain power, complex algorithms, call centres, transmission protocols, breakthrough in optic engineering and all that are the sources of wealth.
4. The writer thinks that many Indians have become Americans because of the outsourcing business. Some have taken actual American names, some imitate the American accent at call centres and some imitate American business techniques at softwares labs.
5. The author feels that the playing field is flat because instead of the world being round it has emerged as a flat competitive field offering an equally advantageous platform to all the countries.

Passage 20

It is not possible to admit that there is life of any sort on the moon. It is a world that is completely dead, a sterile mountainous waste on which during the heat of the day Sun blazes down with fury, but where during the long night the cold is more intense than anything ever experienced on the Earth.

These hard facts are conveniently forgotten by those who believe that it would be possible to shoot a rocket containing human beings to the moon, from which the human explorers could land and explore some portion of the moon's surface.

The explorers would need to be encased in airtight suits and provided with oxygen apparatus to enable them to breathe. Even supposing that they could protect themselves against the great heat by day and the extreme cold at night, a worse fate might be in store for them unless their suits were completely bullet-proof. For they would be in danger of being shot by a shooting star. The average shooting star or meteor, which gives so strongly the impression of a star falling from the sky, is a small fragment of matter, usually smaller than a pea and often no larger than a grain of sand. Space is not empty, but contains great numbers of such fragments. The Earth, in its motion round the Sun meets many of these fragments, which enter the atmosphere at a speed many times greater than that of a rifle bullet.

The meteor, rushing through the air, becomes intensely heated by friction and it is completely vaporised before it has penetrated within a distance of twenty miles from the surface of the Earth. Many millions of these fragments enter our atmosphere in the course of a day, but the atmosphere protects us from them. On the moon, however, they fall to the surface and so great is their number that the lunar explorers would run a considerable risk being hit.

The difficulties that would have to be encountered by any one who attempted to explore the moon would be incomparably greater than those that have to be faced in the endeavour to reach the top of Everest: except in two respects: one, movement would be less fatiguing, because the gravitational pull of the moon is not very great, and two, the moon having no atmosphere, the lunar explorers would have no strong winds, in fact no winds at all, to contend with. [CISF, 2015]

SUBJECTIVE COMPREHENSION

Questions
1. What would an explorer observe on the moon?
2. How should an explorer equip himself on the moon mission?
3. Why can a meteor be dangerous?
4. What happens when a meteor rushes through the air?
5. How is exploring the moon less difficult than climbing Mount Everest?

Answers
1. An explorer will observe it as a world that is completely dead, as a sterile mountain of waste where the days are blazing with fury and nights are colder than any ever experienced on Earth.
2. An explorer shall have to equip himself of an airtight suit and an oxygen apparatus to enable him to breathe. They should also ensure that their suit is bullet proof in order to escape from the shooting stars/meteors.
3. A meteor can be dangerous on moon as they fall directly on the surface of moon unlike being evaporated by the atmosphere of Earth.
4. When a meteor rushes through the air, it becomes immensely heated due to friction and vaporises completely before hitting the surface. Thus, the atmosphere of the Earth protects us from such fragments on everyday basis.
5. Exploring the moon is less difficult than climbing the Mount Everest because of two reasons. First, movement on moon is less exhausting due to the lesser gravitational pull of the moon than that of the Earth. Second, the explorer will not have to face strong winds since moon does not have an atmosphere.

Passage 21

The public sector is at the cross-roads ever since the launch of economic reforms in India. The pendulum has been swinging between survival and surrender. It is the result of a confluence of several factors: a shift in global economic environment, the emergence of the market economy and myths surrounding the performance of the public sector. So virulent has been the onslaught that it is becoming axiomatic that by the very concept, the public sector is inefficient and resource waster whereas private enterprises resource efficient.

The reform programme in India commenced with the policy of restricting of the public sector supported by greater public participation. With the passage of time, the process of liberalisation has shifted to privatisation in a disguised form couched as strategic role. In the wake of the recent hot pursuit of the wholesale privatisation programme a lively debate has emerged. It provides a golden opportunity to introspect and revisit the issue.

At the very outset, it must be made clear that in the worldwide liberalised economic environment and a very high stake of the state in most public sector undertakings disinvest policy seeks to differentiate closed or bankrupt enterprise from the private sector-a fact deliberately overlooked by the champions of privatisation. These undertakings need immediate attention. They are an unnecessary drain on the public exchequer. If these cannot be sold lock, stock and barrel, asset stripping is the only option.

Obviously, the government cannot realise good price from these assets but their disposal will help to stop the drain. If these assets are depreciated or become <u>obsolete</u>, then there is no point in holding on to them indefinitely and take to softer option of selling the vibrant and highly profit-making organisations to reduce the budgetary deficit. Non performers exist both in public and private sectors. Why condemn the public sector as a whole ? Better option will be closure or privatisation of loss making and non-viable units supporting PSUs which could be turned around and become healthy and viable.

Let it be understood that PSUs are a big repository of value and it will take quite some time for privatisation programme to materialise despite the desire to expedite the process.

[CISF, 2015]

Questions

1. What is the debate about in the passage above?
2. What does the author favour and why?
3. What sugesstions are offered to contain/recover losses?
4. How has market economy brought about change in people's thinking about PSUs?
5. Make sentences of the following words used in the passage to bring out their meaning :
   (a) virulent
   (b) axiomatic
   (c) strategic
   (d) obsolete

Answers

1. The passage lays the approach of privatisation of the public undertakings as a whole considering them to be resource inefficient against the private enterprises which people considers to be resource efficient.
2. The author favours supporting the profit making and variable enterprises in both public and private sector and closure/privatisation of non-performing public units for the development of the economy instead of brushing off PSUs completely.
3. The author suggests not holding onto obsolete or depreciated assests, instead the writer favours selling these assets to vibrant and high profit making organisation to reduce bugdetary deficit and recover losses.
4. Market economy has brought change in peoples, thinkings about PSUs. The very defined assumption regarding public sector undertakings has been changed. PSUs now are not as overlooked or underestimated as they used to be earlier.
5. (i) A **virulent** virus has spread across the city killing 50 people so far.
   (ii) It is **axiomatic** that you reap what you sow.
   (iii) A **strategic** planning for the organisation is the most crucial concern of the management.
   (iv) He disposed off all the **obsolete** machinery from his garage.

Passages for Practice

Directions *Read the passages carefully and answers the questions that follow.*

Passage 1

The advances of the scientific age have not been fortuitous. They are the logical outcome of fearless thought, practiced now unfortunately by only a few and even by the few only in limited fields. Imagine, however, the possibilities inherent in the application to the social and political questions of the day of the same style of thought pursued with the same energy and cooperation that went to the production of the atom bomb. Almost without exception, the major problems facing governments and peoples today are technical ones—full production and employment, social security, housing, race-relations, food supplies, agricultural policy, health, war, distribution. The solution of these problems is impossible except by the methods of science.

This complex civilisation, rendered so by science, needs the scientific method in every aspect of the citizen's life. Science is no longer neutral. When the first atomic bomb exploded in New Mexico, it exploded with it all further possibility for science to stand aside. It can no longer be socially irresponsible but the main body of citizens cannot wish to see it become all-powerful. Through no wish of its own, science has been forced to assume a commanding position.

The future of politics is scientific. Only philosophers can now safely guide the destinies of men. This is not a new view. Even Plato, in spite of his insistence on the importance of the expedient, confessed, "I was forced to the condition that only the true philosophy can enable us to discern in all cases what is good for communities and individuals"; and that accordingly the human race will see better days if either those who rightly and genuinely follow philosophy acquire political power, or else the class who have political control become real philosophers.

Science is the learning of the democracies. It has always been so in Greece as in our times; and recent history has shown most clearly that other forms of government can only exit provided that scientific spirit is eliminated even when its technology is retained. Only in a community where the citizens have freedom of action can science flourish and only when science flourishes can the citizens be free. Democracy and science go hand-in-hand. It is not a coincidence that the principles of citizenship were taught in Greece when science flourished and have come into their own again in modern times.

But even in a democracy there will always be forces in opposition to the spread of knowledge and liberty of thoughts among the citizens. The danger of the rising oligarchy is ever present and science is not the learning of the oligarchies—even scientific ones: Rhetoric and tradition are the remnants of oligarchies. The possibility of a scientific oligarchy is now the most imminent of the changes we may have to face.

Science has given to the citizen through technology the power of self-destruction, but has placed alongside it the basic philosophy that has vitalized science itself. On what use he makes of these twin gifts depends the world's future. If, as he has done in the past, he grasps avidly the former and neglects the latter, then Norman Collins is right, "Modern man is obsolete, a self-made anachronism becoming more incongruous by the minute. He has exalted change in everything but himself."

After three centuries, science is now supreme and as a result the world stands at the cross-roads. But if we recognize the need for change, break the chains of habit and indulge in the single-minded pursuit of truth, the new scientific age shall be bright with promise for citizenship and for the citizen on every plane of communal life.

[CAPF, 2009]

Questions

1. How does scientific knowledge affect the political system?
2. How has science rendered modern civilization complex?
3. In what way has science been given a commanding position?
4. When will democracy be changed into oligarchy?
5. How do politics and philosophy complement each other?
6. What can man do to strike balance between inventions and social development?
7. Can a philosopher guide the destiny of man?
8. Explain the portions underlined in the passage, keeping in view the context in which they appear.

Passage 2

According to the findings of a recent Government Survey there are an estimated 33 million registered NGOs working in the country—one for every 400 Indians. Not only has the number of NGOs in India risen dramatically but so has their influence. In some of India's flagship development efforts—the National Rural Employment Guarantee Act, the National Rural Health Mission, the Right to Education or even the draft Right to Food Act—NGOs have been at the forefront both in formulating these laws and policies and in implementing them. NGOs have helped voice the concerns of some of India's most vulnerable groups and focus the attention of the government on critical, social and developmental issues.

They have also spearheaded efforts to expose corruption and maladministration in government bringing in much needed transparency.

But despite the growing influence of NGOs in India today, we know very little about them : their structure, activities, sources of funding and, more importantly, how accountable they are to the people they represent. This is alarming given the crores of rupees in development aid that NGOs receive from the government and from donors every year. Ironically, though NGOs have been watchdogs of the government for many years, there has been little regulation or monitoring of their own activities leading many to ask a very fundamental question : who watches the watchers?

Interestingly, although India as probably the world's highest NGO population, the debate on NGO accountability is still in its nascent stages. Across the world, NGOs have been experimenting with different ways of addressing the issue of accountability; Indian NGOs would do well by learning from these efforts. For example, NGOs in Kenya are legally required to comply with the Code of Conduct for NGOs developed by the National Council of NGOs, a self regulatory body set up under the NGO Coordination Act in 1990. The code ensures that NGOs comply with basic ethical and governance standards. Similarly, in Uganda, the NGO Quality Assurance Mechanism (QuAM) certifies NGOs against a set of quality standards designed to ensure NGO credibility.

SUBJECTIVE COMPREHENSION

In Chile, *Chile Transparente* has developed transparency standards for NGOs which require organisations to publish online information about their mission, vision, activities, staff, details of funding etc. [Civil Services (Mains), 2010]

Questions

1. What are India's important development schemes?
2. How do NGOs help 'Vulnerable Groups' in India?
3. What do we know about the structure, activities and sources of funding of the NGOs in India?
4. Whom does the author describe as watchers? Why?
5. How do the NGOs in other nations deal with the issue of accountability?

Passage 3

The work which Gandhiji had taken in hand was not only the achievement of political freedom but establishment of a social order based on truth and non-violence, unity and peace, equality and universal brotherhood, and maximum freedom for all. The unfinished part of his experiment was perhaps even more difficult to achieve than the achievement of freedom.

In the political struggle the fight was against a foreign power and all could or did either join in it or at least wish it success and give to it their moral support. In establishing the social order of his pattern, there was lively possibility of a conflict arising between groups and classes of our own people.

Experience shows that man values his possessions because here he sees the means of perpetuation and survival through his descendants even after his body is reduced to ashes. That new order cannot be established without radically changing men's mind and attitude towards property and at some stage or other the haves have to yield place to the have nots. We have seen in our time attempts to achieve a kind of egalitarian society. But this was done by and large by the use of physical force. In the result, it is difficult to say that the instinct to possess has been rooted out or that it will not reappear in an even worse form under a different face. It may even be that like gas kept confined within metallic containers under great pressure, or water held behind a big dam, that breaks the barrier, reaction will one day sweep back with violence equal in extent and intensity to what was used to establish and maintain the outward egalitarian form.

This enforced egalitarianism contains in its bosom the seed of its own destruction. The root cause of class-conflict is possessiveness or the acquisitive instinct. So long as the ideal that is held up to be achieved is one of securing the maximum of material satisfaction, possessiveness is neither suppressed nor eliminated but grows by what it feeds upon. Nor does it cease to be such– it is possessiveness still whether it is confined to a few only or is bared by many. If egalitarianism is to endure, it has to be based not on the possession of the maximum of material goods whether by few or by all but on voluntary, enlightened renunciation – denying oneself what cannot be shared by others or can be enjoyed only at the expense of others.

This calls for substitution of spiritual values for purely material ones. Mahatma Gandhi showed us how the acquisitive instinct inherent in man could be transmuted by the adoption of the ideal of trusteeship by those who have for the benefit of all those who have not so that instead of leading to exploitation and conflict it would become a means and incentive to the amelioration and progress of society.

[CAPF, 2011]

Questions

1. What, according to the author was the unfinished part of Gandhiji's experiment?
2. Why is a change in men's attitude to property necessary for establishing a new social order?
3. Why does the author say that enforced egalitarianism contains the seeds of its own destruction?
4. How can the acquisitive instinct of man be made a tool for social progress?

Passage 4

The happy man is the man who lives objectively, who has free affections and wide interests, who secures his happiness through these interests and affections and through the fact that they, in turn, make him an object of interest and affection to many others. To be a recipient of affection is a potent cause of happiness, but the man who demands affection is not the man upon whom it is bestowed. The man who receives affection is, speaking broadly, the man who gives it. But it is useless to attempt to give it as a calculation, in the way in which one might lend money at interest, for a calculated affection is not genuine and is not felt to be so by the recipient.

What then can a man do who is unhappy because he is encased in self? So long as he continues to think about the causes of his unhappiness, he continues to be self-centred and therefore does not get outside the vicious circle, if he is to get outside it, it must be by genuine interests, not by simulated interests adopted merely as a medicine. Although this difficulty is real, there is nevertheless much that he can do if he has rightly diagnosed his trouble. If, for example, his trouble is due to a sense of sin, conscious or unconscious, he can first persuade his conscious mind that he has no reason to feel sinful, and then proceed to plant this rational conviction in his unconscious mind, concerning himself meanwhile with some more or less neutral activity. If he succeeds in dispelling the sense of sin, it is possible that genuine objective interests will arise spontaneously. If his trouble is self-pity, he can deal with it in the same manner after first persuading himself that there is nothing extraordinarily unfortunate in his circumstances.

If fear is his trouble, let him practise exercises designed to give courage. Courage has been recognised from time immemorial as an important virtue, and a great part of the training of boys and young men has been devoted, to producing a type of character capable of fearlessness in battle. But moral courage and intellectual courage have been much less studied; they also, however, have their technique. Admit to yourself every day at least one painful truth, you will find it quite useful. Teach yourself to feel that life will still be worth living even if you were not, as of course you are, immeasurably superior to all your friends in virtue and intelligence. Exercises of this sort prolonged through several years, will at last enable you to admit facts without flinching and will, in so doing, free you from the empire of fear over a very large field.

[CAPF, 2011]

Questions

1. What kind of affection can be a potent cause of happiness?
2. How can a 'self-encased' person get out of his sense of unhappiness?
3. How can a person overcome his feeling of self-pity and fear?
4. Explain the various kinds of courage mentioned by the author.

Passage 5

Recently, I spent several hours sitting under a tree in my garden with the social anthropologist William Ury, a Harvard University professor who specialises in the art of negotiation and wrote the bestselling book, 'Getting to Yes'. He captivated me with his theory that tribalism protects people from their fear of rapid change. He explained that the pillars of tribalism that humans rely on for security would always counter any significant cultural or social change. In this way, he said, change is never allowed to happen too fast. Technology, e.g. is a pillar of society. Ury believes that every time technology moves in a new or radical direction, another pillar such as religion or nationalism will grow stronger-in effect, the traditional and familiar will assume greater importance to compensate for the new and untested. In this manner, human tribes avoid rapid change that leaves people insecure and frightened.

But we have all heard that nothing is as permanent as change. Nothing is guaranteed. Pithy expressions, to be sure, but no more than cliches. As Ury says, people don't live that way from day-to-day. On the contrary, they actively seek certainty and stability. They want to know they will be safe.

Even so we scare ourselves constantly with the idea of change. An IBM CEO once said: We only re-structure for a good reason and if we haven't re-structured in a while, that's a good reason. 'We are scared that competition, technology and the consumer will put us out of business, so we have to change all the time just to stay alive. But if we asked our fathers and grandfathers, would they have said that they lived in a period of little change? Structure may not have changed much. It may just be the speed with which we do things.

Change is over-rated, anyway, consider the automobile. It's an especially valuable example, because the auto industry has spent tens of billions of dollars on research and product development in the last 100 years. Henry Ford's first car had a metal chassis with an internal combustion, gasoline-powered engine, four wheels with rubber tyres, a foot operated clutch assembly and brake system, a steering wheel, and four seats, and it could safely do 18 miles per hour. A hundred years and tens of thousands of research hours later, we drive cars with a metal chasis with an internal combustion gasoline-powered engine, four wheels with rubber tyres, a foot operated clutch assembly and brake system, a steering wheel, four seats and the average speed in London in 2001 was 17.5 miles per hour!

That's not a hell of a lot of return for the money. Ford evidently doesn't have much to teach us about change. The fact that they're still manufacturing cars is not proof that Ford Motor Co is a sound organisation, just proof that it takes very large companies to make cars in great quantities-making for an almost impregnable entry barrier.

50 years after the development of the jet engine, planes are also little changed They've grown bigger, wider and can carry more people. But those are incremental, largely cosmetic changes. Taken together, this lack of real change has come to mean that in travel–whether driving or flying–time and technology have not combined to make things much better. The safety and design have of course accompanied the times and the new volume of cars and flights, but nothing of any significance has changed in the basic assumptions of the final product.

At the same time, moving around in cars or aeroplanes becomes less and less efficient all the time. Not only has there been no great change, but also both forms of transport have deteriorated as more people clamour to use them. The same is true for telephones, which took over hundred years to become mobile, or photographic film which also required an entire century to change.

The only explanation for this is anthropological. Once established in calcified organisations, humans do two things: sabotage changes that might render people dispensable and ensure industry-wide emulation. In the 1960s, German auto companies developed plans to scrap the entire combustion engine for an electrical design. (The same existed in the 1970s in Japan and in the 1980s in France). So, for 40 years, we might have been free of the wasteful and ludicrous dependence on fossil fuels. Why didn't it go anywhere? Because auto executives understood pistons and carburettors and would be loath to cannibalise their expertise, along with most of their factories.

Questions

1. How do humans avoid rapid changes that frighten them?
2. How does the author explain the pillars of tribalism?
3. What can you say by Ford's manufacturing of cars?
4. Is change over-rated according to the author? Why or why not?

Passage 6

Fifty feet away, three male lions lay by the road. They didn't appear to have a hair on their heads. Nothing the colour of their noses (leonine noses darken as they age, from pink to black), Craig estimated that they were 6 years old-young adults. 'This is wonderful' he said, after staring at them for several moments. "This is what we came to see. They really are maneless." Craig, a professor at the University of Minnesota, is arguably the leading expert on the majestic Serengeti lion, whose head is mantled in long, thick hair. He and Peyton West, a doctoral student who has been working with him in Tanzania, had never seen the Tsavo lions that live some 200 miles East of the Serengeti. The scientists had partly suspected that the maneless males were adolescents mistaken for adults by amateur observers. Now they knew better.

The Tasvo research expedition was mostly Peyton's show. She had spent several years in Tanzania compiling the data she needed to answer a question that ought to have been answered long ago: why do lions have manes? It's the only cat, wild or domestic, that displays such ornamentation. In Tsavo, she was attacking the riddle from the opposite angle. Why do its lions not have manes? (Some 'maneless' lions in Tsavo East do have partial manes, but they rarely attain the regal glory of

SUBJECTIVE COMPREHENSION

the Serengeti lions'.) Does environmental adaptation account for the trait? Are the lions of Tsavo, as some people believe, a distinct subspecies of their Serengeti cousins?

The Serengeti lions have been under continuous observation for more than 35 years, beginning with George Schaller's pioneering work in the 1960s. But the lions in Tsavo, Kenya's oldest and largest protected ecosystem have hardly been studied. Consequently, legends have grown up around them. Not only do they look different, according to the myths, they behave differently, displaying greater cunning and aggressiveness. 'Remember too, 'Kenya: The Rough Guide warns, Tsavo's lions have a reputation of ferocity.' Their fearsome image became well-known in 1898, when the males stalled construction of what is now Kenya Railways by allegedly killing and eating 135 Indian and African labourers. A British Army Officer in charge of building a railroad bridge over the Tasavo river, Lt Col JH Paterson, spent 9 months pursuing the pair before he brought them to bay and killed them. Stuffed and mounted, they now glare at visitors to the Field Museum in Chicago. Paterson's account of the leonine reign of terror, The Man-Eaters of Tsavo, was an international bestseller when published in 1907. Still in print, the book has made Tsavo's lions notorious. That annoys some scientists.

"People don't want to give up on mythology." Dennis rang me one day. The zoologist has been working in Tasvo off and on for 4 years. "I am so sick of this man-eater business. Petterson made a helluva lot of money off that story, but Tsavo's lions are no more likely to turn man-eater than lions from elsewhere."

But tales of their savagery and wiliness don't all come from sensationalist authors looking to make a buck. Tsavo lions are generally larger than lions elsewhere, enabling them to take down the predominant prey animal in Tsavo, the Cape buffalo one of the strongest, most aggressive animals of Earth. The buffalo don't give up easily: They often kill or severely injure an attacking lion and a wounded lion might be more likely to turn to cattle and humans for food.

And other prey is less abundant in Tsavo than in other traditional lion haunts. A hungry lion is more likely to attack humans. Safari guides and Kenya Wildlife Service rangers tell of lions attacking Land Rovers, raiding camps, stalking tourists. Tsavo is a tough neighbourhood, they say, and it breeds tougher lions.

But are they really tougher? And if so, is there any connection between their manelessness and their ferocity? An intriguing hypothesis was advanced 2 years ago by Gnoske and Peterhans. Tsavo lions may be similar to the unmaned cave lions of the Pleistocene. The Serengeti variety is among the most evolved of the species the latest model, so to speak-while certain morphological differences in Tsavo lions (bigger bodies, smaller skills and may be even lack of a mane) suggest that they are closer to primitive ancestor of all lions. Craig arid Peyton had serious doubts about this idea, but admitted that Tsavo lions pose a mystery to science.

Questions

1. What did the scientists knew better?
2. Why does the book 'Man-Eaters of Tsavo' annoys some scientists?
3. What can weaken the hypothesis advanced by Gnoske and Peterhans most?
4. What all has contributed to the popular usage of Tsavo lions as savage creatures?

Passage 7

Throughout human history, the leading causes of death have been infection and trauma. Modern medicine has scored significant victories against both and the major causes of ill health and death are now the chronic degenerative diseases, such as coronary artery disease, arthritis, osteoporosis, Alzheimer's, macular degeneration, cataract and cancer. These have a long latency period before symptoms appear and a diagnosis is made. It follows that the majority of apparently healthy people are pre-ill. But are these conditions inevitably degenerative? A truly preventive medicine that focused on the pre-ill, analysing the metabolic errors which lead to clinical illness, might be able to correct them before the first symptom. Genetic risk factors are known for all the chronic degenerative diseases and are important to the individuals who possess them. At the population level, however, migration studies confirm that these illness are linked for the most part to lifestyle factors exercise, smoking and nutrition. Nutrition is the easiest of these to change and the most versatile tool for affecting the metabolic changes needed to tilt the balance away from disease.

Many national surveys reveal that malnutrition is common in developed countries. This is not the calorie and/or micronutrient deficiency associated with developing nations (Type A malnutrition), but multiple micronutrient depletion, usually combined with calorific balance or excess (Type B malnutrition). The incidence and severity of Type B malnutrition will be shown to be worse if newer micronutrient groups such as the essential fatty acids, xanthophylls and flavonoids are included in the surveys. Commonly ingested levels of these micronutrients seem to be far too low in many developed countries.

There is now considerable evidence that Type B malnutrition is a major cause of chronic degenerative diseases. If this is the case, then it is logical to treat such diseases not with drugs but with multiple micronutrient repletion, or pharmaco-nutrition'. This can take the form of pills and capsules–nutraceuticals', or food formats known as functional foods. This approach has been neglected hitherto because it is relatively unprofitable for drug companies–the products are hard to patent and it is a strategy which does not sit easily with modern medical interventionism.

Over the last 100 years, the drug industry has invested huge sums in developing a range of subtle and powerful drugs to treat the many diseases we are subjected to. Medical training is couched in pharmaceutical terms and this approach has provided us with an exceptional range of therapeutic tools in the treatment of disease and in acute medical emergencies. However, the pharmaceutical model has also created an unhealthy dependency culture, in which relatively few of us accept responsibility for maintaining our own health. Instead, we have handed over this responsibility to health professionals who know very little about health maintenance or disease prevention.

One problem for supporters of this argument is lack of the right kind of hard evidence. We have a wealth of epidemiological data linking dietary factors to health profiles/disease risks, and a great deal of information on mechanism: how food factors interact with our biochemistry. But almost all intervention studies with micronutrients, with the notable exception of the Omega 3 fatty acids, have so far produced conflicting or negative results. In other words, our science appears to have no predictive value. Does this invalidate the science? Or are we simply asking the wrong questions?

Based on pharmaceutical thinking, most intervention studies have attempted to measure the impact of a single micronutrient on the incidence of disease. The classical approach says that if you give a compound formula to test subjects and obtain positive results, you cannot know which ingredient is exerting the benefit, so you must test each ingredient individually. But in the field of nutrition, this does not work. Each intervention on its own will hardly make enough difference to be measured. The best therapeutic response must, therefore, combine micronutrients to normalise our internal physiology.

So do we need to analyse each individual's nutritional status and then tailor a formula specifically for him or her? While we do not have the resources to analyse millions of individual cases, there is no need to do so. The vast majority of people are consuming suboptimal amounts of most micronutrients and most of the micronutrients concerned are very safe. Accordingly, a comprehensive and universal programme of micronutrient support is probably the most cost-effective and safest way of improving the general health of the nation.

Questions
1. Why is it not necessary to tailor micronutrient based treatment plans to suit individual deficiency profiles?
2. What does the author recommend micronutrient repletion for and why?
3. Why are large number of apparently healthy people deemed pre-ill?
4. Why is Type B malnutrition a serious concern in developed countries?

Passage 8

Can India make it to a leadership position in the new millennium or will it retain the 'fast train-going-slow' image of the last 50 odd years? Most people believe that the potential for our country to succeed is huge. They are also disappointed at the inability to convert the natural advantages we possess into tangible benefits. The recent success of our infotech industry globally has reinforced the belief that when we put our mind to it we can and do succeed. Now, the expectation is that, this success will be replicated in other areas.

There is no doubt that India's future will be driven by the intellectual capital of its people. Even though many of the billion Indian people are and will continue for the foreseeable future to live in a third-world setting, there are many Indians with the skills, ability and aspiration to prosper and flourish in a first-world environment. It is, therefore, likely that India will, at the same time, belong to both the first and third worlds. That first-world environment will be powered increasingly by knowledge workers and brainware. India clearly has the numbers. It needs to invest in training and skill-building and also encourage entrepreneurship and risk-taking.

I have no magic recipe to convert India's people power into a competitive advantage on global basis. Also, I am nowhere near qualified to address macro issues like universal education and school curricula. Therefore, I have to shrink the issue into a familiar **framework** of 'growing our people.' It is imperative that Indian business pay more than lip service to the empowerment of their employees. We have to break the 'do-as you are are told' mentality which inhibits creativity and promotes the culture of servitude long after our 'foreign masters' are gone. Together with empowerment, there has to be a culture of personal accountability, so that everyone realises the necessity of valuing commitment. In all areas of activity, seniority and hierarchies (if any) must be based purely on merit. **Seniority, like respect, must be earned** and not 'termed,' i.e. based on the length of service.

Future organisations will be based on communities and interaction, between individuals and teams both within and outside the organisation. The work environment both with respect to physical space as well as culture, must be barrierless/boundryless, allowing the **impromptu** and regular and regular interaction across workgroups/teams.

Organisations must accept that empowerment and personal accountability should go hand in hand with a degree of tolerance for mistakes and failures. Mistakes and failures are good learning opportunities for our people and should be regarded as such unless repeated. Tolerance would also provide a safety net for those prepared to take risks, a quality rarely seen among Indian executives today, but crucial to succeed in the new economy. Organisations must be as transparent as possible with their employees. Both good and bad news must be shared. Often organisations and their leadership wrongly believe that the employees aren't interested in certain information, or more arrogantly, decide that information is best withheld as it is beyond the comprehension of their employees.

Knowledge sharing must be pushed at all levels through a carrot-and-stick approach. Those who continuously hoard knowledge must be weeded out. Everyone must come to work thinking that he will learn and add to his skills.

Performance management must be institutionalised to give everyone a clear understanding of organisational goals, team goals, individual's role or goals within a team, rewards which follow from meeting goals and career opportunities in the organisation. Encourage a sense of commitment to the community among your employees. Apart from making them feel good about themselves, it also affords opportunities for them to work as teams in a non-work environment.

Above all, make work fun. If people, however talented, show up at work because it is a job, then they are unlikely to realise their full potential.

The above is not an exhaustive list for each organisation to get the best out of its people. But if each organisation addresses some of these issues then people will grow individually and collectively. This is bound to have a beneficial effect on harnessing and driving their intellectual capital.

Questions
1. What does the author attributes the success of India to?
2. How can the organisations be fairly transparent?
3. Explain the phrase 'fast train going slow' in reference to the passage.
4. What is the predicament of Indian business according to the writer?
5. What factors can inhibit creatively in people?

SUBJECTIVE COMPREHENSION

Passage 9

In modern time, Abraham Lincoln stands as the model of a compassionate statesman. He showed this quality not only in striving for the emancipation of the American blacks, but in the dignity with which he conducted the American Civil War.

Lincoln did not fancy himself as a liberator. He thought it would be better for all if emancipation was a gradual process spread over many years. He proposed compensation for slave-owners in US, bonds and grants for the rehabilitation of blacks- '**colonisation**' as they called it. But fate was to deem otherwise. The haste with which the South wanted to break away from the Union with the North, compelled him to move faster than he expected, perhaps more than most men of his time he had thought through the issue of slavery. 'We must free the slaves, he said, 'or be ourselves subdued.' Before reading, he first draft of the proclamation of emancipation, he told his colleagues. '**In giving freedom to the slaves, we assure freedom to the free**'.

On 22nd September, 1862, Lincoln set his hand on the Proclamation of Emancipation declaring that on the first day of January 1863, all persons held as slaves within any state 'shall be then, and forever free.' Lincoln's revolution for slavery left him without any moral indignation or passion against the slave-owners. The guilt of the slave-owners, he felt, should be shared by the whole country the North and the South, for it seemed to him that everyone in the nation was an accomplice in perpetuating that system. To have whipped up any hatred against slave-owners would, to him, have been an act of malice.

'I shall do nothing in malice', he wrote, 'what I deal with is too vast for malicious dealing'. As the Civil War was coming to a successful conclusion, a Northerner demanded of Lincoln : 'Mr President, how are you going to treat the Southerners when the war is over? Lincoln replied : 'As if they never went to war ?'

When the news came of the Victory of the Northern against the Confederate forces, someone suggested that the head of the Confederation Administration, Jefferson Davies, really ought to be hanged. 'Judge not, that ye be not judged'. Lincoln replied, as to the demand for the prosecution of rebels, Lincoln replied : 'We must extinguish our resentments if we expect harmony and union'. This was his last recorded utterance.

Questions

1. What does the author means by the sentence "In giving freedom to the slave...free"?
2. How can you say that Abraham Lincoln was a passionate statesman?
3. What obstacles did Lincoln face in carrying out emancipation?
4. What does the term 'colonisation' as used in the passage means?

Passage 10

Globalisation, liberalisation and free market are some of the most significant modern trends in economy. **Most economists** in our country seem **captivated** by the spell of the free market. Consequently, nothing seems good or normal that does not accord with the requirements of the free market. A price that is determined by the seller or, for the matter, established by anyone other than the aggregate of consumers seems **pernicious**. Accordingly, it requires a major act of will to think of price-fixing as both normal and having a valuable economic function.

In fact, price fixing is normal in all industrialised societies because the industrial system itself provides as an effortless consequence of its own development, the price fixing that it requires. Modern industrial planning requires and rewards great size. Hence, a comparatively small number of large firms will be competing for the same group of consumers. That each large firm will act with consideration of its own needs and thus avoid selling products for more than its competitors charge, is commonly recognised by **advocates** of free-market economic theories. But each large firm will also act with full consideration of the needs that it has in common with the other large firms competing for the same customers.

Each large firm will thus avoid significant price cutting, because price-cutting will be prejudicial to the common interest in a **stable** demand for products. Most economists do not see price-fixing when it occurs because they expect it to be brought about by a number of **explicit** agreements among large firms; it is not.

Moreover, those economists who argue that allowing the free-market to operate without interference is the most efficient method of establishing prices have not considered the economics of non-socialist countries. Most of these economies employ intentional price-fixing, usually in an **overt** fashion. Formal price-fixing by cartel and informal price-fixing by agreements covering the members of an industry are common place. Were they something peculiarly efficient about the free-market and inefficient about price-fixing, the countries that have avoided the first and used the second would have suffered drastically in their economic development. There is no indication that they have.

Socialist industry also works within a framework of controlled prices. In the early 1970s, the Soviet Union began to give firms and industries some flexibility in adjusting prices that a more informal evolution has accorded the capitalist system. Economists in the USA have hailed the change as a return to the free-market. But the then Soviet firms were not in favour of the prices established by a free-market over which they exercised little influence; rather, Soviet firms acquired some power to fix prices.

Questions

1. What is the authors objective behind the passage?
2. Why is the price fixed by sellers pernicious?
3. What was the result of the Soviet Unions' change in economic policy in the 1970s?
4. Price-fixing in non-socialistic countries beneficial or harmful. Support your answer.

PART C
GRAMMAR SKILLS

Grammar-cum-Translation Method has been in use in our country for teaching and learning English as a second language. In this approach, learning English Grammar becomes an integral syllabus. First grammar and then language is the popular form of learning language. Since traditional Examination Boards and Government Employment Commission have gone very slow in adopting Direct Method of Teaching/Learning English. The value of oral work (reading habits) is far from realised under this system. In the current method 'a word' and not 'a sentence' is the unit of learning. We emphasise translation as means of entering the domain of English do.

At the same time, we have to go by the practical use of English: how can it help us get a good job and status in the society? According to the need of the aspirants sitting for various board, university and government examination bodies learning English Grammar is indispensable. Therefore, the present section on grammar may help the students use the language as well as understand it. The selective contents included in the
book would provide ample guidance and practice in sentence building, indispensable equipment for Comprehension as well as Writing Skills.

CHAPTER 1

The Function of Tenses

A **tense** may be defined as that form of a verb which indicates the time and the state of an action or event.

In this manner, a verb may refer to :

I. Time of an action (Tense)

For example

(i) He goes to school. *(Present time of an action)*
(ii) He went to school. *(Past time of an action)*
(iii) He will go to school. *(Future time of an action)*

From the above sentences, it will be clear to the students that there are three main tenses.

1. The Present tense   2. The Past tense   3. The Future tense

II. State of an action (Function of tenses)

For example

(i) I write letters regularly. *(Present tense, Habitual function)*
(ii) I am writing a letter. *(Present continuous, Progressive function)*
(iii) I have just written a letter. *(Present perfect, Preceding function)*
(iv) I have been writing a letter for some time. *(Present perfect continuous, Time expression)*

The Tenses and their Functions

Tenses

Present
- Present Indefinite
- Present Continuous
- Present Perfect
- Present Perf. Continuous

Past
- Past Indefinite
- Past Continuous
- Past Perfect
- Past Perf. Continuous

Future
- Future Indefinite
- Future Continuous
- Future Perfect
- Future Perf. Continuous

The Present Indefinite Tense —*Habitual Action*

A. This tense is generally used to denote '**habit, custom, practice, repeated action, permanent activity, general truth**' etc.

These ideas are expressed by the adverbs of frequency such as '**often, seldom, usually, never, occasionally, sometimes, normally, generally, always, frequently, rarely, daily**'.

For example
  (i) The old lady goes for a walk in the morning.
  (ii) Parul usually believes everybody.
  (iii) Arnav often gets late for lunch.
  (iv) Suhani always comes in time.

B. This tense is also used to make a statement in the present **showing permanent nature and activity of the subject and eternal** principles. *For example*
  (i) I know him well.
  (ii) He teaches in St Xavier College.
  (iii) The cow gives milk.
  (iv) Rivers freeze at high altitude.

Additional Uses of Present Indefinite Tense

Historical Present
  (i) Now, Netaji enters and addresses the Indian soldiers.
  (ii) Now, Arjun shoots arrows at Bhishma.

Future Arrangement
  (i) The Prime Minister arrives from New York tomorrow.
  (ii) He leaves his job next week.

WORK BOOK EXERCISE (A)

Directions *Make the sentences using* **Present Indefinite** *tense with suitable forms of verbs given in the brackets.*

1. Buses .... on this road every hour. *(run)*
2. .... his son .... to school regularly? *(go)*
3. .... he .... egg curry? *(like)*
4. He .... in the gymnasium daily. *(not practise)*
5. He .... dinner at 8 p.m. *(not have)*
6. He usually .... me at dusk. *(visit)*
7. Neena .... on the stage. *(dance)*
8. She .... cards every afternoon. *(play)*
9. Apples .... ripe in autumn. *(get)*
10. The last bus normally .... at mid night. *(leave)*

The Present Continuous Tense —*Progressive Action*

A. This tense is normally used **for an action in progress** that is temporary in nature (not for a permanent activity) in the present at the time of speaking.

For example
  (i) She is not working. She is swimming in the river.
  (ii) It is raining outside.

B. It also expresses **future action or a definite arrangement in the near future**.

For example
  (i) I am going to the cinema tomorrow.
  (ii) She is coming next week.

Additional Uses of Present Continuous Tense

C. Continuous tense with 'always' may express an idea, which is not to the liking of the speaker. *For example*
  (i) She is always teaching her children.
  (ii) He is always praising his friends.

D. There are some of the verbs, which sometime don't admit of progressive action. Such verbs are called Non-progressive (Stative verbs). *For example*
  (i) **Verbs of Perception** See, taste, smell, hear, prefer, please.
  (ii) **Verbs of Thinking Process** Think, know, mean, mind.
  (iii) **Verbs Showing Possession** Own, have, belong, comprise, possess, contain.
  (iv) **Verbs Expressing Feelings or State of Mind** Believe, like, love, want, wish, desire, hate.
  (v) **Verbs in General** Look, seem, appear, affect, resemble, cost, require, stand, face, become.

(a) Study these sentences carefully:

Incorrect	Correct
1. He is owning a car.	He owns a car.
2. We are hearing the bell.	We hear the bell.
3. This house is belonging to me.	This house belongs to me.
4. I am not hating him.	I don't hate him.
5. Are you forgetting my name?	Have you forgotten my name?
6. I am not meaning this.	I don't mean this.
7. I am having no house to live in.	I have no house to live in.
8. She stands in the shade of a tree.	She is standing in the shade of a tree.
9. The temple is standing in the heart of the city.	The temple stands in the heart of the city.
10. The book is containing good subject-matter.	The book contains good subject-matter.

(b) Mark the difference in the use of stative activity and progressive verbs. (temporary activity)

1. The rose smells sweet. *Stative verb*
2. She is smelling a black rose. *Progressive verb*
3. He lives in Chennai. *Stative verb*

4. She is living in India at present.	*Temporary activity*
5. She has a large house to live in.	*Stative verb*
6. She is having lunch now.	*Progressive verb*
7. It looks it may rain soon.	*Stative verb*
8. She is looking at the sky.	*Temporary activity*
9. I am seeing him next morning.	*Progressive verb*
10. The nurse is feeling her forehead.	*Progressive verb*
11. I think she is a miser.	*Stative verb*
12. I am thinking of leaving Chandigarh.	*Progressive verb*
13. I love my sister.	*Stative verb*
14. She is loving her daughter.	*Progressive activity*

E. 'While, still, at the moment, presently (at present) and now' may help students to express progressive present.

WORK BOOK EXERCISE (B)

Directions *Make the sentences using* **Present Continuous** *tense with suitable forms of verbs given in the brackets.*

1. She ...., she .... chess with her friends. *(not work, play)*
2. She .... for America next year. *(leave)*
3. What .... you .... at present? I .... a poem. *(read, read)*
4. We .... lunch at 2:00 tomorrow as Ram .... a noon train. *(have, catch)*
5. Meena usually does the cooking but I .... it today as she isn't here. *(do)*
6. Mother .... bath now as she always takes bath at noon. *(take)*
7. I can't hear what you ....; the neighbours .... too much noise. *(say, make)*
8. .... she still .... ? *(sing)*
9. She .... to Delhi tomorrow. *(go)*
10. She can't open the door because she .... clothes. *(put on)*

The Present Perfect Tense —*Preceding Action*

A. This tense is a mixture of present and past. At the time of speaking, the action is already completed in the past. It always implies a strong connection with the present though the action took place in the past. Generally, the following adverbs and conjunctions are used to express the **preceding action**.

'Ever, just, recently, already, yet, till (time), so far, of late, lately, before, (by) by the time, after' etc.

Note 'Just' is used in the sense of 'already'. Other meanings of 'just' are 'now' and 'exactly'.
  (i) I have **just** seen that film.
  (ii) I have **already** had my breakfast.
  (iii) **'Ever'** means 'any time in the past' and 'always'.
  (iv) **'So far, yet, till'** means 'upto now', upto this. *(negative implication)*
  (v) **Of late, lately** *(recently, used only in Present Perfect Tense)*

THE FUNCTION OF TENSES

B. Present Perfect + Point of time = Simple Past

It should be noted that point of time in the past indicates that action took place at a point in the past. The point of time in the past is expressed by 'Since, ever since, last, yesterday, the other day, ago, before, back' formerly, (any time in the past) etc.

For example
- (i) She has returned 2 days ago/before. *(omit 'has')*
- (ii) She returned 2 days ago. *(Correct)*

C. Present Indefinite + Time expression = Present Perfect

This tense can also be used with 'since, for, how long, whole, all, throughout, all along' etc to express time expression. *For example*
- (i) He has known me for 2 years.
- (ii) She has owned this parlour since 2002.

Note Look up **Perfect Continuous** tense for details about time expression.

WORK BOOK EXERCISE (C)

Directions *Make the sentences using **Present Perfect** tense with suitable forms of verbs given in the brackets.*

1. In the movie we .... just .... the most extraordinary scene. (see)
2. This is the best book I .... ever .... (read)
3. How long .... you .... him? (know)
4. There are no taxies available because the drivers .... on strike lately. (go)
5. Vinay .... the punctured tyre of his car yet. (mend)
6. The police .... the thief so far and the residents are displeased. (arrest)
7. I shall not go to the movie as I .... already .... it. (see)
8. You can go. Rain .... just .... now. (stop)
9. I .... him since yesterday. (meet)
10. This house .... to me since my birth. (belong)

WORK BOOK EXERCISE (D)

Directions *Complete the sentences by using the **Present Perfect** or the **Simple Past** as the case may be. Remember that*
(a) Present Perfect = Preceding action, (Action in the past used in present)
(b) Present Perfect + Point of time = Simple Past
(c) Present Indefinite + Time expression = Present Perfect

1. Have you taken lunch?
   (a) Yes, I ....   (b) Yes, I .... at 1 pm.
2. Have you prepared your lesson?
   (a) Yes, I ....   (b) Yes, I .... in the morning.
3. Have you seen such a nice movie?
   (a) No, I ....   (b) Yes, I ....
   (c) Yes, I .... last year.

4. Have you opened a bank account?
   Yes, I .... only yesterday.
5. How long have you known this man?
   (a) I .... him since I arrived here.   (b) I .... him when I was at school.
6. When have you learnt driving?
   I .... when I was at Mumbai.
7. Have you ever met him since he left Delhi?
   (a) No, I .... him since.
   (b) Yes, I .... him, when he was in the town last week.
8. Have you written a letter to him?
   Yes, I .... in the morning.
9. Has your scooter stopped?
   No, it .... but the brakes are loose.
10. Has Mr Kapoor ever worked with you?
    Yes, he .... for 5 years. He has recently retired.

The Past Indefinite Tense —*Habitual Action*

A. This tense is used for a past habit, indicated generally by

'Often, seldom, usually, normally, generally, occasionally, sometimes, never, always, frequently, rarely, daily, used to, would' etc.

For example
   (i) They never drank wine.
   (ii) He always carried an umbrella.
   (iii) I used to go to Delhi by train.
   (iv) She would go there daily.

B. This tense is also used for a single act completed in the past. **Definite point of time is denoted by**

'Since, ever since, earlier, ago, back, before, last, yesterday, the other day' (any point of time in the past) etc.

For example
   (i) I met your brother yesterday.
   (ii) She bought a car 2 years ago.

It is wrong to say
   (i) I have met your brother yesterday.   *(remove 'have')*
   (ii) She has bought a car 2 years ago.   *(remove 'has')*

Note Present Perfect + Point of time = Simple Past

'Point of time' denotes the time when the action takes place. (Present, Past, Future Tense). *For example*
   (i) I come here every Sunday.   *(Point of time)*
   (ii) I went to Delhi yesterday.   *(Point of time)*
   (iii) I shall go there tomorrow.   *(Point of time)*

Time Expression For time expression, look up Perfect Continuous Tense.

THE FUNCTION OF TENSES

🔦 WORK BOOK EXERCISE (E)

Directions *Make the sentences using **Past Indefinite** tense with suitable forms of verbs given in the brackets.*

1. We .... a terrifying news last night. *(hear)*
2. They .... their success 2 days ago. *(celebrate)*
3. The police .... the dacoits at 9:00 pm. *(catch)*
4. Seema .... her lost book an hour before. *(not find)*
5. The train .... at 8:00 at the station yesterday. *(not arrive)*
6. My teacher .... a book last year. *(write)*
7. As a boy I often .... to school on foot. *(go)*
8. My friend frequently .... his hometown in the past. *(visit)*
9. He .... to his home every weekend. *(come)*
10. I seldom .... a cheque even when there was balance in my account. *(write)*

The Past Continuous Tense —*Progressive Action*

A. This tense is chiefly used for past action in progress. *For example*
  (i) It was still raining, when I reached there. *(Past action in progress)*
  (ii) He was busy in packing last evening. *(Past action in progress)*

B. It is also used for a definite arrangement for future in the past.
For example
  (i) He was leaving that night. *(Definite arrangement for future in the past)*
  (ii) I asked her what she was doing next Sunday. *(Definite arrangement for future in the past)*

C. As mentioned in the case of the present continuous tense, certain verbs don't admit of progressive action. Please study such verbs carefully. **Refer to such verbs under Present Continuous tense section.**

D. 'While, still, at that moment, then' may help the students to express progressive action in the past.

🔦 WORK BOOK EXERCISE (F)

Directions *Make the sentences using **Past Continuous** tense with suitable forms of verbs given in the brackets.*

1. My cousin wears sandals but when I last saw him he .... boots. *(wear)*
2. On the beach many children .... and many girls .... in the sea. *(play, swim)*
3. Seema was alone in house at that time because her father ..... in the garage then. *(work)*
4. As she .... the stairs, she slipped and fell. *(climb)*
5. The teacher went to see what the students .... in the garden. *(do)*
6. He did not come because he .... a meeting next day. *(attend)*
7. She left study because she .... that year. *(marry)*
8. When I went to see my mother, she .... at that moment. *(sleep)*
9. When I went to bed, my sister .... still .... *(work)*
10. She .... the floor when I called on her. *(sweep)*

The Past Perfect Tense —*Past Preceding*

A. This tense is used, when out of two actions it is necessary to emphasise that the preceding action was completely finished before the succeeding action started.

For example
    (i) I had gone to Delhi last week before my father came. *(Correct)*
    (ii) I had gone to Delhi last week. *(Incorrect, because preceding action is not implied here)*

B. Sometimes preceding action is implied and is indicated by the use of
'**Ever, just, recently, already, yet, so far, till (time), by the time (by), before, after**' etc. *For example*
    (i) I had already taken breakfast.
    (ii) I had finished the book before he came.
    (iii) I had returned from college just then.
    (iv) I finished the book after I had returned from college.

C. This tense is also used as time expression with
'**Since, for, how long, whole, all, throughout, all along**' etc. *For example*
    (i) She had known him for 2 years.
    (ii) He had owned this plaza for 5 years.

Note Look up Perfect Continuous tense for details about time expression.

D. Past Perfect tense used with verbs such as
'**Want, hope, expect, think, suppose, mean, intend**' indicate that the action mentioned did not take place. *For example*
    (i) I had wanted to help my brother. *(but could not help)*
    (ii) I had expected to pass. *(but did not pass)*
    (iii) My sister had hoped that I would send her money. *(unfulfilled hope)*
    (iv) Vishal had intended to set-up his own business. *(but could not)*

💡 WORK BOOK EXERCISE (G)

Directions *Make the sentences using **Past Perfect tense** with suitable forms of verbs given in the brackets.*

1. After the guests .... we did the washing. *(leave)*
2. She .... all the material by last evening. *(type)*
3. We .... shopping before it started raining. *(finish)*
4. The house .... to him since his birth. *(belong)*
5. She was not present because she .... office when her boss called her. *(leave)*
6. She .... this apartment in Mumbai for ten years but never told anyone. *(own)*
7. He .... her for 2 years before he married her. *(know)*
8. People did not believe him because he .... credibility. *(lose)*
9. He could not become a government servant because he .... part in political activities in his college days. *(take)*
10. Many students .... by the time match began. *(arrive)*

The Future Indefinite Tense —*Future Action*

A. This tense expresses an action that is to take place in future. *For example*

'Soon, shortly, in a few moments, tomorrow, presently (soon), next year/ month/ week' etc indicate future action. *For example*

   (i) They will come here shortly.
   (ii) Ritu will take examination next month.

Note **Presently** means (i) soon (ii) at present.

B. It should be noted that there are several ways to express future action in English as given below.

(a) Future action is expressed in the **Present Continuous** tense. But it is more definite action than the action expressed in the future indefinite. *For example*
   (i) They are coming tomorrow.   *(certain to come)*
   (ii) She is marrying soon.   *(certain to marry)*

(b) Future action is also expressed in the **Future Continuous** tense. *For example*
   (i) Sushant will be arriving soon.   *(He will arrive)*
   (ii) I shall be going tomorrow.   *(I shall go)*

(c) Future action is also expressed in the **Present Indefinite** tense. *For example*
   (i) She arrives from the USA next month.   *(will arrive)*
   (ii) The Prime Minister leaves for Lucknow tomorrow.   *(will leave)*

Note   Ordinarily, **'shall'** is used with first person of pronoun 'I' and 'we'. **'Will'** is used with second and third persons.

Besides, there are following uses of 'shall' and 'will':

1. You shall not move.   Order
2. They shall be rewarded.   Assurance/promise
3. I will help my brother.   Determination
4. You shall look after elders.   Duty
5. I will go to Delhi tomorrow.   Intention
6. I shall go to Delhi.   (may or may not go)
7. I shall be drowned.   (may be drowned)
8. I will be drowned.   (determined to be drowned)

WORK BOOK EXERCISE (H)

Directions *Put the verbs in the brackets using either the **Simple Future** or the **Present Continuous/ Future Continuous**.*

1. I .... my friend tomorrow.   *(meet)*
2. You .... college next year.   *(join)*
3. He .... shortly.   *(come)*
4. I am sure he .... in time for the class.   *(come)*
5. You .... English after another 2 months of hard work.   *(speak)*

6. Our college .... up for Diwali next week. *(break)*
7. He .... next month. *(arrive)*
8. My tailor .... my dress tomorrow. *(stitch)*
9. He .... dinner with us tonight. *(take)*
10. He .... money from the bank for his daughter's marriage. *(borrow)*

The Future Continuous Tense —*Future Progressive*

A. This tense is used to express an action that will be in progress with a point of time in future. *For example*
  (i) She will be waiting for me, when I reach her home.
  (ii) What will he be doing, when you visit him?
  (iii) Get home at once. Your mother will be wondering where you are.
  (iv) Probably, it will be raining, when you reach Bhopal.
  (v) Rahul will be watching movie on television now.

B. This tense is also used to express the future indefinite tense or definite future arrangement. *For example*
  (i) He will be going to Pune by car today.
  (ii) She will be arriving tomorrow to meet her husband.

C. As mentioned in the case of the Present Continuous tense certain verbs do not admit of progressive action. Refer to such verbs under Present Continuous tense section.

WORK BOOK EXERCISE (I)

Directions *Make the sentences using **Future Continuous** tense with suitable forms of verbs given in the brackets.*

1. He ...... for Mr Kapoor next week as his own assistant is expected to be on leave. *(work)*
2. In a few years time, we all .... in multi-storeyed houses. *(live)*
3. We .... ourselves in school today as our principal's mood is very upset now-a-days. *(behave)*
4. My brother ...... at the party tonight as mother is likely to be present there. *(not drink)*
5. He surely .... if you visit his room now. *(smoke)*
6. You should finish your tea immediately because your father .... where you are. *(think)*
7. Richa .... food, when her friend arrives. *(cook)*
8. We .... by train this time tomorrow. *(travel)*
9. We .... Physics during next term. *(study)*
10. What .... the servant .... when we reach home? *(do)*

The Future Perfect Tense —*Future Preceding*

A. This tense is used, when out of two actions, it is necessary to emphasise that the preceding action will be completely finished before the succeeding action starts in future. Sometimes, preceding action is implied and indicated by the use of

'Ever, just, already, recently, yet, so far, till (time), before, (by), by the time after'. *For example*
- (i) She will have already prepared food, when I reach home.
- (ii) He will have rung up his wife before he arrives.
- (iii) I think the news will not have been published so far.
- (iv) My assistant will have typed five letters by lunch today.

B. This tense is also used to express time expression.

'Since, for, how long, whole, all, throughout, all long' denote that action started sometime in the past and is continuing into the present. *For example*
- (i) He will have known her for 2 years by next month.
- (ii) He will have suffered a lot by now since his birth.

WORK BOOK EXERCISE (J)

Directions *Make the sentences using **Future Perfect** tense with suitable forms of verbs given in the brackets.*

1. I .... this essay by tomorrow morning. (complete)
2. With the rate he is studying, he .... by next year. (qualify)
3. The ship .... before we reach the harbour. (leave)
4. If he continues with his exercises, he .... 10 kg by the end of this month. (lose)
5. She .... me for 5 years by next month. (know)
6. The teacher .... all the syllabus by the end of the year. (finish)
7. If we don't hurry, the train .... before we reach the station. (leave)
8. By the time, the chief guest arrives, they .... the cultural programme. (finish)
9. When you reach there, he .... bath yet. (take)
10. This house .... to me for 5 years by my next birthday. (belong)

Perfect Continuous : Present, Past, Future
—*Time Expression*

A. Perfect Continuous tense (Present, Past, Future) denotes an action continuing from the past into the present. It implies the duration of an action. (past to present)

The time expression is normally indicated by

'Since, for, how long, whole, all, throughout, all along.'

Note '**For**' is used for a period of time from the past to present. '**Since**' is used for a particular point of time or some event in the past to present.

B. Time expression can be used with both continuous and indefinite tenses as follows:

(a) **Continuous + Time expression = Perfect continuous**
(Present, Past, Future) *(Action is not yet complete)*

(b) **Indefinite + Time expression = Perfect**
(Present, Past, Future) *(Action is complete)*

Note Students should note the difference between point of time and time expression.

(i) She goes to temple every Monday. *(Point of time)*
(ii) She visited her uncle yesterday. *(Point of time)*
(iii) She has completed two letters since last night. *(Time expression)*
(iv) She has been suffering from fever for 2 days. *(Time expression)*
(v) She had been playing Chess the whole day yesterday. *(Time expression)*

WORK BOOK EXERCISE (K)

Directions *Make the sentences using **Perfect Continuous** or **Perfect tense** (Present, Past, Future) with suitable forms of verbs given in the brackets.*

Present

1. She .... me since 2004. *(know)*
2. For the last 10 years, he .... this factory. *(own)*
3. He .... in the same class for the last 3 years. *(study)*
4. Neena .... nutritious food since morning. *(not eat)*
5. It .... for 2 days now. *(rain)*
6. How long .... you .... for the train? *(wait)*
7. I .... it throughout my life. *(believe)*
8. I .... my pocket money since I left school. *(earn)*
9. Many of our friends .... us since we bought the new house. *(visit)*
10. The man and wife in our neighbourhood .... since they got married. *(quarrel)*

Past

11. The whole day long he .... at home and .... a book since yesterday. *(sit, read)*
12. His radio ...... since 8 am yesterday. The neighbours were getting disturbed. *(play)*
13. He .... this building for the last 10 years, when he sold it. *(own)*
14. Yesterday, she .... for her lost dog since morning. *(search)*
15. Last night, the dog .... for a long time. *(bark)*

Future

16. How long .... in this house when the new guests arrive tomorrow? *(stay)*
17. My aunt .... in England for 5 years, when I go there. *(live)*
18. She .... still .... for 2 hours, when they reach there. *(sleep)*
19. She .... as the Principal of that school for 5 years by next month. *(work)*
20. She .... me for 10 years by next month. *(know)*

Cumulative Exercises
(Based on Function of Tenses)

Exercise 1

Directions *Use the correct forms of the verbs given in the brackets and complete the following sentences.*

1. Look! Sara .... to the movies. *(go)*
2. We ...... to London because our friends ...... us. *(go, invite)*
3. Tushar ...... to his hometown in 1994. *(move)*
4. While one group ..... dinner the others ..... wood for the campfire. *(prepare, collect)*
5. They .... the classroom by the end of the hour. *(leave)*
6. I .... English for 7 years now. *(learn)*
7. During my last summer holidays, my parents ...... me on a trip to Greece. *(send)*
8. At the moment Rajeev .... English grammar. *(revise)*
9. She .... all afternoon. *(work)*
10. They .... the treasure. *(not discover)*
11. How many desserts ...... Saurabh ......? *(order)*
12. Builders .... the millennium Dome by the end of the year 2009. *(finish)*
13. Tomorrow at around 7:30 pm, I .... through America. *(drive)*
14. Jasmine .... in love until she .... Aman 2 years ago. *(never fall, meet)*
15. They .... for 6 hours by the end of class. *(study)*
16. When I .... breakfast, the phone suddenly rang. *(have)*
17. Yesterday's power cut .... all our computers crash. *(make)*
18. According to the schedule, the train .... in 20 minutes time. *(leave)*
19. I .... a few girlfriends tonight for a coffee. *(meet)*
20. It's very difficult for us to get jobs here, so we .... emigrating to Canada. *(consider)*
21. Remember that after you .... the contract, you won't be able to change your mind. *(sign)*
22. He .... football all afternoon and needs a shower! *(play)*
23. We .... the car for 6 months, before we discovered it was stolen. *(own)*
24. The police ...... no stone unturned to trace the culprits. *(leave)*
25. This time tomorrow, I .... on the beach. *(lie)*
26. Neha .... to a funeral on Wednesday afternoon. *(go)*
27. I tried the cake to see how it .... *(taste)*
28. .... you .... the electrician yet? *(pay)*

29. Rachel could see that the child .... some time. (cry)
30. I hope, by next summer, I .... enough money for a holiday. (save)
31. I .... she will be late. (not think)
32. 'Is my car ready?' 'No, but we ...... by this evening.' (finish)
33. How much .... you .... to spend, sir? (want)
34. Priyanka's father .... badminton on TV, but he .... cricket. (watch)
35. What .... you ....with your money, Nitin? (do)
36. .... Venesa .... to school by car this morning? (come)
37. .... Sonal and Sonali .... muffins for their party? (bake)
38. How long .... you .... German by the end of this class? (learn)
39. No-one even noticed when I got home. They ...... the big game on TV. (all watch)
40. We ...... really want to ...... and ...... the musical fountain again. (go, see)

Exercise 2

Directions *Make the directed changes in the following sentences without changing their meaning.*

1. I will finish the job by supper time. *(Use future perfect tense)*
2. It is snowing since Tuesday. *(Use present perfect progressive tense)*
3. I have sent ten e-mails yesterday. *(Use simple past tense)*
4. The climate gets warmer. *(Use present progressive tense)*
5. It was raining all night and the grass was very wet. *(Use past perfect tense)*
6. I will wait in the baggage hall, when you come out of customs. *(Use future progressive tense)*
7. The new minister will be making his television debut this evening. *(Use simple present tense)*
8. You will do your homework before you go out with your mates. *(Use present progressive tense)*
9. Avtarit started learning the piano in January. Now it's May. *(Use present perfect progressive tense)*
10. A light passenger plane crashed in London. *(Use present perfect tense)*
11. She didn't write to Samar because she lost his address. *(Use past perfect tense)*
12. When I went out, it rained. *(Use past progressive tense)*
13. When Vikrant arrived, I had waited for 35 minutes. *(Use past perfect continuous)*
14. The boat is full of water. It is sinking. *(Use future indefinite tense)*
15. Next summer, I will be studying French for 4 years. *(Use future perfect progressive)*
16. My sister has been living in New York. *(Use present indefinite tense)*
17. This time tomorrow I will ski. *(Use future progressive tense)*
18. I wonder, if you will be free this evening. *(Use past indefinite tense)*
19. I was making coffee. Would you like a cup? *(Use present perfect tense)*
20. Sahir finished his lunch. He sat down to watch a film. *(Use past perfect tense)*

THE FUNCTION OF TENSES   321

Exercise 3

Directions *Correct the following sentences without changing their meaning. Do not make unnecessary changes in the original sentence.*

1. She is often coming to me on Sundays.
2. She just completed the letter then.
3. It came to my notice lately.
4. My brother has returned from training 2 months back.
5. I know him for the last 20 years.
6. I never met him this morning.
7. She did not write the letter till now.
8. He was having a number of books.
9. The news of his death has been declared so far.
10. The dog was barking the whole night.
11. For the last 6 months, he is working on this problem.
12. Last week, I had met him twice.
13. I found that someone picked my pocket.
14. By the time she returned, he typed all letters.
15. She rang me up after she decided to go.
16. How long is she working in the office?
17. The house is belonging to me for the last 20 years.
18. My house is facing the East.
19. Manav has broken a cup last evening.
20. My mother is rarely sleeping at noons.
21. They still write letters today.
22. I own this plot of land since my youth.
23. They found that the tap ran.
24. I cannot believe that he is wasting time all along his life.
25. They brought him home when he died.
26. We have written the letter last evening.
27. He worked for three hours, when I met him.
28. Mahmood Gazanavi has invaded India many times.
29. When I met her last year, she was married for 3 years.
30. How long will you know Ritu on her next birthday?
31. What did you do since I saw you last night?
32. Where have you been an hour ago?

33. He has written this novel in 1985.
34. I didn't ask her what she is doing since.
35. In the morning, I found it was raining the whole night.
36. The doctor found that he was bitten by a snake.
37. I try to contact you all these days.
38. I saw that Tom stood in a corner at the banquet.
39. She will leave before he comes.
40. She did not complete the composition yet, when I arrived there.
41. How can I come as it still drizzles?
42. By two o'clock yesterday, I called on her twice but she was not at home.
43. It is looking that he may not come tonight.
44. I found that he was recently discharged from the hospital.
45. A little later, I realised that my luggage was stolen.
46. Where are you keeping your money, when you go out?
47. I admired him since the day I met him.
48. When at last we reached school, the bell was already rung.
49. I am sorry that you left your book in the library, when you came here last time.
50. I am leaving for my office early every morning.
51. What do you look at the road? Does something happen there?
52. My wife paints furniture, whenever she had time.
53. Of late, she did not go to any movie.
54. This is the best book that he ever read.
55. I didn't know what she is writing for the last 2 years.
56. By the time she comes, he will complete the work.
57. The book will be written by next year.
58. I saw that the book lay on the table.
59. She will already return home, when he arrives.
60. Don't worry since she just had her breakfast.

Previous Years' Questions

I. Directions *Make the directed changes in the following sentences without changing their meaning.*

1. If it rains, the college will close. [IES, 2013]
   (Use the past tense)
2. John Lennon died while he lived in New York. [IES, 2014]
   (Use progressive or continuous forms)
3. So long as the rain (to continue), I stayed at home. [IFS, 2014]
   (Use the correct tense of the verb)

II. Directions *Use the correct forms of the verbs in brackets.*
[Civil Services (Mains), 2014]

1. His company is greatly .... after. *(seek)*
2. His courage ...... him. *(forsake)*
3. The terrified people ...... to the mountains. *(flee)*
4. The police ...... no stone unturned to trace the culprits. *(leave)*
5. The robber ...... him a blow on the head. *(strike)*

III. Directions *Use the correct forms of the verbs in brackets.*
[Civil Services (Mains), 2015]

1. Your friends ...... for you for over an hour. *(wait)*
2. It is not worth ...... so much money for this concert. *(pay)*
3. When I reached the station, the train .... *(leave)*
4. I .... the Taj Mahal last month. *(visit)*
5. The criminal ...... the victim with a blunt object. *(attack)*

IV. Directions *Use the correct form of verb given in brackets.*
[Civil Services (Mains) 2009]

1. I don't usually .... an umbrella but today I'm .... one. *(carry)*
2. She never .... about her children. *(worry)*
3. The child always .... when he has a bath, listen he's .... now. *(cry)*

Answers

WORK BOOK EXERCISE (A)
1. run
2. Does, go
3. Does, like
4. does not practise
5. does not have
6. visits
7. dances
8. plays
9. get
10. leaves

WORK BOOK EXERCISE (B)
1. is not working, is playing
2. is leaving
3. are, reading, am reading
4. are having, is catching
5. am doing
6. is taking
7. are saying, are making
8. Is, singing
9. is going
10. is putting on

WORK BOOK EXERCISE (C)
1. have, seen
2. have, read
3. have, known
4. have gone
5. has not mended
6. have not arrested
7. have, seen
8. has, stopped
9. have not met
10. has belonged

WORK BOOK EXERCISE (D)
1. (a) have taken (b) took
2. (a) have prepared (b) prepared
3. (a) haven't seen (b) have seen (c) saw
4. opened
5. (a) have known (b) knew
6. learnt
7. (a) have not met (b) met
8. wrote
9. has not stopped
10. has worked

WORK BOOK EXERCISE (E)
1. heard
2. celebrated
3. caught
4. did not find
5. did not arrive
6. wrote
7. went
8. visited
9. came
10. wrote

WORK BOOK EXERCISE (F)
1. was wearing
2. were playing, were swimming
3. was working
4. was climbing
5. were doing
6. was attending
7. was marrying
8. was sleeping
9. was, working
10. was sweeping

WORK BOOK EXERCISE (G)
1. had left
2. had typed
3. had finished
4. had belonged
5. had left
6. had owned
7. had known
8. had lost
9. had taken
10. had arrived

WORK BOOK EXERCISE (H)
1. will meet/am meeting
2. will join/are joining
3. will come/will be coming
4. will come/is coming
5. will speak/will be speaking
6. will break/is breaking
7. will arrive/is arriving
8. will stitch/is stitching
9. will take/is taking
10. will borrow/is borrowing/will be borrowing

WORK BOOK EXERCISE (I)
1. will be working/will work
2. shall be living
3. will be behaving
4. will not be drinking/will not drink
5. will be smoking
6. will be thinking
7. will be cooking
8. will be travelling
9. will be studying
10. will, be doing

THE FUNCTION OF TENSES

WORK BOOK EXERCISE (J)
1. will have completed
2. will have qualified
3. will have left
4. will have lost
5. will have known
6. will have finished
7. will have left
8. will have finished
9. will not have taken
10. will have belonged

WORK BOOK EXERCISE (K)
1. has known
2. has owned
3. has been studying
4. has not eaten
5. has been raining
6. have, been waiting
7. have believed
8. have been earning
9. have been visiting/have visited
10. have been quarrelling
11. had been sitting, had been reading
12. had been playing
13. had owned
14. had been searching
15. had been barking
16. will have they been staying
17. will have been living
18. will have been, sleeping
19. will have been working
20. will have known

Cumulative Exercises
(Based on Function of Tenses)

Exercise 1
1. is going
2. went, had invited
3. moved
4. was preparing, were collecting
5. will have left
6. have been learning
7. sent
8. is revising
9. has been working
10. have not discovered
11. has, ordered
12. had finished
13. will be driving
14. had never fallen, met
15. will have been studying
16. was having
17. made
18. leaves
19. am meeting
20. are considering
21. have signed
22. has been playing
23. had owned
24. left
25. will be lying
26. is going
27. tasted
28. Have, not paid
29. had been crying
30. will have saved
31. don't think
32. will have finished
33. did, want
34. watches, doesn't watch
35. have, done
36. Did, come
37. Do, bake
38. will, have been learning
39. were all watching
40. didn't, go, see

Exercise 2
1. I will have finished the job by supper time.
2. It has been snowing since Tuesday.
3. I sent ten e-mails yesterday.
4. The climate is getting warmer.
5. It had rained all night and the grass was very wet.
6. I will be waiting in the baggage hall, when you come out of customs.
7. The new minister makes his television debut this evening.
8. You are doing your homework before you go out with your mates.
9. Avtarit has been learning the piano for 4 months.
10. A light passenger plane has crashed in London.
11. She didn't write to Samar because she had lost his address.
12. When I went out, it was raining.
13. When Vikrant arrived I had been waiting for 35 minutes.

14. The boat is full of water. It will sink.
15. By next summer, I will have been studying French for 4 years.
16. My sister lives in New York.
17. This time tomorrow I will be skiing.
18. I wondered, if you were free this evening.
19. I have made coffee, would you like a cup?
20. When Sahir had finished his lunch, he sat down to watch a film.

Exercise 3

1. 'often comes' in place of 'is often coming'.
2. 'had just completed' in place of 'just completed'.
3. 'has come' in place of 'came'.
4. Remove 'has'.
5. 'have known' in place of 'know'.
6. 'did not meet' in place of 'never met'.
7. 'has not written' in place of 'did not write'.
8. 'had' in place of 'was having'.
9. Insert 'not' after 'has'.
10. 'had been barking' in place of 'was barking'.
11. 'has been working' in place of 'is working'.
12. Remove 'had'.
13. Insert 'had' after 'someone'.
14. Insert 'had' after 'he'.
15. 'had decided' in place of 'decided'.
16. 'has she been' in place of 'is she'.
17. 'has belonged' in place of 'is belonging'.
18. 'faces' in place of 'is facing'.
19. broke (remove 'has')
20. 'sleeps' in place of 'is sleeping'.
21. 'are still writing' in place of 'write'.
22. 'have owned' in place of 'own'.
23. 'was running' in place of 'ran'.
24. 'has been wasting' in place of 'is wasting'.
25. Insert 'had' after 'he'.
26. 'wrote' in place of 'have written'.
27. 'had been working'/'had worked' in place of 'worked'.
28. Remove 'has'.
29. 'had been married' in place of 'was married'.
30. 'will you have known' in place of 'will you know'.
31. 'have done'/'have been doing' in place of 'did do'.
32. 'were you' in place of 'have you been'.
33. 'wrote' in place of 'has written'.
34. 'had been doing' in place of 'is doing'.
35. 'had been raining' in place of 'was raining'.
36. 'had been bitten' in place of 'was bitten'.
37. 'have been trying' in place of 'try'.
38. 'was standing' in place of 'stood'.
39. 'will have left' in place of 'will leave'.
40. 'had not completed' in place of 'did not complete'.

THE FUNCTION OF TENSES

41. 'is drizzling' in place of 'drizzles'.
42. 'had called' in place of 'called'.
43. 'looks' in place of 'is looking'.
44. 'had been' in place of 'was'.
45. 'had been stolen' in place of 'was stolen'.
46. 'do you keep' in place of 'are you keeping'.
47. 'have admired' in place of 'admired'.
48. 'had been' in place of 'was'.
49. 'had left' in place of 'left'.
50. 'leave' in place of 'am leaving'.
51. 'are you looking' in place of 'do you look', 'Is something happening' in place of 'Does something happen'.
52. 'has' in place of 'had'.
53. 'has not gone' in place of 'did not go'.
54. 'has read' in place of 'read'.
55. 'had been writing' in place of 'is writing'.
56. 'will have completed' in place of 'will complete'.
57. 'will have been written' for 'will be written'.
58. 'was lying' in place of 'lay'.
59. 'will have already returned' in place of 'will already return'.
60. 'has just had' in place of 'had'.

Previous Years' Questions

I. 1. If it had rained, the college would have been closed.
    2. John Lennon died while he was living in New York.
    3. As long as the rain continued, I stayed at home.

II. 1. sought   2. has forsaken   3. had fled
    4. left   5. strike

III. 1. have been waiting 2. paying   3. had left
     4. visited   5. attacked

IV. 1. carry, carrying   2. worries   3. cries, crying

CHAPTER 2

Voice

A verb may tell us about what a person or a thing does. Therefore, a verb is said to be an action on the part of a doer/subject.

For example
- (i) They will **do** the work.
- (ii) The teacher **has punished** the boy.

The verbs 'do, punish' are transitive. The actions of the subjects 'They, The teacher' passes over to the objects 'work, the boy'. Therefore, these verbs are called transitive.

The verb may **also tell us what** is done to a person or a thing.

Now read the following sentences :
- (iii) The work **will be done** by them. *(Passive voice)*
- (iv) The boy **has been punished** by the teacher. *(Passive voice)*

How to Define a Voice?

(a) In active voice, a sentence begins with a subject (They, The teacher) sentence (i) and (ii).

(b) In passive voice, a sentence begins with an object (The work, The boy) sentences (iii) and (iv).

However, sentences only with **transitive verbs** admit of passive expressions.

Now study the following sentences :
- (v) Jaya **came** here.
- (vi) Father **is going** out.

The verbs 'come, go' are **intransitive** because these verbs do not have objects. The effect of the action does not pass over to any object. Therefore, these verbs are called intransitive. Since, they are not used with object, they do not admit of passive expressions.

Therefore, before making a sentence, a student must note carefully, whether the sentence is beginning with subject or object.

How to Make a Passive Voice?

(a) The passive voice of an active voice is formed by using the verb 'to be'. However, the original active verb must be converted into **Past Participle** (PP).

(b) Object may be placed before the verb in passive expression.

Now study the examples:

In conclusion, the construction of these sentences may be represented as follows:

(a) (i) Subject + Transitive verb + Object　　　　　　　　　　　(Active)
　　(ii) Subject + Intransitive verb　　　　　　　　　　　　　　(Active)
(b) Object + To be + PP of Transitive verb + Subject　　　　　　(Passive)

The Verb 'To be' (Study the following table)

The verb 'To be' has following two uses:

1. As an **auxiliary verb**, it is used with other verbs, both in active and passive voice.
2. As an **ordinary/regular verb**, it is used in 'No verb' sentences.

The forms of 'to be'	Tenses	The forms of verb in passive voice	No verb
Be	Infinitive, Modals, Future Indefinite		Noun Pronoun
Is, am, are	Present Indefinite	PP	Adjective
Was, were	Past Indefinite	(Past Participle)	Adverb
Been	Perfect (Present, Past, Future)	of Transitive Verb	
Being	Continuous (Present, Past), Participle/Gerund		

The use of 'To be' in the passive sentences:
Object + be (be + PP of Transitive Verb) + by Subject

(A) Infinitive, (B) Modals, (C) Future Indefinite
　　(i) He doesn't like to be punished.
　　(ii) The young persons should be taught good manners.
　　(iii) He will be punished for his misbehaviour.

(D) Present Indefinite—is, am, are
　　(i) She is taught English daily by her class teacher.
　　(ii) I am often invited to attend party by my friends.
　　(iii) Elections are held every five years.

(E) Past Indefinite—was, were
　　(i) She was punished for her negligence.
　　(ii) Both the friends were selected for senior Hockey team.

(F) Perfect (Present, Past, Future)—been
   (i) He has just been elected as a member of the committee.
   (ii) She had already been admitted to hospital.
   (iii) My friend will have been married by now.

(G) Continuous (Present, Past)—being
   (i) The match is being telecast now.
   (ii) The match was being telecast yesterday.

(H) Participle/Gerund—being
   (i) Nobody likes being cheated.
   (ii) The murderer escaped being hanged.
   (iii) I saw her being taken to hospital.

Note Future continuous and perfect continuous tenses do not admit of passive voice expressions.

WORK BOOK EXERCISE (A)

Directions *Use the verbs given in brackets either in active or passive as the case may be.*

1. The teacher .... with the students yesterday for their misbehaviour. *(annoy)*
2. The criminals should .... at the earliest. *(punish)*
3. I .... then that he .... working hard. *(convince, be)*
4. Prohibition in many states .... lately by the State Governments. *(enforce)*
5. His parents .... , when he did not arrive at the function. *(disappoint)*
6. Our leaders ought to .... honestly in the interest of common people. *(behave)*
7. Children should .... with responsibility to make them feel responsible. *(entrust)*
8. I .... to see my Aunt, when I reached home. *(amaze)*
9. My father .... , when he sees my brother's report card. *(please)*
10. The eldest son .... the burden of the whole family these days. *(bear)*
11. The residents .... to see five cold blooded murders in her house last night. *(alarm)*
12. The parents .... to hear that their son was involved in the theft. *(ashame)*
13. I .... to receive a nice birthday present from my cousin a month ago. *(delight)*
14. We .... to see her behaving in a confident manner last night. *(satisfy)*
15. Yesterday, the police .... to find the door closed from outside. *(perplex)*
16. I .... by the sound of a cracker in the midnight yesterday. *(startle)*
17. The train .... , when you reach station as you are late. *(leave)*
18. The venue of marriage .... still .... , when the guests arrived. *(be, decorate)*
19. The principal .... to see the results of the students tomorrow. *(surprise)*
20. Yesterday, every student .... to find the question-paper out of syllabus. *(confuse)*

Some Rules to Make Passive Voice

Rule I
The objects used in the following sentences are used with verbs, which do not agree with the common rules of verbs. Such nouns are given in chapter on Nouns under Rule (iv) and (v). Study the following sentences:
  (i) He gave me spectacles.
      Spectacles were given to me by him.
  (ii) They play Billiards.
      Billiards is played by them.

In these sentences, the noun 'spectacles' is followed by plural verb and 'Billiards' by singular verb. Students should take note of such misleading nouns.

Rule II
Study carefully the use of interrogative pronoun while changing active sentences into passive.

'Which, what' etc are placed as they are. However, when 'What/Which' is used as a subject, it is changed into 'By what'. But 'Who' is changed into 'By whom' and 'Whom' is changed into 'Who'.

For example
  (i) What are you writing?
      What is being written by you?
  (ii) What makes you angry?
      By what are you made angry?
  (iii) Who teaches you English?
      By whom are you taught English?
          Or
      Who are you taught English by?
  (iv) Whom are you teaching?
      Who is being taught by you?
  (v) Which girl helped you?
      By which girl were you helped?

Rule III
(a) **When the subjects are indefinite/vague pronouns or understood nouns, it is not necessary to use them in passive voice as 'by somebody'.**
  For example
    (i) Somebody has picked my pocket.
        My pocket has beed picked.
    (ii) They will declare the result soon.
        The result will be declared soon.

(b) **Sentences beginning with negative indefinite pronouns are converted into negative.** *For example*
    (i) Nobody can change destiny.
        Destiny cannot be changed.
    (ii) None saw her in the parlour.
        She was not seen in the parlour.

Rule IV

When principle clause is followed by Noun clause as object, the passive voice is made as follows:
- (i) People consider that he is honest.
  It is considered that he is honest.
- (ii) We hope that he will pass.
  It is hoped that he will pass.

Study these verbs carefully, which are followed by Noun clause as object 'consider, believe, understand, suspect, report, say, claim, know, expect, allege, find', learn, require, suppose (Appear, seem)

Rule V

Verbs with two objects—Sometimes verbs are used with two objects in active voice sentences. Passive voice can be made with either of the objects.

For example
- (i) He gave me a book.
  - (a) I was given a book by him.
  - (b) A book was given to me by him.
- (ii) They made him King. (Complement; King is complement of the verb 'make')
  He was made King.

Rule VI

'By' is not used with certain verbs, when making a passive voice, Instead we use at, with, in, to, etc. *For example*
- (i) I know him.
  He is known to me.
- (ii) Her sudden arrival surprised everyone
  Everybody was surprised at her sudden arrival.

Rule VII

Infinitives *For example*
- (i) She is to write a letter.
  A letter is to be written by her.
- (ii) They were to complete the work.
  The work was to be completed by them.
- (iii) My sister has to buy a new car.
  A new car has to be bought by my sister.
- (iv) There is nothing to lose.
  There is nothing to be lost.
- (v) I would like someone to help me.
  I would like to be helped.
- (vi) I am not to blame for the loss. *[Passive sense (responsible for)]*
  I am not to be blamed for the loss.

VOICE   333

Rule VIII

Participles/Gerund *For example*
  (i) I remember my mother taking me to doctor.
      I remember being taken to doctor by my mother.
  (ii) I found his friends laughing at him.
      I found him being laughed at by his friends.

Rule IX

If a preposition or an adverb is used with a verb to convey specific meaning, it should not be removed while making a passive voice. *For example*
  (i) Mothers **look after** their children.
      Children are looked after by their mothers.
  (ii) You should not **look down upon** the poor.
      The poor should not be looked down upon.

Rule X

The Verbs, 'Let, bid, make, help, feel, see, watch, hear', are used with direct infinitive (without to) in active voice.

In passive voice, these verbs are used with Infinitive (to + verb)

'Let' is an exception. 'Let' is followed by direct infinitive, both in active and passive voice sentences.

For example
  (i) I bade him go.
      He was bidden to go.
  (ii) I have made her sing a song.
      She has been made to sing a song.
  (iii) She let me go.
      I was let go by her.

Rule XI

Imperative Sentences

  1. Command and order   2. Permission, Request, Advice

1. Command and Order

  (a) **Passive** When object is given, use Let + object + be + Past Participle.
      For example
      (i) Bring a book.
          Let a book be brought.
      (ii) Turn Payal out.
          Let Payal be turned out.
  (b) **Passive** When no object is given, begin in the sentence with 'You are ordered/commanded to.........'.
      For example
      (i) Go out at once.
          You are ordered to go out at once.
      (ii) Don't stay here.
          You are ordered not to stay here.

2. **Permission, Request, Advice**
   (a) **Passive** When object is given, make passive with object

   Object + Should + Past Participle
   For example
   (i) Obey parents.
   Parents should be obeyed.
   (ii) Listen to me.
   I should be listened to.
   (iii) Prepare for war.
   You should be prepared for war.
   Or
   Be prepared for war.

Note Use of 'let' is avoided in this type of sentences.

   (b) **Passive** When no object is given, begin the sentence with 'You are allowed, requested or advised ....'. *For example*
   (i) Please come soon.
   You are requested to come soon.
   (ii) Please don't talk loudly.
   You are requested not to talk loudly.

Rule XII

Sentences Beginning with Let (Permission & Suggestion)

   (a) **Passive** When object is given, make passive voice as follows. *For example*
   (i) Let me play here (Permission)
   I may be allowed to play here.
   (ii) Let us help him. (Suggestion)
   He should be helped.

   (b) **Passive** When no object is given, begin, the sentence, with ....
   'It is suggested ....'. *For example*
   (i) Let us stay here (Suggestion)
   It is suggested that we should stay here.
   (ii) Let us sleep here.
   It is suggested that we should sleep here.

Rule XIII

'To be' is often allowed in the sense of 'have' in passive voice sentences of the following verbs.

'Fall, rise, come, arrive, go, lose.' *For example*
   (i) Mighty Caeser is fallen.   (*has fallen*)
   (ii) Summer is come.   (*has come*)
   (iii) The book is lost.   (*has been*)
   (iv) The sun is risen.   (*has risen*)
   (v) Golden days are gone.   (*have gone*)

VOICE

Rule XIV

Miscellaneous Sentences
Study these sentences carefully:

1. The police arrested a militant and sent him to jail. (Active)
   A militant was arrested by police and (was) sent to jail. (Passive)
2. It is necessary to help the poor. (Active)
   The poor are required to be helped. (Passive)
3. It is time to wind up business. (Active)
   It is time for the business to be wound up. (Passive)
4. The fruit tastes sweet. (Active)
   The fruit is sweet when (it is) tasted. (Passive)
5. I have to stay here. (Active)
   I am obliged to stay here. (Passive)
6. It is your duty to help your children. (Active)
   You are supposed (bound in duty) to help your children. (Passive)
7. It is impossible to do. (Active)
   It is impossible to be done. (Passive)

The Use of 'To Be' (As An Ordinary/Regular Verb)

As an ordinary verb : It is used to denote a state, condition, existence, quality, time, distance, weather etc.

There is no action in this kind of sentences.
   (i) She **is** a naughty child.   (ii) She **was** healthy.

In these sentences, 'To be' verb has been used alone. It is, itself, an ordinary verb. For our convenience, we may call them 'No verb sentences'.

WORK BOOK EXERCISE (B)

Directions *The use of 'To be' as an ordinary verb.*

1. I wonder where Atul .... lately. (be)
2. Where .... you an hour ago? (be)
3. Of late, there .... great improvements in the city. (be)
4. Mr Bhargava .... our family doctor since long. (be)
5. My friend .... in Mumbai for ten years, when I .... there last month. (be, transfer)
6. Everybody presumes that she may .... present at the time of her brother's marriage next month. (be)
7. He .... ill for the last ten days, when his wife .... him yesterday. (be, visit)
8. He .... 20 now, next year he .... an adult. (be, be)
9. The milkman .... absent since last Sunday. (be)
10. He .... in Delhi for ten years, when I went there. (be)
11. I am convinced now that his political views .... worth listening to. (be)

12. She .... to Mumbai lately with her father for treatment. *(be)*
13. There .... a lot of money for you in this job. *(be)*
14. He .... a petty clerk only ten years ago. *(be)*
15. The dinner .... ready before we arrived. *(be)*

WORK BOOK EXERCISE (C)

Directions *Change the voice according to the corresponding rules explained above.*

Rule I
1. He bought new scissors.
2. They have brought news for you.
3. The minister has issued orders for his transfer.
4. I received summons yesterday.
5. He has repaired his quarters.

Rule II
1. Which book do you like most?
2. Who did this work?
3. What are you teaching?
4. Whom do you like most?
5. Who has taught you English?
6. What is he teaching you?
7. What caused this loss?
8. Which student took you home?

Rule III
1. Nobody can mend this wall.
2. Nobody saw him going out.
3. Somebody has stolen my books.
4. One should do one's duty.
5. Somebody told us to wait outside.
6. We worship God.
7. They say so.
8. Some people have seen the ghosts. (The subject is not vague in this sentence.)
9. The Police arrested the thief.
10. The university will declare the result soon.

Rule IV
1. They hope that he will pass.
2. People believe that he will return soon.
3. We decided that we would leave early.
4. Nobody knows how rich he is.
5. He expects that he will pass.

Rule V
1. He has given me a book.
2. They will ask me a question.
3. They made him Captain.
4. She told me a story.
5. He bought me a scooter.
6. I shall read you this report.
7. They refused him admission to the college.
8. I have offered him a job.
9. I shall show him the library.
10. She did not lend me money.
11. Twenty members comprise the committee.

VOICE

Rule VI
1. I do not expect it from you.
2. The angry mob thronged the roads.
3. A blow of lathi killed the dog.
4. Do you know the lady?
5. The book contains much information.
6. The servant annoyed the master.
7. His behaviour surprised everyone.
8. His insolence has annoyed the teacher.
9. Their jokes disgusted me.
10. Material life always disgusts him.
11. They keep the details on the computers.
12. My sister bore a son last year.
13. Her looks impressed everybody.
14. Their idle talk will vex you.
15. The movie does not interest her.
16. Your explanation will not satisfy your boss.
17. His actions pleased his father.
18. Her behaviour shocked me.
19. His failure in life disappointed his wife.
20. The sound of the blast alarmed the villagers.

Rule VII & VIII
1. Arnav is to help his sister.
2. Shaurya has to distribute sweets.
3. They saw the police chasing a terrorist.
4. She was to write a book on animals.
5. They found him helping the poor.

Rule IX
1. What are you listening to?
2. They were searching for the lost book.
3. The government cannot dispense with computers.
4. I have never heard of such an accident.
5. All his friends will laugh at him.
6. Do not discriminate against the poor.

Rule X
1. I made him write a letter.
2. She let me stay in her home.
3. She bade me leave the room.
4. They heard her sing a song.
5. I saw him go.

Rule XI
1. Obey your teacher.
2. Do it as early as possible.
3. Do not go out.
4. Prevent him from going out.
5. Please enter by this door.
6. Do not insult the weak.
7. Get out of the room.
8. Kindly give me some money.

Rule XII
1. Let me sleep here.
2. Let them watch the match.
3. Let us watch T.V.
4. Let us not hurt anybody.
5. Let us go now.
6. Let us enter college. (request)

Cumulative Exercises

Exercise 1

Directions *Rewrite the following sentences using the passive structure.*
1. We should put this in the fridge.
2. Somebody sent application forms to all the students.
3. The doctors operated on her yesterday morning.
4. Someone handed me a note.
5. The decision has deprived many people of the right to vote.
6. The Chairman held over the last two items until the next committee meeting.
7. The farmer prevented walkers from crossing the field after he fenced it off.
8. Suhani's questions began to irritate Akshay.
9. Tarun has interviewed the Finance Minister.
10. They have made him return the money.
11. Children often look up to strict teachers.
12. Mr Chakravarty has taught Virat to sing for many years.
13. Somebody will give you the questions a week before the exam.
14. Everybody believed (that) the plan would fail.
15. People are blaming climate change for the recent flooding.
16. Somebody had stolen the painting from the gallery.
17. They will have cleared the litter from the pitch before the match starts.
18. It is reported that the damage is extensive.
19. In 1981, it was believed that there were only two experts on disease in the country.
20. An Indian firm designed the software for this project.

Exercise 2

Directions *Rewrite the following sentences using the active structure.*
1. Anyone who misbehaves, will be punished. You won't be told again.
2. Flowers had been left at the accident site by well-wishers.
3. The streets are being cleared for the match by the police.
4. Has your computer been affected by the lightning?
5. The witnesses had been questioned for hours by detectives.
6. Fresh pasta started to be sold by super markets only in the 1990s.
7. Tanya was helped to her feet after the accident.
8. She is looked after by Sanam.
9. Has Mayank been seen (by anyone) this morning?
10. Threatening letters are being sent to him.

Previous Years' Questions

I. **Directions** *Rewrite the following sentences using the passive structure.*
   1. They will not open the shop on Monday. [Civil Services (Mains), 2008]
   2. Mukesh caught the thief at the airport.
   3. Someone has stolen my pen.
   4. One cannot solve this problem.
   5. Rajesh has opened the door.
   6. She gave her sister a car. [Civil Services (Mains), 2010]
   7. I had already shown the suspect's photograph to the policeman.
   8. They believe him to be dangerous.
   9. They made him tell them everything.
   10. They elected me President.

II. **Directions** *Rewrite the following sentences as directed without changing the meaning.*
   1. She is writing a letter.
      (Change into passive voice) [IFS, 2014]
   2. He learnt the alphabet before he could read.
      (Change into passive voice) [IFS, 2015]
   3. People say the bridge is unsafe. *(Change the voice)* [CAPF, 2015]
   4. The one-man committee determined there was no need to take action.
      (Rewrite using passive structure)
   5. Cricket fans filled the streets during the World Cup.
      (Rewrite using passive structure) [Civil Services (Mains), 2013]
   6. They are installing new computers in the office.
      (Change into passive voice) [IFS, 2013]
   7. The people will make him President.
      (Change into passive voice) [Civil Services (Mains), 2015]
   8. My pocket has been picked.
      (Change into active voice) [Civil Services (Mains), 2015]
   9. The audience loudly cheered the Mayor's speech.
      (Change into passive voice) [Civil Services (Mains), 2014]
   10. A reward was given to him by the Governor.
       (Change into active voice) [Civil Services (Mains), 2014]
   11. Give the order. *(Change the voice)* [CAPF, 2013]

III. **Directions** *Make the directed changes in the following sentences without changing their meaning.*
   1. Germany invaded Poland in 1939, thus initiating the Second World War.
      (Change into passive voice) [IES, 2014]
   2. I know him. *(Change into passive voice)* [IES, 2015]
   3. Road accidents injure many people everyday.
      (Change into passive voice) [IES, 2013]

Answers

WORK BOOK EXERCISE (A)
1. was annoyed
2. be punished
3. was convinced, was
4. has been enforced
5. were disappointed
6. behave
7. be entrusted
8. was amazed
9. will be pleased
10. is bearing
11. were alarmed
12. were ashamed
13. was delighted
14. were satisfied
15. were perplexed
16. was startled
17. will have left
18. was, being decorated
19. will be surprised
20. was confused

WORK BOOK EXERCISE (B)
1. has been
2. were
3. have been
4. has been
5. had been, was transferred
6. be
7. had been, visited
8. is, will be
9. has been
10. had been
11. are
12. has been
13. is
14. was
15. had been

WORK BOOK EXERCISE (C)

Rule I
1. New scissors were bought by him.
2. News has been brought for you by them.
3. Orders for his transfer have been issued by the minister.
4. Summons was received by me yesterday.
5. His quarters have been repaired by him.

Rule II
1. Which book is liked most by you?
2. By whom was this work done?

   Or

   Who was this work done by?
3. What is being taught by you?
4. Who is liked most by you?
5. By whom have you been taught English?

   Or

   Who have you been taught English by?
6. What is being taught to you by him?
7. What was this loss caused by?
8. By which student were you taken home?

Rule III
1. This wall cannot be mended.
2. He was not seen going out.
3. My books have been stolen.
4. Duty should be done.
5. We were told to wait outside.
6. God is worshipped.
7. It is said so.
8. The ghosts have been seen by some people.
9. The thief was arrested.
10. The result will be declared soon.

Rule IV
1. It is hoped that he will pass.

   Or

   He hopes to pass.

VOICE

2. It is believed that he will return soon.

   Or

   He is believed to return soon.
3. It was decided that we would leave early.
4. It is not known how rich he is.
5. It is expected that he will pass.

   Or

   He is expected to pass.

Rule V

1. I have been given a book by him.

   Or

   A book has been given to me by him.
2. I will be asked a question by them.

   Or

   A question will be asked of me by them.
3. He was made captain.
4. I was told a story by her.
5. I was bought a scooter by him.

   Or

   A scooter was bought for me by him.
6. This report will be read by me for you.
7. He was refused admission to the college.

   Or

   Admission to the college was refused to him.
8. He has been offered a job by me.

   Or

   A job has been offered to him by me.
9. He will be shown the library by me.

   Or

   The library will be shown to him by me.
10. I was not lent money by her.

    Or

    Money was not lent to me by her.
11. The committee is comprised of twenty members.

Rule VI

1. It is not expected of you by me.
2. The roads were thronged with the angry mob.
3. The dog was killed with a blow of lathi.
4. Is the lady known to you?
5. Much information is contained in the book.
6. The master was annoyed with the servant.
7. Everyone was surprised at his behaviour.
8. The teacher has been annoyed at his insolence.
9. I was disgusted at their jokes.
10. He is always disgusted with material life.
11. The details are kept on computers.
12. A son was born to my sister last year.
13. Everybody was impressed with her looks.
14. You will be vexed at their idle talk.

15. She is not interested in the movie.
16. Your boss will not be satisfied with your explanation.
17. His father was pleased with his actions.
18. I was shocked at her behaviour.
19. His wife was disappointed at his failure in life.
20. The villagers were alarmed at the sound of the blast.

Rule VII & VIII
1. Arnav's sister is to be helped by him.
2. Sweets have to be distributed by Shaurya.
3. A terrorist was seen being chased by the police.
   Or
   The police were seen chasing the terrorist.
4. A book on Animals was to be written by her.
5. The poor were found being helped by them.
   Or
   He was found helping the poor.

Rule IX
1. What is being listened to by you?
2. The lost book was being searched for by them.
3. Computers cannot be dispensed with by the government.
4. Such an accident has never been heard of.
5. He will be laughed at by all his friends.
6. The poor should not be discriminated against.

Rule X
1. He was made to write a letter by me.
2. I was let stay in her home.
3. I was bidden to leave the room by her.
4. She was heard to sing a song by them.
5. He was seen to go by me.

Rule XI
1. Your teacher should be obeyed.
2. It should be done as early as possible.
3. You are ordered not to go out.
   Or
   You are forbidden to go out.
4. He should be prevented from going out.
5. You are requested to enter by this door.
6. The weak should not be insulted.
7. You are ordered to get out of the room.
8. You are requested kindly to give me some money.

Rule XII
1. I may be allowed to sleep here.
2. They may be allowed to watch the match.
3. TV should be watched by us.
4. Nobody should be hurt by us.
5. It is suggested that we should go now.
6. We might be allowed to enter college.

Cumulative Exercises

Exercise 1

1. This should be put in the fridge.
2. All the students were sent application forms.

   Or

   Application forms were sent to all the students.
3. She was operated on yesterday morning.
4. I was handed a note.

   Or

   A note was handed to me.
5. Many people have been deprived of the right to vote (by the decision).
6. The last two items were held over (by the Chairman) until the next committee meeting.
7. Walkers were prevented from crossing the field after it was fenced off (by the farmer).
8. Akshay began to be irritated by Suhani's questions.
9. The finance minister has been interviewed by Tarun.
10. He has been made to return the money.
11. Strict teachers are often looked up to by children.
12. Virat has been taught to sing (by Mr Chakravarty) for many years.
13. You will be given the questions a week before the exam.
14. It was believed that the plan would fail.
15. The recent flooding is being blamed on climate change.

    Or

    Climate change is being blamed for the recent flooding.
16. The painting had been stolen from the gallery.
17. The litter will have been cleared from the pitch before the match starts.

    Or

    The pitch will have been cleared of litter before the match starts.
18. The damage is reported to be extensive.
19. In 1981, there were believed to be only two experts on the disease in the country.
20. The software for this project was designed by an Indian firm.

Exercise 2

1. I shall punish anyone who misbehaves. I won't tell you again.
2. Well wishers had left flowers at the accident site.
3. The police are clearing the streets for the match.
4. Has the lightning affected your computer?
5. Detectives had questioned the witnesses for hours.
6. Supermarkets started to sell fresh pasta only in the 1990s.
7. People helped Tanya to her feet after the accident.
8. Sanam looks after her.
9. Has anyone seen Mayank this morning?
10. Someone is sending him threatening letters.

Previous Years' Questions

I. 1. The shop will not be opened on Monday by them.
    2. The thief was caught at the airport by Mukesh.
    3. My pen has been stolen.
    4. This problem cannot be solved.
    5. The door has been opened by Rajesh.
    6. Her sister was given a car by her.
       Or
       A car was given to her sister by her.
    7. Suspect's photograph had already been shown to the policeman by me.
       Or
       The policeman had already been shown suspect's photograph by me.
    8. He is believed to be dangerous.
    9. He was made to tell them everything.
    10. I was elected President.

II. 1. A letter is being written by her.
    2. The alphabet was learnt by him before he could read.
    3. The bridge is said to be unsafe.
    4. It was determined by the one-man committee that there was no need to take action.
    5. The streets were filled with the cricket fans during the World Cup.
    6. New computers are being installed in the office by them.
    7. He will be made President.
    8. Somebody has picked my pocket.
    9. The mayor's speech was loudly cheered by the audience.
    10. The governor gave him a reward.
    11. Let the order be given.

III. 1. The Second World War was initiated when Poland was invaded by Germany in 1939.
     2. He is known to me.
     3. Many people are injured everyday in road accidents.

CHAPTER 3

Clause Analysis

A number of finite verbs in a sentence determine a number of clauses. Non-finite verbs are not considered for the purpose of clause analysis.

1. In a **simple sentence** there is one finite verb and hence only one clause.
   (a) She **is writing** a novel.
   (b) Pearl **will examine** a patient.
2. In a **complex sentence**, there are more than one clauses as follows:
   (a) Principal/Main clause
   (b) Subordinate clauses
      (i) Noun clause
      (ii) Adjective clause
      (iii) Adverb clause
   These subordinate clauses are joined by subordinating conjunctions.
3. In a **compound sentence**, there are more than one Principal clause/Co-ordinate clause related to each other.
   (a) Principal clause
   (b) Co-ordinate clause
   Co-ordinate clause is joined by co-ordinating conjunctions.

Note However, when co-ordinating conjunction joins two subordinate clauses, the sentence remains a complex sentence.

Now, let us study how to analyse a sentence by pointing out the clauses separately and defining their functions. Before attempting clause analysis of sentences a student must go through chapter on clauses.

Principal Clause

While analysing a sentence, a student is required to find out a **Principal clause**. It is easy to do so because the Principal clause is not introduced by any joining connective. Having found out the **Principal clause** a student is expected to break up the rest of the sentence into **Subordinate/Co-ordinate clauses**.

Study the following examples carefully:

1. He told me that he would help my brother, who needed some money.
   - (a) He told me — Principal clause.
   - (b) that he would help my brother — Noun clause, object of the verb 'told'.
   - (c) who needed some money — Adjective clause, qualifying 'brother.'

   (The sentence is complex)

2. He gave money to the students, who were poor, whenever they asked for it.
   - (a) He gave money to the students — Principal clause
   - (b) who were poor — Adjective clause, qualifying the noun 'Students'
   - (c) whenever they asked for it — Adverb clause of time, modifying verb 'gave'

   (The sentence is complex)

3. He replied that he went to his brother, whenever he liked.
   - (a) He replied — Principal clause
   - (b) that he went to his brother — Noun clause, object to the verb 'replied'
   - (c) whenever he liked — Adverb clause of time, modifying verb 'went'

   (The sentence is complex)

4. Nobody can tell, where he lives because he has not told anybody and nobody has cared to find it out.
   - (a) Nobody can tell — Principal clause
   - (b) where he lives — Noun clause, object to the verb 'tell'
   - (c) because he has not told anybody — Adverb clause of reason, modifying verb 'tell'
   - (d) and nobody has cared to find it out — Co-ordinate clause to Adverb clause

   (The sentence is complex)

5. Although he came late, he was not punished and so was pardoned by the teacher, who himself came late.
   - (a) He was not punished by the teacher — Principal clause
   - (b) Although he came late — Adverb clause of contrast
   - (c) who himself came late — Adjective clause, qualifying the noun 'teacher'
   - (d) and so was pardoned — Co-ordinate to Principal clause

   (The sentence is compound)

Noun Clause

By now, it is clear that a Noun clause is one of the three **subordinate** clauses in a complex sentence. It does the work of a noun. As a rule, students should remember that a noun clause explains/answers a **verb** or a **noun** in the following cases:

CLAUSE ANALYSIS

Function of a Noun Clause
Study the following examples carefully:
1. **The subject of a verb**
   (i) What he did is not desirable.
   (ii) That he will succeed is certain.

   These sentences can also be written in the following manner to show that Noun clauses have been used in place of subject:
   (i) It is not desirable what he did.
   (ii) It is certain that he will succeed.

   Here, Noun clause is in apposition to Pronoun 'it'.

2. **The object of a transitive verb**
   (i) He does not **know** when he will return.
   (ii) She **confessed** that she had met him.

   In the above sentences, noun clauses explain the verb **know** and **confessed**.

3. **The complement of a verb**
   (i) The fact **is** that he is dishonest.
   (ii) His hope **is** that his son will return.

   Noun clause following the verb 'to be' performs the function of a complement
   (in place of predicate)

   To be, become, seem, appear, grow, taste, smell, prove, come, go, feel are some of the verbs followed by a Noun clause as a complement.

4. **The object of a preposition/infinitive**
   (i) There is no sense **in** what you say.
   (ii) Pay heed **to** what your elders say.
   (iii) I was pleased **to note** that he was recovering.

5. **The apposition to a noun/pronoun**
   (i) I have not heard the **news** that he has married her.
   (ii) I do not believe in his **statement** that he was not present there.
   (iii) It is desirable what he did.
   (iv) It is certain that he will succeed.

Adjective Clause

As a subordinate clause in a complex sentence, Adjective clause does the work of an adjective. It qualifies a noun or pronoun in the Principal or any other subordinate clause.

Study the following examples carefully:
1. He is the man, **who is honest**. *(Qualifying the noun 'man')*
2. The time, **when he will come**, is not certain. *(Qualifying the noun 'time')*
3. Those, **who are honest**, succeed in life. *(Qualifying the pronoun 'those')*
4. I gave him the pen, **which I bought for myself**. *(Qualifying the noun 'pen')*
5. I met a man, **I had already known**. *(Qualifying the noun 'man')*
6. He will buy the house, **I built last year**. *(Qualifying the noun 'house')*

In the sentences 5 and 6, the conjunctions **whom** and **which** are understood and **not expressed therefore**.

Adverb Clause

As already described, an Adverb clause is a subordinate clause. It does the work of an adverb. It, therefore, modifies some adjective or verb.

Adverb clauses are classified as follows:

1. **Adverb clause of Time**—Time clause is introduced by conjunctions of time such as *'when, as, while, before, after, by the time, as soon as, until, till, whenever, since, as long as, ever since'*.

2. **Adverb clause of Condition**—
   (a) There are three types of Conditional clauses. Each kind contains a different pair of tenses.
      (i) Present likely condition.
      (ii) Present unlikely condition.
      (iii) Past condition.
   (b) Conditional clauses are introduced with connectives *'if, unless, would that suppose, on condition that, provided, in case.'*

   Sometimes, subordinate conjunction 'if' is omitted in Adverb clause of condition.
   (should, had, were are used instead)

3. **Adverb clause of Purpose**—Adverb clause of Purpose is introduced by conjunctions *'that, so that, in order that and lest.'*

4. **Adverb clause of Place**—Adverb clause of place is introduced by the conjunctions *'where'* and *'wherever'* but Adverb clause of Place does not qualify any place given in the main clause.

5. **Adverb clause of Result**—Adverb clause of Result is expressed by *'that'* in the adverb clause preceded by *'so', 'such'* in the main clause.

6. **Adverb clause of Reason**—Adverb clause of Reason is introduced by *'because, since, as'*. However, *'so'* and *'therefore'* should be avoided in the Main clause.

7. **Adverb clause of Concession or Contrast**—Adverb clause of contrast is introduced by *'although, though, even if, however, whatever, no matter, notwithstanding that, as, whether, even though, much as, even as.'*

8. **Adverb clause of Manner**—Adverb clause of Manner is introduced by *'as, as if and as though.'*

9. **Adverb clause of Comparison**—In Adverb clause of comparison, the use of the case of a pronoun and the objects being compared should be taken note of carefully. Comparison should be between the same case of pronoun or between the same two persons or things being compared. Adverb Clause of comparison is introduced by *'than'* and *'as'*.

The verb in Adverb clause of Comparison is often understood and not mentioned.

Some of the connectives denoting different meanings have been used in the following sentences. As a result of this, they form different clauses:

1. I asked him **when he would go their**. *(Noun clause)*
2. I know the time **when he will come**. *(Adjective clause)*
3. He will give me money **when I go to Bombay**. *(Adverb clause)*
4. I shall not tell you **where he lives**. *(Noun clause)*

CLAUSE ANALYSIS 349

5. I shall go to the place **where my friend lives**. *(Adjective clause)*
6. I shall go **where my friend lives**. *(Adverb clause)*
7. I do not know **if he will come**. *(Noun clause)*
8. You will pass **if you work hard**. *(Adverb clause)*
9. I do not know **who came here last night**. *(Noun clause)*
10. I know the boy **who came here last night**. *(Adjective clause)*
11. I know the man **whom every body likes**. *(Adjective clause)*
12. I do not know **whom she is teaching**. *(Noun clause)*
13. I know **that he will come**. *(Noun clause)*
14. I know the boy **that lives there**. *(Adjective clause)*
15. We come here **that we may study**. *(Adverb clause)*
16. He is so tired **that he cannot run**. *(Adverb clause)*
17. **Since my brother came**, he has been teaching. *(Adverb clause)*
18. **Since she is ill**, she can not go out. *(Adverb clause)*
19. He is such a boy **that does not help any body**. *(Adjective clause)*
20. **As I arrived at the station**, the train left. *(Adverb clause)*
21. **As he was late**, he missed the bus. *(Adverb clause)*
22. She is as intelligent **as his brother is**. *(Adverb clause)*
23. **Rich as he is**, he is not happy. *(Adverb clause)*
24. She did it **as I advised her to do**. *(Adverb clause)*
25. I shall do **whatever he says**. *(Noun clause)*
26. I shall do **whatever you may say**. *(Adverb clause)*
27. I do not know **whether he will come tomorrow**. *(Noun clause)*
28. I shall do it **whether you like it or not**. *(Adverb clause)*
29. **While it was raining**, nobody went out. *(Adverb clause)*
30. She is intelligent **while her brother is dull**. *(Co-ordinate clause)*
31. I cannot say **what he is talking about**. *(Noun clause)*
32. He told me **what his father told him**. *(Noun clause)*

WORK BOOK EXERCISE (A)

Directions *Find out the Noun clause and mention the function as explained in the foregoing examples.*

1. I say that she is intelligent.
2. I can not say if she will go.
3. I did not know whether she would go.
4. It is certain that she will marry him.
5. I do not know what she is doing these days.
6. I shall not do what you want me to do.
7. What he says is not correct.
8. I was pleased by what she did for us.
9. She never believed in his statement that he would get her a job.
10. Everybody was pleased to note that she looked cheerful at the party.
11. She was asked when she would return.
12. The fact is that he is a cheat.
13. That she will succeed is certain.
14. I am certain that he will pass.
15. Listen to what I say.

WORK BOOK EXERCISE (B)

Directions *Below are given the sentences for the students to find out Adjective clause stating the Noun or Pronoun qualified by them.*

1. I know the man who came here.
2. This is my pen which I gave you.
3. I don't know any man that is present here.
4. He is such a man as will never cheat you.
5. I have met all the boys that have been admitted to the hostel.
6. This is the best book that I have ever read.
7. I have invited Mohan whose father is a famous doctor.
8. I have invited Mohan all of us admire.
9. It is the table the leg of which is broken.
10. The news he gave is wrong.
11. I know the time when he arrived.
12. This is the reason why he will not stand by you.
13. It is I who am helping them.
14. He settled in the town where he was born.
15. Let us help only those that are really needy.

WORK BOOK EXERCISE (C)

Directions *Each of the following sentences contain an Adverb clause. Pick out the Adverb clause stating its kind and the word it modifies.*

1. When you write the book, I shall help you.
2. My brother had come before we took our dinner.
3. After we had taken our dinner, my brother came.
4. Since she arrived, she has been suffering from cold.
5. He will not come until you leave this place.
6. Please wait till I leave.
7. He works hard so that he may stand first.
8. Walk carefully lest you should fall.
9. She worked so hard that she could get first class.
10. If you work hard, you will pass.
11. Unless you work hard, you will not pass.
12. Were I a doctor, I would treat him.
13. Although he worked hard, he did not pass.
14. As he is intelligent, he will pass.
15. She talks as if she were rich.
16. She did this work as I told her.
17. He is wiser than she.
18. His shirt is cheaper than mine.
19. She is as good as he.
20. I like her more than him.

Cumulative Exercise

Directions *Analyse the following sentences pointing out the kind of clauses. A student is also required to state their functions.*

1. The boy stated that his brother would not come.
2. The boy, who lives here, said that his brother would not come.
3. The boy, who lives here, told us that his brother, who was a doctor and whom they had called would not come.
4. We don't know, how our ancestors led their lives in great difficulties when there were no comforts of life.
5. We, who live in the present age, do not know how our ancestors led their lives in ancient India.
6. We do not know whether our ancestors led their lives in great difficulties but we are certain of their problems.
7. The house that was constructed by me has been rented to the student, who came yesterday.
8. The persons, who do wrong to others, are always humiliated by those, whom they wrong.
9. Once he said that he could not do the work his brother was doing as he was illiterate.
10. He told us that he had read the book, which was written by Tagore.
11. He was ordered that he would not go out until the rain had stopped.
12. Those, who do not respect others don't know that others will not respect them unless they respect them.
13. I doubt if he said that those, who would not come in time, would not get food.
14. We cannot say anything about any religion unless we agree that all the religions teach us to be compassionate.
15. Those, who do not help others unless their motive is fulfilled, are called selfish.
16. I did not tell him that I would not help those boys, who do not work hard.
17. I don't know how this came to be so although I must confess that if I had inquired I could have found out why he acted so selfishly.
18. He tells everybody that nobody will help and give him money because nobody believes him.
19. She told me that if I gave her book she would be grateful to me.
20. Satya knows very well that when her husband returns from office she will be asked to leave the house.
21. Will you ever forget her, who stood by you, when you were in trouble and will not write to her?
22. She hoped that she would inherit the property of her sister, who had no offspring.

23. The statement that she was absent when the police came was not believed by her friends, who suspected her complicity in the crime.
24. Hardy believed that the forces that govern human destiny are still in the making.
25. The robbers warned him that if he informed the police of the happening, he would be in trouble again.
26. History is a witness to the fact that there had never been a strong central authority to rule over our country that remained under foreign domination for ages.
27. I have no pity for a man, who you know very well, told me that he had lost courage when disaster befell him.
28. Mr Patel asked his party men to find out if they could launch agitation, when the British Government was torn with internal problems.
29. He told the little girl that throwing banana on to a pavement was a bad habit because any pedestrian could slip on it.
30. You should be content and pleased with what you have these days; since to complain of high prices does not speak well of you.
31. He could not utter a single word to his son, who, when he arrived, was in a dejected mood.
32. She knew that as it was dark, she would not be allowed to go to meet her friend she had promised to visit and give money.
33. It is remarkable to meet with success, when one is actually expecting failure because desirable chance happenings are the spice of life.
34. Those, in trouble, should realise that life is not as easy as they thought it to be, though no difficulty is beyond solution.
35. I know that my son, if he had been sent to JNU, would have made a mark in life since the environment for mental make up is no less important than the inborn qualities.
36. The fact is that he is not going to help you because he knows that, as you are unfaithful, you will not stand by him in difficulties.
37. That you are a hard working fellow is well known to those, who have promised to teach you what you want to learn.
38. It is certain that he will succeed and nobody can deny that he will secure good marks.

Answers

WORK BOOK EXERCISE (A)
1. That she is intelligent — N.C., Object to the verb 'say'
2. If she will go — N.C., Object to the verb 'say'
3. Whether she would go — N.C., Object to the verb 'know'
4. That she will marry him — N.C., In apposition to 'it'
5. What she is doing — N.C., Object to the verb 'know'
6. What you want me to do — N.C., Object to the verb 'do'
7. What he says — N.C., Subject of the verb 'is'
8. What she did for us — N.C., Object to the preposition 'by'
9. That he would get her a job — N.C., Case in apposition to the 'statement'
10. That she looked cheerful at the party — N.C., Object to infinitive 'to note'
11. When she would return — N.C., Object to the verb 'asked'
12. That he is a cheat — N.C., Complement of 'is'
13. That she will succeed — N.C., Subject of the verb 'is'
14. That he will pass — N.C., Object to 'certain'
15. What I say — N.C., Object to the preposition 'to'

WORK BOOK EXERCISE (B)
1. Who came here — Adj. C. qualifying the noun 'man'
2. Which I gave you — Adj. C. qualifying the noun 'pen'
3. That is present here — Adj. C. qualifying the noun 'any man'
4. As will never cheat you — Adj. C. qualifying the noun 'such a man'
5. That have been admitted to the hostel — Adj. C. qualifying the noun 'all the boys'
6. That I have ever read — Adj. C. qualifying the noun 'the best book'
7. Whose father is a famous doctor — Adj. C. qualifying the noun 'Mohan'
8. (Whom) all of us admire — Adj. C. qualifying the noun 'Mohan'
9. The leg of which is broken — Adj. C. qualifying the noun 'the table'
10. (That) he gave — Adj. C. qualifying the noun 'the news'
11. When he arrived — Adj. C. qualifying the noun 'Time'
12. Why he will not stand by you — Adj. C. qualifying the noun 'Reason'
13. Who am helping them — Adj. C. qualifying the pronoun 'I'
14. Where he was born — Adj. C. qualifying the noun 'Town'
15. That are really needy — Adj. C. qualifying the pronoun 'those'

WORK BOOK EXERCISE (C)
1. When you write the book — Adv. C. of time, Modifying the verb 'help'
2. Before we took our dinner — Adv. C. of time, Modifying the verb 'had come'
3. After we had taken our dinner — Adv. C. of time, Modifying the verb 'came'
4. Since she arrived — Adv. C. of time, Modifying the verb 'suffering'
5. Until you leave this place — Adv. C. of time, Modifying the verb 'come'
6. Till I leave — Adv. C. of time, Modifying the verb 'wait'
7. So that he may stand first — Adv. C. of purpose, Modifying the verb 'work hard'
8. Lest you should fall — Adv. C. of purpose, Modifying the verb 'walk'
9. That she could get first class — Adv. C. of result, Modifying the verb 'worked'
10. If you work hard — Adv. C. of condition, Modifying the verb 'pass'

11. Unless you work hard — Adv. C. of condition, Modifying the verb 'not pass'
12. Were I a doctor — Adv. C. of condition, Modifying the verb 'treat'
13. Although he worked hard — Adv. C. of contrast, Modifying the verb 'pass'
14. As he is intelligent — Adv. C. of reason, Modifying the verb 'pass'
15. As if she were rich — Adv. C. of manner, Modifying the verb 'talks'
16. As I told her — Adv. C. of manner, Modifying the verb 'did'
17. Than she (is) — Adv. C. of comparison, Modifying the adjective 'wiser'
18. Than mine (is) — Adv. C. of comparison, Modifying the adjective 'cheaper'
19. As he is — Adv. C. of comparison, Modifying the adjective 'good'
20. Than (I like) him — Adv. C. of comparison, Modifying the verb 'like

Cumulative Exercise

1. (a) The boy stated — Principal clause
   (b) that his brother would not come — Noun clause, Object to the transitive verb 'stated'
   (The sentence is complex)
2. (a) The boy said — Principal clause
   (b) who lives here — Adjective clause, Qualifying the noun 'the boy'
   (c) that his brother would not come — Noun clause, Object to the transitive verb 'said'
   (The sentence is complex)
3. (a) The boy told us — Principal clause
   (b) who lives here — Adjective clause, Qualifying the noun 'the boy'
   (c) that his brother would not come — Noun clause, Object to the transitive verb 'told'
   (d) who was a doctor — Adjective clause, Qualifying the noun 'brother'
   (e) and whom they had called — Co-ordinate clause to 'd'   *(The sentence is compound)*
4. (a) We don't know — Principal clause
   (b) how our accestors led their lives in great difficulties — Noun clause, Object to the finite verb 'know'.
   (c) when there were no comforts of life — Adverb clause of time, Modifying the verb 'lead'.
   (The sentence is complex)
5. (a) We do not know — Principal clause
   (b) who live in the present age — Adjective clause, Modifying the pronoun 'We'.
   (c) how our ancestors led their lives in ancient India — Noun clause, Answer to finite verb 'know'.   *(Th sentence is complex)*
6. (a) We do not know — Principal clause
   (b) whether our ancestors led their lives in great difficulties — Noun clause, Answer to the finite verb 'know'.
   (c) but we are certain of their problems — Co-ordinate clause of 'a'
   (The sentence is compound)
7. (a) The house has been rented to the student — Principal clause
   (b) that was constructed by me — Adjective clause, Qualifying the noun 'house'
   (c) who came yesterday — Adjective clause, Qualifying the noun 'student'.
   (The sentence is complex)
8. (a) The persons are always humiliated — Principal clause
   (b) who do wrong to others — Adjective clause, Qualifying the noun 'persons'
   (c) whom (by those) they wrong — Adjective clause, Qualifying the pronoun 'those'
   (The sentence is complex)

CLAUSE ANALYSIS

9. (a) Once he said — Principal clause
   (b) that he could not do the work his brother was doing — Noun clause, Object to the verb 'say'
   (c) as he was illiterate — Adverb clause of reason, Qualifying the verb 'do'.
   (The sentence is complex)

10. (a) He told us — Principal clause
    (b) that he had read the book — Noun clause, Answer to the verb 'told'.
    (c) which was written by Tagore — Adjective clause, Qualifying the noun 'the book''.
    (The sentence is complex)

11. (a) He was ordered — Principal clause
    (b) that he would not go out — Noun clause, Answer to the verb 'ordered'
    (c) until the rain had stopped — Adverb clause of condition, Specifying the condition
    (The sentence is complex)

12. (a) Those don't know — Principal clause
    (b) who don't respect others — Adjective clause, Qualifying the pronoun 'those'.
    (c) that others will not respect them — Noun clause, Answer to the verb 'know'.
    (d) unless they respect them — Adverb clause of condition, Specifying the conditon
    (The sentence is complex)

13. (a) I doubt — Principal clause
    (b) if he said — Adverb clause of condition
    (c) that those who would not come in time would not get food — Noun clause, Answer to the verb 'said'
    (The sentence is complex)

14. (a) We cannot say — Principal clause
    (b) anything about any religion — Noun clause, Answer to verb 'say'
    (c) unless we agree — Adverb clause of condition, Specifying the condition
    (d) that all the religions teach us to be compassionate — Noun clause, Answer to the verb 'agree'
    (The sentence is complex)

15. (a) Those are called selfish — Principal clause
    (b) who do not help others — Adjective clause, Qualifying pronoun 'those'
    (c) unless their motive is fulfilled — Adverb clause, Specifying the condition
    (The sentence is complex)

16. (a) I did not tell him — Principal clause
    (b) that I would not help those boys — Noun clause, Answer to verb 'tell'
    (c) who do not work hard — Adjective clause, Qualifying the noun 'boys'
    (The sentence is complex)

17. (a) I don't know — Principal clause
    (b) how this came to be so — Noun clause, Object to the transitive verb 'know'
    (c) although I must confess — Adverb clause of contrast, Modifying the verb 'don't know'
    (d) that I could have found out — Noun clause, Object to the transitive verb 'confess'
    (e) if I had inquired — Adverb clause of condition, Modifying the verb 'found'
    (f) why he acted so selfishly — Noun clause, Object to the transitive verb 'found'
    (The sentence is complex)

18. (a) He tells everybody — Principal clause
    (b) that nobody will help and give him money — Noun clause, Answer to the finite verb 'tell'
    (c) because nobody believes him — Adverb clause, specifying reason.
    (The sentence is complex)

19. (a) She told me — Principal clause
    (b) that if I gave her book — Noun clause, Answer to verb 'told'.
    (c) she would be grateful to me — Co-ordinate clause   . *(The sentence is compound)*

20. (a) Satya knows very well — Principal clause
    (b) that when her husband returns from office — Noun clause, Answer to verb 'knows'
    (c) she will be asked to leave the house — Co-ordinate clause (The sentence is compound)
21. (a) Will you ever forget her and will not write to her — Principal clause
    (b) who stood by you — Adjective clause, Modifying pronoun 'her'
    (c) when you were in trouble — Adverb clause of time (The sentence is complex)
22. (a) She hoped — Principal clause
    (b) that she would inherit the property of her sister — Noun clause, Answer to the verb 'hope'
    (c) who had no offspring — Adjective clause, Qualifying the noun 'sister'
    (The sentence is complex)
23. (a) The statement was not believed by her friends — Principal clause
    (b) that she was absent — Noun clause, Apposition to the noun 'the statement'
    (c) when the police came — Adverb clause of time, Modifying the verb 'was'
    (d) who suspected her complicity in the crime — Adjective clause, Qualifying the noun 'the friends.'
    (The sentence is complex)
24. (a) Hardy believed — Principal clause
    (b) that the forces are still in the making — Noun clause, answer to verb 'believed'
    (c) that govern the human destiny — Adjective clause qualifying the noun 'forces'
    (The sentence is complex)
25. (a) The robbers warned him — Principal clause
    (b) that if he informed the police of the happening — Noun clause, Object of verb 'warned'
    (c) he would be in trouble again — Co-ordinate clause to 'a'. (The sentence is compound)
26. (a) History is a witness to the fact — Principal clause
    (b) that there had never been a strong central authority to rule over our country — Noun clause, Complement of verb 'to be'
    (c) that remained under foreign domination for ages — Adjective clause, Qualifying the noun 'a strong central authority' (The sentence is complex)
27. (a) I have no pity — Principal clause
    (b) for a man you know very well — Indirect object to verb 'have'
    (c) who told me that he had lost courage — Adjective clause, Qualifying noun 'man'
    (d) when disaster befell him — Adverb clause of time (The sentence is complex)
28. (a) Mr Patel asked the party men to find out — Principal clause
    (b) if they could launch agitation — Noun clause, Object of the infinitive to 'find out'
    (c) when the British Government was torn with internal problems — Adverb clause of time, Modifying the verb 'launch' (The sentence is complex)
29. (a) He told the little girl — Principal clause
    (b) that throwing banana on to a pavement was a bad habit — Noun clause, Object to verb 'told'
    (c) because any pedestrian could slip on it — Adverb clause stating reason
    (The sentence is complex)
30. (a) You should be content with — Principal clause
    (b) and pleased — Co-ordinate to principal clause
    (c) what you have these days — Noun clause, Object to the preposition 'with'
    (d) since to complain of high prices does not speak well of you — Adverb clause of condition, Modifying the verb 'should be' (The sentence is compound)

CLAUSE ANALYSIS 357

31. (a) He could not utter a single word to his son — Principal clause.
    (b) who was in a dejected mood — Adjective clause, Qualifying the noun 'son'
    (c) when he arrived — Adverb clause of time, Modifying the verb 'utter'
    (The sentence is complex)

32. (a) She knew — Principal clause
    (b) that as it was dark she would not be allowed to go to meet her friend — Noun clause, Answer to verb 'knew'
    (c) she had promised to visit and give money — Co-ordinate clause to 'a'
    (The sentence is compound)

33. (a) It is remarkable to meet with success — Principal clause
    (b) when one is actually expecting failure — Adverb clause of time
    (c) because desirable chance happenings are the spice of life — Adverb clause of reason
    (The sentence is complex)

34. (a) Those, in trouble, should realise — Principal clause
    (b) that life is not as easy as they thought it to be — Noun clause, Answer to 'realise'
    (c) though, no difficulty is beyond solution — Adverb clause of contrast
    (The sentence is complex)

35. (a) I know — Principal clause
    (b) that my son would have made a mark in life — Noun clause, Object to the transitive verb 'know'
    (c) If he had been sent to JNU — Adverb clause of condition, Modifying the verb 'made' in (b)
    (d) since the environment for mental make up is no less important — Adverb clause of reason, Modifying the verb 'sent' in (c)
    (e) Than the inborn qualities (are) — Adverb clause of comparison. *(The sentence is complex)*

36. (a) The fact is — Principal clause.
    (b) that he is not going to help you — Noun clause, Complement of verb 'is'
    (c) because he knows — Adverb clause of reason, Modifying the verb 'to help'
    (d) that you will not stand by him in difficulties — Noun clause, Object to the transitive verb 'knows'
    (e) as you are unfaithful — Adverb clause of reason, Modifying the verb 'stand by'
    (The sentence is complex)

37. (a) (It) is well known — Principal clause
    (b) that you are a hard working fellow — Noun clause, Subject of the verb 'is known'
    (c) who (to those) have promised to teach you — Adjective clause, Qualifying the pronoun 'those'
    (d) what you want to learn — Noun clause, Object to infinitive 'to teach'
    (The sentence is complex)

38. (a) It is certain — Principal clause
    (b) that he will succeed — Noun clause, Apposition to pronoun 'it'
    (c) and nobody can deny — Co-ordinate clause to 'a'
    (d) that he will secure good marks — Noun clause, Object to the transitive verb 'deny'
    (The sentence is compound)

CHAPTER 4

Non-Finite Verbs
(Infinitives, Gerunds, Participles)

Study the following sentences carefully:
  (i) I have given him money.
  (ii) I like to give him money today.

In the sentence (i), the verb 'have given' has 'I' as its subject. The verb 'have given' is limited by the number and person of its subject. It is, therefore, called a **finite verb**.

In sentence (ii), 'like' is a finite verb. But 'to give' has no separate subject and is not limited by number and person. It is, therefore, called a **Non-finite verb**.

Forms of Non-Finite Verbs

The Non-finite verbs are divided into three forms:
  I. Infinitives   II. Gerunds   III. Participles

I. Infinitive

Infinitive is a kind of noun with certain features of a verb. 'To' is used with infinitives. However, it is omitted sometimes.

Forms of Infinitive

As used in the following sentences:

  (i) She comes here **to study**. *(Purpose)*
  (ii) Everyone desires **to be admired**. *(Passive voice)*
  (iii) He admitted **to have abused** him. *(Perfect infinitive)*
  (iv) He admitted **to have been arrested** last year. *(Perfect passive)*
  (v) He seems **to be running** out of money. *(Continuous infinitive)*
  (vi) He admitted **to have been spying** for the enemy for sometime.
      (Perfect continuous, time expression)
  (vii) Everyone desires **to be popular**. *('Be' as an ordinary verb)*
  (viii) **To err** is human. *(Subject)*

NON-FINITE VERBS

Rules of Infinitive

Rule I
(A) (Verb/Adjective/Noun) + Infinitive
   (i) She comes here to study.   *(Active voice)*
   (ii) Nobody likes to be cheated.   *(Passive voice)*
   (iii) Everyone desires to be rich.   *(No verb)*
   (iv) To err is human. (It is human to err).   *(Subject)*

(B) Some of the verbs and adjectives are followed by infinitives.
   agree, happy, desire, need, dare, hope, expect, decede, want, wish, refuse, eager, fail, glad, happy, herd, easy.

(C) How + Infinitive
   When Infinitive is used to express manner, the full forms of infinitive is 'how to'. The verbs implying manner/method are—
   '**know, learn, explain, teach, discover, wonder, show, ask, remember, forget**' etc. *For example*
   (v) He knows how to write English.
   (vi) We taught him how to cook food.

Rule II Difference between 'To' and 'For'
   Study the following sentences carefully:
   I went to see him.   *[Correct (purpose)]*
   I went for seeing him.   *(Incorrect)*
   'for seeing' cannot be used for purpose implying future because

(A) For + Gerund is used for actions showing cause. (Action in the past).
   For example
   (i) He will punish you for breaking the pen.
   (ii) He punished you for coming late.

(B) For + Gerund is used for showing purpose for which the subject is used.
   For example
   (i) This book is to read.   *(Say for reading)*
   (ii) This machine is to measure height.   *(Say for measuring)*
   (iii) The house is to let.   *(Correct)*

(C) For + Noun is used for purpose in place of **to + verb** when verb is made to serve as noun.
   For example
   (i) We come here for a drive.
   (ii) Sameer requested for a rest.
   (iii) Esha went for a walk.

(D) To + Gerund is also used with certain verbs and phrases.
   For example
   (i) She is used to swimming at dawn.
   (ii) Esha came here with a view to studying.   *[Refer to Rule III (Gerunds)]*

Rule III Direct Infinitive

In certain cases, the infinitive without 'to' is used. We may call it infinitive without 'to' or Direct Infinitive. Direct Infinitive is used after :

(A) 'Need' and 'Dare' in the negative and interrogative sentences only when they are used as auxiliaries. *For example*
    (i) You need to work hard. *(Affirmative)*
    (ii) You do not need to work hard. *(Negative as ordinary)*
    (iii) He need not work hard. *(Negative as auxiliary)*
    (iv) Do you need to work there now? *(Interrogative as ordinary)*
    (v) Need he work there now? *(Interrogative as auxiliary)*
    (vi) He dares to go outside in dark. *(Affirmative)*
    (vii) He does not dare to go in dark. *(Negative as ordinary)*
    (viii) He dare not go in dark. *(Negative as auxiliary)*
    (ix) Does he dare to go in dark? *(Interrogative as ordinary)*
    (x) Dare he go in dark? *(Interrogative as auxiliary)*

Note 's' is not used with **dare/need** as auxiliary verbs.

(B) 'Direct Infinitive' is used after the verbs—'**let, bid, make, know, help, feel, hear, watch, see**'.

'Direct Infinitive' is used only when these verbs are **used in active voice** (not in passive voice except the verb 'let'.) The verb '**let**' is followed by direct infinitive both in active and passive voice. *For example*
    (i) I made the student write an essay. *(Active voice)*
    (ii) The student was made to write an essay. *(Passive voice)*
    (iii) The teacher let him go out. *(Active voice)*
    (iv) He was let go out by the teacher. *(Passive voice)*

(C) The following phrases are also used with Direct Infinitive 'had better, had rather, would rather, would better, as soon, sooner than (prefer)'. *For example*
    (i) I would/had better leave your house at once.
    (ii) She would/had rather stay than leave now.
    (iii) They had sooner stay than leave.
    (iv) I would as soon stay at home as go. *(with equal willingness)*

(D) Direct Infinitive is used with, '**but, than, and, except, as, or**'. *For example*
    (i) He did nothing but cry. *(correct)*
    (ii) She did no more than sleep the whole day. *(correct)*
    (iii) She had nothing to eat except to drink water. *(remove 'to')*
    (iv) Do you wish to watch TV or to go to bed early. *(remove to)*

(E) Direct infinitive is used with phrases, 'Why not & Why'. *For example*
    (i) Why not rest now? *(Suggestion)*
    (ii) Why not stay here? *(Suggestion)*
    (iii) Why stay here? *(Question)*

(F) 'Have + object' (used in the sense of 'wish') is followed by direct infinitive. *For example*
    (i) I will have him **believe** it. *(I wish him to believe it)*
    (ii) She will have me **recite** this poem.

NON-FINITE VERBS

(G) 'Won't' + have + object + gerund (Used in the sense of won't allow).
For example
   (i) I won't have you talking like that.
   (ii) I won't have you staying at Meerut.

Rule IV Perfective Infinitive

(A) Perfect infinitive should be used if the action expressed by the infinitive precedes the action of the finite verb. *For example*
   (i) Yesterday I intended to have gone to Delhi.   *(Incorrect, say 'to go')*
   (ii) He admitted to have uttered these words against me.   *(Correct)*

In the above sentence (ii), the action 'uttered' is prior to the action of the finite verb. Hence, the use of perfect infinitive is justified.

(B) The verbs where perfect infinitive may be, if needed, used.
'**Deny, confess, admit, recollect, remember, recall, claim, regret, seem, appear, report, believe, understand, say, allege, suspect, learn, require, suppose etc.**
For example
   (i) She denied to have seen him yesterday.
   (ii) He appears to have been rich earlier.
   (iii) I still remember to have met you in Shimla last year.
   (iv) He appears to be poor these days.

Note (i) She denied seeing him yesterday. (Correct - as 'seeing' is an earlier action)
   (ii) She denied having seen him yesterday.   *(Correct)*

Rule V

Use of infinitive after **Adjective and Noun** in active voice should be taken care of

(A) **Adjective**—'enough' is used after adjective or '**very**' before adjective, when infinitive expresses affirmative meaning. 'too' is used before adjective, when infinitive expresses negative meaning. *For example*
   (i) She is too ill **to go out**.   *(cannot go out)*
   (ii) She is good enough **to help me**.   *(can help me)*

(B) **Noun**—Preposition should be used, if required, after the infinitive, when the infinitive qualifies the noun. *For example*
   (i) These days no airlines is safe to travel.   *(Use 'by' after 'travel')*
   (ii) I gave him a pen to write.   *(Use 'with' after 'write')*
   (iii) He gave me a paper to read.   *(No preposition)*
   (iv) I have no house to live.   *(Use 'in' after 'live')*
   (v) I have no book to read.   *(No preposition)*

Rule VI Split Infinitive

'To' should not be separated from its verb by inserting any adverb between the two. **The split infinitive** is grammatically wrong. *For example*
   (i) You are requested to kindly stay for sometime.   *(Use kindly to stay)*
   (ii) You are required at least to obey your parents.   *(Correct)*
   (iii) I advised him to carefully carry the bag.   *(Say to carry carefully)*
   (iv) The students were required to seriously study for examination.
           (Say 'to study seriously')

Rule VII Continuous Infinitive

Continuous Infinitive can be used with the following verbs and Modal auxliaries.
  (a) appear, seem, believe, consider, think, report, happen, arrange, hope, pretend, say etc.
  (b) may be, might be, should be, could be, must be etc.

For example

(i) Malini appears to be running temperature.	*It appears that.........*
(ii) I happened to be sitting with my daughters.	*When I was sitting.........*
(iii) She is reported to be working at Chandigarh.	*It is reported.........*
(iv) She is said to be always cursing her fate.	*It is said that.........*
(v) She pretended not to be overhearing our talk.	*She pretended as if.........*
(vi) I hope to be living in a large house in a few years.	*I hope that I shall.........*
(vii) She may be coming tomorrow.	*Perhaps will come*
(viii) She may be sleeping now	*Perhaps is sleeping*
(ix) He thought she might be waiting for her.	*Perhaps was waiting*
(x) She could be going by car.	*(deduction)*
(xi) She must be waiting for her husband.	*(deduction)*
(xii) You should be sleeping now instead of watching TV.	*(Advice)*

II. Gerund (Verbal Noun)

Gerund is a verb form, which functions as a noun. It is formed by adding 'ing' with a verb. It is used in place of Infinitive in certain cases. *For example*

(i) I do not believe **in talking** rubbish.	*(Preposition + gerund)*
(ii) I do not like **riding**.	*(Direct gerund)*
(iii) She is used **to swimming**.	*(To + gerund)*
(iv) **Smoking** is not good for health.	*(Subject)*

(1) Infinitives and gerunds are easily replaceable. However, certain rules have to be followed for replacing **infinitives** and **gerunds** by each other. *For example*

(i) I like **to swim** today.	*(At a particular time)*
(ii) I like **swimming**.	*(General/habitual statement)*

(2) The difference between **participle** and **gerund**

Gerund is a kind of noun like infinitive. Participle is a verb/adjective (an action in progress). *For example*

(i) I saw him **smoking in** the cinema **hall**.	*(Participle)*
(ii) **Smoking** is injurious to health.	*(Gerund)*
(iii) I am tired **of working** in this place.	*(Gerund)*
(iv) We found him **working** even after the sun had set.	*(Participle)*
(v) He was punished **for playing** carelessly.	*(Gerund, showing 'reason')*
(vi) They were seen **playing**.	*(Participle)*
(vii) **Riding,** he fell off the horse.	*(Participle)*
(viii) I prefer **swimming to riding**.	*(Gerund)*
(ix) My plants need **trimming**.	*(To be trimmed)*
(x) **Barking** dogs seldom bite.	*(Participle)*

Note The verbs, **'need, require, want'**, are followed by gerund in place of passive voice infinitive.

Rules of Gerund

Rule I Preposition + Gerund

Gerund is used after certain verbs/phrases, that are followed by appropriate prepositions instead of 'to'.

        In case of, for + gerund, refer to rule II on Infinitives.

Let us study a few of them

desirous of	intent on	justified in
disqualify from	bent on	hesitate in
refrain from	keen on	a hope of
prevent from	aim at	hope to (infinitive)
debar from	confident of	fortunate in
desist from	confidence in	harm in
restrain from	insist on	assist in
prohibit from	persist in	a chance of
dissuade from	succeed in	fond of
abstain from	successful in	take/feel pleasure in
point in	sense in	give pleasure to (infinitive)
deter from	interested in	

For example
  (i) I prohibited him to go there.   *(Use 'from going' in place of 'to go')*
  (ii) She is bent to harm her friend.   *(Use 'on harming' in place of 'to harm')*
  (iii) She is confident to get success.   *(Use 'of getting' in place of 'to get')*
  (iv) She insisted to pay money to her mother.   *(Use 'on paying' in place of 'to pay')*

Rule II Direct Gerund

(A) The following phrases and certain verbs are followed by **direct gerund:**

'Avoid, mind, detest, can't help, can't bear, resist, enjoy, resent, stop, start, postpone, defer, worth, prefer, consider, practise, finish, risk, pardon, excuse, forgive, it is no use/good, propose, miss, imagine, regret, means, anticipate, love, like, hate, dislike'.

(B) **Phrasal verbs** are also followed by direct gerunds such as **'give up, put off, set about'**, etc.

For example
  (i) We stopped to write.   *(Say 'writing' for 'to write')*
  (ii) He has given up to play hockey.   *(Say 'playing')*
  (iii) She enjoyed to ride on the hills.   *(Use 'riding' in place of 'to ride')*
  (iv) You should avoid to spend extra money.   *(Use 'spending' in place of 'to spend')*
  (v) She cannot help to tell a lie.   *(Use 'telling' in place of 'to tell')*
  (vi) Suhani does not mind helping me.   *(Correct)*
  (vii) It is no use/good waiting for her.   *(Correct)*
  (viii) There is no use/good of spending on luxuries.   *(Correct)*

Note Sentence (v) can also be written as 'She cannot help but tell a lie.' (but tell = telling)

Rule III To + Gerund

Note the use of gerund correctly with—'**be used to, accustomed to, averse to, with a view to, addicted to, devoted to, in addition to, look forward to, object to, owing to, given to, taken to, disposed to, prone to**. *For example*
    (i) He is addicted to smoke heavily.   *(Use 'smoking' for 'smoke')*
    (ii) We go there with a view to study Science.   *(Use 'studying' for 'study')*
    (iii) He is used to getting up early in the morning.   *(Correct)*
    (iv) She used to dance before her marriage.   *(Correct, habit in the past)*

Rule IV

The noun or pronoun before a Gerund (verbal noun) should be in the possessive case. *For example*
    (i) I don't like him wasting time.   *(Use 'his' for 'him')*
    (ii) Geeta insisted on Rohan going with her.   *(Say 'Rohan's' for 'Rohan')*
    (iii) I saw him wasting time.   *('him' is correct 'wasting' is participle.)*

III. Participle

Participle is the form of a verb that ends with **ing, ed, en, t**.
(A) It is used both as a verb (progressive) and an adjective.

Present	Past	Past Participle	Present Participle	Perfect Participle
Burn	burnt	burnt	burning	having burnt

For example
    (i) We found a candle **burning**.   *(Verb, Present Participle)*
    (ii) A **burning** candle was extinguished.   *(Adjective, Present Participle)*
    (iii) A **burnt** paper was discovered.   *(Adjective, Past Participle)*
    (iv) She returned **disappointed**.   *(Past Participle)*
    (v) **Having taken food**, she left for office.   *(Perfect Participle)*

(B) Past participle is used as passive voice of present participle. It is also used to make perfect participles.

A burning candle	—	That is burning.	*(Adjective)*
A burnt paper	—	That is burnt.	*(Adjective)*
Having burnt paper	—	After burning paper.	*(Verb)*
Having been burnt	—	Passive voice.	*(Verb)*

Rules of Participles

Rule I

Participle Clause/Absolute Phrase (Nominative Absolute)

A participle is used as participle clause. It is a kind of clause containing participle in place of a finite verb.

Absolute Phrase/Nominative Absolute is a kind of participle with a **Noun/Pronoun** going before it.
    (i) **Walking in the garden**, I came across an old friend. *(Present Participle, Active voice)*
    (ii) **Surprised at the news**, I rushed to the airport.   *(Past Participle, Passive voice)*

NON-FINITE VERBS

   (iii) **Having taken food,** I left for office. *(Perfect Participle, Active voice)*
   (iv) **Having been arrested, the thief** was taken to prison. *(Perfect Participle, Passive voice)*
   (v) **The Sun having risen**, we left the town. *(Absolute Phrase)*

Rule II
Participles can be changed into following clauses :
- (a) Adverb Clause of Time
- (b) Adverb Clause of Condition
- (c) Adverb Clause of Reason
- (d) Adverb Clause of Contrast
- (e) Adjective Clause
- (f) Co-ordinate Clause

(a) Adverb Clause of Time (while, having, on)
   (i) As I was wandering in the street, I met my old friend.
       (While) wandering in the street, I met my old friend.
   (ii) After I had passed High school, I got a job.
        Having passed High school, I got a job.
   (iii) When she saw me, she called me.
         (On) seeing me, she called me.

(b) Adverb Clause of Condition (by, without, but for)
   (i) If you go out, you will catch cold.
       By going out, you will catch cold.
   (ii) If you don't work hard, you will not pass.
        Without working hard, you will not pass.
   (iii) If you had not worked hard, you would have failed.
         But for working hard you, would have failed.

(c) Adverb Clause of Reason (owing to, because of, on account of)
   (i) As she ran very fast, she was able to overtake me.
       On account of running very fast, she was able to overtake me.
   (ii) Since she was late, she was punished.
        Being late, she was punished.

(d) Adverb Clause of Contrast (Inspite of, despite, notwithstanding, for all)
   (i) Although she came late, she was not punished.
       Inspite of coming late, she was not punished.
   (ii) Though she is rich, she is not happy.
        Despite being rich, she is not happy.
   (iii) Though she was punished, she did not feel sorry.
         Inspite of being punished, she did not feel sorry.

(e) Adjective Clause
   (i) I saw a girl, who was singing a song.
       I saw a girl singing a song.
   (ii) The students, who are studying English here, will be successful.
        The students studying English here, will be successful.
   (iii) The book, which was presented to me by my mother, is very interesting.
         The book presented to me by my mother, is very interesting.
   (iv) A burning candle fell off the table.
        A candle that was burning, fell off the table.

(f) **Co-ordinate Clause** A participle can replace a co-ordinate clause
- (i) He returned and he was smiling.
  He returned smiling.
- (ii) She went out and she was disappointed.
  She went out disappointed.

Rule III

Present participle should be used only to express an action, which coincides with the action of the finite verb.

He left for Mumbai on Monday, reaching there on Tuesday. *(Incorrect, 'reaching' is not a simultaneous action)*

He left for Mumbai on Monday and reached there on Tuesday. *(Correct)*

Rule IV Misrelated/Unrelated Participles

When the participle clause/phrase is not followed by a subject of its own, the participle is called **misrelated, dangling or unattached**.
- (i) Wandering in the street, a dog bit him. *(Wrong)*
- (ii) Wandering in the street, he was bitten by a dog. *(Correct)*

Note 'Wandering' should have a proper subject 'he' and not 'a dog'.

How to Correct a Misrelated Participle?

Misrelated participle can be corrected in three ways:
1. Expand the participle into a clause. *(Already explained in Rule II)*
2. Bring the proper subject immediately after the participle. *(by changing voice)*
3. Place the proper subject before the participle. *(only before 'being' and 'having')*

Let us study the problem by working out some questions :

1. Walking along the road, a scooter knocked him down. *(Incorrect)*
   - (i) While he was walking along the road, a scooter knocked him down. *(Correct)*
   - (ii) Walking along the road, he was knocked down by a scooter. *(Correct)*
2. Having taken food, my father sent me to market. *(Incorrect)*
   - (i) When I had taken food, my father sent me to market. *(Correct)*
   - (ii) I, having taken food, my father sent me to market. *(Absolute Phrase)*
   - (iii) Having taken food, I was sent to market by my father. *(Correct)*
3. Being cloudy, we enjoyed picnic. *(Incorrect)*
   - (i) As it was cloudy, we enjoyed picnic. *(Correct)*
   - (ii) It, being cloudy, we enjoyed picnic. *(Absolute Phrase)*
4. Being honest, the teacher rewarded him. *(Incorrect)*
   - (i) As he was honest, the teacher rewarded him. *(Correct)*
   - (ii) He, being honest, the teacher rewarded him. *(Correct)*
   - (iii) Being honest, he was rewarded by the teacher. *(Correct)*
5. Possessing huge wealth, people do not like him. *(Incorrect)*
   - (i) Although he possesses huge wealth, people do not like him. *(Correct)*
   - (ii) Possessing huge wealth, he is not liked by people. *(Correct)*

NON-FINITE VERBS

Rule V

However, participles such as—'**regarding, concerning, considering, speaking**', do not refer to any particular subject. They can do without agreement with any noun or pronoun.

    (i) Considering his problems, he was advised to leave Jalgaon.   *(Correct)*

    (ii) Roughly speaking, two hundred persons died in the earthquake.   *(Correct)*

In these sentences, the unexpressed subject is indefinite. Therefore, participle need not be in agreement with the Noun or Pronoun it refers to.

Some Important uses of Non-Finites

Study the following sentences carefully and note the difference in their sense:

1. I regret being late/to be late.   *(Present Infinitive)*
2. I regret to have been late/having been late.   *(Perfect Infinitive)*
3. She prided herself on being Indian.   *('Pride' is verb here)*
4. Take Pride in serving your motherland.   *('Pride' is noun here)*
5. I feel pleasure in inviting you to dinner tonight.   *(No difference in meaning)*
6. It gives me pleasure to send you greetings.   *(No difference in meaning)*
7. Leaving home is difficult.   *(Experience)*
8. To leave home is difficult.   *(Opinion)*
9. I would like to attend marriage tomorrow.   *(Enjoy)*
10. I would like you to study.   *(Think it right)*
11. I like to get myself examined.   *(Think it wise)*
12. I like attending marriages.   *(Habit)*
13. My mother loves telling us stories.   *(Habit)*
14. I would love to do it for your sake.   *(Enjoy)*
15. I propose to go there.   *(Intend)*
16. I propose doing it hurriedly.   *(Suggest)*
17. She began (started, commenced) laughing.   *(Progressive)*
18. She began to understand me.   *(Infinitive after began)*
19. The Government means curbing corruption.   *(Intend)*
20. Your orders mean asking me to leave the job.   *(Result)*
21. We must not risk driving in heavy rain.   *(Take chance)*
22. There is no risk of getting late.   *(Possible)*
23. It is no use/good confessing now.   *(Advantage)*
24. There is no use/good of confessing now.   *(Advantage)*
25. I would prefer to wait.   *(For an occasion)*
26. I prefer riding to swimming.   *(Habit)*

WORK BOOK EXERCISE (A)

Directions *Spot the errors, if any, in the following sentences.*
1. The teacher made the students to solve their problems.
2. His aim is no more than to use unfair means to attain success in life.
3. He goes every Sunday to Delhi with a view to buy raw material.
4. The teacher asked them to stop write as soon as the bell rang.
5. She can't help to visit her sister every Sunday.
6. He is rich today but he appears to be poor in the past.
7. The scientists claim to discover cure for AIDS and the medicine will be put on sale very soon.
8. She started to cry when she was left alone.
9. She did not dare enter the room without his permission.
10. I always resent my brother wandering about and doing nothing.
11. You should always aim to achieve higher goal to succeed in life.
12. She was confident to qualify the examination.
13. The civilians were prohibited to attend the shooting competition in the Military area.
14. You are requested to carefully carry the bag because it contains fragile material.
15. Last night, she intended to have left.
16. She was let to do, whatever she liked.
17. She was forbidden from moving out with her friends.
18. He can't tolerate/bear anybody talking nonsense.
19. He is understood to leave India for good last year.
20. How dare he to abuse my friend?
21. Those, who have no house to live, should be provided with accommodation.
22. She does not mind visit her uncle, though he does not treat her well.
23. You must desist to take to unfair means for achieving your ends.
24. The whole night, she did nothing but to read.
25. He is extremely desirous to be educated.
26. He knows swimming.
27. He hardly need to go there.
28. She is not to be blamed for this episode.

WORK BOOK EXERCISE (B)

Directions *Fill in the blanks with the most suitable form of Infinitive/Gerund.*
1. Today everyone wishes .... money quickly. *(earn)*
2. She is very keen .... modelling. *(take)*
3. The director made the officers .... longer than usual. *(wait)*
4. My brother is interested .... in Army. *(serve)*
5. The boys in the hostel are averse .... part in the strike. *(take)*
6. He never minds .... the deserving persons. *(help)*

NON-FINITE VERBS

7. She resented .... late at night. *(return)*
8. I feel pleasure .... you of my success. *(inform)*
9. I don't remember .... in Kashmir last year. *(meet)*
10. Throughout the day, she did nothing but .... illness. *(feign)*
11. The professor insisted .... the essay within allotted time. *(write)*
12. The maid servant was made .... food on time. *(cook)*
13. You are ready, you appear .... food on time. *(cook)*
14. I have known him .... anything for money. *(do)*
15. She intended .... in for teaching profession. *(go)*
16. For modern man, there are a number of diseases .... *(suffer)*
17. You had better .... in her house overnight. *(stay)*
18. You must know .... in society. *(conduct)*
19. It gives me immense pleasure .... you of her engagement. *(inform)*
20. She comes .... me daily in the evening. *(see)*
21. His mother always forbids him .... with Nisha. *(speak)*
22. The carpet needs .... before we use it. *(clean)*
23. The police officer denied .... callous to the undertrial. *(be)*
24. I have ever looked forward .... the President of the District Rotary Club. *(be)*
25. We expected .... to the celebration. *(invite)*
26. She has given up .... on her friend's advice. *(smoke)*
27. Remember, this is not a safe road .... *(travel)*
28. Classical music is worth .... *(listen)*
29. The officer always bade me .... fast. *(work)*
30. He is reported .... Mumbai for good last year. *(leave)*
31. My mother always detests .... with shady children. *(deal)*
32. How dare you .... to your teachers like this? *(talk)*
33. They need not .... for their turn. *(wait)*
34. You don't need .... here any more in the sun. *(stand)*
35. He is rich today, but he seems .... in the past. *(be poor)*
36. He dared.................to his father very rudely. *(talk)*
37. He objected to .... money on cosmetics. *(spend)*
38. The High Court restrained the Lower Court .... any action against him. *(take)*
39. She has postponed .... abroad next year. *(go)*
40. This book is desgined to help you .... for competitive exams. *(prepare)*
41. Netaji is believed .... in air crash. *(die)*
42. She is reported .... today. *(absent)*
43. A robber is alleged .... yesterday. *(arrested)*
44. My friend is expected .... to hospital. *(admit)*
45. His friend is suspected .... Deepak last night. *(kill)*

WORK BOOK EXERCISE (C)

Directions *Use these Participle clauses/Absolute phrase correctly.*

1. Writing a letter, a beggar disturbed her.
2. Being fine, we decided to go on picnic.
3. Being late, the teacher punished her.
4. But for working hard, she would have passed.
5. Inspite of being late, the teacher did not punish her.
6. Climbing up the stairs, her sandal broke and she fell.
7. Having passed B.A. examination, he offered me a job.
8. Inspite of being a miser, everybody likes to spend money on her.
9. While taking admission to a school, a birth certificate must be shown.
10. Cooking my dinner in the kitchen, a strange sound attracted my attention.
11. By going out, you will catch cold.
12. Wounded in an accident, the people took him to hospital.
13. Not following the question, the wrong answer was written in the Examination.
14. While standing under an apple tree, a ripe apple fell on him.
15. Tired of work, the teacher asked him to take rest.
16. Roughly speaking, Delhi is 60 kilometres away from Meerut.
17. Being dissatisfied with the teacher, the student made complaint to the Principal.
18. Having run for two miles, there was no sight of the school yet.
19. He started factory two years ago, achieving target only last month.
20. I saw a dead horse running along the road.

Answers

WORK BOOK EXERCISE (A)

1. Drop 'to' before 'solve'
2. write 'using'
3. 'buying' in place of 'buy'
4. 'writing' in place of 'write'
5. 'visiting' in place of 'visit'
6. 'to have been' in place of 'to be'
7. 'to have discovered' in place of 'to discover'
8. 'crying' in place of 'to cry'
9. 'to enter' in place of 'enter'
10. 'brother's' in place of 'brother'
11. 'at achieving' in place of 'to achieve'
12. 'of qualifying' in place of 'qualify'
13. 'from attending' in place of 'to attend'
14. Say 'to carry the bag carefully'
15. 'to leave' in place of 'to have left'
16. Drop 'to' before 'do'
17. 'to move' in place of 'from moving'
18. 'anybody's in place of 'anybody'
19. 'to have left' in place of 'to leave'
20. Drop 'to' before 'abuse'
21. Insert 'in' after 'live'
22. 'visiting' in place of 'visit'
23. 'from taking' in place of 'to take'
24. Delete 'to'
25. 'of being' in place of 'to be'
26. Say 'how to swim'
27. Drop 'to' before 'go'
28. Say 'to blame'

WORK BOOK EXERCISE (B)

1. to earn
2. on taking up
3. wait
4. in serving
5. to taking
6. helping
7. my returning
8. in informing
9. to have met you
10. feign
11. on writing
12. to cook
13. to have cooked
14. do
15. to go
16. to suffer from
17. not stay
18. how to conduct yourself
19. to inform
20. to see
21. to speak
22. cleaning
23. to have been
24. to being
25. to be invited
26. smoking
27. to travel by
28. listening to
29. work
30. to have left
31. dealing
32. talk
33. wait
34. to stand
35. to have been poor
36. to talk
37. my spending
38. from, taking
39. going
40. prepare
41. to have died
42. to be absent
43. to have been arrested
44. to be admitted
45. to have killed

WORK BOOK EXERCISE (C)

1. While she was writing a letter,
2. Place 'it' before 'being'
3. Place 'she' before 'being' or she was punished by the teacher.
4. Place 'not' after 'would'
5. she was not punished by the teacher
6. While she was climbing
7. Place 'I' before 'having'
8. Although she is a miser.
9. 'When one takes' in place of 'While taking'
10. While I was cooking
11. Correct
12. Say 'he was taken to hospital'
13. As I did not follow
14. While he was standing
15. As he was tired.
16. Correct
17. Correct
18. Even after they had run.
19. 'and achieved target' for 'achieving'
20. Running along the road, I saw a dead horse.

CHAPTER 5

Narration

Direct Narration

Direct narration is a kind of speech which is reported by some other person exactly in the words spoken by the speaker. This speech is placed within inverted commas.

She said to him, "I shall give you money." *(Direct Narration)*

Indirect Narration

Indirect narration is a speech, which is reported by some other person by using certain conjunctions in place of commas and making necessary changes in the verbs and the pronouns of the reported speech.

She told him that she would give him money. *(Indirect Narration)*

For the purpose of changing narration, sentences are divided as follows :

Assertive Sentences

Sentences denoting statements in affirmative and negative.
  (i) You are playing.
  (ii) He did this work.
  (iii) She was not sleeping.
  (iv) They will not write to us.

Interrogative Sentences

(a) Sentences beginning with auxiliary verbs. (Yes or No answer type questions)
  (i) Are you playing?
  (ii) Did he do this work?
  (iii) Was she sleeping?
  (iv) Will they write to us?
(b) Sentences beginning with question words such as .... when, where, why, who, which, what etc.
  (i) When are you playing?
  (ii) Why did he do this work?
  (iii) Where was she sleeping?
  (iv) What will they write to us?

NARRATION

Imperative Sentences

Sentences denoting command, request and advice are called imperative sentences.
 (i) Soldiers, turn to the right.
 (ii) Do not waste time.
 (iii) Please give me something to eat.
 (iv) Let me stay here.

Exclamatory Sentences
Expressing joy, sorrow, wonder etc.
 (i) How nice of him!
 (ii) Ah! It is beautiful locket.
 (iii) What a pretty girl she is!
 (iv) Alas! All is over.

Optative Sentences
Expressing wish, prayer, etc.
 (i) May you live long!
 (ii) Good bye, my daughters!
 (iii) Happy Diwali, children!
 (iv) Fie, what an ughy sight!

Change in Narration

Assertive Sentences

Assertive sentences are changed in indirect narration as follows:

(A) **Reporting Verb** Verb in the Reporting verb is changed into 'tell' or 'told' with an object otherwise 'say' and 'said' are retained.
 'Think'/wonder to oneself can also be used.
 (i) He says, "I am a doctor." *(Direct)*
   He says that he is a doctor. *(Indirect)*
 (ii) She said, "I am a doctor."
   She said that she was a doctor.
 (iii) She says to me, "I am a doctor."
   She tells me that she is a doctor.
 (iv) She thought, "She will not go out with him."
   She thought to herself that she would not go out with him.

(B) **Inverted Commas** 'That' is used in place of inverted commas.
  She said to me, "I am a doctor."
  She told me that she was a doctor.

(C) **Tense**
 (a) If the Reporting verb is in the Present or Future or Reported speech is a universal truth, the tense of Reported speech does not change.
  (i) She says, "I shall go to Delhi."
    She says that she will go to Delhi.
  (ii) I say to her, "I shall give her money."
    I tell her that I shall give her money.
  (iii) Teacher said to the students, "The Sun rises in the East."
    Teacher told the students that the Sun rises in the East.

(b) If the Reporting verb is in the past, the tense of the Reported speech changes into past as follows :

(i) **Present tense changes into past tense**

Present indefinite	Past indefinite
Present Continuous	Past Continuous
Present Perfect	Past Perfect
Present Perfect Continuous	Past Perfect Continuous

(ii) **Past tense changes as follows**

Past indefinite	Past Perfect
Past Continuous	Past Perfect Continuous
Past Perfect	No Change
Past Perfect Continuous	No Change

(iii) **Future tense**
will/shall change into would/should

(iv) **Modals are changed as follows**

May	Might
Can	Could
Have to	Had to
Had to	Had had to
Should	No change
Must	No change

Change of Tenses

Some Hints

1. Need not, used to, would rather, would better, had rather, had better, should, must, subjunctive mood do not change.
2. **Past Continuous :**
   Past continuous changes, when it refers to a **complete action**
   She said to me, "I was thinking of helping him but changed my mind later on."
   She told me that she had been thinking of helping him but changed her mind later on. *(Complete action)*
3. **Past continuous does not change when it is used in time clause :**
   He said to me, "While I was singing, she was dancing."
   He told me that while he was singing, she was dancing.
4. **Past indefinite does not change in the following cases :**
   (a) When it is used in time clause.
      (i) She said to me, "When I met him, he was playing."
          She told me that when she met him he was playing.
      (ii) She said to her mother, "Father had left before/when she reached home."
           She told her mother that father had left before/when she reached home.
   (b) When it expresses two simultaneous actions.
      She said, "I cooked vegetables and he fried rice."
      She said that she cooked vegetables and he fried rice.
   (c) When it expresses historical past.
      He said, "Netaji was born in Kolkata."
      He said that Netaji was born in Kolkata.

NARRATION

Change of 'Will'

'Will' changes into 'should' when the speaker seeks advice or request.

The mother said, "What will I do with so much money, My son!"
The mother asked her son what she should do with so much money.

Change of 'Need'

(i) She said, "Need I write a letter?"
She asked if she had to write a letter.

(ii) She said, "If I am selected, I needn't study further."
She said that if she was selected, she would not have to study further.

Change of 'Could'

'Could' is changed in case of permission.

She said to me, "When I was a student, I could not go out alone."
She told me that when she was a student, she was not allowed to go alone.

Change of 'Must'

(a) 'Must' Normally does not change when it refers to duty or laws of nature.

(i) Rahul said to her, "You must obey your parents."
Rahul said to her that she must obey her parents.

(ii) She said, "We must all die."
She said that we must all die.

(b) 'Must' Changes in the following cases.

(i) She said, "I must leave at once."
She said that she had to leave at once.

(ii) Natasha said, "I must get up early tomorrow."
Natasha said that she would have to get up early the next day.

(iii) Lekha said, "Mansi, You must be silent."
Lekha ordered Mansi to be silent.

Changes of Pronouns in the Reported Speech

1. **First Person** (I, we) in the reported speech change into the subject of the Reporting verb.

    (i) She said to me, "I am unwell."
    She told me that she was unwell.

    (ii) Rohan said to her, "I shall leave Jaipur soon."
    Rohan told her that he would leave Jaipur soon.

    (iii) The Captain said, "we have won at last."
    The Captain told his team mates that they had won at last.

Note 'We' does not change in the following cases.

(a) When 'we' is used in general sense.
(b) When object 'me' is included in the subject.
(c) But 'we' changes into 'It' when 'we' is used by a newspaper or an organisation.

   (i) The saint said, "We are mortals."
   The saint said that we are mortals.

   (ii) She said to me, "We are to leave for temple early."
   She told me that we were to leave for temple early.

   (iii) The Pioneer said, "We are not responsible for any error."
   The Pioneer said that it was not responsible for any error.

2. **Second Person** 'You' in the Reported speech changes into the object of the Reporting verb.
   (i) He said to his mother, "Will you give me money."
   He asked his mother if she would give him some money.
   (ii) The teacher said to the students, "You are not to leave the class without permission."
   The teacher advised the student that they were not to leave the class without permission.
3. **Third Person** (He, She, They, It) in the Reported speech does not change.
   (i) I said to her, "He will not come."
   I told her that he would not come.
   (ii) The boy said to his father, "They have not returned the book."
   The boy told his father that they had not returned the book.
5. **Adverbials of time, place and demonstrative :**
   (i) Adverbials of Time

Now	change into	Then
Ago	,,	Before
Today	,,	That day
Tomorrow	,,	The next day
Yesterday	,,	The Previous day/The day before
Last night	,,	The Previous night/the night before
Next month	,,	The following month
The day before yesterday	,,	Two days before
The day after tomorrow	,,	In two days time

Note Today, Tomorrow, Tonight do not change when the speech is reported the same day.
   (a) This morning he said, "I shall leave Chennai tomorrow."
   This morning he said that he would leave Chennai tomorrow.
   (b) Esha said today, "I am leaving Pune tonight."
   Esha said today that she was leaving Pune tonight.

(ii) Adverbial of Place

Change of 'Here' : 'Here' changes into 'there'.
'Here' changes' to 'there' only when there is reference to place.
We shall meet here again. *(change into there)*
Come here, boys. *(No change)*

(iii) Adverbial of Demonstratives

Change of 'This', 'These'
   (a) Used with time .... changes into 'that', 'those'.

This week	That week
This month	That month

   (b) Used as adjective .... changes into 'the'.

This book	The book
These books	The books

   (c) Used as Pronoun .... changes into 'it'.
   I shall do *this* tomorrow.
   I shall do *it* tomorrow.

NARRATION

(d) Used as subject .... does not change.
'this', 'these', give the sense of the object being near.
This is my book.
These are my books

Examples

Some examples are worked out as follows :

(a) Direct   : Rahul says, "The teacher is ill."
    Indirect : Rahul says that the teacher is ill.
(b) Direct   : She said, "The Sun rises in the East."
    Indirect : She said that the Sun rises in the East.
(c) Direct   : Shashi said, "I have completed my work."
    Indirect : Shashi said that she had completed her work.
(d) Direct   : They said, "We won the match."
    Indirect : They said that they had won the match.
(e) Direct   : You said to her, "I have called my friends."
    Indirect : You told her that you had called your friends.
(f) Direct   : I said, "I shall leave Chennai soon."
    Indirect : I said that I should leave Chennai soon.
(g) Direct   : Jatin said, "I had to leave my village because of poverty."
    Indirect : Jatin said that he had had to leave his village because of poverty.
(h) Direct   : He said, "I shall leave tomorrow."
    Indirect : He said that he would leave the next day.
(i) Direct   : He said to her, "I want to see you now."
    Indirect : He told her that he wanted to see her then.
(j) Direct   : She said, "well, I shall accompany you."
    Indirect : She told me that she would accompany me.
(k) Direct   : She said, "you see, you cannot meet the boss."
    Indirect : She told me that I could not meet the boss.

Note Well, you see, okay, you know, therefore, so, yet, but etc. .... when these words are used in the Reported speech, they do not change.

Interrogative Sentences

1. **Reporting Verb**
   Verb in the Reporting verb is changed into ask/asked or inquire/inquired of or want /wanted to know, demand/demanded, wonder/wondered.
   Mother said to daughter, "Have you completed your home work?"
   Mother asked daughter if she had completed her home work.

2. **Inverted Commas**
   (a) In 'yes' or 'no' Answer type questions 'if' or 'whether' is used in place of inverted commas.
   Father said to me, "Do you know the residence of the doctor?"
   Father asked me if I knew the residence of the doctor.

(b) In the sentences, beginning with Question words, inverted commas are replaced by question word itself (who, when, what etc.)
   The teacher said to Rohan, "Why are you late?"
   The teacher asked Rohan why he was late.

(c) But, if a Clause with Interrogative Pronouns (Question words) is followed by main clause 'that' is used before the question words and this rule also applies to 'if and whether' in 'yes' or 'No' answer type questions.
   (i) She said to me, "When she will come, is not certain?"
      She told me that when she would come, was not certain.
   (ii) I said to him, "whether she will pass, is not certain?"
      I told him that whether she would pass, was not certain.

(d) Tense
(e) Pronouns
(f) Adverbs of time and place

The changes in these parts of the reported speech are made as explained earlier in the case of assertive sentences

Note Students are required to change interrogative sentences into Assertive sentences before changing the Narration. e.g.
Direct : She said to her mother, "Will you take me to temple?"
Indirect : She asked her mother whether/if she would take her to temple.

Examples

Some examples are worked out as follows :

(a) Direct   : Tina said to Rohan, "Will you help me today?"
   Indirect : Tina asked Rohan if he would help her that day.
(b) Direct   : He said to me, "What are you doing?"
   Indirect : He asked me what I was doing.
(c) Direct   : Anil said to me, "Why did you do it?"
   Indirect : Anil inquired of me why I had done it.
(d) Direct   : Pearl said to Riya, "Do you know Rohit?"
   Indirect : Pearl asked Riya if she knew Rohit.
(e) Direct   : The teacher said to the boy, "Have you done your home work?"
   Indirect : The teacher asked the boy if he had done his home work.
(f) Direct   : She said, "How can I do such a foolish work?"
   Indirect : She thought/wondered how she could do such a foolish work.
(g) Direct   : Sonia said to her brother, "When my husband will return tonight, is uncertain."
   Indirect : Sonia told her brother that when her husband would return that night, was uncertain.
(h) Direct   : Nisha said, "Whether (if) you have qualified the test, cannot be confirmed."
   Indirect : Nisha told her sister that whether (if) she would qualify the test, could not be confirmed.
(i) Direct   : Rahul said to Ritesh, "What you are doing, is immoral."
   Indirect : Rahul told Ritesh that what he was doing, was immoral.

NARRATION

(j) **Direct** : She said to her companions, "Why not stay overnight here?"
   Indirect : She suggested to her companion that they should stay overnight there.
(k) **Direct** : Manu said to his friend, "Why help him now?"
   Indirect : Manu told his friend that it was no use helping him then.

Note Could, would, would like used as polite request in interrogative sentences are reported as follows:

Request, Advice + Object + to

(i) She said to her friend, "Could/would you please lend me some money?"
   She requested her friend to lend her some money.
(ii) The captain said to the lady, "Would you like to have dinner with me?"
   The captian requested/invited the lady to have dinner with him.

Imperative Sentences

(a) **Reporting Verb** A verb in the Reporting verb changes into command/order, beg, request, advise, forbid, suggest, propose, assure, ask, remind, warn, agree, refuse, promise, etc.

   (i) She said, "Mohan, please bring me that book."
      She requested Mohan to bring her that book.
   (ii) Mother said to me, "Take umbrella with you, when you go out."
      Mother advised me to take umbrella with me, when I went out.
   (iii) I said to my friend, "Don't go out in dark."
      I forbade my friend to go out in dark.
   (iv) The captain said, "Soldiers, March on till it is dark."
      The captain commanded the soldiers to march on till it was dark.
   (v) The lady said, "Thanks, I shall never forget this kindness, Arnav."
      The lady thanked Arnav and assured him that she would never forget the kindness.
   (vi) Richa said, "Congratulation my son, you have won."
      Richa congratulated her son telling him that he had won.

(b) **Inverted Commas** 'To/not to' is used in place of inverted commas.

   (i) She said to the Postman, "Either go or wait."
      She asked the Postman either to go or wait.
   (ii) The lady said to the soldier, "Please do come sometime."
      The lady requested the soldier to come sometime.
   (iii) Richa said to her friend, "If I were you, I would not care for such a man."
      Richa advised her friend not to care for such a man.
   (iv) The manager ordered the clerk, "Run to the next office and bring some stationery."
      The manager ordered the clerk to run to the next office and bring some stationery.
   (v) She said to the stranger, "You must leave my room at once."
      She ordered stranger to leave her room at once.
   (vi) The teacher said to Suhani, "Will you stop talking now?"
      The teacher ordered Suhani to stop talking then.
   (vii) I said to her, "Would/Could you please help me?"
      I requested her to help me.

(c) **Tense**
(d) **Pronouns**

(e) Adverbs of time and place
The change in these parts of reported speech are made as explained earlier in the case of assertive sentences.

Note It should be noted that when 'to' is used in place of inverted commas, the form of the verb does not change.

> to + 1st form of the verb – 'to go'

Change of 'Let'
Study the following sentences carefully:
(a) 'Let' as a proposal/suggestion
  (i) He said, "Let us go to the movie."
  He proposed that they should go to the movie.
  (ii) I said to Deepa, "Let us buy a new house."
  I suggested to Deepa that we should buy a new house.
  (iii) Reena said to me, "Let us celebrate X-Mas."
  I said, "No, let us not."
  Reena proposed to me that we should celebrate X-Mas. But, I did not agree to her proposal.

(b) 'Let' as a request
  (i) Ravi said to the manager, "Let me go home."
  Ravi requested the manager that he might be allowed to go home.
  Or
  Ravi requested the manager to let him go home.
  (ii) The girls said to the gate keeper, "Let us enter the school."
  The girls requested the gate keeper to let them enter the school.

(c) 'Let' as an order
  The manager said to his assistant, "Let the customers in."
  The manager ordered his assistant to let the customers in.

(d) 'Let' as 'don't care'
  (i) Sawant said, "Let it rain, I have to go."
  Sawant persisted that he did not care for the rain and he had to go.
  (ii) Miss Pillai said, "Let my friends say so."
  Miss Pillai said that she did not care for her friends.

Examples
Some examples are worked out as follows :
  (a) Direct : The Principal said, "Congratulations, My son, you have won."
  Indirect : The principal congratulated the boy telling him that he had won.
  (b) Direct : The lady said, "Thanks, I shall never forget this kindness, Arnav."
  Indirect : The lady thanked Arnav and assured him that she would never forget the kindness.
  (c) Direct : She cried, "God will never pardon you."
  Indirect : She bitterly cursed him that God would never pardon him.
  (d) Direct : The manager said to the assistant, "Let the customer in."
  Indirect : The manager ordered the assistant that the customer might be allowed.
  (e) Direct : The girls said to the gate keeper, "Let us enter the school."
  Indirect : The girls requested the gatekeeper to allow them to enter the school.

NARRATION

    (f) **Direct** : Pearl said to her friends, "Let us go on a long drive."
        Indirect : Pearl suggested to her friends that they should go on a long drive.
    (g) **Direct** : She said, "Let it rain, I have to go."
        Indirect : She persisted that she did not care for the rain and she had to go.
    (h) **Direct** : The son said, "Let my parents say so."
        Indirect : The son said that he did not care for his parents.
    (i) **Direct** : She said to the postman, "Either go or wait."
        Indirect : She asked the postman either to go or wait.
    (j) **Direct** : The lady said to her, "Please do come some time."
        Indirect : The lady requested her to come sometime.
    (k) **Direct** : The mother said to her daughter, "Shut the door, will you?"
        Indirect : The mother asked her daughter to shut the door.
    (l) **Direct** : She said, "You are playing, are not you?"
        Indirect : She asked me if I was not playing.
    (m) **Direct** : The mother asked Arnav, "You did not meet Sonia, did you?"
        Indirect : The mother asked Arnav if he had met Sonia.
    (n) **Direct** : Payal said to Rohan, "I did not go to the movie, did you?"
        Indirect : Payal told Rohan that she had not gone to the movie and asked him if he had gone.
    (o) **Direct** : "Well spoken", The audience cried.
        Indirect : The audience applauded/appreciated his speech that he had spoken well.
    (p) **Direct** : "Beware, there is a danger", the captain warned.
        Indirect : The captain warned the soldiers to beware of the danger.
    (q) **Direct** : "Be sure, I am always with you", said the mother.
        Indirect : The mother assured her daughter that she was always with her.
    (r) **Direct** : "Father", said the son, "The teacher said to me, you are a naughty boy."
        Indirect : The son told his father that the teacher had told him that he was a naughty boy.
    (s) **Direct** : "When I shall learn swimming", said a small girl, "is not certain."
        Indirect : A small girl told me that when she would learn swimming was not certain.

Exclamatory Sentences

(a) **Reporting Verb** Verb in the Reporting verb is changed into 'Exclaim with sorrow,' 'Exclaim with surprise, 'Exclaim with joy', 'Cry out' etc.
    (i) Portia said, "Good Heavens, I am ruined".
        Portia exclaimed with sorrow that she was ruined.
    (ii) The director said, "What a good dance, Suhani! you have won the contest."
        The director remarked with appreciation/applauded that Suhani had danced well and declared that she had won the contest.
    (iii) Mona said, "Hello Sameer, Good Morning!"
        Mona greeted Sameer and wished (bade) him good morning.
    (iv) The king said, "How foolish of me!"
        The king confessed with regret that he was very foolish.

382   DESCRIPTIVE ENGLISH

(b) Inverted Commas 'That' is used in place of inverted commas.

   (i) Tarun said, "How clever I am!"
       Tarun exclaimed that he was very clever.
   (ii) Deepa said, "What a pity! you have not succeeded".
       Deepa exclaimed that it was a pity that he had not succeeded.
   (iii) "So help me Heaven!" He cried, "I shall never cheat anyone".
       He called upon heaven to witness his resolve that he would never cheat anyone.
   (iv) "Be Sure, I am always with you," said the mother.
       The mother assured her daughter that she was always with her.

(c) Tense

(d) Pronoun

(e) Adverb of time and place

The change in these parts of reported speech are made as explained earlier in the case of assertive sentences.

Take care of the following changes:
(i) What, Oh, Ah, Good Heavens, Hurrah— joy, sorrow, surprise
(ii) Bravo—Applause, Appreciation
(iii) Hark—Listen
(iv) Fie/Phooh—Contempt

Note Before changing the narration, exclamatory sentences are first transformed into assertive sentences.

Optative Sentences (Prayer & Wish)

(a) Reporting Verb Verb in the Reporting verb is changed into 'wish' and 'pray'.

   (i) The old man said to his son, "May God bless you!"
       The old man wished/blessed his son that God might bless him.
   (ii) They said, "May God save our country."
       They Prayed that God might save their country.

(b) Inverted Commas 'That' is used in place of inverted commas.

   (i) He said, "May God pardon my sins!"
       He prayed that God might pardon his sins.
   (ii) The beggar said, "May you live long."
       The beggar prayed that she might live long.
   (iii) The old woman said to the child, "God helps you!"
       The old woman prayed that God might help the child.

(c) Tense

(d) Pronouns

(e) Adverb of time and place

The change in these parts of reported speech are made as explained earlier in the case of assertive sentences.

Note Before changing the Narration, optative sentences are first converted to assertive sentences.

NARRATION

🔎 WORK BOOK EXERCISE (A)

1. I said to him, "I will not go there tomorrow."
2. The clerk said to me, "I will not attend the office tomorrow."
3. Hari said to them, "Mohan did not sleep here yesterday."
4. Gita said to Rita, "Will you help me in this work?"
5. Sadhna said to me, "Can you go with me to the station?"
6. Her father said to me, "Do you know where Prem is?"
7. I said to him, "Don't you know that I am your friend?"
8. Ram said to me, "Why do you not go home?"
9. He said, "How is your father?"
10. He said to her, "Go away from here at once."
11. The teacher said to the boys, "work hard."
12. The doctor said to the patient, "Do not eat much to escape from disease."
13. The servant said to him, "Sir, grant me leave for two days."
14. He said, "Let us wait for our friends."
15. He shouted, "Let me go."
16. The spectators said, "Bravo! well done."
17. The captain said, "Hurrah! we have won the match."
18. The doctor said, "Alas! The poor man is no more."
19. The teacher said to me, "What a pity you did not follow my advice."
20. Mohan said, "Ah, what a bloody deed you have done!"
21. She said, "How beautiful the rose is!"
22. She said, "What a lazy fellow you are!"
23. She said, "May God pardon him."
24. Ram said to his friend, "May you succeed in the examination."
25. They said, "Long live the Prime Minister."
26. The minister said, "What a disaster the earthquake is!"
27. The teacher said to the boy, "I shall report the matter to the Principal if you misbehave again."
28. I said, "When it gets dark, light the lamp."
29. "Suppose, you children, go out for a nice long walk", she said.
30. "Doctor," cried the patient, "Please tell me how much time I have."

🔎 WORK BOOK EXERCISE (B)

1. He says to me, "I have never been to your house, I shall go with you."
2. He said to me, "She left Ahmedabad after I had gone."
3. She said to him, "But you are a fool. You do not understand me."
4. Sohan said to me, "I am your friend. I will never desert you."
5. The teacher asked Vina, "What is your name? Where do you come from?"
6. My friend told Rita, "I am going out. Will you go along with me?"

7. Rahul said to me, "Where are you going? Can I accompany you?"
8. The teacher said, "Boys, If you want to pass, you should work hard."
9. The teacher said, "Boys, if you want to pass, why are you not working hard?"
10. The teacher said, "Boys, if you want to pass, work hard."
11. "Will you give me lodging for one night?" asked the weary traveller, "Yes", said my father, "you are very welcome."
12. The Governor of the town asked the slave, "How has this hungry lion forgotten his nature?" The slave replied, "This very lion, which is standing before you, was my friend in the woods."
13. Seema said to Arnav, "Will you go to hospital today?" Arnav said, "No." "Why?" asked Seema, "Because I am feeling better." replied Arnav.
14. The teacher said to Rita, "Did you finish your work yesterday?" Rita said, "No, Sir, my mother was ill."
15. The teacher said, "If you come before school tomorrow, I will explain it." The boys said, "Sir, we shall do as you say."
16. "Go down to the bazar. Bring me some oil and lump of ice," ordered his master.
17. Rameshwar said to his teacher, "Sir, I did not do my work as I was ill."
18. Father said to Mohit, "Dear, why are you sad today?"
19. Father said to Mohit, "Bring me a glass of water."
20. He said, "O! Son, my daughter will marry the strongest and greatest person. There is no one stronger and greater than you. Will you accept her as your wife?"
21. The policeman said to the thief, "Rascal, How could you dare do that? Did you not know the punishment of your crime?"
22. The girl said to the youngman, "Who are you? What do you want from me? I have never seen you before? Please take your seat."
23. A farmer took his sons to the field and said, "There is a treasure hidden here in the earth. If you find it, share it amongst you."
24. The student said, "May I come in, Sir? I am late today." The teacher said, "Yes, you may but this is not your first chance of getting late."
25. The woman said, "All travellers are welcome for the sake of one." "Who is that one," said the king, "for whose sake you make all travellers welcome?" "It is our lawful king, Robert the Bruce.", said the old woman.
26. "How pretty you are!" said the fox to the crow. "I am sure, so beautiful a bird must have a beautiful voice. Cheer up, my dear, will you not sing a few notes for me?"
27. Ram said to me, "Thank you for all your help. I could not have finished the work without your help."
28. He said to the shopkeeper, "You are a fool. You have done the opposite of what I desired you to do. Instead of changing the perfume, you have changed the shaving cream."
29. "I am a dead man, Hardy," said Nelson, "I am going fast, it will be all over with me soon. Let my dear lady have my hair and other things belonging to me."
30. A young prince once asked a lady, "How is it that you are so fascinating?" The lady felt shy and left the room saying, "Beauty lies in the eyes of a beholder."
31. He said, "Yes, I have broken the slate."
32. He said, "No, I have not done this."
33. The candidate said to the boss, "I assure you of my best service."

NARRATION

34. The doctor said to the patient, "I hope you are better now."
35. "Since it is fine, let us go swimming", Juliet said to Arnav.
36. "How steep the hill is!" They said, "We are tired."
37. "Neither a borrower, nor a lender be," said he to his son.
38. "Why have you come to disturb me," said the master, "Go away."
39. Said Shaurya to Sameer, "Be up. It is no use wasting time." "But I have no work to do today." replied Sameer.
40. "Ladies are," said the chaueffer, "waiting out side. They are getting impatient, Sir."
41. "Mohan made this mess. Let him clear it up," said his father.
42. I said, "Let Mohan do his worst, he cannot harm me."
43. "Let's give a party", said Jaya. "Let's not," said her husband.

Cumulative Exercises

Exercise 1

Directions *Change the following sentences into indirect speech.*

1. Socrates said, "Virtue is its own reward."
2. He said to the interviewer, "Could you please repeat the question?"
3. He said, "It used to be a lovely, quiet street."
4. The Prime Minister said, "We shall not allow any one to disturb the peace.
5. The spectators said, "Bravo! well done, players."
6. I said to my friend, "Good Morning, Let us go for a picnic today."
7. The new student asked the old one, "Do you know my name?"
8. I said to her, "I can no longer tolerate your coming late."
9. I said to my mother, "I will certainly take you to Bengaluru this week."
10. "How long does the journey take?" My co-passenger asked me.
11. "How clever of you to have solved the puzzle so quickly." said the mother.
12. He said, "I go for a walk every morning."
13. I reiterated, "I don't care about the job.
14. I said to my brother, "Let us go to some hill station for a change."
15. I said, "How many discoveries go unheeded?"
16. Gopan said to me, "Can you do these sums for me?"
17. The boss said, "It's time we began planning our work."
18. He said to the judge, "I did not commit this crime."
19. Rahul said, "I will do it now or never."

20. Doshi said to his wife, "Please select one of these necklaces."
21. He wrote in his report, "The rainfall has been scanty till now."
22. She said to Rita, "Please help me with my homework."
23. My father once said to me, "If I can't trust my people then I don't want to be doing this."
24. "Govind", said the manager sternly, "I command you to tell me what the old man said."
25. I said to him, "Where have you lost the pen, I brought for you yesterday?"

Exercise 2

Directions *Change the following sentences into direct speech.*

1. Kiran asked me whether I had seen the cricket match on television the earlier night.
2. David told Anna that Mona would leave for her native place the next day.
3. I asked him why he was working so hard.
4. He exclaimed that it was a cold day.
5. The tailor asked him if he would have the suit ready by the next evening.
6. He requested the interviewer to repeat the question.
7. He urged them to be quiet and listen to his words.
8. He told me that he had often told me not to play with fire.
9. The Captain commanded his men to stand at ease.
10. Pawan told me that if he heard any news, he would phone me.
11. The teacher congratulated Mahesh and wished him success in life.
12. The poor examine, invoking God, implored him to take pity on him.
13. I asked where he would be the next day, in case I had to ring him.
14. Seeta asked me if I could give her my pen.
15. The father warned his son that he should beware of him.
16. Manna asked Rohan whether he had sat in a trolley bus earlier.
17. Farhan asked Geeta whether she could lend him a hundred rupees until the next day.
18. He proposed going for a swim as it was quite fine then.
19. He said that I couldn't bathe in that sea as it was very rough.
20. Jagdish said that they had passed by a beautiful lake when they had gone on a trip to Goa.
21. He told me that he expected me to attend the function.
22. He enquired why I had not sent my application to him.
23. Dinesh asked Eliza whether she was going to the party the next day.
24. John asked how long it would take to travel from Germany to South Africa.
25. Ashok asked Anil what he had seen at the South Pole.

Previous Years' Questions

Directions *Change the following sentences into indirect speech.*

I. [Civil Services (Mains), 2005]
   1. He said, "I am too ill to speak now."
   2. The policeman said to the man, "Where are you going?"
   3. She said to her children, "Let me work undisturbed."
   4. He said to the students, "Do not sit here."
   5. He said, "May God pardon the sinner."
   6. The master said to the servant, "Go to the bazar and bring fruits." [CPO, 2003]
   7. The traveller said, "What a beautiful night." [CPO, 2004]

II. [Civil Services (Mains), 2006]
   1. He said, "I will not approve of such a behaviour in future."
   2. He said on the telephone, "We kept on doing our work till late night."
   3. She said, "As your mother is ill, you must go at once."
   4. Ram said to Sita, "Do you intend to come with me to the forest."
   5. The child said to Sherpa, "Why didn't you choose to climb to the moon?"

III. [Civil Services (Mains), 2008]
   1. Amrita said to me, "Why did't you attend my class?"
   2. My father said to me, "Wash your clothes."
   3. Our teacher said, "The earth revolves around the sun."
   4. Meera said, "The plane has landed."
   5. Our English teacher said to Mohan, "Open the window."

IV. [Civil Services (Mains), 2010]
   1. He wrote in his letter, "I saw Poonam at the theatre a couple of days ago."
   2. The forecast says, "It will rain tomorrow."
   3. He said to me, "It would be nice if I could see you again."
   4. I said, "If I had any money I'd buy you a drink."
   5. The teacher said, "Why don't you work harder?"

V. **Directions** *Rewrite the sentences as directed making necessary changes without changing their meanings.*

   A. Change the following sentences into indirect speech.
   1. The children said, "we went to the zoo this morning." [CAPF, 2015]
   2. He shouted, "Let me go." [CAPF, 2013]
   3. "Are you coming home with me?" he asked [IFS, 2014]
   4. He said, "I have passed the examination." [IES, 2014]
   5. The workers said, "We were repairing the road." [IFS, 2015]
   6. The stranger said, "Could you tell me where the post office is?" [IES, 2015]

7. "What a beautiful day!", said the young tourist. [Civil Services (Mains), 2013]
8. The proud father remarked, "What a wonderful batsman my son is!" [Civil Services (Mains), 2013]
9. My mother remarked, "Aren't the children lovely?" [Civil Services (Mains), 2013]
10. Rama said to her daughter, "Please come with me to the doctor's clinic." [Civil Services (Mains), 2014]
11. He said to me, "I have often told you not to play with fire."
12. My father said, "Wait, till I have finished all that I have to say." [IES/ISS, 2013]
13. He said to me, "What is your name?" [Civil Services (Mains), 2015]

B. Change the following sentences into direct speech.
1. She said that they would have a party that night. [CAPF, 2013]
2. He said that he had come to see me. [Civil Services (Mains), 2014]
3. My mother asked me if I had finished my breakfast. [Civil Services (Mains), 2015]

Answers

WORK BOOK EXERCISE (A)
1. I told him that I would not go there the next day.
2. The clerk told me that he would not attend the office the next day.
3. Hari told them that Mohan had not slept there the previous day.
4. Gita asked Rita if she would help her in the work.
5. Sadhna asked me if I could go with her to the station.
6. Her father asked me whether I knew where Prem was.
7. I asked him if he did not know that I was his friend.
8. Ram asked me why I did not go home.
9. He asked me how my father was.
10. He ordered her to go away from there at once.
11. The teacher advised the boys to work hard.
12. The doctor advised the patient not to eat much to escape from disease.
13. The servant requested him to grant him leave for two days.
14. He said that they should wait for their friends.
    Or
    He told me that we should wait for our friends.
15. He shouted to me to let him go.
    Or
    He shouted to me that he might be allowed to go.
16. The spectators applauded them saying that they had done well.
17. The captain exclaimed with joy that they had won the match.
18. The doctor exclaimed with sorrow that the poor man was no more.
19. The teacher expressed regret that it was a great pity that I had not followed his advice.
20. Mohan exclaimed with sorrow that it was a very bloody deed he had done.
21. She exclaimed with wonder that the rose was very beautiful.
22. She exclaimed with pity that he was a very lazy fellow.

NARRATION

23. He prayed that God might pardon him.
24. Ram wished that his friend might succeed in the examination.
25. They prayed that their Prime Minister might live long.
26. The minister exclaimed with sorrow that the earthquake was a terrible disaster.
27. The teacher threatened/warned the boy to report the matter to the Principal if he misbehaved again.
28. I told her to light the lamp when it got dark.

    Or

    I told her that when it got dark she should light the lamp.
29. She proposed that the children went out for a nice long walk.
30. The patient pleaded with the doctor to tell her how much time she had.

Work Book Exercise (B)

1. He tells me that he has never been to my house and therefore, he will go with me.
2. He told me that she left Ahmedabad after he had gone.
3. But she told him that he was a fool because he did not understand her.
4. Sohan told me that he was my friend and therefore, he would never desert me.
5. The teacher asked Vina what her name was and where she came from.
6. My friend told Rita that she was going out and asked her if she would go along with her.
7. Rahul asked me where I was going and if he could accompany me.
8. The teacher told the boys that if they wanted to pass, they should work hard.
9. The teacher asked the boys why they were not working hard, if they wanted to pass.
10. The teacher advised the boys to work hard, if they wanted to pass.

    Or

    The teacher told the boys that if they wanted to pass, they should work hard.
11. The weary traveller asked my father if he would give him lodging for one night. My father replied in affirmative and added that he was very welcome.
12. The Governor of the town asked the slave how the hungry lion had forgotten his nature. To this, the slave replied that very lion, which was standing before him, had been his friend in the woods.
13. Seema asked Arnav if he would go to hospital that day. Arnav replied that he would not. Then Seema asked him why he would not. Arnav replied that he would not go because he was feeling better.
14. The teacher asked Rita if she had finished her work the previous day. Rita replied respectfully that she had not because her mother had been ill.
15. The teacher told the boys that if they came before school the next day, he would explain it. The boys assured him respectfully that they would do as he said.
16. His master ordered the servant to go down to the bazar and bring him some oil and lump of ice.
17. Rameshwar told his teacher respectfully that he had not done his work as he had been ill.
18. Father asked Mohit lovingly why he was sad that day.
19. Father asked Mohit to bring him a glass of water.
20. Addressing him as his son, he told him that his daughter would marry the strongest and greatest person and there was no one stronger and greater than he. So, he asked him if he would accept her as his wife.
21. Calling the thief rascal, the policeman asked him how he could dare do it and if he had known the punishment of his crime.
22. The girl asked the young man, who he was and what he wanted from her. Further she told him that she had never seen him before and requested him to take his seat.

23. A farmer took his sons to the field and told them that there was a treasure hidden there in the earth. He advised them to share it amongst them, if they found it.
24. The student asked the teacher respectfully if he might come in although he was late that day. The teacher replied that he might, but reminded him that that was not his first chance of getting late.
25. The woman, told the king that all travellers were welcome for the sake of one. The king asked the woman, who that one was for whose sake she made all travellers welcome. To this, the old woman replied that it was their, lawful king, Robert the Bruce.
26. The fox flattered the crow saying that he was very pretty, and told him that she was sure that so beautiful a bird must have a beautiful voice. she cheered him up lovingly and asked him if he would not sing a few notes for her.
27. Ram thanked me for all my help (saying that) and said that he could not have finished the work without my help.
28. He reprimanded the shopkeeper saying that he was a fool because he had done the opposite of what he had desired him to do. He informed him that instead of changing the perfume, he had changed the shaving cream.
29. Nelson called Hardy near him and told him that he was a dead man and he was going fast because it would be all over with him soon. So, he requested Hardy to let his dear lady have his hair and other things belonging to him.
30. A young prince once asked a lady how it was that she was so fascinting. She felt shy and left the room saying that beauty lay in eyes of a beholder.
31. He admitted that he had broken the slate.
32. He denied that he had done it.
33. The candidate assured the boss of his best services.
34. The doctor hoped that the patient was better then.
35. Juliet suggested to Arnav that they should go swimming since it was fine.
36. They exclaimed that the hill was very steep and they were tired.
37. He advised his son to be neither a borrower nor a lender.
38. The master scolded his servant for disturbing him and ordered him to go away.
39. Shaurya asked Sameer to be up, as it was no use wasting time. But Sameer replied that he had no work to do that day.
40. The chauffer told his master resentfully that the ladies were waiting outside and they were getting impatient.
41. Mohan's father said that Mohan had made the mess and that he was to clear it.
42. I declared that Mohan might do his worst, he could not harm me.
43. Jaya suggested giving a party (to give a party) but her husband opposed the idea.

Cumulative Exercises

Exercise 1

1. Socrates said that virtue is its own reward.
2. He requested the interviewer if he could repeat the question.
3. He said that it used to be a lovely, quiet street.
4. The Prime Minister said that no one would be allowed to disturb the peace.
5. The spectators applauded the players saying that they had done well.
6. I wished my friend good morning and proposed that we should go for a picnic that day.
7. The new student asked the old one if he knew his name.
8. I warned her that I could no longer tolerate her coming late.

NARRATION

9. I told my mother that I would certainly take her to Bengaluru that week.
10. My co-passenger asked me how long the journey would take.
11. The mother exclaimed admiringly that it was very clever of him to have solved the puzzle so quickly.
12. He said that he went for a walk every morning.
13. I reiterated that I did not care about the job.
14. I suggested to my brother that we should go to some hill station for a change.
15. I wondered how many discoveries went unheeded.
16. Gopan asked me if I could do those sums for him.
17. The boss said that it was time they had begun planning their work.
18. He told the judge that he had not committed that crime.
19. Rahul said that he would do it then or never.
20. Doshi requested his wife to select one of those necklaces.
21. He reported that the rainfall had been scanty till then.
22. She requested Rita to help her with her homework.
23. My father once told me that if he couldn't trust his people then he didn't want to be doing that.
24. The manager commanded Govind to tell him what the old man had said.
25. I asked him where he had lost the pen, I had brought for him the previous day.

Exercise 2

1. Kiran asked me, "Did you see the cricket match on television last night?"
2. David said to Anna, "Mona will leave for her native place tomorrow."
3. I said to him, "Why are you working so hard?"
4. He said to her, "What a cold day!"
5. The tailor said to him, "Will you have the suit ready by tomorrow evening"?
6. He said to the interviewer, "Could you please repeat the question?"
7. He said, "Be quiet and listen to my words."
8. He said to me, "I have often told you not to play with fire."
9. The Captain said to his men, "Stand at ease."
10. Pawan said to me, "If I hear any news, I'll phone you."
11. The teacher said to Mahesh, "Congratulations! Wish you success in life.
12. The poor examinee said, " O God, take pity on me."
13. "Where will you be tomorrow", I said, "in case I have to ring you?"
14. Seeta said to me, "Can you give me your pen?"
15. The father warned his son, "Beware of him".
16. Manna asked Rohan, "Have you sat in a trolley bus before?"
17. Farhan asked Geeta, "Could you lend me a hundred rupees until tomorrow?"
18. "What about going for a swim", he said, "It's quite fine now."
19. "You can't bathe in this sea", he said to me, "It's very rough."
20. Jagdish said, "We passed by a beautiful lake when we went on a trip to Goa."
21. He said to me, "I expect you to attend the function."
22. He said, "Why didn't you send your application to me?"
23. Dinesh asked, "Are you going to the party tomorrow, Eliza?"
24. John asked, "How long will it take to travel from Germany to South Africa?"
25. "What did you see at the South Pole?" Ashok asked Anil.

Previous Years' Questions

I. 1. He said that he was too ill to speak then.
    2. The policeman asked the man where he was going.
    3. She requested her children to let her work undisturbed.
    4. He ordered the students not to sit there.
    5. He prayed that God might pardon the sinner.
    6. The master ordered the servant to go to the bazar and bring fruits.
    7. The traveller exclaimed that it was a very beautiful night.

II. 1. He said (warned) that he would not approve of such a behaviour in future.
    2. He said (informed) on the telephone that they had kept on doing their work till late night.
    3. She told me that as my mother was ill, I must go at once.
    4. Ram asked Sita if she intended to go with him to forest.
    5. The child asked Sherpa why he had not chosen to climb to the moon.

III. 1. Amrita asked me why I had not attended her class.
    2. My father ordered me to wash my clothes.
    3. Our teacher said that the earth revolves around the sun.
    4. Meera said that the plane had landed.
    5. Our English teacher ordered Mohan to open the window.

IV. 1. He wrote in his letter that he had seen Poonam at the theatre a couple of days before.
    2. The forecast says that it will rain tomorrow.
    3. He told me that it would be nice if he could see me again.
    4. I told him that if I had any money, I would buy him a drink.
    5. The teacher asked the student why he did not work harder.

V. A. 1. The children said that they had gone to the zoo that morning.
    2. He shouted to me to let him go.
       Or
       He shouted to me that he might be allowed to go.
    3. He asked me if I was coming home with him.
    4. He said that he had passed the examination.
    5. The workers said that they had been repairing the road.
    6. The stranger asked me if I could tell him, where the post office was.
    7. The young tourist exclaimed with joy that it was a beautiful day.
    8. The proud father remarked with joy that his son was a wonderful batsman.
    9. My mother remarked if the children were not lovely.
    10. Rama requested her daughter to go with her to the doctor's clinic.
    11. He warned me not to play with fire.
    12. My father asked me to wait till he had finished all that he had to say.
    13. He asked me what my name was.

B. 1. She said, "We will have a party tonight."
    2. He said, "I have come to see you".
    3. My mother said, "Have you finished your breakfast?"

CHAPTER 6

Synthesis

Synthesis means the combination of two or more simple sentences into one simple, complex and compound sentence.

Part I : Complex Sentence

A complex sentence is formed by joining two or more simple sentences with the help of subordinate conjunctions as follows:

As stated earlier, a complex sentence consists of more than one clause. Besides a principal clause, one or more subordinate clauses to form a complex sentence. There are three kinds of subordinate clauses joined by their respective subordinating conjunctions. e.g.

   (i) I know **that** he is a good boy. *(Noun clause)*
   (ii) I know the man **who** was here yesterday. *(Adjective clause)*
   (iii) I shall give you money **when** you do this work. *(Adverb clause)*

These sentences contain three kinds of subordinate clauses:
(A) Noun clause
(B) Adjective clause
(C) Adverb clause

A. Noun Clause

I know that he is a good boy.

In the above sentence, 'I know' is a principal clause and 'that he is a good boy' is a Noun clause as it does the work of a noun. Noun clause answers the verb or noun in the principal or any other subordinate clause.

Subordinate conjunctions of Noun clause are– **that, if, whether, when, where, how, why, what, who, whose, whom, which, whatever.**

A set of simple sentences may be combined in the following manner by making noun clause.

(a) **Object to a Transitive Verb**
   (i) I say it. He is a good man.
       I say that he is a good man.
   (ii) I said it. He is a good man.
       I said that he was a good man.
   (iii) I cannot say. Will he come tomorrow?
       I cannot say if/whether he will come tomorrow.
   (iv) I don't know. What is he doing?
       I don't know what he is doing.

(b) **Object of Infinitive, Gerund and Participle**
   (i) Everybody was pleased to know. She was absent.
       Everybody was pleased to know that she was absent.
   (ii) She kept on asking. When will her mother return?
       She kept on asking when her mother would return.

(c) **Object to Preposition**
   (i) I don't believe. She said something.
       I don't believe in what she said.
   (ii) Please listen. Your teacher is telling something.
       Please listen to what your teacher is telling.

(d) **Complement of a Verb**
   (i) The hope is. She will return tomorrow.
       The hope is that she will return tomorrow.
   (ii) The fact is. Nisha has not qualified the test.
       The fact is that Nisha has not qualified the test.

Note Noun clause following the verbs –'to be, become, seem, appear, grow, taste, smell, prove, look, make' etc. –performs the function of a complement of these verbs (in place of a predicate).

(e) **The Case in Apposition to a Noun**
   (i) She never believed in his statement. His father is a doctor.
       She never believed in his statement that his father was a doctor.
   (ii) No one heard the news. The prime minister is coming tomorrow.
       No one heard the news that the prime minister was coming the next day.

(f) **The Case in Apposition to a Pronoun**
   (i) It is true. My brother has left for America.
       It is true that my brother has left for America.
   (ii) It was not known. What is she doing in Indore?
       It was not known what she was doing in Indore.

(g) **The Subject of a Verb**
   (i) It is true. What he knows.
       (a) It is true what he knows.
       (b) What he knows is true. (subject of a verb)

SYNTHESIS

(ii) It is not known. When will she come?
   (a) It is not known when she will come.
   (b) When she will come is not known. (subject of a verb)

Noun clause as a subject may be used in place of pronouns. 'It, this, that,' Noun clause works as a subject in this type of sentences.

Some examples have been worked out for the students :

(i) I say. She is a good woman.
   I say that she is a good woman.

(ii) I said. He is an honest man.
   I said that he was an honest man.

(iii) I cannot say. She will come.
   I cannot say whether/if she will come.

(iv) I did not know. Will he come?
   I did not know if he would come.

(v) I doubt. Can he do it?
   I doubt if he can do it.

(vi) I am certain. She has got through the examination.
   I am certain that she has got through the examination.

(vii) I don't know. He said something.
   I don't know, what he said.

(viii) What you say. I shall not do.
   I shall not do, what you say.

(ix) It is not clear. What he says.
   (a) It is not clear, what he says.
   (b) What he says, is not clear.

(x) It is true. She will succeed.
   (a) That she will succeed, is true.
   (b) It is true that she will succeed.

(xi) She came sometime in the morning. It is a mystery.
   (a) When she came in the morning, is a mystery.
   (b) It is a mystery, when she came in the morning.

(xii) I wonder. How can she pass?
   I wonder, how she can pass.

(xiii) He denied. He has committed theft.
   He denied that he had committed theft.

(xiv) The fact is. He is a hard-working fellow.
   The fact is that he is a hard working fellow.

(xv) The fact is well known. He is an honest person.
   The fact, that he is an honest person, is well known.

(xvi) She came from somewhere in 1970. It is not revealed.
   (a) It is not revealed, where she came from in 1970.
   (b) Where she came from in 1970, is not revealed.

(xvii) Someone misguided him. His parents don't know.
His parents don't know, who misguided him.

(xviii) A certain number of students were admitted. The Principal does not know this number.
The Principal does not know, how many students were admitted.

(xix) Everybody wants to know the reason. The two friends quarrelled yesterday.
Everybody wants to know, why the two friends quarrelled yesterday.

(xx) Do you know the time? The train will arrive at a certain time.
Do you know, when the train will arrive?

WORK BOOK EXERCISE (A)

Directions *Combine the following sentences into complex sentences.*

1. I don't know. He will come.
2. He is going somewhere. I cannot say.
3. He was not guilty. That was the verdict of the bench.
4. There is no doubt in it. He will do it.
5. He is correct. I am sure of it.
6. You gave him stolen money. That was his statement.
7. He may be guilty. I am not certain.
8. Some one arrived late at night. I do not know.
9. I don't believe it. He said something to me.
10. Nobody informed me. My mother went to temple sometime in the evening.
11. Everybody doubts it. He will pass.
12. This is my belief. He will cheat you.
13. My father will come here. I do not know the time.
14. Where have you put my purse? Please tell me.
15. Are you listening? I am saying something.
16. He came late. I cannot tell the reason.
17. The news is wrong. He died last night.
18. He confessed. He had committed murder.
19. It was expected. He will arrive soon.
20. It is believed. Netaji died in air crash.
21. I cannot say. She may be a doctor.
22. What is your attitude to life? All depends on this.
23. My son is anxious to learn. How can one travel to space?
24. The fact is. He is a coward.
25. She declared her intention. She will not marry next year.
26. He wasted a certain amount of money. His wife cannot tell.
27. I cannot rely on it. She has promised me something.
28. The police are trying to inquire. When did she leave the party?

29. She told me the fact. Her father will not allow her to go abroad.
30. Our expectation was. We will succeed.
31. The news is not correct. She has returned from Chennai.
32. She confessed. She went to Delhi last night.
33. My sister kept on asking. When shall I come back from Indore?
34. The verdict of the Judges has been challenged. He is guilty.
35. I cannot tell. She came sometime in the morning.
36. The rumour is baseless. He died last night.
37. She completed this work in a strange manner. Everyone wonders.
38. It is certain. She will arrive today.
39. I heard him telling his mother. He is leaving for America very soon.
40. It cannot be confirmed. Has he married?

B. Adjective Clause

I know the man, who was here yesterday.

In the above sentence, 'I know the man' is a principal clause and 'who was here yesterday' is an Adjective clause. It does the work of an Adjective qualifying noun 'the man'. Adjective clause qualifies noun or pronoun as the case may be.

Subordinate conjunctions of Adjective clause are—"**Who, whose, whom, which, of which, that, as, why, when, where.**"

Some examples have been worked out for the students:

(i) I know the man. He is a doctor.
   I know the man, who is a doctor.

(ii) This is my pen. It is very costly.
   This is my pen, which is very costly.

(iii) I don't know any of the men. They live here.
   I don't know any of the men that live here.

(iv) I have met all the boys. They are studying in the college.
   I have met all the boys that are studying in the college.

(v) The Sanskrit language is not difficult to learn. It is taught in our school.
   The Sanskrit language, that is taught in our school, is not difficult to learn.

(vi) The monster was proud of his power. He was defeated by Hercules.
   The monster, who was proud of his power, was defeated by Hercules.

(vii) He settled in the town. He retired there from service.
   He settled in the town, where he retired from the service.

(viii) It was midnight. The trains collided then.
   It was midnight when the trains collided.

(ix) I had many friends in prosperity. All of them have deserted me now.
   In prosperity, I had many friends, who all have deserted me now.

(x) He has become suddenly rich. I can tell you the reason.
   I can tell you the reason why he has become suddenly rich.

(xi) Shalini bought only one of the flats? These were built by AWHO.
Shalini bought only one of the flats that was built by AWHO.

(xii) I have invited Mohan. Everybody likes him.
I have invited Mohan, whom everybody likes.

(xiii) He bought a new book. Its price is very cheap.
He bought a new book the price of which is very cheap.

(xiv) The book has been found. I lost it yesterday.
The book, which I lost yesterday, has been found.

(xv) He settled in Nagpur. He was born there.
He settled in Nagpur, where he was born.

WORK BOOK EXERCISE (B)

Directions *Combine the following simple sentences into complex sentences.*

1. Shakespeare was a great dramatist. He is the author of a number of plays.
2. You have put my purse somewhere. Please show me the place.
3. This is the college. I studied here.
4. It was 10 o'clock. My father left for office then.
5. Can you tell me the reason? You are wasting time.
6. The boy was present there. The teacher gave him a prize.
7. I bought a pen. I shall give you the same pen.
8. I was the first man. I heard his name on the radio.
9. They were sitting under a tree. Its shade was very cool.
10. I shall go by the Taj Express. It goes to Agra direct.
11. They are reading a book. It is very rare.
12. The news is true. He gave it yesterday.
13. Yesterday I bought a book. It is very cheap.
14. They committed a mistake. It was quite serious.
15. You can not believe such a person. The person is dishonest.
16. We undertook a journey to Gwalior. It was tiring.
17. A soldier was lying in the field. He was wounded.
18. The dog felled the candle. It was burning.
19. They are healthy. The healthy do not need a doctor.
20. The man died last night. He was wounded in an accident.
21. The magic ball was eaten by the jester. It was meant for king.
22. Seema was the last person. She left for home.
23. This is a class room. It is not the place to play.
24. He has a large family. He has to educate them.
25. He has some bills. He must pay them in cash.
26. I have no friend. I cannot talk to him.
27. Childhood is a time. One can teach good habits to children.
28. I know the reason. He could not succeed.

SYNTHESIS

29. The time is not certain. He will come tomorrow.
30. Nobody appreciated the way. She behaved at the party.
31. I was informed of the place. He was living there.
32. I remember very well the year. He retired then.
33. You can have anything. Whatever you like.
34. The students are very hard working. They hail from Bihar.
35. The girl is a cousin of my wife. The girl has long hair.
36. I never visit any of my uncles. They reside in Manekshaw Enclave.
37. The news is true. The Voice of America broadcast it.
38. The players were present at the function. The President awarded them cash prize.
39. Good deeds live after men. They do them in their lives.
40. Kabir was a famous poet. He wrote spiritual poetry.

C. Adverb Clause

I shall give you money when you do this work.

In the above sentence, 'I shall give you money' is a principal clause and 'when you do this work' is an Adverb clause. It does the work of an Adverb. It is required to modify some verb, Adverb or Adjective in some other clause.

Adverb clause may be classified as follows.

Time Clause

Conjunctions When, as, while, as soon as, before, after, by the time, until, till, whenever, small, as long as-

Some examples have been worked out for the students:

(i) He saw the police departing. He immediately got into his car.
   As he saw the police departing, he immediately got into his car.

(ii) I will get money for you. Don't go till then.
   Don't go, until I get money for you.

(iii) I left office. My wife arrived afterwards.
   My wife arrived after I had left office.

(iv) He was going to school. He was caught in the rain.
   While he was going to school, he was caught in the rain.

(v) His father retired last year. He has been idle from that time.
   Since his father retired last year, he has been idle.

Condition Clause

Conjunctions If, unless, suppose, in case, on condition that, provided, I wish, I would, would that, if only. e.g.

(i) Work hard. You will fail.
   If you do not work hard, you will fail.

(ii) We may go tomorrow. It depends on the weather.
   We may go tomorrow if weather permits.

(iii) Do it well. You will be rewarded.
If you do it well, you will be rewarded.

(iv) Work hard. You will fail otherwise.
If you do not work hard, you will fail.

(v) She had laboured. Otherwise she would not have succeeded.
If she had not laboured, She would not have succeeded.

Purpose

Conjunctions So that, lest, in order that, that. e.g.

(i) He went to Delhi. He wanted to meet his mother.
He went to Delhi so that he might meet his mother.

(ii) He is afraid of getting late. He will go by his own car.
He will go by his own car, lest he should get late.

Place

Conjunctions Where, wherever. e.g.

(i) I shall go. He works there in a factory.
I shall go, where he works in a factory.

(ii) You can stay. You can stay anywhere.
You can stay, wherever you like.

Result

Conjunctions 'That' (followed by 'Such', 'So'). e.g.

(i) He grew weaker and weaker. He was admitted to hospital.
He grew so weak that he was admitted to hospital.

(ii) He drove very fast. He soon overtook us.
He drove so fast that he soon overtook us.

Reason

Conjunctions Because, since, as, that, now that. e.g.

(i) The students disobeyed the teacher. He was annoyed.
The teacher was annoyed because the students disobeyed him.

(ii) You are disturbing me. I cannot work.
I cannot work as you are disturbing me.

(iii) He came late. He was punished.
He was punished because he came late.

(iv) It was dark outside. I did not go out.
Since, it was dark outside, I did not go out.

Concession or Contrast

Conjunctions Although, though, as, even if, however, even if, whether, even though, no matter what, no matter that, not withstanding that, much as, whatever. e.g.

(i) He is very old. He can still run very fast.
Although he is very old, he can run very fast.

SYNTHESIS 401

(ii) He has succeeded in life. He is still humble.
Though he has succeeded in life, he is still humble.

(iii) He is lucky. He will not win this match.
However lucky he may be, he will not win this match.

(iv) She is rich. She is not kind.
Rich as she is, she is not kind.

Manner

Conjunctions As, as if, as though. e.g.
(i) I advised him. He acted accordingly.
He acted as I advised him.

(ii) He is not educated. He speaks like an educated person.
He speaks as if he were an educated person.

Comparison

Conjunctions Than, as. e.g.
(i) The tiger is larger. The cat is smaller.
The tiger is larger than the cat.

(ii) Her mother is wise. Richa is equally wise.
Richa is as wise as her mother is.

WORK BOOK EXERCISE (C)

Directions *Combine the following simple sentences into complex sentences.*
1. He ran very quickly. He overtook everybody.
2. You always disturb me. I cannot work.
3. I had left office. My boss called me.
4. The members of the committee arrived. The conference started.
5. You must hurry. Otherwise you will miss the train.
6. It was very sultry noon. I could not go out.
7. I left office. The train started that very moment.
8. He will not leave at night. He cannot bear the idea of being robbed.
9. He came to me. He wanted my help.
10. He found out his mistake. Then he repented very much.
11. Do not sleep outside. You will be ill.
12. I reached the station. The train had left.
13. You left India. You have not written any letter since.
14. The old man walks fast. He walks like a young person.
15. He is rich. He is unhappy.
16. Help others. God will help you.
17. They were playing in the garden. It started raining.
18. No money was given to me. The work was stopped.
19. The patient grew weaker and weaker. He died last night.

20. His brother died. He has been very poor from that time.
21. Everybody will admire him. His being hard working is a condition.
22. Go out. You will catch cold.
23. He was sick. Even then he went out.
24. He was cremated in the village. He settled there after his retirement.
25. He is admired by everybody. He is still not proud.
26. He was sitting on the grass. A snake bit him.
27. She waited for her friend. She waited till her arrival.
28. She came late. Else she would have enjoyed music.
29. Do you want to go to Malabar Hills? Then bring money with you.
30. I shall go. My cousin works there.
31. Water is very cold. No one can drink it.
32. He employed a watch man. He wanted to be safe.
33. They helped me. Otherwise I would not have got success.
34. I would have been glad. I could have given you money.
35. You may go anywhere. You like.
36. He did not stop working. He achieved success.
37. The signal was given. The train started immediately.
38. You can stay here. You wish so.
39. She is beautiful. No other member in her family is so beautiful.
40. Let us wait. The train stops.
41. I make a promise. I stick to it.
42. He is working hard. His aim is to join Army.
43. He fled. He wanted to escape being caught.
44. I will get money for you. Please do not go till then.
45. Everybody will admire you. Your honesty is the condition.
46. He did not receive help in time. He would not have died from burns.
47. He gets more. Then he works more.
48. Do not get into the train. The train must stop.
49. It may rain. The schools may be closed.
50. We shall leave for Shimla. It depends on weather.
51. I should be glad. I could help your husband.
52. He worked hard. He would have failed.
53. I shall be glad. I can help you in getting a job.
54. She treated me in a certain manner. I shall treat her so.
55. My younger sister behaves with me. She behaves like an elder sister.
56. She wrote an essay. She wrote to the best of her ability.
57. She speaks well. She writes better.
58. She is wise. She is more kind.
59. He is not rich. He spends like a rich person.
60. The candidates stayed in the hall. They stayed till the departure of the supervisor.
61. She is wise. Her mother is equally wise.
62. I advised him. He did the work accordingly.
63. He will go by his own car. He is afraid of getting late.
64. The patient grew weaker and weaker. He died at last.

Part II : Simple Sentence

A simple sentence is formed by combining two or more simple sentences into one simple sentence as follows: **Some examples have been worked out for the students.** The following are the usual ways of combining a set of simple sentences into one simple sentence:

A. By using Infinitive

(i) He bought a pen. He wanted to give it to me.
He bought a pen to give it to me.

(ii) The work was very easy for her. She could do it.
The work was very easy (easy enough) for her to do.

(iii) She is very weak. She cannot understand a single word of the letter.
She is too weak to understand a single word of the letter.

(iv) I went to the station. My object was to receive my uncle.
I went to the station to receive my uncle.

(v) I have a lot of money. I would spend it tonight.
I have a lot of money to spend tonight.

(vi) She admitted. She met him last evening.
She admitted to have met him last evening.

(vii) It appears. She is improving in her study.
She appears to be improving in her study.

(viii) It is expected. She will come tomorrow.
She is expected to come tomorrow.

(ix) I advised her. She acted accordingly.
She acted according to my advice.

B. By using Participle (Present, Past, Perfect)

1. Present Participle

(i) She entered the Mall. She was very happy.
Entering the Mall, she was very happy.

(ii) I was hungry. I took my food.
Being hungry, I took my food.

(iii) I reached college. I went direct to my class room.
Reaching college, I went direct to my class room.

2. Past Participle

(i) She was disappointed. She left her study.
Being disappointed, she left her study.

(ii) I gave him a candle. It was burnt.
I gave him a burnt candle.

(iii) I found my pen. It was lost.
I found my lost pen.

3. Perfect Participle

(i) I took food. I went to college.
Having taken food, I went to college.

(ii) He picked my pocket. He fled.
Having picked my pocket, he fled.

C. By using Nominative Absolute

(i) The police arrived. The pick pocket fled.
The police having arrived, the pick pocket fled.

(ii) The picture ended. The audience left.
The picture having ended, the audience left.

D. By using Preposition before Gerund or Noun

(i) She insisted. She would go with me.
She insisted on going with me.

(ii) Suhani persisted. She wanted to live in Hyderabad.
Suhani persisted in living in Hyderabad.

(iii) My brother bought a new house. He bought it for his wife.
My brother bought a new house for his wife.

E. By using Noun or Phrase in Apposition

In such kind of sentences, Noun or Phrase is placed within commas after the Nouns referred to.

(i) My brother went to Shimla. Shimla is a beautiful hill station in Himachal.
My brother went to Shimla, a beautiful hill station in Himachal.

(ii) Kapil Dev was the best bowler. He was the Captain of Indian Cricket team.
Kapil Dev, the Captain of Indian Cricket team, was the best bowler.

F. By using Adjective

(i) I came across a girl in the garden. She was beautiful.
I came across a beautiful girl in the garden.

(ii) They laughed at a small boy. He was hungry.
They laughed at a small hungry boy.

G. By using Conjunction 'And'

(i) I saw a cow. I saw a calf also.
I saw a cow and a calf.

(ii) He bought new books. He bought also old books.
He bought new and old books.

(iii) Nisha went to the movie. Her husband also went with her.
Nisha and her husband went to the movie.

SYNTHESIS

H. **By using Adverbs or Adverbial Phrases**

(i) She went to parlour. She went frequently.
   She went to parlour frequently.

(ii) He was running. His speed was slow.
   He was running slowly.

(iii) I am sure. She will go to the movie.
   I am sure that she will go to the movie.

WORK BOOK EXERCISE (A)

Directions *Combine the following set of simple sentences into one simple sentence.*

By using Infinitive

1. He is very weak. He cannot run.
2. I want a knife. I shall peel the vegetables.
3. He had a large family. He had to support them.
4. She has no pen. She cannot write a cheque.
5. He heard of my success. He was glad of it.
6. It is believed. He died from heart attack.
7. I expect. I shall pass next year.
8. It is reported. She has married lately.

By using Participle

1. He drew the sword. He attacked the enemy.
2. He could not eat nuts. He had no teeth.
3. I was returning home. I saw a black dog.
4. He resolved firmly. He never smoked.
5. She completed the letter. She posted it.
6. He was disappointed. He gave up the job.
7. Turn to the right. You will find my house.
8. She was tired of riding. She went to bed.
9. We heard no answer. We rang the bell again.
10. Ceasar was stabbed. He died from the wounds.

By using Nominative Absolute

1. The sun rose. Fog disappeared.
2. Archana was late. The teacher punished her.
3. The letter was written. I posted it soon.
4. The time was over. We handed our the note books.
5. It was cloudy. We went on picnic.
6. The rain is scanty this year. Sugar is dear in the market.
7. His uncle died. He inherited the property.
8. Rashmi's father was rich. She was not proud of this.
9. The Ganga is our sacred river. We should keep it clean.

By using Preposition before Gerund or Noun
1. He killed his enemy. He was justified in this.
2. She wanted to go to market. She insisted on this.
3. He won praise. He saved the life of the prince.
4. The teacher was absent. We were informed of this.
5. The girl has long hair. The girl is the cousin of my wife.
6. He has stolen my book. There is no doubt about this.
7. He is reading comics. He is fond of them.
8. He was wounded. I heard of this.
9. All returned safe. We all were happy at this.
10. I bought a new house. I paid huge amount for it.

By using Noun or Phrase in Apposition
1. Suniti is the daughter of a doctor. She stood first in the college.
2. Mr. Sinha is an engineer. He works in the Hydel department.
3. Harsh is a famous poet. He writes love poetry.
4. Nanda is a great builder. He has built a number of apartments.
5. He bought a very costly picture. It is a work by a most famous artist of India.

By using Adverbs or Adverbial Phrase
1. He replied back. This took him no time.
2. He saved money. This was wise of him.
3. I escaped from the den of gangster. This was lucky.
4. I got help from my friends. This was not expected.
5. I shall return tonight. It will not be long.
6. I shall get through the examination. There is no doubt about this.
7. She went to college. She was in a hurry.
8. She will go to the states next year. It is certain.

By using Adjective or And
1. I am buying a house next week. It is very costly.
2. A girl entered the room. She was young.
3. She was kind. She was generous.
4. Why are you nervous? Why are you sad?

(A) **Noun Clause** (Simple Sentence)

Some examples have been worked out (Relating to Noun Clause) **for the students:**
(i) There is no doubt in it. He will do it.
   Undoubtedly, he will do it.
(ii) He is correct. I am sure of it.
   I am sure of his being correct.
(iii) Nobody informed me. My father went sometime in the evening.
   Nobody informed me of the time of my father's departure in the evening.

SYNTHESIS

(iv) It is allaged. He committed a murder.
   He is alleged to have committed murder.
(v) It is understood. He is honest.
   He is understood to be honest.
(vi) The news is wrong. That he died.
   The news of his death is wrong.
(vii) They did not inform me. Their mother was ill.
   They did not inform me of their mother's illness.
(viii) He confessed. He had committed the murder.
   He confessed to have committed the murder.
(ix) He hoped. He will succeed.
   He hoped to succeed.
(x) I told you something. You must believe.
   You must believe my statement.
(xi) We believe. The news is true.
   We believe in the truthfulness of the news.
(xii) It is high time. You should start working hard.
   It is high time for you to start working hard.
(xiii) I wish. You should be quiet.
   I wish you to be quiet.
(xiv) You saved money. It was prudent.
   It was prudent of you to save money.
(xv) He will marry her. He is not afraid of it.
   He is not afraid of marrying her.
(xvi) I expect. I will meet you tomorrow.
   I expect to meet you tomorrow.
(xvii) I expect. He will pass with credit.
   (a) I expect him to pass with credit.
   (b) He is expected to pass with credit.
(xviii) It appears. He is rich.
   He appears to be rich.
(xix) It is believed. He is honest.
   He is believed to be honest.
(xx) It is reported. He is doing well in business.
   He is reported to be doing well in business.
(xxi) It appears. He has been cheated.
   He appears to have been cheated.
(xxii) He denies. He met her yesterday.
   He denies to have met her yesterday.
(xxiii) He insisted. He will join college.
   He insisted on joining college.

(xxiv) He will succeed. It is certain.
    (a) He is certain to succeed.
    (b) He will certainly succeed.
(xxv) I do not know. How did he travel to Delhi?
    I do not know the manner of his travelling to Delhi.
(xxvi) I cannot tell the reason. Why did he leave his sister.
    I cannot tell the reason of his leaving his sister.
(xxvii) He left yesterday. No body informed me.
    No body informed me about his leaving yesterday.
(xxviii) He declared. He was innocent.
    He declared his innocence.
(xxix) How long will the war last? It is uncertain.
    The duration of war is uncertain.
(xxx) The king ordered. The murderer should be hanged.
    The king ordered the murderer to be hanged.

WORK BOOK EXERCISE (B)

Directions *Combine the following sentences into simple sentences.*

1. The student admitted. He was absent.
2. I am not aware. What is he?
3. I don't know. What is his name?
4. I cannot recall. Where does he live?
5. I have no faith in his promise. She promised to help me.
6. It is certain. She will succeed.
7. My faith is firm. He will succeed.
8. That makes the offence worse. You were absent.
9. She is sure. She will secure high marks.
10. She persisted. She will continue her study.
11. My father insisted. I should join army.
12. We do not know the reason. She left the party suddenly.
13. The soldiers were told. How could they climb the hill?
14. I expect. He is honest.
15. We hope. We will be invited.
16. He denied. He sold spurious drugs to the customers.
17. It is certain. She has two son.
18. It is expected. She will qualify Entrance Examination.
19. It appears. She is honest.
20. It is believed. Netaji died in air crash.
21. It is alleged. He stole his brother's jewellery.
22. It is likely. She may come late.
23. It is certain. He will be punished tomorrow.
24. He is sure. He will succeed.
25. It is beyond doubt. She will recover from illness.

SYNTHESIS

(B) Adjective Clause to Simple Sentence

Some examples have been worked out (Relating to Adjective Clause) **for the students:**

(i) He gave me money. He gave it to spend.
He gave me money to spend.

(ii) He has a lot of money. He will spend it on books.
He has a lot of money to spend on books.

(iii) In the park we saw children. They were playing base ball.
In the park, we saw children playing base ball.

(iv) I will board a train. It connects Udaipur.
I will board a train connecting Udaipur.

(v) They are watching match. It is very interesting.
They are watching a very interesting match.

(vi) The magic ball was eaten by the jester. It was meant for the king.
The magic ball, meant for the king, was eaten by the jester.

(vii) The soldier lay in the battlefield. He was wounded.
The wounded soldier lay in the battlefield.

(viii) He visited the Taj. It is an artistic building.
He visited the Taj, an artistic building.

(ix) The book is very costly. I purchased it yesterday.
The book purchased by me yesterday, is very costly.

(x) Rathore is our captain. He scored five runs.
Rathore, our captain, scored five runs.

(xi) The girl is cousin of my wife. She has long hair.
The girl, with long hair, is the cousin of my wife.

WORK BOOK EXERCISE (C)

Directions *Combine the following simple sentences into one simple sentence.*

1. She has arrived earlier. Do you know the reason?
2. Kabir was a famous poet. He was a weaver.
3. I bought a house last year. It is quite large.
4. We came across a soldier. He was in trouble.
5. He invented a machine. It is used for stitching.
6. Mr Verma is our teacher. Everybody loves him.
7. This is a class room. It is not the place to play.
8. We committed a mistake. It is quite serious.
9. Do you know the time? Your father left in the morning.
10. The boys are honest. They live near my house.
11. The man could not do work well. The man was tired.
12. We undertook a journey. The journey was tiring.
13. I was the first man. I heard his name on the radio.

14. He has a large family. He has to educate them.
15. He has some bills. He must pay them.
16. They admitted the offence. They committed last night.
17. You cannot believe such a person. The person is dishonest.
18. We undertook a journey to Gwalior. The journey was tiring.
19. In the street, we saw a beggar. He was begging from door to door.
20. The man died last night. He was wounded in an accident.
21. The police discovered the weapon. It was used to kill the victim.
22. Air is the first necessity of life. It is the cheapest thing in the world.
23. Childhood is a time. One can learn good habits during this time.
24. I know the reason. He could not succeed.
25. The time has been announced. He will come tomorrow.
26. I remember very well the year. He retired then?
27. These students are very hard working. They hail from Bihar.
28. The offence is unpardonable. She committed it intentionally.
29. The good deeds live after men. They do them in life.
30. Malini repaid the debt. Her father had incurred it.

(C) Adverb Clause to Simple Sentence

Some examples have been worked out (Relating to Adverb Clause) **for the students:**

(i) She is very poor. She cannot carry on her study.
She is too poor to carry on her study.

(ii) He employs a watchman. He wants to be safe.
He employs a watchman to be safe.

(iii) He heard the news. He fainted.
On hearing the news, he fainted.

(iv) He was sitting on a tree. A snake bit him.
Sitting on a tree, he was bitten by a snake.

(v) The police arrived. The rioters fled.
The police having arrived, the rioters fled.

(vi) She was late. She was punished.
Being late, She was punished.

(vii) She came late, She was not punished.
Inspite of being late, she was not punished.

(viii) Work hard. You will succeed.
By working hard, you will succeed.

(ix) Work hard. You will fail otherwise.
Without working hard, you will fail.

(x) She had laboured hard. Otherwise she would not have succeeded.
But for hard labour, she would not have succeeded.

SYNTHESIS

WORK BOOK EXERCISE (D)

Directions *Combine the following simple sentences into one simple sentence.*

1. I had passed high school examination. I got a job.
2. He takes dinner early. He is afraid of getting ill.
3. The thief saw the police. He fled immediately.
4. He was sitting on the grass. A snake bit him.
5. He was late. He was punished.
6. The weather was unpleasant. We did not go out.
7. She was insulted. She left the room.
8. He was overpowered by the enemy. The enemy stabbed him.
9. He possess huge wealth. He is not happy.
10. Go out. You will catch cold.
11. Work hard. You will fail.
12. Examine the paper carefully. You can not give your opinion.
13. He is very lazy. He is not fit to be a player.
14. We may go tomorrow. It depends on the weather.
15. Every sunday he goes to Delhi. He goes to see his sick brother.
16. He is so weak. He cannot even walk.
17. I advised him. He did the work accordingly.
18. He is working hard. His aim is to join Army.
19. He is very kind. He helps everybody.
20. Permit me. I shall leave the room.
21. The work was done. I was present then.
22. He is very honest. He will not deceive you.
23. Turn to right. You will see a tall building.
24. He was going to school. He was caught in the rain.
25. His father retired last year. He has been idle from that time.
26. He drove very fast. He soon overtook us.
27. He succeeded in life. He is still humble.
28. He is very clever. He can see through your tricks.
29. Your sorrow is too deep. It cannot be expressed in tears.
30. This house is too small. It cannot serve my purpose.

WORK BOOK EXERCISE (E)

(Based on Noun, Adjective and Adverb Clauses)

Directions *Combine the following set of sentences into one simple sentence.*

1. The lady entered the Mall. She went straight to the manager.
2. Archana lost her purse. It was very costly. It contained a lot of cash.
3. He came late. He was punished for this.
4. Small families are not an advantage. It is certain now.

5. Some people drink. This is injurious to health.
6. He has some new clothes. They are in the box.
7. He told a lie. He was not afraid of it.
8. We reached Shimla. We went to our hotel.
9. Yesterday, my brother went to Chandigarh. Rohan went also.
10. She was clever. I could notice it.
11. It was very hot. I did not go out.
12. The train was late. We reached home late.
13. My father did not sell the house. This was wise.
14. They were walking in the garden. They enjoyed themselves.
15. Rohit had no money. He succeeded in his aim.
16. Work hard. You will pass.
17. The speech ended. We went to dinner.
18. He had no house. He could not sell.
19. He fired at his friend. He was arrested for this.
20. She earns a lot of money. She runs a beauty parlour.
21. Ashok was a great Emperor. He become compassionate. It happened after the battle of Kalinga.
22. He was walking in the street. He saw a beggar. The beggar was not able to walk.
23. He arrived at the party. He was pleased. He met all of his friends.
24. We come to the institute. We come to study. We study English.
25. Deepa was driving. She heard Reema's voice. She was humming a song.
26. I am threatened. I will speak the truth. I am not afraid of it.
27. It was dark. He fired at his enemy. He wanted to kill him.
28. He was successful. I was told. I was glad of it.
29. The child had broken window pane. It was tinted. He was playing cricket. He was punished for this.
30. We were delighted. We saw him. He was buying fruit. He was buying mangoes.

Part III : Compound Sentence

We have already studied that a compound sentence contains a co-ordinate clause or more than one main clause. They are joined by co-ordinating conjunctions.

Co-ordinating conjunctions are given as follows:
(A) Illative conjunction are used when one statement is concluded from the other. They express reason.

They are – so, therefore, for
(i) She came late. She was punished.
   She came late, so she was punished.
(ii) I cannot go out. It is very cold outside.
   (a) I cannot go out for it is very cold outside.
   (b) It is very cold out side, therefore, I cannot go outside.

SYNTHESIS

(B) Adversative conjunctions add two statements to make a compound sentence. They express a contrast. They are '**still, nevertheless, but, yet, whereas, while, however**'.

They express contrast.

(i) She is intelligent. She is dishonest.
She is intelligent but dishonest.

(ii) She was ill. She came.
She was ill yet she came.

(C) Alternative conjunctions express a choice between alternatives. They are '**or, nor, otherwise, else, or else**'. They express condition.

(i) Work hard. You will fail.
Work hard or you will fail.

(ii) Do not be angry. Do not be rash.
Be neither angry nor rash.

(D) Cumulative (Copulative) Conjunction add one statement to the other. They are **both-and, not only-but also, as well as, and neither-nor, either-or.**

(i) He is a fool. He is dishonest also.
He is not only a fool but also dishonest.

(ii) He is handsome. He is smart also.
He is not only handsome but also smart.

WORK BOOK EXERCISE (A)

Directions *Combine the set of simple sentences into one compound sentence.*

1. He is intelligent. He is careless.
2. He can succeed. He will not work hard.
3. Morning walk is a good exercise. Everybody should walk.
4. He came late. He would have enjoyed music.
5. Walk fast. You will catch bus.
6. Wait here. He will not meet you.
7. The bus was slow. He reached late.
8. You are a liar. Your brother is a liar.
9. She is smart. She is honest too.
10. Do not be a borrower. Do not be a lender.
11. You may be correct. You may be wrong.
12. She is often late. She comes on foot.
13. Stand outside. Come in
14. Weather was not fair. We went on picnic.
15. She came. She consoled me.

WORK BOOK EXERCISE (B)

Directions *Combine the set of simple sentences into one compound sentence.*
1. She came late. She was punished.
2. I can not go out. It is very cold outside.
3. She is intelligent. She is dishonest.
4. She was ill. She came.
5. Work hard. You will fail.
6. Do not be angry. Do not be rash.
7. He is a fool. He is dishonest also.
8. He is handsome. He is smart.
9. He is intelligent. He is careless.
10. He can succeed. He will not work hard.
11. Morning walk is a good exercise. Everybody should walk.
12. He came late. He would have got the bus.
13. Walk fast. You will catch bus.
14. Wait here. He will not meet you.
15. The bus was slow. He reached late.
16. You play piano. Your brother plays piano.
17. She is obedient. She is polite also.
18. Do not be a borrower. Do not be a lender.
19. Richa cannot sing. Esha cannot sing.
20. Everything decays. Truth Survives.
21. I doubt it. He will pass.
22. I went to Indore. I spent a few days there.
23. I requested her to lend me some money. She refused.
24. You come by car. We shall take you to temple.
25. He took bath. He put on new clothes.
26. He fell off the stairs. He died from injuries.
27. Say one word. I shall kill you.
28. Write to father. Otherwise, I would do so.
29. He is working hard. He wants to pass.
30. Sona cannot sing. Her husband cannot sing.

Cumulative Exercises

Exercise 1

Directions *Combine each set of sentences into one simple sentence.*

1. He was occupied with important matters. He had no leisure to see visitors.
2. The dog bit the man. He was a notorious burglar.
3. The judge gave his decision. The court listened silently.
4. His father was dead. He had to support his widowed mother.
5. The Pathan took out a knife. His intention was to frighten the old man.
6. It must be done. The cost does not count.
7. He must apologise. He will not escape punishment otherwise.
8. He was delighted with the intelligence and brightness of the scholars. He overlooked the fact of their knowing few things by heart.
9. The stable door was open. The horse was stolen.
10. He was not at the meeting. His absence was unavoidable.

Exercise 2

Directions *Combine each set of simple sentences into one compound sentence.*

1. He failed. He persevered.
2. He was obstinate. He was punished.
3. The harvest truly is plenteous. The labourers are few.
4. The train was wrecked. No one was hurt.
5. The river is deep and swift. I am afraid to dive into it.
6. You may play hockey. You may play football. You must do either of the two.
7. A is equal to B. B is equal to C. A is equal to C.
8. We must catch the 6 o'clock train. There is only half an hour left. We must start without further delay.
9. It was a stormy night. We ventured out.
10. A timid dog is dangerous. He always suspects ill-treatment. He tries to protect himself by snapping.

Exercise 3

Directions *Combine each set of simple sentences into one complex sentence.*
1. You are drunk. That aggravates your offence.
2. The game was lost. It was the consequence of his carelessness.
3. She keeps her ornaments in a safe. This is the safe.
4. Let men sow anything. They will reap its fruit.
5. You are strong. I am equally strong.
6. I am very sorry. I cannot adequately express my sorrow.
7. He has many plans for earning money quickly. All of them failed.
8. Life lasts a certain time. Let us be honest during that time.
9. He was quite tired. He could scarcely stand.
10. Honesty is the best policy. Have you never heard it?

Previous Years' Questions

Directions *Rewrite each of the following sentences as directed without changing the meaning.*
1. Radha was the eldest. She had to look after her parents.
   (Combine to form a single sentence) **[Civil Services (Mains), 2013]**
2. She decorated the room. The purpose was to make it look beautiful.
   (Combine using 'so that') **[Civil Services (Mains), 2013]**
3. I could have finished the work. But, I would have had to go out early.
   (Combine into one sentence beginning with 'Had') **[Civil Services (Mains), 2013]**
4. I scored the highest marks in my class. I was given a prize.
   (Combine in one sentence using 'for') **[IFS, 2013]**
5. He drove back home late in the night. He was told not to do so.
   (Combine in one sentence using 'despite') **[IFS, 2013]**
6. The gentleman is sitting in the front row. He is my father.
   (Combine in a complex sentence) **[IFS, 2013]**
7. He is very clever. He cannot be fooled.
   (Combine the two sentences using 'too') **[IFS, 2014]**
8. He was tired of play. He sat down to rest.
   (Combine the two sentences into one) **[IFS, 2014]**
9. It is very hot outside. You cannot go out.
   (Rewrite using 'so') **[IFS, 2015]**
10. My brother is not a doctor. My sister is also not a doctor.
    (Change the sentence using 'neither ... nor') **[IFS, 2015]**
11. The tutor has come. He will teach my son.
    (Combine the two sentences using 'to') **[CAPF, 2015]**
12. The man would not agree to my suggestion. He would not leave me in peace.
    (Make into a single sentence using 'neither ... nor') **[CAPF, 2015]**

SYNTHESIS

13. We enjoyed our holiday. It rained a lot.
    (Join the two simple sentences to make one complex sentence.) [IES, 2015]
14. The engine stopped. It had heated up.
    (Combine these sentences using 'because')
15. They were tired. They worked late into the night.
    (Combine these sentences using 'although')
16. He slept early. He woke up late.
    (Combine these sentences using 'but')
17. He was on medication. He felt drowsy.
    (Combine these sentences using 'so')
18. She was very angry. She said nothing.
    (Combine these sentences using 'yet')
19. The coffee was hot. We could not drink it.
    (Combine the sentences using 'too ... to') [Civil Services (Mains), 2009]
20. The wind was strong. It could blow people away.
    (Combine the sentences using 'enough to')
21. You are not old. You cannot continue to work.
    (Combine the sentences using 'too ... to')
22. The print was clear. We could read it easily.
    (Combine the sentences using 'enough to')
23. The child was very small. It could not walk.
    (Combine the sentences using 'too ... to')
24. It was hot. We could cook food with the sun's rays.
    (Combine the sentences using 'enough to')
25. This book is heavy. I cannot carry it.
    (Combine the sentences using 'too ... to')
26. You are old. You should know better.
    (Combine the sentences using 'enough to')
27. She was shocked. She did not react.
    (Combine the sentences using 'too ... to')
28. The essay was good. It earned full marks.
    (Combine the sentences using 'enough to')

Answers

Part I

WORK BOOK EXERCISE (A)

1. I do not know whether he will come.
2. I cannot say, where he is going.
3. The verdict of the bench was that he was not guilty.
4. There is no doubt that he will do it.
5. I am sure that he is correct.
6. His statement was that you gave him stolen money.

   Or

   That you gave him stolen money, was his statement.
7. I am not certain if he is guilty.
8. I do not know, who arrived late at night.
9. I do not believe in what he said to me.
10. Nobody informed me, when my mother went to temple in the evening.
11. Everybody doubts if he will pass.
12. This is my belief that he will cheat you.

    Or

    That he will cheat you, is my belief.
13. I do not know, when my father will come here.
14. Please tell me, where you have put my purse.
15. Are you listening to what I am saying.
16. I cannot tell, why he came late.
17. The news that he died last night, is wrong.
18. He confessed that he had committed murder.
19. It was expected that he would arrive soon.
20. It is believed that Netaji died in air crash.
21. I cannot say whether/if she is a doctor.
22. All depends on what your attitude to life is.
23. My son is anxious to learn, how one can travel to space.
24. The fact is that he is a coward.
25. She declared her intention that she would not marry the following year.
26. His wife cannot tell, how much money he wasted.
27. I cannot rely on what she has promised to me.
28. The police are trying to inquire, when she left the party.
29. She told me the fact that her father would not allow her to go abroad.
30. Our expectation was that we would succeed.
31. The news that she has returned from Chennai, is not correct.
32. She confessed that she had gone to Delhi the previous night.
33. My sister kept on asking, when I would come back from Indore.
34. The verdict of the Judges, that he is guilty, has been challenged.
35. I cannot tell, when she came in the morning.
36. The rumour, that he died last night, is baseless.
37. Everyone wonders, how she completed this work.
38. It is certain that she will arrive today.
39. I heard him telling his mother that he was leaving for America very soon.
40. It cannot be confirmed whether he has married.

    Or

    Whether he has married, cannot be confirmed.

SYNTHESIS

WORK BOOK EXERCISE (B)

1. Shakespeare, who was a great dramatist, is the author of a number of plays.
2. Please show me the place, where you have put my purse.
3. This is the college, where I studied.
4. It was ten o'clock when my father left for office.
5. Can you tell me the reason why you are wasting time?
6. The boy, whom the teacher gave a prize, was present there.
7. I shall give you the same pen that I bought.
8. I was the first man, who heard his name on the radio.
9. They were sitting under a tree, the shade of which was very cool.
10. I shall go by the Taj express which goes to Agra direct.
11. They are reading a book which is very rare.
12. The news, that he gave yesterday, is true.
13. Yesterday, I bought a book, which is very cheap.
14. They committed a mistake which was quite serious.
15. You cannot believe such a person, who is dishonest.
16. We undertook a journey to Gwalior which was tiring.
17. A soldier, who was wounded, was lying in the field.
18. The dog felled the candle which was burning.
19. Those, who are healthy, do not need a doctor.
20. The man, who was wounded in accident, died last night.
21. The magic ball, which was meant for the king, was eaten by the jester.
22. Seema was the last person who left for home.
23. This is a class room which is not the place to play.
24. He has a large family whom he has to educate.
25. He has some bills which he must pay in cash.
26. I have no friend whom I can talk to.
27. Childhood is a time when one can teach good habits to children.
28. I know the reason, why he could not succeed.
29. The time, when he will came tomorrow, is not certain.
30. Nobody appreciated the way in which she behaved at the party.
31. I was informed of the place, where he was living.
32. I remember very well the year, when he retired.
33. You can have anything that you like.
34. The students, who hail, from Bihar, are very hard working.
35. The girl, who has long hair, is a cousin of my wife.
36. I never visit any of my uncles that reside in Manekshaw Enclave.
37. The news, which the voice of America broadcast, is true.
38. The players, whom the president awarded cash prize, were present at the function.
39. The good deeds, which men do in their lives, live after them.
40. Kabir, who was a famous poet, wrote spiritual poetry.

WORK BOOK EXERCISE (C)

1. He ran so quickly that he overtook everybody.
2. As you always disturb me, I cannot work.
3. When I had left office, my boss called me.
4. When the members of the committee arrived, the conference started.
5. You must hurry lest you should miss the train.
6. I could not go out because it was very sultry noon.

7. As soon as I left office, the rain started.
8. He will not leave at night, lest he should be robbed.
9. He came to me so that I might help him.
10. When he found out his mistake, he repented very much.
11. If you sleep outside, you will be ill.
12. When I reached the station, the train had left.
13. Since you left India, you have not written any letter.
14. The old man walks as fast as a young person.
15. Rich as he is, he is unhappy.
    Or
    Though he is rich, he is unhappy.
16. If you help others, God will help you.
17. While they were playing in the garden, it started raining.
18. The work was stopped because no money was given to me.
19. The patient grew so weak that he died last night.
20. Since his brother died, he has been very poor.
21. Everybody will admire him if he is hard working.
22. If you go out, you will catch cold.
23. Although he was sick, he went out.
24. He was cremated, where he settled after his retirement.
25. Though he is admired by everybody, he is not proud.
26. While he was sitting on the grass, a snake bit him.
27. She waited for her friend, till she arrived.
28. If she had not come late, she would have enjoyed music.
29. If you want to go to Malabar Hills, bring money with you.
30. I shall go, where my cousin works.
31. Water is so cold that no one can drink it.
32. He employed a watchman so that he might be safe.
33. If they had not helped me, I would not have got success.
34. If I had given you money, I would have been glad.
35. You may go, wherever you like.
36. He did not stop working until he achieved success.
37. As soon as the signal was given, the train started.
38. You can stay here if you wish.
39. No other member in her family is as beautiful as she is.
40. Let us wait till the train stops.
41. If I make a promise, I stick to it.
42. He is working hard so that he may join Army.
43. He fled lest he should be caught.
44. Please do not go until I get money for you.
45. Everybody will admire you on condition that you are honest.
46. If he had received help in time, he would not have died from burns.
47. The more he gets, the more he works.
48. Do not get into the train until it stops.
49. If it rains, the schools may be closed.
50. We shall leave for Shimla if weather permits.
51. I should be glad if I could help your husband.
52. If he had not worked hard, he would have failed.
53. I shall be glad if I can help you in getting a job.

SYNTHESIS

54. I shall treat her as she treated me.
55. My younger sister behaves as if she were an elder sister.
56. She wrote an essay as well as she could.
57. She writes better than she speaks.
58. She is more kind than wise.
59. He spends as if he were a rich person.
60. The candidates stayed in the hall till the supervisor departed.
61. She is as wise as her mother is.
62. He did the work as I advised him.
63. He will go by his own car lest he should get late.
64. The patient grew so weak that he died at last.

Part II

WORK BOOK EXERCISE (A)

By using Infinitive

1. He is too weak to run.
2. I want a knife to peel the vegetables.
3. He had a large family to support.
4. She has no pen to write a cheque.
5. He was glad to hear of my success.
6. He is believed to have died from heart attack.
7. I expect to pass next year.
8. She is reported to have married lately.

By using Participle

1. Drawing the sword, he attacked the enemy.
2. Having no teeth, he could not eat nuts.
3. Returning home, I saw a black dog.
4. Having resolved firmly, he never smoked.
5. Having completed the letter, she posted it.
6. Disappointed, he gave up the job.
7. Turning to the right, you will find my house.
8. Tired of riding, she went to bed.
9. Hearing no answer, we rang the bell again.
10. Having been stabbed, Ceasar died from the wounds.

By using Nominative Absolute

1. The sun having risen, fog disappeared.
2. Archna being late, the teacher punished her.
3. The letter having been written, I posted it soon.
4. The time being over, we handed over the note books.
5. It being cloudly, we went on picnic.
6. The rain being scanty this year, sugar is dear in the market.
7. His uncle having died, he inherited the property.
8. Despite her father being rich, Rashmi was not proud.
9. The Ganga being our sacred river, we should keep it clean.

By using Preposition before Gerund or Noun
1. He was justified in killing his enemy.
2. She insisted on going to the market.
3. He won praise for saving the life of the prince.
4. We were informed of the absence of the teacher.
5. The girl with long hair, is the cousin of my wife.
6. There is no doubt about his stealing my book.
7. He is fond of reading comics.
8. I heard of his being wounded.
9. We all were happy at the safe return of all.
10. I paid huge amount for a new house.

By using Noun or Phrase in Apposition
1. Suniti, the daughter of a doctor, stood first in the college.
2. Mr. Sinha, an engineer, works in the Hydel department.
3. Harsh, a famous poet, writes love poetry.
4. Nanda, a great builder, has built a number of apartments.
5. He bought a very costly picture, a work by a most famous artist of India.

By using Adverbs or Adverbial Phrase
1. He replied back in no time.
2. He saved money wisely.
3. I escaped from the den of the gangsters luckily.
4. I got help from my friends unexpectedly.
5. I shall return tonight before long.
6. Undoubtely, I shall get through the examination.
7. She went to college hurriedly.
8. She will certainly go to the states next year.

By using Adjective or And
1. I am buying a very costly house next week.
2. A young girl entered the room.
3. She was kind and generous.
4. Why are you nervous and sad?

WORK BOOK EXERCISE (B)
1. The student admitted to have been absent.
   Or
   The student admitted his absence.
2. I am not aware of his profession.
3. I don't know his name.
4. I cannot recall his residence.
5. I have no faith in her promise to help me.
6. Her success is certain.
   Or
   She will certainly succeed.
7. My faith in his success is firm.
8. Your absence makes the offence worse.
9. She is sure of securing high marks.
10. She persisted in continuing her study.
11. My father insisted on my joining army.
12. We do not know the reason of her leaving the party suddenly.
13. The soldiers were told the manner of climbing the hill.
14. I expect him to be honest.
15. We hope to be invited.

SYNTHESIS

16. He denied to have sold spurious drugs to the customers.
17. She has certainly two sons.
18. She is expected to qualify Entrance Examination.
19. She appears to be honest.
20. Netaji is believed to have died in air crash.
21. He is alleged to have stolen his brother's jewellery.
22. She is likely to come late.
23. He will certainly be punished tomorrow.
24. He is sure to succeed.
25. Undoubtedly, she will recover from illness.

WORK BOOK EXERCISE (C)

1. Do you know the reason of her arrival earlier?
2. Kabir, a famous poet, was a weaver.
3. I bought a quite large house last year.
4. We came across a soldier in trouble.
5. He invented a stitching machine.
    Or
    He invented a machine used for stitching.
6. Mr Verma, our teacher, is loved by everybody.
    Or
    Everybody loves Mr Verma, our teacher.
7. The class room is not a place to play.
8. We committed a quite serious mistake.
9. Do you know the time of your father's departure in the morning?
10. The boys, living near my house, are honest.
11. The tired man could not do work well.
12. We undertook a tiring journey.
13. I was the first man to hear his name on the radio.
14. He has a large family to educate.
15. He has some bills to pay.
16. They admitted the offence committed by them last night.
17. You cannot believe a dishonest person.
18. We undertook a tiring journey to Gwalior.
19. In the street, we saw a beggar begging from door to door.
20. The man wounded in an accident died last night.
21. The police discovered the weapon used to kill the victim.
22. Air, the cheapest thing in the world, is the first necessity of life.
23. Childhood is the time to learn good habits.
24. I know the reason of his failure.
25. The time of his arrival has been announced.
26. I remember very well the year of his retirement.
27. These students hailing from Bihar, are very hard working.
28. The offence, she committed intentionally, is unpardonable.
29. The good deeds, done by men in life, live after them.
30. Malini repaid the debt incurred by her father.

Work Book Exercise (D)

1. After having passed high school examination, I got a job.
2. He takes dinner early to avoid sickness.
   Or
   He takes dinner early so as not to get sick.
3. Seeing the police, the thief fled immediately.
4. While sitting on the grass, he was bitten by a snake.
5. Being late, he was punished.
6. The weather being unpleasant, we did not go out.
7. Being insulted, she left the room.
8. Being over powered by the enemy, he was stabbed.
9. Inspite of possessing huge wealth, he is not happy.
10. By going out, you will catch cold.
11. Without working hard, you will fail.
12. Without examining the paper carefully, you can not give your opinion.
13. He is too lazy to be a player.
14. Depending on the weather, we may go tomorrow.
15. Every sunday he goes to Delhi to see his sick brother.
16. He is too weak to walk.
17. He did the work in accordance with my advice.
18. He is working hard to join the army.
19. He is kind enough to help everybody.
20. I shall leave the room with your permission.
21. The work was done in my presence.
22. He is honest enough not to deceive you.
23. Turning to right, you will see a tall building.
24. While going to school, he was caught in the rain.
25. Since retirement, his father has been idle.
26. He drove fast enough to overtake us.
27. Inspite of success in life, he is humble.
28. He is too clever to see through your tricks.
29. Your sorrow is too deep for tears.
30. This house is so small for me.

Work Book Exercise (E)

1. Entering the Mall, the lady went straight to the manager.
2. Archana lost her very costly purse containing a lot of cash.
3. He was punished for coming late.
4. Small families are certainly not an advantage now.
5. Drinking is injurious to health.
6. He has some new clothes in the box.
7. He was not afraid of telling a lie.
8. Reaching Shimla, we went to our hotel.
9. Yesterday, my brother and Rohan went to Chandigarh.
10. I could notice her cleverness.
11. It being very hot, I did not go out.
12. The train being late, We reached home late.

SYNTHESIS 425

13. My father did not wisely sell the house.
14. While walking in the garden, they enjoyed themselves.
15. Inspite of having no money, Rohit succeeded in his aim.
16. You will pass by working hard.
17. The speech having ended, we went for dinner.
18. He had no house to sell.
19. He was arrested for firing at his friend.
20. She earns a lot of money by running a beauty parlour.
21. Ashoka, a great Emperor, became compassionate after the battle of Kalinga.
22. Walking in the garden, he saw a beggar, unable to walk.
23. Arriving at the party, he was pleased to meet all of his friends.
24. We come to the institute to study English.
25. While driving, Deepa heard Reena humming a song.
26. Inspite of being threatened, I am not afraid of speaking the truth.
27. He fired at his enemy in dark to kill him.
28. I was glad to be told that he was successful.
29. The child was punished for breaking the tinted pane while playing cricket.
30. We were delighted to see him buying mangoes.

Part III

WORK BOOK EXERCISE (A)

1. He is intelligent but careless.
2. He can succeed but he will not work hard.
3. Morning walk is a good exercise, therefore, everybody should walk.
4. He came late otherwise, he would have enjoyed music.
5. Walk fast and you will catch bus.
6. Wait here otherwise, he will not meet you.
7. The bus was slow, so he reached late.
8. You are a liar and so is your brother.
9. She is both smart and honest.
10. Neither be a borrower nor be a lender.
11. You may be either correct or wrong.
12. She comes on foot so she is often late.
13. Stand outside or come in.
14. Weather was not fair yet we went on picnic.
15. She came and consoled me.

WORK BOOK EXERCISE (B)

1. She came late, so she was punished.
2. It is very cold out side, therefore I cannot go.
3. She is intelligent but dishonest.
4. She was ill yet she came.
5. Work hard or you will fail.
6. Be neither angry nor rash.
7. Besides being dishonest, he is a fool.
8. He is handsome as well as smart.
   Or
   He is handsome and smart too.
9. He is intelligent but careless.
10. He can succeed but he will not work hard.
11. Morning walk is a good exercise, therefore, everybody should walk.
12. He came late otherwise, he would have got the bus.

13. Walk fast and you will catch bus.
14. Wait here otherwise, he will not meet you.
15. The bus was slow, so he reached late.
16. You play piano and so does your brother.
17. She is not only obedient but also polite.
18. Be neither a borrower not a lender
19. Both, Richa and Esha cannot sing.
20. Everything decays but truth survives.
21. He will pass and I doubt it.
22. I went to Indore and I spent a few days there.
23. I requested her to lend me some money but she refused.
24. Come by car and we shall take you to temple.
25. He took bath and he put on new clothes.
26. He fell off the stairs and so he died from injuries.
27. One word more and I shall kill you.
28. Either you write or I must write to father.
29. He wants to pass and so he is working hard.
30. Neither Sona nor her husband can sing.

Or

Sona cannot sing and her husband cannot sing either.

Or

Sona cannot sing and neither can her husband.

Cumulative Exercises

Exercise 1

1. Being occupied with important matters, he had no leisure to see visitors.
2. The dog bit the man, a notorious burglar.
3. The court listened silently to the decision given by the judge.
4. His father being dead, he had to support his widowed mother.
5. The Pathan took out a knife to frighten the old man.
6. It must be done at any cost.
7. He must apologise to escape punishment.
8. Delighted with the intelligence and brightness of the scholars, he overlooked the fact of their knowing few things by heart.
9. The stable door being open, the horse was stolen.
10. He was unavoidably absent at the meeting.

Exercise 2

1. He failed, nevertheless he persevered.
2. He was obstinate; therefore, he was punished.
3. The harvest truly is plenteous, but the labourers are few.
4. The train was wrecked, but no one was hurt.
5. The river is deep and swift, so I am afraid to dive into it.
6. You must either play hockey, or you must play football.
7. A is equal to B and B is equal to C, therefore, A is equal to C.
8. We must catch the 6 o'clock train and there being only half an hour left, we must start without further delay.
9. It was a stormy night, yet we ventured out.
10. A timid dog is dangerous, for he always suspects ill-treatment and tries to protect himself by snapping.

SYNTHESIS

Exercise 3

1. That you are drunk, aggravates your offence.
2. The consequence of his carelessness was that the game was lost.
3. This is the safe, where she keeps her ornaments.
4. As men sow, so shall they reap.
5. I am as strong as you are.
6. I cannot adequately express how sorry I am.
7. All the plans, which he has for earning money quickly, have failed.
8. Let us be honest as long as life lasts.
9. He was so tired that he could scarcely stand.
10. Have you never heard that honesty is the best policy.

Previous Years' Questions

1. Being the eldest, Radha had to look after her parents.
2. She decorated the room, so that it might look beautiful.
3. Had I not gone early, the work could have been finished.
4. I was given a prize for scoring the highest marks in my class.
5. Despite being told not to drive back home late in the night, he did so.
6. The gentleman sitting in the front row, is my father.
7. He is too clever to be fooled.
8. Tired of playing, he sat down to rest.
9. It is so hot outside, that you cannot go out.
10. Neither my brother, nor my sister is a doctor.
11. The tutor has come to teach my son.
12. The man would neither agree to my suggestion, nor leave me in peace.
13. Although it rained a lot, yet we enjoyed our holiday.
14. The engine stopped because it had heated up.
15. Although they were tired, they worked late into the night.
16. He slept early but he woke up late.
17. He was on medication so he felt drowsy.
18. She was very angry yet she said nothing.
19. The coffee was too hot for us to drink.
20. The wind was strong enough to blow people away.
21. You are too old to continue to work.
22. The print was clear enough to be read easily.
23. The child was too small to walk.
24. It was hot enough to cook food with the sun's rays.
25. The book is too heavy for me to carry.
26. You are old enough to know better.
27. She was too shocked to react.
28. The essay was good enough to earn full marks.

CHAPTER 7

Transformation

Transformation is a process of changing sentences into various forms given below.

Part I Simple Sentences

Change of a simple sentence to a complex sentence is made by expanding a phrase or words into a subordinate clause.
- (A) Noun phrase/Noun to Noun clause.
- (B) Adjective phrase/Adjective to Adjective clause.
- (C) Adverb phrase/Adverb to Adverb clause.

Part II Complex Sentences

Change of a complex sentence to a simple sentence is made by replacing a subordinate clause into a word or phrase as follows:
- (A) Noun clause to Noun phrase, Noun, Infinitive, Gerund, case in apposition etc.
- (B) Adjective clause to Adjective phrase/Adjective, Participle, Infinitive, case in apposition etc.
- (C) Adverb clause to Adverbial phrase/Adverb, Participle, Infinitive etc.

Part III Compound Sentences
- (A) Change of a simple sentence to a compound sentence.
- (B) Change of a complex sentence to a compound sentence.

Note Students are again reminded of the instructions that all sentences simple, complex and compound have bearing on Inter-relationship of the clauses.

Part IV Miscellaneous Sentences
- (A) Interchange of degree of comparison.
- (B) Interchange of affirmative and negative sentences.
- (C) Interchange of assertive and interrogative sentences.
- (D) Interchange of exclamatory and assertive sentences.
- (E) Sentences expressing condition.   (F) Sentences expressing contrast.
- (G) Removal of adverb 'too'.   (H) Interchange of Parts of Speech.
- (I) Interchange of voice.
- (J) Change of Narration.

(Refer to chapters on Voice and Narration in the book)

Part I : Simple to Complex

A simple sentence can be changed to a complex sentence by expanding phrase or a group of words into a subordinate clause as explained below :
- (A) Noun phrase/Noun to Noun clause.
- (B) Adjective phrase/Adjective to Adjective clause.
- (C) Adverb phrase/Adverb to Adverb clause.

(A) **Noun phrase is a group of words that does the work of a noun (explanation). Study the following examples :**
   (i) He hopes to succeed.   *(object to verb)*
   (ii) Truth cannot perish.   *(subject to verb)*
   (iii) Pay attention to his words.   *(object to preposition)*
   (iv) My faith, about his success, is firm.   *(case in apposition to Noun)*
   (v) It is unfortunate to be cheated by friends.   *(case in apposition to a pronoun 'it')*
   (vi) My wish is to do something useful.   *(complement of a verb 'is')*

   Change of Noun Phrase/Noun to a Noun Clause:
   (i) He hopes <u>that he will succeed</u>.
   (ii) <u>What is true</u> cannot perish.
   (iii) Pay attention <u>to what he says</u>.
   (iv) My faith, <u>that he will succeed</u>, is firm.
   (v) It is unfortunate <u>that one is cheated by friends</u>.
   (vi) My wish is <u>that I should do something useful</u>.

(B) **Adjective phrase is a group of words that does the work of an Adjective (qualification).**

   Study the following examples :
   (i) He is a student <u>of great promise</u>.
   (ii) I met my friend <u>living in Mumbai</u>.
   (iii) They found a dead body <u>covered with a white sheet</u>.
   (iv) He is a man <u>of few words</u>.
   (v) Mohan, <u>with a lot of wealth</u>, is a miser.

   Change of Adjective Phrase/Adjective to an Adjective Clause :
   (i) He is a student, <u>who holds a great promise</u>.
   (ii) I met my friend, <u>who is living in Mumbai</u>.
   (iii) They found a dead body, <u>which was covered with white sheet</u>.
   (iv) He is a man, <u>who speaks a few words</u>.
   (v) Mohan, <u>who has a lot of wealth</u>, is a miser.

(C) **Adverb phrase is a group of words that does the work of an adverb (modification).**

   Study the following examples :
   (i) I shall do it <u>in your presence</u>.
   (ii) Do not go <u>till I return</u>.
   (iii) He went there <u>to buy books</u>.
   (iv) He was blamed <u>for telling a lie</u>.
   (v) <u>For all his wealth</u>, he is unhappy.

Change the Adverbial Phrase/Adverb into Adverb Clause :
(i) I shall do it, <u>when you are present</u>.
(ii) Do not go <u>until I return</u>.
(iii) He went there <u>so that he might buy books</u>.
(iv) He was blamed <u>as he told a lie</u>.
(v) <u>Although he is wealthy</u>, he is unhappy.

Note Subordinate clauses can be introduced by subordinating conjunctions as given in chapter on Clauses.

WORK BOOK EXERCISE (A)
(Simple to Noun Clause)

Directions *Change the following simple sentences into complex sentences by using Noun clause.*

1. He confessed his guilt.
2. All depends on his future.
3. His age is not known.
4. Speak the truth.
5. His silence proved his complicity in the crime.
6. He appears to be running temperature.
7. He denied to have murdered.
8. He is believed to be honest.
9. She informed me of her arrival.
10. The news of his death is wrong.
11. Subhash Chandra Bose is believed to have died in Japan.
12. I have already heard his statement.
13. He is sure to have been punished.
14. He is expected to give me money.
15. Mohit may do anything.
16. I wish you to be successful in life.
17. He wishes to be a very rich person.
18. There is no truth in his remarks.
19. The place of his hiding is likely to be discovered very soon.
20. We believe the news to be true.
21. Your innocence is beyond any doubt.
22. I have long doubted his honesty.
23. I have long suspected his guilt.
24. His father is likely to give him punishment.
25. It is high time to leave India.
26. His resignation is out of the question.

TRANSFORMATION

WORK BOOK EXERCISE (B)

Directions *Change the following complex sentences into simple ones by using Noun clause.*

1. I have long suspected him to be a thief.
2. The news of his arrival has not been intimated.
3. Her remarks about my failure were disgusting.
4. Truth is eternal.
5. She is expected to learn good manners.
6. Pay heed to my instructions.
7. She has a desire to learn swimming.
8. Her wish is to do social work in future.
9. He is reported to have lost his reputation.
10. I kept on wondering about her success.
11. Everybody is responsible for his deeds.
12. His fall is certain.
13. She did not inform me of his profession.
14. Nobody knows his whereabouts.
15. She jumped at my offer.

WORK BOOK EXERCISE (C)
(Simple to Adjective Clause)

Directions *Change the following simple sentences into complex sentences by using Adjective clause.*

1. I bought a very cheap pen yesterday.
2. I saw a beggar begging from door to door.
3. This is my native village.
4. Do you know the reason of his failure?
5. The value of exercise is great.
6. His offence is unpardonable.
7. They came across the students smoking by the road side.
8. A tired man cannot do work well.
9. This is not the manner to please your boss.
10. He gave me money to spend.
11. The pen given by him is very cheap.
12. I have no friend to talk to.
13. He was the last to arrive at the party.
14. He gave me a fake news.
15. How can you believe a dishonest person?

WORK BOOK EXERCISE (D)

Directions *Change the following simple sentences to complex sentences by using Adjective clause.*

1. We committed a quite serious mistake.
2. They found a rare piece of diamond.
3. We undertook quite a tiring journey.
4. The tired man could not do work well.
5. The dog felled the burning candle.
6. The murder committed by him ruined his life.
7. He invented a machine for stitching.
8. He saw a brightly burning candle in the corner.
9. A class room is not the place to play.
10. He has a large family to educate.
11. He was the last man to attend the funeral.
12. Do you know the time of your father's departure?
13. Do you know the reason of her arrival earlier?
14. Nobody appreciated her behaviour at the party.
15. I was informed of his residence.
16. Kabir, a weaver, was a famous poet.
17. Everybody loves Mr Verma, our teacher.
18. The boys living near my house are honest.
19. The place of the cremation of the leader was thronged with people.
20. She told me the reason of her being late.
21. Shakespeare, a great dramatist, wrote a number of plays.
22. The girl with long hair is a cousin of my wife.
23. They live just near the by pass on the outskirts of the city.
24. The players awarded cash prize by the President were present at the function.
25. The offence committed by them intentionally is unpardonable.
26. I paid the debt incurred by my father.

WORK BOOK EXERCISE (E)
(Simple to Adverb Clause)

Directions *Change the following simple sentences into complex sentences by using Adverb clause.*

1. For all his experience he is still not efficient.
2. He cannot succeed without hard work.
3. On being scolded he left the room.
4. The signal having been given the train started.
5. I shall be very glad to help him.
6. He is too simple to win the game.

TRANSFORMATION 433

7. He was punished on account of his mischief.
8. The work was done in my presence.
9. Despite his wealth, he is not respected.
10. You must wait here, till the arrival of your father.
11. Notwithstanding his poverty, he is honest.
12. Do it to the best of your ability.
13. Nobody must expect to become rich without hard work.
14. My heart is too full for words.
15. With a view to continuing his higher study, he borrowed money from the bank.
16. Being very fat, she is undergoing slimming treatment.
17. In comparison with the tiger the cat is swifter.
18. I am thankful to you for helping my brother.
19. But for the timely help, he would have died from burns.
20. She is kind enough to help everybody.
21. He did not stop working before his success.
22. They were afraid of being caught in the shower.
23. You must act in accordance with the rules.
24. Considering his capability, he was promoted.
25. Weather permitting, we shall leave for Shimla.
26. Water is too hot to drink.
27. All being well, I shall meet her parents today.
28. I shall be glad to be invited.
29. I would be glad to be there.
30. I would have been glad to have been there.
31. Your behaviour was too much for the guests.
32. She is too good for me.
33. He was quick enough to overtake me.
34. It, being a junk food, we did not taste it.
35. But for our poverty, we would have been a happy family.

Part II : Complex to Simple

A complex sentence can be changed to simple sentence by contracting a subordinate clause into a phrase or a word.

(A) Noun clause to Noun phrase/Noun, Infinitive, Participle, Gerund, Case in apposition etc.

(B) Adjective clause to Adjective phrase/Adjective (Infinitive/Participle, Case in apposition etc.

(C) Adverb clause to Adverb phrase/Adverb, Participle, Infinitive etc.

Note We have already studied the examples in the foregoing explanation.

WORK BOOK EXERCISE (A)

Directions *Change the following complex sentences to simple sentences by replacing Noun clause.*

1. It is much regretted that she is dishonest.
2. He admitted that his enemy was generous.
3. I know, where your brother lives.
4. Pay heed to what your officers say.
5. Never say what is wrong.
6. We believe that God exists.
7. I expect that he will pass.
8. It is unfortunate that he died young.
9. He asked me, why I gave money to his brother.
10. He confessed that he had met her last evening.
11. I agreed that I would teach him.
12. I informed him that she had gone.
13. It appears that he has been scolded by his father.
14. I ordered him that he should leave the room at once.
15. People are certain that he is honest.

WORK BOOK EXERCISE (B)

Directions *Change the following complex sentences to simple sentences by replacing Noun clause.*

1. He confessed that he was guilty.
2. I do not care for what she has remarked.
3. Mohit may do what he likes.
4. I have long doubted if he is honest.
5. The rumour, that he has died, is baseless.
6. How old he is, is not known.
7. What she said is disgusting.
8. The fact that he was silent, proved his complicity in the crime.
9. He denied that he had murdered.
10. It appears that she is absent today.
11. It was alleged that she had abused him.
12. She wanted to know what his name was.
13. My hope is that I should earn a lot of money.
14. It is sure that he has been punished.
15. It is expected that he will give me money.
16. All depend on what his future is.
17. I don't believe in what she said.
18. I agreed to what he proposed.

TRANSFORMATION

🔎 WORK BOOK EXERCISE (C)

Directions *Change the following complex sentences to simple sentences by replacing Adjective clause.*

1. He is not such a man as can be trusted.
2. A student, who is careless cannot succeed.
3. He is not a man, who will cheat anyone.
4. He has a large house in which he lives.
5. The statement they made is false.
6. You can have anything that you like.
7. Dogs that bark seldom bite.
8. I know the reason, why he could not succeed.
9. Milton, who was a famous poet, wrote 'Paradise Lost'.
10. The train, that connects New Delhi, is late.
11. Childhood is a time when good habits can be learnt.
12. The man, who was wounded, died last night.
13. Those, who are healthy, do not need a doctor.
14. The good deeds that man does, live after him.
15. The place, where the leader was cremated, was thronged with people.

🔎 WORK BOOK EXERCISE (D)

Directions *Change the following complex sentences to simple sentences by replacing Adjective clause.*

1. Yesterday, I bought a book, which is very cheap.
2. You cannot believe a person, who is dishonest.
3. Those, who are hard working, succeed in life.
4. A soldier, who was wounded, was lying in the field.
5. The players, who were tired, could not perform well.
6. The monster, who was proud of his power, was defeated by Hercules.
7. In the street we saw a beggar, who was begging from door-to-door.
8. The man, who was wounded in the accident, died last night.
9. The police discovered the weapon, which was used to kill the victim.
10. The magic ball, which was meant for the king, was eaten by the jester.
11. Seema was the last person, who left for home.
12. My uncle was the first man, who heard her name on the radio.
13. He has some bills, which he must pay in cash.
14. I have no friend, whom I can talk to.
15. Childhood is a time, when one can teach good habits to children.
16. The time, when he will come tomorrow, is not certain.
17. All of us were told the reason, why he had become rich suddenly.
18. I remember very well the year, when he retired.

19. The people, who reside in our colony, were shouting for justice.
20. Rathore, who is our captain, scored fifty runs.
21. Edison, who was a great scientist, invented electricity.
22. We visited the Taj, which is a unique building.
23. I shall travel by the Taj Express, which goes to Agra direct.
24. The students, who hail from Bihar, are very hard working.
25. Tomorrow, I will board a train, which connects Udaipur.
26. The news, which the Voice of America broadcast, is true.
27. I met a poet, whom I had already known.
28. Mr. Gupta will buy the house, which I built only last year.
29. The book, which I had lost, has been found out.
30. Those, who live in glass houses, should not throw stones at others.

WORK BOOK EXERCISE (E)

Directions *Change the following complex sentences to simple sentences by replacing Adverb clause.*

1. He did as I wished.
2. We get up when it is morning.
3. When we had finished work, we went home.
4. As he saw me, he ran away.
5. While she was walking in the garden, a stranger addressed her.
6. He is so kind that he helps everybody.
7. We went home after the teacher had arrived.
8. He wrote as fast as he could.
9. He will not return money, unless he is threatned.
10. I succeeded better than I expected.
11. When the thief was found out, he was arrested.
12. Although she was punished, she was not ashamed.
13. You can talk as much as you like.
14. Poor as he is, he is honest.
15. Notwithstanding that he is honest, he is not hard working.
16. If they had not helped me, I would not have gained success.
17. He ran fast so that he might catch taxi.
18. As she ran fast, the teacher declared her first.
19. As he is poor, we will help him.
20. If God wills, you will succeed.
21. If I make a promise, I will stick to it.
22. Everybody complimented him because he had succeeded.
23. He has come to Chandigarh so that capable doctors may treat him.
24. As it was fine, we left for picnic.
25. While they were watching TV, their friends visited them.

TRANSFORMATION

26. While she was crossing the road, a scooter knocked her down.
27. Sania is so slow that she cannot be a good tennis player.
28. She is too clever to see through your tricks.
29. Her sorrow is so deep that it cannot be expressed in tears.
30. He will stick to his job lest he should starve.
31. When the signal was given, the train started.
32. Since I arrived in Chennai, I have not had any rest.
33. The project was not launched because no money was given to me.
34. This house is so small that I cannot live in it.
35. Since the weather was very pleasant, we went on a long drive.

Part III : Simple and Complex to Compound

(A) Change of simple sentences to compound sentences.
(B) Change of complex sentences to compound sentences.

(A) Simple sentence can be converted to compound sentence by changing phrase and a co-ordinating clause:
   (i) Noun phrase/Noun to co-ordinate clause.
   (ii) Adjective phrase/Adjective to co-ordinate clause.
   (iii) Adverb phrase/Adverb to co-ordinate clause.

(B) Complex sentence can be converted to compound sentences by changing subordinate clause to co-ordinating clause :
   (i) Noun clause to co-ordinate clause.
   (ii) Adjective clause to co-ordinate clause.
   (iii) Adverb clause to co-ordinate clause.

Note (a) Co-ordinate clause is also called Independent clause.
   (b) We have already studied co-ordinating conjunctions in chapter on Clauses and Synthesis.
   They are : and, but, yet, still, nevertheless, whereas, while, or, otherwise, else, or else, nor, as well as.

A. Change of Simple Sentences into Compound

Some examples have been worked out for the students:
1. Climbing up the stairs, he fell down.
   He was climbing up the stairs and he fell down.
2. Being disappointed, he left the job.
   He was disappointed, so he left the job.
3. Having taken bath, he put on new clothes.
   He had taken bath and put on new clothes.
4. Inspite of being rich, he is not happy.
   He is rich but he is not happy.
5. By running very fast, you can catch the bus.
   Run very fast and catch the bus.

6. It being very hot we left for Nainital.
   (a) We left for Nainital for it was very hot.
   (b) It was very hot so, we left for Nainital.
7. Arriving at home, she found her son missing.
   She arrived at home and she found her son missing.
8. Without respecting others, you will not be respected.
   Respect others otherwise, you will not be respected.
9. For all his knowledge, he could not earn money.
   He had knowledge but he could not earn money.
10. Being stabbed fatally, he died.
    He was stabbed fatally, so he died.

WORK BOOK EXERCISE (A)

Directions *Change the following simple sentences into compound sentences.*

1. I shall leave the room with your permission.
2. For all his knowledge, he is a fool.
3. He was punished on account of his fault.
4. Despite his wealth, he is not respected.
5. He worked hard to secure high percentage of marks.
6. On his return, we asked him many questions.
7. In addition to Mathematics, he also teaches Hindi.
8. I am thankful to you for sending me money.
9. Besides being rich, he is learned also.
10. Notwithstanding my request, he left Jhansi.
11. He was sitting in the drawing room watching TV.
12. With all his contacts, he never used unfair means.
13. He must admit his fault on pain of punishment.
14. He must work hard to secure high percentage of marks.
15. He was dismissed for embezzlement.
16. The weather being very fine, we left for swimming.
17. In the event of his death, his son will inherit the property.
18. He did not follow the rules out of ignorance.
19. To my surprise, he could not qualify examination.
20. Only the rich can afford such a costly treatment.
21. Do this to escape suffering.
22. He went by car fearing rain.
23. Without being invited, I shall not go.
24. Neither of the statements is correct.
25. Do not desire without deserving.

TRANSFORMATION

(B) Change of Complex Sentences into Compound

Some examples have been worked out for the students:

1. When she arrived at home, she found her son missing.
   She arrived at home and found her son missing.
2. While he was climbing up the stairs, he fell down.
   He was climbing up the stairs and fell down.
3. As he was disappointed, he left the job.
   He was disappointed so he left the job.
4. When he had taken bath, he put on new clothes.
   He had taken bath and put on new clothes.
5. Although he is rich, he is not happy.
   He is rich but he is not happy.
6. If you run very fast, you can catch the bus.
   Run very fast and catch the bus.
7. As it was very hot, we left for Nainital.
   (a) We left for Nainital for it was very hot.
   (b) It was very hot so, we left for Nainital.
8. If you do not respect others, you will not be respected.
   Respect others otherwise, you will not be respected.
9. Although he had knowledge, he could not earn money.
   He had knowledge but he could not earn money.
10. As he was stabbed fatally, he died.
    He was stabbed fatally, so he died.

WORK BOOK EXERCISE (B)

Directions *Change the following complex sentences to simple sentences replacing Subordinate clause.*

1. Although she is sick, she will come.
2. If you come by car, we will take you to temple.
3. As it was cold, we did not go out.
4. When the thief was found out, he was arrested.
5. When she arrived, everybody welcomed her.
6. If you do not stop smoking, you will suffer from lung disease.
7. I shall not go, unless I am invited.
8. If you listen seriously, I will tell you all.
9. I am glad that he has recovered from illness.
10. I have found the pen that I had lost.
11. He had a dog that was very faithful.
12. Unlucky as he is, he is never disappointed.
13. (a) Do this lest you should suffer.
    (b) If you do not do this, you will suffer.
14. However intelligent he may be, he cannot succeed.
15. If he had not given me money, I would not have started business.

16. If he were at home, I would meet him.
17. If he is at home, I shall give him money.
18. In case he dies, his son will inherit his property.
19. He must work hard so that he may pass.
20. He could afford to spend something but he spent more.

Part IV : Interchange of Sentences

(A) Interchange of Degree
(B) Interchange of Affirmative and Negative Sentence
(C) Interchange of Assertive and Interrogative Sentence
(D) Interchange of Exclamatory and Assertive Sentence
(E) Sentences Expressing Condition
(F) Sentences Expressing Contrast
(G) Removal of Adverb 'too'
(H) Interchange of Parts of Speech

A. Interchange of Degrees without Changing the Meaning

Rule I

1. Comparative – She is more intelligent than her brother is.
   Positive – Her brother is not so intelligent as she is.
2. Comparative – She is not more intelligent than her brother is.
   Positive – Her brother is as intelligent as she is.
3. Positive – She is not so intelligent as he.
   Comparative – He is more intelligent than she.

Rule II

4. Positive – Very few writers in India are as famous as RK Narayan.
   Comparative – RK Narayan is more famous than most of the Indian writers.
   Superlative – RK Narayan is one of the most famous Indian writers.

Rule III

5. Positive – No other writer in India is so famous as RK Narayan.
   Comparative – RK Narayan is more famous than any other writer in India.
   Superlative – RK Narayan is the most famous of all the writers in India.
6. Positive – No other bowler in India is so famous as Kapil Dev.
   Comparative – Kapil Dev is more famous than any other bowler in India.
   Superlative – Kapil Dev is the most famous of all the bowlers in India.

Rule IV

7. Superlative – Varanasi is not the oldest of all the cities in UP.
   Comparative – Varanasi is not older than some other cities in UP.
   Positive – Some other cities in UP are at least as old as Varanasi.

TRANSFORMATION

More Solved Examples

1. Positive – Rustam was as powerful as his brother.
   Comparative – Rustam's brother was not more powerful than Rustam.
2. Superlative – Shivaji was one of the greatest warriors of India.
   Comparative – Shivaji was greater than most of the warriors in India.
3. Positive – Very few countries are as rich in heritage as India.
   Comparative – India is richer in heritage than most of the countries.
4. Comparative – Eagle flies higher than any other bird.
   Positive – No other bird flies as high as eagle.
   Superlative – Eagle flies highest of all the birds.
5. Positive – No one else is so honest as our principal.
   Comparative – Our principal is more honest than anybody else.
   Superlative – Our principal is the most honest of all.
6. Superlative – She is the most successful teacher in our college.
   Positive – No other teacher in our college is as successful as she is.
   Comparative – She is more successful than any other teacher in our college.
7. Superlative – She is one of the most successful business women in our country.
   Comparative – She is more successful than most of the business women in our country.
   Positive – Very few business women in our country are as successful as she is.
8. Comparative – It is better to lend than borrow.
   Positive – Borrowing is not as good as lending.
9. Superlative – The Ambanis are not the richest of all the Indian industrialist.
   Comparative – The Ambanis are not richer than some other Indian Industrialists.
   Positive – Some other Indian industrialists are at least as rich as the Ambanis.
10. Positive – No other legendary hero was so valorous as Arjun.
    Superlative – Arjun was the most valorous of all the legendary heroes.

B. Interchange of Affirmative and Negative Sentences

Study the following examples:

1. Affirmative – Only he is responsible for my failure in life.
   Negative – None, but he, is responsible for my failure in life.
2. Negative – He could not climb up the tree.
   Affirmative – He failed to climb up the tree.
3. Affirmative – As soon as she arrived, she went to bed.
   Negative – No sooner did she arrive than she went to bed.

4.	Negative	– If you do not work hard, You will fail.
	Affirmative	– Unless you work hard, you will fail.
5.	Affirmative	– He is an honest person.
	Negative	– He is not a dishonest person.
6.	Affirmative	– I was doubtful of his success.
	Negative	– I was not sure of his success.
7.	Affirmative	– She is more intelligent than he.
	Negative	– He is not so intelligent as she.
8.	Affirmative	– Netaji was a greater freedom fighter than any other leader.
	Negative	– No other leader was so great freedom fighter as Netaji.
9.	Affirmative	– She is too clever to be cheated.
	Negative	– She is so clever that she cannot be cheated.
10.	Affirmative	– He is sometimes angry.
	Negative	– He is not always angry.
11.	Affirmative	– Everybody admits that he is very helpful.
	Negative	– Nobody denies that he is very helpful.
12.	Affirmative	– You must have given money to your poor friend.
	Negative	– You must not have failed to give money to your friend.
13.	Affirmative	– I will always remember you in my life.
	Negative	– I will never forget you in my life.
14.	Affirmative	– It is unlikely that he will give you money.
	Negative	– It is not likely that he will give you money.
15.	Affirmative	– Everybody cried.
	Negative	– (a) There was none, who did not cry.
		(b) There was none, but cried.
16.	Affirmative	– I love my children.
	Negative	– I am not without love for my children.
17.	Affirmative	– He is bound to succeed.
	Negative	– He cannot but succeed.
18.	Affirmative	– It always pours, when it rains.
	Negative	– It never rains but pours.
19.	Affirmative	– I saw her last, when I visited Pune.
	Negative	– I have not seen her, since I visited Pune.
20.	Affirmative	– I met him in 2009.
	Negative	– I have not met him since 2009.
21.	Affirmative	– The fort was burnt before it was surrendered.
	Negative	– The fort was not surrendered until it was burnt.
22.	Affirmative	– It is often difficult.
	Negative	– It is not always easy.
23.	Affirmative	– Look before you leap.
	Negative	– Don't leap before you look.

TRANSFORMATION

24. Affirmative   – I met Malini five years ago.
    Negative   – I have not met Malini for five years.
25. Affirmative   – Always speak the truth.
    Negative   – Never tell a lie.
26. Affirmative   – Every one has feelings.
    Negative   – There is no man, who has no feelings.
27. Affirmative   – He always began a job, which he completed.
    Negative   – He never began a job, which he did not complete.
28. Negative   – There is no smoke without fire.
    Affirmative   – Fire causes smoke.
29. Negative   – There is no rose without a thorn.
    Affirmative   – Every rose has a thorn.
30. Affirmative   – All those boys are intelligent.
    Negative   – None of the boys is/are dull.
31. Affirmative   – We found a few students.
    Negative   – We did not find many students.
32. Affirmative   – I am very tired.
    Negative   – I am not a little tired.
33. Affirmative   – She accepted my offer.
    Negative   – She did not refuse my offer.
34. Negative   – If you had not helped me, I would have failed.
    Affirmative   – But for your help, I would have failed.
35. Affirmative   – Work or perish.
    Negative   – If you do not work, you will perish.
36. Negative   – If you do not pay, you will be refused admission.
    Affirmative   – Unless you pay, you will be refused admission.
37. Affirmative   – If Leena were at home, I would meet her.
    Negative   – Leena is not at home otherwise I would meet her.
38. Affirmative   – She was forbidden to loiter in the gallery.
    Negative   – She was asked not to loiter in the gallery.
39. Affirmative   – Sushma loves her father as much as she loves her mother.
    Negative   – Sushma loves her father no less than her mother.
40. Affirmative   – Raghu has more wealth than common sense.
    Negative   – Raghu does not have as much common sense as he has wealth.
41. Affirmative   – You know her nature as well as her husband does.
    Negative   – Her husband does not know her nature better than you.
42. Affirmative   – He was more worthy of a praise than anyone else.
    Negative   – None else was as worthy of praise as he was.

C. Interchange of Assertive and Interrogative Sentences

Study the following sentences:

1. Assertive   – I gave you money to buy a bike.
   Interrogative   – Did I not give you money to buy a bike?

2. **Interrogative** – Was he not kind to help you?
   Assertive – He was kind enough to help you.
3. **Interrogative** – Who does not like to be praised?
   Assertive – Everybody likes to be praised.
4. **Interrogative** – Who can forget their sacrifice?
   Assertive – Nobody can forget their sacrifice.
5. **Interrogative** – Why waste money on luxuries?
   Assertive – It is foolish to waste money on luxuries.
6. **Assertive** – He could not have achieved success without your help.
   Interrogative – Could he have achieved success without your help?
7. **Assertive** – That is not the manner to do this work.
   Interrogative – Is this the manner to do this work?
8. **Assertive** – No one can be expected to do wrong to his parents.
   Interrogative – Who can be expected to do wrong to his parents?
9. **Interrogative** – What though I have lost a friend for your sake?
   Assertive – It does not matter that I have lost a friend for your sake.
10. **Assertive** – Their glory can never fade.
    Interrogative – When can their glory fade?
11. **Interrogative** – Have I ever refused to give you money?
    Assertive – I have never refused to give you money.
12. **Interrogative** – Why not stay here tonight?
    Assertive – It is better, we should stay here tonight.
13. **Interrogative** – What is the use of going there?
    Assertive – (a) It is no use going there.
    (b) There is no use of going there.
14. **Interrogative** – If you stab him, will he not die?
    Assertive – If you stab him, he will die.
15. **Interrogative** – Why blame him?
    Assertive – It is no use blaming him.
16. **Interrogative** – What is that to me?
    Assertive – It does not matter to me.

D. Interchange of Exclamatory and Assertive Sentences

Study the following sentences:

1. **Exclamatory** – How smart she is!
   Assertive – She is very smart.
2. **Exclamatory** – What a pretty girl she is!
   Assertive – She is a very pretty girl.
3. **Exclamatory** – Oh that, I were a doctor!
   Assertive – I wish, I were a doctor.
4. **Exclamatory** – Alas! He died so young.
   Assertive – It is sad (to think) that he died so young.

TRANSFORMATION

5. Exclamatory – Would that she were here!
   Assertive – I wish, she were here.
6. Exclamatory – Had you but completed your education!
   Assertive – I wish you had completed your education.
7. Assertive – It is very foolish of me to ask for money.
   Exclamatory – How foolish of me to ask for money!
8. Assertive – I wish, I had come here last year.
   Exclamatory – Would that I had come here last year!
9. Exclamatory – Hurrah! we have won the match.
   Assertive – It is a matter of joy that we have won the match.
10. Exclamatory – To think of our living together!
    Assertive – It is strange that we think of living together.
11. Exclamatory – If only I could meet her now!
    Assertive – I wish, I could meet her now.
12. Exclamatory – Alas! we have lost today!
    Assertive – It is sad that we have lost today.
13. Exclamatory – Bravo, well done!
    Assertive – It is brave of you to have done well.
14. Exclamatory – To think of our meeting here!
    Assertive – I never thought of meeting you here.
15. Exclamatory – What a piece of work is man!
    Assertive – Man is a wonderful piece of work.
16. Exclamatory – How wise of you!
    Assertive – It is very wise of you.
17. Exclamatory – Oh to be a queen!
    Assertive – I wish, I were a queen.
18. Exclamatory – Oh to have been a prince!
    Assertive – I wish, I had been a prince!
19. Exclamatory – Our Prime Minister and so weak!
    Assertive – It is shocking that our Prime Minister is so weak.
20. Exclamatory – Such a man and my husband.
    Assertive – It is shocking that such a man is my husband.
21. Exclamatory – What a pity! you have lost.
    Assertive – It is a great pity you have lost.
22. Exclamatory – A child and so bold at this age!
    Assertive – It is wonderful that a child is so bold at this age.
23. Exclamatory – O for a small house to live in Mumbai!
    Assertive – I ardently wish to have a small house to live in Mumbai.
24. Exclamatory – Fie, Fie! you are a cheat.
    Assertive – It is contemptible that you are a cheat.
25. Exclamatory – Alas! that ever a friend should be false.
    Assertive – It is sad that a friend should be false.

E. Sentences Expressing Conditions

1. If/In case you work hard, you will get through.
2. Unless you take medicine, you will not get well.
3. You will get well only if you take medicine.
4. Should you help me, I shall succeed.
5. Were I a doctor, I should treat you.
6. Had you gone there, you would have met her.
7. Supposing you win lottery, how will you spend money?
8. I shall go to the movie provided you allow me.
9. Do it and you will be awarded a prize.
10. Do not be late otherwise /or you will be punished.
11. Have you paid for this book? Then take it.
12. One more game and we will play in the finals.
13. Without investing money, you can't earn profit.
14. By going out, you will catch cold.
15. But for examining me, the doctor could not have diagnosed my illness.
16. I shall give you information, in the event of your keeping it secret.
17. I shall give you information, on the condition that you will not reveal it.

F. Sentences Expressing Contrast

1. Although she is poor, she is honest.
2. Even though she came late, she was not punished.
3. Notwithstanding that she is wealthy, she is a miser.
4. Rich as she is, she is not honest.
5. Admitting that she is learned, she is not proud.
6. However hard you may try, you cannot compete with him.
7. However intelligent she may be, she cannot pass.
8. I shall do it whatever you may say.
9. She was tired, all the same she did not go to bed.
10. He is very strict at the same time, he is loving by Nature.
11. For all that he may say, nobody trusts him.
12. It was raining nevertheless she went away.
13. Even if you run fast, you will not get the train.
14. He was weak indeed, but he could walk.
15. She has married indeed, but she is not happy.
16. Come what may, she will not desist from playing tricks.
17. Much as I would have liked to give her money, I had no means.
18. No matter what they said, he married a girl of her choice.
19. No matter where she is, she will call me up as usual.
20. I must go whether you come with me or not.

TRANSFORMATION

G. Removal of Adverb 'too'

Rewrite the following sentences removing the Adverb 'too':

1. He is too tired to walk.
   He is so tired that he cannot walk.
2. She is too anxious for the safety of her husband.
   She is over anxious for the safety of her husband.
3. It is too cold to go on picnic.
   It is so cold that one cannot go on picnic.
4. The shirt is too loose for my body.
   The shirt is so loose that it does not fit my body.
5. It is too hot.
   It is excessively hot.
6. He is too eager for praise.
   He is over eager for praise.
7. The fort is too high for anyone to climb.
   The fort is so high that no one can climb it.
8. He was too selfish.
   He was selfish beyond limit.
9. My heart is too full for words.
   My heart is so full that I cannot utter a word.
10. He is too fast not to catch up with you any moment.
    He is so fast that he can catch up with you any moment.
11. She is too good for me.
    She is so good that I am no match for her.
12. This house is too small for me.
    This house is so small that it cannot serve my purpose.
13. This adversity is too much for anyone.
    This adversity is so harsh that no one can bear it.
14. My teacher is too fat.
    My teacher is fatter than she should be.
15. As a child, Suhani was too active.
    As a child, Suhani was more active than she should have been.

H. Interchange of Parts of Speech

Following interchanges of one part of speech for another are made :

1. Noun
   - (a) Noun   into   Verb
   - (b) Noun   into   Adjective
   - (c) Noun   into   Adverb
2. Verb
   - (a) Verb   into   Noun
   - (b) Verb   into   Adjective
   - (c) Verb   into   Adverb

3. Adjective
   (a) Adjective into Noun
   (b) Adjective into Verb
   (c) Adjective into Adverb
4. Adverb
   (a) Adverb into Noun
   (b) Adverb into Verb
   (c) Adverb into Adjective

WORK BOOK EXERCISES

Nouns

(a) **Nouns into Verbs**

Directions *Replace the nouns in Italics in the following sentences by verbs.*

1. She got *success* in the examination.
2. Her *intention* was to harm me.
3. He gave me *advice*.
4. They can not get *admission* without documents.
5. I have a *disinclination* for work in office.
6. The *taste* of these oranges is sour.
7. They have made an *agreement* to complete this work in time.
8. I have no *inclination* of going to the movie.
9. He is a *disgrace* on his family.
10. The *cost* of this refrigerator is very high.

(b) **Nouns into Adjectives**

Directions *Replace the Nouns in Italics in the following sentences by Adjectives.*

1. She admitted her *guilt*.
2. The room was full of *dust*.
3. He is a man of great *courage*.
4. They do work with *skill*.
5. He is living in *peace* these days.
6. He was punished for his *negligence*.

(c) **Nouns into Adverbs**

Directions *Replace the Nouns in Italics in the following sentences by Adverbs.*

1. She left the room in *anger*.
2. Please carry it with *care*.
3. She survived because of *luck*.
4. She is living in *peace* with her only son.
5. She listened to me with *patience*.
6. She listened to me with *attention*.
7. She left the room in a *hurry*.
8. He goes to Chandigarh every *week*.

TRANSFORMATION

Verbs

(a) Verbs into Nouns
Directions *Replace the Verbs in Italics in the following sentences by Nouns.*
1. My brother promised to help me.
2. This computer is made in India.
3. She accepted all that I proposed.
4. She was bathing.
5. She signed the documents.
6. I need money.
7. Please help me.
8. She was so intelligent that we admired her.

(b) Verbs into Adjectives
Directions *Replace the Verbs in Italics in the following sentences by Adjectives.*
1. She differs with me in her views.
2. She always obeys her brother.
3. He has succeeded in her work.
4. He hoped to succeed.
5. I doubt your honesty.
6. His success has astonished me.

(c) Verbs into Adverbs
Directions *Replace the Verbs in Italics in the following sentences by Adverbs.*
1. She hurried to the bus stop.
2. I forced him to leave.
3. She succeeded in her task.
4. She attended to my advice.
5. They helped me in difficulties.
6. She cares for her duty.

Adjectives

(a) Adjectives into Nouns
Directions *Replace the Adjectives in Italics in the following sentences by Nouns.*
1. Exercise makes body strong.
2. Her actions are careful.
3. She is very wise in spending money.
4. Their expedition was successful.
5. He is a courageous man.
6. We are proud of our country.
7. The room is dusty.

(b) Adjectives into Verbs

Directions *Replace the Adjectives in Italics in the following sentences by Verbs.*

1. You have given me pleasant news.
2. Her favour was intentional.
3. She was successful in her job.
4. He is careful of his health.
5. Your behaviour was annoying to your wife.
6. We are proud of your success.

(c) Adjectives into Adverbs

Directions *Replace the Adjectives in Italics in the following sentences by Adverbs.*

1. She is leading a peaceful life with her daughter.
2. Be careful in your work.
3. She is attentive in learning computers.
4. His handwriting is neat.
5. I am comfortable in my seat.
6. He is a slow driver.
7. Her action is intentional.
8. I am certain that I will pass.

Adverbs

(a) Adverbs into Nouns

Directions *Replace the Adverbs in Italics in the following sentences by Nouns.*

1. Do not talk with children angrily.
2. Do your work attentively.
3. Enter the room carefully.
4. They did it successfully.
5. Stock-taking is done annually.

(b) Adverbs into Verbs

Directions *Replace the Adverbs in Italics in the following sentences by Verbs.*

1. She went to the airport in a taxi hurriedly.
2. They always act obediently.
3. She does her duty carefully.
4. They served me helpfully.
5. She listened to my advice attentively.

(c) Adverbs into Adjectives

Directions *Replace the Adverbs in Italics in the following sentences by Adjectives.*

1. Fortunately, they succeeded in the difficult task.
2. She is walking gracefully.
3. She behaved with me disgracefully.
4. She solved the problem successfully.
5. Probably, she will succeed.
6. She was dressed elegantly.

Cumulative Exercise

Directions *Rewrite the following sentences as directed.*

1. His .... with the strangers astonished everybody. (use noun of 'familiar')
2. India is richer in heritage than most of the countries. (use 'rich' in place of 'richer')
3. A student of our school is a .... leader. (use adjective of 'fame')
4. We were disappointed when our tour was cancelled. (make noun of 'cancel')
5. He was happy to leave the house. (use 'happily' in the sentence)
6. It is better to starve than beg. (make gerund of 'to starve')
7. There is possibility of his being late. (use modal 'may')
8. She looks just as smart in saari as she does in jeans. (use 'whether' in the sentence)
9. None in their correct senses will ever do it. (begin the sentence with 'none but')
10. Our principal is the most honest of all in the college.
    (make the sentence comparative)
11. Suresh thought of a new plan. (change voice)
12. He could not complete the race as he had injured his foot.
    (rewrite by using verb 'prevent')
13. Shivaji was one of the greatest warriors of India. (change into comparative degree)
14. Sheena returned a month ago. (begin the sentence with 'It is')
15. For more information contact the Secretary. (begin the sentence with 'Should')
16. You remembered to buy a pen for me. didn't you?
    (begin the sentences with 'you did not')
17. You have nothing to complain of. (begin the sentence with 'There is')
18. Please read this letter. (use phrasal verb beginning with 'go')
19. He has refused to help me. (begin the sentence with 'He said')
20. It is better to lend than borrow. (use gerund for infinitive)
21. The price of milk has risen steadily. (make sentence using 'steady')
22. The judge punished the guilty. (make sentence using 'fail')
23. If you do not come, I will not go to the movie. (use 'unless' for 'if')
24. His victory surprised me. (make sentence using 'take')
25. The driver lost the job for rash driving. (begin the sentence with 'Had')
26. He gives me the same love as he gives her. (rewrite the sentence using 'no less')
27. Her failure in life disappointed her parents. (make noun of 'disappoint')
28. We did not have good time because it was too cold. (begin the sentence with 'If')
29. Of what use is this book to you? (begin the sentence with 'This book')
30. She is not such a wise lady as she is known. (make a comparative degree of 'wise')
31. Put your tools away. People may fall over them. (combine the sentences)
32. I would rather die than flatter. (rewrite the sentence using 'prefer')
33. Nobody will deny that she is honest. (use 'admit' in the sentence)

34. If you cannot face the music, I will have to. *(make the sentence by using 'or')*
35. Although she was too young, the commission appointed her.
    (use 'despite' for 'although')
36. She is not so much wise as beautiful. *(make comparative of 'wise')*
37. This should be of the greatest value to mankind. *(make positive degree of 'great')*
38. The storm, which had been a threat since Monday, at last broke out with great fury. *(rewrite the sentence by using 'Threaten')*
39. Waste not, want not. *(begin the sentence with 'If')*
40. I accept your offer. *(use 'acceptable' in this sentence)*
41. Reena has more money than brain. *(write the sentence in 'positive degree')*
42. It is normal for a child to eat four times a day.
    (make adverb of 'normal' in the sentence)
43. I caught a train and went to Amravati. *(make a sentence with 'Perfect Participle')*
44. I was not sure that it was you. *(use 'doubtful' for 'not sure')*
45. I do not know her nature any better than you. *(use positive degree)*
46. She complained that the room was hot. *(make a simple sentence)*
47. Tanya is the most punctual of all the boys in her class.
    (make a comparative degree)
48. What long hair you have! *(end the sentence with 'is')*
49. Even if you try hard, you cannot earn much. *(use 'however' in the sentence)*
50. Do they believe in God? *(end the sentence with 'exists')*
51. Who replaced the player after he was injured? *(use 'substitute' for replace)*
52. She has not met me for years. *(make the sentence using 'ago')*
53. Only my friends are responsible for my adversity. *(make negative)*
54. All the athletes complained that amenities provided were far from satisfactory. *(make sentence with 'complain of')*
55. It is unlikely that he will help you. *(make the sentence using 'not')*
56. He attended the function. No one raised any objection.
    (combine the sentence using 'gerund attending')
57. The girls were not permitted to go on picnic. *(make sentence using 'let')*
58. I have not a map, I can't guide you. *(make the sentence using 'if')*
59. They found little sugar in the kitchen. *(make a 'negative sentence')*
60. Sunil had visited Mohan only once before but he remembered the route.
    (make the sentence using 'although')
61. I met him last, when his father died. *(use 'since' for 'when')*
62. If only I could meet her again. *(begin the sentence with 'Would that')*
63. The situation was filled with high drama. *(use 'dramatic' in the sentence)*
64. The sun rose and the fog disappeared. *(make the sentence with 'nominative' absolute)*
65. O for a small place to live in the hills! *(begin the sentence with 'I wish')*
66. We worried about his attitude to the poor. *(begin the sentence with 'His attitude')*
67. It is sad that a friend should be false. *(make sentence using 'Alas')*

TRANSFORMATION

68. This is the last time, you will ever sit in this room.
    (begin with 'Never' in the sentence)
69. This sum is too difficult for me. *(make a complex sentence)*
70. It is wonderful that such a child is bold. *(begin the sentence with 'How')*
71. He refused to allow the late comers in and this annoyed them.
    (begin the sentence with 'His refusal')
72. Fie Fie! you are a cheat. *(change into 'assertive sentence')*
73. Fairies do not exist. *(make the sentence 'using out of the question.)*
74. This plane flies direct from Srinagar to Delhi. *(rewrite the sentence using 'flight')*
75. What is that to you? *(make the sentence 'negative')*
76. This is the greatest discovery that the world has ever known.
    (begin the sentence with 'Never')
77. Eat few rich dinners and you will need few medicines. *(rewrite the sentence with 'if')*
78. He will be angry if you come late. *(use 'and' in the sentence)*
79. The brilliant student surprised every one. *(use 'brilliance' in the sentence)*
80. It is no use blaming him. *(begin the sentence with 'There')*
81. I was so sure that I could depend on him. *(use 'dependence' in the sentence)*
82. You will have to write legibily. *(write using prefix 'it' before legibily)*
83. Shall we ever forget these happy days. *(rewrite using 'never')*
84. This is not the manner to do this work. *(write a clause after manner)*
85. His prompt reply will able us to take timely action. *(rewrite the correct sentence)*
86. As it was a recess time, the students were playing. *(begin the sentence with 'It')*
87. Who does not like to be praised? *(change the sentence into assertive)*
88. That was not my meaning at all. *(rewrite using the verb 'mean')*
89. If you listen seriously, I will tell you all. *(rewrite the sentence using 'in the event of')*
90. I am glad that he has recovered from illness. *(rewrite the sentence using 'recovery')*
91. Do this to escape sufferings. *(make the sentence using 'lest')*
92. It is likely that he will help you. *(rewrite the sentence beginning with 'He')*
93. Mr Rahul is on leave, Mrs Deepa ... English these days. *(fill in the form of verb 'teach')*
94. Please sit down. *(change the voice)*
95. Gold jewellery is bought and sold here. *(change the voice)*
96. He is said to be a spy. *(begin the sentence with 'It')*
97. She denied to have visited the multiplex yesterday.
    (begin the sentence with 'She denied that')
98. This computer is made in India. *(use noun of 'made' in the sentence)*
99. Every one wept, when he departed. *(use 'but wept' in the sentence)*
100. If you had not worked hard, you would have wasted this year.
    (use 'hard work' in the sentence)
101. Although she is glamorous, she is modest. *(use 'as' in the sentence)*

Previous Years' Questions

I. Directions *Rewrite each of the following sentences as directed without changing the meaning.*

1. He is too arrogant to listen to advice.
   (change into a complex sentence) [Civil Services (Mains), 2015]
2. He confessed that he was guilty.
   (change into a simple sentence) [Civil Services (Mains), 2015]
3. He finished his exercise and put away his books.
   (change into simple sentence) [Civil Services (Mains), 2014]
4. In the event of his being late, he will be punished.
   (change into compound sentence) [Civil Services (Mains), 2014]
5. Although there is inflation, the standard of living has gone up.
   (change into simple sentence) [CAPF, 2015]
6. Notwithstanding his hard work, he did not succeed.
   (change into compound sentence) [CAPF, 2015]
7. He felt confident to pass his driving test *(change into a complex sentence)* (IFS, 2015)
8. We are sure of his honesty. *(change into a complex sentence)*
9. She bought a house last year. The house is white. *(change into simple sentence)*
10. She confessed that she was guilty. *(change into a simple sentence)*
11. He had to sing or be executed.
    (turn into complex sentence) [Civil Services (Mains), 2006]

II. Directions *Rewrite each of the following sentences as directed without changing the meaning.*

1. No one dares to criticise her for what she says.
   (rewrite the sentence starting with 'No matter') [Civil Services (Mains), 2013]
2. It would be wonderful if we would go to Shimla.
   (change into an exclamatory sentence using 'how') [Civil Services (Mains), 2013]
3. He drove too fast for the police to catch.
   (Remove 'too') [Civil Services (Mains), 2014]
4. Sita is not one of the cleverest girls in the class.
   (change into comparative degree) [Civil Services (Mains), 2014]
5. I was doubtful whether it was you.
   (change into negative form) [Civil Services (Mains), 2014]
6. It is sad to think that youth should pass away.
   (change into exclamatory sentence) [Civil Services (Mains), 2014]
7. He ran fast to reach the bus stop.
   (change into an interrogative sentence) [Civil Services (Mains), 2015]
8. To the best of my knowledge, he is a vegetarian.
   (begin the sentence: As far as ....) [Civil Services (Mains), 2015]
9. AR Rehman is a versatile music composer, ...?
   (supply an appropriate tag question) [Civil Services (Mains), 2015]
10. It is a pity that a noble person should suffer.
    (change into an exclamatory sentence) [Civil Services (Mains), 2015]
11. This is one of his more readable books. *(use the superlative degree)* [IES, 2013]

TRANSFORMATION

    12. Our generation is modern.   *(use the superlative)* **[IES/ISS, 2014]**
    13. I did not spend as much money as you. *(change into comparative degree)* **[IES/ISS, 2015]**
    14. You are allowed into the club only if you are a member.
        (rewrite the sentence using 'Unless') **[IES/ISS, 2015]**

III. Directions *Rewrite each of the following sentences as directed without changing the meaning.*

    1. As soon as the bell rang, the train started.
        (rewrite the sentence using 'No sooner') **[CAPF, 2013]**
    2. If it does not stop raining, we cannot play.   *(begin with 'Unless')* **[CAPF, 2013]**
    3. Notwithstanding his hard work, he did not succeed.
        (rewrite the sentence using 'yet') **[CAPF, 2013]**
    4. Durga is a brave girl.   *(change to exclamatory sentence)* **[CAPF, 2013]**
    5. He is as strong as his brother.
        (change the degree of comparison without changing the meaning) **[CAPF, 2013]**
    6. No sooner did the Sun rise than the rain stopped.
        (rewrite using 'As soon as') **[CAPF, 2015]**
    7. He was more sly than a fox.   *(change from affirmative to negative)* **[CAPF, 2015]**

IV. Directions *Rewrite each of the following sentences as directed without changing the meaning.* **[Civil Services (Mains), 2000]**

    1. "Shut the door after you." She told him curtly.   *(change into indirect form)*
    2. Did he commit all the mistakes?   *(change into passive voice)*
    3. Many difficulties are <u>impossible to overcome</u>.
        (use a single word for the underlined phrase)
    4. Hard as he tried, the old man failed to find a buyer for his bicycle. *(Use 'Though')*
    5. She is so good that cannot beat her.   *(replace 'so' by 'too')*

V. Directions *Rewrite each of the following sentences as directed without changing the meaning.* **[Civil Services (Mains), 2001]**

    1. You are too early for the show.   *(use 'enough')*
    2. The Mahanadi is not so long as the Ganga.   *(use the comparative degree)*
    3. Sarita said, "Don't open the window."   *(change into the indirect form)*

VI. Directions *Rewrite each of the following sentences as directed without changing the meaning.* **[Civil Services (Mains), 2002]**

    1. "Do not make a noise." said the teacher to his student.   *(change into indirect)*
    2. Hari is so short that he cannot touch the ceiling.   *(replace 'so' by 'too')*
    3. I gave him a ten-rupee note yesterday.   *(change into passive voice)*
    4. Hard as he worked, he failed in the examination.   *(use 'though')*

VII. Directions *Rewrite each of the following sentences as directed without changing the meaning.* **[Civil Services (Mains), 2003]**

    1. No metal is as costly as gold.   *(use comparative degree of 'costly')*

2. I doubt, if you have done it. *(change into negative without changing the meaning)*
3. He was elected leader. *(change into active voice)*
4. She said, "Can you write a poem." *(change into indirect speech)*

VIII. Directions *Rewrite each of the following sentences as directed without changing the meaning.*   **[Civil Services (Mains), 2006]**
1. Give the order. *(change into passive form)*
2. I was doubtful whether it was you. *(turn into negative)*
3. He has <u>disgraced</u> his family. *(use the noun form of 'disgrace')*
4. He was so tired that he could not stand.
   (turn into a simple sentence replacing 'so' by 'too')

IX. Directions *Rewire the following sentences using 'it' at the beginning of the sentence.*   **[Civil Services (Mains), 2013]**
1. Impressing Ramesh Mohan would be a piece of cake.
2. Visiting old people in hospitals is a very good idea.
3. To smoke 20 cigarettes a day is bad for your health.
4. Chatting with strangers on the computer can be very dangerous.
5. My father says, keeping the computer on all day is a waste of electricity.

X. Direction *Rewrite the following sentences using 'it' at the beginning of the sentence.*   **[Civil Services (Mains), 2009]**
1. To talk like that is silly.
2. To hear your voice is good.
3. To tell the truth is essential.
4. To have a friend is better than money.
5. To talk yourself is difficult.

XI. Direction *Rewrite the following sentences using 'it' at the beginning of the sentence.*
1. To make mistakes is easy.   **[Civil Services (Mains), 2010]**
2. To wait for people, who were late made him angry.
3. My ambition was to retire at thirty.
4. Your task is to get across the river without being seen.
5. For you, to ask Ramesh, would be a big mistake.

XII. Directions *Change the following into their corresponding.*
(a) Negatives and   (b) Questions.   **[Civil Services (Mains), 2007]**
1. Ram resembles his father.
2. Raju studied French.
3. The bicycle cost ₹ 500.
4. The thief broke the window open.
5. My mother has a beautiful umbrella.

XIII. Directions *Change each one of the following sentences into their corresponding.*
(a) *Negatives* and   (b) *Wh-questions.*   **[Civil Services (Mains), 2008]**
1. Rakhi has passed the MA examination.
2. India played twenty matches last year.
3. Her father constructed this building.
4. This car runs on CNG.
5. Kirti studies in this college.

Answers
Part I

WORK BOOK EXERCISE (A)
1. He confessed that he was guilty.
2. All depends on what his future is.
3. How old he is, is not known.
4. Speak, what the truth is.
5. The fact that he was silent, proved his complicity in the crime.
6. It appears that he is running temperature.
7. He denied that he had murdered.
8. It is believed that he is honest.
9. She informed me that she had arrived.
10. The news, that he died, is wrong.
11. It is believed that Subhash Chandra Bose died in Japan.
12. I have already heard what he has said.
13. It is sure that he has been punished.
14. It is expected that he will give me money.
15. Mohit may do what he likes.
16. I wish that you may be successful in life.
17. He wishes that he should be a very rich person.
18. There is no truth in what he says.
19. (a) Where he is hiding, is likely to be discovered very soon.
    (b) It is likely that his place of hiding, will be discovered very soon.
20. We believe that the news is true.
21. That you are innocent, is beyond any doubt.
22. I have long doubted if he is honest.
23. I have long suspected that he is guilty.
24. It is likely that his father will give him punishment.
25. (a) It is high time that I should leave India. (b) It is high time, I left India.
26. That he will resign, is out of the question.

WORK BOOK EXERCISE (B)
1. I have long suspected that he is a thief.
2. The news that he has arrived, has not been intimated.
3. Her remarks that I had failed, were disgusting.
4. What is true, is eternal.
5. It is expected that she will learn good manners.
6. Pay heed to what I have instructed.
7. She has a desire that she should learn swimming.
8. Her wish is that she should do social work in future.
9. It is reported that he has lost his reputation.
10. I kept on wondering if she would succeed.
11. Everybody is responsible for what he does.
12. That he will fall, is certain.
13. She did not inform me what she was.
14. Nobody knows where he is.
15. She jumped at what I offered her.

Work Book Exercise (C)

1. Yesterday, I bought a pen, which is very cheap.
2. I saw a beggar, who was begging from door to door.
3. This is the village, where I was born.
4. Do you know the reason, why he has failed?
5. The value, of exercise that we take, is great.
6. The offence, which he committed, is not pardonable.
7. They come across the students, who were smoking by the road side.
8. A man, who is tired, cannot work well.
9. (a) It is not the manner, which you use to please your boss.
   (b) It is not the manner, how you please your boss.
10. He gave me money, which I could spend.
11. The pen, which is given by him, is very cheap.
12. I have no friend, whom I can talk to.
13. He was the last man, who arrived at the party.
14. He gave me a news that was fake.
15. How can you believe a person, who is dishonest.

Work Book Exercise (D)

1. We committed a mistake, which was quite serious.
2. They found a piece of diamond, which is rare.
3. We undertook a journey, which was quite tiring.
4. The man, who was tired, could not do work well.
5. The dog felled the candle, which was burning.
6. The murder, which he committed, ruined his life.
7. He invented a machine, which is used for stitching.
8. He saw a candle, which was burning brightly.
9. This is a class room, which is not the place to play.
10. He has a large family, whom he has to educate.
11. He was the last man, who attended the funeral.
12. Do you know the time, when your father went.
13. Do you know the reason, why she arrived earlier.
14. Nobody appreciated the way in which she behaved at the party.
15. I was informed of the place, where he was living.
16. Kabir, who was a weaver, was a famous poet.
17. Everybody loves Mr Verma, who is our teacher.
18. The boys, who live near my house, are honest.
19. The place, where the leader was cremated, was thronged with people.
20. She told me the reason why she was late.
21. Shakespeare, who was a great dramatist, wrote a number of plays.
22. The girl, who has long hair, is a cousin of my wife.
23. They live just near the by pass, which is on the outskirts of the city.
24. The players, whom the President awardeed cash prize, were present at the function.
25. The offence, which they committed intentionally, is unpardonable.
26. I paid the debt, which my father incurred.

Work Book Exercise (E)

1. Although he is experienced, he is not efficient.
2. Unless he works hard, he cannot succeed.
3. When he was scolded, he left the room.

TRANSFORMATION

4. When the signal was given, the train started.
5. I shall be very glad if I help him.
6. He is so simple that he cannot win the game.
7. As he did mischief, he was punished.
8. The work was done, when I was present.
9. Though he is wealthy, he is not respected.
10. You must wait here, till your father arrives.
11. Although he is poor, yet he is honest.
12. Do it as best as you can.
13. Nobody must expect to become rich, unless he works hard.
14. My heart is so full that I cannot utter a word.
15. He borrowed money from the bank so that he might continue his higher study.
16. She is undergoing slimming treatment because she is very fat.
17. The cat is swifter than the tiger.
18. I am thankful to you because you helped my brother.
19. If he had not got timely help, he would have died from burns.
20. She is so kind that she helps everybody.
21. He did not stop working, until he got success.
22. They were afraid lest they should be caught in the shower.
23. You must act as the rules say.
24. He was promoted because he was very capable.
25. We shall leave for Shimla if weather permits.
26. Water is so hot that no one can drink it.
27. If all is well, I shall meet her parents today.
28. I shall be glad if I am invited.
29. I would be glad if I were there.
30. I would have been glad if I had been there.
31. Your behaviour was so bad that the guests could not bear it.
32. She is so good that I am no match for her.
33. He was so quick that he could overtake me.
34. As it was a junk food, we did not taste it.
35. If we had not been poor, we would have been a happy family.

Part II

WORK BOOK EXERCISE (A)

1. Her dishonesty is much regretted.
2. He admitted his enemy's generosity.
3. I know the residence of your brother.
4. You must pay heed to the words of your officers.
5. Never say anything wrong.
6. We believe in God's existence.
7. I expect him to pass.
8. Unfortunately, he died young.
9. He asked me the reason for giving money to his brother.
10. He confessed meeting her last night.
    He confused to have met her last night.
    He confessed having met her last night.
11. I agreed to teach him.

12. I informed him of her departure.
13. He appears to have been scolded by his father.
14. I ordered him to leave the room at once.
15. People are certain of his honesty.

WORK BOOK EXERCISE (B)
1. He confessed his guilt.
2. I do not care for her remarks.
3. Mohit may do anything.
4. I have long doubted his honesty.
5. The rumour of his death is baseless.
6. His age is not known.
7. Her statement is disgusting.
8. His silence proved his complicity in the crime.
9. He denied to have murdered.
10. She appears to be absent today.
11. She was alleged to have abused him.
12. She wanted to know his name.
13. My hope is to earn a lot of money.
14. He is sure to have been punished.
15. He is expected to give me money.
16. All depends on his future.
17. I don't believe in his statement.
18. I agreed to his proposal.

WORK BOOK EXERCISE (C)
1. (a) He is not a trust worthy man.
   (b) He is not a man to be trusted.
2. A careless student cannot succeed.
3. He is not a man to cheat anyone.
4. He has a large house to live in.
5. They made a false statement.
6. You can have anything of your choice.
7. Barking dogs seldom bite.
8. I know the reason of his failure.
9. Milton, a famous poet, wrote 'Paradise Lost'.
10. The train connecting New Delhi is late.
11. Childhood is a time to learn good habits.
12. The wounded man died last night.
13. Healthy people do not need a doctor.
14. Good deeds done by a man live after him.
15. The place of cremation of the leader was thronged with people.

WORK BOOK EXERCISE (D)
1. Yesterday, I bought a very cheap book.
2. You cannot believe a dishonest person.
3. The hard working persons succeed in life.
4. A wounded soldier was lying in the field.
5. The tired players could not perform well.
6. The monster proud of his power, was defeated by Hercules.

TRANSFORMATION

7. In the street, we saw a beggar begging from door to door.
8. The man wounded in the accident, died last night.
9. The police discovered the weapon used to kill the victim.
10. The magic ball meant for the king, was eaten by the jester.
11. Seema was the last person to leave for home.
12. My uncle was the first man to hear her name on the radio.
13. He has some bills to pay in cash.
14. I have no friend to talk to.
15. Childhood is a time to teach good habits to children.
16. The time of his arrival tomorrow, is not certain.
17. All of us were told the reason of his becoming rich suddenly.
18. I remember very well the year of his retirement.
19. The residents of our colony were shouting for justice.
20. Rathore, our captain, scored fifty runs.
21. Edison, a great scientist, invented electricity.
22. We visited the Taj, a unique building.
23. I shall travel by the Taj Express going to Agra direct.
24. The students hailing from Bihar are very hard working.
25. Tomorrow, I will board a train connecting Udaipur.
26. The news broadcast by the Voice of America is true.
27. I met a poet already known to me.
28. Mr Gupta will buy the house built by me only last year.
29. The book, lost by me yesterday, has been found out.
30. Those living in glass houses, should not throw stones at others.

WORK BOOK EXERCISE (E)

1. He did in accordance with my wish.
2. We get up in the morning.
3. After having finished our work, we went home.
4. Seeing me, he ran away.
5. Walking in the garden, she was addressed by a stranger.
6. He is kind enough to help everybody.
7. We went home after the arrival of the teacher.
8. He wrote fast to the best of his ability.
9. Without being threatened, he will not return money.
10. I succeeded beyond my expectations.
11. On being found out, the thief was arrested.
12. Despite being punished, she was not ashamed.
13. You can talk to your liking.
14. Inspite of being poor, he is honest.
15. Despite being honest, he is not hard working.
16. But for their help, I would not have gained success.
17. He ran fast to catch taxi.
18. On account of running fast, she was declared first by the teacher.
19. He being poor, we will help him.
20. God willing, you will succeed.
21. I make a promise to stick to it.
22. He was complimented because of his success.
23. He has come to Chandigarh to be treated by capable doctors.

24. It, being fine, we left for picnic.
25. While watching TV, they were visited by their friends.
26. Crossing the road, she was knocked down by a scooter.
27. Sonia is too slow for a good tennis player.
28. She is so clever that she can see through your tricks.
29. Her sorrow is too deep for tears.
30. He will stick to his job so as to escape starvation.
31. The signal having been given, the train started.
32. I have not had any rest since my arrival in Chennai.
33. No money having been given to me, the project was not launched.
34. The house is too small for me to live in.
35. The weather being very pleasant, we went on a long drive.

Part III

Work Book Exercise (A)

1. You permit me and I shall leave the room.
2. He is a man of knowledge but he is a fool.
3. He committed a fault so he was punished.
4. He is wealthy but he is not respected.
5. He worked hard and secured high percentage of marks.
6. He returned and we asked him many questions.
7. He teaches Mathematics and Hindi also.
8. You sent me money so, I am thankful to you.
9. He is not only rich but also learned.
10. He did not accept my request but left Jhansi.
11. He was sitting in the drawing room and watching TV.
12. He had many contacts but never used unfair means.
13. He must admit his fault otherwise he will be punished.
14. He must work hard and will secure high percentage of marks.
15. He was dismissed for he embezzled money.
16. The weather was very fine so we left for swimming.
17. He will die and his son will inherit the property.
18. He was ignorant so he did not follow the rules.
19. He could not qualify examination and I was much surprised.
20. (a) This treatment is very costly so, only the rich can afford it.
    (b) None, but the rich, can afford this treatment.
21. Do this or suffer.
22. He feared rain and went by car.
23. I am not invited and so I shall not go.
24. Neither this statement nor that statement is correct.
25. First desire and then deserve.

Work Book Exercise (B)

1. She is sick but she will come.
2. Come by car and we will take you to temple.
3. It was cold so we did not go out.
4. The thief was found out and he was arrested.
5. She arrived and everybody welcomed her.

TRANSFORMATION

6. You must stop smoking otherwise, you will suffer from lung disease.
7. I am not invited so I shall not go.
8. Listen seriously and I will tell you all.
9. He has recovered from illness so I am glad.
10. I had lost the pen but I have found it.
11. He had a dog and that was very faithful.
12. He is unlucky but he is never disappointed.
13. Do this otherwise, you will suffer.
14. He is very intelligent but he cannot succeed.
15. He gave me money and I started business.
16. He is not at home otherwise, I would meet him.
17. He may be at home and in that case I will give him money.
18. He will die and his son will inherit his property.
19. He must work hard and he will pass.
20. He spent more than he could afford.

Part IV
WORK BOOK EXERCISES

Nouns
(a) Nouns into Verbs
1. She succeeded in the examination.
2. She intended to harm me.
3. He advised me.
4. They cannot be admitted without documents.
5. I am disinclined to work in office.
6. These oranges taste sour.
7. They have agreed to complete this work in time.
8. I am not inclined to go to the movie.
9. He has disgraced his family.
10. This refrigerator costs a lot.

(b) Nouns into Adjectives
1. She admitted that she was guilty.
2. The room was dusty.
3. He is a courageous man.
4. They are skillful workers.
5. His life is peaceful these days.
6. He was punished, for he was negligent.

(c) Nouns into Adverbs
1. She left the room angrily.
2. Please carry it carefully.
3. She survived luckily.
4. She is living with her only son peacefully.
5. She listened to me patiently.
6. She listened to me attentively.
7. She left the room hurriedly.
8. He goes to Chandigarh weekly.

Verbs
(a) Verbs into Nouns
1. My brother made a promise to help me.
2. This computer is of Indian make.
3. She accepted all my proposals.
4. She was taking bath.
5. She put signature on the documents.
6. I am in need of money.
7. Please provide me help.
8. Her intelligence won our admiration.

(b) **Verbs into Adjectives**
1. Her views are different from mine.
2. She is obedient to her brother.
3. He has been successful in her work.
4. He was hopeful of success.
5. I am doubtful of your honesty.
6. His success is astonishing to me.

(c) **Verbs into Adverbs**
1. She left for the bus stop hurriedly.
2. I turned him out forcibly.
3. She did her task successfully.
4. She listened to my advice attentively.
5. They served me in difficulties helpfully.
6. She does her duty carefully.

Adjectives

(a) **Adjectives into Nouns**
1. Exercise gives strength to our body.
2. She acts with care.
3. She spends money with wisdom.
4. They achieved success in their expedition.
5. He is a man of courage.
6. We take pride in our country.
7. The room is full of dust.

(b) **Adjectives into Verbs**
1. Your news has pleased me.
2. She intended to favour me.
3. She succeeded in her job.
4. He cares about his health.
5. Your wife was annoyed with your behaviour.
6. We pride ourselves in your success.

(c) **Adjectives into Adverbs**
1. She is living with her daughter peacefully.
2. Do your work carefully.
3. She is learning computers attentively.
4. He writes neatly.
5. I am sitting comfortably.
6. He drives slowly.
7. She did it intentionally.
8. I will certainly pass.

Adverbs

(a) **Adverbs into Nouns**
1. Do not talk with children in anger.
2. Do your work with attention.
3. Enter the room with care.
4. They got success in doing this.
5. Stock-taking is done every year.

(b) **Adverbs into Verbs**
1. She hurried to the airport in a taxi.
2. They always obey.
3. She cares for her duty.
4. They helped me in difficulty.
5. She attended to my advice.

(c) **Adverbs into Adjectives**
1. It is fortunate that they succeeded in the difficult task.
2. Her gait was graceful.
3. Her behaviour was disgraceful to me.
4. She was successful in solving the problem.
5. It is probable, she may succeed.
6. Her dress was elegant.

Cumulative Exercise

1. His familiarity with the strangers astonished everybody.
2. Very few countries are as rich in heritage as India.
3. A student of our school, is a famous leader.
4. The cancellation of our tour disappointed us.
5. He left the house happily.
6. Starving is better than begging.
7. He may be late.
8. She looks smart whether she wears saari or Jeans.
9. None but in their correct senses will ever do it.
10. Our principal is more honest than anybody else in the college.
11. New plan was thought of by Suresh.
12. His injured foot prevented him from completing the race.
13. Shivaji was greater than most of the warriors in India.
14. It is a month since Sheena returned.
15. Should you require more information, contact the Secretary of the club.
16. You did not forget to buy a pen for me, did you?
17. There is nothing to complain of.
18. Please go through this letter.
19. He said that he would not help me.
20. Borrowing is not as good as lending.
21. There is a steady rise in the price of milk.
22. The judge did not fail to punish the guilty.
23. Unless you come, I will not go to the movie.
24. (a) His victory took me by surprise
    (b) I was taken by surprise at his victory.
25. Had the driver not driven rashly, he would not have lost the job.
26. He loves me no less than he loves her.
27. Her failure in life caused disappointment to her parents.
28. If it had not been cold, we would have had good time.
29. This book is of no use to you.
30. She is not wiser than she is known to be.
31. Put your tools away lest people should fall over them.
32. I would prefer to die rather than flatter.
33. Everybody will admit that she is honest.
34. Face the music or I will have to.
35. Despite being young, she was appointed by the Commission.
36. She is more wise than beautiful.
37. Nothing else is of as great value to mankind as this is.
38. The storm, which had threatened since Monday, at last broke out with great fury.
39. If you do not waste, you will not want.
40. Your offer is acceptable to me.
41. Reena has not as much brain as she has money.
42. Normally, a child should eat four times a day.
43. Having caught a train, I went to Amravati.
44. I was doubtful if it was you.
45. You know her nature as well as I.
46. She complained of the room being hot.
47. Tanya is more punctual than any boy in the class.
48. How long your hair is!

49. However hard you may try, you cannot earn much.
50. Do they believe that God exists?
51. Who was substituted for the injured player?
52. She met me years ago.
53. None, but my friends are responsible for my adversity.
54. All the athletes complained of unsatisfactory amenities.
55. It is not likely that he will help you.
56. No one raised any objection to his attending the function.
57. The girls were not let go on Picnic.
58. If I had a map, I could guide you.
59. They found no sugar in the kitchen.
60. Although Sunil had visited Mohan only once before, he remembered the route.
61. I have not met him since his father died.
62. Would that, I could meet her again.
63. The situation was highly dramatic.
64. The Sun having risen, the fog disappeared.
65. (a) I wish to have a small place in the hills to live in.
    (b) I wish, I had a small place in the hills to live in.
66. His attitude to the poor worried us.
67. Alas! a friend should be false.
68. Never will you sit in this room again.
69. This sum is so difficult that I cannot solve.
70. How bold such a child is!
71. His refusal to allow the late comers annoyed them.
72. It is contemptible that you are a cheat.
73. Existence of fairies is out of the question.
74. The flight of the plane from Srinagar to Delhi is direct.
75. It does not matter to you.
76. Never has the world known such a great discovery.
77. If you eat few rich dinners, you will need few medicines.
78. He will be angry at your coming late.
79. The brilliance of the student surprised everyone.
80. There is no use of blaming him.
81. I was sure of my dependence on him.
82. You will not have to write illegibly.
83. We shall never forget these happy days.
84. This is not the manner how you should do this work.
85. His prompt reply will enable us to take timely action.
86. It was a recess time and the students were playing.
87. Everybody likes to be praised.
88. I did not mean it at all.
89. In the event of your listening seriously, I will tell you all.
90. His recovery from illness has made me glad.
91. Do this lest you should suffer.
92. He is likely to help you.
93. Mr Rahul is on leave. Mrs Deepa is teaching English these days.
94. You are requested to sit down.
95. We buy and sell gold jewellery.
96. It is said that he is a spy.
97. She denied that she had visited the multiplex yesterday.

TRANSFORMATION

98. This computer is of Indian make.
99. There was none but wept when he departed.
100. But for hard work, you would have wasted this year.
101. Glamorous as she is, she is modest.

Previous Years' Questions

I.
1. He is so arrogant that he does not listen to advice.
2. He confessed his guilt.
3. Having finished his exercise, he put away his books.
4. He must not be late, or he will be punished.
5. The standard of living has gone up despite inflation.
6. He worked hard, yet he did not succeed.
7. He felt confident about passing his driving test.
8. We are sure that he is honest.
9. She bought a white house last year.
10. She confessed her guilt.
11. If he had not sung, he would have been executed.

II.
1. No matter what she says, no one dares to criticise her.
2. How wonderful it would be going to Shimla!
3. He drove so fast that the police could not catch him.
4. Some girls of the class are cleverer than Sita.
5. I was not sure whether it was you.
6. Alas! The youth should pass away!
7. Did he run fast to reach the bus stop?
8. As far as I know, he is a vegetarian.
9. Isn't he?
10. What a pity! A noble person should suffer.
11. This is his most readable book of all.
12. Ours is one of the most modern generation.
13. I did not spend more money than you.
14. Unless you are a member, you are not allowed into the club.

III.
1. No sooner had the bell rang, than the train started.
2. Unless it stops raining, we cannot play.
3. He worked hard, yet he did not succeed.
4. Bravo, Durga!
5. His brother is not stronger than him.
6. As soon as the Sun rose, the rain stopped.
7. A fox was not so sly as him.

IV.
1. She ordered him curtly to shut the door after him.
2. Were all the mistakes committed by him?
3. Many difficulties are invincible.
4. Though the old man tried hard, he failed to find a buyer for his bicycle.
5. She is too good to beat her.

V.
1. You are early enough for the show.
2. The Ganga is longer than the Mahanadi.
3. Sarita ordered me not to open the window.

VI.
1. The teacher ordered his student not to make a noise.
2. Hari is too short to touch the ceiling.

3. He was given a ten-rupee note by me.
4. Though he worked hard, he failed in the examination.

VII. 1. Gold is costlier/more costly than any other metal.
2. I am certain that you have done it.
3. They elected him leader.
4. She asked me if I could write a poem.

VIII. 1. Let the order be given.
2. I was certain that it was not you.
3. He has brought disgrace on his family.
4. He was too tired to stand.

IX. 1. It would be a piece of cake to impress Ramesh Mohan.
2. It is a very good idea to visit old people in hospitals.
3. It is bad for your health to smoke 20 cigarettes.
4. It can be very dangerous to chat with strangers on the computer.
5. It is a waste of electricity to keep the computer on all day according to my father.

X. 1. It is silly to talk like that.
2. It is good to hear your voice.
3. It is essential to tell the truth.
4. It is better to have a friend than money.
5. It is difficult to talk yourself.

XI. 1. It is easy to make mistakes.
2. It made him angry to wait for people, who were late.
3. It was my ambition to retire at thirty.
4. It is your task to get across the river without being seen.
5. It would be a big mistake for you to ask Ramesh.

XII. 1. (a) Ram does not resemble his father.
   (b) Does Ram resemble his father?
2. (a) Raju did not study French.
   (b) Did Raju study French?
3. (a) The bicycle did not cost ₹ 500.
   (b) Did the bicycle cost ₹ 500?
4. (a) The thief did not break the window open.
   (b) Did the thief break the window open?
5. (a) My mother does not have a beautiful umbrella.
   (b) Does my mother have a beautiful umbrella.

XIII. 1. (a) Rakhi has not passed the MA examination.
   (b) When has Rakhi passed the MA examination?
2. (a) India did not play 20 matches last year.
   (b) When did India play 20 matches?
3. (a) Her father has not constructed this building.
   (b) What her father has constructed?
4. (a) This car does not run on CNG.
   (b) What does this car run on?
5. (a) Kirti does not study in this college.
   (b) Where does Kirti study?

CHAPTER 8

Prepositions

What is a Preposition?

The word **Preposition** (as is indicated by prefix **'Pre'**) is a word or a group of words that is placed before a noun or pronoun to indicate direction, method, place, source etc. In other words, the noun or pronoun is shown to have a kind of relation with regard to something else with the help of a Preposition. e.g.

    (i) The Preposition may join one noun to another.
        Sheena was in the **kitchen**.   (*'Sheena' and 'kitchen'*)
    (ii) It may join noun to a verb.
        She **slipped** off the **stairs**.   (*'slipped' and 'stairs'*)
    (iii) It may join noun to an adjective.
        We are **proud** of our **country**.   (*'proud' and 'country'*)

1. **'At, in, on, of, off, through, below, with'** etc., are some of the prepositions.
2. The noun or pronoun used with the preposition is in the **accusative case.** e.g.
   (i) The book is on the **table**.
   (ii) I did not talk to **him**.
   Here **'table'** and **'him'** have been used in the accusative case because these are words, the objects, of the preposition.
3. A Preposition sometimes may have more than one object. e.g.
   (i) I gave money to Ritu and her brother.
   (ii) Distribute the mangoes among the boys and the girls.
4. A clause can also be the object to a preposition. e.g.
   (i) I was pleased with what she did for me.
   (ii) Pay attention to what your parents say.
5. Adverbs of time and place can also be the object of preposition. e.g.
   (i) I don't like to go from here.
   (ii) She had returned by then.
6. When verbs are placed after prepositions (other than 'to'), they should be in the gerund form except when they are used in infinitive form. e.g.
   (i) I am confident of winning her love.
   (ii) She does not believe in wasting time.
   (iii) She insisted on going to Pune.

Prepositions before Particular Words

(A) Travel and movement
(a) From, to, at, in, by, on, into, onto, off, out, out of. e.g.
  We travel daily from Meerut to Delhi.
(b) Arrive at/in, get to (reach). e.g.
  (i) They arrived in India in March.
  (ii) I arrived at Patel Bridge.
  (iii) I go to the Bus stand late.
(c) Home (Without preposition) e.g.
  (i) They went home by bus. *(Without Preposition)*
  (ii) She returned to her home late. *(With Preposition)*

(B) Above and over
(a) 'Above', 'over' mean higher than
(b) But 'over' can also mean 'covering on the other side of', across, from one side to the other and in every part of the region. e.g.
  (i) We put a sheet over his body.
  (ii) There is a bridge over the river.
  (iii) He has friends all over the world.

(C) Under, below, beneath
(a) 'Below', 'under', mean lower than, but 'under' can indicate contact. e.g.
  (i) She kept money under the bed.
  (ii) The old man was crushed under the car.
(b) However, 'below' is used, when there is a space between the two surfaces. e.g.
  They live below us. (We live above them)
(c) 'Under' can mean junior in ranks. e.g.
  He is under me. (I am his superior, below doesn't have this meaning)
(d) 'Beneath' has the same meaning as under, but it is better to use it for abstract meanings. e.g.
  He would think it beneath him to do such a small work. (Unworthy of him)

(D) Time and date (Use at, on, by, in)
At dusk, at noon, at dawn, at midnight, at midday, at sixteen (the age) at night, at six, at 7:30, in/on the morning/afternoon/evening/night (of a certain date). e.g.
  We left on the evening of the sixth at 5:30 pm.
  We left in the evening/afternoon.

(E) On time, in time, in good time
(a) 'On time' (at time arranged, neither before nor after). e.g.
  The train is running on time.
(b) 'In time' (not late). e.g.
  Passengers should be in time for their train.
(c) 'In good time' (with comfortable margin). e.g.
  I arrived at the theatre in good time.

PREPOSITIONS

(F) At the beginning/at the end, in the beginning/in the end, at first, at last
  (a) At the beginning of a book, there is a foreword. (Literally at the beginning)
  (b) At the end, (of the book) there may be an index.
  (c) 'In the beginning/at first' = In the early stage. It implies that later there was a change. e.g.
  In the beginning, we used hand tools, later we had machines.
  (d) 'In the end/At last' = eventually/after sometime. e.g.
  At first, he opposed marriage, but in the end, he gave his consent.
  (e) in, on, at, the back of
    (i) What is there at the back of the table. *(behind)*
    (ii) There is glossary at the back of the book. *(few pages)*
    (iii) There is a room on the back of the house. *(back of as part/area)*
    (iv) He was stabbed in the back.

(G) By, before
  By time/date (not later than). e.g.
  (i) Please be at home by 8:00 pm.
  (ii) By the end of this year, my study will have finished.

Rules of Preposition

Rule I

A preposition is usually placed before its object but sometimes it is placed after it in the following cases :

(A) When the object in the interrogative pronoun is understood. e.g.
  (i) To whom are you talking? *(Incorrect)*
     Who are you talking to? *(Correct)*
     Whom are you talking to? *(Correct)*
  (ii) About what are you talking? *(Incorrect)*
     What are you talking about? *(Correct)*
  (iii) For what are you looking? *(Incorrect)*
     What are you looking for? *(Correct)*
  (iv) For what are you waiting? *(Incorrect)*
     What are you waiting for? *(Correct)*

(B) When the object of the preposition is a relative pronoun 'that'. e.g.
  (i) This is the book for that I have been looking. *(Incorrect)*
     This is the book that I have been looking for. *(Correct)*
  (ii) This is the picture of that she always talks. *(Incorrect)*
     This is the picture that she always talks of. *(Correct)*

(C) When an infinitive qualifies a noun, the preposition should be placed after the infinitive, if required. e.g.
  (i) It is not a safe place to live. *(Say 'live in')*
  (ii) He gave me a pen to write. *(Say 'write with')*
  (iii) He gave me money to spend. *(Correct)*

Rule II

(A) As a rule, no preposition is placed after the following verbs, when these verbs are used in active voice.

'Stress, emphasise, discuss (matter), investigate, comprise, accompany, consider, violate, demand, resemble, pervade, precede, succeed, reach (at), resign (post), attack, invade, resist, enter (come into), eschew, befall, order, direct, join, sign, affect, ensure, board, describe, await, lack, regret, concern. e.g.

(i) The police are investigating into the case.	(Drop 'into')
(ii) The teacher emphasised on the need of discipline in life.	(Drop 'on')
(iii) I have ordered for his transfer.	(Drop 'for')
(iv) I shall discuss about the problem with you.	(Drop 'about')
(v) Soni resembles with her mother.	(Drop 'with')
(vi) Our college comprises of class rooms.	(Drop 'of')
(vii) India has never attacked on any country.	(Drop 'on')
(viii) She promised to accompany with me to the park.	(Drop 'with')
(ix) The Committee is comprised of five members.	(Correct)

(B) Omission of 'to' with verbs of communication before the object, 'advise, tell, ask, beg, command, encourage, request, inform, order, urge. e.g.

(i) I advised to him to go.	(Drop 'to')
(ii) I informed to the police of the accident.	(Drop 'to')
(iii) I enquired of him.	(Correct)

Rule III

Use of preposition in relation to its object

(A) Omission of preposition before Indirect Object.

Study the following verbs :

'bring, give, lend, promise, leave, sell, buy, show, take, fetch, tell, hand, send, sing, read, cost, play (an instrument), find, get, ask, offer etc.' e.g.

(i) I shall fetch you books from market.
   Or
   I shall fetch books for you from market.
(ii) Her father left him large property.
   Or
   Her father left large property to him.
(iii) I shall buy you this necklace.
   Or
   I shall buy this necklace for you.
(iv) I shall find Robin a nice job.
   Or
   I shall find a nice job for Robin.
(v) Will you sing me a song?
   Or
   Will you sing a song for me?

PREPOSITIONS

(B) Note the placement of proper object (Direct/Indirect) with the use of the following verbs with special reference to the preposition.

The use of verbs **'provide, supply, furnish, entrust, present'**. e.g.

I provided him money.	*(Incorrect)*
I provided him with money.	*(Correct)*
Or	
I provided money to him.	*(Correct)*

(C) The correct use of **'rob, fine, inform, explain, recommend, compensate, suggest, propose'**, in relation to objects. e.g.

(a) Rob a person of something.
(b) Fine someone (ten rupees etc).
(c) Inform someone of something.
(d) Explain something to a person.
(e) Recommend/Suggest/Propose something/some-body to others.
(f) Compensate someone for something.

Some examples have been worked out to the students:

(i) He robbed the old woman of all her ornaments.
(ii) The teacher fined him ten rupees.
(iii) We informed the police of the accident.
(iv) The teacher explained the meaning of the poem to us.
(v) He recommended me for promotion to the Principal.
(vi) He recommended this book to his students.
(vii) I shall compensate you for the loss.

Rule IV

A student should take special note of the following Prepositions :

(A) 'Than and but' as Preposition :

'Than and but' are usually conjunctions. However, they may be sometimes used as Prepositions. e.g.

(i) I did not see any other person than your brother.
(ii) I did not see any body else but your brother.

(B) **'A'** in the following sentences has been used as a Preposition, though in a weakened form of (in). e.g.

(i) He earns fifty rupees a day.
(ii) She visits me once a month.

(C) Between, Among

'Between' is used while referring to two persons/things. It may also be used for two or more in choice.

'Among' is used while referring to more than two persons/things. e.g.

(i) The two brothers divided the property between themselves.
(ii) The two brothers and their sisters divided the property among themselves.

> **Note** Between the students in the class, which is the best?
> (between is correct in choice for more than two)

(D) **Beside, Besides**
   '**Beside**' means 'by the side of'.
   '**Besides**' means 'in addition to'. e.g.
   (i) Besides studying, he is also working somewhere.
   (ii) She sat beside him at the party.

(E) **By, With**
   '**By**' is used for 'doer' of the action.
   '**With**' is used to denote the instrument. e.g.
   (i) He struck the dog with a stick.
   (ii) A dog was struck by him.

(F) **Since** (as a preposition)
   (a) **'Since' is used for time expression** (time from the past to the present)
   Since is used for a definite time in the past or some past occasion. e.g.
   since birth, since last Sunday, since Diwali, since 2 o'clock.
   (i) I have not met him since last month. *(From last month till now)*
   (ii) She has been doing home work since morning. *(From morning till now)*

   (b) **'Since' as a conjunction**
   (i) It is ten years, since I saw him. *(or has been)*
   (ii) I have not met him, since he came back.

   (c) **'Since' as an adverb**
   (i) She went to the USA in 2003 and I have not seen her since. *(From 2003 till now)*
   (ii) It was indeed a shock but she has since recovered from it. *(Long before now.)*

(G) '**For**' is used for time expression (indefinite) and a specific period of time (for two months/six years/two hours etc.) e.g.
   (i) I shall go to Delhi for two weeks. *(Period of time)*
   (ii) He stayed with me for two hours daily.
   (iii) She has been sleeping for two hours. *(Time expression)*
   (iv) She has been in Delhi for one week.

(H) **From, Between**
   '**From**' is normally used with '**to/till/until**'.
   '**Between**' is used with '**and**'. e.g.
   (i) He works in the office from ten to five.
   (ii) The reception will be held between 5 pm and 9 pm.

(I) **Before, Ago**
   '**Before**' denotes the preceding action and can also be used in place of '**Ago**'.
   '**Ago**' refers to the past action. e.g.
   (i) She left India two days ago/before. *(Conjunction)*
   (ii) She had left India before she was married. *(Preceding action)*

(J) **In, At**
   '**In**' refers to towns, cities and countries in a wider sense while '**at**' is used for speaking of comparatively smaller places. e.g.
   (i) He lives in Delhi.
   (ii) He lives at Rohini in Delhi.

PREPOSITIONS

(K) In, Into

'**In**' denotes position whereas '**into**' shows movement and entrance. e.g.
- (i) The students are in the classroom.
- (ii) The students came into the classroom.

(L) On, Upon

'**On**' denotes position, '**upon**' denotes movement. e.g.
- (i) The book is on the table.
- (ii) He threw the book upon the table.

(M) Within, In, On, In good time

'**Within**' means before the end of time, '**In**' means at the end of time while denoting a period of time. e.g.
- (i) He will return in ten minutes.
- (ii) He will return within ten minutes.
- (iii) The train is running on time. *(Neither before nor after)*

(N) Till, To (upto)

'**Till**' is used for time.

'**To**' (upto) is used of place/distance. e.g.
- (i) He studied till 11 pm.
- (ii) I went upto Rani Bagh.

Rule V

When two words or adjectives require different prepositions, appropriate prepositions should be used with both the words. e.g.
- (i) He is senior and older than I. *(Use 'to' after 'senior')*
- (ii) His dress is different and cheaper than mine. *(Use 'from' after 'different')*
- (iii) She is younger and taller than her sister. *(Correct)*

Important Prepositions

	Preposition	Meaning and Use
1.	**Abound in (V)**	(*rich in*) Uttar Pradesh *abounds in* water resources.
2.	**Abound with (Adj.)**	(*full of*) The forest is *abound with* streams. (teeming with)
3.	**Absolve from**	(*declare free from guilt, promise, duty etc.*) The court has *absolved* him *from* the crime.
4.	**Absorb in**	(*busy in work*) He is completely *absorbed in* his work.
5.	**Abstain from**	(*hold oneself back, used for food habits*) His doctor asked him to *abstain from* drinks.
6.	**Abstemious in**	(*eating and drinking*) Those, who are *abstemious in* food habits, enjoy good health.
7.	**Accede to**	(*a request or proposal*) He *acceded to* my request.
8.	**Access to**	(*means of reaching, approaching*) I have no *access to* the Prime Minister.
9.	**Adhere to**	(*stick to*) We decided to *adhere to* the programme already agreed upon.

10.	**Approve of**	(*give one's approval*) She *approved of* my proposal in no time.
11.	**Assent to**	(*official agreement e.g. to a proposal*) The President has given *assent to* the Bill.
12.	**Abhorrent of**	(*abhor, to hate*) He is *abhorrent of* dowry system.
13.	**Acquaint with**	(*familiar with*) I am not *acquainted with* this lady.
14.	**Addicted to**	(*be given to something harmful*) He is *addicted to* alcohol.
15.	**Assured of**	(*positive about*) I am *assured of* his help in need.
16.	**Attain to**	(*arrive at a position/post*) He *attained to* this status after hard struggle.
17.	**Attraction for**	(*a thing or person*) He has *attraction for* her.
18.	**Attracted to**	(*thing or person*) He was *attracted to* her at first sight.
19.	**Avail of**	(*take advantage of*) She *availed* herself *of* this opportunity and got success.
20.	**Aloof from**	(*keep from*) Keep *aloof from* bad boys.
21.	**Advance for**	(*mature*) He is *advanced for* his years.
22.	**Advance by**	(*prepone by*) The visit of Viru has been *advanced by* two days.
23.	**Abide by**	(*rules, comply with*) You should *abide by* the rules laid down by the committee.
24.	**Accused of**	(*a crime, charge with*) He was *accused of* theft and convicted.
25.	**Acquit of**	(*crime, fault*) He was *acquitted of* the crime.
26.	**Admit to**	(*admission*) He was *admitted to* the school on merit.
27.	**Admit of**	(*scope for*) Your crime does not *admit of* any excuse.
28.	**Admit into**	(*admittance*) He was *admitted into* the room of the Principal.
29.	**Alight on**	(*the ground*) The birds *alighted on* the roof of my house.
30.	**Alight from**	(*a bus, car, train*) When he *alighted from* the car, he was welcomed with open arms.
31.	**Alight at**	(*site, a place*) The birds *alighted at* the antenna.
32.	**Annoy with**	(*a person*) Noddy was *annoyed with* his friends on account of their misbehaviour.
33.	**Annoy at**	(*an act*) Suhani was *annoyed at* the misbehaviour of her friends.
34.	**Aspire after**	(*fame*) It is human nature to *aspire after* fame.
35.	**Aspire to**	(*the post*) All the candidates *aspire to* the post of commissioned officers.
36.	**Amuse at**	(*mock at, laugh at*) Everyone was greatly *amused at* his awkward behaviour during the cermony.
37.	**Amuse with**	(*enjoy*) They *amused* themselves *with* playing video games.
38.	**Answer (to)**	(*a person*) What will you *answer* to your father? (a) She did not *answer* my question. (b) She did not give *answer to* my question. (Used as a noun)
39.	**Answer for**	(*explain, account for*) You will have to *answer for* your misdeeds.
40.	**Account for**	(*explain*) You should *account for* your absence from the office.
41.	**Antipathy to**	(*averse to a thing*) I have great *antipathy to* wine.
42.	**Antipathy against**	(*a person*) We should not have *antipathy against* the poor.
43.	**Ask for**	(*demand*) I *asked* him *for* help but he refused.
44.	**Affiliated to**	(*a university or board*) Agra college is *affiliated to* the BR Ambedkar University.
45.	**Affiliated with**	(*a party*) Indian communists are *affiliated with* the Communist Parties of Russia and China.

PREPOSITIONS

46. **Attend to** — (*pay attention to*) He did not *attend to* what his mother advised him.
47. **Attend upon** — (*serve, wait upon*) He has no servant to *attend upon* him in old age.
48. **Antidote to** — (*that counteracts the effect of poison*) There is no effective *antidote to* poison.
49. **Antidote against** — (*cure for*) Quinine is an effective *antidote against* Malaria.
50. **Agree with** — (*a person*) I do not *agree with* you.
51. **Agree on** — (*a point*) After much discussion they *agreed on* the terms of Partnership.
52. **Agree to** — (*views*) He *agreed to* all my views but his father did not.
53. **Afflicted with** — (*disease, problem, mental trouble*) India is *afflicted with* extreme poverty.
54. **Allowance for** — (*allow for*) Always make *allowance for* the mistake of others and pardon them.
55. **Atone for** — (*a fault, sin*) The Hindus go to the Ganga to *atone for* their sins.
56. **Aptitude for** — (*talent*) He shows some *aptitude for* languages.
57. **Alliance with** — (*joined or united*) China has entered into *alliance with* Pakistan against India.
58. **Acquiesce in** — (*accept passively*) I had no alternative but to *acquiesce in* his unfair demand.
59. **Apprise of** — (*inform*) I *apprised* him *of* the serious food situation in the state.
60. **Act upon** — (*comply with*) Always *act upon* the advice of your elders.
61. **Adept in** — (*proficient in*) He is *adept in* the art of dancing.
62. **Adept at** — (*thing*) My brother is *adept at* classical music.
63. **Adapt to** — (*make suitable*) You must *adapt* yourself *to* new situations for attaining to high position in life.
64. **Accustomed to** — (*be used to*) I am *accustomed to* early rising.
65. **Akin to** — (*similar to*) Your behaviour of indifference is *akin to* jealousy.
66. **Alien to** — (*foreign to*) French is *alien to* me because I have never studied it.
67. **Alive to** — (*aware of*) He is fully *alive to* the danger of the situation.
68. **Amenable to** — (*advice, willing to be guided*) Now-a-days, majority of the student are not *amenable to* discipline.
69. **Analogous to** — (*similar to*) Jahanara's wisdom was *analogous to* her beauty.
70. **Aware of** — (*know about*) I am *aware of* your success.
71. **Beware of** — (*cautious*) *Beware of* dogs lest you should be bitten.
72. **Blush at** — (*praise*) She *blushed at* the mention of her qualities.
73. **Blush for** — (*a fault, ashamed of*) I *blush for* the vices of my son, who has disgraced the family.
74. **Blind in** — (*the eye*) He is *blind in* left eye and needs major surgery.
75. **Blind to** — (*defects*) We should not be *blind to* the fault of our children.
76. **Born of** — (*parents*) She was *born of* a beautiful parents.
77. **Born to** — (*passive voice*) A son was *born to* her.
78. **Bearing on** — (*relation to*) Your speech has no *bearing on* the subject that we are discussing.
79. **Beset with** — (*surrounded with*) India is *beset with* many problems these days.
80. **Believe in** — (*to have faith*) I *believe in* him because he is honest.
81. **Believe** — (*regard as true*) I *believe* him because he is speaking the truth.
82. **Benefit by** — (*verb*) You should *benefit by* the experience of others.
83. **Benefit from** — (*noun*) You should derive *benefit from* the experience of others.

84.	**Compensate for**	(*give something to make up*) He *compensated* me *for* the damage to my scooter.
85.	**Cure of**	(*a disease*) He is *cured of* illness after the long treatment.
86.	**Cure for**	(*treatment*) There is no *cure for* AIDS yet.
87.	**Compete with**	(*person*) He will *compete with* me for the first position in the college.
88.	**Compete for**	(*trophy etc*) Our team will not *compete for* Roman Trophy.
89.	**Conformity with**	(*views*) I acted in *conformity with* the opinion of the majority.
90.	**Conformity to**	(*rules, according to*) I did that in *conformity to* the traditions of the family.
91.	**Cling to**	(*to hold tight*) The child was *clinging to* her mother.
92.	**Comply with**	(*act in accordance with*) You must *comply with* the rules laid down by the committee.
93.	**Condemn to**	(*punishment*) The accused was *condemned to* death.
94.	**Congratulate on**	(*success*) Arnav *congratulated* his friend *on* success.
95.	**Certain of**	(*sure of*) Those, who work hard, should be *certain of* their success.
96.	**Confident of**	(*success*) My sister is always *confident of* success.
97.	**Count on**	(*depend on*) You should never *count on* unreliable persons.
98.	**Charge of**	(*noun*-crime) *Charge of* murder was framed against him.
99.	**Charge with**	(*verb*-crime) He was *charged with* the murder of his neighbour.
100.	**Cope with**	(*manage work*) My advocate cannot *cope with* heavy court work.
101.	**Contrast to**	(*noun*) Her character is a *contrast to* her husband's.
102.	**Contrast with**	(*verb*) They tried to *contrast* the character of their father *with* mine.
103.	**Cash in on**	(*avail of*) Every body of them was trying to *cash in on* reservation of posts announced for the community.
104.	**Contribute to**	(*add to a thing*) Every Indian should *contribute to* the success of Indian economy.
105.	**Complain against**	(*a person*) He *complained* to the Principal *against* me.
106.	**Complain of**	(*a thing*) The teacher *complained of* his rude behaviour.
107.	**Cordone off**	(*protect*) The dias of the PM was *cordoned off*.
108.	**Commit to**	(*a promise, pledge, sentence*) He has *committed* himself *to* the service of the society.
109.	**Confide in**	(*a person*) I have always *confided in* him and he has never deceived me.
110.	**Confide to**	(*a person*) Do not *confide* your secrets *to* unreliable friends.
111.	**Consist in**	(*remain*) Beauty *consists in* the character of a person.
112.	**Consist of**	(*comprise*) The house *consists of* four rooms.
113.	**Commence**	(*on a day, at time, in a month*) The examinations will *commence* on Monday next at 10 o'clock.
114.	**Commence with**	(*as first item*) He *commenced with* grammar, when he started teaching English.
115.	**Clamour for**	(*demand*) The labourers are *clamouring for* the rise in their wages.
116.	**Clamour against**	(*complain against*) The residents are *clamouring against* the negligence of the police.
117.	**Cause for**	(*reason for*) There is no *cause for* anxiety.
118.	**Cause of**	(*result from*) The *cause of* cancer is still unknown.
119.	**Concerned for**	(*worried*) I am greatly *concerned for* the safety of his money.
120.	**Concerned with**	(*have anything to do*) I am not *concerned with* his business.
121.	**Condole with**	(*a person*) I *condoled with* my friend in the death of his father.

PREPOSITIONS

122.	**Disappoint of**	(*hopes*) I was *disappointed of* my success in the new venture.
123.	**Despair of**	(*hopes*) He was *despaired of* the hope of early marriage of her daughter.
124.	**Dabble in/at**	(*art, politics etc*) Though he belonged to the family of politicians, he never *dabbled in* politics.
125.	**Destined for**	(*some future*) He is *destined for* the post of DM and is expected to be promoted soon.
126.	**Disgrace on**	(*dishonourable*) He is a *disgrace on* his family.
127.	**Dwell on/upon**	(*speak/write in detail*) The teacher *dwelt on* the need of discipline.
128.	**Die of**	(*a disease*) He *died of* malaria after a few days' illness.
129.	**Die from**	(*some cause*) He *died from* over work because hard work had affected his health adversely.
130.	**Differ with**	(*a person in views*) I *differ with* you on the views of life.
131.	**Differ from**	(*in something*) She *differs from* me both in habits and looks.
132.	**Deal in**	(*trade in*) My friend *deals in* cloth.
133.	**Deal with**	(*a matter, a person*) You must learn how to *deal with* customers.
134.	**Dispense with**	(*to remove, to do without*) You cannot *dispense with* the use of fan in summer.
135.	**Dispense**	(*to deal out, distribute*) As a judge, he *dispenses* equal justice to all and one.
136.	**Dispose of**	(*sell*) I shall *dispose of* my old furniture and buy new one.
137.	**Disposed to**	(*inclined to*) He is *disposed to* travelling abroad.
138.	**Decamp with**	(*booty*) The robbers had *decamped with* the booty before the police arrived.
139.	**Disgust with**	(*person, life*) Being spiritual, he is *disgusted with* materialistic lie life.
140.	**Disgust at**	(*an act*) Every one felt *disgusted at* his jokes.
141.	**Discriminate against**	(*not to treat well*) No one should *discriminate against* the poor.
142.	**Discriminate between**	(*difference between*) We should always *discriminate between* right and wrong.
143.	**Embark on**	(*venture, undertake*) He has decided to *embark on* new business undertaking.
144.	**Enter**	(*place, no preposition*) He *entered* my room without my permission.
145.	**Enter into**	(*alliance, agreement*) India and America have *entered into* various agreements.
146.	**Enter upon/on**	(*undertake*) My brother has decided to *enter upon* expansion programme of his business.
147.	**Enlarge on/upon**	(*write or say more*) I need not *enlarge on* the problem and waste your time.
148.	**Endowed with**	(*gifted with*) His wife is *endowed with* both charms and talents.
149.	**Enamoured with**	(*a person*) Rosalind was *enamoured with* Orlando at first sight.
150.	**Enamoured of**	(*a thing*) Though it was their first meeting, he was *enamoured of* her talents.
151.	**Enrage at**	(*a thing, an act*) The teacher was *enraged at* the student's insolence.
152.	**Enrage with**	(*a person*) The teacher was *enraged with* the student for his insolence.
153.	**Exult over**	[*enjoy (bad sense)*] The spectators *exulted over* the defeat of Pakistani team.

#	Phrase	Meaning & Example
154.	**Exult at**	(*enjoy*) The spectators *exulted at* the victory of Indian team.
155.	**Eligible for**	(*a post*) Only graduates are *eligible for* the post.
156.	**Familiar to**	(*to know*) Her face is quite *familiar to* everyone.
157.	**Familiar with**	(*knowledge*) I am not very *familiar with* botanical names.
158.	**False of**	(*heart*) He is not *false of* heart.
159.	**False to**	(*friends or principles*) We should not be *false to* our friends.
160.	**Fascinated by**	(*a thing*) The children were *fascinated by* all the toys in the shop windows.
161.	**Fascinated with**	(*a person*) I was *fascinated with* her because of her admirable manners.
162.	**Fly into**	(*anger*) On hearing my remarks, she *flew into* a rage.
163.	**Feed on**	(*live on*) Carnivorous animals *feed on* flesh.
164.	**Fondness for**	(*liking for*) He has *fondness for* classical music.
165.	**Fond of**	(*linking for*) He is *fond of* classical music.
166.	**For lack of/ For want of/ For short of/**	(*something*) *For lack of* money, he could not continue study further.
167.	**Grieve for**	(*a person*) He *grieved for* the victims of the storm.
168.	**Grieve over**	(*a thing*) He *grieved over* the loss of money in business.
169.	**Grieve at**	(*an event*) He *grieved at* my father's death, when I informed him of my personal tragedy.
170.	**Guard against**	(*mistakes, temptations*) You should *guard against* the wrong use of words.
171.	**Guard from**	(*a danger, of a thing etc*) You should *guard from* him because he is false of heart.
172.	**Glance at**	(*take a quick look*) He *glanced at* her face and started noting down her address.
173.	**Glance through**	(*go through*) He *glanced through* the letter in a hurry and handed it back to me.
174.	**Good at**	(*expert*) He is *good at* piano.
175.	**Good for**	(*nothing*) He is *good for* nothing fellow.
176.	**Hear from**	(*a person*) I have not *heard from* you for a long time.
177.	**Hear of**	(*something*) I *heard of* this event in Mumbai and rushed back to Delhi.
178.	**Hear by**	(*post, through communication*) I *heard by* a letter about his success.
179.	**Hard by**	(*near*) The college is *hard by* and I go to college on foot.
180.	**Hard up**	(*financially tight*) He is *hard up* these days.
181.	**Hanker after**	(*run after, hunger after*) Don't *hanker after* money and fame.
182.	**Healed of**	(*a disease, cured of*) He is *healed of* illness after long treatment.
183.	**Infer from**	(*statement*) You cannot *infer* anything *from* his statement.
184.	**Insight into**	(*reality, situation*) Wise persons have *insight into* the reality of life.
185.	**Impress upon**	(*a person, advice*) The Principal *impressed upon* the students the need of discipline.
186.	**Impress with**	(*with a thing*) He *impressed* me very much *with* his good manners.
187.	**Inquire for/about**	(*a thing*) He has just gone to *inquire for* the supply of rations.
188.	**Inquire after**	(*welfare, ask after*) I *inquired after* his father's health.
189.	**Inquire of**	(*ask a person*) I *inquired of* him the name of his father.
190.	**Inquired into**	(*investigate*) The police are *inquiring into* the case.
191.	**Interfere in**	(*a thing*) Don't *interfere in* my private affairs.

PREPOSITIONS

192.	Interfere with	(*hinder*) Refrain from *interfering with* the course of justice.
193.	Invest with	(*authority*) The Principal was *invested with* powers to deal with this problem.
194.	Influence with	(*a person*) He has immense *influence with* the police.
195.	Influence over	(*the people*) The PM has great *influence over* the people of tribal regions.
196.	Influence on	(*a thing*) The *influence* of books *on* young children is great.
197.	Intrude into	(*forcibly*) He *intruded into* the room but was turned out.
198.	Intrude on	(*privacy*) Don't *intrude on* the privacy of anyone.
199.	Intimate with	(*friendly*) She is *intimate with* my family.
200.	Irritated at	(*thing*) He seems greatly *irritated at* my refusal.
201.	Incensed at	(*thing*) He was greatly *incensed at* his conduct.
202.	Indignant at	(*thing*) Instead of being happy, he is *indignant at* my offer.
203.	Judge of	(*give opinion*) Don't *judge of* things by their outward appearance.
204.	Judge by	(*test by*) He was *judged by* his academic qualifications.
205.	Jump to	(*conclusion*) Don't *jump to* conclusion without giving due consideration to the facts.
206.	Jump at	(*an offer*) He *jumped at* the offer and was highly pleased.
207.	Jeer at	(*an act, a person*) The spectators *jeered at* their team on their fourth defeat.
208.	Jest at	(*an act, a person*) Never *jest at* those, who are in trouble.
209.	Known to	(*passive voice*) You are *known to* her very well.
210.	Known by	(*recognise*) A man is *known by* the company he keeps.
211.	Known for	(*a quality*) Arnav is well-*known for* his benevolence.
212.	Knocked at	(*the door*) I *knocked at* the door but there was no reply.
213.	Knock on	(*noun*) Mala heard a *knock on* the door.
214.	Key to	(*success*) Hard work is *key to* success.
215.	Lean on	(*depend on*) I had to *lean on* him in difficulties.
216.	Lean to	(*inclined towards*) He seems to *lean* more *to* his daughter than his son.
217.	Live in	(*region, area, country*) He is *living in* America.
218.	Live at	(*indicate the place*) He is *living at* Agra.
219.	Live on	(*food*) He *lives* entirely *on* vegetables these days.
220.	Live by	(*livelihood, manner*) I have to *live by* the labour of my own hands.
221.	Live off	(*source*) Now-a-days, he is *living off* rental income.
222.	Listen to	(*advice*) You should *listen to* my advice.
223.	Liable for	(*responsible for*) I hold you *liable for* the murder.
224.	Liable to	(*deserve*) He is *liable to* imprisonment and fine.
225.	Laugh with	(*enjoy with others*) It is better to *laugh with* than to laugh at others.
226.	Laugh at	(*an act, person*) Never *laugh at* the old persons.
227.	Lacking in	(*something, wanting in*) Even educated persons were *lacking in* table manner.
228.	(Have) Liking for	(*a person, a thing*) She has great *liking for* children.
229.	(Take) Liking to	(*a person, a thing*) My friend took *liking to* Arnav and married him.
230.	Likeness between	(*similarity*) There is *likeness between* the Chinese and the Koreans.
231.	Limit to	(*extent*) There is always a *limit to* friendship.
232.	Move to	(*tears*) On listening to the tale of my sufferings, Pearl was *moved to* tears.

#	Phrase	Usage
233.	**Move with**	(*pity*) Pearl was *moved with* pity at his plight.
234.	**Move by**	(*condition*) We were *moved by* her pathetic condition.
235.	**Married to**	(*a woman*) Arnav was *married to* a famous doctor.
236.	**Married with**	(*a man*) She was *married with* Arnav.
237.	**Mix with**	(*a thing*) Please don't *mix* water *with* milk.
238.	**Menace to**	(*treat to*) Terrorists are *menace to* the security of the country.
239.	**Match for**	(*a person in quality*) His father is no *match for* my uncle.
240.	**Mock at**	(*an act, a person*) Never *mock at* the poverty of others.
241.	**Meditate on**	(*past act*) She was in tears, when she *meditated on* her humilation.
242.	**Meditate**	(*future act*) She is *meditating* revenge for her humiliation.
243.	**Neglectful of**	(*a person, work, a thing*) He has been *neglectful of* his business.
244.	**Negligent in**	(*careless in duty*) Don't be *negligent in* your duty.
245.	**Need for**	(*something*) There is no *need for* further action in the matter.
246.	**(in) need of**	(*something*) I am not in *need of* money (feelings).
247.	**Originate in**	(*place as a source*) Modern civilisation *originated in* Europe.
248.	**Originate with**	(*a person*) This scheme *originated with* the Finance Minister.
249.	**Occupied in**	(*doing a thing*) I am just now *occupied in* solving the problems.
250.	**Occupied with**	(*a thing*) My father is *occupied with* the expansion of his business.
251.	**Operate on/upon**	(*in the sense of operation*) The doctor decided to *operate on* her leg immediately.
252.	**Oblivious of**	(*having no memory, ignorant of*) *Oblivious of* danger, they kept on marching ahead.
253.	**Offend at**	(*thing*) He was *offended at* my words.
254.	**Offend with**	(*person*) Please don't get *offended with* her as she is honest.
255.	**Overwhelm with**	(*feelings*) Her mother was *overwhelmed with* love for his son.
256.	**Overwhelm by**	(*defeated by*) The enemy was *overwhelmed by* our army.
257.	**Part with**	(*a thing*) A miser cannot *part with* a single penny.
258.	**Part from**	(*a person*) I *parted from* my friend in Delhi.
259.	**Preface to**	(*a book*) He wrote a *preface to* his book.
260.	**Profit by**	(*learn*) You will *profit by* experience.
261.	**Profit from**	(*gain*) We may *profit from* new pension policy.
262.	**Partiality for**	(*a thing, liking*) She has *partiality for* sweets.
263.	**Partiality to**	(*a person's favour*) He always shows *partiality to* his relatives.
264.	**Prone to**	(*inclined to*) Thickly populated areas are *prone to* riots and diseases.
265.	**Perish by**	(*destroy, famine, sword*) The tyrants *perish by* sword.
266.	**Perish with**	(*suffer from*) They are *perishing with* starvation.
267.	**Prevail against**	(*a thing, face*) They *prevailed against* all odds in life.
268.	**Prevail on/upon**	(*a person, to compel*) I have *prevailed on* him to come to attend the function.
269.	**Point out**	(*reveal*) I *pointed out* his errors and he got annoyed with me.
270.	**Point at**	(*blame*) No one can *point at* his character because he is quite honest.
271.	**Point to**	(*refer to*) His speech *pointed to* a few problems relating to poverty.
272.	**Preside at**	(*a party, chief guest*) The Governor *presided at* the feast.
273.	**Preside over**	(*meeting, president*) He *presided over* the meeting in the absence of the Chairman.
274.	**Provided against**	(*adversity*) We should always *provide against* a rainy day.

PREPOSITIONS

275.	**Provided for**	(*arrange what is necessary*) He died without *providing for* his family.
276.	**Popular for**	(*a good quality*) He is *popular for* his honesty.
277.	**Popular with**	(*the people*) He is *popular with* the students of the class.
278.	**Pine for**	(*crave for a person*) She is *pining for* the return of her lost son.
279.	**Pine away**	(*die away with grief*) She *pined away* in the memory of her lost son.
280.	**Play at**	(*cards*) We are *playing at* cards.
281.	**Play upon**	(*a musical instrument*) She is *playing upon* the piano.
282.	**Partake of**	(*share any thing*) They *partook of* our food and were satisfied.
283.	**Prey on**	(*exploit*) The rich *prey on* the poor.
284.	**Passion for**	(*strong desire*) He has *passion for* writing poetry.
285.	**Peculiar to**	(*particular*) This habit is *peculiar to* my father.
286.	**Pity for**	(*a man*) We should feel *pity for* the poor.
287.	**Pity on**	(*a man*) He should take *pity on* the poor.
288.	**Pity**	(*used as a verb*) We should *pity* the poor.
289.	**Pride on**	(*used as a verb*) They *prided* themselves *on* their wealth.
290.	**Pride in**	(*an object of importance*) They take *pride in* their wealth.
291.	**Proud of**	(*people, nation*) We should be *proud of* our country.
292.	**Prompt in**	(*quick in*) You should be *prompt in* doing your duty.
293.	**Quick at**	(*a thing*) The dog is *quick at* smelling.
294.	**Quick in**	(*doing a thing*) The boy is *quick in* working out the problems.
295.	**Quick of**	(*understanding*) The child is very *quick of* understanding.
296.	**Quarrel over**	(*a thing*) They *quarrelled over* the division of their ancesteral property.
297.	**Quarrel with**	(*a person*) Don't *quarrel with* your friends over trifles.
298.	**Reputation for**	(*a quality*) My brother has a *reputation for* honesty.
299.	**Remorse for**	(*wrong doing*) She felt *remorse* later on *for* neglecting her old parents.
300.	**Respite from**	(*relief from*) People have felt no *respite from* cold wave.
301.	**Replace by**	(*a new object*) Old furniture will be *replaced by* new one.
302.	**Repent of**	(*an action*) He *repented of* the misdeeds of his youth.
303.	**Recourse to**	(*resort to, adopt as means*) They took *recourse to* wrong means for success.
304.	**Revenge oneself on**	(*used as verb*) (*a person*) He *revenged himself on* his enemy for the murder of his brother.
305.	**Revenge for**	(*used as noun*) (*an injury*) She took *revenge* on him *for* his misdeeds.
306.	**Reconcile oneself to**	(*a thing*) You must *reconcile yourself to* the circumstances and endure them.
307.	**Reconcile with**	(*a person*) He has not yet been *reconciled with* his wife.
308.	**Reason with**	(*a person*) I *reasoned with* him but could not bring him round.
309.	**Reckon on/upon**	(*depend on*) You can safely *reckon upon* the books for advice.
310.	**Remonstrate with**	(*a person*) The players *remonstrated with* the umpire against his LBW decision.
311.	**Remiss in**	(*duty*) Those who are found *remiss in* duty, will be punished.
312.	**Sure of**	(*a thing*) We are *sure of* victory in the game.
313.	**Sequel to**	(*as a result*) *Sequel to* success in life, he become extremely rich.
314.	**Smile at**	(*mock at*) All his friends *smiled* mockingly *at* his failure.
315.	**Smile on**	(*favour*) At last, fate *smiled on* him and he was successful.

#	Phrase	Meaning & Example
316.	Slow at	(*doing something*) On account of her old age, she is *slow at* cooking.
317.	Substitute for	(*old thing*) New furniture will be *substituted for* old one.
318.	Scare of	(*afraid of*) I got *scared of* the sound of bomb blast.
319.	Shoot at, strike at, catch at, hit at	(*used for unsuccessful attempt*) The police *shot at* the thief, who escaped in darkness.
320.	Shoot, Strike, Catch, Hit	(*used for successful attempt*) The police *shot* the robber dead.
321.	Speak for	(*favour*) I shall *speak for* you to the Commander.
322.	Speak of	(*praise*) There is no scenic spot here to *speak of*.
323.	Start on	(*journey*) He *started on* journey for Mumbai, though, he did not have enough money.
324.	Strive for	(*try for*) It is futile to *strive for* permanent joy in life.
325.	Strive with	(*compete with*) Don't *strive with* the rich and the powerful.
326.	Side with	(*verb*) (*favour*) He would never *side with* those, who are unjust.
327.	Search for	(*a thing*) He is still *searching for* a good house.
328.	Search	(*frisk*) He was *searching* his pocket.
329.	Seek	(*try to find*) He *sought* shelter in the house of his friend, when there were riots.
330.	Seek after	(*in demand*) He is much *sought after* actor these days.
331.	Seek for	(*try to win*) He always *sought for* his aim in his life.
332.	Seething with	(*anger, discontent*) The residents of the locality were *seething with* anger over the apathy of the police.
333.	Suffer	(*loss*) He *suffered* heavy loss in business.
334.	Suffer from	(*disease*) He is *suffering from* cancer and is not likely to survive long.
335.	Show off	(*display*) The modest persons do not *show off* their wealth.
336.	Sentence to	(*punishment*) Madho was *sentenced to* death by the judge.
337.	Spark off	(*give rise to, trigger off*) Communal speech will *spark off* riots in the town.
338.	Think of	(*remember a subject*) *Think of* a plan and let me know tomorrow.
339.	Think over	(*to consider*) I will *think over* your case after sometime.
340.	Tantamount to	(*equal in effect*) His remarks are *tantamount to* insult.
341.	Tired of	(*sick of, fed up with, weary*) I am *tired of* listening to his flattering words.
342.	Treat of	(*a subject, deal with*) You should *treat of* this problem patiently.
343.	Tresspass on	(*encroach on, land*) Do not *tresspass on* government land.
344.	Tresspass against	(*law*) He was punished for *tresspassing against* the rules of the road.
345.	Triumph over	(*difficulties*) At last, he *triumphed over* his difficulties.
346.	Trifle with	(*make fun of*) Don't *trifle with* the feelings of the poor.
347.	Usher in	(*begin, bring out*) Globalisation has *ushered in* an era of market economy.
348.	Verse in	(*thing, expert in*) She is *versed in* the art of cooking.
349.	Vote for	(*a person*) I don't *vote for* worthless politicians.
350.	Vote on	(*resolution*) The members *voted on* the resolution, which was passed by majority.
351.	Vote to	(*win*) He was *voted to* power with thumping majority.
352.	Venture upon	(*an undertaking*) He did not dare to *venture upon* new enterprise.
353.	Vain of	(*proud of*) Though rich, she is not *vain of* her wealth.
354.	Vexed with	(*person*) Don't get *vexed with* me.

PREPOSITIONS

355.	Vexed at	(*a thing*) I am *vexed at* my brother's absence.
356.	Wait upon	(*attend upon, to serve*) Who is *waiting* upon this table?
357.	Wait for	(*person, thing*) He is *waiting for* her.
358.	Weary of	(*a thing*) He was *weary of* study and retired to bed.
359.	Warn against	(*fault, danger*) I have already *warned* you *against* your carelessness.
360.	Warn of	(*danger*) He *warned* the nation *of* financial crisis.
361.	Wish for	(*a thing*) I dont *wish for* anything in life.
362.	Worthy of	(*praise, note*) Your remarks are really *worthy of* note.
363.	Wanting in	(*lacking in*) She is *wanting in* common sense.
364.	Ward off	(*keep at a distance*) Hindus believe in many rituals to *ward* the evils *off*.
365.	Wary of	(*something, chary of*) We should be *wary of* strangers.
366.	Yearn for	(*acute desire, long for*) She *yearned for* the return to her own home.
367.	Zealous for/about	(*a thing*) A good soldier is always *zealous for* his country's honour.

WORK BOOK EXERCISE (A)

Directions *Spot the errors, if any, in the following sentences.*

1. We should always listen the advice of our well wishers.
2. He closely resembles with his father in facial features.
3. While taking examinations, always write with dark ink.
4. The Insurance Company has promised to compensate the damage to my house.
5. You must revise your answer sheet again.
6. He suffered from heart attack last year.
7. Everybody complains against callous treatment of the police.
8. She is very popular among her friends and relatives.
9. The highway robbers robbed all their belongings.
10. Would you please ring me up on next Monday?
11. Don't quarrel on trifles with your friends.
12. My house comprises of five rooms and is spacious enough for two families.
13. There is no cause of anxiety about his health.
14. Children should be taught to write by a fountain pen.
15. Pakistan invaded on India in 1965.
16. His employers were compelled to dispense his services.
17. On Diwali, he will order for a new pair of shoes.
18. You should at least congratulate your friend for his grand success in the elections.
19. The accused was bound by a chain and taken to prison.
20. My father has assured me to present me a new scooter on my next birthday.
21. The charge with murder against him, could not be proved.
22. In vain, you are searching your lost purse.
23. For coming late, the teacher fined ten rupees on him.
24. It is very different and costlier than your shirt.
25. Don't laugh on the poor if they can't afford comforts of life.

26. Fragrance pervaded in the garden and we enjoyed our evening stroll.
27. Due to lack of common sense, he cannot succeed in life.
28. He parted with his wife in tears.
29. It is not his nature to pick up a quarrel with his neighbours.
30. The residents informed the tragedy to the police long ago.
31. The reforms must come from up.
32. She never wavered from her loyalty to me.
33. Please do not play into the hands of criminals.
34. She has aversion for senseless TV serials.
35. Your remarks are worthy to note.

WORK BOOK EXERCISE (B)

Directions *Spot the errors, if any, in the following sentences.*

1. In a democratic society, no one should be discriminated because of caste and creed.
2. A summons was served to him last week.
3. As a responsible officer, you should dispense with justice to the poor and the needy.
4. Whenever she goes out, her chaperon accompanies with her.
5. The meeting began at about 2 pm and he had arrived quite earlier.
6. The news of the Prime Minister's death spread in all over the country.
7. He always travelled in second class with a view to understanding the pulse of his countrymen.
8. She was admitted in the hospital when she met with a serious accident.
9. After his death, his wife and children died of misery and starvation.
10. While going to college, I met my old friends in the way.
11. My friends entrusted me his valuables, when he went abroad.
12. Our neighbour was charged of murder last year.
13. You must comply by the orders of your seniors.
14. The father of my friend deals with medicine.
15. She has been ill from fever since Monday.
16. Real beauty consists of good character.
17. The dacoits set fire on the house.
18. There was warning on the notice board "No admission without permission."
19. While returning back from Delhi, he lost his purse.
20. He was overwhelmed by grief on the demise of his father.
21. It is very difficult to resist against the prevailing system and traditions.
22. My father did not agree to me on this point.
23. The show will commence from 3 pm.
24. Two terrorists were shot, but were able to escape through the dense forest.
25. Those, who violate against the law of the country, should be sent behind the bars.

PREPOSITIONS

26. You are not eligible to the post because you don't have the experience required by the company.
27. He aspires for fame in whatever field he takes up a job.
28. Though recently married, they are not pulling on well with each other these days.
29. They are working with heart and soul and are sure to succeed in the long run.
30. She stayed at home in whole day because she felt sick.
31. What is time in your watch?
32. My uncle went to abroad last year.
33. The train is running in time.
34. His character is a contrast to my sister's.
35. He is not able to cope up with heavy work.
36. We suffer because we mistake the unreal as real.
37. There is tendency of leaving work undone on the part of children.
38. Please tear away this letter.

WORK BOOK EXERCISE (C)

Directions *Spot the errors, if any, in the following sentences.*

1. She is very arrogant because she comes from a rich family.
2. He has not come to meet me, although he came back before a week.
3. I saw him climbing on the tree to pluck mangoes.
4. Everybody knows what for Kanpur is famous.
5. He has never wished any reward, although he has served suffering humanity throughout his life.
6. Do you know, he will be operated tomorrow in a Delhi hospital?
7. Six teams are competing the Singer World Cup.
8. They were talking something but I don't know what they were talking.
9. She prays God everyday for the safe return of her son.
10. In a short time, the new staff will be substituted by those, who are on long leave.
11. You should not leave now because this road is not safe to travel.
12. My father has promised to provide me a scooter next year.
13. He always differs from his friends in views on life.
14. Indians should learn to remain united together.
15. She has a great liking to sweets.
16. He is wanting of honesty and nobody trusts him.
17. In accordance to my advice, she did not go there.
18. After he had struggled, fate smiled at him at last.
19. Such a glorious success has never been dreamt by us.
20. In the meanwhile, she kept on waiting outside.
21. I can't say, to whom she was talking on phone yesterday.
22. She has been crying from morning.
23. He is not in fault and so he should be excused.

24. Always side those, who are just and honest.
25. Selfish persons always seek after cheap popularity.
26. Please fill water in the bucket.
27. Kashmir is to the north of India.
28. He will wait here until 5 o'clock.
29. The DM will preside over the feast.
30. He was moved with tears on her condition.
31. They went to home soon after the accident.
32. It is a saying in the Kashmiries.
33. He does not seem to be aware as to his qualities.
34. His behaviour cannot be called into question.
35. The banquet to all accounts was lavish.
36. You must learn to tackle with complex problems.
37. I regret for my absurd remarks.

WORK BOOK EXERCISE (D)

Directions *Fill up the blanks with suitable prepositions.*

1. His professional ability proves that he is cut .... for this job.
2. The history of Hindu religion dates .... ancient times.
3. Now, government servants have the day .... every Saturday.
4. Nothing can deter him .... pursuing his aim of life.
5. After the death of his father, the responsibility has devolved .... him.
6. In accordance with the advice of a doctor, she is .... diet.
7. Normally, he stays .... until 11 p.m. these days.
8. No one believes him because he is false .... heart.
9. The officials have the habit of fawning .... ministers.
10. The problem of communal harmony cannot be glossed .... by government.
11. Kanishka was initiated .... Buddhism by Buddhist monks.
12. Consequent upon heavy loss, he is worse .... these days.
13. Co-operation between friends stems .... mutual consideration.
14. Many Russians name their children .... Indians.
15. Indians have pinned their hopes .... the emergence of some superman.
16. She could not muster .... courage to stand against the maltreatment.
17. Strangely, her name did not occur .... me on the second meeting.
18. The whole town was plunged .... sorrow after the massacre of the students.
19. On seeing a robber, he at once reached .... his pistol in his pocket.
20. The government acted judiciously to stave .... the crisis.
21. The boys were seen hanging .... girls' hostel.
22. There is a tendency to trump ...... charges against opposition leaders in every country.
23. In fact, there is no library in our town to speak ....
24. To my surprise, even well to do persons have no scruple .... cheating others.

PREPOSITIONS

25. You should not mind his .... the cuff remarks.
26. The court has yet to serve summons .... him for the suit filed against him.
27. The court has yet to serve him .... summons for the suit filed against him.
28. He is 5' 1" and he is tall .... his age.
29. He stared me .... the face as if he would devour me.
30. Don't stare .... the girls as long as you are in the class.

WORK BOOK EXERCISE (E)

Directions *Fill up the blanks with suitable prepositions.*

1. You cannot expect respect from him because he is lost .... sense of shame.
2. You have not to get up because the book is lying .... hand.
3. After all, hard work has come to tell .... your health.
4. Dishonesty is always detrimental .... progress in life.
5. He made insulting remarks that are derogatory .... his reputation.
6. In the long run, drinking proved fatal both .... his reputation & health.
7. The rich are not inured .... manual labour.
8. Disintegration of the country is inimical .... the progress of the people.
9. The court has absolved him .... all the charges levelled against him.
10. Children, by the force of habit, are attracted .... anything that glitters.
11. Anyone, who comes in contact with him, is enamoured .... his charismatic personality.
12. Encouraged by the success of his ventures, he has decided to embark .... the expansion programme.
13. At the sight of his former wife he, flew .... a rage.
14. Now-a-days, there is rage .... pop music among the Indian youth.
15. Most of the family members dissented .... the suggestion he made.
16. The President dwelt .... the problems facing the country.
17. The robbers not only injured the landlord but also decamped .... booty.
18. The labourers are clamouring .... hike in their wages.
19. On the eve of the Prime Minister's visit, Civil Line has been cordoned ....
20. .... the campus, there is much indiscipline for want of proper management.
21. He has great antipathy .... those, who are hypocrites.
22. Quinine is an effective antidote .... Malaria.
23. As a dancer, she has aptitude .... Classical system.
24. One should never acquiesce .... unjustified demands of the employees.
25. She blushed .... the mention of her lover's name.
26. He is born .... an intelligent mother.
27. Your remarks don't have any bearing .... the communal problem.
28. He was vexed .... the belated reply from his son.
29. The lady was greatly incensed .... the misbehaviour of the bus conductor.
30. He decided to enter .... a new course of life.

WORK BOOK EXERCISE (F)

Directions *Fill up the blanks with suitable prepositions.*

1. As a step to renovation, he has decided to replace old furniture .... new one.
2. During the course of speech, the Principal enlarged .... the need of improving college library.
3. He was in a hurry and just glanced .... the letter.
4. Now-a-days, the rich persons enjoy influence .... the police authorities.
5. Nobody likes anyone to intrude .... his privacy.
6. Think over the matter. Please don't jump .... conclusions in a hurry.
7. The scheme of Rozgar Yojna originated .... the Prime Minister.
8. We must not show partiality .... our relatives.
9. The Hindus believe in many rituals to ward .... evils.
10. There is no limit .... the wants of man.
11. The mosquito is a menace .... the health of mankind.
12. Don't think that there is any exception .... the rules of moral conduct.
13. Cold climate is conducive .... working conditions for man.
14. We have decided to adhere .... the original programme.
15. Those, abstemious .... habits, are known to live long.
16. Don't mix with those, who don't approve .... your style of living.
17. The visit of the PM has been advanced .... two days.
18. Since her failure in the exams, she prefers to remain aloof .... her friends.
19. Everyone was greatly amused .... her ignorance of simple facts of life.
20. We have the habit of exulting .... the discomfiture of our rivals.

WORK BOOK EXERCISE (G)

Directions *Fill up the blanks with appropriate prepositions.*

1. Disruptive forces in the country are fatal .... the integrity of the nation.
2. Politeness is a quality that is alien .... Mrs. Kapoor.
3. Liquor is not the best means to gain respite .... sufferings in life.
4. I think his long silence is tantamount .... a refusal.
5. Never in life has he been beset .... grave financial problems.
6. Heedless .... consequences he remained deaf .... her request.
7. Temperance in life is conducive .... health.
8. As a literary artist, he is indifferent .... praise or blame.
9. There is no need .... helping a reckless fellow like him.
10. For want .... experience, he was easily taken in by his sweet words.
11. The newspaper will issue a supplement .... the issue of 15th August.
12. Pollution is growing as a potential menace .... human survival.

PREPOSITIONS

13. Sequal .... the announcement of new fiscal policy, the industrial sector has started looking up.
14. Pakistan has ever been hostile .... India since it came .... being.
15. The Yadavs claim their descent .... the clan of Lord Krishna.
16. As an educated lady, she is very much alive .... her rights.
17. Afflicted .... penury, he died a miserable death.
18. Pre-independent India had given birth to a number of sons fired .... patriotism.
19. She was overcome .... fatigue and went to bed.
20. How can a highly successful person like him be devoid .... common sense.
21. She is destined .... a career higher than you expect.
22. The youngman eligible .... marriage can apply to the Matron of the Rescue Home.
23. As a policy of the office, he is not fit .... the post, he is holding.
24. After straying/digressing .... the main subject he reverted .... it again.
25. The two injured persons succumbed .... their injuries in the District Hospital.
26. At dusk, the intruder emerged .... behind the bushes.
27. Although it is an exaggerated statement, it does not detract .... the truth.
28. The players remonstrated .... the umpire .... his partiality.
29. Learn to grapple .... the problems of life.
30. This fellow is good .... nothing.

WORK BOOK EXERCISE (H)

Directions *Fill up the blanks with appropriate prepositions.*

1. He is always distrustful .... the prejudicial motives of his partners.
2. The attitude of the fanatics is always prejudicial .... other religion.
3. The way she uses cosmetics, is offensive .... good taste.
4. The competitive exams should never be allowed to coincide .... university examinations.
5. At the fag end of his life, he was bereft .... wealth and home.
6. Extremism is detrimental .... the progress of a country.
7. The minister has decided to sue the newspaper .... libellous writing.
8. You have no right to trespass .... the law of the land.
9. The government has decided to impose enhanced excise duty .... luxury goods.
10. Aurangzeb divested Shahjahan .... royal powers.
11. He is a cosmopolitan and tolerant .... the religious views of others.
12. Your behaviour of indifference smacks .... jealousy.
13. Now-a-days, the majority of students are not amenable .... discipline.
14. The DM has consented to preside .... the function.
15. The rich are always susceptible .... flattery.

16. Since the death of his son, he remains confined .... his home.
17. This year, the result is contrary .... the expectations of everyone.
18. The thickly populated localities are prone .... communal riots.
19. "Have compassion .... every creature", preached Buddha.
20. Those found remiss .... duty will not be pardoned.
21. The climate of Mumbai does not agree .... me.
22. He is still smarting .... humiliating behaviour of his boss.
23. Your future plans rest .... imaginary ideas.
24. The jewellery, recovered from the robbers, has not yet been restored .... him.
25. The police had to resort .... lathi charge .... extreme provocation.
26. The question of unemployment bristles .... insurmountable difficulties.
27. The godowns of the FCI are infested .... rats.
28. Her house is adjacent .... Amitabh's.
29. Never do any thing, that is incompatible .... national interests.
30. He treated .... religious communalism in India exhaustively.

Cumulative Exercise

Directions *Fill up the blanks with appropriate prepositions.*

1. Don't side .... those, who act contrary .... national interests.
2. She took exception .... his oblique reference to her parents.
3. Mr. Narayan has been overwhelmed .... grief, since his young son met with a fatal accident.
4. At last, she acceded .... his proposal of marriage after long courtship.
5. The team was elated .... joy .... their victory.
6. Despite financial programme, they could not adhere .... it.
7. The emergency meeting of the college staff approved .... the budget proposals for the coming year.
8. They have apprised the authorities concerned .... the failure of the plan.
9. Never judge .... a metal .... its glitter as all that glitters is not gold.
10. My guest had to pay for lunch, since I had no money .... me.
11. His head is teeming .... brilliant ideas.
12. At present, the country is agog .... rumours of civil war.
13. You must account .... your absence .... the hostel warden.
14. "Who is waiting .... this table?". The customer asked.
15. At present, India is beset .... many problems.

PREPOSITIONS

16. He is dead .... all sense of honour.
17. No noble act is prompted .... selfish motives.
18. She is proficient .... the art of cooking.
19. Now-a-days, material values take precedence .... spiritual values.
20. Mr Kakkar has a retinue of servants working .... him.
21. He fell .... the horse and sustained injuries.
22. We have not yet decided .... the venue of the meeting.
23. I have done .... her, as she is impervious .... reasonable advice.
24. Don't despair .... your efforts despite failure.
25. How come, you are getting negligent .... your duty.
26. Your apprehensions about your wife borders .... lunacy.
27. Have you caught up .... your pending work?
28. Sitting idle and living .... rental, income does not agree .... my taste.
29. He smelled .... liqour, when he entered the banquet hall.
30. The visit of the Prime Minister has been preponed .... ten days.

Previous Years' Questions

Directions *Fill in the blanks with appropriate preposition/participle and rewrite the completed sentences.*

I.
[Civil Services (Mains), 2006]
1. I told him that he could not catch a big fish .... a small rod.
2. He was taken .... task for shortage in cash balance.
3. The father pulled .... his son for his extravagant habits.
4. He is so clever, it is difficult to see .... his tricks.
5. I have been invited by my friend .... tea.

II.
[Civil Services (Mains), 2009]
1. The shopkeeper refused to bargain .... the customer.
2. He did not believe .... bargaining.
3. He had already decided .... a fair price.
4. The customer was looking .... a bargain.
5. They argued .... the price for a long time.

III.
[Civil Services (Mains), 2010]
1. I am angry .... her .... lying.
2. I was red .... anger at his remarks.
3. Could you explain this rule .... me, please.
4. People have always been kind .... me.

IV. [CAPF, 2011]
1. Try to cut it .... a sharp knife.
2. He was accused .... theft.
3. She threw the ball .... me.
4. He is suffering .... a chronic disease.
5. I congratulated her .... her wedding.

V. [CAPF, 2015]
1. The post office will compensate us .... the loss.
2. The scene .... of us is magnificent, isn't it?
3. It is against my nature to pick a quarrel .... anyone.
4. I can't climb .... that high roof.
5. I haven't seen a movie .... the end of February.

VI. [CAPF, 2014]
1. The beauty of Venice consists .... the style of its ancient buildings.
2. My insomnia was bad enough .... me to seek advice .... a psychiatrist.
3. The method I was taught came .... a girl guide.
4. He owns a mansion girdled .... a black path.

VII. [CAPF, 2013]
1. She swims everyday .... the summer.
2. World War II lasted .... more than 5 years.
3. They work everyday .... 7 am.
4. He spoke .... me.
5. India became a Republic .... 1950.

Answers

WORK BOOK EXERCISE (A)
1. Listen to
2. Drop 'with'
3. Write in dark ink
4. Compensate me for damage
5. Drop 'again'
6. Drop 'from'
7. 'Of' in place of 'against'
8. 'With' in place of 'among'
9. Robbed them all of the belongings
10. Drop 'on'
11. 'Over' in place of 'on'
12. Drop 'of'
13. 'For' in place of 'of'
14. Write with
15. Invaded India
16. Dispense with
17. Drop 'for' after 'order'
18. On his grand success
19. 'Bound with' in place of 'bound by'
20. Present me with a new scooter
21. 'Of' in place of 'with'
22. Searching for your lost purse
23. Fined him ten rupees
24. Different from
25. Laugh at the poor
26. Drop 'in' after pervaded
27. 'For' in place of 'Due to'
28. Parted from his wife
29. To pick a quarrel
30. Informed the police of
31. 'From above'
32. 'Waver in'
33. 'Play in the hands'
34. 'Aversion to'
35. 'Worthy of'

WORK BOOK EXERCISE (B)
1. Discriminated against
2. 'On' in place of 'to'
3. Dispense justice
4. Accompanies her
5. Began at 2 pm/about 2 pm
6. Spread all over the country
7. Travelled second class
8. Admitted to the hospital
9. Died from
10. On the way
11. Entrusted me with his valuables
12. 'With' in place of 'of'
13. 'With' in place of 'by'
14. 'In' in place of 'with'
15. 'With' in place of 'from'
16. 'In' in place of 'of'
17. 'To' in place of 'on'/set house on fire
18. Say 'admittance'
19. Drop 'back'
20. 'With' in place of 'by'
21. Remove 'against'
22. 'With' in place of 'to'
23. 'At' in place of 'from'
24. 'At' after 'shot'
25. Remove 'against'
26. 'For' in place of 'to'
27. 'After' in place of 'for'
28. Remove 'on'
29. Remove 'with'
30. Remove 'in'
31. By your watch
32. Delete 'to'
33. Say 'on time'
34. No error
35. Remove 'up'
36. 'Unreal for'
37. 'Tendency for'
38. 'Tear up'

WORK BOOK EXERCISE (C)
1. 'Of' in place of 'from'
2. A week before/ago
3. 'Up' in place of 'on'
4. What Kanpur is famous for
5. Insert 'for' after 'wished'
6. 'On/upon' after 'operated'
7. Insert 'for' after 'competing'
8. Insert 'about' after 'talking' on both the cases.
9. Insert 'to' after 'prays'
10. 'For' in place of 'by'

11. Insert 'by' after 'travel'
12. Insert 'with' after 'me'
13. 'With' in place of 'from'
14. Remove 'together'
15. 'For' in place of 'to'
16. 'In' in place of 'of'
17. 'With' in place of 'to'
18. 'On' in place of 'at' after 'smiled'
19. Insert 'of' after 'dreamt'
20. Delete 'In the'
21. Who she was talking to
22. 'Since' in place of 'from'
23. 'At' in place of 'in'
24. Insert 'with' after 'side'
25. 'For' in place of 'after'
26. Fill the bucket with water
27. Use 'in' for 'to'
28. Say 'till'
29. Use 'at'
30. Use 'to' in place of 'with'
31. 'Went home'
32. 'Saying among'
33. 'Aware of'
34. 'Call in question'
35. 'For all accounts'
36. 'Tackle problems'
37. Delete 'for'

WORK BOOK EXERCISE (D)

1. out	2. from	3. off	4. from
5. on	6. on	7. up	8. of
9. on	10. over	11. into	12. off
13. from	14. after	15. on	16. up
17. to	18. into	19. for	20. off
21. about	22. up	23. of	24. in
25. off	26. on	27. with	28. for
29. in	30. at		

WORK BOOK EXERCISE (E)

1. to	2. at	3. upon	4. to
5. to	6. to	7. to	8. to
9. from	10. to	11. of	12. upon
13. into	14. for	15. from	16. on
17. with	18. for	19. off	20. on
21. against	22. against	23. for	24. in
25. at	26. of	27. on	28. at
29. at	30. upon		

WORK BOOK EXERCISE (F)

1. by	2. upon	3. through	4. with
5. on	6. to	7. with	8. to
9. off	10. to	11. to	12. to
13. to	14. to	15. in	16. of
17. by	18. from	19. at	20. over

WORK BOOK EXERCISE (G)

1. to	2. to	3. from	4. to
5. with	6. of, to	7. to	8. to
9. for	10. of	11. to	12. to
13. to	14. to, into	15. from	16. to
17. with	18. with	19. by	20. of
21. for	22. for	23. for	24. from, to
25. to	26. from	27. from	28. with, against
29. with	30. for		

PREPOSITIONS

WORK BOOK EXERCISE (H)

1. of	2. to	3. to	4. with
5. of	6. to	7. for	8. against
9. on	10. of	11. of	12. of
13. to	14. at	15. to	16. to
17. to	18. to	19. for	20. in
21. with	22. under	23. on	24. to
25. to, under	26. with	27. with	28. to
29. with	30. of		

Cumulative Exercise

1. with, to	2. to	3. with	4. to
5. with, over	6. to	7. of	8. with
9. of, by	10. on	11. with	12. with
13. for, to	14. on	15. with	16. to
17. by	18. in	19. over	20. for
21. off	22. on	23. with, to	24. of
25. in	26. on	27. with	28. off, with
29. of	30. by		

Previous Years' Questions

I.	1. with	2. to	3. up	4. through	5. to
II.	1. with	2. in	3. on	4. into	5. over
III.	1. with, for	2. with	3. to	4. to	
IV.	1. with	2. of	3. at	4. from	5. on
V.	1. for	2. in front	3. with	4. up	5. since
VI.	1. of	2. for, from	3. from	4. with	
VII.	1. during	2. for	3. from	4. to	5. in

CHAPTER 9

Miscellaneous

Exercise 1

Directions *Rewrite/Correct the following sentences without changing their meaning. Do not make unnecessary changes in the original sentence.*

1. It's high time we play a match.
2. Rarely ever does the captain make a statement about the poor performance of the team.
3. People has decided to meet over a cup of coffee.
4. Despite of the hardships, he came out very successfully.
5. He was surrounded by a crowd of well wishers.
6. The construction of this building require additional people to work for.
7. On the time of his entry, he was crying for no good reason.
8. The principal has made compulsory for the teachers come at 7 am.
9. She made me wait two agonising hours.
10. I could neither contact Amit nor Aashna.
11. Hardly had she left the hospital, then it began to rain.
12. Our all members are very cooperative.
13. The construction of new hotel stopped.
14. His kindness and benevolence are well-known to everyone.
15. Better to reign in hell than to serve in heaven.
16. Anyone of the two girls can solve this puzzle.
17. Indian Government wants to build strong India.
18. She refrains to do this work.
19. I will meet you before I shall leave for home.
20. They had better died than surrender before the enemy.
21. She takes generally her breakfast at 8 am.
22. The teacher punished the boy for disobedience.
23. They have been residing here since 4 years.

MISCELLANEOUS

24. After the chef complete the demonstration, she left the students to clean the kitchen.
25. It can rain, it is so sultry.
26. So absurdly he spoke that everybody was shocked.
27. Do you dare refuse me?
28. Would you mind to work with me?
29. Every man and every woman has his own fascinations.
30. You cannot prevent me to go to the market.

Exercise 2

1. She is as much noted for her beauty as for her wisdom.
2. None of these two books is useful.
3. If you run fast, you would have won the race.
4. You must work hard to win the first prize.
5. Hurrah! we have won the match !
6. The train arrived before we reached there.
7. She forgot locking the door, when she went to market.
8. A variety of subjects are taught in this school.
9. Move fast lest you would miss the bus.
10. One month after another have passed.
11. I shall be glad meeting you.
12. Having opened the drawer, she took out a knife.
13. This is the same shirt, which I saw in the shop.
14. One must be conscientious about his dental hygiene.
15. She persisted to write again.
16. Is there any doubt whether she will come?
17. The valley goes deep and deep after this point.
18. No one hardly goes to church daily.
19. No building in our town is so beautiful as this.
20. He was tired that he could not do anything.
21. Are you hearing a strange noise?
22. He will have finish the work by 9 pm.
23. She neither could nor will help him.
24. Under no circumstances, I shall accept my transfer.
25. It is not the teachers, but the principal, who decide this issue.
26. Will you be so kind as sanction my leave?
27. Being a rainy day, the school remained closed.
28. I can rely on your words, not somebody else's.
29. Only those employees should be promoted, whom are sincere.
30. In this article, the author has described about poverty.

Exercise 3

1. This is a good hotel to stay in.
2. Will he has completed his work by tomorrow?
3. A lot of books and magazines was destroyed in the fire.
4. She was known having hidden the jewellery box.
5. Each of the employees have to arrange their own vehicle.
6. She is desirous to leave the place.
7. I have never seen her nor heard of her.
8. He is braver than stronger.
9. The story is much interesting.
10. Smoking is injurious for health.
11. If I was you, I would dismiss him.
12. We eat because we may live.
13. He has completed his book yesterday.
14. I written to her day before yesterday.
15. A prudent person will never become extravagant despite of the fact he has enough resources.
16. A brave man does not fear dying.
17. Standing near the gate, a dog caught her.
18. You and I are responsible for this loss.
19. He kept away from the function.
20. Man is a mortal.
21. He intends to go to Bhopal.
22. He is neither ashamed nor sorry for his misdeeds.
23. I hope that you are well now.
24. It was both, a long ceremony and very tedious.
25. He is the best of the two students.
26. I drive seldom after sunset.
27. Let's pray to God, do we?
28. If you will heat ice, it may turn to water.
29. I took medicine, because I might get well soon.
30. He told me that I have made a mistake.

Exercise 4

1. The sum could be solved by you.
2. She will be gone to market at this time.
3. The house was white, unless we painted it.
4. The jury was divided in their opinion in that case.

MISCELLANEOUS

5. She left yesterday, isn't she?
6. He learned to operate the machine.
7. Waiting for the train, a brick fell on my feet.
8. I have read Milton's poems, who was a romantic poet.
9. The girls, who was late, was fined.
10. We should prevent damage and theft of public property.
11. If I won a lottery, I will buy a big house.
12. But his behaviour, however, has not changed.
13. He is more wiser than you.
14. Do you know him? No, I do.
15. I am elder to you, am I?
16. Until you work hard, you can't beat him.
17. She went to Delhi the tomorrow morning.
18. Have the books returned by him?
19. The patient had fainted then the doctor came.
20. He have been living in Kolkata for 7 years.
21. None of those reasons are valid.
22. Some people prefer to spend money to earn it.
23. Being a cold morning, I didn't go to office.
24. I want to purchase ten knifes.
25. My wife's secretary's mother has expired.
26. What is his opinion about the work, which you have completed?
27. The train arrives at the platform 7.
28. She neither objected nor approved of it.
29. He ordered for a cup of tea.
30. Either you must grant his request or incur his ill will.

Exercise 5

1. We are seeing with our eyes.
2. The students will have left the class before the teacher came.
3. Her brother like bananas, but she like peaches.
4. His mother die 3 months ago.
5. I might try again, if you wish.
6. More than one girl were killed in the accident.
7. Suman went to church, so am I.
8. She avoids to do her duties seriously.
9. I am thinking to leave my job and going back to my native place.
10. The ship has sunken.
11. The first inning is going to over now.

12. That is one of the interesting books that has appeared this year.
13. Rajat and myself are responsible for this decision.
14. To who do you wish to speak?
15. These are Chairman's instructions that must be followed.
16. He is from United States.
17. Vikrant has no interest or passion for cricket.
18. He informed to me yesterday.
19. Take an umbrella, in case it may rain.
20. A time not for words, but action.
21. Tushar came prior than me.
22. We were very delighted to get the news.
23. She doesn't like men, who are too tall.
24. I am sure that he is doing his best.
25. We have not met before, have we?
26. Until he comes back, wait for him.
27. The days pass happily.
28. She ran as fast as she could to catch the train.
29. Shyam respectfully wished his teacher Good Morning.
30. The stranger exclaimed with surprise what he saw before him.

Exercise 6

1. He would have reached here before the Sun set.
2. When the contestant complete the first test, she received another clue.
3. Does it rain all the year here?
4. I possess two brothers.
5. He did came here yesterday.
6. Neither of these questions are right.
7. Slow and steady win the race.
8. Nothing, but birds, are seen.
9. I will have you to remember me.
10. To drink being his habit, we didn't go with him.
11. When using this machine, it must be remembered to unlock it first.
12. My sympathies are always with the poor.
13. Let me take your leave.
14. Each of the students are ready to do their duty.
15. Young will support the motion.
16. We travelled mostly by the night.
17. She criticised upon my action without logic.

MISCELLANEOUS

18. As she started late, she will miss the train.
19. I agree your proposal is very good.
20. Arnav is one of the strongest person, if not the strongest, in the town.
21. Life in the country is different from the city.
22. Hemant was fortunately not available in the hostel.
23. Breathe deeply, when you walk.
24. No other man in our village is very poor as Naman.
25. The Sun having rose, the fog disappeared.
26. No one voted against the bill, had they?
27. Without his help, Nitin would have been ruined.
28. Amit discussed the matter with so many another fellows.
29. Have you talked to her latterly?
30. He said to the President, "Please give me one chance."

Exercise 7

1. Let the poor not be teased.
2. On yesterday, I went shopping and found some great outfits for spring.
3. No culture can live, if it attempt to be exclusive.
4. I wish, I was a millionaire.
5. He will has been waiting for you for three days.
6. Suhana is being collecting stamps since childhood.
7. Have you the alarm for the morning?
8. I had have my work completed by him.
9. He could pay you on Monday.
10. Much of the time were wasted by the students.
11. So absurd did he spoke that everyone was offended.
12. Could you tell me to explain the situation?
13. It is totally useless to cry over the spilt milk.
14. She has committed not one but many mischiefs.
15. None of the two girls could complete the job.
16. Let us ourselves rest at the bed.
17. He has thousand rupees.
18. The Sun rises in East and sets in West.
19. He is bent to fight again.
20. It is a year since I have met her.
21. He seems, as he hadn't had a nice meal for many days.
22. This is longest river in the world.
23. Iron is harder than any metal.
24. Akansha came quicker than I expected.

25. You are forbidden not to write on the table.
26. Is that music enough loud?
27. As soon as, he see the monkey, he flew.
28. The moment once lost, is forever lost.
29. He is so weak that he cannot run.
30. You are always punctual, are you?

Exercise 8

1. She used to go to temple, wasn't she?
2. If he had telephoned me, I would have gave him the address.
3. If I were you, I will forgive him.
4. Both he is a philosopher and a teacher.
5. As my neighbourers are very co-operative, I do not have any problem here.
6. I enjoyed fully.
7. She seems very much reduced.
8. I am very much tired after my walk.
9. He said, "What a pitiful scene"?
10. Dessert aren't supposed to be made by them.
11. My father assured me that he will buy a bike for me.
12. She has been cooking meal from 8 a.m.
13. Either the mother or the daughter have made this pudding.
14. You may not hurry, there is plenty of time.
15. Yesterday only he did buy that car.
16. I observed him to play.
17. She is enough matured to go alone.
18. A novice can't learnt to spelling without being help.
19. The chair's legs are broken.
20. Ships after ships were sailing by those days.
21. One should respect not only his own parents but also others.
22. There was no one that didn't support the cause.
23. One night, there was terrible earthquake.
24. The police investigated into the case.
25. We were paralysed by fear.
26. Soon, I got a call afterwards.
27. He failed in the examination; moreover, he didn't lose heart.
28. She has both a good education and she has good work habits.
29. This custom has been observed since immemorial time.
30. I am very satisfied with her conduct.

Exercise 9

1. Pratham walks rather fast but Pranav walks rather slowly.
2. Although hard she may work, she will not succeed.
3. His silence proves his guilt.
4. Few people know that you are an artist, aren't they?
5. If for the food, I would have arrived here yesterday.
6. This man maintains his livelihood by hard work.
7. She said to me, "Is it still drizzling?"
8. Have the assignment been finished by you?
9. The campers hidden inside the cabin, when they saw the bear.
10. Should God give you courage to face it!
11. So suspicious she became that she couldn't talk to her husband for several days.
12. Will you be so kind as sanction by leave?
13. I happened looking towards the road, when their car stopped.
14. There are many news published in local paper.
15. How many cattles do you have?
16. Everyones concern is no one concern.
17. Either of these roads lead to the hospital.
18. If one fails, then he must try again.
19. Honesty is a best policy.
20. Aakash is waiting for you on the bus stop.
21. Nothing, except the best, is sold in our shop.
22. If I had wings, I will fly to London.
23. I had rather read than wasting my time here.
24. She peacefully died yesterday.
25. He strolled the park twice before supper.
26. She not only makes a promise and also keeps it.
27. Please record my dissent on this matter.
28. You can eat so much you like.
29. The house needs immediate repairing, isn't it?
30. I shall attend the meeting, provides he also attends.

Exercise 10

1. If I had an umbrella, I would have lend it to you.
2. Nowadays, she is living in foreign but her husband is in India.
3. Do you know swimming?
4. She said that her uncle had come yesterday.
5. The sum could has been solved by you.

6. I have already taken tea, have I?
7. He is considered to support the liberals.
8. He switched on the light before he open the door.
9. He pass all the tests without fail.
10. Did the doctor came to see you yesterday?
11. She neither talked nor will speak to him.
12. Every young and every old were happy to receive a gift.
13. On no account, this switch must be put on.
14. She did not visit the Punjab, not did I.
15. The act is easy to be performed.
16. He seemed to be a great musician.
17. I heard someone crying but failed seeing anyone.
18. Sleeping in the house, a thief entered their house.
19. There are a few peoples, who are really honest.
20. My son's in law sister is coming tomorrow.

Previous Years' Questions

Directions *Rewrite/Correct the following sentences after making necessary corrections. Please do not make unnecessary changes in the original sentence.*

I.   [Civil Services (Mains), 2014]

1. School is very near my home.
2. They never fail, who die in great cause.
3. It rained an hour before.
4. He wrote a most complete account of his travels.
5. Either of these three answers is incorrect.
6. You will be late, until you hurry.
7. He is seldom or ever absent from school.
8. The colours so passed off one another that she could not distinguish them.
9. The general as well as his soldiers were killed in the battle.
10. The boat was drowned.

II.   [Civil Services (Mains), 2015]

1. He enjoyed during the holidays.
2. Whoever works hard, he will win.
3. The man, who knocked at the door, was stranger.
4. I asked my colleague, when was he going to his home town.
5. Besides clothes, the shopkeeper deals with cosmetics too.
6. He is desirous for joining the army.

MISCELLANEOUS

7. The judge said that the truth always triumphed.
8. One should help his friend in difficulty.
9. Sachin Tendulkar is the best batsman India has produced, isn't it?
10. More you read, less you understand.

III. [Civil Services (Mains), 2013]
1. One must do what he thinks best.
2. He will surely not do that, did he?
3. Can I leave the room now, Sir?
4. My neighbour, along with two friends, were pushing his car, which is stalled.
5. I thought to help him, but he did not welcome my suggestion.
6. When I was a child, I enjoyed to eat ice-cream in the bench.
7. The principal, along with the teachers, are planning to apply for a leave.
8. Do you have an idea, who is that man?
9. Unemployment, as well as poverty, influence the votes.
10. When I woke up, the man already disappeared after committing murder in the running train.

IV. [IES, 2013]
1. Nobody likes to be cheated, isn't it?
2. Choose only such friends, whom you can trust.
3. He is a MA is Geology.
4. They had left yesterday.
5. We are looking forward to see you soon.
6. One of the file is lost.
7. If he came early, you could have met him.
8. It was so cold that the water freezed.
9. Are there some more papers left to be signed?
10. We will be going to the church for Sunday Mass.

V. [IES, 2014]
1. I would rather die than begging alms.
2. Neither of the five players was selected.
3. The fisherman held several fish from the sea.
4. I asked him that how many brothers had he.
5. He cannot dare to come here.
6. This is the man, which killed his father.
7. No sooner had she arrived, when the telegram came.
8. John is a tall boy, isn't it?
9. They have disposed off their farm house.
10. My handwriting is superior than any of yours.

VI. [IES, 2015]

1. Despite of repeated reminders, the company has not responded.
2. All the students will attend the function, wouldn't they?
3. This is one of the best books that has been recently purchased for the library.
4. Flying on the Northern part of India, we could see the peak of the Everest.
5. Your friend is waiting for you since morning.
6. People expect a lot from an university scholar.
7. The Sun is rising in the East everyday.
8. When we arrived at the station, the train already left.
9. Neither the officer, nor his PS were in the office.
10. The minister, along with his wife, are leaving for London.

VII. [IFS, 2013]

1. He works hard lest he does not lose his job.
2. This cloth is inferior than that.
3. He made me to apply for the job.
4. Did he told you, when he would return?
5. I need little sugar for tea.
6. My older brother does not play hockey.
7. I enjoy to tell jokes.
8. His uncle deals with pre-owned cars.
9. The officer came in just we were about to leave.
10. Haven't you got nobody to help you?

VIII. [IFS, 2014]

1. The apples are grown in many countries.
2. The chief, with all his men, were massacred.
3. One of his friend has been injured in an accident.
4. The food that I dislike mostly is cabbage.
5. I shall not stay long than I can help.
6. The Prime Minister lives in 7 Race Course Road.
7. I have seen the film last week.
8. You have done a mistake.
9. We have finished our work, have we?
10. He asked me, what I want.

IX. [IFS, 2015]

1. How long is he wearing glasses?
2. The new bridge had been opened 6 months ago.
3. I'm afraid he did a mistake in the calculation.
4. His uncle did not arrive yet.
5. A good curry is my most favourite meal.
6. He asked the gardener whether either of the ladies were at home.

MISCELLANEOUS

7. Every nation and every government are engaged in an economic war.
8. The sceneries of the Himalayas are unrivalled.
9. The patient died, before the doctor arrived.
10. Though he was busy, but he talked to me.

X. Both of them did not partake in the function. [CAPF, 2013]

XI. [CAPF, 2014]
1. The retention of a major portion of our earnings have helped build our new house.
2. Geeta suspects Seeta for stealing the pen.
3. She's used to get up early.
4. Jane thought she can win the prize.
5. The gardener picked up flowers in the garden.
6. I wish, I was as tall as my leader.
7. Sharmas will start after the breakfast.
8. I look forward to see him soon.
9. Each boy and each girl was in their best dress.
10. Why is Ruby appearing so sad.

XII. You may either have an apple or an orange. [CAPF, 2015]

Answers

Exercise 1

1. It's high time we played a match.
2. Seldom, if ever, does the captain make a statement about the poor performance of the team.
3. People have decided to meet over a cup of coffee.
4. Despite the hardships, he came out very successfully.
5. He was surrounded with a crowd of well wishers.
6. The construction of this building requires additional people to work for.
7. At the time of his entry, he was crying for no good reason.
8. The principal has made it compulsory for the teachers to come at 7 am.
9. She made me wait for two agonising hours.
10. I could contact neither Amit nor Aashna.
11. Hardly had she left the hospital, when it began to rain.
12. All our members are very cooperative.
13. The construction of new hotel has stopped.
14. His kindness and benevolence is well-known to everyone.
15. Better reign in hell than serve in heaven.
16. Either of the two girls can solve this puzzle.
17. Indian Government wants to build a strong India.
18. She refrains from doing this work.
19. I will meet you before I leave for home.
20. They had better die than surrender before the enemy.

21. Generally, she takes her breakfast at 8 am.
22. The teacher punished the boy for his disobedience.
23. They have been residing here for 4 years.
24. After the chef completed the demonstration, she left the students to clean the kitchen.
25. It may rain, it is so sultry.
26. So absurdly did he speak that everybody was shocked.
27. Do you dare to refuse me?
28. Would you mind working with me?
29. Every man and every woman have their own fascinations.
30. You cannot prevent me from going to the market.

Exercise 2

1. She is noted as much for her beauty as for her wisdom.
2. Neither of these books is useful.
3. Had you run fast, you would have won the race.
4. You must work hard so that you may win the first prize.
5. It is a matter of joy that we have won the match.
6. The train had arrived before we reached there.
7. She forgot to lock the door, when she went to market.
8. A variety of subjects is taught in this school.
9. Move fast lest you should miss the bus.
10. One month after another has passed.
11. I shall be glad to meet you.
12. Opening the drawer, she took out a knife.
13. This is the same shirt that I saw in the shop.
14. One must be conscientious about one's dental hygiene.
15. She persisted on writing again.
16. Is there any doubt that she will come?
17. The valley goes deeper and deeper after this point.
18. Hardly, any one goes to church daily.
19. No other building in our town is so beautiful as this.
20. He was so tired that he could not do anything.
21. Do you hear a strange noise?
22. He will have finished the work by 9 pm.
23. She could not and will not help him.
24. Under no circumstances, shall I accept my transfer.
25. It is not the teachers, but the principal, who decides this issue.
26. Will you be so kind as to sanction my leave?
27. It being a rainy day, the school remained closed.
28. I can rely on your words, not somebody else's.
29. Only those employees should be promoted, who are sincere.
30. In this article, the author has described poverty.

Exercise 3

1. This is a good hotel to stay at.
2. Will he have completed his work by tomorrow?
3. A lot of books and magazines were destroyed in the fire.
4. She was known to have hidden the jewellery box.

MISCELLANEOUS

5. Each of the employees has to arrange his own vehicle.
6. She is desirous of leaving the place.
7. I have never seen her or heard of her.
8. He is more brave than strong.
9. The story is very interesting.
10. Smoking is injurious to health.
11. If I were you, I would dismiss him.
12. We eat so that we may live.
13. He completed his book yesterday.
14. I wrote to her the day before yesterday.
15. A prudent person will never be extravagant despite the fact he has enough resources.
16. A brave man does not fear to die.
17. While she was standing near the gate, a dog caught her.
18. I and you are responsible for this loss.
19. He kept himself away from the function.
20. Man is mortal.
21. He intends going to Bhopal.
22. He is neither ashamed of nor sorry for his misdeeds.
23. I hope you are well now.
24. The ceremony was both, long and tedious.
25. He is the better of the two students.
26. I seldom drive after sunset.
27. Let's pray to God, shall we?
28. If you heat ice, it turns to water.
29. I took medicine, in order that I might get well soon.
30. He told me that I had made a mistake.

Exercise 4

1. The sum cold have been solved by you.
2. She will be going to market at this time.
3. The house was white, until we painted it.
4. The jury were divided in their opinion in that case.
5. She left yesterday, didn't she?
6. He learned how to operate the machine.
7. While I was waiting for the train, a brick fell on my feet.
8. I have read poems of Milton, who was a romantic poet.
9. The girls, who were late, were fined.
10. We should prevent damage to and theft of public property.
11. If I won a lottery, I would buy a big house.
12. His behaviour however, has not changed.
13. He is wiser than you.
14. Do you know him? No, I don't.
15. I am elder to you, aren't I?
16. Unless you work hard, you can't beat him.
17. She went to Delhi the next morning.
18. Have the books been returned by him?
19. The patient had fainted before the doctor came.

20. He has been living in Kolkata for 7 years.
21. None of those reasons is valid.
22. Some people prefer spending money to earning it.
23. It being a cold morning, I didn't go to office.
24. I want to purchase ten knives.
25. The mother of my wife's secretary has expired.
26. What is his opinion about the work that you have completed?
27. The train arrives at platform 7.
28. She neither objected to nor approved of it.
29. He ordered a cup of tea.
30. You must either grant his request or incur his ill will.

Exercise 5

1. We see with our eyes.
2. The students will have left the class before the teacher comes.
3. Her brother likes bananas, but she likes peaches.
4. His mother died 3 months ago.
5. I will try again, if you wish.
6. More girls than one were killed in the accident.
7. Suman went to Church, so did I.
8. She avoids doing her duties seriously.
9. I am thinking of leaving my job and going back to my native place.
10. The ship has sunk.
11. The first innings is going to be over now.
12. That is one of the interesting books that have appeared this year.
13. Rajat and I are responsible for this decision.
14. To whom, do you wish to speak?
    Or
    Whom do you wish to speak to?
15. These are the instructions of the chairman that must be followed.
16. He is from the United States.
17. Vikrant has no interest in or passion for cricket.
18. He informed me yesterday.
19. Take an umbrella, in case it rains.
20. A time not for words, but for action.
21. Tushar came prior to me.
22. We were much delightful to get the news.
23. She doesn't like a man too tall.
24. I am sure, he is doing his best.
25. The sentence is already correct.
26. Unless he comes back, wait for him.
27. The days pass off happily.
28. The sentence is already correct.
29. Respectfully, Shyam wished his teacher Good Morning.
30. The stranger exclaimed with surprise what he had seen before him.

MISCELLANEOUS

Exercise 6

1. He will have reached here before the Sun sets.
2. When the contestant completed the first test, she received another clue.
3. Does it rain here all the year.
4. I have two brothers.
5. He came here yesterday.
6. Neither of these questions is right.
7. Slow and steady wins the race.
8. Nothing, but birds, is seen.
9. I will have you remember me.
10. Drinking being his habit, we didn't go with him.
11. When using this machine, you must remember to unlock it first.
12. My sympathy is always with the poor.
13. Let me take leave of you.
14. Each of the students is ready to do his duty.
15. Youth will support the motion.
16. We travelled mostly during the night.
17. She criticised my action without logic.
18. As she started late, she missed the train.
19. I agree that your proposal is very good.
20. Arnav is one of the strongest persons, if not the strongest, in the town.
21. Life in the country is different from the life in the city.
22. Fortunately, Hemant was not available in the hostel.
23. Breathe deep, when you walk.
24. No other man in our village is as poor as Naman.
25. The Sun having risen, the fog disappeared.
26. No one voted against the bill, did they?
27. But for his help, Nitin would have been ruined.
28. Amit discussed the matter with many other fellows.
29. Have you talked to her lately?
30. He requested the President to give him a chance.

Exercise 7

1. Do not tease the poor.
2. Yesterday, I went shopping and found some great outfits for spring.
3. No culture can live, if it attempts to be exclusive.
4. I wish, I were a millionaire.
5. He will have been waiting for you for three days.
6. Suhana has been collecting stamps since childhood.
7. Have you set the alarm for the morning?
8. I had my work completed by him.
9. He could have paid you on Monday.
10. Much of the time was wasted by the students.
11. So absurdly did he speak that everyone was offended.
12. Could you tell me how to explain the situation?
13. It is totally useless crying over the spilt milk.
14. She has committed not one but many acts of mischief.

15. Neither of the girls could complete the job.
16. Let us rest at the bed.
17. He has a thousand rupees.
18. The Sun rises in the East and sets in the West.
19. He is bent on fighting again.
20. It is a year since I met her.
21. He seems, as though, he hadn't had a nice meal for many days.
22. This is the longest river in the world.
23. Iron is harder than any other metal.
24. Akansha came quickly than I expected.
25. You are forbidden to write on the table.
26. Is that music loud enough?
27. As soon as, he saw the monkey, he fled.
28. The moment once lost, is lost forever.
29. He is too weak to run.
30. You are always punctual, aren't you?

Exercise 8

1. She used to go to temple, usedn't she?
2. If he had telephoned me, I would have given him the address.
3. If I were you, I would have forgiven him.
4. He is both, a philosopher and a teacher.
5. As my neighbours are very co-operative, I do not have any problem here.
6. I enjoyed myself fully.
7. She looks much thinner.
     Or
   She looks very thin.
8. I am very tired after my walk.
9. He exclaimed that it was a pitiful scene.
10. Dessert isn't supposed to be made by them.
11. My father assured me that he would buy a bike for me.
12. She has been cooking meal since 8 a.m.
13. Either the mother or the daughter has made this pudding.
14. You need not hurry, there is plenty of time.
15. Only yesterday, did he buy that car.
16. I observed him playing.
17. She is matured enough to go alone.
18. A novice can't learn to spell without being helped.
19. The legs of the chair are broken.
20. Ship after ship was sailing by those days.
21. One should respect not only one's own parents but also other's.
22. There was none that didn't support the cause.
23. One night, there was a terrible earthquake.
24. The police investigated the case.
25. We were paralysed with fear.
26. Soon afterwards, I got a call.

MISCELLANEOUS

27. He failed in the examination; nevertheless, he didn't lose heart.
28. She has both, a good education and good work habits.
29. This custom has been observed since time immemorial.
30. I am much satisfied with her conduct.

Exercise 9

1. Pratham walks fairly fast but Pranav walks rather slowly.
2. However hard she may work, she will not succeed.
3. The fact that he is silent, proves his guilt.
4. Few people know that you are an artist, don't they?
5. But for the flood, I would have arrived here yesterday.
6. This man obtains his livelihood by hard work.
7. She asked me if it was drizzling, till then.
8. Has the assignment been finished by you?
9. The campers hid inside the cabin, when they saw the bear.
10. May God give you courage to face it!
11. So suspicious did she become that she couldn't talk to her husband for several days.
12. Will you be so kind as to sanction my leave?
13. I happened to be looking towards the road, when their car stopped.
14. There are many items of news published in the local paper.
15. How many cattle do you have?
16. Everyone's concern is no one's concern.
17. Either of these roads leads to the hospital.
18. If one fails, then one must try again.
19. Honesty is the best policy.
20. Aakash is waiting for you at the bus stop.
21. Nothing, but the best, is sold in our shop.
22. If I had wings, I would fly to London.
23. I had rather read than waste my time here.
24. Yesterday, she died peacefully.
25. He strolled round the park twice before supper.
26. She not only makes a promise but also keeps it.
27. Please record my dissent in this matter.
28. You can eat as much as you like.
29. The house needs immediate repairing, doesn't it?
30. I shall attend the meeting, provided he also attends.

Exercise 10

1. If I had an umbrella, I would lend it to you.
2. Now-a-days, she is living abroad but her husband is in India.
3. Do you know how to swim?
4. She said that her uncle had come the previous day.
5. The sum could have been solved by you.
6. I have already taken tea, haven't I?
7. He is considered to be supporting the liberals.
8. He switched on the light before he opened the door.
9. He passed all the tests without failing.

10. Did the doctor come to see you yesterday?
11. She didn't talk and will not speak to him.
12. Every young and every old was happy to receive a gift.
13. On no account, must this switch be put on.
14. She did not visit Punjab, neither did I.
15. The act is easy to perform.
16. He seemed to have been a great musician.
17. I heard someone cry but failed to see anyone.
18. While they were sleeping in the house, a thief entered their house.
19. There are few people, who are really honest.
20. The sister of my son-in-law, is coming tomorrow.

Previous Years' Questions

I. 1. The school is very near to my home.
    2. Those, who die in great cause, never fail.
         Or
       They never fail, who die in a great cause.
    3. It rained an hour ago.
    4. He wrote a complete account of his travels.
    5. Either of these answers is incorrect.
    6. Unless you hurry, you will be late.
    7. He is seldom or never absent from school.
    8. The colours passed off one another such that she could not distinguish them.
    9. The general as well as his soldiers was killed in the battle.
    10. The boat sank.

II. 1. He enjoyed himself during the holidays.
    2. Whoever works hard, will win.
    3. The man, who knocked at the door, was a stranger.
    4. I asked my colleague, when he was going to his home town.
    5. Besides clothes, the shopkeeper also deals in cosmetics.
    6. He is desirous of joining the army.
    7. The judge remarked that the truth always triumph.
    8. One should help one's friend in difficulty.
    9. Sachin Tendulkar is the best batsman India has ever produced, isn't it?
    10. The more you read, the less you understand.

III. 1. One must do what one thinks best.
     2. He will surely not do that, will he?
     3. May I leave the room now, Sir?
     4. My neighbour, along with his two friends, was pushing his car, which is stalled.
     5. I thought of helping him, but he did not welcome my suggestion.
     6. When I was a child, I enjoyed eating ice-cream on the bench.
     7. The principal, along with the teachers, is planning to apply for leave.
     8. Do you an idea about that man?
     9. Both, unemployment and poverty, influence the votes.
     10. When I woke up, the man had already disappeared after committing a murder in the running train.

MISCELLANEOUS

IV.
1. Nobody likes to be cheated upon, do they?
2. Choose only such friends that you can trust.
3. He is an MA in Geology.
4. They left yesterday.
5. We are looking forward to seeing you soon.
6. One of the files is lost.
7. If he had come early, you could have met him.
8. It was so cold that the water froze.
9. Are there any more papers to be signed?
10. We will be going to the church for the Sunday Mass.

V.
1. I would rather die than beg.
2. None of the five players was selected.
3. The fisherman caught several fish from the sea.
4. I asked him how many brothers he had.
5. He dare not come here.
6. This is the man, who killed his father.
7. No sooner had she arrived, than the telegram came.
8. John is a tall boy, isn't he?
9. They disposed off their farm house.
10. My handwriting is superior to any of yours.

VI.
1. Despite repeated reminders, the company has not responded.
2. All the students would attend the function, wouldn't they?
3. This is one of the best books that have been purchased recently for the library.
4. Flying over the Northern part of India, we could see the peak of the Everest.
5. Your friend has been waiting for you since morning.
6. People expect a lot from a university scholar.
7. The Sun rises in the East everyday.
8. When we arrived at the station, the train had already left.
9. Neither the officer nor his PS was in the office.
10. The minister, alongwith his wife, is leaving for London.

VII.
1. He works hard lest he should lose his job.
2. The cloth is inferior to that.
3. He made me apply for the job.
4. Did he tell you, when he would return?
5. I need some sugar for tea.
6. My elder brother does not play hockey.
7. I enjoy telling jokes.
8. His uncle deals in pre-owned cars.
9. The officer came in just, when we were about to leave.
10. Haven't you got somebody to help you?

VIII.
1. Apples are grown in many countries.
2. The chief, with all his men, was massacred.
3. One of his friends has been injured in an accident.
4. The food that I dislike most is cabbage.
5. I shall not stay longer than I can help.
6. The Prime Minister lives on the 7 Race Course Road.

7. I saw the film last walk.
8. You have committed a mistake.
9. We have finished our work, haven't we?
10. He asked me, what I wanted.

IX. 1. Since how long is he wearing glasses?
2. The new bridge was opened 6 months ago.
3. I'm afraid he might have made a mistake in the calculation.
4. His uncle has not arrived yet.
5. A good curry is my favourite meal.
6. He asked the gardener whether either of the ladies was at home.
7. Every nation and every government is engaged in an economic war.
8. The scenery of the Himalayas are unrivalled.
9. The patient had died, before the doctor arrived.
10. Though he was busy, he talked to me.

X. None of them partake in the function.

XI. 1. The retention of a major portion of our earnings has helped to build our new house.
2. Geeta suspects Seeta for stealing her pen.
3. She is used to getting up early.
4. Jane thought that she could win the prize.
5. The gardener picked up flowers from the garden.
6. I wish, I could be as tall as my leader.
7. The Sharmas will start after the breakfast.
8. I am looking forward to seeing him soon.
9. Every boy and every girl was in their best dress.
10. Why does Ruby appear so sad?

XII. You may have either an apple or an orange.

PART D
VERBAL SKILLS

Verbal Ability' is synonymous with 'Word Power'. A student's comprehension skills, writing skills and communication skills depend on his verbal skills. In written examinations, the verbal skills of an examinee is tested by way of his comprehension skills.

This section of the book provides students with a large number of words and expressions. It would be presumptuous to claim that the words and expressions included in the book are sufficient. However we have taken every care to avoid superfluity. There is no tendency on our part to include a word just because nobody has ever heard of it. Only such words and their figurative expressions as are currently in vogue have been dealt within the ensuing chapters to help students meet with the challenge confidently in this sphere.

Every care has been taken that the words selected should serve the purpose of various class of aspirants attempting different competitions such as Civil Services (Mains), IFS, IES, CAPF, State PCS & PCS (J), TGT & PGT (English) and other organisations. In fact, this section will equip the students with 'Word Power' for every occasion.

CHAPTER 1

Paronyms and Homonyms

Confusion is often caused in understanding the meanings of certain words because they are either similar in meaning and form or similar in their sound of pronunciation. The words which are different in meaning or use but are similar in form or derivations are called **Paronyms**.

On the other hand, **Homonyms** are similar in their sound or pronunciation but different in meaning. They are also called **Homophones** (different in spelling and meaning but pronounced alike). In Modern English, Paronyms and Homonyms (Homophones) are not much distinguished.

1. **Access** *(approach)* It is very difficult to have an *access* to the Prime Minister.
   Accession *(coming to throne)* The *accession* of the prince to the throne was welcomed by the people.
   Excess *(more than desired)* *Excess* of everything is bad.
2. **Accept** *(to take)* The teachers *accepted* the invitation of the students on the Teacher's Day.
   Except *(leaving out)* Everybody *except* Rahul was invited to the party.
   Expect *(hope)* I never *expected* that my friends would desert me in the lurch.
3. **Alter** *(change)* Mohan is so obstinate that no one can *alter* his views.
   Altar *(place of worship)* When I visited temple, I saw him kneeling at the *altar*.
4. **Assent** *(agree)* I got *assent* of my father to study in a boarding school.
   Ascent *(climbing up)* The *ascent* to Kargil hills is very arduous.
5. **Adopt** *(take up)* One should not *adopt* the bad habits of others.
   Adapt *(adjust)* One must learn to *adapt* oneself to the circumstances of life.
   Adept *(expert)* Shruti is *adept* in the art of dancing.
6. **Amicable** *(friendly)* Finally the two brothers came to an *amicable* settlement.
   Amiable *(lovable, obliging)* Being an *amiable* house wife she is liked by her kith and kin.

7. **Accede** *(accept)* The director was kind enough to *accede* to the request of the labourers.
   Exceed *(surpass)* Your essay should not *exceed* three hundred words.
   Concede *(agree)* The prisoner did not *concede* to the argument of the jailor.
8. **Alteration** *(change)* There is no *alteration* in the programme yet.
   Altercation *(wordy quarrel)* There was an *altercation* between the shop keeper and my brother.
9. **Apposite** *(suitable)* Her remarks about the character of her friends are quite *apposite*.
   Opposite *(contrary)* Sita's behaviour is *opposite* to that of her brother.
10. **Affect** (verb) *(to influence, to pretend)* Continuous attack of asthma has *affected* his health.
    Effect (noun) *(influence)* Excessive hard work in life had adverse *effect* on her health.
11. **Allusion** *(reference)* The poem is explained properly by the help of many *allusions*.
    Illusion *(unreal)* According to the Vedantists life is an *illusion*.
12. **Ail** *(suffer)* Rohit is getting weaker day by day, we don't know what *ails* him.
    Ale *(intoxicating drink)* He visits *ale* house daily even against the advice of doctors.
13. **Apprehend** *(fear, perceive, arrest)* The soothsayer *apprehended* the day of Rohit's death.
    Comprehend *(understand)* She could not *comprehend* the meaning of the passage.
14. **Admission** *(to get admitted, acceptance)* These days in order to get *admission* to convent schools, you must give a lot of money.
    Admittance *(entry)* No *admittance* without permission.
15. **Antique** *(of ancient times)* There are many *antique* pieces in the museum.
    Antic *(odd, tricks)* *Antics* of the juggler regaled the children.
16. **Alternate** *(by turns)* We have a moral science class on every *alternate* day.
    Alternative *(one of the two choices)* There is no *alternative* to honesty in dealing with the people.
17. **Artful** *(clever)* She was able to change the behaviour of her in laws towards her by *artful* means.
    Artistic *(pertaining to art)* Everybody admires her for *artistic* temperament.
18. **Artist** *(one who practises fine art)* He is a frivolous *artist*.
    Artiste *(performing)* There was no security for the *artiste*, who had come to perform for the charity show.
    Artisan *(one who does handicraft)* The *artisans* of Moradabad are very skillful.
19. **Affection** *(love, kindly feeling)* My mother is held in high *affection* and respect by all the members of the family.
    Affectation *(unnatural behaviour, pretence)* I always feel vexed at her *affectation*.
20. **Abstain** *[keep from things (eating, drinking, voting)]* We should *abstain* from drinking.
    Refrain *(keep from bad habits)* You should *refrain* from telling a lie.

PARONYMS AND HOMONYMS

21. **Avenge** *(just punishment)* Hamlet delayed *avenging* the murder of his father.
    Revenge *(to punish out of personal grudge)* He *revenged* himself on his enemy by abducting his minor child.
22. **Adulteration** *(making impure)* The owners of the milk dairy were charged with *adulteration* of milk.
    Adultery *(having extra marital relations)* Her husband accused her of *adultery* and deserted her.
23. **Aspersion** *(slander)* We should not cast *aspersions* on our friends.
    Aspiration *(ambition, desire)* You can attain your *aspiration* only by hard work.
24. **Avert** *(to check)* A little common sense *averted* a major mishap.
    Advert *(refer to)* He *adverted* to the problem of Indian security in his speech.
25. **Birth** *(to be born)* The exact date of the *birth* of a person is known from his *birth* certificate.
    Berth *(a seat in a train)* I have got two *berths* booked in the Rajdhani Express.
26. **Bridle** *(reins)* It is very difficult to control a horse without a *bridle*.
    Bridal *(of bride)* The *bridal* dress must have cost a lot.
27. **Barbaric** *(savage, simple)* She was selected to play the part of a village damsel because of her *barbaric* beauty.
    Barbarous *(inhuman)* The muslim invaders were *barbarous* in their wars.
28. **Barbarity** *(cruelty)* Hitler's *barbarity* is too terrible to be related.
    Barbarism *(uncivilised conditions)* *Barbarism* still prevails in most of the tribal regions of the world.
29. **Beneficial** *(useful)* Nutritious food is *beneficial* for health.
    Beneficent *(kind)* Everybody paid rich tribute to the king as he was *beneficent* to all and sundry.
30. **Beside** *(by the side of)* He sat *beside* her father.
    Besides *(in addition to)* *Besides* English she is also learning French.
31. **Bear** *(tolerate, carry, give birth)* Mohan cannot *bear* being insulted by his boss.
    Bare *(naked)* He was bitten by a snake as he was *bare* foot.
32. **Borne** *(carried)* The dead body was *borne* by his friends.
    Born *(take birth)* Pearl was *born* in Ashwini Hospital at Mumbai.
33. **Bail** *(security)* His application for release on *bail* was rejected.
    Bale *(bundle of cloth)* He was carrying a *bale* of cotton on his head.
34. **Beatific** *(feeling joy and peace)* The saints are always in a *beatific* state of mind.
    Beatitude *(state of bliss, blessedness)* He experienced *beatitude* before he died.
35. **Caste** *(class of society)* In ancient times people were divided into different *castes* according to the work they did.
    Cast *(throw)* We *cast* away old clothes and buy new ones.
    Cost *(price)* The *cost* of living has risen a lot.
36. **Childlike** *(simple, innocent as a child)* Her *childlike* face has won over many hearts.
    Childish *(silly)* No body likes him for his *childish* habits.

37. **Canvass** *(propagate)* Because of approaching elections people are *canvassing* for their candidates.
   Canvas *(rough cloth)* While jogging he always wears *canvas* shoes.
38. **Cite** *(to quote)* The advocate *cited* many examples to prove his case.
   Site *(place)* It is a very spacious *site* for constructing a nursing home.
   Sight *(scenery, vision)* The mutilated body of a child was a ghastly *sight*.
39. **Continuous** *(without break)* He has been sleeping for an hour *continuously*.
   Continual *(continuity with break)* It has been drizzling *continually* since last night.
40. **Cemetery** *(burial place)* The dead body was taken to the *cemetery* for burial.
   Symmetry *(quality of harmony or balance in size and design)* The building looks exquisite only because of its remarkable *symmetry*.
41. **Career** *(vocation, profession)* If we want to make a good *career* we must work.
   Carrier *(that one carries)* The goods were taken to the destination on public *carrier*.
42. **Confident** *(certain, sure)* I am very *confident* of my friend's success in the interview.
   Confidant *(one who shares a secret)* Once his *confidant*, now Dinesh is the arch enemy of his mentor.
43. **Compliment** *(regards)* I *complimented* my friend on her success.
   Complement *(that completes)* Both husband and wife are *complement* to each other.
44. **Cannon** *(big gun)* Hundreds of *cannons* were shot in the battlefield.
   Canon *(principle, a law)* *Canons* of any religion are not easy to follow.
45. **Creditable** *(praiseworthy)* It is really *creditable* for a village boy to have topped the university.
   Credible *(believable)* Your excuse is not *credible*.
   Credulous *(simple, artless)* Children are *credulous* by nature.
46. **Coma** *(state of unconsciousness)* After the accident my friend had been in state of *coma* for several hours.
   Comma *(a mark of punctuation)* *Comma* is a very important part of learning punctuation.
47. **Corporal** *(physical)* In our school the children are not given *corporal* punishment.
   Corporeal *(having body, material)* Ghosts are not *corporeal* beings.
48. **Comprehensive** *(exhaustive, extensive)* *Comprehensive* steps have been taken to meet with unforeseen emergency.
   Comprehensible *(understandable)* The talk of the new student in our class was not *comprehensible* to us at all.
49. **Contagious** *(that spreads by contact)* Small pox is a *contagious* disease.
   Contiguous *(adjacent)* New Delhi and Noida are *contiguous*.
50. **Censure** *(blame, criticise)* *Censure* motion tabled by the opposition fell through.
   Censor *(examination of films and plays)* The film 'The Bandit Queen' has not been approved of by the *censor* board.

PARONYMS AND HOMONYMS 525

51. **Collision** *[striking against (face to face)]* Due to heavy fog the car met with a *collision*.
    Collusion *(nexus)* There was a *collusion* between the smugglers and the political leaders.
52. **Contemptible** *(deserving contempt)* The conduct of the taxi driver was highly mean and *contemptible*.
    Contemptuous *(expressing contempt)* She dismissed the servant with *contemptuous* gesture.
53. **Considerable** *(large, to great extent)* The industrialist spent *considerable* amount of money to uplift the living conditions of his workers.
    Considerate *(thoughtful of others)* He is beneficent and *considerate* to his subordinates.
54. **Ceremonious** *(formal)* One should not be very *ceremonious* in the marriage of daughters.
    Ceremonial *(of ceremony)* I could not attend the *ceremonial* function of his marriage.
55. **Complaisant** *(pleasing, obliging)* He is popular with his friends on account of his *complaisant* nature.
    Complacent *(self satisfied)* Most of the students of my class are *complacent* in their outlook and will not revolt against the principal.
56. **Conscious** *(aware)* We should always be *conscious* of what is going on around the world.
    Conscience *(inner voice)* I always act according to my *conscience*.
    Consensus *(general agreement)* Government should be run by *consensus*.
    Conscientious *(honest, scrupulous)* Being a *conscientious* worker he never shirks work.
57. **Coherent** *(intelligible)* She was so nervous that her words were not *coherent*.
    Inherent *(inborn quality)* Sincerity is *inherent* in her character.
58. **Collaborate** *(work together)* Indian industries are compelled to *collaborate* with multinational companies for survival.
    Corroborate *(confirm)* The principal *corroborated* the teacher's statement made to the police.
59. **Casual** *(occasional)* He is on *casual* leave today.
    Causal *(relating to cause)* There is definite *causal* relationship between population and poverty.
60. **Council** *(an assembly)* The Legislative *Council* has passed the Bill.
    Counsel *(advice)* His *counsel* proved very beneficial in the end.
61. **Councillor** *(member of council)* He is a *councillor* of the Legislative Council.
    Counsellor *(adviser)* I have engaged a noted *counsellor* to defend my case.
62. **Corpse** *(dead body)* A mutilated *corpse* was found in a locked house.
    Corps *(body of troops)* He is serving in Army Ordnance *Corps*.
    Carcass *(dead body of animal)* A *carcass* of a dog was lying in the road.
63. **Coarse** *(rough)* Though he is quite rich, he wears *coarse* clothes.
    Course *(line of action)* He has given up immoral *course* of life.

64. **Century** *(one hundred)* Twentieth *century* will be known as the age of science.
    Centenary *(100th anniversary)* *Centenary* of Indian National Movement was celebrated in 1985 AD.
65. **Conservation** *(preservation)* *Conservation* of forests is very important for our survival.
    Conservatism *(orthodox ideas)* I am quite liberal and do not believe in *conservatism*.
66. **Conform** *(adhere to)* You must *conform* to the rules laid down by your company.
    Confirm *(ratify)* I shall *confirm* my programme tomorrow.
67. **Capacity** *(ability to contain)* The hall has a seating *capacity* for five hundred students.
    Capability *(power of doing things)* My friend has *capability* to do any difficult task.
68. **Commonplace** *(ordinary, usual)* We are fed up with the *commonplace* speeches of our leaders.
    Common place *(place for all)* The street is a *common place* for everyone.
69. **Commandeer** *(seize for military purpose)* When martial law was imposed in Pakistan huge area of vacant land was *commandeered* for building air strip.
    Commander *(one who commands)* The *commander* of the army ordered the soldiers to capture the fort.
70. **Disease** *(illness)* My friend is suffering from an incurable *disease*.
    Decease *(death)* On account of the *decease* of his father, the burden of the family fell on his shoulders.
71. **Deny** *[refers to past (action, knowledge)]* She *denied* that she had gone to watch the movie last night.
    Refuse *[refers to future (request, order)]* Meeta *refused* that she would not return the money.
72. **Duel** *(fight between two persons)* In ancient times many *duels* were fought in order to settle disputes.
    Dual *(double)* She follows *dual* policy and misguides her husband.
73. **Deference** *(regards)* All children should have *deference* for their elders.
    Difference *(distinction)* There is no *difference* among the basic concepts of all the religions.
    Deferment *(postponement)* His application for *deferment* of hearing was turned down.
74. **Decent** *(right and suitable)* She always wears *decent* clothes.
    Descent *(coming down)* The *descent* of the hill is very dangerous.
    Dissent *(disagreement)* Only a few members expressed *dissent* to my suggestion.
75. **Desert** (noun) *(sandy land)* The government has greatly solved the problem of pure drinking water in the *desert*.
    Desert (verb) *(leave)* She was *deserted* by her husband.
    Dessert *(sweet dish)* *Dessert* was served after dinner.
76. **Dominant** *(dominating)* Sohan is very *dominant* in our class.
    Domineer *(to dominate)* Mothers-in-law try to *domineer* over their daughters-in-law.

PARONYMS AND HOMONYMS

77. **Drought** *(lack of rain)* Last year most of the areas of Uttar Pradesh suffered from a severe *drought*.
    Draught *(current of wind, quantity of liquid)* A *draught* of cool wind was very refreshing.

78. **Defective** *(having defect)* As he met with a severe accident last year, one of his legs is *defective*.
    Deficient *(lacking)* Though young he is *deficient* in common sense.

79. **Diverse** *(different)* The two children of one family may have *diverse* temperaments.
    Divers *(several)* (i) He has consulted *divers* doctors about his disease.
    (ii) Those, who dive into river/sea, are *divers*.

80. **Deduce** *(infer)* It is difficult to *deduce* any conclusion from your ambiguous remarks.
    Deduct *(subtract)* Two days' wages will be *deducted* from your monthly salary.

81. **Deliverance** *(freedom, emancipation)* Lord Buddha preached eight fold path to attain *deliverance* from sorrows of life.
    Delivery *(giving letters etc)* The *delivery* of the letter was just in time.

82. **Decry** *(criticise)* The foreign policy of the Congress party has always been *decried*.
    Descry *(dimly seen)* We could *descry* only a traveller in the bleak evening.

83. **Defy** *(violate)* How dare you *defy* my orders?
    Deify *(to worship)* Swami Vivekananda is *deified* by every Indian.

84. **Doze** *(sleep)* The teacher caught him *dozing* in the class.
    Dose *(of medicine)* You should not take heavy *dose* of medicine.

85. **Dam** *(barrier built to reserve water)* A *dam* has been built on the river.
    Damn *(condemn)* The book was *damned* by the critics.

86. **Diversion** *(change in direction)* There is a *diversion* on the road ahead.
    Diversity *(variety)* *Diversity* is the chief feature of our civilisation.

87. **Enviable** *(causing envy)* All the people are jealous because of his *enviable* position in the society.
    Envious *(feeling of envy)* Her friends were *envious* of her success in the medical entrance examination.

88. **Exception** *(objection)* There are always *exceptions* to rules in every language.
    Exceptional *(rare, to a large extent)* In his own class Rohit is a boy of *exceptional* abilities.
    Exceptionable *(objectionable)* I objected to her *exceptionable* remarks against my parents.

89. **Eminent** *(famous)* Shakespeare was an *eminent* playwright.
    Imminent *(impending)* Third world war is *imminent*.
    Immanent *(present everywhere)* Divine force is *immanent* in universe.

90. **Eligible** *(fit to be chosen)* Untrustworthy people are not *eligible* for responsible posts.
    Illegible *(that cannot be read)* I can't read this letter as her handwriting is *illegible*.

91. **Exceedingly** *[to a great extent (good sense)]* One of my cousins is an *exceedingly* rich person.
    Excessively *[to a great extent (bad sense)]* They spent money on the feast lavishly and *excessively*.

92. **Exhausting** *(tiring)* Teaching nursery classes is a very *exhausting* job.
    Exhaustive *(detailed, comprehensive)* The teacher gave to the students *exhaustive* notes on English Grammar.
    Exhausted *(tired)* He was *exhausted* and went to bed immediately.

93. **Economical** *(frugal)* A housewife should always be *economical* if she wants to run her house smoothly.
    Economic *(pertaining to economy)* India is yet to cross many hurdles to overcome *economic* crisis.
    Economics *(a subject)* *Economics* is an interesting subject.

94. **Elude** *(escape)* Sohan was so clever that he *eluded* the police and escaped from the prison.
    Allude *(refer, cite)* The speaker *alluded* to many examples from the Gita.

95. **Excite** *(stir up feelings)* The people got very *excited* when the police refused to take any action against the culprits.
    Incite *(rousing to action)* The communal speech of the leader *incited* the mob to violence.
    Insight *(ability to see the truth)* India needs leaders of great *insight*.

96. **Envelop** *(cover, wrap)* As the dark clouds covered the sky, the whole town was *enveloped* in darkness.
    Envelope *(a letter cover)* Please put the letter in the *envelope*.

97. **Expeditious** *(quick, prompt)* Dattu is very *expeditious* in answering letters.
    Expedient *(practical, contrary to principles)* Selfish persons are always *expedient* in their approach to life.
    Expedition *(a journey to unknown place)* They will go on an *expedition* to Everest.

98. **Esteem** *(respect)* As Mahesh is very sociable, he is held in high *esteem* by his friends.
    Estimate *(calculate)* Can you give me the *estimate*, of the cost of the house?
    Estimation *(opinion, judgement)* In my *estimation*, he is the fool of the first water.

99. **Exposure** *(reveal, exposed to heat or cold)* She will not attend office today as she is suffering from *exposure*.
    Exposition *(explanation)* Tilak's *exposition* of the Gita is remarkable.

100. **Egotist** *(one who talks a lot of oneself)* It is difficult to stand the company of an *egotist*.
     Egoist *(one who believes in self interest, proud)* An *egoist* is moved only by self-interest while helping others.

101. **Emerge** *(come out)* It is hoped that he will *emerge* successful out of these trying conditions.
     Immerse *(plunge into, absorb in)* Being a man of contemplative nature, he is always *immersed* in pensive mood.

PARONYMS AND HOMONYMS

102. **Eruption** *(bursting)* The *eruption* of volcano caused heavy destruction on the island.
 Irruption *(attack)* The *irruption* of Pakistan Army was successfully repulsed.
103. **Elemental** *(of nature, elements)* Inspite of *elemental* hardships, Columbus discovered America.
 Elementary *(beginning, introductory)* You must have *elementary* knowledge of science.
104. **Excursion** *(picnic)* The students will go on *excursion* tomorrow.
 Incursion *(sudden attack)* *Incursions* by Pakistan and China, into our borders, speak of our weakness.
105. **Entrance** *(opening, gate)* The *entrance* to the fair by this route has been blocked up.
 Entry *(coming into)* The *entry* of student leaders into college premises is banned.
106. **Expensive** *(costing much money)* She bought a less *expensive* dress.
 Valuable *(useful)* The book provides *valuable* data for further study.
107. **Fatal** *(causing death)* On his way to school, he met with an accident and received a *fatal* wound in the leg.
 Fateful *(very significant)* The formation of I.N.A. was a *fateful* event.
 Fatalist *(believer in fate)* Indians are *fatalists* by nature.
108. **Forceful** *(strong and powerful)* Netaji had a *forceful* personality.
 Forcible *(by force, compulsion)* He was evicted from the house *forcibly*.
109. **Feign** *(pretend)* In order to save himself the accused *feigned* madness in the court.
 Fain *(gladly)* She would *fain* do anything for her friends.
110. **Forgo** *(give up)* Parents *forgo* their own comforts for the sake of their children.
 Forego *(go before)* This point has been dealt with in detail in the *foregoing* passage.
111. **Facility** *(convenience, dexterity)* The hotel provides all kinds of *facilities* to its customers.
 Felicity *(apt expression, joy)* May God bless you with *felicity*!
112. **Facilitate** *(make easy)* The new agreement will *facilitate* the development of the trade.
 Felicitate *(to congratulate)* I *felicitated* him on his success.
113. **Fair** *(a show, just, colour)* Let us go to Nauchandi *fair*.
 Fare *(passage money, meal)* There is a steep rise in railway *fare*.
114. **Formality** *(show ceremony)* True friends never observe *formality* with each other.
 Formalism *(observance of rites)* Swami Dayanand taught the Hindus to shun *formalism* in religion.
115. **Fiscal** *(of public revenue)* Government is trying to bring down the *fiscal* deficit in the next budget.
 Financial *(monetary)* He suffered huge *financial* loss in the business.
116. **Gentle** *(not harsh)* We should be *gentle* and polite to our elders.
 Genteel *(well mannered, of the upper class)* People belonging to middle class try to maintain the style of *genteel* class of society.

117. **Gamble** *(to play for stake)* On the occasion of Diwali people *gamble* and are ruined.
Gambol *(to frisk)* It is a beautiful sight to see a deer *gamboling* in a forest.
118. **Graceful** *(beautiful)* She has a *graceful* gait.
Gracious *(kind, merciful)* God is *gracious*.
119. **Gate** *(door)* The dacoits entered the house through the main *gate*.
Gait *(manner of walking)* Her *gait* is graceful.
120. **Gravitation** *(pulling towards, attracting)* Theory of *gravitation* was invented by Newton.
Gravity *(quality of being serious)* One must observe *gravity* on solemn occasions.
121. **Hoard** *(amass, to store)* As he is a smuggler, he has a *hoard* of gold and silver in his house.
Horde *(a gang)* A *horde* of militants intruded into Indian territory.
122. **Historic** *(likely to be famous in history)* Kapil Dev scored *historic* victory by winning the World Cup in 1983.
Histrionic *(art of acting)* Rekha is known for her *histrionic* talents.
Historical *(of history)* I visited many *historical* buildings in Delhi, while I was in school.
123. **Humility** *(politeness)* *Humility* in victory is a rare virtue.
Humiliation *(insult, disgrace)* All respectable persons prefer death to *humiliation*.
124. **Honorary** *(unpaid)* My sister taught in a college as an *honorary* tutor.
Honourable *(deserving honour)* He is regarded *honourable* member of the club.
125. **Human** *(race of man)* On account of ecological disturbances, the existence of *human* beings is endangered.
Humane *(kind)* Doctors are supposed to be considerate and *humane*.
126. **Hail** *(belong to, welcome, frozen rain)* Those *hailing* from Bangladesh are living illegally in this country.
Hale *(healthy)* He is *hale* and hearty and enjoys life to his fill.
127. **Healthy** *(having health)* In spite of his old age he is quite *healthy*.
Healthful *(promoting health)* The climate of hill stations is *healthful*.
128. **Hypocritical** *(guilty of hypocrisy)* I do not like his *hypocritical* attitude towards his friends.
Hypercritical *(too critical)* It does not pay in life to be *hypercritical* of trivial matters.
129. **Humanity** *(mankind, quality of being kind)* One must act in the larger interest of *humanity*.
Humanism *(devotion to human interest)* Act of *humanism* is always appreciated.
130. **Hollow** *(not solid, with a hole, false)* The stick is *hollow*; nothing is inside it.
Hallow *(ed)* *(sacred)* The *hallowed* shrine is visited by the devotees throughout the year.
Halo *(circle of light around the head)* Holy men are painted with *halo* around their heads.

PARONYMS AND HOMONYMS   531

131. **Industrial** *(pertaining to industry)* *Industrial* progress in India has not been rapid.
     Industrious *(hard working)* My friend is an *industrious* man and he achieved success in life.

132. **Impossible** *(that is not possible)* If we make up our mind and work hard, nothing is *impossible* in this world.
     Impassable *(that cannot be passed through)* Many passes in the Himalayas are *impassable* during winter.

133. **Ingenious** *(skilful, clever)* She devised an *ingenious* scheme to hoodwink the police.
     Ingenuous *(frank, innocent)* Children are liked for their *ingenuous* nature.

134. **Imaginary** *(fanciful, unreal)* Don't be daunted by *imaginary* troubles.
     Imaginative *(contemplative)* Poets and artists are *imaginative* by temperament.

135. **Intelligible** *(understandable)* Your remarks are not *intelligible* to me.
     Intelligent *(wise and sensible)* Only *intelligent* students are found to succeed in this world of stiff competition.

136. **Immoral** *(not according to morality)* An *immoral* person suffers in the long run.
     Unmoral *(non-moral, amoral)* *Unmoral* persons are not concerned with morality or the immorality of an action.

137. **Incomparable** *(without equal)* She was a damsel of *incomparable* beauty.
     Uncomparable *(having no similarity)* The security problems of India and Pakistan are *uncomparable*.

138. **Invert** *(to put upside down)* Put this statement in *inverted* commas.
     Inert *(passive)* *Inert* gases are without active chemical properties.

139. **Inept** *(incompetent)* *Inept* handling of situation resulted in riots.
     Inapt *(unsuitable)* The title of the story is *inapt*.

140. **Incidental** *(happening as natural or a part of)* The risk of loss is always *incidental* to any business.
     Accidental *(by chance)* It was just an *accidental* meeting between the two school mates.

141. **Jealous** *(full of jealousy)* All his friends are *jealous* of him.
     Zealous *(enthusiastic)* My brother is very *zealous* about his new appointment.

142. **Judicious** *(wise, thoughtful)* We must be *judicious* in the choice of our career.
     Judicial *(pertaining to judiciary)* He was sent to *judicial* lock up by the Magistrate.

143. **Kindly** *(acts, feelings)* I shall never forget your *kindly* act.
     Kind *(tender, pitiful)* He is a *kind* man who helps every body.

144. **Lightning** *(flash of light)* *Lightning* struck his house and set the whole house on fire.
     Lightening *(make light)* He is always interested in *lightening* the financial burden of his father.

145. **Luxurious** *(pertaining to luxury)* As she is the daughter of a rich industrialist, she lives a very *luxurious* life.
     Luxuriant *(rich in growth)* The hills of Uttarakhand are teeming with *luxuriant* forests.

146. **Loathe** *(detest)* The rich should not *loathe* the poor.
     Loth (loath) *(unwilling)* She was *loth* to go with him alone.
147. **Limit** *(extent)* You must spend within your *limits*.
     Limitation *(shortcomings)* There are many *limitations* in Parliamentary form of government in backward countries.
148. **Loud** *(loud sound)* Everyone was alarmed when there was a *loud* blast in the locality.
     Loudly *(in a loud manner)* The teacher forbade them to speak *loudly*.
     Aloud *(audible)* The students requested the teacher to speak *aloud*.
149. **Learned** *(erudite, educated)* He is not only rich, but also *learned* and wise.
     Learnt *(past of learn)* He *learnt* his lesson very well.
150. **Literal** *(expressed in words)* Most of the words are used in *literal* and figurative sense.
     Literary *(of literature)* He is a *literary* man and reads a lot of books.
151. **Maze** *(winding paths)* The walled city is full of *mazes*.
     Maize *(a kind of corn)* *Maize* grows in abundance in Africa.
152. **Memorable** *(worthy of remembering)* In the plays of Shakespeare we find a lot of *memorable* quotations.
     Memorial *(statue or anything in the memory of)* We collected money to erect *memorial* in the memory of war heroes.
     Immemorial *(longer than people can remember)* The religious rites of the Hindus are *immemorial* tradition.
153. **Momentary** *(short lived)* One should not run after the wordly pleasures as they are *momentary*.
     Momentous *(very important)* 'Operation Shakti' at Pokhran was the *momentous* event in the history of independent India.
154. **Morale** *(the state of spirit, confidence)* The *morale* of the army should always be high.
     Moral *(sense of right and wrong, lesson)* We are advised to pursue a *moral* course of life.
155. **Maritime** *(relating to sea, or ships)* Once Britain was a great *maritime* power.
     Marine *(found in the sea/trade by sea)* India should develop *marine* trade to earn foreign exchange.
156. **Manifest** *(obvious, evident)* It should be *manifest* to all by now that China and Pakistan are inciting trouble on our borders.
     Manifestation *(act or desire that makes obvious)* Indiscipline among the youth is just a *manifestation* of serious national evil.
157. **Negligible** *(unimportant)* The dacoits attacked his house yesterday night but his loss is *negligible*.
     Negligent *(careless in duty)* We should not be *negligent* in our duty.
     Neglectful *(careless)* He is so *neglectful* that he doesn't care for his family's interest.
158. **Notable** *(creditable)* India has made a *notable* progress in the field of agriculture.
     Noticeable *(easy to notice)* There is *noticeable* improvement in the patient.
     Notorious *[famous (unfavourable)]* Our political leaders are *notorious* for their apathy to public interest.
     Noted *(famous)* The leader is *noted* for his honesty.

PARONYMS AND HOMONYMS

159. **Observance** *(compliance)* In order to remain healthy *observance* of certain simple rules is required.
   Observation *(notice)* Children have very keen *observation* power.
160. **Ordinance** *(a government order)* The government has issued an *ordinance* against the people who do not pay the taxes on time.
   Ordnance *(a gun)* There is an *ordnance* factory at Kanpur.
161. **Official** *(pertaining to office)* You are bound to maintain *official* secrecy.
   Officious *(ready to offer services, flatterer)* Beware of *officious* fellows.
162. **Organisation** *(institution)* He is working in a non-government *organisation*.
   Organism *(living beings with parts working together)* Human *organism* is a complex system.
   Organic *(of an organ)* *Organic* diseases destroy the organs.
163. **Petrol** *(fuel)* *Petrol* is very costly these days.
   Patrol *(go round)* The *patrol* van is regularly moving on the highway day and night for our protection.
164. **Providential** *(divine)* My friend's *providential* escape at the critical moment saved his life.
   Provident *(frugal, thrifty)* She is quite *provident* and economical in household expenses.
   Providence *(divine force)* Trust in *providence* for good days.
165. **Practical** *(not theoretical)* The scientist gave a *practical* demonstration of his experiment.
   Practicable *(capable of being practised)* Only *practicable* schemes are adopted by our Managing Director.
166. **Proscribe** *(ban, prohibit)* Indecent books are generally *proscribed* by he government.
   Prescribe *(recommend, advise)* Doctor has *prescribed* a very efficacious medicine for the treatment of the disease.
167. **Popular** *(admirable)* As Mrs Neena is a very kind teacher, she is very *popular* with her students.
   Populous *(thickly populated)* China is the most *populous* country in the world.
168. **Pale** *(bloodless, yellowish)* Due to his prolonged sickness he looks very *pale* now.
   Pail *(container)* A *pail* full of milk was lying in the kitchen.
169. **Pair** *(double of a thing)* I gave a *pair* of new shoes to my brother on his birthday.
   Pare *(trim)* Please *pare* your finger nails regularly.
170. **Pane** *(window glass)* Our window *pane* was broken by the children who were playing Cricket outside our house.
   Pain *(suffering of mind or body)* She was feeling *pain* in her neck.
171. **Peel** *(to remove the skin)* Please wash the mangoes before you *peel* them.
   Peal *(a loud sound)* On hearing his jokes all of us went into a *peal* of laughter.
172. **Personal** *(private)* We were asked to express our *personal* views on this subject in the debate.
   Personnel *(persons employed)* The *personnel* department has issued termination notice to Sachin.

173. **Punctual** *(at fixed time)* *Punctual* students alone deserve a splendid success.
Punctilious *(very careful in duty)* We are taught to be very *punctilious* in our work in the school.
174. **Prudent** *(wise, careful, foresight)* It is *prudent* on her part to break with selfish friends.
Prudential *(of prudent actions, policy)* The *prudential* actions of my father saved the family from financial crisis.
175. **Precedent** *(previous examples)* The lawyer cited many *precedents* in support of his case.
President *(Head of Institution)* Indian *President* is only de jure head of the government.
176. **Physique** *(physical health)* He is a smart youngman with a good *physique*.
Physic *(medicine)* No *physic* has yet been discovered to cure cancer.
Physics *(a subject)* *Physics* is my favourite subject.
177. **Prey** *(hunt and kill)* As a national bird the Peacock is not a bird of *prey*.
Pray *(offer prayer)* He *prays* to God daily.
178. **Proceed** *(to move forward)* Inspite of difficulties he *proceeded* with is enterprise.
Precede *(to go before)* I have mentioned every detail in the *preceding* passage.
179. **Politic** *(prudent, wise)* It is not *politic* to flog the dead horse.
Political *(of politics)* The *political* parties in India have no concern for the poor.
180. **Prosecute** *(file a suit in the court)* You are likely to be *prosecuted* in the court for violation of rules.
Persecute *(oppress)* She was mercilessly *persecuted* for not bringing a car in dowry.
181. **Pitiable** *(deserving pity)* The condition of the family is *pitiable* on account of poverty.
Pitiful *(making one feel pity)* It was a *pitiful* sight to see a beggar woman suffering from cancer.
182. **Polity** *(form of government)* Indian *polity* is not in a healthy state these days.
Policy *(plan of action)* Honesty is the best *policy*.
183. **Proscription** *(prohibition)* The *proscription* of the newspaper was resented by the people.
Prescription *(recommendation)* The *prescription* of medicine by the doctor proved very useful.
184. **Putrefy** *(to rot)* Many unclaimed dead bodies lay *putrefying* in the field.
Petrify *(turn into stone, stun)* We were *petrified* with terror to see the ghastly sight of the carnage.
185. **Righteous** *(just, truthful)* The Principal's anger was *righteous* for he could not tolerate the indiscipline in the college.
Rightful *(having right)* He is the *rightful* owner of the property.
186. **Raise** *(increase)* The traders have *raised* the prices of food grains.
Raze *(wipe out)* All the huts of the poor were *razed* to the ground as they needed land to build a five star hotel.

PARONYMS AND HOMONYMS 535

187. **Reign** *(rule)* The *reign* of Gupta dynasty is known as golden period in the history of India.
Rein *(bridle of horse)* He *reined* the horse and escaped a fall.

188. **Rite** *(ceremony)* The marriage was performed according to Hindu *rites*.
Wright *(give a shape)* He is a great play *wright*.
Write *(compose)* Please *write* in the note-book.

189. **Rout** *(put to defeat)* The enemy was *routed* by Indian forces.
Route *(path)* You should not go by long *route*.

190. **Respective** *(belonging to each)* After the match we left for our *respective* homes.
Respectable *(enjoying respect)* His father is a *respectable* man of the city.
Respectful *(showing respect)* You must be *respectful* to your elders.

191. **Rapt** *(fully attentive)* They listened to the speech of the Prime Minister with *rapt* attention.
Wrapt *(lost in, absorbed)* She did not notice my arrival as she was *wrapt* in her thoughts.

192. **Recourse** *(means of action)* I do not advise you to have *recourse* to legal action in this matter.
Resource *(means, raw material)* India is a land teeming with natural *resources*.

193. **Symbol** *(sign, to represent something)* Vinoba Bhave was a *symbol* of simplicity and honesty.
Cymbal *(a musical instrument)* The melodious sound of the *cymbals* impressed every body.

194. **Stationery** *(writing material)* His father deals in office *stationery*.
Stationary *(static, fixed)* The Sun is *stationary*.

195. **Soar** *(rise, fly)* Birds are *soaring* in the sky.
Sore *(wound, painful)* People are *sore* because the prices are soaring.
Sour *(bitter)* The grapes are *sour*.

196. **Suspect** *(to think to be true)* The whole class *suspects* Rohan to have stolen Rita's money.
Doubt *(to think to be untrue)* I *doubt* if she will get through the examination.

197. **Sociable** *(fond of mixing with people)* Because of her *sociable* behaviour she is liked by all the members of her family.
Social *(pertaining to society)* Man is a *social* animal.

198. **Sensual** *(voluptuous, exciting senses)* We should not indulge in *sensual* pleasures or we will repent later on.
Sensuous *(that affects the senses)* John Keats' poetry is *sensuous*.

199. **Spacious** *(having large space)* My house contains many *spacious* rooms.
Specious *(outwardly attractive)* No body was impressed with his *specious* arguments.

200. **Spiritual** *(opposed to material, of spirit)* Indians should not give up their *spiritual* heritage.
Spirituous *(containing intoxicating drink)* Excessive consumption of *spirituous* drinks is injurious to health.

201. **Stimulant** *(that which stimulates)* Tea is a *stimulant* for a worker after a day's hard work.
     Stimulus *(incentive)* Man hardly acts if there is no *stimulus* before him.
202. **Special** *(specific)* He came here on a *special* mission to bring about reconciliation between the two parties.
     Especial *(to a great degree)* It is *especially* hot these days.
203. **Storey** *(upper part of a building)* He lives in the second *storey* of the house.
     Story *(tale)* It is a very interesting *story*.
204. **Suit** *(a set of clothes, a lawsuit)* He presented me with a woollen *suit*.
     Suite *(a set of rooms)* He has booked a *suite* in the hotel.
205. **Sham** *(pretend to be, pretence)* What he says is all *sham*.
     Shame *(feeling of humiliation)* He felt *shame* at having told a lie.
206. **Severe** *(violent, rigorous)* She is suffering from *severe* headache.
     Sever *(separate)* You can never *sever* relations with your family.
207. **Statue** *(figure of animal/man in stone or wood)* The *statue* of Dr. Ambedkar was unveiled by the President.
     Statute *(law passed by law making bodies)* The *statute* was passed by the Parliament unanimously.
208. **Temperance** *(moderation in habits)* We should observe *temperance* in eating and drinking habits because it leads to healthy way of life.
     Temperament *(disposition, nature)* Always keep from persons of choleric *temperament*.
209. **Tolerable** *(bearable)* The food that was served in his daughter's marriage was *tolerable*.
     Tolerant *(liberal in ideas)* Every religion teaches us to be *tolerant* of the religious views held by others.
210. **Temporal** *(worldly, physical)* We should not hanker after *temporal* glory.
     Temporary *(lasting for short time)* He was given the job on the *temporary* basis only.
211. **Tamper** *(meddle with)* Please do not *tamper* with my papers.
     Temper *(emotional state of mind, soften)* One must not lose one's *temper*.
212. **Teem** *(full of)* India is a country *teeming* with natural resources.
     Team *(group of players)* His name has not been included in the college cricket *team*.
213. **Uninterested** *(having no interest)* Gaurav is *uninterested* in the study of science.
     Disinterested *(free from personal motive)* A *disinterested* leader of the party always commands respect from his followers.
214. **Variation** *(change)* *Variation* in his blood pressure worried the doctors.
     Variance *(opposite)* My views are always at *variance* with my father's.
215. **Vocation** *(profession)* Singing is both his *vocation* and avocation.
     Avocation *(hobby)* Gardening is a very favourite *avocation* of my father.
216. **Virtuous** *(having virtues)* She is a *virtuous* and devoted house wife.
     Virtual *(real)* Her mother is the *virtual* head of the family.

PARONYMS AND HOMONYMS

217. **Voracity** *(greed)* He is detested on account of his *voracity* for wealth.
 Veracity *(truthfulness)* It is very difficult to verify the *veracity* of her statement since she is very clever.
218. **Vane** *(weather cock)* The wind *vane* points to the direction of the wind.
 Vain *(proud, useless)* She is *vain* of her wealth.
 Wane *(decline)* His popularity as a political leader is on the *wane*.
 Vein *(a blood vein)* All the *veins* carry blood to heart.
219. **Vassal** *(a slave)* In ancient times prisoners of war were made *vassals*.
 Vessel *(a small ship, utensil)* Empty *vessels* make much noise.
220. **Venal** *(corruptible)* The *venal* leaders are bane of Indian polity.
 Venial *(to be forgiven)* The fault is so slight that it is thought to be *venial*.
221. **Wreak** *(take revenge)* At last he *wreaked* vengeance by killing his enemy.
 Wreck *(destroy)* The fury of the storm *wrecked* many houses.
222. **Wither** *(fade)* The plants kept in the shade will *wither* for want of Sun and light.
 Whither *(where)* Modern man is so much confused that he does not know *whither* he is heading for.
223. **Willing** *(ready)* We should always be *willing* to help the needy.
 Wilful *(deliberate)* His marriage was a total failure on account of his *wilful* nature.
224. **Wave** *(sea or river wave)* The *waves* rose sky high when the storm blew up.
 Waive *(remove, forgo)* Government has at last agreed to *waive* excise duty on cloth.
225. **Wrest** *(snatch by force)* The enemy *wrested* his gun and killed him.
 Rest *(peace)* Please go and take *rest* now.
226. **Womanly** *[of woman (good sense)]* My mother has *womanly* virtues.
 Womanish *[of woman (bad sense)]* His voice is *womanish* as it is quite shrill.
227. **Whet** *(increase interest)* Lemon will *whet* your appetite for more food.
 Vet *(screening)* The candidates were *vetted* for security reasons.
 Wet *(covered with water/liquid)* He got *wet* in the rain and is not well.

Previous Years' Questions

I. Directions *Fill in the blanks with the help of appropriate word given in brackets.*
                                                                        [Civil Services (Mains), 2003]

1. Nehruji made a .... speech in Parliament on this occasion. *(historical, historic)*
2. Such heavy responsibilities cannot be .... easily. *(born, borne)*
3. The doctor visits him on .... days. *(alternative, alternate)*
4. I do not know why he is .... towards me. *(contemptuous, contemptible)*
5. To do work for more than eight hours is quite .... *(exhaustive, exhausting)*
6. Democracy does not allow the .... of the minorities. *(prosecution, persecution)*
7. No meeting of the .... of ministers has been scheduled for tomorrow.
                                                                        (council, cabinet)
8. All worldly pleasures are considered to be .... by saints.
                                                                        (momentary, momentous)
9. Any .... of secret documents is punishable by law. *(tempering, tampering)*
10. He is an .... person to work with. *(amiable, amenable)*

II. Directions *Fill in the blanks with the help of appropriate word given in brackets.*
                                                                        [Civil Services (Mains), 2004]

1. She has a .... appearance. *(gracious, graceful)*
2. Our principal is a man of kind and .... nature. *(judicious, judicial)*
3. He was offered a .... job. *(temporal, temporary)*
4. He is .... to both praise and blame. *(sensible, sensitive)*
5. Gandhiji was the .... head of Congress party. *(virtuous, virtual)*
6. I do not regard his scheme as .... *(practicable, practical)*
7. The equator is an .... line round the world. *(imaginative, imaginary)*
8. The ship sailed in spite of .... difficulties. *(elemental, elementary)*
9. Act of .... negligence are punishable by law. *(willing, wilful)*
10. I am the .... owner of the house. *(rightful, righteous)*

III. Directions *Which of the two words within brackets in the following sentences is correct in the context?*
                                                                        [Civil Services (Mains), 2005]

1. Poets often .... (*sore/soar*) to great heights of imagination.
2. Knowledge .... (*proceeds/precedes*) from the Goddess of learning.
3. The tower was struck by .... (*lightning/lightening*) and fell down.
4. Kanpur lies on the air .... (*rout/route*) to Kolkata.
5. Everyone is .... (*jealous/zealous*) of him.

PARONYMS AND HOMONYMS 539

6. He was found in .... (*collusion/collision*) with the plotters.
7. Wicked persons are not .... (*illegible/eligible*) for responsible posts.
8. The crocodile emerged from the river and .... (*seized/ceased*) a goat.
9. He is a man of .... (*lose/loose*) character.
10. The emperor is staying at the royal .... (*mansion/mention*)

IV. Directions *Use the following homonyms in sentences so as to bring out the difference in meaning clearly without changing the form.*

1. (a) Compliment   Complement
   (b) Canvas   Canvass
   (c) Device   Devise
   (d) Ghostly   Ghastly
   (e) Cite   Site   [IES, 2015]

2. (a) Impetus   Impetuous
   (b) Allusion   Illusion
   (c) Collision   Collusion
   (d) Official   Officious
   (e) Imminent   Eminent   [CAPF, 2015]

3. (a) Coast   Beach
   (b) Contagious   Infectious
   (c) Famous   Famed
   (d) Incident   Accident
   (e) Price   Cost   [CAPF, 2014]

4. (a) Rest   Wrest
   (b) Precis   Precise
   (c) Confident   Confidant
   (d) Glove   Glow
   (e) Knotty   Naughty   [IFS, 2015]

5. (a) Share   Sheer
   (b) Raise   Rage
   (c) Fear   Fair
   (d) Cattle   Kettle
   (e) Pair   Pare   [IFS, 2014]

6. (a) Moral   Morale
   (b) Access   Axis
   (c) Forcible   Forceful
   (d) Flair   Flare
   (e) Metal   Mettle   [IFS, 2013]

V. Directions *Choose the appropriate word to fill in the blanks.*

A.   [Civil Services (Mains), 2013]

1. My teacher said that I need to .... (*practice, practise*) more.
2. The hot weather .... (*affects, effects*) people in different ways.
3. Wouldn't it be nice if we had to work only on .... (*alternative, alternate*) days?

4. Our politicians are known to .... (*avoid, evade*) taxes.
5. The principal .... (*complimented, complemented*) the students on their fine performance.

B. **[Civil Services (Mains), 2015]**
1. Slow and .... wins the race. (*study/steady*)
2. The farm scientists have discovered a new .... to combat soil erosion. (*device/devise*)
3. Going back on your word is a .... of trust. (*breach/break*)
4. A .... of cars was following the minister. (*fleet/float*)
5. The businessman tried to .... a deal with the inspector. (*strike/stroke*)

C. 1. He got a .... blow from his enemy. (*deadly/deathly*)
2. The .... of his speech was very lucid and natural. (*delivery/deliverance*)
3. I do not know how to express my gratitude; you have been .... to me. (*beneficial/beneficent*)
4. My friend will .... me to the hospital. (*accompany/escort*)
5. We sat in the .... of a tree and relaxed a while. (*shadow/shade*)

Answers

I. 1. historic   2. borne   3. alternate   4. contemptuous
   5. exhausting   6. persecution   7. council   8. momentary
   9. tampering   10. amiable

II. 1. graceful   2. judicious   3. temporary   4. sensitive
    5. virtual   6. practicable   7. imaginary   8. elemental
    9. wilful   10. rightful

III. 1. soar   2. proceeds   3. lightning   4. route
     5. jealous   6. collusion   7. eligible   8. seized
     9. loose   10. mansion

IV. 1. (a) **Compliment** (*a remark that expresses praise*) She *complimented* me on my grammatical skills.
    Complement (*something that completes or makes perfect*) A good wine is a *complement* to a good meal.
    (b) **Canvas** (*a closely woven, heavy cloth of cotton, hemp or linen, used for tents, sails, etc*) I picked up the brush and painted a picture on the *canvas*.
    Canvass (*to solicit votes, opinions, or the like*) The President spent most of his time *canvassing* for votes for the elections.
    (c) **Device** (*a tool or technique used to do a task*) He handed the *device* to her.
    Devise (*to plan or create*) A new system has been *devised* to control traffic in the city.
    (d) **Ghostly** (*looking or sounding like a ghost*) A *ghostly* figure emerged from the churchyard.
    Ghastly (*very frightening and unpleasant*) The weather was *ghastly*.

PARONYMS AND HOMONYMS

(e) **Cite** (*to mention some thing as a reason or an example*) He *cited* his heavy workload as the reason for his breakdown.
Site (*a place where a building, town, etc was, is or will be located*) All the materials are on *site* so that work can start immediately.

2. (a) **Impetus** (*something that encourages a process or activity to develop more quickly*) The debate seems to have lost much of its initial *impetus*.
Impetuous (*rash or impulsive*) We made an *impetuous* decision to go swimming in the lake in December.

(b) **Allusion** (*reference*) The poem is explained properly with the help of many *allusions*.
Illusion (*unreal*) The idea of absolute personal freedom is an *illusion*.

(c) **Collision** (*striking against face to face*) Due to heavy fog, the car met with a *collision*.
Collusion (*nexus*) There was a *collusion* between the smugglers and the political leaders.

(d) **Official** (*pertaining to office*) You are bound to maintain *official* secrecy.
Officious (*assertive of authority in a domineering way*) The security people were very *officious*.

(e) **Imminent** (*about to happen*) They were in *imminent* danger of being swept away.
Eminent (*distinguished or renowned*) He is one of the world's most *eminent* statisticians.

3. (a) **Coast** (*seashore*) The ship sailed along the West *coast* of Africa.
Beach (*a pebbly or sandy shore, especially by the sea*) Goa has fabulous sandy *beaches*.

(b) **Contagious** (*infectious, communicable*) Cold and cough is a *contagious* disease.
Infectious (*likely to spread or influence others in a rapid manner*) It is important to isolate patients with *infectious* diseases so that others will not become sick.

(c) **Famous** (*well-known*) Priyanka Chopra is a *famous* actress.
Famed (*noted*) He is *famed* for his eccentricities.

(d) **Incident** (*event or happening*) A memorable *incident* occurred at one of these meetings.
Accident (*mishap or disaster*) He met with an *accident* at the factory.

(e) **Price** (*amount of money expected or given in payment*) The land was sold for a high *price*.
Cost (*an amount that has to be paid or spent to buy or obtain something*) We are able to cover the *cost* of the event.

4. (a) **Rest** (*relax, take a break*) He needed to *rest* after the feverish activity.
Wrest (*take or remove by force*) Anaira tried to *wrest* her arm from his hold.

(b) **Precis** (*a summary or abstract of a text or speech*) From some book of her own Miss Shanaya, the English teacher, had given a lengthy paragraph for *precis* work.
Precise (*exact or accurate*) The director was *precise* with his camera positions.

(c) **Confident** (*self-assured*) She is a *confident*, outgoing girl.
Confidant (*close friend or companion*) The diary was her close *confidant* with whom she shared her innermost secrets.

(d) **Glove** (*a covering for the hand worn for protection against cold or dirt*) Tanya put on some rubber *gloves*, so that she wouldn't leave fingerprints.
Glow (*radiance, light*) The setting Sun cast a deep red *glow* over the city.

(e) **Knotty** (*extremely difficult or complex*) It was a *knotty* legal problem.
Naughty (*disobedient*) You've been a really *naughty* boy.

5. (a) **Share** (*portion, division*) Under the proposals, investors would pay a greater *share* of the annual fees required.
Sheer (*absolute, complete*) She giggled with *sheer* delight.

(b) **Raise** (*rise increment*) He wants a *raise* and some perks.
Rage (*violent uncontrollable anger*) Her face was distorted with *rage*.

(c) **Fear** (*terror, panic*) I cowered in *fear* as bullets whizzed past.
   Fair (*just, equitable*) The group has achieved *fair* and equal representation for all its members.
(d) **Cattle** (*animals of a group related to domestic cattle, including cows, bulls, buffaloes etc*) *Cattles* are usually seen grazing in the field.
   Kettle (*a metal or plastic container used for boiling water*) Sameer put some water into the *kettle* and put it on the stove.
(e) **Pair** (*a set of two things used together*) She bought a *pair* of socks.
   Pare (*trim by cutting away outer edges*) Samrat *pared* his thumbnails with a knife.

6. (a) **Moral** (*lesson, message*) The *moral* of this story was that one must see the beauty in what one has.
   Morale (*confidence*) The teams' *morale* was high.
(b) **Access** (*entrance, means of entry*) The staircase gives *access* to the top floor.
   Axis (*an imaginary line about which a body rotates*) The Earth revolves on *its axis* once every 24 hours.
(c) **Forcible** (*vigorous and strong*) They could only be deterred by *forcible* appeals.
   Forceful (*powerful*) She was a *forceful* personality.
(d) **Flair** (*talent*) She had a *flair* for languages.
   Flare (*blaze, burst*) The *flare* of the match lit up his face.
(e) **Metal** (*a solid material which is typically hard, shiny with good electrical and thermal conductivity*) Iron is a useful *metal*.
   Mettle (*determination, courage*) The team showed their true *mettle* in the second half.

V. **A.** 1. practise   2. affects   3. alternate
     4. evade   5. complimented

   B. 1. steady   2. device   3. breach
     4. fleet   5. strike

   C. 1. deadly   2. delivery   3. beneficent
     4. accompany   5. shade

CHAPTER 2

One Word Substitutions

One Word Substitutions (Substitutes) may be defined as single words that are used in place of a group of words to denote a person, an object, a place, a state of mind, a profession etc. In common parlance they are termed as single words used to make an expression brief and pertinent. Polonius in 'Hamlet', a play by Shakespeare, aptly remarks :

"Therefore since brevity in the soul of wit.

The tediousness the limbs and outward flourishes I will be brief :"

As such the use of one word substitutions tend to obviate the repetition of unnecessary words avoiding verbosity and ambiguity. Rambling style speaks of a rambling state of mind whereas brevity conveys telling effect.

Moreover, one word substitutions are indispensable while writing a precis of a given passage. A student is required not to exceed the limit of words. They come in handy in such situations. Hence their significance cannot be gainsaid and students are advised to learn them very seriously.

A few of one word substitutes are given below for the benefit of the students.

A. One Word Denoting Person

1. Agnostic — one who is not sure about God's existence
2. Altruist — a lover of mankind (*Syn.*–Philanthropist)
3. Amateur — one who does a thing for pleasure and not as a profession
4. Ambidexterous — one who can use either hand with ease
5. Anarchist — one who is out to destroy all governments, peace and order
6. Apostate — a person who has changed his faith
7. Arbitrator — a person appointed by two parties to solve a dispute
8. Ascetic — one who leads an austere life
9. Atheist — a person who does not believe in God (*Ant.*–Theist)

10.	Bankrupt	– one who is unable to pay his debts (*Syn.*–Insolvent)
11.	Bigot	– one who is filled with excessive enthusiasm in religious matters (*Syn.*–Fanatic)
12.	Bohemian	– an unconventional style of living
13.	Cacographist	– one who is bad in spellings
14.	Cannibal	– one who feeds on human flesh
15.	Carnivorous	– one who feeds on flesh
16.	Chauvinist	– a person who is blindly devoted to an idea
17.	Connoisseur	– a critical judge of any art and craft
18.	Contemporaries	– persons living at the same time
19.	Convalescent	– one who is recovering health after illness
20.	Coquette	– a girl/woman who flirts with men
21.	Cosmopolitan	– a person who regards the whole world as his country
22.	Cynosure	– one who is a centre of attraction
23.	Cynic	– one who sneers at the beliefs of others
24.	Debonair	– suave (polished and light hearted person)
25.	Demagogue	– a leader who sways his followers by his oratory
26.	Dilettante	– a dabbler (not serious) in art, science and literature
27.	Effeminate	– a man who is womanish in his habits
28.	Egoist	– a lover of oneself, of one's advancement
29.	Egotist	– one who often talks of his achievements
30.	Emigrant	– a person who leaves his country to settle in another country (*Ant.*–Immigrant)
31.	Epicure	– one who is for pleasure of eating and drinking
32.	Fastidious	– one hard to please (very selective in his habits)
33.	Fatalist	– one who believes in fate
34.	Feminist	– one who works for the welfare of women (*Syn.*–Philogynist)
35.	Fugitive	– one who runs away from justice (*Syn.*–Absconding person)
36.	Gourmand	– a lover of good food
37.	Gourmet	– a connoisseur of food
38.	Henpecked	– a husband ruled by his wife
39.	Hedonist	– one who believes that sensual pleasure is the chief good
40.	Heretic	– one who acts against religion
41.	Herbivorous	– one that lives on herbs
42.	Honorary	– one who holds a post without any salary
43.	Highbrow	– a person considering himself to be superior in culture and intellect (*Syn.*–Snob)
44.	Hypochondriac	– one who is over anxious about his health
45.	Iconoclast	– one who is breaker of images and traditions
46.	Illiterate	– one who does not know reading or writing (*Ant.*–Literate)
47.	Immigrant	– a person who comes to a country from his own country for set-tling (*Ant.*–Emigrant)
48.	Impregnable	– that cannot be entered by force (*Ant.*–Pregnable)
49.	Impostor	– one who pretends to be somebody else

ONE WORD SUBSTITUTIONS

50.	**Indefatigable**	– one who does not tire easily
51.	**Introvert**	– one who does not express himself freely (*Ant.*–Extrovert)
52.	**Insolvent**	– a person who is unable to pay his debts (*Syn.*–Bankrupt)
53.	**Itinerant**	– one who journeys from place to place (Nomadic)
54.	**Invincible**	– one too strong to be defeated (*Ant.*–Vincible)
55.	**Invulnerable**	– one that cannot be harmed/wounded (*Ant.*–Vulnerable)
56.	**Libertine**	– a person who leads an immoral life (*Syn.*–Lecher)
57.	**Martyr**	– one who dies for a noble cause
58.	**Mercenary**	– one who does something for the sake of money (bad sense)
59.	**Misanthrope**	– one who hates mankind (*Ant.*–Philanthropist)
60.	**Misogamist**	– one who hates the institution of marriage
61.	**Misologist**	– one who hates knowledge (*Ant.*–Bibliologist)
62.	**Namesake**	– a person having the same name as another
63.	**Narcissist**	– Lover of self
64.	**Novice**	– one who is inexperienced in anything (*Syn.*–Tyro)
65.	**Numismatist**	– one who collects coins
66.	**Omnivorous**	– one who eats everything
67.	**Optimist**	– a person who looks at the bright side of things (*Ant.*–Pessimist)
68.	**Orphan**	– one who has lost one's parents
69.	**Philanthropist**	– one who loves mankind (*Ant.*–Misanthrope)
70.	**Philogynist**	– one who works for the welfare of women (*Ant.*–Misogynist)
71.	**Polyglot**	– one who speaks many languages (*Syn.*–Linguist)
72.	**Pacifist**	– one who hates war, loves peace
73.	**Pessimist**	– one who looks at the dark side of life (*Ant.*–Optimist)
74.	**Philanderer**	– one who amuses oneself by love making
75.	**Philistine**	– one who does not care for art and literature
76.	**Posthumous**	– a child born after the death of father Or a book published after the death of the author Or an award received after the death of the recepient
77.	**Philatelist**	– one who collects stamps
78.	**Pedestrian**	– one who goes on foot
79.	**Recluse**	– one who lives in seclusion
80.	**Sadist**	– a person who feels pleasure by hurting others
81.	**Samaritan**	– one who helps the needy and the helpless
82.	**Somnambulist**	– a person who walks in sleep
83.	**Somniloquist**	– a person who talks in sleep
84.	**Stoic**	– a person who is indifferent to pain and pleasures of life
85.	**Swashbuckler**	– a boastful fellow
86.	**Teetotaller**	– one who does not take any intoxicating drugs
87.	**Termagant**	– a noisy quarrelsome woman, a shrew

88.	Truant	– one who remains absent from duty without permission
89.	Toper/Sot	– one who is a habitual drunkard
90.	Uxorious	– one extremely fond of one's wife
91.	Veteran	– one who has a long experience of any occupation
92.	Versatile	– one who adapts oneself readily to various situations
93.	Virtuoso	– one who is brilliant performer on stage (specially music)
94.	Volunteer	– one who offers one's services
95.	Verbose	– a style face of difficult words (maestro)

B. One Word Denoting General Object

1.	Abdication	– voluntary giving up of throne in favour of someone
2.	Almanac	– an annual calendar with position of stars
3.	Amphibian	– animal that live both on land and sea
4.	Allegory	– a story that expresses ideas through symbols
5.	Anomaly	– departure from common rule
6.	Aquatic	– animals that live in water
7.	Autobiography	– the life history of a person written by himself
8.	Axiom	– a statement accepted as true without proof
9.	Anonymous	– bearing no name
10.	Belligerent	– one that is in a war-like mood (*Syn.*–Bellicose)
11.	Biography	– the life history of a person (written by some other person)
12.	Biopsy	– examination of living tissue
13.	Blasphemy	– an act of speaking against religion (Heresy)
14.	Chronology	– events presented in order of occurrence
15.	Conscription	– compulsory enlistment for military service
16.	Crusade	– a religious war
17.	Drawn	– a game that results neither in victory nor in defeat
18.	Eatable	– anything to be eaten
19.	Edible	– fit to be eaten
20.	Encyclopaedia	– a book that contains information on various subjects
21.	Ephemeral	– lasting for a very short time/a day
22.	Epilogue	– a concluding speech/comment at the end of the play (*Ant.*–Prologue)
23.	Extempore	– a speech made without preparation (*Syn.*–Impromptu)
24.	Fable	– a story relating to birds/animals with a moral in the end
25.	Facsimile	– an exact copy of handwriting, printing (*Syn.*–Xerox)
26.	Fatal	– that causes death
27.	Fauna	– the animals of a particular region
28.	Flora	– the flowers of a particular region
29.	Fragile	– that can be easily broken
30.	Gregarious	– animals which live in a flock, used for human beings also (*Syn.*–Sociable)
31.	Illegible	– incapable of being read (*Ant.*–Legible)

ONE WORD SUBSTITUTIONS

32. **Inaccessible** – a person/place that cannot be easily approached (*Ant.*–Accessible)
33. **Impracticable** – incapable of being practised (*Ant.*–Practicable)
34. **Inaudible** – a sound that cannot be heard (*Ant.*–Audible)
35. **Incorrigible** – incapable of being corrected (*Ant.*–Corrigible)
36. **Irreparable** – incapable of being repaired (*Ant.*–Reparable)
37. **Indelible** – a mark that cannot be erased (*Ant.*–Delible)
38. **Infallible** – one who is free from all mistakes and failures (*Ant.*–Fallible)
39. **Inedible** – not fit to eat (*Ant.*–Edible)
40. **Inflammable** – liable to catch fire easily (*Ant.*–Non-inflammable)
41. **Inevitable** – that cannot be avoided (*Ant.*–Evitable)
42. **Indispensable** – that cannot be dispensed with, removed (*Ant.*–Dispensable)
43. **Interregnum** – a period of interval between two regimes and governments
44. **Intelligible** – that can be understood (*Ant.*–Unintelligible)
45. **Lunar** – of the moon
46. **Maiden** – a speech or an attempt made by a person for the first time
47. **Mammal** – an animal that gives milk
48. **Manuscript** – a matter written by hand
49. **Nostalgia** – home sickness, memories of the past
50. **Omnipresent** – one who is present everywhere
51. **Omnipotent** – one who is all powerful
52. **Omniscient** – one who knows all
53. **Parable** – a short story with a moral
54. **Parole** – pledge given by a prisoner for temporary release not to escape
55. **Panacea** – a remedy for all ills
56. **Pantheism** – the belief that God pervades nature
57. **Pedantic** – a style meant to display one's knowledge
58. **Plagiarism** – literary theft or passing off an author's original work as one's own
59. **Platonic** – something spiritual (love)
60. **Portable** – that can be carried in hand
61. **Potable** – fit to drink
62. **Plebiscite** – a decision made by public voting
63. **Pseudonym** – an imaginary name assumed by an author
64. **Quarantine** – an act of separation from a person to avoid infection
65. **Quadruped** – an animal with four feet
66. **Refrendum** – general vote of the public to decide a question (*Syn.*–Plebiscite)
67. **Red-tapism** – official formality resulting in delay
68. **Regalia** – dress with medals, ribbons worn at official ceremonies
69. **Sacrilege** – violating the sanctity of religious places/objects (*Syn.*–Desecration)

70.	Sinecure	– a job with high salary but a little responsibility
71.	Soliloquy	– a speech made when one is alone
72.	Soporific	– a medicine that induces sleep
73.	Souvenir	– a thing kept in memory of an event
74.	Swan song	– the last literary work of a writer/an artist
75.	Solar	– of the sun
76.	Transparent	– that can be seen through (*Ant.*–Opaque)
77.	Venial	– a slight fault that can be forgiven
78.	Verbatim	– repetition of a speech or a writing word for word
79.	Utopia	– an imaginary land with perfect social order
80.	Zodiac	– a diagram showing the path of planets

C. One Word Denoting Place

1.	Abattoir	– a place where animals are slaughtered for the market
2.	Apiary	– a place where bees are kept
3.	Aquarium	– a tank for fishes
4.	Arena	– a place for wrestling
5.	Arsenal	– a place for ammunition and weapons
6.	Asylum	– a place for lunatics, and political refugees
7.	Aviary	– a place where birds are kept
8.	Archives	– a place where government records are kept
9.	Burrow	– the dwelling place of an animal underground
10.	Cache	– a place where ammunition is hidden
11.	Cage	– a place for birds
12.	Casino	– a place with gambling tables etc.
13.	Cemetery	– a graveyard where the dead are burried
14.	Cloakroom	– a place for luggage at a railway station
15.	Convent	– a residence for nuns
16.	Creche	– a nursery where children of working parents are cared for while their parents are at work
17.	Crematorium	– a cremation ground where the last funeral rites are performed
18.	Decanter	– an ornamental glass bottle for holding wine or other alcoholic drinks
19.	Dormitory	– the sleeping rooms in a college or public institution
20.	Drey	– a squirrel's home
21.	Elysium	– a paradise with perfect bliss
22.	Gymnasium	– a place where atheletic exercises are performed
23.	Granary	– a place for storing grain
24.	Hangar	– a place for housing aeroplanes
25.	Hive	– a place for bees
26.	Hutch	– a wooden box with a front of wire for rabbits
27.	Infirmary	– a home for old persons
28.	Kennel	– a house of shelter for a dog

ONE WORD SUBSTITUTIONS

29.	Lair/Den	– the resting place of a wild animal
30.	Mint	– a place where money is coined
31.	Menagerie	– a place for wild animals and birds (Sanctuary)
32.	Monastery	– a residence for monks or priests
33.	Morgue	– a place where dead bodies are kept for identification
34.	Mortuary	– a place where dead bodies are kept for post-mortem
35.	Orchard	– a place where fruit trees are grown
36.	Orphanage	– a place where orphans are housed
37.	Pantry	– a place for provisions etc. in the house
38.	Portfolio	– a portable case for holding papers, drawing etc
39.	Reservoir	– a place where water is collected and stored
40.	Resort	– a place frequented for reasons of pleasure or health
41.	Stable	– a house of shelter for a horse
42.	Sty	– a place where pigs are kept
43.	Scullery	– a place where plates, dishes, pots and other cooking utensils are washed up
44.	Sheath, Scabbard	– a case in which the blade of a sword is kept
45.	Sanatorium	– a place for the sick to recover health
46.	Tannery	– a place where leather is tanned
47.	Wardrobe	– a place for clothes

D. One Word Denoting Profession

1.	Anchor	– a person who presents a radio/television programme
2.	Anthropologist	– one who studies the evolution of mankind
3.	Astronaut	– a person, who travels in spacecraft
4.	Calligraphist	– a person who writes beautiful writing
5.	Cartographer	– one who draws maps
6.	Choreographer	– one who teaches art of dancing
7.	Chauffeur	– one who drives a motor car
8.	Compere	– one who introduces performing artistes on the stage programmes
9.	Curator	– one who is incharge of a museum/a cricket pitch
10.	Florist	– one who deals in flowers
11.	Invigilator	– one who supervises in the examination hall
12.	Laxicographer	– one who compiles a dictionary
13.	Radio Jockey	– one who presents a radio programme
14.	Psephologist	– one who studies the pattern of voting in elections
15.	Sculptor	– one who gives shape to stone
16.	Usurer	– one who lends money at very high rates

E. One Word Denoting Kind of Government

1.	Anarchy	– absence of Government
2.	Aristocracy	– Government by the nobles/lords
3.	Autocracy	– Government by one person (Syn.–Dictatorship)

4. **Autonomy** – the right of self-government
5. **Bureaucracy** – Government run by officials
6. **Democracy** – Government by the people
7. **Gerontocracy** – Government by old men
8. **Kekistocracy** – Government by the worst citizen
9. **Neocracy** – Government by the inexperienced persons
10. **Ochlocracy** – Government by mob (*Syn.*–Mobocracy)
11. **Oligarchy** – Government by a few persons
12. **Panarchy** – Government run universally
13. **Plutocracy** – Government by the rich
14. **Secular** – Government not by the laws of religion
15. **Monarchy** – Government by a King/Queen
16. **Thearchy** – Government by the Gods
17. **Theocracy** – Government by the laws of religion

F. One Word Denoting Killing/Death of Persons

1. **Cemetery** – a graveyard where the dead are burried
2. **Cortege** – a funeral procession comprising a number of mourners
3. **Cremation** – a place where the last funeral rites are performed ground/Crematorium
4. **Obituary** – an account in the newspaper about the funeral of the deceased
5. **Elegy** – a poem of lamentation on the death of someone loved and admired
6. **Epitaph** – words inscribed on the grave/tomb in the memory of the one burried
7. **Filicide** – murder of one's children
8. **Foeticide** – murder of a foetus
9. **Fratricide** – murder of one's brother
10. **Genocide** – murder of race
11. **Homicide** – murder of a man/woman
12. **Infanticide** – murder of an infant
13. **Matricide** – murder of one's mother
14. **Parricide** – murder of one's parents
15. **Patricide** – murder of one's father
16. **Regicide** – murder of king or queen
17. **Suicide** – murder of oneself
18. **Uxoricide** – murder of one's wife
19. **Sororicide** – murder of one's sister
20. **Mortuary** – a place where dead bodies are kept for postmortem
21. **Morgue** – a place where bodies are kept for identification
22. **Postmortem** – Medical Examination of a dead body (*Syn.*–Autopsy)

ONE WORD SUBSTITUTIONS 551

G. One Word Denoting Marriage

1. Adultery — the practice of having extra-marital relations
2. Alimony — an allowance paid to wife on divorce
3. Bigamy — the practice of having two wives or husbands at a time
4. Celibacy — a state of abstention from marriage
5. Concubinage — live-in relationship–a man and a woman living without being married
6. Misogamist — one who hates marriage
7. Matrimony — a state of being married
8. Monogamy — the practice of marrying one at a time
9. Polygamy — the practice of marrying more than one wife at a time
10. Polyandry — the practice of marrying more than one husband at a time
11. Spinister — an older woman who is not married

H. One Word Denoting Time Period

1. Annual — happening once in a year
2. Biennial — happening in two years
3. Triennial — happening in three years
4. Quadrennial — happening in four years
5. Quinquennial — happening in five years
6. Decennial — happening in ten years
7. Semicentennial — 50th anniversary
8. Centennial (Centenary) — 100th anniversary
9. Sesquicentennial — 150th anniversary
10. Bicentennial (bicentenary) — 200th anniversary
11. Trientennial (Tercentenary) — 300th anniversary
12. Tetra centennial — 400th anniversary
13. Pentacentennial — 500th anniversary
14. Sexagenarian — one who is in sixties
15. Septuagenarian — one who is in seventies
16. Octagenarian — one who is in eighties
17. Nonagenarian — one who is in nineties
18. Centenarian — one who is hundred years old
19. Century — a period of hundred years
20. Millennium — a period of thousand years

I. One Word Denoting Group (People, Animals, Birds and Things)

1. Agenda — a list of business matters at a meeting
2. Alliance — a state of relationship formed between states, powers etc
3. Anthology — a collection of poems

4.	**Attendance/ Retinue**	– a number of servants, persons present with a person in authority
5.	**Audience**	– a number of people gathered to listen
6.	**Band**	– a group of musicians, followers
7.	**Batch**	– a group of pupils
8.	**Battery**	– a group of heavy guns
9.	**Bale**	– a large quantity of cotton tied in a bundle
10.	**Bench**	– the office of judges or magistrates
11.	**Bevy**	– a large group of girls/ladies
12.	**Block**	– a group of houses or buildings bounded by four sides
13.	**Bouquet**	– a bunch of flowers
14.	**Brood**	– a family of young-ones
15.	**Brace**	– a pair of pigeons
16.	**Board**	– decision-making body of directors
17.	**Cache**	– of arms, store house for hiding
18.	**Caravan**	– a group of people travelling with their vehicles or animals
19.	**Catalogue**	– a list of books
20.	**Caucus**	– of inner circle of members of government
21.	**Clique**	– a small group of persons belonging to a body
22.	**Circle**	– a group of friends
23.	**Claque**	– a group of applauders i.e. paid to clap
24.	**Cloud**	– of locusts
25.	**Cluster**	– a group of islands
26.	**Code**	– a systematic collection of laws
27.	**Colony/column**	– a group of people of one race moving in the same direction
28.	**Constellation**	– a series of stars
29.	**Chest**	– of drawers
30.	**Congress**	– a meeting of delegates
31.	**Convoy**	– a group of trucks/lorries travelling together under protection
32.	**Cortege**	– a funeral procession
33.	**Course**	– a series of lectures or lessons
34.	**Conference**	– a meeting of preachers, delegates
35.	**Congregation**	– a group of worshippers
36.	**Crew**	– of sailors manning ships
37.	**Drove**	– a flock of cattle (being driven)
38.	**Flight**	– the action of flying of birds
39.	(a) **Flotilla**	– a small fleet of boats
	(b) **Fleet**	– of ships
40.	**Galaxy**	– a system of millions of stars, beauties
41.	**Gallery**	– a room that contains pictures and statues displayed for sale.
42.	**Grove**	– a small orchard of trees
43.	**Hamlet**	– a group of houses in a village
44.	**Haul**	– a number of fish (in a net) caught at one time

ONE WORD SUBSTITUTIONS

45.	Heap	– a number of ruins, stones
46.	Herd	– a large group of animals that live together
47.	Hive	– (swarm) of bees
48.	Host	– a large number of people, reasons, considerations
49.	Horde	– of people, robbers
50.	Jumble	– an untidy collection of things
51.	Litter	– of young pigs, dogs at birth
52.	Lock	– a section of hair
53.	Order	– a society of knights, monks living under the same rule
54.	Panel	– a small group of inspectors, examiners for investigation
55.	Poultry	– of fowls, ducks etc
56.	Posse	– a group of policemen
57.	Rosary	– a string of beads
58.	School	– a group of thinkers, or learned men sharing similar ideas
59.	Sea	– of troubles, difficulties, cares
60.	Series	– a number of similar events, matches, lectures
61.	Shoal	– a large number of fish swimming together
62.	Sheaf	– of corn, wheat
63.	String	– a sequence of similar items
64.	Stream	– a continuous flow of people/visitors
65.	Suite	– a set of followers, rooms, furniture
66.	Suit	– a set of clothes made of same fabric
67.	Syllabus	– the topics of studies
68.	Swarm	– of flies or locusts, bees, ants
69.	Truss	– a frame work of rafters, posts and bars
70.	Syndicate	– a group of merchants
71.	Team	– a group of players, horses, oxen
72.	Throng	– a large crowd of people
73.	Tissue	– of lies or crimes
74.	Troupe	– a group of artists, dancers or acrobats
75.	Torrent	– of abusive invecties, of rain
76.	Tuft	– of grass, hair
77.	Union	– a political unit containing a number of states
78.	Barrage	– of questions
79.	Volley	– a number of arrows, stones, abuses
80.	World	– of cares, troubles

J. One Word Denoting Science and Arts

1.	Acoustics	– the study of sound
2.	Aeronautics	– the science or art of flight
3.	Aesthetics	– the philosophy of fine arts
4.	Agronomy	– the science of soil management and the production of field crops

5. **Alchemy** — Chemistry in ancient times
6. **Bibliography** — the study of history of a list of books on a subject
7. **Anatomy** — the science dealing with the structure of animals, plants or human body
8. **Anthropology** — the science that deals with the origin, physical and cultural development of mankind
9. **Arboriculture** — cultivation of trees and vegetables
10. **Astrology** — the ancient art of predicting the course of human destinies with the help of indications deduced from the position and movement of the heavenly bodies
11. **Bacteriology** — the study of bacteria
12. **Botany** — the study of plants
13. **Calligraphy** — the art of beautiful handwriting
14. **Ceramics, Pottery** — the art and technology of making objects from clay etc.
15. **Chronobiology** — the study of duration of life
16. **Chronology** — the science of arranging time in periods and ascertaining the dates and historical order of the past events
17. **Chromatics** — the art of making fireworks
18. **Cosmogony** — the science of the nature of heavenly bodies
19. **Cosmography** — the science that describes and maps the main features of the universe
20. **Cosmology** — the science of the nature, origin and history of the universe
21. **Cryogenics** — the science of dealing with the production control and the application of very low temperatures
22. **Cypher** — the art of secret writings
23. **Cytology** — the study of cells, especially their formation, structure and functions
24. **Dactylography** — the study of finger prints for the purpose of identification
25. **Dactylology** — the technique of communication by signs made with the fingers. It is generally used by the deaf
26. **Demography** — the study of human population with the help of the records of the number of births and deaths
27. **Ecology** — the study of the relation of animals and plants to their surroundings, animate and inanimate
28. **Entomology** — the study of insects
29. **Epigraphy** — the study of inscriptions
30. **Ethnology** — the study of human races
31. **Ethology** — the study of animal behaviour
32. **Etymology** — the study of origin and history of words (Morphology)
33. **Eugenics** — the study of production of better offspring by the careful selection of parents
34. **Ergonomy** — the study of effect of environment on workers
35. **Ganealogy** — the study of family ancestries and histories

ONE WORD SUBSTITUTIONS

36.	Genetics	– the branch of biology dealing with the phenomenon of heredity and the laws governing it
37.	Geology	– the science that deals with the physical history of the earth
38.	Gymnastics	– the art of performing acrobatics feats
39.	Heliotherapy	– the sun cure
40.	Histology	– the study of tissues
41.	Horticulture	– the cultivation of flowers, fruits, vegetables and ornamental plants
42.	Hydropathy	– the treatment of diseases by the internal and external use of water
43.	Hagiology	– Study of the lives of saints
44.	Iconography	– teaching with the aid of pictures and models
45.	Iconology	– the study of symbolic representations
46.	Jurisprudence	– the science of law
47.	Lexicography	– the writing or compiling of dictionaries
48.	Numismatics	– the study of coins and metals
49.	Odontology	– the scientific study of the teeth
50.	Ornithology	– the study of birds
51.	Orthoepy	– the study of correct pronunciation
52.	Pedagogy	– the art or method of teaching
53.	Petrology	– the study of rocks/crust
54.	Philately	– the collection and study of postage/revenue stamps etc
55.	Philology	– the study of written records, their authenticity etc
56.	Phonetics	– the study of speech sounds, and the production, transmission, reception
57.	Physiognomy	– the study of human face
58.	Paleography	– the study of ancient writings
59.	Rhetoric	– the art of elegant speech or writing
60.	Sericulture	– the raising of silk worms for the production of raw silk
61.	Seismology	– the study of earthquakes and the phenomenon associated with it
62.	Spelelogy	– the study of caves
63.	Telepathy	– communication between minds by some means other than sensory perception
64.	Zoology	– the study of animal life

K. One Word Denoting Phobia/Mental Disorder

The word 'phobia' comes from 'Phobus' a minor Roman God (Son of Mars and Aphrodite) who accompanied his war God Father into the battle to spread fear among the enemy. Warriors carried shields bearing Phobus to reinforce the power of this fear God.

1.	Acrophobia	– high places
2.	Aerophobia	– fear of air
3.	Aglophobia	– of pain

4.	Altiphobia	–	of altitude
5.	Anorexia	–	fear of getting fat makes young girls stop eating resulting in harmful effect
6.	Agorophobia	–	of public/place open
7.	Androphobia	–	of males
8.	Autophobia	–	of solitude
9.	Bathophobia	–	of depths
10.	Biblophobia	–	of books
11.	Cacophobia	–	of ugliness
12.	Catrophobia	–	of doctors
13.	Cellophobia	–	extreme fear about beauty
14.	Chronophobia	–	of time
15.	Cynophobia	–	of dogs
16.	Claustrophobia	–	of being confined to small place
17.	Dipsophobia	–	of thirst
18.	Dipsomania	–	morbid compulsion to drink
19.	Demonomania	–	delusion of being under evil spirits
20.	Entomophobia	–	of insects
21.	Ergophobia	–	of work
22.	Gamophobia	–	of marriage
23.	Genophobia	–	of birth
24.	Geraphobia	–	of old age
25.	Gnosiophobia	–	of knowledge
26.	Graphophobia	–	of writing
27.	Gynaephobia	–	of women
28.	Haemetophobia	–	of blood
29.	Hedonophobia	–	of pleasure
30.	Hodophobia	–	of travel
31.	Hydrophobia	–	of water
32.	Kleptophobia	–	of stealing/thieves
33.	Kleptomania	–	a compulsive desire to steal
34.	Lipophobia	–	of getting fat
35.	Logophobia	–	of study
36.	Logomania	–	mania for talking
37.	Maieusiophobia	–	of childbirth
38.	Metrophobia	–	of motherhood
39.	Menemophobia	–	of old memories
40.	Monophobia	–	of loneliness, of being alone
41.	Mysophobia	–	of filth, contamination
42.	Magalomania	–	delusion about one's greatness
43.	Nyctophobia	–	of darkness
44.	Ophthalmophobia	–	of eyes
45.	Ochlophobia	–	of crowds/mobs

ONE WORD SUBSTITUTIONS

46. **Paedophobia** – of children
47. **Pathophobia** – of disease/sickness
48. **Peniophobia** – of poverty/money problem
49. **Pharmacophobia** – of medicine
50. **Phasmophobia** – of ghosts
51. **Xenophobia** – of foreigners
52. **Pyrophobia** – of fire
53. **Thanatophobia** – of death
54. **Scelerophobia** – of burglars
55. **Theophobia** – of God
56. **Toxicophobia** – of poison
57. **Triskaidekaphobia** – of number thirteen
58. **Theomania** – a delusion that one is God

L. *One Word Denoting Young-one*

	Adult	Young-one		Adult	Young-one
1.	Ass	Foal	14.	Frog (toad)	Tadpole
2.	Bird	Nestling	15.	Goat	Kid
3.	Butterfly, moth	Caterpillar	16.	Goose	Gosling
4.	Cat	Kitten	17.	Hare	Leveret
5.	Cock	Cockerel	18.	Hen	Pullet
6.	Cow	Calf	19.	Horse	Foal, colt
7.	Cow	Heifer	20.	Lion, Bear, Fox	Cub
8.	Deer	Fawn	21.	Mare	Filly
9.	Dog	Puppy	22.	Owl	Owlet
10.	Duck	Duckling	23.	Pig	Piglet
11.	Eagle	Eaglet	24.	Sheep	Lamb
12.	Elephant	Calf	25.	Stallion (horse)	Colt or Foal
13.	Fowl	Chicken	26.	Swan	Cygnet

M. *One Word Denoting Distinctive Sound*

	Animal	Sound		Animal	Sound
1.	Apes	Gibber	13.	Cats	Mew
2.	Arms	Clang	14.	Chains	Clank
3.	Asses	Bray	15.	Coins	Jingle/tinkle
4.	A person in agony	Moan	16.	Corks	Pop
5.	Babies	Lisp	17.	Cocks	Crow
6.	Bees	Hum	18.	Crows	Crow, caw
7.	Beetles	Drone	19.	Deer	Bell
8.	Bells	Jingle/chime	20.	Dogs	Bark
9.	Birds	Chirp, warble	21.	Doors	Creak/bang
10.	Brakes	Screech	22.	Doves	Coo
11.	Cattle	Low	23.	Duck	Quack
12.	Camels	Grunt	24.	Elephants	Trumpet

	Animal	Sound		Animal	Sound
25.	Fire	Crackle	43.	Owls	Hoot
26.	Flies	Buzz	44.	Oxen/cow	Low
27.	Frogs	Croak	45.	Paper	Crinkle
28.	Glasses	Tinkle	46.	Parrots	Talk
29.	Goats	Bleat	47.	Pigeons	Coo
30.	Guns	Roar	48.	Pigs	Squeal
31.	Hens	Cackle	49.	Ravens	Croak
32.	Hoofs	Clatter	50.	Rain	Patter
33.	Horses	Neigh	51.	Rivers	Murmur
34.	Silk	Rustle	52.	Serpents	Hiss
35.	Hyenas	Laugh	53.	Silk	Rustle
36.	Jackals	Howl	54.	Teeth	Chatter
37.	Larks	Sing, warble	55.	Tigers	Roar
38.	Leaves	Rustle	56.	Trees	Sigh
39.	Lions	Roar	57.	Water	Ripple
40.	Mice	Squeak	58.	Whip	Crack
41.	Monkeys	Gibber	59.	Wind	Whistle
42.	Nightingales	Sing, warble	60.	Wings	Flap

N. **One Word Denoting Diminutive**

'Diminutives' are the words that indicate smallness. Such words are often used as an expression of affection or contempt. Diminutives are normally formed by the use of suffixes such as 'Let' etc. For example the diminutive of the book may be formed by the use of 'let'—Booklet.

	Word	Diminutive		Word	Diminutive
1.	Ankle	Anklet	21.	Latch	Latchet
2.	Babe	Baby	22.	Leaf	Leaflet
3.	Ball	Ballet, Bullet	23.	Lock	Locket
4.	Baron	Baronet	24.	Nest	Nestling
5.	Book	Booklet	25.	Nose	Nozzle
6.	Brace	Bracelet	26.	Part	Particle
7.	Brook	Brooklet	27.	Poet	Poetaster
8.	Car	Chariot	28.	Pouch	Pocket
9.	Cask	Casket	29.	Ring	Ringlet
10.	City	Citadel	30.	River	Rivulet
11.	Cigar	Cigarette	31.	Sack	Satchel
12.	Corn	Kernel	32.	Star	Starlet, Asterisk
13.	Crown	Coronet	33.	Statue	Statuette
14.	Dear	Darling	34.	Stream	Streamlet
15.	Grain	Granule	35.	Table	Tablet
16.	Hill	Hillock	36.	Top	Tip
17.	Home	Hamlet	37.	Tower	Turret
18.	Ice	Icicle	38.	Umbrella	Parasol
19.	Isle	Islet	39.	Weak	Weakling
20.	Lady Purse	Reticule			

O. *One Word Denoting Comparison*

1. As *blind* as a bat.
2. As *bitter* as gall, hemlock.
3. As *cheerful* as a lark.
4. As *cunning*, sly, wily as a fox.
5. As *fair* as a rose.
6. As *fast* as a hare, light, storm, eagle.
7. As *firm* as a rock.
8. As *flat* as a board, or a pancake.
9. As *free* as air.
10. As *fresh* as a daisy or a rose.
11. As *grave* as a judge.
12. As *greedy* as a dog, or a wolf.
13. As *gentle* as a lamb.
14. As *hard* as a flint, or a stone.
15. As *harmless* as a dove.
16. As *hungry* as a horse, or a hunter.
17. As *light* as a feather.
18. As *merry* as a cricket.
19. As *obstinate* as a mule.
20. As *pale* as death, or ghost.
21. As *playful* as a butterfly, or a kitten or a squirrel.
22. As *proud* as a peacock.
23. As *slippery* as an eel.
24. As *soft* as butter.
25. As *silent* as the dead, or stars.
26. As *tricky* as a monkey.
27. As *true* as steel.
28. As *wise* as a serpent or Solomon.
29. As *yielding* as wax.
30. As *agile* as a cat, monkey.
31. As *far* apart as the poles.
32. As *black* as ebony/coal.
33. As *blithe* as May.
34. As *boisterous* as stormy sea winds.
35. As *bounteous* as nature.
36. As *brief* as time–as a dream.
37. As *brittle* as glass.
38. As *candid* as mirrors.
39. As *chaste* as Minerva.
40. As *constant* as the sun.
41. As *cool* as cucumber.
42. As *cosy* as the nest of a bird.
43. As *dangerous* as machine-guns.
44. As *deceptive* as the mirage of the desert.
45. As *docile* as a lamb.
46. As *fit* as a fiddle.
47. As *fresh* as dew, as a sea breeze, rose.
48. As *grim* as death.
49. As *haggard* as spectres, ghosts.
50. As *harsh* as truth.
51. As *heavy* as lead.
52. As *inconsistent* as the moon, as the waves.
53. As *industrious* as an ant.
54. As *inevitable* as death/fate.
55. As *mad* as a hatter, as a March hare.
56. As *mean* as a miser.
57. As *meek* as a dove, mouse.
58. As *nervous* as a mouse.
59. As *resistless* as wind.
60. As *restless* as ambition, as the sea.
61. As *secure* as the grave.
62. As *slow* as a snail.
63. As *solitary* as a tomb.
64. As *talkative* as a magpie.
65. As *transparent* as glass.
66. As *treacherous* as memory.
67. As *vain* as a peacock.
68. As *vigilant* as stars.
69. As *zig-zag* as lightning.
70. As *uncertain* as the weather.
71. As *white* as snow.
72. As hungry as church mouse.
73. As *dear* as life.
74. As *straight* as an arrow.
75. As *impatient* as a lover.
76. As *swift* as an arrow.
77. As *old* as hills.
78. As *cold* as marble.
79. As *sharp* as razor.
80. As *busy* as a bee.

CHAPTER 3

Synonyms and Antonyms

Against each keyword are given the lists of 'Synonyms and Antonyms' separately. A student is required to study the words given in the list carefully. These words will add to the 'Thesaurus' comprising words and phrases that they have already learnt. If need be, they may look up a word in the dictionary for correct reference.

A

Abjure
    Syn : forsake, renounce, retract, revoke
    Ant : approve, sanction, patronise, adopt

Abject
    Syn : despicable, servile, base, contemptible
    Ant : exalted, commendable, praiseworthy, imposing

Aversion
    Syn : dislike, hatred, indifferent, apathy
    Ant : affection, fondness, niceness, liking

Authentic
    Syn : genuine, reliable, valid, guaranteed
    Ant : fictitious, counterfeit, unreal, false

Audacity
    Syn : boldness, arrogance, insolence, haughtiness
    Ant : mildness, humility, cowardice, submission

Astute
    Syn : clever, intelligent, wise, brilliant
    Ant : dull, unintelligent, shallow, solid

SYNONYMS AND ANTONYMS

Abettor
- *Syn* : assistant, accomplice, colleague, associate
- *Ant* : opponent, adversary, antagonist, rival

Abate
- *Syn* : moderate, mitigate, lessen, decrease
- *Ant* : aggravate, intensify, augment, supplement

Arraign
- *Syn* : charge, blame, accuse, complain
- *Ant* : exculpate, pardon, condone, exonerate

Apathy
- *Syn* : unconcern, indifference, insensitivity, aloofness
- *Ant* : concern, care, anxiety, eagerness

Alien
- *Syn* : foreigner, outsider, stranger, emigrant
- *Ant* : native, citizen, resident, occupant

Alacrity
- *Syn* : swiftness, briskness, promptness, speed
- *Ant* : laziness, sluggishness, indolence, lethargy

Affront
- *Syn* : provoke, exasperate, indignity, irreverence
- *Ant* : conciliate, appease, mollify, assuage

Adversity
- *Syn* : misfortune, calamity, misery, affliction
- *Ant* : prosperity, fortune, assistance, favour

Antique
- *Syn* : ancient, old fashioned, primitive, of past
- *Ant* : modern, recent, novelty, vogue

Antipathy
- *Syn* : hostility, aversion, disillusion, dislike
- *Ant* : admiration, approval, fascination, devotion

Amplify
- *Syn* : enlarge, extend, dialation, elevate
- *Ant* : curtail, lessen, diminution, contraction

Amass
- *Syn* : gather, accumulate, store, collect
- *Ant* : disperse, dissipate, spend, scatter

Alleviate
- *Syn* : abate, relieve, mitigate, lessen
- *Ant* : intensify, augment, aggravate, enhance

Admonish
    Syn : counsel, reprove, warn, chastise
    Ant : approve, applaud, praise, flattery

Adjacent
    Syn : adjoining, beside, proximity, closeness
    Ant : distant, separate, remoteness, aloofness

Adherent
    Syn : follower, disciple, dependent, supporter
    Ant : rival, adversary, opponent, antagonist

Accomplish
    Syn : attain, succeed, triumph, exploit
    Ant : forsake, deter, disappoint, collapse

Absolve
    Syn : pardon, forgive, reprieve, relent
    Ant : compel, accuse, charge, bind

Acrimony
    Syn : harshness, bitterness, inhumanity, enmity
    Ant : sweetness, courtesy, humanity, benevolence

Accumulation
    Syn : store, amass, preservation, conservation
    Ant : scattering, dissipation, separation, division

B

Bustle
    Syn : haste, tumult, stir, flurry
    Ant : slowness, sluggishness, quiet, inertness

Brittle
    Syn : frail, fragile, delicate, breakable
    Ant : tough, enduring, unbreakable, strong

Blemish
    Syn : fault, smirch, stigma, stain
    Ant : purity, impeccable, spotless, stainless

Bleak
    Syn : dismal, gloomy, chilly, dreary
    Ant : bright, pleasant, balmy, cheerful

Blame
    Syn : reprove, upbraid, censure, reproach
    Ant : commend, applaud, laud, praise

SYNONYMS AND ANTONYMS

Benevolence
- *Syn* : humanity, generosity, charity, liberality
- *Ant* : malevolence, inhumanity, malignity, unkindness

Barbarous
- *Syn* : uncivilised, savage, untamed, brutal
- *Ant* : cultured, humane, refined, gentle

Baffle
- *Syn* : confound, elude, frustrate, perplex
- *Ant* : poise, composure, facilitate, cooperate

Bewitching
- *Syn* : magical, fascinating, tantalising, spell binding
- *Ant* : repulsive, repugnant, nauseating, disgusting

C

Contrary
- *Syn* : dissimilar, conflicting, contradictory, opposite
- *Ant* : similar, alike, homogeneous, resembling

Contradict
- *Syn* : impugn, deny, oppose, confront
- *Ant* : approve, confirm, sanction, endorse

Contempt
- *Syn* : scorn, disregard, disdain, despicable
- *Ant* : regard, approval, praise, recommend

Consternation
- *Syn* : fear, disappointment, dismay, hopelessness
- *Ant* : peace, repose, calm, fearless

Conspicuous
- *Syn* : distinguished, prominent, obvious, visible
- *Ant* : concealed, obscure, hidden, unapparent

Consolidate
- *Syn* : combine, condense, compact, strong
- *Ant* : separate, sever, weak, scattering

Consequence
- *Syn* : effect, outcome, repercussion, result
- *Ant* : origin, start, beginning, incipient

Consent
- *Syn* : agree, permit, accede, assent
- *Ant* : object, disagree, dissent, differ

Conscious
- *Syn* : aware, apprised, knowledge, informed
- *Ant* : unaware, ignorant, unfeeling, faint

Concede
- *Syn* : yield, assent, permit, sanction
- *Ant* : deny, reject, dissent, disallow

Comprise
- *Syn* : include, contain, consist, compose
- *Ant* : reject, lack, exclude, except

Compassion
- *Syn* : kindness, sympathy, clemency, commiseration
- *Ant* : cruelty, barbarity, persecution, apathy

Concur
- *Syn* : approve, agree, consent, endorse
- *Ant* : differ, disagree, dissent, oppose

Commodious
- *Syn* : convenient, suitable, roomy, comfortable
- *Ant* : inconvenient, unsuitable, uncomfortable, confined

Collision
- *Syn* : encounter, clash, conflict, dissenting
- *Ant* : agreement, harmony, compatible, union

Cherish
- *Syn* : nurture, treasure, foster, encourage
- *Ant* : abandon, forsake, renounce, discard

Chastise
- *Syn* : punish, admonish, scold, reprove
- *Ant* : cheer, comfort, encourage, stimulate

Cavity
- *Syn* : depth, depression, hole, aperture
- *Ant* : elevation, projection, mound, height

Cease
- *Syn* : terminate, pause, desist, discontinue
- *Ant* : commence, continue, initiate, originate

Circumlocution
- *Syn* : redundancy, verbosity, tediousness, verbiage
- *Ant* : terseness, compression, directness, brevity

Commotion
- *Syn* : turmoil, disturbance, agitation, excitement
- *Ant* : tranquility, stillness, quietness, calm

D

Delusion
- *Syn* : deception, hallucination, illusion, fallacy
- *Ant* : reality, certainty, veracity, fact

Delicious
- *Syn* : palatable, tasteful, appetising, dainty
- *Ant* : distasteful, unsavoury, tolerable, inedible

Deliberate
- *Syn* : ponder, intentional, meditate, consider
- *Ant* : rash, sudden, indifferent, random

Degradation
- *Syn* : disgrace, dishonour, humiliation, debase
- *Ant* : exaltation, praise, triumphant, honour

Defray
- *Syn* : meet, bear, spend, pay
- *Ant* : declaim, decline, refuse, abjure

Defile
- *Syn* : contaminate, pollute, profane, desecrate
- *Ant* : purify, sanctity, cleanse, disinfect

Deficient
- *Syn* : scanty, inadequate, lacking, wanting
- *Ant* : adequate, ample, sufficient, abundant

Defer
- *Syn* : prolong, suspend, postpone, delay
- *Ant* : accelerate, expedite, stimulate, hasten

Default
- *Syn* : failure, omission, negligence, lapse
- *Ant* : perfection, vigilance, attentive, observance

Dedicate
- *Syn* : devote, consecrate, loyal, surrender
- *Ant* : refuse, negate, prohibit, reject

Decipher
- *Syn* : interpret, reveal, decode, transcribe
- *Ant* : misinterpret, distort, confuse, pervert

Deceit
- *Syn* : deception, artifice, treachery, duplicity
- *Ant* : veracity, sincerity, truth, honesty

Decay
    Syn : collapse, decomposition, deteriorate, putrefaction
    Ant : flourish, progress, growth, development

E

Evident
    Syn : obvious, apparent, distinct, conspicuous
    Ant : obscure, concealed, hidden, invisible

Evade
    Syn : avoid, elude, dodge, shun
    Ant : acknowledge, confront, verify, confirm

Eternal
    Syn : perpetual, endless, imperishable, immortal
    Ant : temporary, momentary, transient, fleeting

Esteem
    Syn : respect, regards, honour, reverence
    Ant : ridicule, spurn, despise, humilitate

Eradicate
    Syn : destroy, exterminate, abolish, remove
    Ant : secure, plant, restore, revive

Equivocal
    Syn : uncertain, hazy, ambiguous, vague
    Ant : obvious, lucid, clear, plain

Eliminate
    Syn : expel, oust, exclude, remove
    Ant : restore, accept, retain, include

Elevate
    Syn : dignify, heighten, promote, raise
    Ant : deprecate, denounce, lower, decline

Elegant
    Syn : graceful, distinguished, refined, polished
    Ant : obnoxious, unrefined, ridiculous, coarse

Elation
    Syn : joy, exaltation, delight, enthusiasm
    Ant : gloom, despair, depression, melancholy

Efface
    Syn : destroy, obliterate, annihilate, abolish
    Ant : retain, maintain, regenerate, resurrect

SYNONYMS AND ANTONYMS

Ecstasy
- Syn : delight, exultation, overjoy, rapture
- Ant : despair, calamity, doldrums, depression

Eccentric
- Syn : strange, abnormal, cranky, odd
- Ant : natural, conventional, uniform, methodical

Earnest
- Syn : ardent, sincere, resolute, determined
- Ant : unheeding, frivolous, negligent, careless

Evasion
- Syn : prevaricate, avoid, neglect, pretext
- Ant : response, defence, compliance, action

F

Frantic
- Syn : violent, agitated, frenzied, wild
- Ant : subdued, gentle, lucid, coherent

Franchise
- Syn : suffrage, right, privilege, patronise
- Ant : bondage, oppression, serfdom, irresolute

Fragments
- Syn : scraps, residue, segment, section
- Ant : total, entire, gross, aggregate

Fragile
- Syn : weak, infirm, brittle, frail
- Ant : enduring, tough, robust, tenacious

Forsake
- Syn : desert, renounce, relinquish, disown
- Ant : hold, maintain, retain, claim

Formidable
- Syn : dangerous, invincible, redoubtable, dreadful
- Ant : harmless, insignificant, weak, feeble

Forerunner
- Syn : precursor, predecessor, ancestor, pioneer
- Ant : descendant, follower, heir, successor

Foe
- Syn : opponent, antagonist, adversary, contender
- Ant : comrade, helper, friend, fellow

Fluent
- Syn : fast, smooth, voluble, glib
- Ant : hesitant, slow, sluggish, halting

Fluctuate
- Syn : deflect, vacillate, vary, deviate
- Ant : stable, resolute, constant, inalterable

Flourish
- Syn : Prosper, triumph, thrive, blossom
- Ant : decay, collapse, wither, deteriorate

Flimsy
- Syn : trifling, transparent, brittle, unsubstantial
- Ant : firm, tenacious, durable, retentive

Fleeting
- Syn : transient, temporary, ephemeral, transitory
- Ant : enduring, eternal, perpetual, unceasing

G

Guile
- Syn : cunning, deceit, duplicity, chicanery
- Ant : honesty, frankness, sincerity, integrity

Grudge
- Syn : hatred, aversion, unwilling, objection
- Ant : benevolence, affection, goodwill, kindness

Grisly
- Syn : disgusting, atrocious, monstrous, loathsome
- Ant : pleasing, attractive, beautiful, alluring

Gracious
- Syn : courteous, beneficent, magnificent, dignified
- Ant : rude, unforgiving, discourteous, uncourtly

Gorgeous
- Syn : magnificent, dazzling, brilliant, grand
- Ant : dull, unpretentious, modest, plain

Glut
- Syn : stuff, satiate, overflow, cram
- Ant : reduce, abstain, moderate, restrain

Gloom
- Syn : obscurity, darkness, dejection, disillusion
- Ant : delight, mirth, joviality, bright

SYNONYMS AND ANTONYMS

Gigantic
- Syn : huge, enormous, immense, monstrous
- Ant : small, diminutive, miniature, slight

Genuine
- Syn : real, authentic, creative, original
- Ant : deceptive, spurious, imitative, derivative

Genial
- Syn : cheerful, pleasant, joyful, affable
- Ant : sullen, dismal, morose, melancholy

Generous
- Syn : liberal, unselfish, benevolent, hospitable
- Ant : miserly, stingy, covetous, greedy

Garrulous
- Syn : loquacious, talkative, communicative, informative
- Ant : reserved, quiet, taciturn, reticent

H

Heretic
- Syn : non-conformist, secularist, dissident, offender
- Ant : conformable, adaptable, religious, believer

Hazard
- Syn : presumption, danger, peril, risk, presume
- Ant : conviction, security, assurance, certainty

Haughty
- Syn : arrogant, pompous, obstinate, imperious
- Ant : humble, submissive, modest, inoffensive

Harass
- Syn : irritable, molest, suppress, tyranny
- Ant : assist, comfort, tolerant, connive

Hapless
- Syn : unfortunate, ill-fated, hostile, doomed
- Ant : fortunate, lucky, favoured, satisfied

Haphazard
- Syn : random, sudden, unsorted, reckless
- Ant : deliberate, considered, thoughtful, discerning

Hamper
- Syn : retard, prevent, hinder, obstruct
- Ant : promote, facilitate, foster, assist

Haggard
- Syn : exhausted, lean, emaciated, gaunt
- Ant : exuberant, active, lively, robust

Homely
- Syn : plain, coarse, unadorned, simple
- Ant : sauve, polished, dignified, refined

Hail
- Syn : greet, welcome, acclaim, honour
- Ant : disregard, belittle, avoid, despise

Heinous
- Syn : outrageous, vile, awful, wicked
- Ant : righteous, pleasing, exquisite, appealing

I

Intrigue
- Syn : scheme, conspiracy, manipulation, counterplot
- Ant : candour, sincerity, bluntness, honesty

Intrinsic
- Syn : genuine, fundamental, inherent, congenital
- Ant : extraneous, incidental, extrinsic, derived

Invective
- Syn : accusation, censure, malediction, denunciation
- Ant : approval, acclamation, admiration, approbation

Instil
- Syn : inculcate, inject, infuse, implant
- Ant : eradicate, extract, eliminate, expel

Insolvent
- Syn : indigent, destitute, bankrupt, defaulter
- Ant : wealthy, solvent, affluent, substantial

Insipid
- Syn : tasteless, vapid, savourless, unflavoured
- Ant : delicious, luscious, pungent, piquant

Insinuate
- Syn : communicate, allude, hint, suggest
- Ant : conceal, camouflage, suppress, mask

Inquisitive
- Syn : inquiring, curious, searching, studious
- Ant : distracted, negligent, indifferent, impassive

SYNONYMS AND ANTONYMS

Innocuous
- *Syn* : salutary, wholesome, innocent, harmless
- *Ant* : deleterious, baneful, insanitary, injurious

Indignation
- *Syn* : resentment, ire, wrath, rage
- *Ant* : modesty, tranquility, forbearance, equanimity

Indigence
- *Syn* : privation, destitution, insolvency, penury
- *Ant* : affluence, abundance, opulence, luxury

Incongruous
- *Syn* : inappropriate, absurd, ridiculous, awkward
- *Ant* : compatible, harmonious, homogeneous, consistent

Incompetent
- *Syn* : inefficient, unskilled, immature, unqualified
- *Ant* : dexterous, skilled, ingenious, competent

Inclination
- *Syn* : disposition, affection, proneness, propensity
- *Ant* : neutrality, indifference, apathy, unresponsive

Incite
- *Syn* : instigate, provoke, motivate, arouse
- *Ant* : deter, discourage, restrain, dissuade

Incentive
- *Syn* : motivation, allurement, inducement, spur
- *Ant* : dissuasion, reluctance, deterrent, discouragement

Impute
- *Syn* : attribute, ascribe, charge, indict
- *Ant* : exculpate, support, vindicate, excuse

Impudence
- *Syn* : sauciness, impertinence, insolence, arrogance
- *Ant* : submissiveness, modesty, humility, meekness

Impious
- *Syn* : irreligious, unholy, irreverent, hypocritical
- *Ant* : pious, devout, spiritual, venerate

Impetuous
- *Syn* : violent, impulsive, imprudence, indiscretion
- *Ant* : considerate, composed, discretion, prudence

Impediment
- *Syn* : hurdle, obstruction, hindrance, retardation
- *Ant* : assistance, concurrence, deliverance, aid

J

Juvenile
- Syn : young, tender, youthful, adolescent
- Ant : dotage, antiquated, senile, old

Justify
- Syn : defend, exculpate, warrant, vindicate
- Ant : impute, arraigne, accuse, incriminate

Just
- Syn : honest, impartial, righteous, upright
- Ant : unequal, unfair, discriminatory, unseasonable

Judicious
- Syn : thoughtful, prudent, discerning, discriminating
- Ant : irrational, foolish, misconception, fatuous

Jubilant
- Syn : rejoicing, triumphant, gay, cheerful
- Ant : melancholy, depressing, gloomy, despondent

Jovial
- Syn : frolicsome, cheerful, merry, exultant
- Ant : solemn, morose, malcontent, sad

Jaded
- Syn : tired, exhausted, fatigued, languish
- Ant : renewal, recreation, restorative, refreshed

Jejune
- Syn : dull, boring, uninteresting, monotonous
- Ant : interesting, exciting, piquant, thrilling

K

Kindred
- Syn : relation, species, relative, affinity
- Ant : unrelated, dissimilar, hetrogeneous, disparate

Keen
- Syn : sharp, poignant, eager, acute
- Ant : vapid, insipid, blunt, undesiring

Knave
- Syn : dishonest, scoundrel, vagabond, rogue
- Ant : paragon, innocent, benefactor, idealist

Knell
- Syn : death knell, last blow, demolish, suppress
- Ant : reconstruction, rediscovery, procreation, resurrection

SYNONYMS AND ANTONYMS

Knotty
- *Syn* : complicated, difficult, arduous, onerous
- *Ant* : simple, manageable, tractable, flexible

L

Luxuriant
- *Syn* : profuse, abundant, dense, plentiful
- *Ant* : scanty, meagre, inadequate, deficient

Luscious
- *Syn* : palatable, delicious, delectable, delightful
- *Ant* : unsavoury, tart, sharp, sour

Lure
- *Syn* : attract, entice, tempt, induce
- *Ant* : repel, dissuade, confute, threaten

Lunacy
- *Syn* : delusion, insanity, madness, imbecility
- *Ant* : normalcy, sanity, sagacity, shrewdness

Ludicrous
- *Syn* : absurd, bizarre, preposterous, grotesque
- *Ant* : balanced, congruous, consistent, solemn

Lucid
- *Syn* : sound, rational, coherent, sane
- *Ant* : obscure, hidden, incomprehensible, unintelligible

Listless
- *Syn* : lazy, inattentive spiritless, incurious
- *Ant* : brisk, attentive, diligent, agile

Linger
- *Syn* : loiter, prolong, hesitate, delay
- *Ant* : hasten, quicken, dart, hurry

Liberate
- *Syn* : emancipate, rescue, unshackle, absolve
- *Ant* : suppress, menacle, obstruct, detain

Liberal
- *Syn* : magnanimous, hospitality, generous, benevolence
- *Ant* : stingy, niggardly, malevolent, malicious

Liable
- *Syn* : accountable, bound, responsible, likely
- *Ant* : unaccountable, apt to, irresponsible, exempt

Lenient
- *Syn* : compassionate, merciful, moderate, tolerant
- *Ant* : cruel, severe, violent, vehement

Lax
- *Syn* : slack, careless, negligence, indifferent
- *Ant* : firm, reliable, meticulous, scruplous

Lavish
- *Syn* : abundant, excessive, profuse, extravagant
- *Ant* : scarce, deficient, frugal, conserve

M

Mutual
- *Syn* : joint, identical, correlative, reciprocal
- *Ant* : separate, distinct, divergent, individual

Mutinous
- *Syn* : recalcitrant, insurgent, unruly, revolutionary
- *Ant* : submissive, faithful, compliant, loyal

Murky
- *Syn* : dusky, dreary, dismal, bleak
- *Ant* : bright, shining, luminous, radiant

Munificent
- *Syn* : liberal, hospitable, benevolent, kind
- *Ant* : frugal, penurious, moderate, economical

Multitude
- *Syn* : crowd, throng, mass, swarm
- *Ant* : minority, handful, paucity, scarcity

Morose
- *Syn* : surly, sulky, sullen, depressed
- *Ant* : sprightly, animated, buoyant, blithe

Monotonous
- *Syn* : irksome, tedious, humdrum, insipid
- *Ant* : varied, pleasant, appealing, captivating

Momentous
- *Syn* : notable, eventful, consequential, stirring
- *Ant* : trivial, insignificant, commonplace, immaterial

Mollify
- *Syn* : appease, assuage, relieve, mitigate
- *Ant* : irritate, infuriate, aggravate, exasperate

Molest
- *Syn* : pester, harass, vex, misbehave
- *Ant* : console, soothe, comfort, cheer

N

Novice
- *Syn* : tyro, beginner, debutant, apprentice
- *Ant* : veteran, ingenious, experienced, mentor

Nourish
- *Syn* : sustain, nurture, tend, foster
- *Ant* : exhaust, starve, weaken, enervate

Nonchalant
- *Syn* : indifferent, negligent, uncaring, heedless
- *Ant* : attentive, considerate, vigilant, scrupulous

Nimble
- *Syn* : prompt, brisk, lively, agile
- *Ant* : sluggish, languid, weary, tardy

Niggardly
- *Syn* : miserly, covetous, inadequacy, deficiency
- *Ant* : generous, profuse, redundant, excessive

Negligent
- *Syn* : inattentive, careless, heedless, perfunctory
- *Ant* : vigilant, careful, considerate, alert

Nefarious
- *Syn* : detestable, atrocious, heinous, unlawful
- *Ant* : commendable, worthy, upright, inoffensive

Nauseous
- *Syn* : unsavoury, loathsome, abominable, repellent
- *Ant* : commendable, worthy, benevolent, inoffensive

Native
- *Syn* : original, vernacular, indigenous, aboriginal
- *Ant* : alien, extraneous, exotic, foreign

Nasty
- *Syn* : offensive, defiled, malevolent, malignant
- *Ant* : pleasing, gratifying, benevolent, attractive

Nominal
- *Syn* : trifling, insubstantial, bare, negligible
- *Ant* : substantial, considerable, excessive, exorbitant

O

Outbreak
- Syn : eruption, insurrection, explosion, outburst
- Ant : compliance, subjection, passivity, harmony

Ostentation
- Syn : display, pretension, vaunt, pomposity
- Ant : modesty, constraint, diffidence, economy

Ostensible
- Syn : apparent, evident, obvious, overt
- Ant : concealed, covert, obscure, vague

Ornamental
- Syn : decorative, adorned, glamorous, picturesque
- Ant : unseemly, plain, blemished, disfigured

Ordain
- Syn : order, impose, prescribe, proclaim
- Ant : revoke, abolish, violate, abrogate

Oracular
- Syn : cryptic, vague, enigmatic, profound
- Ant : lucid, distinct, intelligible, unambiguous

Opaque
- Syn : filmy, dim, obscure, shady
- Ant : transparent, bright, translucent, revealing

Onerous
- Syn : arduous, troublesome, inconvenient, formidable
- Ant : facile, agreeable, uncomlicated, flexible

Ominous
- Syn : threatening, inauspicious, forebode, menacing
- Ant : consoling, auspicious, propitious, comforting

Offspring
- Syn : descendants, siblings, posterity, progeny
- Ant : ancestors, forefathers, pedigree, progenitors

Offensive
- Syn : abhorrent, arrogant, insolent, impudent
- Ant : docile, compliant, courteous, captivating

Odious
- Syn : abhorrent, obnoxious, prejudice, malevolent
- Ant : engaging, fascinating, endearing, captivating

Occult
- *Syn* : latent, ambiguous, esoteric, elusive
- *Ant* : intelligible, transparent, fathomable, scrutable

P

Proscribe
- *Syn* : prohibit, exclude, ban, forbid
- *Ant* : solicit, include, permit, sanction

Propitiate
- *Syn* : appease, soothe, pacify, placate
- *Ant* : aggravate, annoy, scorn, displease

Promulgate
- *Syn* : declare, proclaim, notify, announce
- *Ant* : reserve, suppress, disguise, withhold

Promiscuous
- *Syn* : confused, indiscriminate, casual, random
- *Ant* : regular, discriminate, orderly, select

Profuse
- *Syn* : lavish, abundant, generous, plentiful
- *Ant* : scarce, scanty, meagre, paucity

Profligate
- *Syn* : dissolute, degenerate, immoral, flagitious
- *Ant* : virtuous, upright, moral, ethical

Prodigy
- *Syn* : miracle, marvel, wonder, extraordinary
- *Ant* : normal, average, mediocre, common

Prodigious
- *Syn* : vast, enormous, immense, huge
- *Ant* : unimpressive, diminutive, slight, puny

Presumptuous
- *Syn* : presuming, arrogant, affected, insolent
- *Ant* : unassuming, modest, bashful, unobtrusive

Premature
- *Syn* : precious, untimely, mistimed, inopportune
- *Ant* : belated, opportune, timely, mellow

Predicament
- *Syn* : plight, dilemma, fix, quandary
- *Ant* : resolution, confidence, firmness, certainty

Precarious
    Syn : doubtful, insecure, unreliable, uncertain
    Ant : assured, undeniable, reliable, substantial

Pompous
    Syn : haughty, arrogant, flamboyant, florid
    Ant : unpretentious, humble, coy, modest

Perpetual
    Syn : uninterrupted, lasting, perennial, incessant
    Ant : passing, transient, ephemeral, fleeting

Peril
    Syn : hazard, danger, jeopardy, compulsory
    Ant : caution, security, safety, assurance

Peremptory
    Syn : overbearing, absolute, arbitrary, compulsory
    Ant : tolerant, indecisive, optional, indulgent

Penetrate
    Syn : pierce, perforate, insert, infiltrate
    Ant : discharge, leak, seep, emerge

Peevish
    Syn : perverse, sullen, irritable, fretful
    Ant : suave, amiable, polite, pleasant

Peerless
    Syn : matchless, unrivalled, unique, surpassing
    Ant : mediocre, commonplace, inferior, imperfect

Paramount
    Syn : foremost, eminent, supreme, unrivalled
    Ant : trivial, inferior, subsidiary, ordinary

Panic
    Syn : apprehension, dismay, alarm, dread
    Ant : calm, confidence, security, tranquility

Pamper
    Syn : spoil, indulge, flatter, please
    Ant : chasten, correct, deny, disparage

Palpable
    Syn : distinct, prominent, plain, concrete
    Ant : concealed, obscure, intangible, covert

Palliate
    Syn : extenuate, moderate, alleviate, soften
    Ant : denounce, condemn, reproach, reprehend

SYNONYMS AND ANTONYMS

Placid
Syn : tranquil, calm, compose, unruffled
Ant : turbulent, hostile, agitated, volatile

Q

Questionable
Syn : uncertain, disputable, dubious, unverifiable
Ant : positive, authentic, reliable, substantial

Quell
Syn : subdue, reduce, supress, extinguish
Ant : exacerbate, agitate, foment, instigate

Quaint
Syn : queer, strange, odd, ridiculous
Ant : familiar, usual, common, normal

Quack
Syn : impostor, deceiver, dissembler, knave
Ant : upright, unfeigned, trained, genuine

Quibble
Syn : equivocate, prevaricate, evade, dissemble
Ant : unfeign, plain, scrupulous, conscientious

Quash
Syn : abrogate, annul, cancel, revoke
Ant : uphold, empower, authorise, permit

Quarantine
Syn : isolate, separate, seclude, screened
Ant : gregarious, amiable, sociable, companionable

R

Reverence
Syn : respect, esteem, regards, veneration
Ant : disrespect, dishonour, affront, offence

Reveal
Syn : disclose, expose, unfold, divulge
Ant : hide, conceal, confine, cover

Retract
Syn : recant, repudiate, revoke, withdraw
Ant : confirm, assert, declare, affirm

Remote
- *Syn* : inaccessible, farther, distant, slight
- *Ant* : adjoining, adjacent, proximate, contiguous

Remorse
- *Syn* : regret, penitence, deplore, lament
- *Ant* : ruthless, obduracy, pitiless, relentless

Resentment
- *Syn* : displeasure, wrath, ire, bitterness
- *Ant* : content, cheer, pleasure, agreement

Rescind
- *Syn* : annul, abrogate, revoke, repeal
- *Ant* : delegate, permit, authorize, propose

Repulsive
- *Syn* : repellent, forbidding, hideous, detestable
- *Ant* : agreeable, enticing, attractive, alluring

Repugnant
- *Syn* : hostile, offensive, disagreeable, distasteful
- *Ant* : agreeable, pleasant, friendly, tasteful

Remonstrate
- *Syn* : censure, protest, argue, expostulate
- *Ant* : agree, laud, endorse, commend

Remnant
- *Syn* : residue, piece, part, remainder
- *Ant* : entire, whole, complete, unbroken

Relinquish
- *Syn* : forsake, abandon, surrender, abdicate
- *Ant* : persist, continue, occupy, hold

Redress
- *Syn* : relief, restoration, remedy, repair
- *Ant* : retribution, forfeiture, harm, degenerate

S

Sycophant
- *Syn* : parasite, flatterer, cringing, servile
- *Ant* : devoted, loyal, truthful, faithful

Sway
- *Syn* : influence, control, command, power
- *Ant* : impotence, futility, disability, incapacity

SYNONYMS AND ANTONYMS

Superfluous
- Syn : excessive, surplus, redundant, unnecessary
- Ant : scanty, inadequate, dearth, scarce

Stupor
- Syn : lethargy, insensibility, unconsciousness, coma
- Ant : consciousness, sensibility, sensitive, feeling

Stern
- Syn : harsh, severe, austere, rigorous
- Ant : lenient, considerate, benevolent, generous

Stain
- Syn : blemish, tarnish, disgrace, stigma
- Ant : honour, purify, virtuous, noble

Stable
- Syn : abiding, lasting, steadfast, constant
- Ant : erratic, wavering, unsteady, restless

Squalid
- Syn : dirty, soiled, filthy, odious
- Ant : attractive, tidy, polished, spruce

Spurious
- Syn : counterfeit, adulterated, fake, frandulent
- Ant : genuine, positive, original, sincere

Sporadic
- Syn : intermittent, scattered, isolated, infrequent
- Ant : incessant, frequent, constant, regular

Spontaneous
- Syn : unforced, instinctive, sudden, unintentional
- Ant : intended, devised, premeditated, intentional

Solicit
- Syn : entreat, implore, approach, accost
- Ant : protest, oppose, prohibit, disapprove

Sneer
- Syn : mock, scorn, spurn, condemn
- Ant : flatter, praise, encourage, laud

Slander
- Syn : defame, malign, detract, despise
- Ant : applaud, approve, commend, exalt

Sinister
- Syn : woeful, disastrous, evil, ruinous
- Ant : auspicious, fortunate, propitious, harmless

Shrewd
    Syn : running, observant, crafty, artful
    Ant : thoughtless, rash, simple, imbecile

Shallow
    Syn : trivial, slight, superficial, insubstantial
    Ant : profound, wise, substantial, deep

Shabby
    Syn : miserable, impoverished, deteriorated, impaired
    Ant : prosperous, thriving, restoring, flourishing

Scanty
    Syn : scarce, insufficient, paucity, sparseness
    Ant : lavish, luxuriant, multitude, several

T

Tyro
    Syn : beginner, learner, novice, debutant
    Ant : proficient, veteran, adept, connoisseur

Tumultuous
    Syn : uproarious, violent, disorderly, riotous
    Ant : peaceful, passive, orderly, harmonious

Trivial
    Syn : trifling, insignificant, frivolous, worthless
    Ant : significant, important, consequential, essential

Trite
    Syn : ordinary, commonplace, stale, hackneyed
    Ant : interesting, extraordinary, becoming, proper

Trenchant
    Syn : assertive, forceful, sharp, spirited
    Ant : feeble, ambiguous, shallow, vacillating

Treacherous
    Syn : faithless, deceitful, disloyal, unreliable
    Ant : faithful, reliable, dependable, trustworthy

Transient
    Syn : temporal, transitory, fleeting, passing
    Ant : lasting, enduring, perpetual, immortal

Tranquil
    Syn : peaceful, composed, calm, placid
    Ant : violent, furious, restless, distracting

SYNONYMS AND ANTONYMS

Torture
- *Syn* : torment, agony, pang, oppress
- *Ant* : comfort, consolation, pleasure, delight

U

Utterly
- *Syn* : completely, entirely, extremely, wholly
- *Ant* : deficient, incomplete, insufficient, partial

Usurp
- *Syn* : seize, wrest, encroach, coup
- *Ant* : restore, compensate, grant, reinstate

Unseemly
- *Syn* : undesirable, inappropriate, uncouth, awkward
- *Ant* : becoming, acceptable, decorous, admirable

Ungainly
- *Syn* : clumsy, unskilled, immature, slovenly
- *Ant* : active, expert, skilful, dexterous

Uncouth
- *Syn* : awkward, ungraceful, inelegant, vulgar
- : elegant, graceful, distinguished, shapely

Umbrage
- *Syn* : resentment, bitterness, dissatisfaction, offence
- *Ant* : sympathy, goodwill, amity, esteem

V

Vulgar
- *Syn* : inelegant, offensive, nasty, ungraceful
- *Ant* : refined, graceful, elegant, civil

Vouch
- *Syn* : confirm, consent, approve, endorse
- *Ant* : repudiate, prohibit, recant, retract

Volatile
- *Syn* : light, changing, transient, temporal
- *Ant* : heavy, ponderous, perpetual, stable

Vigilant
- *Syn* : cautious, alert, wary, circumspect
- *Ant* : careless, negligent, inattentive, casual

Vicious
- Syn : corrupt, obnoxious, degraded, demoralised
- Ant : noble, virtuous, innocent, underfiled

Vibrate
- Syn : swing, oscillate, fluctuate, undulate
- Ant : cease, pause, rest, discontinue

Venom
- Syn : poison, resentment, malevolence, rancour
- Ant : antidote, remedy, benevolent, sympathetic

Venerable
- Syn : esteemed, honoured, respectable, worthy
- Ant : unworthy, immature, degrade, degenerate

W

Waive
- Syn : relinquish, remove, abjure, renounce
- Ant : impose, clamp, grasp, retain

Wary
- Syn : cautious, circumspect, prudent, chary
- Ant : heedless, negligent, impulsive, reckless

Wicked
- Syn : immoral, dissolute, vicious, nefarious
- Ant : virtuous, ethical, innocent, noble

Withhold
- Syn : reserve, restrain, hamper, retard
- Ant : emancipate, liberate, dispense, release

Wane
- Syn : decline, dwindle, decrease, deteriorate
- Ant : ameliorate, rise, revive, wax

Y

Yoke
- Syn : connect, harness, hitch, shackle
- Ant : liberate, release, detach, disconnect

Yield
- Syn : surrender, abdicate, succumb, consent
- Ant : resist, protest, prohibit, forbid

SYNONYMS AND ANTONYMS

Yell
- Syn : shout, shriek, exclaim, gesticulate
- Ant : suppress, whisper, muffled, muted

Yearn
- Syn : languish, crave, require, pine
- Ant : content, unwanted, satisfied, gratified

Yawn
- Syn : gape, sleepy, slumber, doze
- Ant : close, active, brisk, wakeful

Z

Zigzag
- Syn : oblique, crooked, winding, wayward
- Ant : straight, even, direct, unbent

Zest
- Syn : delight, enthusiasm, various, energetic
- Ant : disgust, passive, detriment, languid

Zenith
- Syn : summit, apex, maximum, pinnacle
- Ant : nadir, base, bottom, floor

Zealot
- Syn : fanatic, partisan, bigot, chauvinist
- Ant : tolerant, liberal, blasphemy, impious

Zeal
- Syn : eagerness, fervour, enthusiasm, ardour
- Ant : apathy, lethargy, indifference, reluctant

Cumulative Exercise 1
(Based on Synonyms)

Directions *Write the synonyms of the following words.*

Exercise (A)

1. Vigilant
2. Encounter
3. Obstreperous
4. Meddle
5. Incensed
6. Relinquished
7. Misgivings
8. Consonance
9. Contrite
10. Conspicuous
11. Abandon
12. Dynamic
13. Allow
14. Ratified
15. Imponderable
16. Harness
17. Callous
18. Utter
19. Exasperation
20. Facile
21. Furtive
22. Ostentation
23. Salient
24. Restive
25. Queer

Exercise (B)

1. Clamouring
2. Attune
3. Jaded
4. Stagnant
5. Brimming
6. Intriguing
7. Perpetual
8. Ostensible
9. Rebellion
10. Vague
11. Upbraided
12. Pensive
13. Nuptial
14. Pious
15. Dishonourable
16. Drawn
17. Haughty
18. Hapless
19. Penchant
20. Paucity
21. Lethal
22. Unlawful
23. Knave
24. Flimsy
25. Captive

Exercise (C)

1. Spectacular
2. Deteriorating
3. Refurbished
4. Ramifications
5. Supercilious
6. Momentous
7. Stalemate
8. Anxiety
9. Lucrative
10. Forthrightness
11. Reprimand
12. Punctilious
13. Discreet
14. Famished
15. Gimcrack
16. Envious
17. Leap
18. Abashed
19. Inexorable
20. Acerbic
21. Astute
22. Disparate
23. Self-possessed
24. Aplomb
25. Lucid

SYNONYMS AND ANTONYMS

Exercise (D)

1. Expeditiously
2. Devious
3. Impertinent
4. Inexorable
5. Intertwined
6. Long-winded
7. Misleading
8. Munificent
9. Trenchant
10. Vigorous
11. Panacea
12. Tactical
13. Acumen
14. Industrious
15. Surplus
16. Amicable
17. Fiery
18. Unequivocally
19. Excerpts
20. Exasperating
21. Disgruntled
22. Garrulous
23. Temperance
24. Jettison
25. Remorse

Cumulative Exercise 2

(Based on Antonyms)

Directions *Write the antonyms/opposites of the following words.*

Exercise (A)

1. Fragments
2. Abetting
3. Candid
4. Deteriorating
5. Alleviating
6. Deferred
7. Desecrate
8. Frugality
9. Endeavoured
10. Formidable
11. Benevolent
12. Apathy
13. Civilised
14. Squalid
15. Novice
16. Trivial
17. Barren
18. Irksome
19. Hectic
20. Laudable
21. Fetters
22. Feud
23. Fickle
24. Fervent
25. Lackadaisical

Exercise (B)

1. Feebleness
2. Sycophants
3. Clemency
4. Fatigue
5. Encomium
6. Laconic
7. Languid
8. Obligatory
9. Blemish
10. Retreat
11. Disgusted
12. Thrift
13. Lunatic
14. Dismal
15. Distress
16. Disparaging
17. Dessipate
18. Straight
19. Modesty
20. Elated
21. Reunion
22. Counterfeit
23. Serious
24. Confirms
25. Nepotism

Exercise (C)

1. Obscured
2. Craftiness
3. Placate
4. Infiltrated
5. Fastidious
6. Garrulous
7. Fortuitous
8. Zealous
9. Dreadful
10. Perfunctorily
11. Immaculate
12. Fastidious
13. Mitigate
14. Genuine
15. Facetious
16. Pernicious
17. Precarious
18. Recklessly
19. Adversaries
20. Cogent
21. Zeal
22. Garrulous
23. Defiled
24. Glavanised
25. Fortuitious

Exercise (D)

1. Perspicacious
2. Perpetual
3. Imperious
4. Impenitent
5. Stoical
6. Dauntless
7. Rickety
8. Profligate
9. Jettison
10. Flummoxed
11. Doleful
12. Senility
13. Terse
14. Ungainly
15. Vanity
16. Warily
17. Sporadic
18. Overstrung
19. Superficial
20. Grumpy
21. Diverse
22. Succumbed
23. Mammoth
24. Despises
25. Callous

Previous Years' Questions

I. Directions *Write the antonyms of the following words.*

1. (i) Amateur (ii) Modesty (iii) Shallow
   (iv) Conceited (v) Atheist
   [Civil Services (Mains), 2013]

2. (i) Ability (ii) Precise (iii) Constructive
   (iv) Extravagant (v) Pretentious
   [Civil Services (Mains), 2014]

3. (i) Arrival (ii) Introvert (iii) Ascend
   (iv) Save (v) Mortal
   [Civil Services (Mains), 2015]

4. (i) Notorious (ii) Legitimate (iii) Responsible
   (iv) Satisfaction (v) Promotion
   [Civil Services (Mains), 2011]

5. (i) Useful (ii) Active (iii) Encourage
   (iv) Rational (v) Timely
   [Civil Services (Mains), 2012]

II. Directions *Write the synonyms of the following words.*

(i) Lethargy (ii) Emaciated (iii) Latent
(iv) Sporadic (v) Compendium
[CLAT, 2012]

Answers

Cumulative Exercise 1
(Based on Synonyms)

Exercise (A)

1. Watchful
2. Face
3. Unruly
4. Interfere
5. Enraged
6. Give up
7. Doubt
8. Agreement
9. Penitent
10. Prominent
11. Forsake
12. Energetic
13. Permit
14. Confirmed
15. Incalculable
16. Utilise
17. Hard hearted
18. Total
19. Irritation
20. Easy
21. Secret
22. Display
23. Prominent
24. Restless
25. Odd

Exercise (B)

1. Protesting
2. Adapt
3. Fatigued
4. Motionless
5. Overflowing
6. Curious
7. Never ending
8. Apparent
9. Mutiny
10. Indistinct
11. Scolded
12. Thoughtful
13. Bridal
14. Holy
15. Discreditable
16. Deduced
17. Arrogant
18. Unfortunate
19. Inclination
20. Scarcity
21. Deadly
22. Nefarious
23. Villain
24. Trivial
25. Prisoner

Exercise (C)

1. Remarkable
2. Worsening
3. Renovated
4. Consequences
5. Contemptuous
6. Important
7. Deadlock
8. Anguish
9. Profitable
10. Outspokenness
11. Punishment
12. Careful
13. Prudent
14. Hungry
15. Worthless
16. Jealous
17. Jump
18. Embarrassed
19. Relentless
20. Bitter
21. Shrewd
22. Different
23. Confident
24. Poise
25. Clear

Exercise (D)

1. Speedily
2. Winding
3. Rude
4. Relentless
5. Linked
6. Circumlocutory
7. Deceptive
8. Generous
9. Incisive
10. Lively
11. Medicine
12. Strategic
13. Sharpness
14. Diligent
15. Excess
16. Friendly
17. Passionate
18. Plainly
19. Extracts
20. Irritating
21. Discontented
22. Talkative
23. Moderation
24. Discard
25. Regret

Cumulative Exercise 2
(Based on Antonyms)

Exercise (A)

1. Whole
2. Baffle
3. Ambiguous
4. Ameliorating
5. Aggravating
6. Expedited
7. Deify
8. Extravagance
9. Shirked
10. Facile
11. Malevolent
12. Sympathy
13. Savage
14. Clean
15. Veteran
16. Important
17. Productive
18. Pleasant
19. Unhurried
20. Disreputable
21. Freedom
22. Brotherhood
23. Stable
24. Impassive
25. Enthusiastic

Exercise (B)

1. Strength
2. Detractors
3. Callousness
4. Energy
5. Denunciation
6. Copious
7. Brisk
8. Voluntary
9. Adornment
10. Advance
11. Pleased
12. Extravagant
13. Sane
14. Cheerful
15. Prosperity
16. Lauding
17. Conserve
18. Distort
19. Boldness
20. Dejected
21. Parting
22. Silent
23. Insincere
24. Contradicts
25. Impartiality

Exercise (C)

1. Clarified
2. Simplicity
3. Infuriate
4. Expelled
5. Amiable
6. Tongue-tied
7. Unlucky
8. Indifferent
9. Comfortable
10. Carefully
11. Flawed
12. Thoughtless
13. Augment
14. Imitation
15. Grave
16. Beneficial
17. Secure
18. Carefully
19. Allies
20. Unconvincing
21. Indifference
22. Unkind
23. Purified
24. Dampened
25. Unfortunate

Exercise (D)

1. Unreliable
2. Intermittent
3. Submissive
4. Repentant
5. Flinching
6. Cowardly
7. Stable
8. Thrifty
9. Accept
10. Comfortable
11. Cheerful
12. Virility
13. Verbose
14. Graceful
15. Humility
16. Cautiously
17. Frequent
18. Calm
19. Deep
20. Pleasant
21. Uniform
22. Overcome
23. Small
24. Appreciates
25. Sensitive

Previous Years' Questions

I. 1. (i) Professional, expert
(ii) Confidence, immorality, boldness
(iii) Deep, significant, full
(iv) Humble, modest, self-conscious
(v) Believer

2. (i) Inability, incompetence, incapability
(ii) Inaccurate, imprecise
(iii) Unproductive, fruitless
(iv) Moderate, reasonable
(v) Genuine, honest, simple

3. (i) Departure, disappearance
(ii) Extrovert
(iii) Descend, decline
(iv) Waste, squander
(v) Immortal, permanent

4. (i) Famous
(ii) Illegitimate
(iii) Irresponsible
(iv) Dissatisfaction
(v) Demotion

5. (i) Useless
(ii) Inert/Idle
(iii) Discourage
(iv) Irrational
(v) Untimely

II. (i) Listlessness
(ii) Very thin/slim
(iii) Concealed
(iv) Occasional
(v) Summary

CHAPTER 4

Foreign Words and Expressions

These words belong to European languages other than English which are often used in English.

Word	Meaning
1. a' la mode	in the fashion, in vogue
2. albeit	although
3. avant garde	pioneer in movement of art/literature
4. ab initio	from very beginning
5. ad hoc	arranged for special purpose
6. au revoir	until we meet again
7. ad interim	meanwhile
8. alma mater	mother institution a person attended
9. ad valorem	according to value
10. annus mirabilis	a wonderful year in which great events take place
11. a'propos	to the point, with reference to
12. alibi	false plea of absence
13. ad nauseam	to offensive limit
14. alter ego	a bosom friend, one's other self
15. alumni	ex students of an institution (alumnus–singular)
16. ante meridiem	time between midnight and noon (a.m.)
17. animus	bad intention
18. a priori	deductive, to infer fact from cause
19. amicus curiae	friend of the court in any judicial proceeding
20. ad infinitum	for indefinite period, for even
21. alpha and omega	from beginning to end
22. alias	otherwise, nick name

23.	amour propre	self love, vanity
24.	Anno Domini	in the Christian era (AD) after the death of
25.	agent provocateur	a secret agent employed to find the suspected criminals
26.	blitzkreig	lightning attack
27.	bona fide	in a good faith, sincere
28.	bon voyage	pleasant journey to you
29.	bourgeoisie	middle class
30.	bete noire	an object of dislike
31.	bonhomie	pleasantness of manners
32.	carte blanche	full freedom of action
33.	communique	official intimation or note
34.	casus belli	act/event leading to war
35.	coup d' etat	violent or unconstitutional change in government
36.	circa	about (born circa 150 BC)
37.	chaperon	a person (usually elderly lady) who accompanies a young girl
38.	commune bonum	the common good
39.	coiffeur	hair dresser
40.	charge d' affairs	one who acts as an ambassador
41.	coup de grace	the final blow
42.	coiffure	style of hair dressing
43.	couturier	man dress designer
44.	couturiere	woman dress designer
45.	canard	a rumour, a hoax
46.	cuisine	the brand of cooked food
47.	cause celebre	a very notable trial
48.	detenu	a prisoner
49.	de tour	indirect way
50.	de novo	afresh
51.	debut	first appearance on stage or in any event
52.	debutant	one making first appearance (male)
53.	debutante	one making first appearance (female)
54.	detente	easing of strained relations
55.	de jure	according to law, by right
56.	de facto	in fact, real
57.	demarche	a political step/presentation
58.	deja vu	a feeling that something has happened before
59.	denoument	final conclusion in a play
60.	dramatis personae	characters in a play
61.	emeritus	retired but retaining honorary title on merit

FOREIGN WORDS AND EXPRESSIONS

62. elite — select, choice
63. en bloc — in a group, collectively
64. entrenous — between ourselves
65. en masse — in a mass
66. ex gratia — as a matter of grace, favour
67. ex post facto — by subsequent act
68. en route — on the way to
69. esprit de corps — spirit of belonging to one organisation
70. ex officio — by virtue of one's post
71. ennui — boredome
72. ex parte — done not in the presence of other
73. elan — dashing spirit
74. et al — and other people
75. exempli gratia — e.g., for example
76. enfant terrible — one who is a source of trouble
77. entente — understanding between the two states
78. entourage — a person's subordinates
79. forte — a person's special talent
80. fait accompli — an accomplished fact
81. fiance — a man to whom one is engaged to marry
82. fiancee — a woman to whom one is engaged to marry
83. gratis — free of charge
84. genre — a style, a particular kind
85. hauteur — haughtiness
86. hors de combat — out of combat, disabled
87. homo sapiens — men as thinking people
88. ipso facto — really, by that very fact
89. ibid — in the same book/chapter
90. impasse — deadlock
91. id est — i.e. (that is to say)
92. infra dig — below one's dignity
93. inter alia — among other things
94. in camera — not open to public
95. instant — of this month
96. joie de vivre — joy of living
97. laissez faire — free from government control/interference
98. locus standi — right to be heard, to interfere
99. lingua franca — common language spoken by people
100. literatur — literary person
101. literati — literary persons

102.	lacuna	shortcoming, gap
103.	leitmolif	a recurring theme
104.	melange	mixture, blending, medley
105.	mutatis mutandis	with necessary changes
106.	menage	household, domestic
107.	mala fide	in bad faith
108.	modus vivandi	way of living
109.	modus operandi	method of dealing with work
110.	magnum opus	a great book, a work of art
111.	melee	mixed fight, stampede
112.	matinee	morning (after noon)
113.	nouveaux riches	people who are newly rich
114.	nota bene	take note
115.	nom de plume	pen name, assumed name
116.	nexus	bond, link, connection
117.	non pareil	incomparable, unparallel
118.	nee	name used after the name of married woman to indicate father's family name
119.	outre	exaggerated
120.	obiter dictum	passing remark
121.	persona non grata	a person not acceptable
122.	persona grata	a person acceptable
123.	pro rata	in proportion
124.	per se	by itself
125.	par excellence	excellent, superb
126.	pot pourri	mixture, musical, medley
127.	post meridiem	afternoon (p.m.)
128.	prima facie	based on the first impression
129.	proletarian	a member of poor class
130.	pari passu	at an equal rate/pace
131.	parole	prisoner's word of honour
132.	protege	one who is patronised by others
133.	quid pro quo	something given or returned as an equivalent of something (tit for tat)
134.	raison d'etre	reason for existence, real purpose
135.	rendezvous	private meeting place
136.	reposte	repartee, retort
137.	RSVP	respondez's ilvous plait (reply, if you please)
138.	religio loci	the religious feeling of a place
139.	resume	a summary, an abstract

FOREIGN WORDS AND EXPRESSIONS

140.	sang froid	coolness in trying condition
141.	status quo	the same position
142.	sine die	for an indefinite period
143.	sub judice	under consideration
144.	sobriquet	pseudonym
145.	summum bonum	chief good
146.	sans	without, deprived of
147.	sine qua non	indispensable condition to achieve something
148.	sanctum sanctorum	the holy of holies
149.	son et lu miere	a historical play staged with sound and light
150.	suo moto	on one's own
151.	tour de force	a feat of strength or skill
152.	tete o tete	a private conversation, face-to-face
153.	ultra vires	beyond one's authority
154.	via	through
155.	versus	against
156.	viva voce	an oral test
157.	viz	namely, that is to say
158.	vice versa	in opposite ways
159.	vide	see, refer
160.	via media	middle course
161.	vox populi von dei	voice of the people is the voice of God
162.	vox populi	voice of the people
163.	vendetta	family feud
164.	vis-a-vis	directly opposite to
165.	volte face	a complete turn about, reversal of policy
166.	xerox	a photocopy
167.	zeitgeist	contemporary spirit

Previous Years' Questions

A. Directions *Given below are a few foreign language phrases which are commonly used. Write the correct meaning for each of the phrases.*

I. 1. Ex officio   2. Ultra vires   3. Quid pro quo   **[CLAT, 2014]**
    4. Inter vivos   5. Corpus juris

II. 1. El-Dorado   2. Quantum comifactus   3. Corpus delicti   **[CLAT, 2013]**
     4. Vis-a-vis   5. Carte blanche

III. 1. Mala fide   2. Tabula rasa   3. De jure   **[CLAT, 2012]**
      4. Raison d'etre

B. Directions *Write short sentences using each of these.*   **[IFS, 2010]**
    1. Prima facia   2. Sub judice   3. De jure
    4. Fait accompli   5. Status quo ante

Answers

A. I. 1. 'Ex officio' means by virtue of one's post.
     2. 'Ultra vires' means beyond one's legal power or authority.
     3. 'Quid pro quo' means gift, favour, etc, exchanged for another.
     4. 'Inter vivos' means among the living.
     5. 'Corpus juris' means body of law.

   II. 1. 'El-Dorado' means the golden one. *or* A place of fabulous wealth or opportunity.
      2. 'Quantum comifactus' means the amount of damage received.
      3. 'Corpus delicti' means an evidence which constitute an offence.
      4. 'Vis-a-vis' means face to face. *or* As compared with.
      5. 'Carte blanche' means full freedom of action.

   III. 1. 'Mala fide' means in bad faith.
       2. 'Tabula rasa' means clean slate.
       3. 'De jure' means concerning law.
       4. 'Raison d'etre' means reason for existence.

B. 1. This seems like a planned murder prima facia.
   2. The proposed model for the plan is sub judice to the committee.
   3. Ragging is immoral from the point of view of values but a crime de jure.
   4. It is a fait accompli that truth can be hindered but never subdued.
   5. The riot affected area is in status quo ante as it was earlier as no relief has reached there.

CHAPTER 5
Legal Vocabulary

Legal glossary is of great significant for the students appearing in Judiciary examinations because rendering Hindi passages into English (translation part) forms an indispensable part of the question-papers. Students, therefore, should look them up very carefully.

A

1. **Abandon** To surrender, control or possession.
2. **Abatement** Curtailment, reduction.
3. **Abduction** To take away a person unlawfully and by force.
4. **Abet** To instigate for committing an offence.
5. **Abettor** One who abets the commission of a crime.
6. **Abeyance** A state of suspension.
7. **Abolish** To put an end to.
8. **Abrogate** To annul/abolish a law.
9. **Abscond** Hide away in order to avoid legal process or to escape arrest.
10. **Abstain** Not to participate in action. Abstain from voting, drinking or smoking etc.
11. **Abstract** A summary of something.
12. **Abuse of the process** (of court) The misuse of legal process for obtaining an unfair advantage.
13. **Access to records or documents** Power to approach the documents.
14. **Accession** Coming to the throne or some office. Acquiring some property.
15. **Accidental omission** To omit something by chance.
16. **Accidental slip** Mistake by accident (without intention).
17. **Accommodation** Provision of what is needed for convenience.
18. **Accomplice** An associate in the commission of crime/offence.

19. **Accomplished** Completed.
20. **Accounting year** A year for which accounts are separately maintained.
21. **Accountrement** A kit, equipment.
22. **Accredited** Having official credentials, recognised officially.
23. **Accrue** To add as a natural growth or increase (benefit, advantage).
24. **Accusation** To charge a person with some offence.
25. **Acknowledge** To admit something as correct or valid in law.
26. **Acquiesce** To give passive assent (without protest).
27. **Acquisition** The act of becoming the owner of.
28. **Acquittal** The act of setting someone free from a charge of an offence after trial.
29. **Act** A thing done, action, a law made by a competent authorities.
30. **Acting in concert** Act in arrangement with others.
31. **Action** A thing done, a judicial action for enforcing law.
32. **Actionable wrong** An offence for which an action can be taken in law.
33. **Active concealment** An act of concealing knowingly.
34. **Actuary** A person who determines the value of life and damages caused in the case of insurance.
35. **Address** Speak to a person or court.
36. **Adduce evidence** Put forward as proof, or reason.
37. **Ad hoc** Concerned with a particular purpose.
38. **Adjourn** To put off proceedings to another day.
39. **Adjuournment** An action of adjourning.
40. **Adjudge** To decide judicially.
41. **Adjudicate** To try and determine judicially.
42. **Adjustment of suits** The settlement of the claim by a lawful agreement.
43. **Administer** To manage the property of other person who dies intesetate (without a will).
44. **Administration of justice** Doing or dispensing justice.
45. **Admit to bail** To accept bail.
46. **Admissible** What is allowed as judicial proof, admissibility of proof.
47. **Admission of appeal** The acceptance by court of an appeal for consideration.
48. **Admonition** An expression of warning in lieu of punishment.
49. **Adolescent** A person grown from childhood to maturity (from 12-18 years).
50. **Adoption** The action of adopting a child.
51. **Adult** Having reached the age of maturity.
52. **Adultery** Voluntary unlawful sexual relations.
53. **Adulterate** Make impure by adding some foreign substance.
54. **Adverse** Acting in an opposing direction.
55. **Affidavit** A written statement signed and sworn by the deponent.
56. **Affiliated** Attached as a member or branch.
57. **Affirmation** A solemn declaration without oath.

LEGAL VOCABULARY

58. **Agnate** A descendant from a common male ancestor.
59. **Agreement of indemnity** An agreement by which one party agrees to save the other from loss or damage.
60. **Alien enemy** A person owing allegiance to a country which is at war with India.
61. **Alimony** Money payable by the husband or wife on separation.
62. **Allegiance** Lawful and faithful obedience to the state and its constitution.
63. **Annuity** An amount of money payable yearly for a certain or uncertain period.
64. **Annual** To make without effect or void.
65. **Anomaly** Deviation from the common order.
66. **Appellant** One who makes an appeal.
67. **Appellate** Pertaining to appeal.
68. **Appendix** An addition subjoined to a document or a book.
69. **Appertaining** Belonging as a part to the whole.
70. **Application for restitution** The application for restoration of a former position.
71. **Apportion** To divide proportionately.
72. **Apprehend** To seize in the name of law. Anticipate something adverse.
73. **Appurtenant** Annexed or belonging legally to something.
74. **Arbitrary** Depending on will or pleasure.
75. **Arbitration** Determination of a matter in dispute by arbitrators.
76. **Armistice** A short truce (stopping of fighting for sometime).
77. **Arrest** To restrain the liberty of a person.
78. **Arson** Wilful and malicious burning of property.
79. **Articles of partnership** Rules governing the conduct of partnership.
80. **As to** Regarding.
81. **Assessee** One upon whom a payment is assessed.
82. **Assumption** The act of assuming or seizing.
83. **At the instance of** On being urged by.
84. **At variance with** Opposed to.
85. **Attach** To take property into the custody of law.
86. **Attestation** The action of affirming to be true or genuine.
87. **Authenticate** To give legal validity.
88. **Aver** To declare in a positive manner.
89. **Award compensation** Determine compensation.
90. **Award** A decision given by an arbitrator or umpire.

B

1. **Bad character** A person whose general conduct is bad.
2. **Bad Debt** A debt considered to be unrecoverable.
3. **Bad faith** Act with some interested fraud or design.
4. **Bailable** An offence in which bail can be granted as a matter of right.

5. **Bailiff** An officer for executing warrants or making arrest.
6. **Bar of jurisdiction** Excluded from consideration by law.
7. **Barrister** A member of one of the four Inns of Court and who has the privilege of pleading in the higher courts.
8. **Barter** An exchange of goods for goods.
9. **Bearing on** Having relation with.
10. **Become enforceable** To come into force.
11. **Belligerent rights** Rights pertaining to war.
12. **Belongings** Personal things.
13. **Bench** A court to decide particular matter or matters.
14. **Beneficially entitled** Entitled to receive and appropriate.
15. **Bequeath** Leaving property by a will.
16. **Beyond authority** Not within power.
17. **Bicameral** A legislature having two chambers.
18. **Binding upon** Obligatory.
19. **Bound by law** Obliged by law.
20. **Breach** Breaking of law.
21. **Breach of contract** Breaking of agreement.
22. **Brother by half blood** A brother by the same father but different mother's.
23. **Burden of proof** Responsibility to prove something.
24. **By virtue of** By authority of.

C

1. **Calling** Profession.
2. **Candidature** The act of being a candidate.
3. **Capacity** (official capacity) Capable by law.
4. **Capital offence** A crime punishable with death.
5. **Capital punishment** Punishment of death.
6. **Captor** One who captures a prisoner.
7. **Capture** The act of taking forcibly.
8. **Case law** Law established by judicial decisions.
9. **Cause** A suit or litigation.
10. **Caveat** A notice given to some officer not to do anything until the opposition party is heard.
11. **Cease to have effect** To discontinue.
12. **Cessation** Discontinuance or stoppage.
13. **Charge** Accusation of a crime which preceeds a formal trial.
14. **Charged with liability** Having responsibility.
15. **Cheating by personation** Impersonation.
16. **Circular** A written directive circulated among many persons.
17. **Civic interest** Interest of the citizens.

LEGAL VOCABULARY

18. **Civil proceedings** A suit filed for the prevention of a private wrong.
19. **Claimant** One who makes a claim.
20. **Client** A person who engages a lawyer.
21. **Code of conduct** Code according to law framed by legal authority.
22. **Cognizable** Capable of being taken cognizance of.
23. **Cognizance** Legal right to try a case.
24. **Cognizable offence** An offence for which police may arrest without warrant.
25. **Collateral security** An additional security.
26. **Collusion** A secret agreement for deceitful purpose.
27. **Come into force** Become enforceable.
28. **Commit for trial** To entrust for trial.
29. **Commutation (of punishment)** The substitution of a lesser punishment for a greater one.
30. **Compensatory** Giving compensation.
31. **Competant** Legally sufficient.
32. **Complicity** The stage of being an accomplice in a crime.
33. **Composition deed** A deed by which a debtor compounds with his creditor.
34. **Compound** To forbear from prosecution for consideration of any private motive.
35. **Compoundable offence** An offence which is capable of being compounded.
36. **Conceal** To hide or keep secret.
37. **Concealment** The action of concealing.
38. **Conclusive proof** Proved in a conclusive manner.
39. **Conditional** Limited by conditions.
40. **Confession** The action of confessing guilt.
41. **Confinement** The action of confining.
42. **Confiscate** Forfeit property to the state.
43. **Connivance** Passive consent.
44. **Consequent failure of** Failure as a result of.
45. **Consignee** A person to whom goods are consigned.
46. **Contempt of court** A wilful disobedience of court.
47. **Contraband** Prohibited by law.
48. **Contingency** An event thought of as possible in the near future.
49. **Contract of indemnity** A contract for compensation.
50. **Contracting party** A party that has entered into contract.
51. **Contravention** The action of violation.
52. **Criminal tresspass** Violation of law amounting to crime.
53. **Covenant** An agreement between two or more persons to comply with certain conditions.
54. **Counter-feit** Immitated with intention to deceive.
55. **Corresponding law** A law having the same object.
56. **Co-opt** To elect into a body by the votes of its existing members.

57. **Court** A place where justice is administered.
58. **Culpable homicide** Criminal murder.
59. **Custody** The detaining of a person by virtue of law.
60. **Custom's tariff** Duty paid on goods imported or exported.

D

1. **Dacoity** Robbery with violence committed by a gang.
2. **Damages** The sum claimed as compensation.
3. **Damages (pecuniary)** Monetary claim.
4. **Dealing authorities** One who deals with the matter.
5. **Dealt with (in the report)** Described in the report.
6. **Debar** To exclude from admission or rights.
7. **Deceased** A dead person.
8. **Decree for damages** To pass a decree for the payment of damages.
9. **Deemed to affect** Regarded as having affect.
10. **Defamatory** That defames.
11. **Default in the payment** Failure to make payment.
12. **Defence** The action of defending in a suit.
13. **Defiance** Action of contempt.
14. **Defray expenses** To meet the expenses.
15. **Deligate** To commit a person with authority.
16. **Deliberate** Pre-mediated.
17. **Demarcation** Making of boundaries.
18. **Deponent** One who deposes or give evidence.
19. **Deportation** The lawful expulsion of a person from the state.
20. **Depredation** Plundering, looting.
21. **Descendant** One descended from an ancestor.
22. **Desist** To discontinue or to stop doing something.
23. **Detain** To keep in confinement or custody.
24. **Deter** To terrify.
25. **Designated** Described by the name of office.
26. **Determination** The action of determining or deciding.
27. **Deteriment** Damage done to or suffered by a person.
28. **Devolution** The passing of property to another on the death of a person.
29. **Disability** The absence of legal capacity to enjoy legal rights.
30. **Disapprobation** The act of disapproval.
31. **Discharge a debt** To pay the debt.
32. **Discharge of the liability** The act of freeing from obligation.
33. **Disclaimer** Formal refusal to undertake the office or duties.
34. **Discretion** The power to decide what is right and proper.

LEGAL VOCABULARY

35. **Discretionary** Left to descretion of somebody.
36. **Disgraceful conduct** Shameful behaviour.
37. **Dispauper** To disqualify from filing a suit without payment of court fee.
38. **Disposal** The action of settling the matter.
39. **Dispose of an appeal** To settle a matter finally.
40. **Dispossession** The action of dispossessing.
41. **Dissolution** The breaking up of any constituted body.
42. **Dissolution of marriage** Breaking up of marriage.
43. **Distinct** Different in quality or kind.
44. **Distinct ground** On a different basis.
45. **Disturb the public tranquility** Disturbing the peace of the people as a whole.
46. **Document of title** A document that confers a title.
47. **Domicile** The place of permanent residence.
48. **Dominion** A self-governing state.
49. **Due course** The logical course of events.
50. **Due proclamation** Official formal public announcement.
51. **Duly** In due manner.
52. **Duplicate** Consisting of or existing in two corresponding or identical parts.
53. **Dying declaration** A statement by a person as to the cause of his own death.

E

1. **Easement** An easement is a right which the owner of a property possesses in respect of other property not his own.
2. **Effective implementation** A productive or useful implementation.
3. **Efficacious** Certain to produce the intended effect.
4. **Electoral college** A body of persons entitled to vote at an election.
5. **Electorate** The whole body of those entitled to vote at an election.
6. **Eligible** Fit or qualified to be chosen.
7. **Empanel** To enter the name on a panel.
8. **Enact** To make into an act.
9. **Encumbrance** A claim or liability attached to property, as mortgage etc.
10. **Enforceable** Capable of being enforced.
11. **Enjoyment** The action or state of enjoying a right.
12. **Ensuing** Next, following.
13. **Entertain** To admit in order to deal with.
14. **Entitled as of right** Having a titles as a matter of right.
15. **Escheat** The lapsing of property to state on the death of the owner without heir and intestate.
16. **Essential commodity** An indispensable object.
17. **Estate** The interest which anyone has in lands. A landed property.
18. **Evacuee** A person removed from his home in the time of war.

19. **Evade the payment** To avoid making payment.
20. **Evasion** The action of evading or escaping.
21. **Evasive denial** A denial in an ambigous language.
22. **Evidence (documentary evidence)** All documents considered as evidence by the court.
23. **Excess of his powers, in** Exceeding one's powers.
24. **Ex-communication** (from any caste or community) The action of excluding an offender from community.
25. **Ex-officio** By virtue of office.
26. **Ex-parte** From one side
27. **Execution** The action of bringing into effect.
28. **Executor** A person appointed by the court to execute the will of the deceased.
29. **Exercise of power** The use of power.
30. **Exigency** Such necessity as belongs to the occasion.
31. **Expendient** Suitable to the circumstances.
32. **Expiration** The coming to the end.
33. **Express condition** Expressed condition.
34. **Expressly** Expressed in words.
35. **Extenuating** That reduces culpability.
36. **Extortion** The action of extorting money by force.
37. **Extradiction** The action of giving up an absconding criminal to the country in which the crime was committed.
38. **Extra-territorial offence** An offence committed beyond the territory of the state.

F

1. **Fabricate** To forge, manipulate.
2. **Face value** The value indicated on the face of a document.
3. **Facsimile** An exact copy of some document, counter part or representation.
4. **Fair trial** A trial in which law has been used fairly.
5. **False personation** Pretending to be some other person.
6. **Fatal** Deadly, resulting in death.
7. **Forbear** To abstain from.
8. **Foreclose** To debar a person from his right to redeem a mortgage.
9. **Forensic** Medical knowledge as needed in legal matters.
10. **Forfeit** To lose the right.
11. **Forge** To do the act of forgery to fabricate.
12. **Fraud** Criminal deception.

LEGAL VOCABULARY

G

1. **Garnishee** A person in whose hands a debt is attached.
2. **General intent** Collective intention.
3. **Generality** Total applicability.
4. **Give effect** To bring into effect.
5. **Give intelligence to the enemy** To be an informer of the enemy.
6. **Grant exemption** Act of granting immunity from liability.
7. **Grant of lease** Grant real estate on contract for a certain period.
8. **Gratification** (by corrupt means) Bribery.
9. **Gratuitous** Without legal consideration.
10. **Grave provocation** Provoking a person intensely.
11. **Gross misconduct** Flagrant misbehaviour.
12. **Ground of appeal** Basis for appeal.
13. **Guarantee** The action of securing.
14. **Guarantor** One who gives a guarantee.
15. **Guardian** One who has or is entitled to the custody of the person or property of a minor or an incapable person.
16. **Guilty** One who has committed a guilt.

H

1. **Habeas Corpus** A writ to produce a person in custody before the court.
2. **Habitual offender** A person used to lead a criminal life.
3. **Hand** (under my hand) In my signatures.
4. **Have a retrospective effect from a date** having effect from a past time.
5. **Heard in person** A statement made by a person himself.
6. **Hearing** Listening to arguments in a court of law.
7. **Hearsay evidence** Evidence heard by the witness.
8. **Herein contained** Contained in this document.
9. **Hereto annexed** Enclosed to this document.
10. **Heretofore** Before this time.
11. **Highly probable** Very probable.
12. **Hostile witness** A witness that has changed evidence in the court.
13. **House breaking** The offence of entering the house by force.
14. **House trespass** Enter the house by force.
15. **Hurt** A bodily injury.
16. **Hypothecation** Mortgaging something for taking loan.

I

1. **Identification parade** A parade conducted in order to test if a witness is able to identify the accused.
2. **Ignorance** Want of knowledge.
3. **Immunity** Freedom from liability.
4. **Impeach** To bring a charge against.
5. **Impair** To reduce the value of something.
6. **Implementation** Giving practical effect.
7. **Implied consent** Consent not given in express words.
8. **Implied warranty** A warranty given to the buyer but not in express words.
9. **Impose** To levy a tax or duty.
10. **Impound** To take something in legal custody.
11. **Improper admission of evidence** Receiving evidence which is not capable of admission.
12. **Imputation** Something attributed against someone.
13. **In an exemplary manner** In a manner worthy of being an example.
14. **In breach of contract** Breaking of contract.
15. **In conformity with** In accordance with.
16. **In conjunction with** Alongwith.
17. **In consultation with** By consulting somebody else.
18. **In contravention of** In violation of.
19. **In furtherance of** In promoting.
20. **In issue** In dispute.
21. **In kind** In the form of goods.
22. **In person** In the presence of.
23. **In pursuance of** Acting in accordance with the power granted.
24. **In transit** On the way.
25. **Inadvertent slip** An omission by accident.
26. **Inchoate** Begun but not completed.
27. **Incompetent** Not having requisite capacity or qualification.
28. **Inconclusive proof** A proof that is incomplete.
29. **Inconsistent** Contrary to one another.
30. **Incumbrance** A claim, lien or liability attached to property.
31. **Indemnify** To make good a loss.
32. **Indemnity** Security against loss or damage.
33. **Indict** To accuse someone before a court.
34. **Inducement** Something attractive which leads a person to action.
35. **Inequitable** Not fair and right.
36. **Inexpedient** Undesirable.
37. **Inference** A conclusion drawn from non-facts.
38. **Infringement** Breach of a law.

LEGAL VOCABULARY

39. **Ingredient** A component part.
40. **Insolvent** One who is unable to pay his debt.
41. **Intangible** Not cognizable by the sense of touch.
42. **Intent to deceive** With an intention of deceiving.
43. **Intended** Designed with an intention.
44. **Interlocutory application** An application made in the course of an action.
45. **Inter vivos** From one living person to another.
46. **Interim** Intended to last for only a short time until somebody/something more permanent is found.
47. **Invalidate** To make invalid.
48. **Involuntary** Not done willingly or by choice.
49. **Irrespective of** Without respect or regard to.

J

1. **Jail** A place for confinement of persons committed by process of law.
2. **Jointly and severally bound** In a joint and individual manner.
3. **Judge** One invested with authority to determine any cause or question in court of law.
4. **Judicial process** Proceedings in the court.
5. **Jurisdiction** Legal power or authority.
6. **Just ground** On the basis according to law.
7. **Juvenile offender** A child who has committed an offence.

K

Kidnapping An act of stealing, abducting or carrying away a person by force or fraud.

L

1. **Laid down** Expounded or stated positively.
2. **Laid on the table of Parliament** To show something to the members.
3. **Law and order** General peace.
4. **Law in force** Existing law.
5. **Lawful custody** Custody according to law.
6. **Leasehold** A tenure by way of lease.
7. **Leave of absence** Permission to be absent from duty.
8. **Legal proceeding** Proceedings in the court.
9. **Legally competent** Competent according to law.
10. **Legatee** A person to receive any property under a will.
11. **Legitimate** In accordance with law.
12. **Lessee** A person to whom a lease is made.

13. **Lessor** A person by whom a lease is made.
14. **Levy** To impose a tax or fine.
15. **Liable** Subject to an obligation.
16. **Liable to pay** Responsible for payment.
17. **Libel** Any published statement in writing damaging the reputation of a person.
18. **Licence** A formal authority to do a certain act.
19. **Litigation** The action of carrying on a suit in law.
20. **Loanee company** A company that has received loan.
21. **Lock out** Strike in industrial establishment.
22. **Lump sum** In one instalment.
23. **Lunatic** Affected with lunacy or of unsound mind.

M

1. **Magistrate** An officer charged with criminal jurisdiction of the first instance.
2. **Maim** To cripple.
3. **Malicious** Given to ill will.
4. **Malignantly** Showing intense ill will.
5. **Malinger** To pretend illness in order to escape duty.
6. **Mandatory injunction** An injunction to do a thing.
7. **Marital misbehaviour** Misconduct in marital affairs.
8. **Material fact** Significant truth.
9. **Material question** Substantial question.
10. **Matrimonial** Pertaining to marriage.
11. **Matter in dispute** Something which is the subject of dispute.
12. **Matter of law** A matter relating to law.
13. **Mental infirmity** Unsoundness of mind.
14. **Minutes** The record of the proceedings of a meeting.
15. **Miscarriage** Untimely delivery (of a child).
16. **Misrepresentation** A statement that gives wrong impression.
17. **Modesty** Properiety of behaviour of women.
18. **Moral turpitude** Immoral act.
19. **Moratorium** A legal order to a debtor to postpone payment.
20. **Mortal wound** A fatal wound.
21. **Mutilate** To destroy a part of a body.
22. **Mutual agreement** A reciprocal agreement.

LEGAL VOCABULARY

N

1. **Namely** That is to say.
2. **Narcotic drugs** Drugs having power to induce stuper, sleep or insensibility.
3. **Negligence** Lack of proper care in doing something.
4. **Non-liability** The absence of liability.
5. **Non-observance** A failure to observe rules/orders.
6. **Non-statutory body** A body not established by status/law.
7. **Noting** Something noted in writing.
8. **Notary** A person publically authorised to draw up or attest documents.
9. **Notice** Intimation.
10. **Noxious matter** An injurious matter.
11. **Null and void** That is declared invalid.

O

1. **Oath** An act of swearing.
2. **Oath of allegiance** Appeal to God in witness for loyalty.
3. **Obscene** Something depraved or offensive to modesty or decency.
4. **Obsolete** That is no longer in practice or use.
5. **Obviate** To prevent by anticipatory measures.
6. **Occasioned by omission** Caused just by neglect.
7. **Occupant** A person holding in actual possession.
8. **Officiating** Acting temporarily in an official capacity.
9. **On a conviction** As a result of sentence following a criminal trial.
10. **On probation of good conduct** On a test of good personal behaviour.
11. **Order in writing** Written order.
12. **Order of forfeiture** The order for deprivation of property as a penalty.
13. **Order of remand** An order for sending back a person to custody; sending back the case for retrial.
14. **Original jurisdiction** The jurisdiction of first instance.
15. **Ostensible** Apparent, opposed to real.
16. **Outraging the religious feelings** Hurt religious feelings.
17. **Outside wedlock** Without marrying.
18. **Outstanding claim** A claim that has not been settled.
19. **Overriding** Subordinating all others to itself.
20. **Overrule** To set aside.
21. **Ownership** The fact or state of being on owner.

P

1. **Parole** A conditional and revocable release of a prisoner.
2. **Part payment** Payment to be made in part.
3. **Pass sentence** Pronounce punishment after a trial.
4. **Patent** A grant from the government as an exclusive privilege for a certain tenure.
5. **Pawn** A thing kept as a security for a debt.
6. **Pecuniary liability** An obligation to pay in cash.
7. **Pendency** The state of being pending.
8. **Perjury** Violation of a promise made on oath.
9. **Personate** To create a false appearance of being someone other than oneself.
10. **Pervert** To make use in a wrong way.
11. **Petition writer** A person who writes petitions.
12. **Pillage** Plunder, loot.
13. **Piracy** Robbery in the high seas.
14. **Plaint** A written statement in which a relief is claimed.
15. **Plaintiff** The party who files a suit.
16. **Plea** That is demanded by pleading.
17. **Plead guilty** To admit one's guilt.
18. **Power of attorney** A formal instrument by which one person empowers another to act on his behalf.
19. **Preclude** To exclude someone or something.
20. **Prejudice** Injurious effect on a right or claim.
21. **Preliminary investigation** Introductory leading upto final investigation.
22. **Presiding officer** The judicial officer who presides over the court.
23. **Presume** To regard as proved until evidence to the contrary is forthcoming.
24. **Pretence** Professed rather than real intention.
25. **Privation** Deprivation.
26. **Privilege** A right or immunity granted as a peculiar benefit.
27. **Privy to the offence** A partner in any action or matter.
28. **Probate of will** The officially verified copy of a will.
29. **Probation** The action or process of testing or putting to proof.
30. **Proclaimed offender** An officially declared offender.
31. **Proclamation** An official and formal public announcement.
32. **Promulgation** The official publication of a new law.
33. **Proprietary** Relating to property.
34. **Propriety** Conformity with requirement.
35. **Prosecution** Carrying on of the legal proceedings against a person.
36. **Prosecution witness** A witness appearing on behalf of the prosecution.
37. **Prospecting stage** The stage at which exploratory investigations are going on.
38. **Prospectively** Being operative with regard to the future.

LEGAL VOCABULARY

39. **Prospects** Expectation for something to come.
40. **Proviso** A clause in a legal document upon the observance of which the document becomes valid.
41. **Provocation** The action of exciting anger, resentment or irritation.
42. **Proxy** One acting for the other.
43. **Public good** Anything conductive to the welfare of the community.
44. **Public, make** To declare some policy.
45. **Public office** Position involving exercise of governmental functions.

Q

1. **Quantum** Quantity, a certain amount.
2. **Quash** To annul, to make null and void.
3. **Quasi judicial** Sharing and approximating to what is judicial.
4. **Quorum** The required number of members legally competent to transact business.
5. **Quota** A regulated quantity maintained by governmental rules.

R

1. **Ransoming** To procure the release of a person by payment of the sum.
2. **Ratification** Approval by word or conduct, formal sanction.
3. **Reasonable** Being in agreement with right judgement.
4. **Reasonable charges** Charges that are agreeable to reason.
5. **Rebut** To refute charges.
6. **Reciprocating** Mutually, giving and receiving.
7. **Redeem** To free mortgaged property, fulfil some obligation.
8. **Redress** Reparation of, compensation for a wrong done to someone.
9. **Reinstating** To restore to an original position.
10. **Relevant** Pertinent, relating to the subject.
11. **Relinquish** To give up control of.
12. **Remain in force** Remain operative.
13. **Remuneration** Payment for services rendered.
14. **Repeal** Abrogation of any law.
15. **Repudiation** The act of a denial of a charge.
16. **Requisite** Required by the circumstances.
17. **Requisition** A requirement, the act of taking of possession.
18. **Rescind** To cancel, annul.
19. **Resort** Public place, use as a means.
20. **Respective** Proper, relating to a particular person.
21. **Respondent** A party called upon to respond or answer a petition.
22. **Restitution** The act of restoring.

23. **Retain** To continue to hold.
24. **Retention** To keep in one's own possession.
25. **Retrospective effect** Having effect from a past time.
26. **Revocable** That can be revoked or cancelled.
27. **Riot** An outbreak of active lawlessness.

S

1. **Sabotage** Destruction or damage to property.
2. **Secession** Unlawful activities leading to cede from state or country.
3. **Sedition** Activities tending to treason.
4. **Seduction** The action of seducing a woman for immoral act.
5. **Sentence** The judicial determination of the punishment for a convicted person.
6. **Set aside** To annul, quash an order.
7. **Set out** Laid down, established as law.
8. **Slander** Defamatory words spoken of another.
9. **Solitary confinement** The imprisonment during which a convict is segregated from others and kept alone.
10. **Specific provision** A law enacted for specific purpose.
11. **Specify** To mention definitely.
12. **Standing counsel** Permanent legal advisor.
13. **Statute** A code of law.
14. **Stipulated** As stated or arranged.
15. **Subject to** Under the control.
16. **Subpoena** A judicial write commanding appearance of a person as a witness.
17. **Substantial** Of importance or value.
18. **Suit for damages** A suit filed for claiming compensation.
19. **Summary** Done without delay, summary trial.
20. **Superannuation** (age of) Age of retirement of service.
21. **Superadded** Added over and above.
22. **Superseded** Set aside, replaced by.
23. **Surety** A person who binds himself for the payment of a sum of money for another.

T

1. **Table of mortality** A list of dead persons.
2. **Tampering** Interfering with
3. **Tangible** That can be touched with
4. **Title** A legal right to the possession of the property.
5. **Tenor** The exact words of documents, the time between the date of issue or acceptance of a note.
6. **Termination of the trial** The closure of a trial.

LEGAL VOCABULARY

7. **Traffic** Engage in illegal trade in business or human beings.
8. **Transfer in perpetuity** A transfer for all times to come.
9. **Transferee** One to whom transfer is made.
10. **Trespass** Encroachment or illegal intrusion.
11. **Trial** A judicial examination of a cause either civil or criminal.
12. **Tribunal** A judicial assembly or authority.

U

1. **Ulterior** Subsequent in time, beyond what is seen or stated.
2. **Unauthorised act** An act for which there is no authority.
3. **Unclaimed** Not claimed.
4. **Unconscionable** That cannot be justified with what is right or reasonable.
5. **Unicameral legislature** A legislative body with one house.
6. **Unlawful assembly** An assembly of persons that is not legal.
7. **Unqualified** Not modified, restricted or limited.
8. **Unrebutted** That has not been rebuted or challenged.
9. **Unrepealed** Not repealed or revoked.
10. **Unsustainable** That which cannot be sustained or supported.
11. **Until further orders** Upto the time of any other order.
12. **Usage** (having force of law) A practice supported by law.
13. **Utrine blood** Being descended from a common female but different males.

V

1. **Vacant** Unoccupied.
2. **Valid** Good or adequate in law.
3. **Validate** To make valid.
4. **Vested interest** Implied interest of a person.
5. **Volition** One's interest or decision made after consideration or deliberation.
6. **Voluntary** Of one's free will, impulse or choice.
7. **Vouched** Declared to be true.

W

1. **Warrant** A order empowering someone to make arrest, seizure etc.
2. **Wilful** Intentional, not accidental.
3. **Will** Desire or wish to do anything.
4. **Witness** One who gives evidence in a cause.
5. **Wrongful act** An unjust or injurious act.

CHAPTER 6

Phrasal Verbs

What are Phrasal Verbs?

English language abounds with the use of verbs with prepositions or adverbs to obtain a variety of meanings. The verbs used with prepositions, adverbs or both are defined as phrasal verbs and they denote idiomatic meaning only when taken as a whole. These prepositions and adverbs are known in grammar as particles. e.g.

    (i) Set in .... start.   (*verb + preposition*)
    (ii) Set up .... establish.   (*verb + adverb*)
    (iii) Put up with .... tolerate.   (*verb + adverb + preposition*)

Note These expressions are to be taken **as a whole** .... verb + particles.

When particle is separated from its verb, both verb and particle revert to their individual meanings separately.
    (i) Set, in
    (ii) Set, up
    (iii) Put, up, with

Expressions of Phrasal Verbs

There are two types of expressions of phrasal verbs :
    1. Transitive Expressions
    2. Intransitive Expressions

Transitive Expressions

I. Nouns (as direct objects) are usually placed at the end of transitive expressions or immediately after the verb and before the particle. e.g.
    (i) She **took off** her apron.
    (ii) She **took her apron** off.

II. Pronoun objects are more often used after the verb or before the short words 'off, on, up, down, in, out, away' etc. e.g.
    (i) I went to **see him off**.
    (ii) She **brought him up**.

PHRASAL VERBS 615

III. Pronoun objects are placed at the end of such expressions when verbs cannot be split such as 'look for, account for, call at, call on, look after' etc. e.g.
   (i) I am **looking for** him.
   (ii) You should **look after** her.
   (iii) I **called on** him yesterday.
   (iv) You have to **stand by** me.

Intransitive Expressions

Intransitive expressions of phrasal verbs **do not** admit of any object. e.g.
   (i) She **broke down** in the court.
   (ii) His father **came round** at last.
   (iii) Their marriage **comes off** next month.
   (iv) The meeting **broke up** suddenly.

Phrasal Verbs Currently in Use

1. **Account for** *(explain the reason, answer for)* I can't *account for* his unusual behaviour in this matter.
2. **Ask after** *(ask about the welfare, inquire after)* I met your brother at the party, he *asked after* you.
3. **Ask for** *(request for)* She *asked for* a glass of water.
   Back out *(go back on, withdraw from promise)* He agreed to help but *backed out* at the last moment.
5. **Be in for** [*about to take place (unpleasant)*] On account of his bad habits, he is *in for* trouble.
6. **Bear away** *(win)* Suhani *bore away* the first prize in the dance competition.
7. **Bear on/upon** [*relevant (bearing on)*] Your remarks have no *bearing on* the main problem.
8. **Bear out** *(support the argument, corroborate)* I am sure my classmates will *bear out* my statement.
9. **Bear with** *(to show patience, cooperate)* In view of the heavy losses suffered by the company, the shareholders were requested to *bear with*.
10. **Blow out** *(extinguish)* The candle *blew out* as the gust of wind came in.
11. **Blow over** *(pass off without harm, come to an end)* Don't worry, the crisis are likely to *blow over*.
12. **Blow up** *(explode, start suddenly)* The plan of the enemy to *blow up* the fly-over was foiled by the police.
13. **Break down** *(emotional collapse, stop functioning)* While giving evidence in the court, she *broke down*.
14. **Break into** *(enter by force)* The robbers *broke into* his house last night.
15. **Break off** *(come to an end, unsuccessfully)* The talks between India and China *broke off*.
16. **Break out** [*spread (war, epidemic, fire, riots)*] The fear that aids has *broken out* in India is not unfounded.

17. **Break through** *(discover a secret, major achievement)* There is no hope of *break through* in the murder case.
18. **Break up** [*terminate (meeting, school, session)*] The college will *break up* next week for summer vacation.
19. **Break up with** *(quarrel)* After long and fruitful friendship, the two friends *broken up with* each other.
20. **Break open** *(open by force)* The thief *broke open* the lock and stole money.
21. **Bring about** *(cause to happen)* The administration helped to *bring about* a peaceful settlement.
22. **Bring out** *(explain the meaning, publish)* When asked to explain, she could not *bring out* the meaning of the poem.
23. **Bring round** *(to make one agree, bring to senses)* I was able to *bring* my mother *round* to my views with great difficulty.
24. **Bring up** *(rear, educate)* Fathers are beginning to play a bigger role in *bringing up* their children.
25. **Call at** *(visit a place to meet)* I was *called at* the residence of my boss yesterday.
26. **Call for** *(necessary, require)* For the unity of the country discipline among the people is *called for*.
27. **Call in/Call out** *(send for help)* The police were *called in* without delay by the residents.
28. **Call off** *(suspend or abandon)* We decided to *call off* the strike.
29. **Call on** *(go and visit a person)* It is a protocol for the Prime Minister to call *on* the President.
30. **Call out** *(ask to come for help)* The National Guards has been *called out*.
31. **Call up** *(to telephone, recall)* Many of my friends *called* me *up* to congratulate me.
32. **Call upon** *(appeal, exhort)* He was *called upon* to prove the correctness of the press reports.
33. **Carry away by** *(lose control)* On hearing the news of his success, he was *carried away by* joy.
34. **Carry on** *(continue)* Now it is difficult to *carry on* this business in the teeth of stiff competition.
35. **Carry out** *(implement, obey, execute)* It is not likely that your father will *carry out* the threat of disinheriting you.
36. **Cast away** *(throw away as useless)* We usually give our servants the old clothes, which we *cast away*.
37. **Cast down** *(dejected, downcast)* Now-a-days, he is *cast down* as a result of his failure in the examination.
38. **Cast off** *(release, remove)* Organisation must *cast off* old fashioned practices in order to survive.
39. **Catch up with** *(make up for deficiency, overtake)* He remained ill for many days but *caught up with* the pending work very soon.
40. **Come about** *(happen)* It is not good that such an unfortunate accident *came about*.

PHRASAL VERBS

41. **Come across** *(meet by chance)* I *came across* my old friend in the market yesterday.
42. **Come by** *(get)* How have you *come by* such a precious diamond?
43. **Come of** *(belong to)* Reeta *comes of* a family of freedom fighters.
44. **Come off** *(take place as arranged, fade, get separated)* I was surprised to see that plaster had *come off* the walls.
45. **Come over** *(get over, overcome)* You can *come over* your problems by honest means.
46. **Come round** *(agree, recover from illness)* My father at first refused to let me continue study but he *came round* in the end.
47. **Come upon** *(come across, get by chance)* My friend *came upon* the evidence just by chance.
48. **Cope with** *(manage)* They *coped with* all their problems cheerfully.
49. **Cut down** *(curtail, reduce)* Since you are out of job these days, you must *cut down* your expenditure.
50. **Cut off** *(discontinue, die, remove)* Gas supplies have now been *cut off*.
51. **(Be) cut out for** *(suitable)* He is *cut out for* an administrative career.
52. **Cut out** *(to take a piece from the whole)* He *cut out* a piece of the cake and put it in my plate.
53. **Cut up** *(distressed, cut into small pieces)* She was *cut up* because she had been scolded by her teacher.
54. **Die down** [*gradually disappear (riots, excitement, storm etc.)*] The wind has *died down*.
55. **Die out** *(become out of use or existence)* He thought that the custom had *died out* a long time ago.
56. **Dispose of** *(sell off)* She has decided to *dispose of* her old house.
57. **Dispose to** *(willing, inclined favourably)* My friend is *disposed to* discussing the problems thoroughly.
58. **Do away with** *(eradicate)* We should *do away with* social evils.
59. **Do for** *(serve the purpose)* This book will *do for* the SSC examination.
60. **(have) Done with** *(have no relation)* I *have done with* him because of his dishonesty.
61. **Do without** *(dispense with, to manage without)* We cannot *do without* fan in summer.
62. **Done for/Done in** *(be ruined)* He appears to be *done for* since he has lost heavily in gambling.
63. **Draw up** *(to write, compose, draft)* I was busy *drawing up* plans for the new course.
64. **Draw on/upon** *(to get money from)* He was able to *draw on* vast reserves of talent.
65. **Drop in** *(to pay a short visit)* I thought I'd just *drop in* and see how you were.
66. **Drop out** *(retire in the midst of doing something)* She could not qualify for the selection as she *dropped out* while the race was in progress.

67. **Fall back** *(retreat)* The rioters *fell back* when the police arrived.
68. **Fall back on** *(depend on)* You must save money to *fall back on* it in the old age.
69. **Fall off** *(decrease in number, get separated)* In the wake of roof tragedy, the admissions in the school have *fallen off*.
70. **Fall out** *(quarrel)* The two friends appear to have *fallen out* over a minor issue.
71. **Fall in with** *(agree with)* Instead of challenging the lie, she *fell in with* their views.
72. **Fall through** *(to remain incomplete, fail)* For want of sufficient funds, your new project is likely to *fall through*.
73. **Follow up** *(pursue after the first attempt)* The idea has been *followed up* by a group of researchers.
74. **Get ahead** *(go forward)* You can *get ahead* of your rivals only by hard work.
75. **Get along** *(be friendly)* They just can't *get along* together because of temperamental differences.
76. **Get at** *(reach, understand)* It is very difficult to *get at* the truth.
77. **Get away** *(escape)* They *got away* on scooter.
78. **Get away with** *(without being punished or with little punishment)* Although his fault was serious, he *got away with* light punishment.
79. **Get on** *(progress)* How is your son *getting on* with his study?
80. **Get on with** *(live together, pull with)* Both, husband and wife, are *getting on* well *with* each other.
81. **Get over** *(recover from illness or shock, come over)* He is still trying to *get over* the financial crises.
82. **Get through** *(pass through, succeed)* It is not possible to *get through* the examination without labour.
83. **Get up** *(rise from bed, dressed)* The woman *got up* from her chair with the baby in her arms.
84. **Give away** *(distribute)* She has *given away* jewellery, worth thousands of Rupees.
85. **Give in** *(surrender, agree)* At first she was adamant but at last she *gave in* to the request of her friend.
86. **Give out** *(announce verbally, emit)* It was *given out* that she had failed.
87. **Give up** *(stop, abstain from)* He *gave up* smoking to save money.
88. **Give way** *(collapse under pressure, break)* The contractor was charged with negligence, when the roof of a new building *gave way*.
89. **Given to** *(accustomed to)* He is *given to* smoking.
90. **Go back on** *(withdraw, back out)* One should not *go back on* one's promise.
91. **Go down** *(be believed)* Your excuse will not *go down*.
92. **Go in for** *(buy, practise, to enter a contest)* I thought of *going in for* teaching.
93. **Go off** *(explode and be discharged)* When he was cleaning his gun, it *went off* and killed him.

PHRASAL VERBS

94. **Go on** *(continue)* There is no need to *go on* arguing about it.
95. **Go over** *(examine carefully, look over)* On *going over* the balance sheet of the company, the auditors have found serious mistakes.
96. **Go through** *(read hurriedly, endure)* He didn't lend me the newspaper because he was *going through* it.
97. **Go up** *(rise, increase)* As a result of a sharp rise in prices, the price of washing soap has *gone up*.
98. **Hand out** *(distribute)* *Hand out* the books to the students.
99. **Hand over** *(give charge or authority)* He has not *handed over* the charge to the new manager.
100. **Hang about** *(stay waiting, roam about)* The boys *hanging about* girls' hostel were rounded up by the police.
101. **Hold on** *(carry on, bear difficulties, persist)* Inspite of financial difficulties, he *held on* and succeeded in the long run.
102. **Hold out** *(resist)* When the robbers ran short of ammunition, they could no longer *hold out*.
103. **Hold over** *(postpone)* Most of the bills are *held over* till the next session of the Parliament.
104. **Hold up** *(to stop in order to rob, delay)* The terrorists *held up* the motor car and kept the ladies as hostages.
105. **Jump at** *(accept happily)* He *jumped at* the offer of his boss to accept the job abroad.
106. **Jump to** [*arrive suddenly (conclusion)*] You should never *jump to* conclusions.
107. **Keep from** *(refrain from, not to mix with)* Always *keep from* selfish people because they can harm you anytime.
108. **Keep off** *(keep at a distance)* There was a notice at the site, "*Keep off* the bushes."
109. **Keep on** *(continue)* She *kept on* crying inspite of my assurance of help.
110. **Keep up** *(maintain)* Always try to *keep up* the standard of life even in the face of crises.
111. **Keep up with** *(try to move with, not to fall behind)* Young men should *keep up with* the latest development in international field.
112. **Lay by** *(save money)* The wise men always *lay by* money for their old age.
113. **(Be) laid up with** *(confined to bed)* She is not going out as she *is laid up with* the flu.
114. **Lay down** *(establish a rule, sacrifice, surrender)* The conditions *laid down* by the Department of Health were violated by the nursing homes.
115. **Lay off** *(to discontinue work, dismiss temporarily)* The workers have been *laid off* for want of raw material.
116. **Lay out** *(plan a building, garden etc.)* A number of gardens were *laid out* by the Moghuls.
117. **Let down** *(humiliate, to lower down)* We should never *let down* our friends.
118. **Let into** *(allow to enter)* After repeated requests, he was *let into* the classroom.

119. **Let off** *(to free from punishment, pardon)* She was *let off* by the Principal with light punishment.
120. **Let (somebody) in on** *(share a secret)* I will not *let* her *in on* my plans.
121. **Let up** *(cessation, respite)* There is no *let up* in heat during May.
122. **Live on** *(depend for food (staple food)* The lion is carnivorous and *lives on* flesh.
123. **Live by** *(means/manner)* You must learn to *live by* honest means.
124. **Live off** *(source of income)* They were *living off* rental income.
125. **Look about** *(in search of, on the watch)* The thirsty crow was *looking about* water here and there.
126. **Look after** *(take care of)* In her old age, she has no one to *look after* her.
127. **Look at** *(see carefully)* The boys are *looking at* the sky.
128. **Look back on** *(to think of the past)* People can often *look back* and reflect *on* happy childhood memories.
129. **Look for** *(search for a lost thing)* She was *looking for* her lost books.
130. **Look down upon** *(hate, despise)* It is folly on your part to *look down upon* the poor students.
131. **Look into** *(investigate the matter)* A committee was set up to *look into* the problem.
132. **Look on** *(to see as a spectator)* His parents *looked on* with a triumphant smile.
133. **Look over** *(examine carefully, go over)* The examiner has yet to *look over* practice note books.
134. **Look out** *(watch out, careful, beware)* *Look out*, there is a snake under the bush.
135. **Look out for** *(in search of, on the watch)* He is *looking out for* a decent job.
136. **Look to** *(rely upon, be careful)* The poor *look to* financial help from the government.
137. **Look up** *(consult some book for a word, rise)* Please *look up* this word in the dictionary.
138. **Look upto** *(respect)* His younger brother *looks upto* him and obeys his every order.
139. **Look upon** *(consider, regard)* We must *look upon* social evils as nuisance.
140. **Make off with/away with** *(run away, destroy)* They *made off with* the cash and fled.
141. **Make out** *(understand the meaning)* The police could not *make out* the coded message they intercepted.
142. **Make over** *(transfer possession, convert)* Since she had no legal heir, she *made over* her house in charity.
143. **Make up** [*to end (quarrel), compose*] You should make an effort to *make up* the quarrel with your friend.
144. **Make up for** *(compensate for)* After her long illness, she is trying her best to *make up for* her deficiency in study.

PHRASAL VERBS

145. **Pass away** *(die, expire)* On the *passing away* of his father, I sent him a message of condolence.
146. **Pass for** *(regarded to be)* The Tatas *pass for* philanthropists in the country.
147. **Pass off** *(take place)* The elections are likely to *pass off* peacefully.
148. **Pass oneself off** *(show off)* The hypocrites always *pass themselves off* as honest persons.
149. **Pass through** *(go through, undergo, endure)* He is *passing through* financial difficulties these days.
150. **Pass out** *(leave after completing education)* The cadets will *pass out* next month after completing their training.
151. **Pull down** *(demolish a structure)* Why did they *pull* the shops *down*?
152. **Pull off** *(succeed)* India *pulled off* victory in the last stage of the match.
153. **Pull through** *(recover from illness)* I think she'll *pull through* her serious illness very soon.
154. **Pull up** *(stop, scold)* The students were *pulled up* by the Principal for their misbehaviour with the class teacher.
155. **Pull with** *(live together, get on with)* He is *pulling* well *with* his wife these days.
156. **Put down** *(crush, keep down)* The riots were *put down* by the local police.
157. **Put off** *(postpone, avoid, discourage)* The meeting had to be *put off* because the President could not come.
158. **Put on** *(wear, pretend)* It is difficult to *put on* the appearance of innocence for a long time.
159. **Put out** *(extinguish)* The fire was *put out* suddenly.
160. **Put up** *(stays, question)* He is *putting up* at a hostel these days.
161. **Put up with** *(tolerate patiently)* For an honourable person, it is difficult to *put up with* the haughty behaviour of the Directors.
162. **Round up** *(arrest)* The police *rounded up* anti-social elements last night.
163. **Run after** *(pursue, hanker after)* We should not *run after* money.
164. **Run down** *(criticise, poor health)* As a result of long illness, she has *run down* a lot.
165. **Run into** *(come across, meet by chance)* While walking along the roadside, I *ran into* my old schoolmates.
166. **Run out** *(come to an end)* When the rations *ran out*, the head office was informed.
167. **Run over** *(crush under)* He was *run over* by a speeding car.
168. **Run through** *(waste money)* It is a pity that he has *run through* his fortune over gambling and drinking.
169. **See off** *(to escort a guest for his departure)* His friends were present at the station to *see him off*.
170. **See through** *(discover something hidden, motive)* Man has grown so clever that it is difficult to *see through* his tricks.
171. **Send for** *(summon)* She *sent for* a doctor, when her husband fell ill.

172. **Set about** *(start doing)* As soon as she reached home, she *set about* calling up her friends.
173. **Set aside** *(allocate, strike down, turn down)* The High court *set aside* the verdict of the lower court in this sensitive matter.
174. **Set in** *(begin)* As soon as the summer *sets in*, the reptiles come out of hibernation.
175. **Set off** *(to start a series of events, process, improve)*
    (i) Cosmetics *set off* the natural grace.
    (ii) Privatisation has *set off* the process of liberalisation in foreign trade.
176. **Set up** *(establish)* The factory was *set up* by his uncle.
177. **Set forth** *(start on a journey, explain)* The party will *set forth* its views on globalisation at a public rally.
178. **Set out** *(start on a journey, set forth)* No sooner was the hunter informed of a lion's presence in the forest, than he *set out*.
179. **Sit back** *(relax)* He believes that he has the right to *sit back* while others should work hard.
180. **Sit up** *(stay out of bed, stay up)* She *sat up* till her son returned.
181. **Stand by** *(support, help)* Although he promised to *stand by* me in difficulties, he did not live up to it.
182. **Stand for** *(represent)* TEC *stands for* Technical Education Certificate.
183. **Stand out** *(to be conspicuous)* She *stood out* from the crowd because of her amiable manners.
184. **Stand up for** *(defend)* It is your duty to *stand up* always *for* the poor.
185. **Strike off** *(remove from the list)* His name has been *struck off* the admission list.
186. **Take after** *(resemble)* She always reminds me of her mother since she *takes after* her.
187. **Take down** *(write)* She was busy in *taking down* the dictation, which the teacher was giving.
188. **Take off** *(remove, leave the ground, improve)* It is difficult for Indian economy to *take off* in the absence of heavy investment.
189. **Take over** *(take up responsibility)* The agency tried to *take over* another company.
190. **(Be) Taken to** *(form a habit)* He *took to* wearing black leather jackets.
191. **Take up** *(start a hobby or study, occupy)* He has *taken up* modeling as a career.
192. **Tell upon** *(affect adversely)* I have warned him that heavy work will *tell upon* his health.
193. **(Be) taken in** *(be deceived)* For all your intelligence, you are likely to *be taken in* by impostors.
194. **Take for** *(supposed to be, identify)* I *took* the scoundrel *for* a noble person.
195. **(Be) taken aback** *(be surprised)* I *was taken aback* to hear of the news of his failure.
196. **Talk over** *(discuss a matter)* I agreed to go home and *talk over* the matter.

PHRASAL VERBS

197. **Turn down** *(reject, strike down)* I *turned down* the request of my friend to go to Simla.
198. **Turn off** *(stop, switch off)* Please make it a point to *turn off* water tap before you go out.
199. **Turn on** *(switch on, start)* She *turned on* the shower to take bath.
200. **Turn over** *(change, capsize, upset)* The boat *turned over* and ten persons were drowned.
201. **Turn out** *(prove, reveal, expel)* Nothing ever *turned out* right for me in life.
202. **Turn up** *(arrive, take place)* Who can say what will *turn up* next?
203. **Watch out** *(look out, careful)* If you do not *watch out*, he might harm you.
204. **Wipe away** *(cleanse, remove)* The marks of blood were *wiped away* by the accused.
205. **Wipe out** *(destroy completely)* We must try to *wipe out* poverty from the country.
206. **Wind up** *(bring to an end)* We were forced to *wind up* the business on account of the heavy loss.
207. **Work out** *(solve the problem)* He is very intelligent and can *work out* any difficult problem.
208. **Work up** *(incite, instigate)* The politicians should not try to *work up* communal frenzy.
209. **Work upon** *(influence)* The leader tried to *work upon* the mob.
210. **Hang of something** *(learn about)* As I entered the conference hall, I got the *hang of conspiracy*.
211. **Hang together** *(fit together)* Your present statement does not *hang together* with the past one.
212. **Hang round with** *(spend time together)* I used to *hang round with* my friends on the Mall Road.
213. **Pull in** *(enter)* As the train *pulled in*, the passengers ran here and there.
214. **Set to** *(determined)* If we really *set to*, we can get the work done within time.
215. **Break with** *(tradition and customs)* It is very difficult to *break with* past customers.

Phrasal Verbs Used as Nouns, Verbs and Adjectives

Break

- **Breakout** [noun *(escape from prison)*] The news of prison *breakout* has been confirmed.
- **Outbreak** [noun *(beginning)*] The *outbreak* of the third world war will prove to be a universal disaster.
- **Breakdown** [noun *(of machinery, mental collapse)*] The *breakdown* of the car delayed our departure.
- **Break-through** [noun *(major achievement)*] There is no sign of any *break-through* in the negotiations.

Beat

Offbeat [adjective *(different, unusual)*] They like *offbeat* themes of the novels.

Bring

Upbringing [noun *(bringing up of a person)*] His *upbringing* has been very simple.

Call

Call-up [noun *(a summon for military service)*] He avoided *call-up* pretending illness.

Come

- **Outcome** [noun *(result of an action)*] We are not aware of the *outcome* of the meeting.
- **Overcome** [verb *(solve problem, succeed, defeat)*] Have you *overcome* your financial problems?

Fall

Fall-out [noun *(dangerous radioactive dust, bad result)*] The *fall-out* of globalisation has not proved a blessing for the common man.

Hold

- **Hold-up** [noun *(attempt for robbery)*] The news of *hold-up* made us turn our route.
- **Uphold** [verb *(support what is right, confirm)*] We should *uphold* the dignity of our profession.

Keep

Upkeep [noun *(maintenance)*] The *upkeep* of my office costs me a lot these days.

Let

Outlet [noun *(way of expressing feelings of energy, a place for selling goods)*] Children must have *outlet* to spend their energy.

Lay

- **Layout** [noun *(the way a building or a book is planned)*] He does not like the *layout* of this building.
- **Outlay** [noun *(expenditure)*] The *outlay* on the plan is exorbitant.
- **Lay-off** [noun *(a period when labour is unemployed, an account of no work)*] There is 6 months *lay-off* in our sugar factory.

Look

- **Look-out** [noun *(on watch)*] He is on the *look-out* for a good job.
- **Outlook** [noun *(attitude to life and the world)*] You must have optimistic *outlook*.
- **Overlook** [verb *(fail to see, pardon)*] He was kind enough to *overlook* my fault.

Make

Make-up [noun *(use of cosmetics)*] It takes her long to put on her *make-up*.

PHRASAL VERBS

Mix

Mix-up [noun *(confusion)*] The *mix-up* of the luggage in the cloak room caused the confusion.

Round

Round-up [noun *(bringing people together, arrest)*] The government ordered a *round-up* of the miscreants.

Run

Runaway [noun, adjective *(one who has escaped)*]
- Noun : The *runaways* from the prison were arrested again.
- Adjective : The *runaway* prisoners were arrested again.

Sell

Sell-out [noun *(not a single article left)*] The new edition of the book has been a complete *sell-out*.

Set

- **Outset** [noun *(start, beginning)*] The trainees were warned of the danger at the *outset*.
- **Offset** [verb *(do something to reduce the effect of others)*] The rise in income is generally *offset* by Income Tax.
- **Upset** [noun, verb *(an unexpected situation, unhappy, anxious)*]
  - Noun : The *upset* in the semi finals has completely dashed our hopes.
  - Verb : The behaviour of her daughter has *upset* her.

Take

- **Intake** [noun *(the quantity or number taken in a period)*] The famous institute in our city has a yearly *intake* of 1,500 students.
- **Take-off** [noun *(leaving ground plane)*] The *take-off* of the aeroplane has been delayed.
- **Take-over** [noun *(an offer to buy company)*] The *take-over* of Sahara Airlines has been finalised.
- **Overtake** [verb *(to go past a vehicle)*] *Overtaking* heavy vehicles is sometimes fatal.

Turn

- **Turnover** [noun *(amount received for sale)*] He has a *turnover* of about 5 lakh a year.
- **Overturn** [noun *(capsize)*] The boat *overturned* and sank.
- **Turn-out** [noun *(attendance)*] There was a heavy *turn-out* for the opening ceremony.

Cumulative Exercise

Directions *Use the following phrasal verbs in sentences of your own.*

1. Act up	2. Act upon	3. Add up
4. Ask out	5. Back off	6. Back up
7. Beg off	8. Bear down	9. Beat off
10. Bone up on	11. Brush up on	12. Burn down
13. Butt in	14. Butter up	15. Calm down
16. Catch on	17. Check in (to)	18. Cheer up
19. Chicken out	20. Chip in	21. Count on
22. Cut back (on)	23. Drag on	24. Drop by
25. Eat out	26. Figure out	27. Fill in
28. Get rid of	29. Goof off	30. Grow up
31. Hang up	32. Iron out	33. Jack up
34. Knock out	35. Look forward to	36. Look over
37. Mix up	38. Nod off	39. Pitch in
40. Rip off	41. Slip up	42. Show up
43. Tell (someone) off	44. Throw away	45. Try out
46. Wait on	47. Watch out for	48. Wear out
49. Wrap up	50. Zonk out	

Previous Years' Questions

I. Directions *Use the following phrasal verbs in sentences of your own.* [CAPF, 2013]

1. To do away with
2. To put up with
3. Turn down
4. Do without
5. Fall back upon

II. Directions *Use the following phrasal verbs in sentences of your own so as to bring out their correct meaning.* [CAPF, 2012]

1. Put up with
2. Fall out [CAPF, 2011]
3. Make out [CAPF, 2011]
4. Deal in [CAPF, 2011]
5. Call on
6. Get off
7. Hold back

Answers

Cumulative Exercise

1. **Act up** [*misbehave (for people); not work properly (for machines)*]
   (i) The babysitter had a difficult time. The children *acted up* all evening.
   (ii) I guess I'd better take my car to the garage. It's been *acting up* lately.

2. **Act upon** *(in accordance with)* The captain, *acting upon* the secret information, caught the militants.

3. **Add up** *(logically fit together)*
   (i) His theory is hard to believe, but his research *adds up*.
   Note *This phrasal verb is often negative.*
   (ii) His theory seems, at first, to be plausible, but the facts in his research don't *add up*.

4. **Ask out** *(ask for a date)* Shalu has a new boy friend. Johny *asked* her *out* last night.

5. **Back off** *(move away to avoid problem)* They *backed off* in horror.

6. **Back up** *(move backward; move in reverse)*
   (i) You missed the lines in the parking space. You'll have to *back up* and try again.
   (ii) The people waiting in line are too close to the door. We won't be able to open it unless they *back up*.

7. **Beg off** *(decline an invitation; ask to be excused from doing something)* At first, Lily said she would be at the party. Later she *begged off*.

8. **Bear down** *(to crush by force)* She was successful in *bearing down* the opposition group.

9. **Beat off** *(to repulse, to drive back)* Indian Army successfully *beat off* the enemy forces.

10. **Bone up on** *(review/study thoroughly for a short time)* If you're going to travely to the UK, you'd better *bone up on* your English.

11. **Brush up on** *(review/study thoroughly for a short time)* If you're going to travel to the UK, you'd better *brush up on* your English.

12. **Burn down** *(become destroyed/consumed by fire)* Lightning struck Mr Kalhan's barn last night. It *burned down* before the fire fighters arrived.

13. **Butt in** [*impolitely interrupt (a conversation, an action)*] Hey, you! Don't *butt in*! Wait for your turn!

14. **Butter up** *(praise someone excessively with the hope of getting some benefit)* I guess Mohan really wants to be promoted. He has been *buttering* his boss *up* all the week.

15. **Calm down** *(become calm/less agitated or upset; help someone become calm/less agitated or upset)* "Why are you so upset? Sheela didn't intend to spill orange juice on you. *Calm down!* I know Raju is upset, but can you *calm* him *down*? He's making so much noise that is irritating everyone in the office."

16. **Catch on** *(develop understanding or knowledge of something)* Bholu had never used a computer until he took this class, but he *caught on* very quickly and is now one of the best students.

17. **Check in** (to) *(register for/at a hotel, conference, etc; let someone know officially that you have arrived)* My plane will arrive around 5:00 pm. I should be able to *check into* the hotel by 6:00 or 6:30.

18. **Cheer up** *(help someone feel less worried/depressed/sad)* Shalu's brother was depressed about not getting a promotion, so she sent him a funny card *to cheer* him *up*.

19. **Chicken out** *(lose the courage or confidence to do something-often at the last minute)* Sahu said he was going to ask Tili for a date, but later on *chickened out*.

20. **Chip in** [*contribute/donate (often money) to/for something done by a group*] We're going to buy a birthday cake for our boss and I'm collecting donations. Do you want to *chip in*?

21. **Count on** *(depend on; trust that something will happen or that someone will do as expected)* I'm *counting on* you to wake me up tomorrow. I know I won't hear the alarm.
22. **Cut back (on)** *(use less of something)* "You drink too much coffee. You should *cut back*." "You should *cut back on* the amount of coffee that you drink".
23. **Drag on** *(last much longer than expected or is necessary)* I thought the meeting would be a short one, but it *dragged on* for more than three hours.
24. **Drop by** [*visit informally (and usually without scheduling a specific time)*] If you're in town next month, we'd love to see you. Please try to *drop by* the house.
25. **Eat out** *(have a meal in a restaurant)* I'm too tired to cook. Why don't we *eat out*?
26. **Figure out** *(logically find the answer to a problem; solve a problem by thinking about it carefully)* For a long time, I couldn't understand the last problem, but I finally *figured* it *out*.
27. **Fill in** *(add information to a form)* The office needs to know your home address and phone number. Could you *fill* them *in* on this form?
28. **Get rid of** *(dismiss someone; fire someone from a job; cause someone to leave)* The treasurer of the ABC company was spending too much money, so the company President *got rid of* him.
29. **Goof off** *(be lazy; do nothing in particular)* "Do you have any special plans for your vacation?" "No. I'm just going to stay home and *goof off*."
30. **Grow up** *(behave responsibly; behave as an adult, not as a child)* "Lee really irritates me sometimes. He's really silly and childish." "I agree. I wish he would *grow up*."
31. **Hang up** *(end a phone conversation by replacing the receiver)* I'd like to talk longer, but I'd better *hang up*. My sister needs to make a call.
32. **Iron out** *(mutually reach an agreement; mutually resolve difficulties)* Yes, I know, we disagree on lots of things, Susan, but we can *iron* them *out*.
33. **Jack up** *(raise/lift by using a jack)* We'll have to *jack* the back of the car *up* before we can change the tire.
34. **Knock out** *(make unconscious)*
    (i) The boxing match ended, when one boxer *knocked* the other one *out*.
    (ii) That medicine really *knocked* me *out*. I slept for 14 hours straight!
35. **Look forward to** *(anticipate pleasantly; think about a pleasant thing before it happens)* I'm really '*looking forward*' to vacation. I can't wait for it to begin!
36. **Look over** *(check; review)* I think, I may have some typos (typing errors) in this report. Could you *look* it *over*?
37. **Mix up** *(cause to become confused)* I didn't complete the assignment because I didn't know how. The directions *mixed* me *up*.
38. **Nod off** [*fall sleep (usually unintentionally)*] The speech was so boring that several people in the audience *nodded off* before it was finished.
39. **Pitch in** *(help; join together to accomplish something)* We'll be finished soon, if everyone *pitches in*.
40. **Rip off** *(cheat; take advantage of; charge too much)* Don't even think about buying a car there. They'll *rip* you *off*.
41. **Slip up** *(make a mistake)* You *slipped* up here. The amount should be ₹ 54172.00, not ₹ 54127.00.
42. **Show up** *(arrive; appear)* The boss was very upset, when you didn't *show up* for the meeting. What happened?
43. **Tell (someone) off** *(speak to someone bluntly and negatively, saying exactly what she/he did wrong)* Julie was really angry at Bob, she *told him off* in front of all of us.
44. **Throw away** *(discard; put in the garbage)* You shouldn't *throw* those newspaper *away*; they're recyclable.

PHRASAL VERBS

45. **Try out** *(use a machine briefly to determine how well it works)* I really like the way this car looks. May I *try* it *out*?

46. **Wait on** [*serve (usually customers in a restaurant, shop, etc)*] I want to make a complaint. The person, who just *waited on* me was very impolite.

47. **Watch out for** *(be careful of; beware of)*
    (i) There's a school at the end of this block. *Watch* out *for* children crossing the street.
    (ii) If you take that road, *watch out for* ice during the winter.

48. **Wear out** *(cause to become exhausted; cause to become very tired)* I had four different meetings today. They *wore* me *out*.

49. **Wrap up** *(finish something; bring something to a conclusion)* We've been talking about the problem for nearly three hours. I hope we'll be able to *wrap* the discussion *up* soon.

50. **Zonk out** *(fall asleep quickly because of exhaustion)* I intended to go shopping after work, but I was so tired that I *zonked out* as soon as I got home.

Previous Years' Questions

I. 1. **To do away with** *(eradicate)* We should *do away with* social evils.
   2. **To put up with** *(tolerate patiently)* For an honourable person, it is difficult *to put up with* the haughty behaviour of the Directors.
   3. **Turn down** *(reject, strike down)* I *turned down* the request of my friend to go to Goa.
   4. **Do without** *(dispense with, to manage without)* We cannot *do without* Air Conditioner in summer.
   5. **Fall back upon** *(depend on)* She has saved much money to *fall back upon* in old age.

II. 1. **Put up with** *(bear someone)* I could not *put up with* her and broke-up.
    2. **Fall out** *(to quarrel)* The two girls *fell out* over the trifle and it became worse.
    3. **Make out** *(understand)* She spoke so softly in my ear that I could not *make out* what she said.
    4. **Deal in** *(to do a business of)* His father *deals in* shares.
    5. **Call on** *(to go and visit someone)* I was *called on* by my friend to his home.
    6. **Get off** *(begin something)* India *got off* to a flying start in the last match.
    7. **Hold back** *(to resist)* I *held* myself *back* during the tense situation.

CHAPTER 7

Idioms and Phrases

The command of idiomatic expressions in any language is pre-requisite for expressive writing and comprehension. Phrasal verbs, idiomatic adjectives and noun phrases and idiomatic pairs of nouns, adjectives and adverbs comprise such a vast portion of idiomatic expressions that it is nearly impossible to deal with them comprehensively in such a short space. However, this chapter contains the most important usages that are indispensable for many competitive examination. Students would do well to consult the dictionary for further improvement in this field.

A

1. **At one's wit's end** (*perplexed*) Sohan was *at his wit's end* to find that his younger brother has taken poison.
2. **At one's fingertips** (*complete knowledge*) All the rules of synthesis are *at his fingertips*.
3. **At the spur of the moment** (*without delay*) In an interview, we must reply *at the spur of the moment*.
4. **All in all** (*most important*) As he was the only son in a big family, he was *all in all* in his home.
5. **At close quarters** (*close examinations*) Many of my friends proved selfish *at close quarters*.
6. **Apple-pie order** (*in perfect order*) On the eve of inspection, everything was kept in *apple-pie order*.
7. **Above board** (*honest and straightforward*) He is known for his *above board* conduct.
8. **Above all** (*before everything else*) *Above all*, he is blunt and dare devil.
9. **As fit as a fiddle** (*strong and healthy*) He has recovered from illness and now he is *as fit as a fiddle*.

IDIOMS AND PHRASES

10. **At random** *(aimlessly)* The militants fired *at random* killing a lot of innocent persons.
11. **At a loose end** *(unoccupied, idle)* Now-a-days, he is *at a loose end* because he has wound up his business.
12. **At logger heads** *(to be at strife)* The partners of our firm are *at logger heads* these days.
13. **At odds** *(in dispute)* The members of the group were *at odds* over the selection procedure.
14. **An apple of discord** *(cause of quarrel)* Ancestral property is *an apple of discord* between the two sisters.
15. **At cross purposes** *(have conflicting intentions)* How can there be peace in their family, when husband and wife are *at cross purposes*.
16. **After one's own heart** *(to one's liking)* When Deepa met a man *after her own heart*, she got married to him.
17. **At the bottom of** *(to be mainly responsible for)* It was found later that Shanu was *at the bottom of* the whole trouble.
18. **At a loss** *(to be unable to decide)* I am *at a loss* to know what to do.
19. **At dagger's drawn** *(to have bitter enmity)* The quarrel between the two brothers has grown more bitter now and they are *at dagger's drawn*.
20. **At large** *(abscond, to keep unchained)* People keep their dogs *at large* at night.
21. **At sea** *(applied to a person confused)* My sister is quite *at sea* in Maths; she cannot solve a single problem.
22. **Add fuel to the flame or fire** *(to make matter worse)* The attempt to suppress the agitation of the strikers only *added fuel to the flame*.
23. **At sixes and sevens** *(in disorder)* There was a robbery in our neighbourhood last night and when I entered the house to inquire, everything was *at sixes and sevens*.
24. **Assume airs** *(to pretend superiority)* The rich are in the habit of *assuming airs* in the presence of their poor relatives.
25. **Argus eyed** *(careful, observant)* As a politician, he is *Argus eyed* and never overlooks even a small matter.
26. **At a stone's throw** *(very close)* My friend's house is *at a stone's throw* from mine.

B

1. **By hook or by crook** *(by one means or another)* He is determined to obtain first division in his class *by hook or by crook*.
2. **Bear the brunt of** *(to bear the main shock of)* The poor have to *bear the brunt of* increasing prices.
3. **Bell the cat** *(to take first step at personal risk)* Many people can boast of their bravery, but very few can *bell the cat*.

4. **Bid defiance** *(to ignore)*—Rohan *bade defiance* to his father's wish of becoming a doctor and instead became an engineer.
5. **Blow one's trumpet** *(to praise oneself)* No one likes to talk to those, who are always *blowing their own trumpet*.
6. **Break the news** *(to give bad news)* He *broke the news* of her husband's death very gently so as to lessen the intensity of the shock.
7. **Burn a hole in one's pocket** *(money spent quickly)* Money given to a spendthrift only *burns a hole in his pocket*.
8. **Bury the hatchet** *(to make peace)* India and Pakistan must *bury the hatchet* to bring about peace to the region.
9. **Beside oneself** *(to feel excessively)* Due to the accidental death of his wife, he was *beside himself* with grief.
10. **Bad blood** *(bitter relations)* The riots have created *bad blood* between the two communities in India.
11. **Black and blue** *(to beat mercilessly)* The thief was beaten *black and blue* by the police.
12. **Beat about the bush** *(to talk in a round about manner)* We should always come to the point and should not *beat about the bush*.
13. **Beat the air** *(to make useless efforts)*—Some speakers merely *beat the air* in speech while preaching.
14. **Build castles in the air** *(to make visionary schemes)*—Many people, who live in dreams *build castles in the air* and do not succeed in life.
15. **Break the ice** *(to speak first after prolonged silence)* In the meeting, Rajesh *broke the ice* and suggested the plan to solve the problem.
16. **Bring to book** *(to punish, to call to account)* The manager was *brought to book* for his negligence.
17. **Breathe one's last** *(to die)* He *breathed his last* in the prime of his life.
18. **Back stairs influence** *(by unfair means)* These days many persons are given good posts through *back stairs influence*.
19. **Bird's eye view** *(concise view)* We had a *bird's eye view* of the whole fair from the top of a giant wheel.
20. **Bolt from the blue** *(sudden or unexpected shock)* The news of her husband's death in the air crash came to her as a *bolt from the blue*.
21. **Burn one's boats** *(point of no return)* We had *burnt our boats* by declaring that we were not going to sign CTBT.
22. **By the by** *(by the way)* *By the by*, what is your age?
23. **Be upto** *(to be equal to)* He *is upto* all the tricks of the trade to grind his own axe.
24. **Bated breath** *(in anxiety, expectancy)* The fate of the match hung in balance and every body waited for the result with *bated breath*.
25. **Bandy words** *(to wrangle, to argue)* Obedient children don't *bandy words* with their parents, when they are advised.

IDIOMS AND PHRASES

26. **Bee in one's bonnet** *(to be fussy)* She seems to have a *bee in her bonnet* because she is always finding faults with others.
27. **Bite the dust** *(to be defeated)* Pakistan had to *bite the dust* in the final of the World Cup.
28. **Blue stocking** *(educated but pedantic lady)* No body likes to mix with her because she is a *blue stocking*.
29. **Book worm** *(a person in the habit of pouring over books)* He has no time for social activities because he is *a book worm*.
30. **Bring down the house** *(receive applause)* Though it was his maiden speech, he *brought down the house* because of his oratory skill.
31. **Brow beat** *(to bully)* The President of the college union always tries to *brow beat* the students opposing him.
32. **Bad egg** *(a worthless)* He comes of a noble family but he himself is a *bad egg*.
33. **Beside the mark** *(irrelevant)* No body agreed with him because his arguments were *beside the mark*.
34. **Burn one's fingers** *(to get into trouble)* Those, who interfere in the affairs of others, often *burn their fingers*.
35. **Brown study** *(reverie, day-dream)* He could not follow the significance of my offer. He was in *brown study*.
36. **Bank on** *(depend on, count on)* The rich always *bank on* money to get things done.
37. **Blaze the trail** *(to start a movement)* Surinder Nath Bannerjee *blazed the trail* of Indian National Movement.
38. **Bull in a China shop** *(one, who causes damage)* Most of the leaders of the freedom struggle have proved *bulls in a China shop*.
39. **By the rule of thumb** *(according to practical experience)* In older times, business was run *by the rule of thumb*.
40. **Big draw** *(a huge attraction)* The match between India and Pakistan is always a *big draw*.
41. **Broken reed** *(support that failed)* When he needed help, his friend proved a *broken reed*.
42. **By the skin of the teeth** *(narrowly)* He escaped death in the accident *by the skin of the teeth*.
43. **Bone of contention** *(cause of quarrel)* Since India has got independence, Kashmir has been a *bone of contention* between India and Pakistan.
44. **Bit/Piece of one's mind** *(to scold)* My father wrote to my brother giving a *piece of his mind* about his insulting conduct.
45. **Born with silver spoon** *(to be born in a rich family)* My friend does not have to worry about spending any amount of money as she is *born with a silver spoon* in her mouth.
46. **Burn candle at both ends** *(squander)* After the death of his father, he is *burning candle at both ends*.
47. **By fits and starts** *(irregularly)* If we study *by fits and starts*, we can never be successful in our exams.

48. **By dint of** *(by force of)* He achieved success in life *by dint of* hard work.
49. **Blow hot and cold** *(to speak in favour and against at the same time)* Do not trust those, who *blow hot and cold* in the same breath.
50. **By and by** *(gradually)* He is recovering *by and by* after long illness.
51. **Blue blood** *(aristocratic blood)* Though my friend has *blue blood,* yet her conduct is very mean and vulgar.

C

1. **Carry matters with a high hand** *(to deal with a person strictly)* The owner of the industry *carried matters with a high hand* and expelled two workers, who were caught doing mischief in the office.
2. **Clip one's wings** *(to weaken the power)* My elder sister is very ambitious but my mother will surely *clip her wings.*
3. **Come home to** *(to understand)* Seema wanted to be a teacher in the college but soon it *came home to* her that she was not fit for the job as she was only a graduate.
4. **Come to a standstill** *(come to a sudden stop)* When we were going to Mussourie yesterday, our car *came to a standstill* right in the middle of the journey.
5. **Come off with flying colours** *(to come out successfully)* The final football match was very crucial but finally we won and *came off with flying colours.*
6. **Cross one's mind** *(to occur to oneself)* In the examination hall, it *crossed my mind* that I had left my pen outside on the table.
7. **Cry for the moon** *(to wish for something impossible)* The hope of winning the lottery amounting to lakhs of rupees is simply *crying for the moon.*
8. **Carry favour with** *(win favour of somebody)* Neena gave a lot of costly presents to her science teacher to *carry favour with* him.
9. **Call a spade a spade** *(to speak plainly)* People often get angry, when one *calls a spade a spade.*
10. **Carry the day** *(to win a victory)* After initial setback, India *carried the day* in the Test match.
11. **Cut a sorry figure** *(to give a poor show)* The speaker *cut a sorry figure* in the meeting.
12. **Cry over spilt milk** *(repent)* Careless students often have to *cry over spilt milk* during the exams.
13. **Cut one's coat according to one's cloth** *(to live within one's means)* A wise man always *cuts his coat according to his cloth,* if he wants to be successful in his life.
14. **Call names** *(to abuse)* Neeta *called* me *names,* so she was severely punished by the teacher.
15. **Curtain lecture** *(a reproof by wife to her husband)* My brother never pays any attention to his wife's *curtain lecture* and does what he thinks.

IDIOMS AND PHRASES

16. **Chip of the old block** *(resembling one's parents in habits)* My friend is quite helpful like her father, so she is a *chip of the old block*.
17. **Cave in** *(yield)* Although our team fought bravely, yet had to *cave in* before the superior power play of the opposite team.
18. **Cloven hoof** *(the evil intention)* The Chinese showed the *cloven hoof* in 1962.
19. **Cut throat** *(tough)* It is very difficult for Indian Industry to survive in the teeth of international *cut throat* competition.
20. **Call in question** *(doubt)* You should not *call in question* my honesty.
21. **Cheek by jowl** *(close together)* In metropolitan cities it is common that affluence and poverty exist *cheek by jowl*.
22. **Come to a pass** *(a difficult situation)* The things have *come to* such *a* pretty *pass* that he is financially ruined.
23. **Close shave** *(a narrow escape)* As he was driving recklessly in a crowded street, he had a *close shave*.
24. **Cut and dried** *(readymade form)* There is no *cut and dried* formula for success in life.
25. **Clinch the issue** *(decide the matter)* When he agreed to leave the house for good, it *clinched the issue* in favour of his wife.
26. **Carry one's point** *(win approval)* After heated discussion, he was able to *carry his point*.
27. **Chequered/Checkered career** *(full of ups and downs)* Politicians have generally *chequered career* all along.
28. **Cut both ends** *(argue in favour of both sides)* He is ambiguous because he always *cuts both ends*.
29. **Cock sure** *(very sure and certain)* He was so *cock sure* of his success that he applied for the job before the declaration of the result.
30. **Cock a snook** *(to show impudent contempt)* She is so proud of her wealth that she always *cocks a snook* at the acts of her husband.
31. **Chapter and verse** *(in full detail, to give proof)* He has such a sharp memory that he can narrate the story *chapter and verse*.
32. **Cool one's heels** *(to be kept waiting)* He had to *cool his heels* before he could meet the President of the party.
33. **Carrot and stick policy** *(reward and punishment)* A successful businessman follows the *carrot and stick policy* towards his employees.
34. **Come in handy** *(to be useful)* Take some woollen clothes. They may *come in handy* in Simla.

D

1. **Dig the grave** *(to tarnish, to destroy)* By taking side of the culprit he *dug the grave* of his reputation.
2. **Draw the long bow** *(exaggerate)* By calling him the best politician of the world, his followers *draw the long bow*.

3. **Die in harness** *(die while working)* Our Principal *died in harness*.
4. **Dutch courage** *(bravery under alcoholic influence)* Drunkards often indulge in *Dutch courage* and boast of their imaginary qualities.
5. **Dare devil** *(fearless person)* Only *a dare devil* can face the land mafia.
6. **Dead broke** *(penniless)* On account of reckless spending he is *dead broke* these days.
7. **Down and out** *(poor and ruined)* After a slump in share market, he is *down and out* these days.
8. **Draconian law** *(extremely severe law)* During emergency in 1975 the Government imposed *Draconian laws* to subdue opposition.
9. **Die-hard** *(persistent in struggle)* He is a *die-hard* person and will not easily surrender.
10. **Days of reckoning** *(time to answer for one's actions)* You may commit crime after crime but *days of reckoning* are never far off.
11. **Down in the mouth** *(out of elements)* Now-a-days, he is *down in the mouth* because he has suffered heavy loss in business.
12. **Dog in the manger** *(a person, who prevents others from enjoying what he himself cannot)* By disrupting Parliament Session, the Congress is following a *dog in the manger* policy.
13. **Damp squib** *(complete failure)* The visit of our Foreign Minister to China proved a *damp squib* on border issue.

E

1. **Eat humble pie** *(to apologise)* Inspite of his constant bragging, he lost the match and had to *eat humble pie*.
2. **Eat one's words** *(take a statement back)* I warned my friend to be very careful in her speech otherwise she would have *to eat her own words*.
3. **End in smoke/fiasco** *(come to nothing)* He spoke a lot about his new film but it all *ended in smoke* and it flopped on the box office.
4. **Egg on** *(to urge somebody)* The Captain *egged* the players *on* to continue to play foul till the end of the match.
5. **Eke out** *(supplement income)* To *eke out* his income, he also works as a part time accountant in the evening.
6. **Every dog has his day** *(good fortune comes sooner or later)* Don't be disappointed. It is truly said that *every dog has his day*.
7. **Ever and Anon** *(now and then, sometimes)* He visits his parents *ever and anon*.
8. **(An) eye wash** *(a pretence)* My friend's promise to help me just proved *an eye-wash*.

IDIOMS AND PHRASES

F

1. **Flesh and blood** *(human nature)* People in some villages are so poor that their sufferings are more than a *flesh and blood* can endure.
2. **Fish in troubled waters** *(to take advantage of the trouble of others)* Shrewd businessmen *fish in troubled waters,* when there is scarcity of things.
3. **Follow suit** *(to act in a like manner)* If you do not obey your elders, your children will *follow suit.*
4. **Fall flat** *(to have no effect)* The minister's speech *fell flat* on the audience.
5. **Fight shy of** *(to attempt to avoid a thing or a person)* I generally *fight shy of* confronting my elder sister as she is in the habit of making sickening comments.
6. **Fabian policy** *(policy of delaying decisions)* Politicians generally follow a *Fabian policy* in order to keep everyone satisfied.
7. **For no rhyme or reason** *(any reason whatsoever)* Seema did not appear for her final examinations *for no rhyme or reason.*
8. **Fight to the finish** *(fight to the end)* Indian Army has vowed to *fight to the finish* and turn every intruder out of Indian Territory.
9. **Few and far between** *(very rare)* His visits to his home town are *few and far between* because of his expanding business.
10. **Flog a dead horse** *(to revive interest in old matters)* The rivals always *flog a dead horse* to insult their enemies.
11. **Fool's errand** *(useless undertaking)* His visit to the States to earn money proved to be a *fool's errand.*
12. **Fall foul of** *(to quarrel)* They were once bosom friends, but now they have *fallen foul of* each other.
13. **Fly off the handle** *(to lose one's temper)* When his father questioned him about money, he *flew off the handle.*
14. **French leave** *(to be absent without permission)* Those, who take *French leave,* should not be pardoned.
15. **Fair and square** *(upright)* My father advised me to be *fair and square* in business dealings.
16. **Feather one's own nest** *(to provide first for oneself)* Our leaders are busy *feathering* their *own nests* and have no concern for the poor.
17. **From pillar to post** *(rush in all directions and suffer much harassment)* You may rush *from pillar to post,* but you stand no chance of getting what you want without a bribe.
18. **Foot the bill** *(bear expenses)* Although he hosted the feast, his brother had to *foot the bill.*
19. **Fair weather friend** *(selfish friend)* A *fair weather friend* will never stand by you in difficulty.
20. **Flash in the pan** *(sudden success)* The success of Indian cricket team is never constant and steady. It is generally a *flash in the pan.*

21. **Fit to hold a candle to** *(match for, equal in quality)* He is the son of a famous writer, but he is not *fit to hold a candle to* his father.
22. **The Fourth Estate** *(the press)* The newspaper is regarded as *the Fourth Estate* of the state.
23. **Feather in one's cap** *(additional success)* His success in his MA exams has added a new *feather in his cap*.
24. **Fly in the face of** *(to defy)* It is disobedience on their part to *fly in the face of* the orders of the Principal.

G

1. **Gain ground** *(to succeed slowly and steadily)* The belief in the abolition of dowry system is *gaining ground*.
2. **Get off scot free** *(to escape without punishment)* A murderer can also very easily *get off scot free* for lack of evidence.
3. **Grease the palm** *(to bribe)* Now-a-days, if you want to get your work done, you will have to *grease the palm* of someone or the other.
4. **Gird up the loins** *(to prepare for hard work)* Indians must *gird up the loins* to face any foreign attack on their country.
5. **Go to the dogs** *(to be ruined)* The rich industrialist will *go to the dogs* because of his son's bad habits.
6. **Get oneself into a mess** *(to drift into trouble)* Due to sheer ignorance, Vijay seems to have *got himself into a mess* in his office.
7. **Give a wide berth** *(to avoid)* We should always *give a wide berth* to all selfish and mean persons.
8. **Gentleman at large** *(an unreliable person)* We must not believe a *gentleman at large*.
9. **Good Samaritan** *(one, who helps strangers)* He is *a good Samaritan* because he always comes to the help of the old and the children in difficulties.
10. **Give a good account of oneself** *(to act creditably)* As the eldest son of his family, he *gave a good account of himself* when calamity befell the family.
11. **Give the devil his due** *(give credit to a worthless person for his good qualities)* We should *give the devil his due* for his good qualities.
12. **Green horn** *(inexperienced)* Though a *green horn* in political field, he appears to have a bright future.
13. **Give up the ghost** *(pass away, die)* After long illness, he *gave up the ghost* last week.
14. **Go the whole hog** *(to do something thoroughly)* You will have to *go the whole hog* to come out of this mess.
15. **Get into a scrape** *(awkward situation)* He *got into a scrape* when his wife refused to let him help his sister.
16. **Go broke** *(become bankrupt)* As a result of heavy gambling, he had to *go broke* in the long-run.

IDIOMS AND PHRASES

17. **Get into hot waters** *(get into trouble)* He *got into hot waters* by marrying a girl of another caste.
18. **Give currency** *(to make publicly known)* The government has refused *to give currency* to a number of scams.
19. **Great hand** *(expert)* He is a *great hand* at organising social parties.
20. **Get down to brass tacks** *(to deal with the matter straight)* Instead of wasting time in discussion, please *get down to brass tacks*.
21. **Give one a long rope** *(to let someone commit mistakes)* He never *gives* his employees *a long rope*.
22. **Good turn** *(an act of kindness)* He did me a *good turn* by recommending me for the post of Vice-President.

H

1. **Hold water** *(sound, tenable)* His statement will not *hold water* as it is not based on facts.
2. **Hang together** *(support one another)* The two statements delivered by the leader of the party do not *hang together*.
3. **Hope against hope** *(hope inspite of disappointment)* Sohan's case is very weak and everybody knows that finally he will lose, but he is still *hoping against hope*.
4. **Have an axe to grind** *(to have a selfish interest)* Reema is very selfish, but the way she is being polite with everyone gives the impression that she *has an axe to grind*.
5. **Have the gift of the gab** *(art of speaking)* Meena is not highly qualified, but she *has the gift of the gab*.
6. **Hit below the belt** *(to strike unfairly)* We should always face the enemy boldly and never *hit* him *below the belt*.
7. **Hold one's tongue** *(to keep quiet)* We should always *hold our tongue* before our elders.
8. **Herculean task** *(very difficult)* It is a *Herculean task* to root out corruption in India.
9. **Haul over the coals** *(to take to task)* She was *hauled over the coals* by her parents for her misconduct.
10. **Have one's finger in everyone's pie** *(to partake of something)* My best friend likes to *have her finger in everyone's pie* as she is in the habit of meddling with the affairs of others.
11. **Halcyon days** *(peaceful days)* The days we spend in our school life are the *halcyon days* of our life.
12. **Have an iron will** *(strong will)* If we have to live among the mean and selfish people, we must *have an iron will*.
13. **Hold out an olive branch** *(offer of peace)* The terrorists are not prepared to *hold out an olive branch* to the Government of India.

14. **Hanky Panky** *(jugglery)* None of this *hanky panky*, tell me the truth.
15. **Have feet of clay** *(full of faults)* The CBI inquiry has revealed that many ministers *have a feet of clay*.
16. **Heart and soul** *(devotedly)* He took part in the annual function *heart and soul*.
17. **Hard and fast** *(strict)* No *hard and fast* rule is laid down about being regular in the college.
18. **Hang fire** *(remain unsolved)* Kashmir problem has been *hanging fire* for many years.
19. **High and dry** *(a difficult situation)* He was left *high and dry* by his business partners.
20. **Hit the nail on the head** *(to do the right thing at the right time)* He *hit the nail on the head* by resigning his job.
21. **Hobson's choice** *(no alternative)* The employees in the private sector have *Hobson's choice* because they are forced to accept what they are ordered to do.
22. **Have too many irons in the fire** *(doing many things at a time)* He is fickle minded and *has too many irons in the fire*.
23. **Hold in abeyance** *(postpone)* For lack of funds the district administration has *held* the construction of road *in abeyance*.
24. **High and mighty** *(proud persons)* The *high and mighty* forget that everything in the world is transient.
25. **Hard nosed attitude** *(aggressive)* I don't know why my teacher always has a *hard nosed attitude* towards me.
26. **Hold in leash** *(to restrain)* As a responsible leader of a party you must *hold* criticism of party workers *in leash*.
27. **Head and shoulders** *(superior)* Shri Atal Behari Vajpayee is *head and shoulder* above his predecessors.
28. **Hold a brief** *(to defend someone)* It is very improper for parents to *hold a brief* for their children who are in the wrong.
29. **Hush money** *(a bribe)* He managed to escape punishment by paying *hush money*.
30. **Hold at bay** *(to prevent enemy from coming)* Maharana Partap could not *hold* the Mughal army *at bay* for long.
31. **Hit the jack pot** *(unexpected success)* He *hit the jack pot* by investing his money in shares.
32. **Helter skelter** *(here and there)* When the police arrived the rioters ran *helter skelter*.
33. **Have a brush with** *(to have encounter)* Our principal *had a brush with* the Vice Chancellor over the appointment of a lecturer.
34. **Hornet's nest** *(raise controversy)* The speaker stirred up *hornet's nest* by referring to impending changes in the rules.
35. **Hold somebody to ransom** *(to demand concession by making someone captive)* It is a pity that a handful of militants are *holding* the nation *to ransom*.
36. **Hole and corner** *(secret)* I have come to know of your *hole and corner* method of dealing with people.

IDIOMS AND PHRASES

I

1. **Ill at ease** *(uncomfortable)* A student is often *ill at ease* when he has to see the Principal after he has done something wrong.
2. **In a fix** *(in a dilemma)* The whole police department is *in a fix* about the threatening letters written by the kidnappers.
3. **In a fair way** *(hopeful)* The doctor feels that patient is *in a fair way* on to recovery.
4. **In the good books of** *(to be in favour with a person)* Sunita's brilliant success in her final examination has led her to be *in the good books of* her teachers.
5. **In tune** *(in a mood)* The teacher asked the students if they were *in tune* for study.
6. **In the lurch** *(to leave a friend in difficulty)* You must never leave your best friend *in the lurch*.
7. **Ins and outs** *(secrets)* The servants are generally familiar with the *ins and outs* of the family.
8. **In the blues** *(in dumps, depressed)* After his failure in the examination, he is *in the blues* these days.
9. **In the red** *(suffer a loss)* Most of our Public Sector Undertakings are *in the red* for lack of efficient administration.
10. **In the limelight** *(prominent)* After being out of favour with the leader of the party, he is again *in the limelight* these days.
11. **In the teeth of** *(inspite of bitter opposition)* Hindu Code Bill was passed *in the teeth* of opposition by various organisations.
12. **In a tight corner** *(in difficult situation)* After losing in gambling heavily, he is *in a tight corner*.
13. **In cold blood** *(to do something deliberately)* The child was murdered *in cold blood*.
14. **In doldrums** *(to be depressed)* After his failure in the examination, he is *in doldrums* these days.
15. **In the family way** *(pregnant)* She has been advised complete rest because she is *in the family way*.
16. **Ivory tower** *(imaginary world)* Those who talk of non-violence as a useful tool in international politics live in *ivory tower*.
17. **In the dumps** *(in low spirits)* Her visit cheered me up as I was *in the dumps* before her visit.
18. **In a flutter** *(excited)* My sister is *in a flutter* today because she is going for the interview.

J

Jaundiced eye *(prejudice)* You must not evaluate the success of your rivals with a *jaundiced eye*.

K

1. **Keep body and soul together** *(to maintain life)* These days because of rising prices, it is difficult to *keep body and soul together*.
2. **Keep at an arm's length** *(to keep at a distance)* Selfish people should always be *kept at an arm's length*.
3. **Keep the wolf from the door** *(to avoid starvation)* In India, millions of people struggle hard to *keep the wolf from the door*.
4. **Kith and kin** *(blood relation)* If we have no love for our *kith and kin*, we cannot be expected to love humanity.
5. **Knit the brow** *(to frown)* Her mother-in-law always *knits the brow* at everything she does.
6. **Kick the bucket** *(to die)* He *kicked the bucket* after long illness in the prime of his life.
7. **Keep up appearances** *(to maintain outward show)* Though he is in financial crisis, he is able to *keep up appearances*.
8. **Keep one's fingers crossed** *(to wait expectantly)* We had to *keep our fingers crossed* till the last ball was bowled.
9. **Keep the pot boiling** *(earn hardly enough for living)* He is earning only to *keep the pot boiling*.
10. **Kick one's heels** *(to waste time in waiting)* As the train was late we had to *kick our heels* at the station.
11. **Keep abreast of** *(not to fall behind)* It is very important for the young persons to *keep abreast of* political developments in the country.

L

1. **Lost in the clouds** *(confused)* My psychology teacher is often *lost in the clouds* as she sometimes is unable to explain the questions clearly.
2. **Lose ground** *(fail to keep position)* The belief in prophecies and horoscopes is *losing ground* these days.
3. **Laugh in one's sleeves** *(to laugh secretly)* The students *laughed in their sleeves* at the teacher's ignorance of the subject.
4. **Leave no stone unturned** *(to make all possible efforts)* The minister assured the poor that he shall *leave no stone unturned* to uplift their condition.
5. **Leap in the dark** *(to take a risk deliberately)* You must not *leap in the dark* by entering the business without experience.
6. **Look sharp** *(to make haste)* *Look sharp*, the bus is moving.
7. **Let the cat out of the bag** *(to disclose)* Sunita has, at last, *let the cat out of the bag*, by confessing that she had stolen her brother's money.
8. **Live in a fool's paradise** *(false hope)* My brother is *living in a fool's paradise*, if he thinks that he can be a rich man without working hard.

IDIOMS AND PHRASES

9. **Lion's share** *(large part)* Generally the sons as compared to daughters have a *lion's share* of their mother's affection.
10. **Loaves and Fishes** *(material benefit)* Most of the ministers are more concerned with the *loaves and fishes* of office than the service of man.
11. **Live-wire** *(energetic)* India needs *live-wire* political leaders, who can put the country on the right track.
12. **Look a gift horse in the mouth** *(criticise a gift)* One should not *look a gift horse in the mouth* because it is given out of love and regards.
13. **Lose one's head** *(to be carried away)* One should not *lose one's head* even in such a victory.
14. **Long and short** *(in brief)* The *long and short* of the principal's speech was that examination would be held on time.
15. **Latin and Greek** *(incomprehensible)* The speech of literary persons is always *Latin and Greek* to illiterate persons.
16. **Last nail in the coffin** *(causing ruin)* Second world war proved to be a *last nail in the coffin* of British imperialism.
17. **Lead up the garden path** *(to cheat)* The traders *lead* the credulous customers *up the garden path* by assuring them of warranty.
18. **Leaps and bounds** *(rapidly)* In comparison to India, China has progressed by *leaps and bounds* in every field.
19. **Last straw** *(the final trial of patience)* The Rowlet Act was the *last straw* on the Camel's back and the whole India rose in protest against the British rule.
20. **Let the grass grow under feet** *(to delay the matters)* We are bound to suffer if we *let the grass grow under feet* by postponing action.

M

1. **Make both ends meet** *(to live within one's means)* As my uncle has to bring up five children, he finds it difficult to *make both ends meet*.
2. **Mend one's fences** *(to make peace)* It is high time for the two brothers to bury the hatchet and *mend their fences*.
3. **Make a clean breast** *(to confess)* When asked by the Magistrate sternly, the thief *made a clean breast* of the whole crime.
4. **Make amends** *(to give compensation)* The government *made amends* to the family for the loss of their earning member in the war.
5. **Make the most of** *(to utilise time)* Students should *make the most of* their time if they want to get an administrative job.
6. **Move heaven and earth** *(to try utmost)* Ramesh *moved heaven and earth* to gain his end but failed.
7. **Make sure** *(to ascertain)* We went to the office to *make sure* if our exams would start in the next week.
8. **Make neither head nor tail** *(not to understand)* The students can *make neither head nor tail* of what Mr Dev teaches them.

9. **Moot point** *(a debatable point, undecided)* The question of abolition of child marriage is a *moot point* as far as Indians are concerned.
10. **Meet one's waterloo** *(to face final defeat)* Tipu Sultan *met his waterloo* in the fourth battle of Mysore.
11. **Man of letters** *(literary person)* Dr Radhakrishnan was *a man of letters*.
12. **Make light of** *(not to care)* He is in the habit *of making light of* the advice of his parents.
13. **Midas touch** *(a touch which turns anything into gold)* Our manager seems to be gifted with *Midas touch* because he is capable of selling every product.
14. **Man of parts** *(a man of qualities)* Our Principal is a *man of parts* and is respected by all and one.
15. **Mealy mouthed** *(soft spoken)* A *mealy mouthed* shopkeeper is always successful.
16. **Man of straw** *(a weak person)* The king being *a man of straw*, his orders were often disobeyed.
17. **Mince matters** *(hide the truth and pretend)* Tell the truth to your parents because it does not pay *to mince matters*.
18. **Mare's nest** *(a false invention)* The involvement of teachers in the scheme proved to be a *mare's nest*.

N

1. **Null and void** *(ineffective)* Strangely, the laws made by the British in India are not yet *null and void*.
2. **Next to nothing** *(almost nothing)* The thieves made off with everything from the kitchen and there was *next to nothing* left.
3. **Neck and crop** *(completely)* The decoits finished him off *neck and crop* beyond recognition.
4. **No love lost** *(intense dislike)* There is *no love lost* between the two neighbours.
5. **Nip in the bud** *(to destroy in the very beginning)* The evils of the society must be *nipped in the bud*.
6. **Not worth one's salt** *(not deserving)* We should not help the persons who are *not worth their salt*.

O

1. **Off hand** *(without preparation or delay)* I am very poor in English grammar and can't answer all the questions *off hand*.
2. **Over head and ears** *(excessively)* Mohan is *over head and ears* in love with Neena.
3. **Out of question** *(certain)* His success is *out of question* because he is working hard these days.

IDIOMS AND PHRASES

4. **Out of the question** *(unlikely, uncertain)* His success is *out of the question* because he is not working hard these days.
5. **Out of the woods** *(out of danger)* The patient is not *out of the woods* yet.
6. **Order of the day** *(in fashion)* It is difficult to get any work done without bribery because bribery is the *order of the day*.
7. **On the score of** *(on the grounds of)* He was debarred from appearing in the examination *on the score* of indiscipline.
8. **On that score** *(for the reason)* You need not worry *on that score*.
9. **Over and above** *(moreover, besides)* I shall lend you books *over and above* what I have promised to give you in cash.
10. **Out and out** *(completely)* Shri Bhagat Singh was a patriot *out and out*.
11. **Off and on** [*occasionally (now and then)*] Since she is over busy these days, she visits me *off and on*.
12. **One's Achilles heel** *(a weak point)* Howsoever powerful a person may be, he is vulnerable because of *his Achilles' heel*.
13. **Off colour** *(not in usual form)* Once a glamorous actress, she is *off colour* these days.
14. **Odds and ends** *(scattered things)* The thief made away with the *odds and ends* lying about the drawing room.
15. **Off the hook** *(out of trouble)* He is not yet *off the hook* because Income Tax department is making a thorough inquiry into his financial status.
16. **Oily tongue** *(flattering words)* He has often won over the enemies by his *oily tongue*.
17. **On the horns of dilemma** *(in a fix)* He is *on the horns of dilemma* in the matter of his marriage.
18. **One's cup of tea** *(to one's liking)* Teaching is not my *cup of tea*.
19. **Out of sorts** *(to be unwell)* Sohan had been *out of sorts* the whole day and could not do his office work properly.
20. **On its last legs** *(about to collapse)* In many sections of Indian society, the system of child marriage is *on its last legs*.
21. **On the carpet** *(to be under consideration)* What is *on the carpet* these days is in the newspapers.

P

1. (A) **Past master** *(an expert)* He is a *past master* in befooling the people by his oily tongue.
2. **Palmy days** *(prosperous, affluent days)* We still remember the *palmy days* of our life when we had nothing much to do and still got everything to fulfil our needs.
3. **Part and parcel** *(inseparable part)* Every Indian citizen living in India must regard himself as *part and parcel* of a larger whole.

4. **Pass the buck** *(to blame each other)* Political parties *pass the buck* on to one another for failure on economic front.
5. **Pay off old scores** *(to take revenge)* The way he is treating his younger brother makes it quite obvious that he is *paying off old scores*.
6. **Pay through one's nose** *(to pay dearly)* A hapless customer has to *pay through his nose* when there is shortage of goods in the market.
7. **Pay lip service** *(pretend to regard)* Most of the political parties *pay lip service* to the plight of the poor.
8. **Pay one back in the same coin** *(tit for tat)* We should not hesitate in *paying* China and Pakistan *back in their own coins*.
9. **Pin-money** *(allowance given to housewife for personal use)* She is frugal and saves even out of *pin-money*.
10. **Pell-mell** *(great confusion)* After the thieves had ransacked the house, every thing was *pell-mell*.
11. **Play fast and loose** *(repeatedly change one's attitude)* No one can trust Rohan as he is used to *playing fast and loose* with his friends.
12. **Play second fiddle to** *(to play a subordinate part)* A self-respecting man can never *play second fiddle to* anyone.
13. **Play truant** *(to be absent from duty without permission)* It is a very bad habit of the employees to *play truant* from office.
14. **Play to the gallery** *(to gain cheap popularity)* The speeches of our leaders are not sincere; they are intended to *play to the gallery*.
15. **Play ducks and drakes** *(to squander money)* After the death of his father he got into heavy debt by *playing ducks and drakes* with money.
16. **Play foul** *(to do something wrong)* Don't *play foul* with your well-wishers.
17. **Plough the sands** *(futile labour)* He cannot make money because he appears to be *ploughing the sands*.
18. **Pour oil on troubled waters** *(to pacify the matters)* The two good friends exchanged hot words but the intervention of their teacher *poured oil on troubled waters*.
19. **Pull a long face** *(to look sad)* Seema *pulled a long face* when she was scolded by her teacher for her carelssness.
20. **Pull one's socks up** *(work hard)* You must *pull your socks up* to get over financial problems.
21. **Pull strings** *(to exercise influence secretly)* He managed his promotion by *pulling strings*.
22. **Put heads together** *(consult seriously)* Our leaders should *put* their *heads together* to solve national problems.
23. **Put a spoke in a wheel** *(to obstruct)* He would not like me to succeed; so he always *put a spoke in a wheel*.

IDIOMS AND PHRASES

24. **Put the cart before the horse** *(to do wrong thing first)* Our leaders *put the cart before the horse* by neglecting villages in the name of industrial progress.
25. **Pros and cons** *(for and against a thing)* We must always consider the *pros and cons* of any new project that we take in hand.
26. **Pyrrhic victory** *(victory at a high cost)* Greek victory over Trojans proved to be *pyrrhic victory*.
27. **Pick holes** *(to find fault with)* He is always *picking holes* in every project.

Q

1. **Queer fish** *(strange person)* One cannot make anything out of Sohan's attitude as he is such a *queer fish*.
2. **Quixotic project** *(foolishly ideal)* Being not worldly wise, he wasted his money in *quixotic projects*.

R

1. **Rise to the occasion** *(to act as the occasion demands)* To face critical situations boldly you should *rise to the occasion*.
2. **Run short of** *(shortage)* These days due to some financial crises my friend is *running short of* money.
3. **Rank and file** *(common man)* If we want our country to progress in every field, we must improve the economic lot of the *rank and file*.
4. **Red tapism** *(official delay)* *Red tapism* is a bane of Indian bureaucracy.
5. **Rest on one's laurels** *(complacent, self satisfied)* Ambitious persons never *rest on their laurels* because they dream of unending achievements.
6. **Rock the boat** *(upset the balance)* If your party withdraws the support from the Government, it may *rock the boat*.
7. **Red herring** *(something to distract attention)* The demand of inquiry into his conduct is just *a red herring* as there is no truth in it.
8. **Rip up old sores** *(to revive forgotten quarrel)* Rahul and his wife can't live in peace; they are always *ripping up old sores*.
9. **Read between the lines** *(to understand the hidden meaning)* If her essay is *read between the lines*, we will find that she has made comments against the government.
10. **Rule the roost** *(to dominate)* Today the rich *rule the roost*.
11. **Red rag to a bull** *(anything that provokes)* The law against the dowry system is, for the greedy persons, like a *red rag to a bull*.
12. **Ride rough shod over** *(to treat in a high handed fashion)* Don't *ride rough shod over* a person when he is down and out.
13. **Rub one the wrong way** *(annoy)* If you *rub him the wrong way*, he is bound to react.

S

1. **Sit on the fence** *(not to commit oneself)* When the party split Ramesh was accused of *sitting on the fence*.
2. **Smell a rat** *(to be suspicious)* I *smelt a rat* in the bargain that my uncle made with my father.
3. **Shed crocodile tears** *(to show false sorrow)* The mother *shed crocodile tears* on the death of her step daughter.
4. **Split hair** *(to indulge in over refined arguments)* We should not try to *split hair* with our elders.
5. **Stand in good stead** *(to be helpful in need)* During the time of distress, the advice of elders always *stands in good stead*.
6. **Show white feather** *(to show cowardice)* Brave people never *show white feather* in the face of difficulties.
7. **See eye to eye** *(to agree)* Neema could never *see eye to eye* with her elder brother.
8. **Set store by** *(to value)* I have always *set store by* my father's opinion.
9. **Snap one's fingers at** *(to show contempt)* The industry owner feels that he may *snap his fingers at* the demands of his workers, but he is greatly mistaken.
10. **Speak volumes for** *(to have abundant proof)* The amount of sacrifice made by Reena's friend *speaks volumes for* her true love for her friend.
11. **Steal a march** *(to get ahead secretly)* Rohan *stole a march* on my brother in business and is very rich today.
12. **Steer clear of** *(to avoid)* Everyone, if possible, should *steer clear of* selfish people.
13. **Swan song** *(last creation)* 'Lament' was the *swan song* of Shelley.
14. **Snake in the grass** *(a secret enemy)* The country is always betrayed by the *snakes in the grass*.
15. **Sword of Damocles** *(facing imminent danger)* A *sword of Damocles* is always hanging over the head of a soldier in the event of war.
16. **Sail under false colours** *(a hypocrite)* We should not believe our leaders because they *sail under false colours*.
17. **Spartan life** *(life of ascetic)* Swami Vivekanand led a *spartan life* for promoting health of mind and body.
18. **Save one's face** *(to avoid disgrace)* He is making lame excuses to *save his face* because he could not qualify the examination.
19. **A scarlet woman** *(a woman with loose morals)* Being *a scarlet woman* she is looked down upon by her neighbours.
20. **Set people by ears** *(to incite people)* The communal speeches *set people by ears*.
21. **To Set Thames on fire** *(to achieve something impossible)* Qualifying Civil Services examination for you is like *setting Thames on fire*.
22. **Sweat of the brow** *(hard labour)* The honest persons live by *sweat of the brow*.

IDIOMS AND PHRASES

23. **Steal someone's thunder** *(make a better impression)* The young actor performed so well that he *stole his rival's thunder.*
24. **Straight from the shoulders** *(candidly)* My lawyer told me *straight from the shoulders* that my case was weak.
25. **Shop lifter** *(one who steals from the shop)* A *shop lifter* often visits a shop as a customer.
26. **Spick and span** *(in order)* Her house looked *spick and span* because everything was in its place.
27. **Shot in the arm** *(encouraging)* A victory in Kargil war proved a *shot in the arm* of our Defence Forces.
28. **Something up one's sleeve** *(a secret plan)* She is quite a mischievous lady. There is always *something up her sleeve.*
29. **Send about one's business** *(to dismiss)* His employees *sent* him *about his business* when he behaved insolently.
30. **Stand one's ground** *(remain firm)* He did not yield to pressure and *stood his ground* till the end.
31. **Small fry** *(insignificant person)* Who cares for him, he is a *small fry* in the office.
32. **Seamy side of life** *(immoral side of society)* The picture depicts realism and presents the *seamy side of life* in modern India.
33. **Sow wild oats** *(irresponsible pleasure seeking)* After *sowing* his *wild oats*, Ram has decided to stick to the straight and narrow path in future.
34. **Spill the beans** *(to give information)* Continuous interrogation finally made the man *spill the beans* and the disaster was averted.
35. **A stalking horse** *(pretence)* The trade union's seemingly rightful demand is only *a stalking horse* to black-mail the management.

T

1. **Turn the tables** *(to reverse the condition)* A batsman often *turns the table* on the opposite team by his good batting.
2. **Turn up one's nose** *(to take lightly with contempt)* Meena has failed twice in her class and yet she *turns up her nose* at my advice.
3. **Turn coat** *(one who changes political affiliations)* Anti-defection bill is aimed at checking the evil practices indulged in by *turn coats.*
4. **Take up the cudgels** *(to support or defend)* One of my lawyer friends *took up the cudgels* on my behalf to defend me.
5. **Turn the corner** *(to pass a critical stage)* After long illness, at last my friend *turned the corner* and was completely out of danger.
6. **Tall talk** *(exaggerate the matters)* No one likes to be in the company of Neema as she always indulges in *tall talk.*
7. **Tooth and nail** *(violently)* All the students revolted *tooth and nail* against the partiality of the teachers towards some students.

8. **Throw in a towel** *(to be defeated)* When the wrestler could not resist the opponent, he had to *throw in a towel*.
9. **Take with a pinch of salt** *(to accept with doubt)* Everybody *takes* Rahul's problems *with a pinch of salt* because he is an unreliable person.
10. **Turn a hair** *(show any reaction)* Although his friends provoked him against Rohit, he did not *turn a hair* and remained calm.
11. **Tall stories** *(exaggerated stories)* Since he retired from Army, he has been famous for his *tall stories* which regale the villagers.
12. **Take the floor** *(make a speech)* When the Prime Minister *took the floor* in the cabinet meeting, there was pin drop silence.
13. **Take lying down** *(accept insult)* It is impossible for me to *take* his remarks *lying down*. It amounts to meek surrender.
14. **Turn to account** *(turn to advantage)* The brave *turn* their failures *to account*.
15. **Take heart** *(feel bold)* You must *take heart* and face life boldly.
16. **Take to heart** *(feel excessively)* He *took* his failure *to heart* and lost interest in worldly affairs.
17. **Take bull by horns** *(to meet the danger boldly)* You can succeed in life only if you have courage to *take bull by horns*.
18. **Through and through** *(entirely)* He was drenched in the rain *through and through*.
19. **To the back bone** *(thoroughly)* We need leaders who are selfless *to the back bone*.
20. **Take wind out of another's sails** *(to gain advantage by anticipation)* Farsighted Generals can win war by *taking wind out of enemy's sails*.
21. **Throw down the glove/gauntlet** *(to challenge)* China had *thrown down the glove* by not recognising Sikkim as part of India.
22. **Take leaf out of somebody's book** *(to emulate)* The young should *take leaf out of great men's books*.
23. **Take people by storm** *(to surprise unexpectedly)* The successful launching of GSLV-1 *took the nation by storm*.
24. **Tall order** *(something difficult)* It is a *tall order* to check population explosion in India.
25. **Throw a spanner** *(to sabotage a plan)* He refused to finance my project and so *threw a spanner* in it.
26. **Take to task** *(punish, ask for explanation, to scold)* To *took* my younger sister *to task* for not obeying her elders.
27. **Turn a deaf ear** *(not to pay attention to, refuse to listen)* All the party members *turned a deaf ear* to their leader.
28. **Throw out of gear** *(not working properly)* Many of our small scale industries have been *thrown out of gear* because of lack of finance.
29. **Take to heels** *(to run away)* The students making mischief *took to* their *heels* on seeing the Principal.

IDIOMS AND PHRASES

30. **Throw cold water** *(to discourage)* Instead of encouraging me my business partner *threw cold water* on my plans.
31. **Turn over a new leaf** *(to be entirely changed)* After the sudden death of his father Rajesh *turned over a new leaf* and took all the responsibilities of the family on himself.
32. **Take somebody for a ride** *(to deceive a person)* The traders *take the customers for a ride* by selling fake foreign goods to them.
33. **Take up arms** *(to fight)* The tribals of this region have *taken up arms* against the government.
34. **To and fro** *(forward and backward)* He was strolling in the garden *to and fro*.
35. **Throw up the sponge** *(surrender)* He never *threw up the sponge* and at last got over his problems.

U

1. **Uphill task** *(difficult task)* The problem of holding exams on time is an *uphill task* for the VC of Ch Charan Singh University.
2. **Ups and downs** *(change in fortune)* My uncle has experienced many *ups and downs* in his furniture business.
3. **Under the rose** *(secretly)* When the parents of Amul did not agree to the marriage of their son, he married Meeta *under the rose*.
4. **Up and doing** *(active)* A labourer should be *up and doing* daily if he has to earn his living.
5. **Under a cloud** *(to be under suspicion)* His secret connections with the smugglers have brought him *under a cloud*.
6. **Upto the mark** *(as good as should be)* Your speech was *upto the mark*.

W

1. **With open arms** *(cordially, warmly)* When my cousin came back from England after 10 years, he was welcomed *with open arms* by all the relatives.
2. **Win laurels** *(to win distinction)* Dr Tagore *won laurels* in the world of literature.
3. **White elephant** *(anything with less utility and more expenditure)* The Public Sector Undertakings have proved *white elephants* to our economy.
4. **Well disposed to** *(friendly or helpful to somebody)* One is always *well disposed to* those who are honest and hard working.
5. **Writing on the wall** *(signal, warning)* The factory owner read the *writing on the wall* and closed down the factory.
6. **When the crunch comes** *(the moment of decision)* Brave persons never despair *when the crunch comes*.
7. **Willy-Nilly** *(whether one wishes or not) Willy-Nilly*, she has to agree to the views of her husband all the time.

8. **Window shopping** *(to look at goods displayed but not for buying)* Though I did not have any mind to make purchases, I just went out *window shopping* in the evening.
9. **Wear and tear** *(damage caused by use)* *Wear and tear* of the machinery is known as depreciation in accountancy.
10. **Weal and woe** *(joy and sorrow)* We must learn to bear *weal and woe* of life patiently.
11. **Wash hands of** *(to have nothing to do)* I have *washed hands of* your affairs because you do not take me seriously.
12. **Wide berth** *(keep away)* We should give a *wide berth* to bad characters.
13. **Will o' the wisp** *(elusive, unreal)* To Romantic poets reality appears to be *will o' the wisp*.
14. **Wry face** *(disappointed look)* He made a *wry face* when he was refused admission to the college of his choice.
15. **Win hands down** *(win easily)* Australia *won hands down* in the Davis Cup finals.
16. **Within an ace of** *(close to something)* When our team was *within an ace of* victory, Iraq scored a last minute goal to draw the game.
17. **Wear the trousers** *(dominant)* It is Leena who *wears the trousers* and her husband simply obeys her.
18. **Wee hours** *(at dawn)* The old couple was murdered in the *wee hours of* the day.
19. **With a high hand** *(oppressively)* He was a king who ruled his subjects *with a high hand*.
20. **Wet blanket** *(any person that dampens enthusiasm)* The principal proved a *wet blanket* while the students were on picnic.
21. **Wild-goose chase** *(unprofitable)* All the efforts of the government to remove illiteracy in India is like *a wild-goose chase*.
22. **Wind fall** *(sudden gain)* The legacy left by his uncle proved a *wind fall* for Arnav.
23. **Wide berth** *(keep away)* We should give a *wide berth* to bad characters.
24. **Wrangle over an ass' shadow** *(to quarrel over trifles)* Their long friendship ended because they *wrangled over an ass' shadow*.

Y

1. **Yellow press** *(newspaper publishing sensational news)* In recent times there is a spurt of sensational newspapers making *yellow press* popular.
2. **Yeoman's service** *(excellent work)* Sardar Patel did a *Yeoman's service* by welding numberless States into one strong nation.

IDIOMS AND PHRASES

WORK BOOK EXERCISE (A)

Directions *Use these idioms/phrases in sentences of your own to bring out their meaning clearly. Do not change the form of the words.*

1. Turn a deaf ear
2. Give a wide berth
3. Look high and low
4. Rush from pillar to postlar
5. In high spirits
6. Point blank
7. Green eyed
8. Pot calling the kettle black
9. Tooth and nail
10. On the wane
11. Flesh creep
12. Queer fish
13. Mare's nest
14. Threw down the gauntlet
15. Elbow room
16. At odds
17. No love lost
18. Talking through his hat
19. Feather in your cap
20. Rub the wrong way
21. Rank and file
22. Burning question
23. On my nerves
24. Wearing their heart on their sleeve
25. Turned the corner

WORK BOOK EXERCISE (B)

1. High and dry
2. Lying down
3. In the offing
4. Die in harness
5. Cut out
6. Snake in the grass
7. Gift of the gab
8. Bird's eye view
9. Sowing his wild oats
10. A white elephant
11. Inspired to draw the long bow
12. With a high hand
13. On the wane
14. Did me a good turn
15. Eat his heart out
16. Still a moot point
17. Cut me dead
18. Hole and corner
19. Spill the beans
20. Stalking horse
21. As good as his word
22. Take my word for it
23. Thin end of the wedge
24. Picking holes
25. To foot the bill

WORK BOOK EXERCISE (C)

1. Done to death
2. Breathing down
3. Not worth a salt
4. At a loose end
5. To be in doldrums
6. To make head or tail
7. Sang froid
8. To strain every nerve
9. As ugly as sin
10. To bid fair
11. To give a cold shoulder
12. To put a spoke in someone's wheel
13. At stake
14. On the cards
15. On one's own accord
16. Down in the mouth
17. To face the music
18. Small talk
19. Carried off one's feet
20. Held in camera
21. In a brown study
22. To take someone to task
23. To pull someone's leg
24. In a nutshell

WORK BOOK EXERCISE (D)

1. To call a spade a spade
2. To be a cut above
3. Put one's foot down
4. Paint the town red
5. To speak volumes
6. Chew the cud
7. Left handed compliment
8. Stuck one's neck
9. To burn fingers
10. Took to heels
11. To come to a head
12. Bee in bonnet
13. Bygone be bygones
14. Hair-breadth escape
15. A far cry
16. Make no bones
17. Elbow grease
18. Something fishy
19. To bank on
20. To plough a lonely furrow
21. Cut and dry (unalterable)
22. To run into rough weather
23. In a soup
24. To make both ends meet
25. To lay down arms

Previous Years' Questions

Directions *Use these idioms/phrases in sentences of your own to bring out their meaning clearly. Do not change the form of the words.*

I. 1. In spite of   2. A bed of roses
    3. Cold war   4. To rule with an iron hand
    5. To make haste   [Civil Services (Mains), 2015]

II. 1. According to   2. All of a sudden
    3. Ready money   4. A burning question
    5. Ins and outs   [Civil Services (Mains), 2014]

III. 1. Give the game away   2. To face the music
     3. Hand in glove   4. In deep water
     5. To leave in the lurch   [IFS, 2013]

IV. 1. To run with the hare and hunt with the hound
    2. Between the devil and the deep sea
    3. A wild goose chase
    4. Make hay while the sun shines
    5. To be on tenter hooks   [IFS, 2014]

V. 1. To pay off old scores   2. To let the cat out of the bag
    2. To smell a rat   4. At daggers drawn
                                                        [IFS, 2015]

Directions *Use the following idioms/phrases in a sentence to bring its meaning clearly.*

I.   1. To make clean breast of   2. A man of straw
     3. Put on the market   4. To meet someone half-way
                                                        [CLAT, 2014]

II. 1. To blaze a trail   2. A snake in the grass
     3. Have too many irons in the fire   4. A fair weather friend
     5. A panacea   [CLAT, 2013]

III. 1. To burn one's fingers   2. To feather one's own nest
     3. To be in blues   4. A fish out of water
     5. Ride the high horse   [CLAT, 2012]

IV. 1. The lion's share   2. Close shave
     4. To die in harness   5. To eat one's words
                                           [Civil Services (Mains), 2007]

V.   1. Bell the cat   2. Thank one's stars
     4. True to one's salt   5. Come out with flying colours
                                           [Civil Services (Mains), 2006]

VI. 1. Look a gift-horse in the mouth   2. Lame duck
     3. Achilles heel   4. Blow hot and cold
     5. Keep a stiff upper lip   [IFS, 2010]

Answers

WORK BOOK EXERCISE (A)

1. **Turn a deaf ear** (*did not pay any attention*) The boy *turned a deaf ear* to the pleadings of all his well-wishers.
2. **Give a wide berth** (*keep away from*) We should *give a wide berth* to bad characters.
3. **Look high and low** (*everywhere*) Sumit had to *look high and low* before he could find his scooter key.
4. **Rush from pillar to postlar** (*rush in all directions and suffer much harassment*) You may *rush from pillar to post*, but you stand no chance of getting what you want without a bribe.
5. **In high spirits** (*cheerful*) At a party, he is always *in high spirits*.
6. **Point blank** (*directly*) She rejected his proposal of marriage *point blank*.
7. **Green-eyed** (*jealous*) We should guard against our *green-eyed* friends.
8. **Pot calling the kettle black** (*someone criticising another for a fault which he himself has*) It was clearly a case of the *pot calling the kettle black* when Jagjit said that Ramu was a thief.
9. **Tooth and nail** (*with strength and fury*) Rahul fought *tooth and nail* to save his company.
10. **On the wane** (*growing less*) The popularity of the yester year's superstar is *on the wane*.
11. **Flesh creep** (*frightened me*) The sight of the accident made my *flesh creep*.
12. **Queer fish** (*strange person*) He is a *queer fish*. I have failed to understand him.
13. **Mare's nest** (*a false invention*) The involvement of teachers in the scheme of education proved to be a *mare's nest*.
14. **Threw down the gauntlet** (*threw the challenge*) Chandu used very ugly words against his kind uncle; he *threw down the gauntlet* before him.
15. **Elbow room** (*freedom*) The present undergraduate syllabus leaves very little *elbow room* for teachers to be innovative.
16. **At odds** (*in dispute*) The members of the group were *at odds* over the selection procedure.
17. **No love lost** (*intense dislike*) There is *no love lost* between the two neighbours.
18. **Talking through his hat** (*talking nonsense*) I did not mind what he was saying, he was only *talking through his hat*.
19. **Feather in your cap** (*additional achievement*) If you pass this difficult examination, it will be a *feather in your cap*.
20. **Rub the wrong way** (*annoy him*) If you *rub* him *the wrong way*, he is bound to react.
21. **Rank and file** (*the ordinary members*) There was opposition to the new policy by the *rank and file* of the government.
22. **Burning question** (*a widely debated issue*) Dowry is a *burning question* of the day.
23. **On my nerves** (*irritates me*) His voice gets *on my nerves*.
24. **Wearing their heart on their sleeve** (*exposing their innermost feelings to others*) Some people have a habit of *wearing their heart on their sleeve*.
25. **Turned the corner** (*passed the crisis*) The doctor says that the patient has *turned the corner*.

WORK BOOK EXERCISE (B)

1. **High and dry** (*isolated*) Komal was left *high and dry* by her friends when she lost all her money.
2. **Lying down** (*to show no reaction*) The party stalwarts have advised the President to take it *lying down* for a while.
3. **In the offing** (*about to start*) A movement for the world unity is *in the offing*.
4. **Die in harness** (*die while still working*) In the Armed Forces, it is considered a great privilege to *die in harness*.
5. **Cut out** (*suitable*) Sita is not *cut out* for this kind of work.
6. **Snake in the grass** (*a hidden enemy*) His most trusted friend proved to be a *snake in the grass*.

IDIOMS AND PHRASES

7. **Gift of the gab** (*a talent for speaking*) A good teacher should have the *gift of the gab*.
8. **Bird's eye view** (*a general view*) The speaker gave a *bird's eye view* of the political conditions in the country.
9. **Sowing his wild oats** (*going through a period of irresponsible pleasure seeking*) After *sowing his wild oats*, Ram has decided to stick to the straight and narrow path in future.
10. **A white elephant** (*an expensive one*) They sold their house because it was *a white elephant*.
11. **Inspired to draw the long bow** (*exaggerate*) When he tells stories about himself, he is *inspired to draw the long bow*.
12. **With a high hand** (*oppressively*) He was a king who ruled his subjects *with a high hand*.
13. **On the wane** (*declining*) Discipline is *on the wane* in schools and colleges these days.
14. **Did me a good turn** (*did an act of kindness*) He *did me a good turn* by recommending me for the post of Vice-president.
15. **Eat his heart out** (*suffer silently*) Being an introvert, he will only *eat his heart out*.
16. **Still a moot point** (*undecided*) The question of abolition of private property is *still a moot point*.
17. **Cut me dead** (*treated me as a complete stranger*) Sumit and I have known each other for a long time, but when I met him the other day for some unknown reason, he *cut me dead*.
18. **Hole and corner** (*secret*) I have come to know of your *hole and corner* method of dealing with people.
19. **Spill the beans** (*to give information*) Continuous interrogation finally made the man *spill the beans* and the disaster was averted.
20. **Stalking horse** (*pretence*) The trade union's seemingly rightful demand is only a *stalking horse* to blackmail the management.
21. **As good as his word** (*ready to fulfil his promise*) The teacher was as *good as his word*.
22. **Take my word for it** (*believe what I say*) The reporter said to the editor, "You need not consult anyone. You can *take my word for it.*"
23. **Thin end of the wedge** (*the beginning of further concessions*) If we give them this concession, it will be the *thin end of the wedge*.
24. **Picking holes** (*finding fault with*) He is always *picking holes* in every project.
25. **To foot the bill** (*to pay*) After the dinner was over, she refused *to foot the bill*.

WORK BOOK EXERCISE (C)

1. **Done to death** (*murdered*) Caesar was *done to death* by the conspirators.
2. **Breathing down** (*watching all his actions closely*) His boss was always *breathing down* his neck.
3. **Not worth a salt** (*quite worthless*) He is *not worth* his *salt* if he fails at this juncture.
4. **At a loose end** (*with nothing to do*) After having finished the last project, I find myself *at a loose end*.
5. **To be in doldrums** (*uncertain*) With the existing management, the future of the company is *in doldrums*.
6. **To make head or tail** (*understand it*) It was such a strange affair that I would not *make head or tail* of it.
7. **Sang froid** (*composure*) She exhibited remarkable *sang froid* during the crisis.
8. **To strain every nerve** (*worked very hard*) My father *strained every nerve* to enable me to get settled in life.
9. **As ugly as sin** (*exceptionally ugly*) Though she herself was *as ugly as sin*, she had the audacity to criticise the looks of her companion.
10. **To bid fair** (*seems likely*) He *bids fair* to be an excellent cricketer.
11. **To give a cold shoulder** (*tries to be unfriendly by taking no notice of her*) He does not like to be friendly with Sarla. He always *gives* her *a cold shoulder*.
12. **To put a spoke in someone's wheel** (*thwarted the execution of the plan*) It was he who *put a spoke in my wheel*.

13. **At stake** (*in danger*) The captain played with determination because the honour of the team was *at stake*.
14. **On the cards** (*certain*) His promotion is *on the cards*.
15. **On one's own accord** (*voluntarily and willingly*) He resigned the post of *his own accord*.
16. **Down in the mouth** (*out of spirits*) Being out of job, he is *down in the mouth* these days.
17. **To face the music** (*faced reprimand*) He *faced the music* for reaching home late.
18. **Small talk** (*light conversation*) While the ladies continued their *small talk* in the drawing room he felt bored.
19. **Carried off one's feet** (*was wild with excitement*) He was *carried off his feet* when he was declared to have won the prize.
20. **Held in camera** (*not open to the public*) The trial was so important that the entire proceedings were *held in camera*.
21. **In a brown study** (*reverie*) She was *in a brown study* and not notice my entrance.
22. **To take someone to task** (*reprimanded him*) The authorities took *him to task* for his negligence.
23. **To pull someone's leg** (*befooling me*) I did not know that he was *pulling my leg* all the time.
24. **In a nutshell** (*in simple and brief manner*) To tell you *in a nutshell*, lust for power and money has almost spoiled him.

WORK BOOK EXERCISE (D)

1. **To call a spade a spade** (*desist from making controversial statement*) He is a plain, simple and sincere man. He will always *call a spade a spade*.
2. **To be a cut above** (*superior*) She is *a cut above* other teachers in the schools.
3. **Put one's foot down** (*not to yield*) Harassed by repeated acts of injustice, he decided to *put his foot down*.
4. **Paint the town red** (*have a lively time*) At Christmas, even the elderly fathers *paint the town red*.
5. **To speak volumes** (*serve as strong testimony*) His letters to his ward *speak volumes* for his forbearance and good sense.
6. **Chew the cud** (*to muse on*) He is in the habit of *chewing the cud*.
7. **Left handed compliment** (*an insincere*) I just paid him a *left handed compliment*.
8. **Stuck one's neck** (*took a risk*) The new CM *stuck his neck* out today and promised 10 kgs free wheat a month for all rural families.
9. **To burn fingers** (*got himself into trouble*) He *burnt his fingers* by interfering in his neighbour's affairs.
10. **Took to heels** (*took to flight*) When the police came, the thieves *took to* their *heels*.
11. **To come to a head** (*reached a crisis*) The dispute regarding the emoluments of junior doctors *came to a head* this week.
12. **Bee in bonnet** (*an obsession about something*) He is a strange fellow, it is very difficult to deal with him, it seems that he has a *bee in* his *bonnet*.
13. **Bygone be bygones** (*ignore the past*) It will be wise on your part to let the *bygones be bygones*.
14. **Hair-breadth escape** (*narrow*) The boy had a *hair-breadth escape* from a street accident.
15. **A far cry** (*an impracticable idea*) Inspite of the efforts of all peace loving people, world peace is still *a far cry*.
16. **Make no bones** (*did not consult anyone*) The management dismissed him and *made no bones* about it.
17. **Elbow grease** (*his hard work*) He has reached present position in his job through *elbow grease*.
18. **Something fishy** (*black at the bottom*) I am afraid there is *something fishy* about the Bofors deal.
19. **To bank on** (*relying on*) Ram could not get to Kolkata for vacation since he was *banking on* his arrears of pay which he did not get in time.
20. **To plough a lonely furrow** (*do without the help of others*) In the organised society of today no individual or nation can *plough a lonely furrow*.
21. **Cut and dry** (*unalterable*) He always follows *cut and dried* religious dogmas.

IDIOMS AND PHRASES

22. **To run into rough weather** (*encounter difficulties*) The new economic policy is likely *to run into rough weather*.
23. **In a soup** (*in trouble*) Sumit thought he was very clever but found himself *in a soup*.
24. **To make both ends meet** (*earn enough*) He cannot *make both ends meet*.
25. **To lay down arms** (*surrendered*) The soldiers *laid down* their *arms*.

Previous Years' Questions

I. 1. **In spite of** (*regardless of*) He was suddenly cold *in spite of* the Sun.
   2. **A bed of roses** (*an easy and peaceful life*) Life is not always *a bed of roses*.
   3. **Cold war** (*rivalry and tension between people or factions*) A *cold war* has been continuing between India and Pakistan since long.
   4. **To rule with an iron hand** (*to control a group of people very firmly*) My uncle *rules* the family business *with an iron hand*.
   5. **To make haste** (*to hasten, to hurry*) *Make haste* or you will miss the train.

II. 1. **According to** (*as said or indicated by someone or something*) *According to* the weather forecast, it should be a beautiful day.
    2. **All of a sudden** (*very quickly and unexpectedly*) *All of a sudden* we heard a loud explosion that shook the building.
    3. **Ready money** (*money in the form of cash that is immediately available*) You might find yourself without the *ready money* you need to snap up a bargain.
    4. **A burning question** (*an urgent or anucial issue under heated discussion*) Real Estate taxes are always *a burning question* for the town leaders.
    5. **Ins and outs** (*full detail*) Before starting any business, you must know all *ins and outs* of it.

III. 1. **Give the game away** (*to reveal a plan or strategy*) We were trying to pretend we didn't know it was her birthday, but Ramesh *gave the game away*.
     2. **To face the music** (*to admit error and accept reprimand or punishment as a consquence for having failed or having done something wrong*) As soon as he broke the window with the football, Aryan know he would have *to face the music*.
     3. **Hand in glove** (*in close cooperation*) They work *hand in glove*.
     4. **In deep water** (*in a dangerous or vulnerable situation*) Many families are *in deep water* because of the mortgage crisis, and some might even lose their homes.
     5. **To leave in the lurch** (*to desert someone in trouble*) Our best salesperson *left* use *in the lurch* at the peak of the busy season.

IV. 1. **To run with the hare and hunt with the hound** (*to support both sides of a dispute*) She never takes a clear position in any dispute, she always tries *to run with the have and hunt with the hounds*.
    2. **Between the devil and the deep sea** (*having only two very unpleasant choices*) For must people a visit to the dentist is the result of a choice *between the devil and the deep blue sea* if you go you suffer, and if you dont go you suffer.
    3. **A wild goose chase** (*searching for a thing that has no chance of being found*) The police went to Assam in search of the killers, but the journey proved to be *a wild goose chase*.
    4. **Make hay while the Sun shines** (*take advantage of a favourable opportunity till it lasts*) He is a successful businessman. He believes in *making hay while the Sun shines*.
    5. **To be on tenter hooks** (*to be in a state of distress*) When police caught him with stolen money, he was on the *tenter hooks*.

V. 1. **To pay off old scores** (*to have revenge*) From her attitude it is clear that she wants *to pay off old scores*.
   2. **To let the cat out of the bag** (*reveal a secret carelessly or by mistake*) Amazingly not one of the people who knew about the surprise *let the cat out of the bag*.

3. **To smell a rat** (*to be suspicious*) I *smelt a rat* in the bargain that my uncle made with my father.
4. **At daggers drawn** (*to have bitter enmity*) The quarrel between the two brothers has grown more bitter now and they are *at dagger's drawn*.

I.
1. **To make clean breast of** (*to confess something*) The man *made a clean breast* of his crime.
2. **A man of straw** (*a weak character*) You should not trust a man of straw.
3. **Put on the market** (*to put for sale*) We put our house on the market at ₹ 20 lacs.
4. **To meet someone half-way** (*to accomplish in between*) I was working on the project alone but I *met him half-way* and did it.

II.
1. **To blaze a trail** (*to be hopeful*) He is always *blazing a trail* about his success.
2. **A snake in the grass** (*a hidden enemy*) One should always be aware of *a snake in the grass*.
3. **Have too many irons in the fire** (*doing many works at the same time*) One can never succeed if one *is having too many irons in the fire*.
4. **A fair weather friend** (*a friend in good times only*) I keep myself from *a fair weather friend*.
5. **A panacea** (*cure to all ailments*) Cramming is a *panacea* for some rote learners.

III.
1. **To burn one's fingers** (*to harm oneself*) Abusing is *burning one's fingers* when comes to character.
2. **To feather one's own nest** (*to think of own profit*) Leaders are doing what, they are *feathering their nest* only.
3. **To be in blues** (*being depressed*) I am in *blues* due to familiar issues.
4. **A fish out of water** (*restless*) Candidates are like *a fish out of water* during result days.
5. **Ride the high horse** (*appear arrogant*) I do not intend to talk to those who *ride the high horse*.

IV.
1. **The lion's share** (*a big share*) Manager intended to take *the lion's share* in the embezzled money.
2. **Close shave** (*escaping with a close margin*) He made a *close shave* in the accident.
4. **To die in harness** (*to die while working*) It is always good *to die in harness*.
5. **To eat one's words** (*to resist oneself*) I was desperate to scold him but I have *to eat my words*.

V.
1. **Bell the cat** (*to take the risk*) Reservation has become such an issue that no party is ready *to bell the cat*.
2. **Thank one's stars** (*to thank one's fortune*) I am *thanking any stars* that I got a government job.
4. **True to one's salt** (*being loyal to someone*) I shall be *true to your salt* if you help me out this time.
5. **Come out with flying colours** (*being successful*) Despite the adversities, he *came out with flying colours*.

VI.
1. **Look a gift-horse in the mouth** (*to anticipate without work*) Results can't be *looked like a gift-horse in the mouth* but you have to work.
2. **Lame duck** (*good for nothing*) I assigned him a task but he turned out to be a lame duck.
3. **Achilles heel** (*a weak point*) Fear from exams is his *achilles heels*.
4. **Blow hot and cold** (*being angry*) His being late, made his boss blow hot and cold.
5. **Keep a stiff upper lip** (*hard to please*) Nothing can make his *stiff upper lip* get relaxed as he is nowhere to take pleasure.

CHAPTER 8

Words Used as Verbs, Nouns and Adjectives

A

Arm
- N – His *arm* was so badly injured that doctors had to amputate it.
- V – The terrorists were *armed* with automatic Machine-guns.
- Adj. – If we wished to make war, we certainly would not want to fight soldiers *armed* with blades such as these.

Age
- N – At a very young *age*, he became addicted to drugs.
- V – He is *ageing* fast because of illness.
- Adj. – She made mesit with two other people: a man who appeared to be *ageless*, and a woman who was very elegant and probably in her mid-thirties.

Aim
- N – He used to torture his wife with the *aim* of extorting money from his in-laws.
- V – The company is *aiming* at increasing exports
- Adj. – I like to jump around, and would lead a fairly serene and *aimless* existence if it weren't for my friends always getting into trouble.

Air
- N – We all must sit in the open to get fresh *air*.
- V – For the first time in an interview, Hillary Clinton *aired* her complaints against Bill Clinton.
- Adj. – The area operates and maintains unmanned *aerial* vehicles.

Attempt
- N — My desperate *attempts* at qualifying a competitive exam were unsuccessful.
- V — The terrorists *attempted* an attack, but failed.
- Adj. — The question given in the sheet was *attentable*.

Alarm
- N — The news of the murder filled the residents with *alarm*.
- V — The residents were *alarmed* by the sound of a bomb-blast.
- Adj. — I found the whole programme extremely interesting in some ways, yet *alarming* in others.

Alert
- N — A red *alert* was sounded on the eve of Independence Day.
- V — The police were *alerted* about the activities of the smugglers.
- Adj. — There are signs that Congress is at least somewhat *alert* to these dangers.

Ally
- N — America and its *allies* attacked Iraq.
- V — Britain has *allied* itself with America for political power.

Anger
- N — She showed *anger* at the misbehaviour of the students.
- V — She was *angered* by my remarks.
- Adj. — He always seems *angry* with the world, and often comes over as tetchy in interviews.

Answer
- N — Her *answer* was not polite.
- V — She *answered* very politely.
- Adj. — The Attorney General is *answerable* only to Parliament for his decisions.

Appeal
- N — The High Court rejected her *appeal* for mercy.
- V — She *appealed* to me for mercy.
- Adj. — Village life is somehow more *appealing* than the city life because of the serenity it offers.

Approach
- N — His *approach* to life is practical.
- V — I *approached* him for help.
- Adj. — We want our nation-builders to be open, *approachable*, and easy to communicate with.

Array
- N — She appeared in a very costly *array*.
- V — The priest was *arrayed* in ceremonial dress.

WORDS USED AS VERBS, NOUNS AND ADJECTIVES

Arrest
- N — The news of his *arrest* was not true.
- V — He was *arrested* on the charge of murder.

Attribute
- N — My friend's most admirable *attribute* is his patience.
- V — She *attributed* her success to her mother.
- Adj. — 43 per cent of all deaths in Ireland were attributable to cardiovascular disease.

Author
- N — She is a very renowned *author*.
- V — She is said to have *authored* many novels.
- Adj. — No *authorial* voice interferes to colour the scene for us.

Avail
- N — My request for help was of no *avail*.
- V — She *availed* herself of every chance.
- Adj. — No doctor is available on Sunday.

Award
- N — She was happy on receiving a handsome *award*.
- V — He was *awarded* a gold medal.

Axe
- N — He used an *axe* to murder her.
- V — She was *axed* from her job.

B

Blind
- N — This is a school for the *blind*.
- V — She eloped with him as she was *blinded* by his love.
- Adj. — I had a little Chihuahua named Carlos that had some kind of skin disease and was totally *blind*.

Bid
- N — India succeeded in its *bid* to draw attention of the world towards terrorism in Kashmir.
- V — She *bid* ₹ 5,000 for the antique flower-vase in an auction.

Bark
- N — The *bark* of his dog disturbed his sleep.
- V — Dogs always *bark* at strangers.

Book
- N — He is fond of reading *books*.
- V — The police *booked* him in a murder case.
- Adj. — The war proved the deepest trauma of a largely *bookish* life.

Blow
- **N** – The loss of their only son came as a terrible *blow*.
- **V** – The police station was *blown* up in a bomb blast.

Break
- **N** – She has been working since morning without a *break*.
- **V** – He fell off the horse and *broke* his leg.
- **Adj.** – An encrypted password feature as introduced by a social messenger application recently is not easily *breakable*.

Bridge
- **N** – Standing on the *bridge*, she was watching the river.
- **V** – She is trying to *bridge* the gap between her estranged parents.

Blood
- **N** – The dead body was found lying in the pool of *blood*.
- **V** – The party workers were *blooded* by the speech of their leaders.
- **Adj.** – Criminologists say that despite her cold-*blooded* killing, she does not fit the serial-killer mould.

Bound
- **N** – Please do not cross the *bound* of decency.
- **V** – Police *bound* the hands of thief with a handcuff.
- **Adj** – I am *bound* in honour to help my brother.

Board
- **N** – He was sitting at the back and so couldn't see the *board* properly.
- **V** – She *boarded* the bus at Roorkee.

Back
- **N** – Something was written on the *back* of the paper.
- **V** – Her parents *backed* her proposals to go abroad.
- **Adj.** – India's military strength, *backed* by a nuclear deterrent, is growing.

Bite
- **N** – She took a *bite* from his cake.
- **V** – The snake *bit* Alka and she died.

Better
- **N** – We should respect our *betters* in life.
- **V** – The union leader is forcing the management to *better* the working conditions of the workers.
- **Adj.** – To keep oneself silent is *better* than an argument.

Burn
- **N** – She succumbed to the *burns* she received in the car accident.
- **V** – We must not *burn* dry leaves.
- **Adj.** – The firestorm raged for about 3 hours and only subsided when all *burnable* material was consumed.

WORDS USED AS VERBS, NOUNS AND ADJECTIVES

Beat
- N — Everyone was dancing to the *beats* of the drum.
- V — He often *beats* animals.
- Adj. — They are *beatable*, he stated, 'just like any other team'.

Burst
- N — The *burst* of cloud caused heavy rains.
- V — She *burst* into anger at my delayed arrival.

Bag
- N — She carried books in her *bag*.
- V — She has *bagged* this prestigious award.

Bail
- N — He was released on *bail*.
- V — His friends *bailed* him out of difficulties.
- Adj. — Why is it so easy for a judge to issue a *bailable* warrant for arrest, before any investigation has been conducted?

Balanced
- N — For peace, there should be *balance* of power in politics.
- V — It was difficult for her to *balance* on her legs because of weakness.
- Adj. — We have brought more youngsters into the team and the team has a more *balanced* look about it now.

Bank
- N — She opened an account in the *bank*.
- V — You must not *bank* on her help.
- Adj. — Before the industry can blossom, good and *bankable* business models are needed.

Bang
- N — The bomb exploded with a *bang*.
- V — He *banged* the door open.

Bar
- N — She opened the lock with an iron *bar*.
- V — The police *barred* the road for the motorists.

Bargain
- N — He made a profitable *bargain*.
- V — Ladies are in the habit of *bargaining*.
- Adj. — The product seems to be *bargainable* as its shelf life is almost over.

Barter
- N — In olden times, *barter* system was in practice.
- V — She has *bartered* away a profitable chance.

Bear
- N — A *bear* was spotted in a forest.
- V — It is hard to *bear* the difficulties in life.
- Adj. — You have made life in this strange existence almost *bearable* and you must accept my apologies.

Benefit
- N — *Benefits* of hard work are many.
- V — He *benefitted* from his father's experience.
- Adj. — The more positive one is in his thoughts, the more he is *beneficial* to himself and the society.

Bend
- N — He touched my feet without *bending*.
- V — There is a dangerous *bend* on the road ahead.
- Adj. — His limbs and fingers were extraordinarily long and *bendable*, as if made of rubber.

Bent
- N — He has a *bent* of mind for literature.
- V — She *bent* to lift the books from the ground.

C

Chair
- N — He offered a *chair* and requested me to sit down.
- V — He was surprised to find a young woman *chairing* the meeting.
- Adj. — He was elected as the *chairman* of the society which helps the poor.

Call
- N — He was happy to receive a *call* for interview.
- V — She *called* the children as it was getting dark.

Cover
- N — When it started raining, they all ran for *cover*.
- V — He *covered* the car to protect it from Sun and dust.
- Adj. — There seemed to be too many issues to be *coverable* in one post.

Court
- N — He was fined for the contempt of *court*.
- V — He has been *courting* Richa for three months.

Calm
- N — He never loses his *calm* of mind.
- V — The news that he was alive *calmed* all our fears.
- Adj. — Everyone knew her time had come, but they tried to keep *calm* faces for her sake.

Cut
- N — Blood was oozing from the deep *cut* on his hand.
- V — She *cut* out big pieces of cake for her children.

Chance
- N — India has a good *chance* to solve the problem of terrorism.
- V — She *chanced* upon her old papers in the cupboard.
- Adj. — She now runs a boutique and recounts how a *chance* encounter changed her life.

WORDS USED AS VERBS, NOUNS AND ADJECTIVES

Close
- N – The meeting came to a *close* before time.
- V – On Sundays, he *closes* his shop somewhat earlier.
- Adj. – You're facing the situation with a *closed* mind.

Copy
- N – The boss asked her to make two duplicate *copies* of the letter.
- V – It is not easy to *copy* the style of other writers.

Conduct
- N – All his teachers appreciate him for his good *conduct*.
- V – You should learn to *conduct* yourself properly in the class.
- Adj. – As long as the material is electrically *conductible*, the machine can work with it.

Corner
- N – The baby was crying in the *corner* of the room.
- V – The chain snatcher, at last, was *cornered* after a long chase.
- Adj. – Nothing is more dangerous than a *cornered* wild beast.

Chain
- N – The dacoits pulled the *chain* and got off the train.
- V – She was relieved to find that the dog was *chained*.

Crop
- N – The farmers are expecting a good *crop* this year.
- V – You should try to solve the problem that may *crop* up.

Cast
- N – The *cast* of the movie is yet to be decided.
- V – The annoyed father *cast* a furious glance at his daughter.

Catch
- N – The Narcotics Department seized a huge *catch* of brown sugar.
- V – The thief was *caught* red handed.
- Adj. – I walk out of movies and plays, and I never accept invitations to operas that have no *catchy* tunes in them.

Cloud
- N – The sky was overcast with *clouds*.
- V – Her eyes were *clouded* with tears.
- Adj. – The weather there is often foggy and skies are *cloudy*.

D

Drive
- N – It was half an hour's *drive*.
- V – She *drives* very well.
- Adj. – It is legally *drivable* in the streets and can cruise on freeways at the speed of a regular car.

Drink
- N – He offered her a *drink* but she politely declined.
- V – He *drinks* only in parties.
- Adj. – In rural areas, very few people have access to *drinkable* water.

Down
- N – You should face ups and *downs* of life bravely.
- V – The workers *downed* tools in protest.

Dog
- N – He loves *dogs*.
- V – His married life was *dogged* by misfortune.
- Adj. – Today the slender *doglike* creatures with pointy ears and bushy tails can be found in every state except Hawaii.

Discipline
- N – Their kids are intelligent but they lack *discipline*.
- V – Corporal punishment in schools was used to *discipline* the students.
- Adj. – It is an example of the *disciplined* financial controls which have built up the funds the country needs for public works and poverty relief.

Design
- N – The *design* of the table is very attractive.
- V – He *designed* the table in a novel style.

Deal
- N – He is happy to finalise this *deal*.
- V – A good salesman *deals* with his customers very tactfully.

Date
- N – The *date* of his surgery is yet to be fixed.
- V – These days he is *dating* the most beautiful girl of the town.
- Adj. – They looked all wrong in their *dated* glass case.

Delay
- N – He gave his consent without any *delay*.
- V – The flights have been *delayed* due to dense fog.

Deck
- N – He was waiting for her on the *deck* of the ship.
- V – The roads were *decked* with flags.
- Adj. – The master bedroom leads on to a *decked* balcony.

Dash
- N – He drove off at a *dash*.
- V – He *dashed* into the room without permission.
- Adj. – Biography, as Bertie Wooster might have put it, is a *dashed* tricky business.

Dawn
- N – He left Delhi at *dawn*.
- V – At last, truth *dawned* upon him.

WORDS USED AS VERBS, NOUNS AND ADJECTIVES

Delight
- N — We felt extreme *delight* at her success.
- V — We were *delighted* to hear of her success.
- Adj. — Instead of being rewarded with a *delighted* smile, there was an awkward, bitter smirk.

Deposit
- N — He has a large amount in bank *deposits*.
- V — He *deposited* money in the bank.

E

Effect
- N — Smoking has adverse *effect* on health.
- V — Only those with progressive ideas can *effect* change in society.
- Adj. — A container deposit system is also *effective* in increasing environmental awareness.

Eye
- N — Last year, she got her *eyes* tested.
- V — She *eyed* the stranger with suspicion.

Elbow
- N — His *elbow* was injured.
- V — He *elbowed* his way through the crowd.

Exercise
- N — He does physical *exercise* daily.
- V — I know how to *exercise* my powers.
- Adj. — It is often said that the degree of compassion and principle that are *exercisable* in politics are inversely related to proximity to power.

Encounter
- N — He was killed in police *encounter*.
- V — He *encountered* many difficulties in life.
- Adj. — Inspector Days Nayak is best known as encounter specialist in the society.

End
- N — He completed the book from beginning to *end*.
- V — She *ended* her life by hanging.

Endeavour
- N — He made every *endeavour* to succeed in life.
- V — She *endeavoured* to please everyone.

Envy
- N — He was filled with *envy* at my success.
- V — Even friends *envy* your success.
- Adj. — The firm is in the *enviable* position of having a full order book.

Essay
- N — He wrote a good *essay*.
- V — He *essayed* a very difficult task.

Esteem
- N — He is held in *esteem* by everybody.
- V — I *esteem* my teachers.
- Adj. — Lal Krishna Advani is one of the esteemed leader of India.

F

Find
- N — She is the sensational *find* in the world of modelling.
- V — We all are trying to *find* a solution to his financial problem.
- Adj. — In an age where everything is searchable and *findable*, some news organisations have chosen to make their archives available only to paying customers.

Fill
- N — The food was so delicious that I had it to my *fill*.
- V — He *filled* my glass to the brim.

Function
- N — He avoids attending wedding *functions*.
- V — My washing machine has stopped *functioning*.

Fool
- N — He was a *fool* enough to believe his enemy.
- V — He can't *fool* me anymore.
- Adj. — He was *foolish* enough to confide in his friends.

Fan
- N — I am a great *fan* of Raj Kapoor.
- V — Some anti-social elements are *fanning* the rumours of communal riots in the city.
- Adj. — In came with a strange *fan-like* contraption which turns out to be a reflector for the flash bulb.

Fish
- N — He is fond of eating fried *fish*.
- V — Don't *fish* in troubled waters.
- Adj. — The river has been above normal level for most of the week, but is now falling back to a *fishable* condition.

Face
- N — Her *face* was badly bruised.
- V — He couldn't *face* the problems of life.
- Adj. — The earlier Door Gods were depicted with fearful *facial* features and expressions.

WORDS USED AS VERBS, NOUNS AND ADJECTIVES

Fall
- N – Last night, Shimla received a snow *fall*.
- V – He *fell* off the horse and was injured.

Floor
- N – The baby was sitting on the *floor*.
- V – Indian Army completely *floored* the enemies in Kargil War.

Favour
- N – She was clever enough to win her boss' *favour*.
- V – He is an orthodox and doesn't *favour* inter-caste marriages.
- Adj. – The exhibitions received *favourable* reviews.

Field
- N – In villages, one can see children working in the *fields* along with their parents.
- V – A good cricketer should also *field* well.
- Adj. – A good organisation always does its *field* work before launching its products.

Fire
- N – Curtains caught *fire* from the burning cigarette.
- V – The police *fired* in the air to disperse the crowd.

Fare
- N – Hike in railway *fare* is not a welcome policy.
- V – He didn't *fare* well this year in his final examinations.

Fast
- N – He is on *fast*.
- V – He has been *fasting* for the last two days.
- Adj. – Jamie was into speed, he liked *fast* cars and the adrenaline rush of living life on the edge.

Fix
- N – On hearing the news of his accident, I was in a *fix*.
- V – I have *fixed* the meeting at 6 in the evening.
- Adj. – These mortgages are primarily priced at a *fixed* rate.

Fly
- N – The *flies* were hovering over the uncovered sweets.
- V – The children waved at the plane *flying* overhead.
- Adj. – If an aircrew makes errors in evaluating an engine failure, they can lose a perfectly *flyable* aircraft.

File
- N – He is looking for his medical *file*.
- V – She *filed* case against the tenant.

Fold
- N – The sheep was taken back to its *fold*.
- V – Having read the newspaper, he *folded* it neatly.
- Adj. – The *foldable* IOLs became popular in the 1990s.

Flood
- N – Many houses were swept away by the *flood*.
- V – Whenever it rains heavily, this region is *flooded* by the river.

Foot
- N – She fell off the horse and got her *foot* hurt.
- V – He was responsible for the damage and so he had to *foot* the bill for the repairs.

Freeze
- N – The government has imposed *freeze* on the salaries of the employees.
- V – It's so cold that water has *frozen* in the pipelines.
- Adj. – It was a huge communal place where, for a rental fee, you stored *freezable* perishables - fish and meat.

Feather
- N – Birds of a *feather* flock together.
- V – The politicians are busy in *feathering* their own nests.
- Adj. – She looks preety in the *feathered* hat.

Feast
- N – The *feast* was very delicious.
- V – He is always happy in *feasting* his friends.

Frown
- N – There was a *frown* of disapproval on her face.
- V – She *frowned* upon the proposal with disapproval.

G

Grant
- N – He received *grant* for higher education from the university.
- V – My father *granted* me permission to attend a late night party.
- Adj. – You should be able to develop most applications with just the user *grantable* capabilities.

Grave
- N – On every death anniversary of his son, he visits his *grave*.
- V – The epitaph *graven* on his tomb is very touching.
- Adj. – The condition of the patients in government hospital is being *grave* day by day.

Ground
- N – Children are playing cricket in the *ground*.
- V – All aircrafts were *grounded* on account of fog yesterday.
- Adj. – In both cases, the fear was neither *groundless* nor unreasonable.

Guess
- N – Our *guess* about his character proved wrong.
- V – Can you *guess* the meaning of this word?
- Adj. – The other book is easily *guessable* from the cover design.

WORDS USED AS VERBS, NOUNS AND ADJECTIVES

Guard
- N — You should always be on *guard* against your enemies.
- V — Try to *guard* your secrets.

Guide
- N — He is working as a *guide* in this historical town.
- V — You must be *guided* by your common sense.

Grasp
- N — Our fate is in the *grasp* of our thoughtless politicians.
- V — You must *grasp* at every chance.
- Adj. — It's a *grasping*, greedy society, fuelled by educational expectation and privilege.

Gaze
- N — She looked at his behaviour with surprised *gaze*.
- V — She *gazed* at the sight thoughtfully.

Glare
- N — She looked at him with angry *glare*.
- V — She *glared* at him and left the room.

H

Hand
- N — You should not talk to your elders with *hands* in your pocket.
- V — The thief was *handed* over to the police.
- Adj. — To help enrich your enjoyment, here is a *handy* glossary of useful terms.

Hold
- N — The management has complete *hold* over the union leader.
- V — While crossing the road, the boy was *holding* his mother's hand very tight.
- Adj. — There are apparently two sorts of fishing licenses *holdable* by motor boats.

Help
- N — She is in a dire need of *help* at this stage of life.
- V — Everybody is ready to *help* her at this juncture.
- Adj. — As well as having elegant rooms, the hotel also had extremely friendly and *helpful* staff.

Head
- N — He is the *Head* of the English Department.
- V — We were *heading* towards our home when our car met with an accident.
- Adj. — Officers say two *headless* birds were found on farmland, and another pair had their necks snapped.

Hedge
- N — Their lawn is surrounded by a well maintained *hedge*.
- V — His decision of sending his son to the army is *hedged* with doubt.

Hurry
- N — I noticed that she was in a *hurry* this morning.
- V — My father asked us to *hurry* up lest we should miss our flight.
- Adj. — Amit left early, after a *hurried* breakfast.

Hire
- N — Please *hire* a taxi at once.
- V — You can get furniture on *hire*.

Host
- N — The *host* arrived late at the party.
- V — The party was *hosted* by her friends.

Heed
- N — You must pay *heed* to my words.
- V — He never *heeded* to the advice of his parents.
- Adj. — There's lots to try if you are feeling a little more *heedless*, though.

Herd
- N — A *herd* of cattle was grazing.
- V — The passengers sat *herded* in the bus.

Hit
- N — He made a *hit* in his new dress.
- V — He was *hit* with a stone.
- Adj. — In the past, Pirates hitters have been too eager to hack at the first *hittable* pitch.

J

Judge
- N — He is a *Judge* in the lower court.
- V — A person is *judged* by his deeds.
- Adj. — The case tangled and not *judgeable*.

Jump
- N — He won gold medal in long *jump*.
- V — Please do not *jump* to conclusions.
- Adj. — There are plenty of *jumpable* walls around the garden, after all.

Jerk
- N — The bus stopped with a sudden *jerk*.
- V — The cart *jerked* along the road.

K

Knot
- N — After a long period of courtship, they both decided to tie the *knot*.
- V — He *knotted* the scarf round his neck.
- Adj. — In freshwater fishing, I use a *knotless* tapered leader.

WORDS USED AS VERBS, NOUNS AND ADJECTIVES

Knock
- N — There was a *knock* on the door.
- V — She *knocked* at the door.

Know
- N — She was already in the *know* of the matter.
- V — I *know* him very well.
- Adj. — Virat Kohli is well *known* cricketer now-a-days.

Kid
- N — He is just a *kid* of twelve years.
- V — Why are you *kidding* your friends?

Key
- N — He always keeps his *keys* in the drawers.
- V — The country is *keyed* up on the eve of the final match.
- Adj. — *Key* facts are the most important facts.

L

Light
- N — He left the *lights* on.
- V — He *lighted* the candle in the room.
- Adj. — In summer, we should wear *light* coloured clothes.

Lock
- N — Before leaving for office, he checks the *locks* of his house twice.
- V — He *locks* all the doors and windows before going to bed.
- Adj. — Despite the *lockless* connecting door, Mel was quite satisfied with the room assigned.

Look
- N — I knew that he won't agree but still I insisted on his having a *look* at the proposal.
- V — He is still *looking* for his lost keys.

Love
- N — He is the *love* of her life.
- V — God *loves* everyone.
- Adj. — All children need love and praise to feel confident and *lovable*.

Lack
- N — *Lack* of confidence will never let you progress in life.
- V — He *lacks* determination.

Last
- N — We offered him the *last* of the food as he came very late.
- V — These shoes won't *last* long.
- Adj. — He was not able to establish a *lasting* dialogue with the United States at that point.

Level
- N — He is a swimming champion at national *level*.
- V — The farmers were *levelling* the fields.
- Adj. — I quickened my pace so that I was *level* with her.

Laugh
- N — The cynical *laugh* of that stranger sent shivers through my spine.
- V — He is too kind to *laugh* at the poor.
- Adj. — The idea that Liz wanted to pick a fight with her family was almost *laughable* if not insane.

Like
- N — I have never met the *like* of her in my life.
- V — She *likes* light music.
- Adj. — Often times I have noted that it is very popular and *likeable* people that die young.

Live
- N — Two *lives* were lost in the flood.
- V — He *lives* in a big mansion.
- Adj. — When I lived in India, I was appalled at the lack of respect for a *liveable* life we all displayed.

Lead
- N — India gained *lead* in the first innings.
- V — The consumer culture is *leading* us nowhere.
- Adj. — Who played the *lead* role in the movie.

Load
- N — The driver was fined for over *load*.
- V — I know how to *load* a gun.
- Adj. — The boy was playing with a *loaded* gun.

M

Make
- N — Both of my radios are of the same *make*.
- V — She has *made* a cake.

Master
- N — He is loyal to his *master*.
- V — She has *mastered* the rules of grammar.

Man
- N — My father is a *man* of principles.
- V — The first space flight was *manned* by the Russians.

Move
- N — Diplomatic *moves* are required to settle the dispute between India and Pakistan.
- V — I think we are *moving* in the wrong direction.
- Adj. — The synovial joints are the most freely *movable* joints.

WORDS USED AS VERBS, NOUNS AND ADJECTIVES

Measure
- N – Government has introduced certain *measures* to tackle the problem of unemployment.
- V – Thermometer is used to *measure* the body temperature.
- Adj. – He believed in having goals that were achievable and *measurable*, and he believed that you needed to be prepared in order to do what you set out to do.

Mail
- N – The *mail* has not been delivered yet.
- V – I have *mailed* greetings to her.

Manoeuvre
- N – Troops on *manoeuvre* were detected by the enemy.
- V – She is *manoeuvring* to get high post in this firm.

Manure
- N – We use *manure* to get high yield.
- V – The field has not been properly *manured*.

March
- N – Many smaller countries have stolen *march* on India.
- V – The army *marched* into enemy's territory.

Mark
- N – He made a *mark* in life.
- V – He *marked* a wrong answer.
- Adj. – The teacher asked the student to read the *marked* pages.

Market
- N – He has just gone to *market*.
- V – He is expert in *marketing* consumer product.

Match
- N – They won the *match* by two goals.
- V – The colour of your shirt does not *match* your coat.
- Adj. – Zoom forward to today, and there is nothing at all that is of *matchable* relevance.

Master
- N – He is *master* in the art of cheating.
- V – He has *mastered* the art of cheating others.

Mean
- N – He is a man of rich *means*.
- V – What do you *mean* by this?
- Adj. – She didn't know why, but for some reason she couldn't be spiteful or *mean* to this man anymore.

Mention
- N — He did not made any *mention* of you.
- V — He *mentioned* your name in the letter.
- Adj. — The first computer based tutorial has animated lessons, rhymes and stories, which certainly are of *mentionable* quality.

Mind
- N — He is a man of strong *mind*.
- V — I don't *mind* helping you.
- Adj. — Heaven preserve us from all these repetitive, *mindless* tasks.

N

Name
- N — I do not know his *name*.
- V — She has been *named* in the F.I.R.
- Adj. — He had two fights against *name* opponents where a win would have propelled him into the limelight.

Need
- N — I helped him in *need*.
- V — She does not *need* my help.
- Adj. — She gave her money away to *needful* people.

Nap
- N — He was having noon *nap*.
- V — He was caught *napping* at duty.

Nod
- N — He gave me a *nod* as he passed by me.
- V — He *nodded* his approval to me.

Note
- N — I took *note* of his misbehaviour.
- V — I *noted* his name in my diary.
- Adj. — The gardens are *notable* for their collection of magnolias and camellias.

Notice
- N — A *notice* by the police was issued to him.
- V — I *noticed* something wrong in her behaviour.
- Adj. — There is a *noticeable* increase in confidence among staff who have been able to come back to work holding their heads high.

Number
- N — The *number* of students was small.
- V — Today the students *number* smaller in the class.
- Adj. — Passwords must have at least six characters and contain a combination of alpha and *numeric* characters.

Nurse
- N — She is a very kind *nurse*.
- V — She *nursed* her husband in his sickness.

WORDS USED AS VERBS, NOUNS AND ADJECTIVES

O

Open
- N — I like to be out in the *open*.
- V — She *opened* the letter hastily.
- Adj. — He climbed through the *open* window.

Object
- N — Wordsworth found solace in the inanimate *objects* of nature.
- V — Her mother didn't *object* to her going out late in the night.

Oily
- N — It is very effective *oil* for pain.
- V — The machine has been well *oiled*.
- Adj. — Omega - 3 fatty acids, such as those in *oily* fish and flaxseed oil, can relieve dry eyes by easing inflammation and stimulating tear production.

P

Process
- N — Chemotherapy is a long and painful *process*.
- V — India does not have enough recycling plants to *process* the waste materials.
- Adj. — From the 1970s, the scientific focus shifted away from cellulose to the more *processable* biopolymer, starch.

Pen
- N — This is the *pen* that my grandfather gave to me on my birthday.
- V — She has *penned* many short stories.

Pride
- N — He looked with *pride* at his daughter playing on piano.
- V — He always *prides* himself on his wealth.
- Adj. — Truly great people are those who are grateful rather than *prideful*.

Pocket
- N — We found to our surprise that somebody had picked his *pocket*.
- V — The boy quickly *pocketed* the chocolates.
- Adj. — The hidden keyboard means that the huge screen is easily accommodated, but it would still be nicer to have a more *pocketable* device.

Produce
- N — The farmers are happy with the *produce* this year.
- V — Hard work will definitely *produce* good results.
- Adj. — The other two legs - commercial industry and government research organisations - play key roles in turning the seeds of science into *producible*, deployable fruits.

Phone
- N — My *phone* is out of order.
- V — I have *phoned* you up to cancel the dinner.

Pin
- **N** — There was a *pin* drop silence in the room.
- **V** — She *pinned* up her hair very neatly.

Pack
- **N** — He bought a *pack* of cards.
- **V** — He has just *packed* her luggage.
- **Adj.** — Ubiquitous for good reason, collapsible doggie bowls are virtually spill-free in the car, totally leakproof, and *packable*.

Pain
- **N** — He cried with *pain*.
- **V** — His behaviour *pained* his parents.
- **Adj.** — Physicians are believed to know how to ensure a *painless* death, and they are in a position to offer palliative care knowledgeably.

Palm
- **N** — I got the work done by greasing the *palm*.
- **V** — He *palmed* off spurious drugs.

Part
- **N** — This is a *part* of the last lesson.
- **V** — She *parted* from her parents sorrowfully.
- **Adj.** — The paper gave a distorted and very *partial* view of the situation.

Park
- **N** — This is a spacious *park*.
- **V** — Please *park* your cars here.

Pass
- **N** — Things have come to a pretty *pass*.
- **V** — Please let me *pass*.

R

Rise
- **N** — His awkward behaviour gave *rise* to my suspicion.
- **V** — She *rises* early in the morning.
- **Adj.** — Alia Bhatt is a *rising* star.

Rest
- **N** — He is overworked and needs *rest*.
- **V** — He is *resting* in his room.
- **Adj.** — The rooms on the hotel were so airy and *restful*.

Reach
- **N** — Good medical treatment is out of *reach* of a middle class man.
- **V** — He *reached* there quite late and missed the opportunity.
- **Adj.** — News organisations rely upon easily *reachable* government officials.

WORDS USED AS VERBS, NOUNS AND ADJECTIVES

Refuse
- N — Industrial *refuse* is a major water pollutant.
- V — She *refused* his offer of help.

Resume
- N — He was much impressed by *resume* of his career.
- V — She is determined *to resume* her studies.
- Adj. — The receive location will remain enabled, with error messages being suspended in a *resumable* state.

Right
- N — You are too young to differentiate between *right* and wrong.
- V — If you give him some time, he will definitely *right* his faults.
- Adj. — They are determined to take their *rightful* place in a new South Africa.

Record
- N — He broke all previous *records* by attaining highest percentage of marks.
- V — I have *recorded* each and every moment of your birthday celebrations.
- Adj. — As with *recordable* blank CDs and DVDs, the manufacturers will make the products but accept no liability for what you might do with them.

Round
- N — The doctor is not available as he is on his *round*.
- V — The police *rounded* up anti-social elements.
- Adj. — She was seated at a small, *round* table.

Ride
- N — He gave me a *ride* in his car.
- V — He *rode* his horse into the dense forest.
- Adj. — Has anyone in the known or unknown universe bought one of these supremely useless, blisteringly overhyped, *rideable* vacuum cleaners?

Rule
- N — I always follow *rules* of my college.
- V — Her admission was *ruled* out.
- Adj. — Those who like crisp rules tend to think *rules* are needed to have real law and think *ruleless* 'judgment' is not law.

Rumour
- N — He spread false *rumour*.
- V — It is widely *rumoured* that she will marry soon.

Resort
- N — There is a good health *resort* in Shimla.
- V — You should *resort* to honest means.

Rear
- N — She was standing in the *rear* of her house.
- V — She *reared* her family well in spite of many problems.
- Adj. — The back end was completely crumpled and the *rear* window was shattered.

Reason
- N – I do not know the *reason* of their quarrel.
- V – It is difficult to *reason* with her because she is obstinate.
- Adj. – Without that step, it's a giant, *reasonless* pain that I'd rather not deal with.

Refrain
- N – All of them joined in singing *refrain*.
- V – You should *refrain* from telling a lie.

S

Sense
- N – She has a good *sense* of humour.
- V – She was wise enough to *sense* that her marriage was on the rocks.
- Adj. – He was a *sensible* and capable boy.

Still
- N – The atmosphere is calm and *still*.
- V – The voice of the poor is *stilled* by the rich.
- Adj. – The sheriff commanded him to stand *still* and drop the gun.

Stay
- N – We thoroughly enjoyed our *stay* at her farmhouse.
- V – I can't *stay* here for long.

Slow
- N – Her recovery is very *slow*.
- V – She asked her husband to *slow* down the car.
- Adj. – She was rather a *slow* reader.

Stand
- N – India must never leave its tough *stand* on terrorism problem under any pressure.
- V – I can not *stand* injustice.

Second
- N – He finished *second* in 100 metres race.
- V – The proposal was flawless and we all *seconded* it.
- Adj. – I have been given a *second*-chance to appear in Civil Services' interview.

Silence
- N – His *silence* on the matter is disturbing me.
- V – His threats *silenced* her.

Spring
- N – *Spring* is the season that infuses new spirit into everything.
- V – The police *sprang* into action and caught the murderers.
- Adj. – It was a bright, almost *springlike* Saturday afternoon.

WORDS USED AS VERBS, NOUNS AND ADJECTIVES

Shoulder
- N — He has broad *shoulders*.
- V — He is *shouldering* the responsibility of his brother's education

Set
- N — He bought a *set* of dining chairs.
- V — He *set* everything right in a short time.
- Adj. — Iris was staring in front of her with a *set* expression.

Sway
- N — The *sway* of public opinion cannot be discounted.
- V — Your opinion about him cannot *sway* me from my decision of marrying him.

Sigh
- N — She heaved a *sigh* of relief on finding her car keys.
- V — She *sighed* at the sight of poverty in slums.

Spell
- N — He has achieved much in such a short *spell*.
- V — This year heavy rainfall *spelt* disaster to the crops.
- Adj. — They are all very *spellable* words. You just probably haven't heard them before.

Subject
- N — I don't want to discuss this *subject* any more.
- V — At her in-law's place she was *subjected* to harassment.
- Adj. — The proposed merger is *subject* to the approval of the shareholders.

Sandwich
- N — He was getting late for office, he hurriedly gulped down his *sandwich*.
- V — He is *sandwiched* between his wife and his parents.

Spoon
- N — The baby is learning to eat with a *spoon*.
- V — The boy was greedily *spooning* up his ice-cream.

Sound
- N — I heard *sound* of someone walking.
- V — I *sounded* her about her bad habits.
- Adj. — Its environs consisted of silent plains and *soundless* forests.

Say
- N — I do not have a *say* in the matter.
- V — I cannot *say* anything about his character.
- Adj. — What someone from one culture is thinking may not be fully *sayable* in the language of another culture.

T

Table
- N – The dog is sitting under the *table*.
- V – We will *table* our proposal in the next meeting.

Touch
- N – The painting needs a final *touch*.
- V – Don't *touch* the live wire.
- Adj. – Canadians spend so much time agonising over our lack of solid, *touchable*, definable identity that it has practically become a national pastime.

Temper
- N – He is a man of good *temper*.
- V – A good *tempered* iron has been used in the furniture.

Turn
- N – You have taken a wrong *turn*.
- V – Now *turn* to your right.

Trade
- N – In the past few years, India's *trade* relations with America has substantially increased.
- V – Our firm is *trading* at a loss.
- Adj. – His current research interests include the use of *tradeable* permits and other economic incentives.

Time
- N – It is high *time* you started working hard.
- V – The move for talks with Pakistan is not well *timed*.
- Adj. – Antiques add to the *timeless* atmosphere of the dining room.

Tide
- N – It is a time for spring *tide*.
- V – He could *tide* over his problems manfully.
- Adj. – Many seas are *tideless*, and the waters of some are saline only in a very slight degree.

Toil
- N – He earned money with sweat and *toil*.
- V – He *toiled* very hard in life.

Tour
- N – He is on *tour* to Europe.
- V – He has *toured* every part of Kashmir valley.

W

Watch
- N – The guard was on *watch* when the burglars broke in.
- V – India is carefully *watching* the diplomatic moves of Pakistan.
- Adj. – They attended dances under the *watchful* eye of their father

WORDS USED AS VERBS, NOUNS AND ADJECTIVES

Well
- N – The water level of the *wells* has gone down.
- V – Tears *welled* up in her eyes.
- Adj. – I do hope all is *well* with you and your family.

While
- N – I worked in my friend's Company for a *while* before going abroad.
- V – Instead of studying he is *whiling* away his precious time.

Work
- N – She does most of her *work* on her computer.
- V – My computer is not *working*.
- Adj. – By bringing *workless* people closer to the labour market and making them more effective at competing for jobs, total employment can be increased.

Want
- N – She couldn't resume her studies for *want* of money.
- V – She never *wanted* to leave her job.
- Adj. – In this area, Morrison was found *wanting* time and time again.

Wrong
- N – You must know the difference between right and *wrong*.
- V – Do not *wrong* just persons.
- Adj. – The doctor may regard the patient's decision as *wrong*.

Water
- N – He is spending his father's hard earned money like *water*.
- V – She is *watering* the plants.
- Adj. – The wanderer is like a dehydrated traveller in a *waterless* desert, or a lover longing to see the distant beloved

Walk
- N – We had a pleasant *walk* along the beach.
- V – *Walking* is a good exercise to keep fit.
- Adj. – This hotel is *walkable* from the bus station.

Will
- N – He is a man of strong *will*.
- V – God has *willed* it so.
- Adj. – He was quite *willing* to compromise.

Y

Yield
- N – The *yield* of wheat per acre in Punjab is very high.
- V – He *yielded* to my request at last.
- Adj. – She dropped on to the *yielding* cushions.

Yoke
- N – No body likes *yoke* of slavery.
- V – The bullocks were *yoked* together.

Cumulative Exercise

Exercise 1

Directions *Make adjectives from the following words.*

1. Craziness
2. Familiarity
3. Misery
4. Offence
5. Zeal
6. Read
7. Wind
8. Width
9. Illness
10. Slave
11. Sport
12. Poverty
13. Silence
14. Freedom
15. Judge
16. Falsehood
17. Analysis
18. Error
19. Tire
20. Abound
21. Provide
22. Grieve
23. Deceive
24. Cure
25. Defend
26. Accident
27. Essence
28. Coward
29. Envy
30. Lustre
31. Sense
32. Burden
33. Life
34. Praise
35. Awe
36. Drama
37. Tragedy
38. Earth
39. Custom
40. Fortune
41. Society
42. Emperor
43. Need
44. Palace
45. Poet
46. War
47. Educate
48. Moment
49. Pride
50. North

Exercise 2

Directions *Make nouns from the following words.*

1. Broker
2. Betray
3. Ignore
4. Confer
5. Mercy
6. Busy
7. Contribute
8. Receive
9. Repeat
10. Martyr
11. Coward
12. Loyal
13. Civil
14. Rogue
15. Knit
16. Close
17. Consult
18. Art
19. Scholar
20. Brother
21. Weigh
22. Lie
23. Abide
24. Grand
25. Weave
26. Conceal
27. Hate
28. Learn
29. Tell
30. Generous
31. Pious
32. Young
33. Exemplify
34. Try
35. Allot
36. Exempt
37. Solve
38. Mortal
39. Hero

WORDS USED AS VERBS, NOUNS AND ADJECTIVES

40. Fly	41. Magic	42. Resident
43. Secret	44. Agree	45. Idle
46. Special	47. Please	48. Trust
49. Err	50. Strive	

Previous Years' Questions

I. Directions *Make adjectives from the following words.*

1. (i) Devastate (ii) Economics
   (iii) Flow (iv) Learn
   (v) Moron [IFS, 2015]
2. (i) Nation (ii) Caution
   (iii) Child (iv) Glue
   (v) Move [IFS, 2014]
3. (i) Imagine (ii) Value
   (iii) Art (iv) Like
   (v) Comfort [IFS, 2013]

II. Directions *Make nouns from the following words.*

1. (i) Pretend (ii) Phenomenal
   (iii) Oriental (iv) Neutral
   (v) Invade [IFS, 2015]
2. (i) Extract (ii) Sad
   (iii) Pray (iv) Undertake
   (v) Dark [IFS, 2014]
3. (i) Submit (ii) Deliver
   (iii) Complain (iv) Wise
   (v) Hope [IFS, 2013]

III. Directions *Make sentences using the following words as directed so as to bring out the meaning.* [IAS Mains, 2006]

   (i) Pitch (as noun and verb) (ii) Mirror (as noun and verb)
   (iii) Humble (as adjective and verb) (iv) In (as adverb and preposition)

IV. Directions *Make verbs from these nouns.* [IAS Mains, 2007]

   (i) Courage (ii) Memory
   (iii) Prison (iv) Class
   (v) Friend

V. Directions *Use each of the following words in two separate sentences, first as a noun then as a verb.* [IAS Mains, 2007]

   (i) Bank (ii) Battle
   (iii) Bite (iv) Brave
   (v) Brush

Answers

Cumulative Exercises

Exercise 1

1. Crazy
2. Familiar
3. Miserable
4. Offensive
5. Zealous
6. Readable
7. Windy
8. Wide
9. Ill
10. Slavish
11. Sporting
12. Poor
13. Silent
14. Free
15. Judicious
16. False
17. Analytical
18. Erratic
19. Tiresome
20. Abundant
21. Provisional
22. Grievous
23. Deceptive
24. Curative
25. Defensive
26. Accidental
27. Essential
28. Cowardly
29. Envious
30. Lustrous
31. Sensible
32. Burdensome
33. Lifelike, lifeless
34. Praiseworthy
35. Awful
36. Dramatic
37. Tragic
38. Earthen
39. Customary
40. Fortunate
41. Social
42. Imperial
43. Needy
44. Palatial
45. Poetical, Poetic
46. Warlike
47. Educative
48. Momentary
49. Proud
50. Northern

Exercise 2

1. Brokerage
2. Betrayal
3. Ignorance
4. Conference
5. Merriment
6. Business
7. Contribution
8. Reception
9. Repetition
10. Martyrdom
11. Cowardice
12. Loyalty
13. Civility
14. Roguery
15. Knitting
16. Closure
17. Consultant
18. Artist
19. Scholarship
20. Brotherhood
21. Weight
22. Liar
23. Abode
24. Grandeur
25. Web
26. Concealment
27. Hatred
28. Learning
29. Tale
30. Generosity
31. Piety
32. Youth
33. Example
34. Trial
35. Allotment
36. Exemption
37. Solution
38. Mortality
39. Heroism
40. Flight
41. Magician
42. Residence
43. Secrecy
44. Agreement
45. Idleness
46. Speciality
47. Pleasure
45. Trustee
49. Error
50. Strife

Previous Years' Questions

I. 1. (i) Devastating (ii) Economical (iii) Flowing (iv) Learned
    (v) Moronic

2. (i) National (ii) Cautious (iii) Childish (iv) Gluey
   (v) Movable

3. (i) Imaginary (ii) Valuable (iii) Artistic (iv) Like
   (v) Comfortable

WORDS USED AS VERBS, NOUNS AND ADJECTIVES 689

II. 1. (i) Pretence (ii) Phenomenon (iii) Oriental (iv) Neutral
    (v) Invasion
  2. (i) Extraction (ii) Sadness (iii) Prayer (iv) Undertaking
    (v) Darkness
  3. (i) Submission (ii) Delivery (iii) Complaint (iv) Wisdom
    (v) Hope

III. (i) **Pitch** *(Noun)* The *pitch* of girls is higher than that of boys.
       Pitch *(Verb)* The bowler *pitched* the ball infront of the batsman.
  (ii) **Mirror** *(Noun)* I try to admire myself in *mirror*.
       Mirror *(Verb)* Rape cases *mirror* the society of its cruel face.
  (iii) **Humble** *(Adjective)* He made a *humble* request.
        Humble *(Verb)* She *humbled* me for any helps.
  (iv) **In** *(Adverb)* He was not allowed to come *in*.
       In *(Preposition)* He did not come *in* the party.

IV. (i) Encourage (ii) Memorise (iii) Prison (iv) Classify
   (v) Befriend

V. (i) **Bank** *(Noun)* I have no account in *bank*.
      Bank *(Verb)* I *bank* with SBI always.
  (ii) **Battle** *(Noun)* Many kings avoided a *battle*.
       Battle *(Verb)* I am *battling* with my career.
  (iii) **Bite** *(Noun)* He took a *bite* from my cake.
        Bite *(Verb)* The dog *bite* me seriously.
  (iv) **Brave** *(Noun)* He is a fellow known for his *bravery*.
       Brave *(Verb)* He *braved* all the difficulties single-handedly.
  (v) **Brush** *(Noun)* I painted the house with the help of a *brush*.
      Brush *(Verb)* I *brushed* my teeth in the morning.

CHAPTER 9

Miscellaneous

Directions Use the following words to make sentences that bring out their meaning clearly. Do not change the form of the words.

1. Aegis
2. Aggrandisement
3. Anachronism
4. Bedraggled
5. Blandishment
6. Buffoon
7. Churlish
8. Clandestine
9. Conundrum
10. Deleterious
11. Disputatious
12. Delirium
13. Egregious
14. Enshroud
15. Extemporaneous
16. Fastidious
17. Faux pas
18. Flabbergasted
19. Gratuitous
20. Grueling
21. Hackneyed
22. Hubris
23. Imposter
24. Innuendo
25. Irrevocable
26. Jargon
27. Juggernaut
28. Knave
29. Labyrinth
30. Leverage
31. Lurch
32. Magnanimous
33. Morass
34. Mosaic
35. Narcissistic
36. Nebula
37. Nihilism
38. Obloquy
39. Outlandish
40. Overtly
41. Palatable
42. Portentous
43. Protocol
44. Quintessential
45. Quixotic
46. Raucous
47. Relinquish
48. Repertoire
49. Sacrosanct
50. Scapegoat
51. Supercalifragilisticexpialidocious
52. Talisman
53. Touché
54. Unassailable
55. Vendetta
56. Wanderlust
57. Woebegone
58. Yore
59. Zeitgeist
60. Ziggurat

Previous Years' Questions

Directions *Use the following words to make sentences that bring out their meaning clearly. Do not change the form of the words.*

I 1. Drought   2. Profitable   3. Plunge
    4. Deformity   5. Restraint
                                                      [Civil Services (Mains), 2015]

II 1. Gratitude   2. Flavour   3. Explosion
    4. Dismal   5. Clumsy
                                                      [Civil Services (Mains), 2014]

III 1. Desultory   2. Grapevine   3. Holistic
    4. Insidious   5. Intransigence   6. Paradigm
    7. Susceptible   8. Ubiquitous   9. Voracious
    10. Venerable
                                                      [Civil Services (Mains), 2013]

IV 1. Loquacious   2. Topsy-turvy   3. Mentor
    4. Enigmatic   5. Nefarious
                                                                 [IES/ISS, 2015]

V 1. Quagmire   2. Remuneration   3. Penchant
    4. Verbiage   5. Niche
                                                                 [IES/ISS, 2014]

VI 1. Inflammatory   2. Zenith   3. Utopia
    4. Exodus   5. Dissenter
                                                                 [IES/ISS, 2013]

VII 1. Channel   2. Canal   3. Gesture
    4. Jester   5. Emigrant   6. Immigrant
    7. Scheme   8. Skim   9. Alternative
    10. Alternate   11. Penury   12. Precarious
    13. Mortify   14. Proscribe   15. Confidant
                                                                 [IFS, 2010]

VIII 1. Conscientious   2. Deleterious   3. Nebulous
    4. Perseverance   5. Wistful
                                                                   [IES, 2012]

IX 1. Corpus   2. Insidious   3. Lateral
    4. Servile   5. Rubric
                                                                   [IES, 2011]

X 1. Alleviate   2. Obfuscation   3. Succinct
    4. Grapevine   5. Dissimulation
                                                                   [IES, 2009]

XI 1. Meltdown   2. Imbroglio   3. Cerebral
    4. Convergence   5. Obligation
                                                                   [IES, 2010]

Answers

1. **Aegis** *(under the influence or protection of a specific individual, body or government)* The knight was under the *aegis* of the king so he was not punished for his crimes against the villagers.
2. **Aggrandisement** *(an increase in power, importance or reputation that is undeserved)* Suzan suggests that *aggrandisement* of one's self-worth may be a desperate attempt to boost one's low self-esteem.
3. **Anachronism** *(something that doesn't fit its time period)* Soon physical books will be completely replaced by e-books and will represent nothing more than an *anachronism*.
4. **Bedraggled** *(messy and filthy)* After playing a game in the rain, the players were *bedraggled* and eager for a shower.
5. **Blandishment** *(the use of flattery (sweet-talk) and enticements to persuade somebody gently to do something)* Even though the salesman produced every *blandishment* he could think of from his bag of tricks, his prospect wouldn't be budged by his flattery.
6. **Buffoon** *(a silly person who tries to be humorous but comes across as foolish)* Since you are making a *buffoon* of yourself, you should go sit quietly in a corner before you embarrass me further!
7. **Churlish** *(rude; impolite)* Maria is a very efficient nurse, but her patients find her bedside manner to be *churlish* and unpleasant.
8. **Clandestine** *(done in an unobtrusive manner to avoid detection)* The robbers' midnight entry into the bank was *clandestine* and went completely unnoticed by the authorities.
9. **Conundrum** *(a difficult problem that seems to have no solution)* Although the mechanic tried to identify the *conundrum* with the car, he was unable to pinpoint the issue.
10. **Deleterious** *(harmful)* It has been medically proven that smoking is *deleterious* to your health.
11. **Disputatious** *(taking pleasure in arguments)* John's *disputatious* personality makes him a great lawyer.
12. **Delirium** *(a condition of extreme happiness and excitement)* As soon as the young girl saw all of her birthday presents, she leaped in *delirium*.
13. **Egregious** *(really bad or offensive)* Unwilling to put up with misbehaviour in her class, the teacher sent the *egregious* student into the hall.
14. **Enshroud** *(to make something hidden)* Wrapping a gift is the perfect way to *enshroud* it from curious eyes.
15. **Extemporaneous** *(completed without any type of advance preparation)* Instead of giving his prepared speech, the minister delivered an *extemporaneous* statement about the recent terrorist attacks.
16. **Fastidious** *(concerned about accuracy and detail; hard to please)* My mother-in-law is the most *fastidious* person on this planet.
17. **Faux pas** *(a social blunder that is quite embarrassing)* Cathy committed a huge *faux pas* when she licked the spoon and put it back in the cake batter.
18. **Flabbergasted** *(overwhelmed by amazement)* The burglar was *flabbergasted* when he broke into the house and found himself surrounded by police officers.
19. **Gratuitous** *(uncalled for; unwarranted; unnecessary)* Even though I had been looking forward to seeing the movie, I walked out of the theater after 30 minutes because of so much *gratuitous* foul language.
20. **Grueling** *(requiring great effort; extremely tiring)* As a traveling salesman, Jim has a *grueling* calendar that keeps him moving from city to city.
21. **Hackneyed** *(repeated too often; overused)* Every time my internet goes down, the cable company gives me a *hackneyed* explanation.

MISCELLANEOUS

22. **Hubris** *(an excess of confidence; having too much pride and personal worth)* Most politicians are so inflated by their own *hubris* they cannot understand the needs of their communities.
23. **Imposter** *(a person who pretends to be someone else in order to trick and deceive people)* Bruce is an *imposter* who deceives others by claiming to be one of their relatives.
24. **Innuendo** *(a statement that indirectly suggests someone has done something immoral, improper, etc.)* The company president refused to respond to the *innuendo* about fraud charges.
25. **Irrevocable** *(not able to be changed, reversed or recovered; final)* Once the President signs the treaty, it will be binding and *irrevocable*.
26. **Jargon** *(communication that a person cannot comprehend)* If you include legal *jargon* in the article, only law students and lawyers will be able to understand your position.
27. **Juggernaut** *(a large item that is seen as unstoppable and can destroy anything in its way)* With the reveal of its best-selling innovation, the software company has become a *juggernaut* in the tech industry.
28. **Knave** *(a dishonest individual)* Jason is a *knave* who will not hesitate to steal money from his family members.
29. **Labyrinth** *(a complicated irregular network of passages or paths in which it is difficult to find one's way; a maze)* At the farm, I found it very easy to get lost in the *labyrinth* of corn stalks.
30. **Leverage** *(something that can be used to sway a negotiation)* The *leverage* I have against Bob should force him to vote for me as the next company president.
31. **Lurch** *(to move around in a sneaky manner)* The cat will *lurch* around the corner to spy on the sleeping dog.
32. **Magnanimous** *(very generous or forgiving; unselfish)* Even though the defendant had broken the law, the *magnanimous* judge gave him the lightest sentence possible.
33. **Morass** *(a complicated or confusing situation)* Even the smartest lawyer will find it difficult to find a solution for this legal *morass*.
34. **Mosaic** *(a hard embellishment that is created by pushing tiny segments of dyed glass or stone into a pliable substance)* The little girl was fascinated by the colorful *mosaic* that comprised the church's window.
35. **Narcissistic** *(obsessed with one's importance and/or physical appearance)* The *narcissistic* teenager cannot walk more than fifty feet without checking her appearance in her pocket mirror.
36. **Nebula** *(a space cloud consisting of gas or dust)* I like to imagine living in a spaceship, drifting around in some massive *nebula*, lost forever in space.
37. **Nihilism** *(the idea that societal rules are worthless and should be eliminated)* The rebels urged the people to grab hold of *nihilism* and remove all government officials from office.
38. **Obloquy** *(shame from public disapproval)* The teacher killed himself after a false accusation of child molestation brought great *obloquy* to his name.
39. **Outlandish** *(very unusual)* When the boy was asked about his report, he created an *outlandish* story about aliens stealing his work.
40. **Overtly** *(publicly, openly)* Although Nancy's boss is not *overtly* racist, he does make some questionable remarks when annoyed.
41. **Palatable** *(satisfactory; suitable)* We found the warm sunny weather quite *palatable* for our picnic.
42. **Portentous** *(foreboding, ominous or threatening)* The woman called the police and complained about the *portentous* man who would not stop following her.
43. **Protocol** *(guidelines for conduct in specific environments as well as for diplomats and heads of state)* The new teacher violated school *protocol* by going directly to the principal instead of first seeking out her grade level chair.

44. **Quintessential** *(a model example of a specific quality)* The critics love the director's latest film and consider it to be the *quintessential* horror movie.
45. **Quixotic** *(unrealistic and impractical)* The idea of an obese person participating in a triathlon is a *quixotic* notion.
46. **Raucous** *(behaving in a noisy and disorderly way)* Without a second thought, the bus driver ordered the *raucous* group to get off at the next stop.
47. **Relinquish** *(to give up, abandon)* Once the terrorists had been cornered, the agents ordered them to *relinquish* their weapons.
48. **Repertoire** *(a set of skills or types of behaviour that a person uses regularly)* As long as the piano player continues to strum through a boring *repertoire* of tunes, he will never keep a large audience.
49. **Sacrosanct** *(too important or respected to be criticised or changed)* The award-winning filmmaker felt his movies were too *sacrosanct* to be criticised by the media.
50. **Scapegoat** *(a person or group made to bear the blame for others or to suffer in their place)* Because the detectives could not catch the real killer, they arrested a vagrant as a *scapegoat* to calm the worried public.
51. **Supercalifragilisticexpialidocious** *(incredible; extremely pleasing)* The amazing view from my hotel balcony was *supercalifragilisticexpialidocious*.
52. **Talisman** *(a charm worn or kept to bring good fortune and ward off evil; lucky charm)* The gambler would not play a single game unless his *talisman* was in his shirt pocket.
53. **Touché** *(recognition given when someone makes a clever statement or when a fencer hits his target)* Sarah's verbal comeback to my smart comment earned her a complimentary "*Touché*."
54. **Unassailable** *(safe from being overtaken)* No one imagined the *unassailable* beverage company would one day be purchased by a more successful entity.
55. **Vendetta** *(a series of actions taken to get back at or harm someone)* When the rapper made fun of his rival in a song, he let everyone know the *vendetta* had not been resolved.
56. **Wanderlust** *(a deep urge to travel)* Even though I had sprained my ankle, I could not resist my *wanderlust* and used crutches to walk to the beach with my friends.
57. **Woebegone** *(sad, tearful, or miserable in appearance)* All of the children were *woebegone* at the loss of their dog.
58. **Yore** *(a very long time ago)* In the days of *yore*, the internet did not exist.
59. **Zeitgeist** *(the spirit or identity of a specific time period)* The classic book about slavery depicts the *zeitgeist* of an era in which men felt entitled to own other men as property.
60. **Ziggurat** *(a tower that is tiered and rectangular in shape and occasionally topped by a holy place)* Before the old man died, he wanted to visit the *ziggurat* to say his final prayer.

Previous Years' Questions

I. 1. **Drought** *(a long period of time when there is no rain)* The district is exposed to *drought* and also to destructive floods.
   2. **Profitable** *(yielding profit, gain or benefit)* He owns a professionally run and *profitable* company.
   3. **Plunge** *(jump or dive quickly and energetically)* The plane exploded and *plunged* into the ocean, killing all the people on board.
   4. **Deformity** *(a deformed condition, disfigurement)* Drugs taken during pregnancy may cause physical *deformity* in babies.
   5. **Restraint** *(self-control)* The police appealed to the crowd for *restraint*.

II. 1. **Gratitude** *(the feeling of being grateful and wanting to express thanks)* I would like to express my *gratitude* to everyone for their hard work.

2. **Flavour** *(taste)* The tomatoes give extra *flavour* to the sauce.
3. **Explosion** *(the sudden violent bursting and loud noise of a bomb exploding)* There were two loud *explosions* and then the building burst into flames.
4. **Dismal** *(not skillful or successful)* The singer gave a *dismal* performance of some old songs.
5. **Clumsy** *(moving or doing things in a very awkward way)* His *clumsy* fingers couldn't untie the knot.

III.
1. **Desultory** *(going from one thing to another, without a definite plan and without enthusiasm)* I wandered about in a *desultory* fashion.
2. **Grapevine** *(rumour or unofficial information)* Aanchal heard through the *grapevine* that Avinagh had got admission into Harvard.
3. **Holistic** *(considering a whole thing)* According to the *holistic* view of good health, a person will not heal if the mind is injured.
4. **Insidious** *(spreading gradually but causing severe harm)* He experienced the *insidious* influence of the corporate culture.
5. **Intransigence** *(stubborn)* No agreement was reached because of *intransigence* on both sides.
6. **Paradigm** *(a typical example or pattern)* The war was a *paradigm* of the destructive side of human nature.
7. **Susceptible** *(very likely to be influenced or harmed)* Some of these plants are more *susceptible* to frost damage than others.
8. **Ubiquitous** *(very common)* Paresh Rawal is an *ubiquitous* movie star.
9. **Voracious** *(greedy)* She has a *voracious* appetite.
10. **Venerable** *(deserving respect)* Mr Amitabh Bachchan is a *venerable* old man.

IV.
1. **Loquacious** *(talkative)* He was the most *loquacious* guest at dinner.
2. **Topsy-turvy** *(in a state of great confusion)* Everything is *topsy-turvy* in my life at the moment.
3. **Mentor** *(an experienced person who advises or helps somebody with less experience)* She spent 10 years as a *mentor* to junior employees.
4. **Enigmatic** *(mysterious and difficult to understand)* This is the most *enigmatic* book I have ever read.
5. **Nefarious** *(criminal, immoral)* Racism in the 21st century is still a *nefarious* reality in the world.

V.
1. **Quagmire** *(a difficult or dangerous situation)* Most young people do not realise the *quagmire* to which occasional drug use can lead.
2. **Remuneration** *(an amount of money that is paid to someone for the work they have done)* The salary earned by teachers is not enough *remuneration* for all the work they do on a daily basis.
3. **Penchant** *(a special liking for something)* She has a *penchant* for champagne.
4. **Verbiage** *(the use of too many words or too difficult words than are needed, to express an idea)* In an attempt to confuse the jury, the attorney used a lot of legal *verbiage*.
5. **Niche** *(a comfortable or suitable role)* He eventually found his *niche* in sports journalism.

VI.
1. **Inflammatory** *(intended to cause very strong feelings of anger)* After a short period of freedom, she was again arrested for making *inflammatory* speeches.
2. **Zenith** *(The time when something is strongest and most successful)* The singer reached her *zenith* when she sold over 12 million records in 2015.
3. **Utopia** *(an imaginary place or state in which everything is perfect)* The book's main setting is a *utopia* in which everyone is satisfied with what he or she has.

4. **Exodus** *(a situation in which many people leave a place at the same time)* Tired of the hardships of farming, many families have made an *exodus* from the country to the city.
5. **Dissenter** *(a person who does not agree with opinions that are officially or generally accepted)* It is a teacher's job to challenge her students and to urge them to be *dissenters* against theories that cannot be proven.

VII
1. **Channel** *(pathways)* Candidates are advised to apply through proper *channel*.
2. **Canal** *(waterways like that of a small river)* Agriculture can be boosted through the building of *canals*.
3. **Gesture** *(motion as communication)* All his *gestures* were incomprehensible to me.
4. **Jester** *(person who jokes)* I love the company of *jesters*.
5. **Emigrant** *(person who leaves his country)* Mr Goyal has become an *emigrant* these days.
6. **Immigrant** *(person from a foreign)* *Immigrants* love to see the architecture of India.
7. **Scheme** *(plan of action)* The *scheme* launched by the government is beneficial.
8. **Skim** *(to take from the top layer)* Cream is obtained by *skimming* the milk.
9. **Alternative** *(options)* There was no *alternative* than to surrender.
10. **Alternate** *(one after other with a successive gap)* He works in *alternate* days only.
11. **Penury** *(poverty)* Pakistan must devise plans to alleviate *penury*.
12. **Precarious** *(doubtful)* I am always *precarious* about his plans and schemes.
13. **Mortify** *(disgrace)* His comments were so *mortifying* that I couldn't bear that.
14. **Proscribe** *(prohibit)* This project was *proscribed* due to its inefficiency in returning.
15. **Confidant** *(close friend)* I love to spend my time with my *confidant*.

VIII
1. **Conscientious** *(careful)* One must be very *conscientious* in the selection of one's friends.
2. **Deleterious** *(damaging)* Smoking has a very *deleterious* effect on our body.
3. **Nebulous** *(confused)* A *nebulous* person will be unable to guide you.
4. **Perseverance** *(forbearance)* A soldier is a man with *perseverance*.
5. **Wistful** *(longing)* Boys are highly *wistful* of possessing luxuries.

IX
1. **Corpus** *(collection)* All his *corpus* seems to be useful from examination point of view.
2. **Insidious** *(tricky)* I can easily see through his *insidious* remarks.
3. **Lateral** *(sideways)* His standing *lateral* and doing nothing is highly reproachable.
4. **Servile** *(mean)* Rape is a *servile* deed.
5. **Rubric** *(rule)* The *rubric* of life lies in being disciplined.

X
1. **Alleviate** *(to remove)* Government is trying hard to *alleviate* poverty.
2. **Obfuscation** *(bafflement)* In a fit of *obfuscation*, he forgot the train tickets.
3. **Succinct** *(brief)* There was a *succinct* appearance of the actress.
4. **Grapevine** *(private source of information)* The ladies are supposed to be *grapevine* in their locality.
5. **Dissimulation** *(hypocricy)* Why don't we call the Babas the tauts for their *dissimilation*.

XI
1. **Meltdown** *(unhappy conclusion)* Everything was going fine but the *meltdown* took all the pleasure.
2. **Imbroglio** *(argument/fight)* Prudent people avoid falling in an *imbroglio*.
3. **Cerebral** *(analytical)* He is quite *cerebral* in the business affairs.
4. **Convergence** *(union)* The college invited its alumni in a convergence yesterday.
5. **Obligation** *(responsibility)* Married ones have many *obligations* to meet.